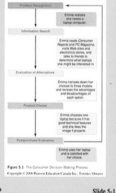

MyMarketingLab includes a wide variety of additional interactive material that allow for further exploration.

INTERACTIVE LEARNING RESOURCES!

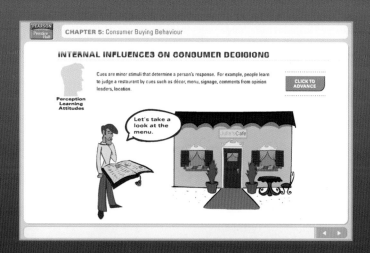

Marketing Toolkit

This tool contains a series of interactive modules, animations, and quizzes that will help you review and master important marketing concepts.

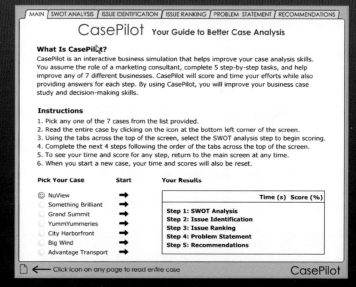

CasePilot

This interactive business simulation is designed to help you improve your case analysis skills. Assume the role of a marketer and work through five step-by-step tasks that align with the case analysis process.

Research Navigator™

This tool provides the easiest way for you to start a research assignment. Complete with extensive help on the research process and four exclusive databases of credible and reliable source material, you can quickly and efficiently make the most of your research time.

The MyMarketingLab Study Plan is based on your specific learning needs.

PERSONALIZED LEARNING!

Auto-Graded Tests and Assignments

MyMarketingLab comes with two pre-loaded Sample Tests for each chapter so you can self-assess your understanding of the material.

Personalized Study Plan

A Study Plan is generated based on your results on Sample Tests and instructor assignments. You can clearly see which topics you have mastered and, more importantly, which you need to work on!

eText

Each problem in the Study Plan links to the eText page discussing the very concept being applied—no searching through pages of text to find the exact reference you need to further explore the problem.

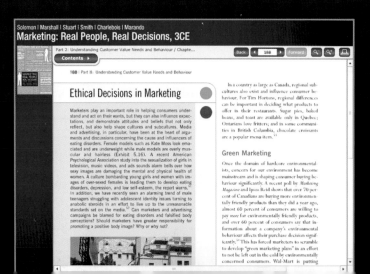

MARKETING
REAL PEOPLE
REAL DECISIONS
THIRD CANADIAN EDITION

MICHAEL R. SOLOMON
SAINT JOSEPH'S UNIVERSITY

GREG W. MARSHALL
ROLLINS COLLEGE

ELNORA W. STUART
THE AMERICAN UNIVERSITY IN CAIRO

J. BROCK SMITH
UNIVERSITY OF VICTORIA

SYLVAIN CHARLEBOIS
UNIVERSITY OF REGINA

MARIANNE MARANDO
SENECA COLLEGE

PEARSON

Prentice
Hall

Toronto

Library and Archives Canada Cataloguing in Publication

Marketing: real people, real decisions / Michael R. Solomon … [et al.].—3rd Canadian ed.

Includes bibliographical references and index.
ISBN 978-0-13-514557-9

1. Marketing—Textbooks. I. Solomon, Michael R.

HF5415.M3696 2008	658.8	C2008-901225-9

ISBN-13: 978-0-13-514557-9
ISBN-10: 0-13-514557-0

Vice President, Editorial Director: Gary Bennett
Acquisitions Editor: Don Thompson
Senior Marketing Manager: Leigh-Anne Graham
Senior Developmental Editor: Paul Donnelly
Production Editor: Cheryl Jackson
Copy Editor: Catharine Haggert
Proofreaders: Karen Alliston, Ann McInnis
Production Coordinator: Patricia Ciardullo
Compositor: ICC Macmillan Inc.
Photo and Permissions Researchers: Dawn du Quesnay, Christina Nair
Art Director: Julia Hall
Cover and Interior Designer: Jennifer Stimson

1 2 3 4 5   12 11 10 09 08

Printed and bound in the United States of America.

BRIEF CONTENTS

CONTENTS

PART III   Creating the Value Proposition   237

Chapter 7   Product Strategy   239

Chapter 14   Developing and Implementing a Marketing Plan   **501**

Appendix   Marketing Plan: j.love handbags   **527**

PREFACE

The complexity of the decisions faced by Canadian marketers in today's technology-intensive, hyper-competitive global business environment is both exciting and challenging. The main goal of this textbook is to help students develop the skills necessary to meet these challenges by immersing them in experiences in marketing decision making.

Unlike other introductory marketing textbooks, *Marketing: Real People, Real Decisions*, Third Canadian Edition, focuses on marketing decision making and the decision *maker*, not just on marketing theory, concepts, and principles. Students practise making and supporting *real* marketing decisions and learn from decisions made by others—experienced and successful international marketers in a variety of industries, companies, and contexts. We believe that this combination of learning by doing and learning from others will engage students in active learning and excite them about careers in marketing, both in Canada and internationally.

Marketing in the Canadian context is not simply a scaled-down version of U.S. practices. In this book, we have captured the uniqueness of the Canadian marketing environment in which students will be working. The discussion of multicultural marketing in Chapter 5, for instance, presents a uniquely Canadian perspective. In addition, most of the examples, exhibits, vignettes, and cases in the book are specifically Canadian, but these are balanced with the need for Canadians to have an international perspective and understand international decision environments. The examples, exhibits, vignettes, and cases have also been chosen to represent a variety of industries to give students a broad perspective on marketing contexts: for-profit and not-for-profit; large established firms and entrepreneurial start-ups; services, durable-goods, packaged-goods, retail, and e tail businesses.

The text has been updated to reflect the rapidly changing technological context of marketing decisions, particularly as it relates to the way Canadian companies use the Internet. Additionally, the role of marketing in small- and medium-sized businesses is well integrated throughout the book in recognition of the importance of these businesses to the Canadian economy. Much has happened since the appearance of the first Canadian edition. Domestic and global events have had a profound effect on how we think about marketing and our marketing decisions. To ensure the book's currency and, where possible, to deepen its international perspective, we have made some significant changes to the text. Here are the highlights:

- The text is more strategic in focus, introducing strategic marketing concepts such as the development of market-driven strategies, positioning strategies, and sources of sustainable competitive advantage. This allows students to fully appreciate the strategic nature and implications of their decisions.

- At the same time, the text focuses on decision making by taking marketing managers' perspectives and showing students how core marketing concepts, theories, and principles are used to make key marketing decisions.

- New to this edition is an organizing framework that illustrates how all of the decisions marketers make relate to each other. The material in the text is now presented in the order illustrated in the framework, making it easier for readers to relate concepts to the "bigger picture."

- Also new to this edition is a feature called **Marketing Metrics** where text boxes provide examples of how marketers specify and measure outcomes.

- The text is more concise, streamlined, and manageable for a one-semester course. The chapter on Customer Satisfaction and Retention has been removed and this material has been integrated into the discussions of marketing strategy and consumer and organizational buying.

- There are six new **Real People** profiles and nine new **Marketing in Action** cases to bring marketing concepts to life in relevant contexts for the readers.

- A total of 10 video cases are available for this edition. Eight of them, six of which are new, appear in the textbook—two at the end of each part. Two bonus video cases are included in the instructor's manual.

- We continue to integrate material on international marketing, ethics, and the use of technology throughout the text, but pay particular attention to ethical issues through a text box in each chapter called "Ethical Decisions in Marketing" in which students are asked to consider their perspective on a decision made by a marketing manager.

We have enhanced the text with the following new content:

- Chapter 1 (What Is Marketing?) introduces an organizing framework that provides students with a summary of the marketing planning process. We have placed a greater focus on value creation through a more detailed discussion of value creation and by using value creation as a theme throughout the text. Material is better organized, more streamlined, and better integrated with Chapter 2.

- The discussion of SWOT analysis in Chapter 2 (Making Strategic Marketing Decisions) has been enhanced, including an example of a SWOT analysis based on the Real People profile and a figure illustrating how SWOT analysis can be used to generate strategic alternatives.

- In Chapter 3 (Market Segmentation and Positioning), we have put greater focus on defending positioning strategies and on developing brand personality.

- In Chapter 4 (Marketing Research), we have updated the section on marketing intelligence, including updated examples. We have also provided a more comprehensive discussion of customer satisfaction measurement and expanded the discussion of interactive and online marketing research.

- In Chapter 5 (Consumer Buying Behaviour), we have enhanced our discussion of brand loyalty and the FCB grid. We have also added a new discussion of both female buying behaviour and green marketing, and we have provided a new section discussing "tipping point" concepts. We have updated our discussion of technology with a new section on blogs and blogging and RSS feeds.

- In Chapter 6 (Organizational Buying Behaviour), we have provided a new section on Customer Relationship Management and made our discussion of the use of technology in managing these relationships more current.

- In Chapter 7 (Product Strategy), we have revised the discussion of the layers of the product concept to be consistent with the approach most instructors expect. A discussion of product classifications has been added to the chapter and "tipping point" concepts are applied. We have also modified the structure of the chapter to fit the organization framework presented in Chapter 1.

- In Chapter 8 (Product Management), we have added a new section on service strategy and modified the structure of the chapter to fit the new organizing framework.

- In Chapter 9 (Pricing Strategy), we have streamlined the presentation of the material and made it easier to read by moving more of the marketing math concepts and examples to the Chapter Appendix.

- In Chapter 10 (Channels and Supply Chain Strategy), we have enhanced our discussion of channel management with new section on motivating channel partners. We have also updated our discussion of supply chain management with new examples.

- In Chapter 11 (Retailing and E-tailing), we have updated our discussion, facts, and figures relating to e-tailing and we have added a discussion of the marketing implications of social networking sites like YouTube, MySpace, and Facebook.

- In Chapter 12 (Integrated Marketing Communications), we have added new sections discussing Characteristics of IMC, Database Marketing, buzz marketing, guerilla marketing, event marketing, and viral marketing.

- In Chapter 13 (Communication Mix and Tactics), we have expanded our discussion of Internet advertising, added a new section on mobile marketing and SMS, and added a new section on Search Engine Marketing and Search Engine Optimization. We have also added a discussion of technology to our treatment of personal selling.

- Finally, in Chapter 14 (Developing and Implementing a Marketing Plan), we have provided a much more detailed discussion of marketing planning and how to write a marketing plan. A new sample marketing plan that follows the prescribed marketing plan outline has been included in the appendix.

APPROACH AND ORGANIZATION

The text is organized into 14 chapters that are grouped in four parts.

Part I (Identifying and Specifying Value Opportunities) provides an overview of the world of marketing (Chapter 1) and strategic marketing decisions (Chapter 2), and it introduces students to the key concepts of market segmentation and positioning (Chapter 3). These chapters help students understand the situational context, identify creative segmentation schemes, develop rich segment profiles, and evaluate the appropriateness of alternative targeting strategies.

Part II (Understanding Customer Value Needs and Behaviour) provides students with foundational tools and concepts for understanding the decision context, conducting industry and competitive analysis, and understanding customers. This section includes discussion of marketing research (Chapter 4), consumer buying behaviour (Chapter 5), and organizational buying behaviour (Chapter 6).

Part III (Creating the Value Proposition) provides students with the tools and concepts relating to product strategies (Chapter 7), product management (Chapter 8), and pricing strategy (Chapter 9). These chapters focus on tailoring product and pricing decisions to suit the target market profile and strategic context.

Part IV (Delivering, Communicating, and Implementing the Value) introduces students to channels and supply chain strategy (Chapter 10), retailing and e-tailing (Chapter 11), integrated marketing communications (Chapter 12), communications mix and tactics (Chapter 13), and developing and implementing a marketing plan (Chapter 14).

Each chapter starts with a profile of a marketing decision maker who works in a position students might expect to have within a few years after graduation. A decision that the marketer has recently faced is described, and alternative courses of action are proposed. At this point, students are asked to step into the shoes of the profiled marketer, evaluate the alternatives, and recommend and defend a course of action. At the end of the chapter, we discuss what decision the marketer made and why, and provide a summary of the known consequences of that decision.

We try to make it clear that the decision made by the marketer is not necessarily the most appropriate one. Our aim is to show the rationale underpinning the decision and to help students understand how that rationale is informed by the decision maker's perspective. This format allows students to take an active role in applying the marketing concepts they are learning.

We have included decision makers from a variety of organizations, ranging from large, well-known companies like Molson and IBM, to smaller regional businesses like Coast Tire, to small family businesses like Yellow Point Lodge. This allows students to see how marketing issues and decisions differ across organizations, and also how they are similar.

One of our objectives for this book is to be as current as possible so that the content is relevant for the marketplace that students will face when they graduate. To that end, we have integrated Internet marketing throughout the book and devoted a major part of Chapter 11 (Retailing and E-tailing) to business and consumer electronic commerce.

KEY FEATURES

This book contains many special features that facilitate learning and enhance understanding of core concepts and their applications:

- **Chapter Objectives** at the beginning of each chapter clearly summarize the core concepts explored in that chapter.

- **Key Terms** are boldfaced where they are defined in the text and listed at the end of each chapter for easy reference.

- **Figures, Tables,** and **Exhibits** throughout the book each carry explanatory captions.

- **Real People, Real Decisions** vignettes frame each chapter by introducing a decision maker and dilemma faced at the beginning and discussing the decision reached at the end.

- **Spotlight on Real People** boxes profile entrepreneurs in small- and medium-sized businesses. Wherever possible, we have highlighted the activities of young Canadian entrepreneurs to whom students can relate as peers.

- **Ethical Decisions in Marketing** boxes recognize that ethics play a crucial role in marketing and business. This feature prompts students to consider ethical dilemmas faced by decision makers.

- **Marketing Metrics** boxes illustrate how marketers specify and measure desired outcomes.

- **Marketing in Action** cases at the end of each chapter provide an opportunity for students to make marketing decisions related to key chapter concepts in up-to-date, relevant decision situations.

- **Video Cases** (at the end of each part of the text) are based on segments from the CBC shows *Venture* and *Marketplace* that deal topically with the practice of marketing, often in a small business context.

- Extensive **Chapter Summary** material helps students understand chapter concepts and issues. **Testing Your Knowledge** and **Discussing Choices and Issues** questions stimulate recall and critical thinking. **Applying What You've Learned** exercises ask students to assume the role of marketing professional and apply concepts and theory to marketing decisions. **Learning by Doing** activities invite students to learn outside the classroom by talking with marketing professionals, observing phenomena in the marketplace, or conducting primary and secondary research.

- **Real People, Real Surfers** exercises help students learn about resources available on the Internet and encourage them to explore first-hand the many permutations of Web-based marketing.

- The **appendix** offers a sample marketing plan integrated with the marketing plan template in Chapter 14.

SUPPLEMENTS

The Instructor's Resource CD-ROM contains the following five components.

- The *Instructor's Manual* provides an overview of each chapter's suggested activities, projects, and topics for class discussions. Moreover, it offers direction on overcoming barriers to effective learning, assigning in-class projects, and developing class plans. It also includes teaching notes for the end-of-chapter cases and end-of-part CBC video cases.

- PowerPoint® Presentations incorporate exhibits and weblinks from the text.

- The *Pearson Education Canada TestGen*, containing over 2700 questions, has been thoroughly revised to provide the optimum number of questions of each format (true/false, multiple choice, and short answer), degree of difficulty (easy, moderate, difficult), and type of cognitive skill tested (recall/application). The TestGen program enables instructors to edit existing questions, add new questions, and generate tests.

- *CBC/Pearson Education Canada Video Library* is a compilation of video segments drawn from the CBC's *Venture* and *Marketplace* programs upon which the video cases in the book are based.

- *Digital Image Gallery* consists of figures and exhibits featured in the book.

MyMarketingLab

To instructors and students alike, we are pleased to introduce MyMarketingLab. It combines multimedia tutorials, animations, tests, quizzes, cases, and an eText to make learning fun! MyMarketingLab is flexible: robust enough to administer an online course, useful as a supplement to a lecture course for marks, or helpful for students as a study tool.

ACKNOWLEDGMENTS

We would first like to express our thanks to the U.S. authors of this text, Michael R. Solomon, Greg W. Marshall, and Elnora W. Stuart, for their vision of a marketing text that reflects the activities and priorities of real marketers. Their student-centred approach to the text continues to inspire, and we hope we have maintained their vision in the third Canadian edition.

We would also like to thank the many other people who have made significant contributions to this book. We greatly appreciate the time that each of the "real people" generously spent to help us write the **Real People, Real Decisions** profiles. Without their willingness to be involved, we could not have provided students with the decision-maker focus that is so central to this book.

We would also like to thank the people at Pearson Education Canada who worked so hard on the preparation of the book, especially Don Thompson, Leigh-Anne Graham, Paul Donnelly, Cheryl Jackson, Trish Ciardullo, and Jennifer Stimson.

We are grateful to the following reviewers, instructors, and real marketers who provided valuable feedback during the development of this edition:

Marc Boivin, University of Calgary
Arun Bhardwaj, NAIT
Paul F. Dunne, College of the North Atlantic
Bill Garbarino, Algonquin College
Sara Holding, Malaspina University College
Kerry Jarvis, Seneca College
Gordon D. MacFarlane, Langara College
Judith Nash, SAIT
David Nowell, Sheridan College
Jean-Paul Olivier, Red River College
Ray Rodda, Cambrian College
Deborah Sauer, Capilano College
Mark Valvasori, Mohawk College

Our families also deserve a great deal of appreciation for enduring with us through the writing process and for being understanding in spite of too many evenings and weekends spent working. We thank you all for your patience and support.

Finally, we have had the privilege, through many combined years of teaching, to interact with outstanding students of marketing. Those students have provided much of the inspiration for this book. We wish to thank all of our previous and current students for motivating us to do this book, and for helping us better understand what students need and want in a marketing textbook.

J. Brock Smith, *University of Victoria*
Sylvain Charlebois, *University of Regina*
Marianne Marando, *Seneca College*

MARKETING
REAL PEOPLE
REAL DECISIONS
THIRD CANADIAN EDITION

PART I

Identifying and Specifying Value Opportunities

Marketing. The term conjures up two common misconceptions. Some people will tell you that marketing is all about advertising. Others tend to equate marketing with selling something to someone. As you will learn in this part, marketing is first and foremost a decision-making process—one that is focused on identifying, creating, and delivering value for customers and other stakeholders. At the end of Part I you will also recognize that leading businesses achieve their success not only by creating economic value, but also by creating social and environmental value.

Yellow Point Lodge
...it's about time

about us | history | environment | where we are

About Us

Yellow Point Lodge has been one of Vancouver Island's favorite rustic retreats for over 60 years. The massive log lodge and variety of cabins are surrounded by 165 acres of private, mostly first growth coastal rainforest with over a mile and a half of waterfront facing the Gulf Islands.

Meals are taken communally in the large dining room and are included in your room rate. Three extra 'tea times' with homemade goodies are featured daily as well. The rate also includes full use of our recreational facilities. These feature our 180 foot saltwater swimming pool, two tennis courts surrounded by forest, our cruiser bicycles and practically untippable kayaks.

amenities | local interests | meals | rooms/cabins | friends of yellow point | photos

3700 Yellow Point Road, Ladysmith, BC, Canada V9G 1E8   Phone (250) 245-7422

click here to get the book

Music selection is an excerpt of "Waltz for Sally" from the Simon Kendall CD "Sweet Compulsion". Please visit http://www.simonkendall.com
Click your browser's STOP button to stop the music

Artwork & design by Farm Fresh Design Studio ::::: Hosting by Coexist Design

CHAPTER 1
What Is Marketing?

CHAPTER OBJECTIVES

WHEN YOU HAVE COMPLETED YOUR STUDY OF THIS CHAPTER, YOU SHOULD BE ABLE TO

1. Define the marketing concept.
2. Describe what tools marketers use to create value for customers: the marketing mix.
3. Outline the basics of marketing planning.
4. Explain the New Era orientation of marketing.
5. Explain marketing's role in creating value.

Visit the MyMarketingLab website at **www.pearsoned.ca/mymarketinglab**. This online homework and tutorial system puts you in control of your own learning with study and practice tools directly correlated to this chapter's content.

Real People, Real Decisions

Meet **Richard Hill,** Owner, Operator of Yellow Point Lodge

Richard Hill learned the hospitality business at the knee of a master, his father Gerry Hill, the original "custodian" of Yellow Point Lodge. In the mid-1930s Gerry Hill started the Yellow Point Lodge near Ladysmith, British Columbia, with seven tiny cabins, a small cookhouse, and a dining room. The lodge was built on the north end of 185 acres overlooking a pristine, rocky promontory of land, with a 270-degree view of the Pacific Ocean and some of the Gulf Islands. Richard grew up at Yellow Point but left after high school to pursue a career in rock and roll.

Richard returned to Yellow Point in 1984 to help his father run the Lodge and learn the family business. Richard Hill is now the owner and manager of Yellow Point Lodge and has assumed the mantle of "custodian" of this unique property. In 1990 he married Sandi Bastian, a friend from his teens, and together they are raising their children with the same values with which Richard was raised.

Yellow Point Lodge is a rustic, all-inclusive camp for adults seeking to get away from the city for rest and relaxation. The menu has not changed in 50 years and the customers like it that way. Roast beef on Friday nights, seafood on Saturday, roast turkey on Sundays—and if you don't eat your veggies, you don't get dessert. This isn't a luxury resort; accommodations range from a basic lodge room to cabins that sleep two, four, six, or eight people, to beach-front shacks with bathroom facilities up the hill and outdoor showers designed for reasonable modesty. For the more adventuresome there is a salt water swimming pool, a hot tub, tennis courts, mountain bikes, and kayaks. For those who just want to curl up with a good book there is a large open room with a huge fireplace, lots of overstuffed chairs and couches, and shelves of good books and board games. The concept isn't for everyone, but those who like it, like it a lot.

Situated just 40 minutes south of the BC Ferry terminal at Nanaimo, Yellow Point Lodge is fully booked from May through September, and has good occupancy the rest of the year. At about $100 a night per person, all in, Yellow Point Lodge guests are intensely loyal. Most guests have been coming to Yellow Point for the same week, or part of a week, every year for 20 or more years, with some not having missed a year in over 50. For these guests, Yellow Point is their summer cabin, which Richard just happens to look after the other weeks of the year. Guests are so devoted to what Richard offers that they formed a society, "The Friends of Yellow Point," who organize work parties to help Richard maintain the property to keep his costs down. When the old lodge burned down in October 1985, the Friends of Yellow Point helped Richard, his father, and a professional crew rebuild it.

With soaring property values, Richard's 185 acres are now worth more than 20 million dollars and Richard's tax bill for holding this land has increased substantially. Other cost pressures are also making it difficult to maintain the value proposition so dearly loved by his guests. However, almost all of the guests are long-time guests and a lot of the value they receive from Richard's offering is the memories they have of summers past and the long-standing relationships they have with the other guests, who all go their separate ways, but once a year get together at Yellow Point. These guests don't like change and are quick to let Richard know if something isn't quite right—by which they mean, it isn't like it used to be. In light of this situation, Richard considered four options to generate greater revenue to offset the increasing costs:

Option 1: Raise the price.

One option is to simply raise the prices. With such strong demand for the Yellow Point experience, and fierce loyalty by the long-time guests, Richard thought that he might be able to raise prices by 10 or 15 percent to match the cost increases. This would be a relatively unobtrusive option, as the experience would not change for the guests. The challenge, however, is that most of Richard's guests are middle-class professionals, such as teachers or government employees, and many are retired and on a fixed income. Richard wondered at what price point the Yellow Point experience would be considered too expensive. As soon as some of the regular guests stop coming, the value of those long-standing relationships erodes, and there is less incentive to return. It could become just another place where you don't know anyone. With higher prices, the Lodge might attract a different clientele, but those people might have higher expectations for luxury accommodation that Richard could not easily provide.

Option 2: Increase capacity.

Richard could develop the property by adding more cabins or extending the "main lodge" to accommodate more visitors. Yellow Point Lodge has easy access for visitors. It isn't too far for anyone, whether they fly into Victoria or Nanaimo, or drive. Richard thought that there was sufficient demand for expansion, given that he was almost fully booked for six months of the year, and guests joked that they had put "their" weeks in their wills. However, expansion would erode the value proposition for the current guests who liked knowing each other and liked the feeling that the facility was all theirs. With 200 guests spread around the current facility, there was a feeling of spaciousness and it was quite easy to find a quiet spot to be by yourself.

Option 3: Sell some of the land.

Would-be developers have been pestering Richard for years. He has been sitting on what they would call a "gold mine." The property is prime for development. Other than the lodge and a few cabins, the land has never been touched. Local amenities are close, and the Duncan-to-Nanaimo region of Vancouver Island has seen unprecedented growth from retirees from across Canada and the United States. Other developments in the area have sold 1/3 acre lots for $300 000 or more for waterfront. This option would sacrifice some of the wilderness aspect of the surroundings, but the proceeds would provide a financial foundation to keep intact the integrity of the rest of the property. It would also provide a significant financial base for his family. This wouldn't, however, be in keeping with his father's vision. Gerry Hill loved this land and wanted to protect all of it from such development. Richard also wondered what his customers would think of this, as many were long-time friends of his father.

Option 4: Protect the land and decrease its value.

The forth option Richard looked at was to find a way to decrease his tax obligation while still maintaining the integrity of the resort. Relatively new tax law made the option of protecting some or all of the land with an ecological covenant a viable alternative. A covenant would prevent Richard, or anyone else in the future, from cutting trees (other than for

safety) on the land. The land would be much less valuable with such a covenant placed on it, reducing Richard's tax liability. Richard would still own the land and his guests would have use of the trails, and the old growth forest, part of a rapidly diminishing coastal Douglas fir zone, would be preserved in perpetuity. Richard still wanted to be able to maintain the lodge and his cabins and expand those facilities if appropriate, so he could not put a covenant on all the land. This was a viable option, but it would mean reducing the value of his very valuable land forever. By doing this, Richard would be taking the decision out the hands of his kids. This would make their lives easier, because they wouldn't be forced to decide, and it might keep family relationships intact in case his kids didn't agree on the best course of action. On the other hand, it would be decreasing their financial inheritance.

WELCOME TO A BRANDED WORLD

I have a TV screen of some 32 inches

TV dinner and an easy chair

From where I view a disaster

And switch the channel fast

And thank my lucky star I wasn't there

The world's in a hurry but I don't have to worry

There's a movie on with a happy end

I've seen it before but I can see it some more

So I don't have to go out and pretend

Alex wakes up with a groan as the Hellacopters blare out a song from the next bedroom. Why does her roommate have to download these loud ringtones onto her cellphone and then leave it on so early in the morning? She throws back the Laura Ashley sheets and rolls out of her new Sleep Number mattress that she bought at Sleep Country Canada. As Alex stumbles across the room in her Dalia Cami pyjamas by La Vie en Rose, her senses are further assaulted as she catches a waft of Amanda's trademark Magic by Celine perfume. She pours herself a steaming cup of Starbucks Verona Blend and stirs in a heaping mound of Splenda. As she starts to grab a Yoplait from the SubZero, she checks her BlackBerry and gets reminded of her job interview with lululemon athletica—yeah for Monster.ca! Good thing she IM'd her friends last night to get advice on what to wear. Alex does a quick scan of *The Globe and Mail* Online, then Googles the manager who will be interviewing her. Hopefully he won't look her up on MySpace—some of those photos aren't exactly professional. Alex slips into her Ann Taylor suit, slides on her Prada shoes, grabs her Coach briefcase, and climbs into her Scion. Traffic is a bear—but she doesn't care, she has her iTunes.

Welcome to Branded You

Marketing is all around us. Indeed, some might say we live in a branded world. Like Alex, you have encounters with many marketers even before you leave for the day via products, ads, the web, charitable causes, podcasts, and other ways you receive information or interact with brands.

What's more, like Alex, *you* are a product. That may sound a bit weird, but companies like Monster and Facebook couldn't exist if you were not a product with value. We are going to use that word a LOT in this book, so let's define it now: **Value** refers to the benefits a

value The benefits a customer receives from buying and using a good or service in relation to the costs and sacrifices of buying and using it.

Exhibit 1.1

Marketing concepts apply to the branding of people, like Avril Lavigne, Sid Crosby, and you.

customer receives from buying and using a good or service in relation to the costs and sacrifices of buying and using it.

You have "market value" as a person—you have qualities that set you apart from others and abilities other people want and need. After you finish this course, you'll have even more value because you'll know about the field of marketing and how this field relates to you as a future business person and a consumer. Although our main focus is understanding how to make effective marketing decisions for organizations, what you learn here equally applies to "brand you"—and hopefully you will get some ideas about what you can do to increase your value to employers, partners, and maybe even to society. You probably already knew that celebrities like Sidney Crosby, Mike Meyers, and Avril Lavigne (Exhibit 1.1) are "brands"—but so is everyone else (albeit not quite as effectively). We "position" ourselves for job interviews; we are "on the market" when we break up with a boyfriend or girlfriend; some people hire image consultants to devise a "marketing strategy" for them; while others undergo plastic surgery or makeovers to improve their "product image." So, the principles of marketing apply to you, just as they apply to coffee, cars, computers, and produce. While there are some differences in how we go about marketing each of these, the basic ideas are the same. Marketing is a fundamental part of our lives both as consumers and as business people. We are going to take you behind the scenes so you can learn what goes on before consumers can make their goods and service choices. Before we talk about the "what and how," let's start with the "who and where."

THE WHO AND WHERE OF MARKETING

This book is about marketing, and more specifically about making effective marketing decisions that create value for others. But who makes these decisions? Marketers come from many different places. Although many have earned marketing degrees, others have all sorts of backgrounds, sometimes with formal training and sometimes without. You will see this in the Real People profiles that are featured in each chapter of the text. Fashion retailers may have training in design. Advertising creative executives often have a fine arts background while copywriters often have degrees in English. E-marketers who design interactive webpages for products and companies may have studied computer science. Even accountants often end up in marketing roles, as someone needs to make marketing decisions for accounting firms.

Marketers work in a variety of locations. They work in consumer goods companies such as Mega Bloks or Black & Decker or at service companies like Yellow Point Lodge, Intrawest (Exhibit 1.2), or the Bank of Montreal. You will see them in retail organizations like lululemon athletica

Exhibit 1.2

Marketing is important to service companies like Intrawest, as well as in most contexts you can think of.

or Frontrunners and at companies that manufacture products for other companies like Bombardier or Nortel. You will see them in government organizations like the Canadian Tourism Commission, not-for-profit organizations like the Canadian Cancer Society, large organizations like IBM Canada, and small startups like TeamPages, a website for intramural and other amateur sports teams to coordinate and communicate their activities. Marketing principles are also used to get people to endorse ideas or to change their behaviours in positive ways. Many organizations work hard to convince consumers to use seat belts, engage in safe sex, not litter, not smoke, and not drink and drive. Finally, sports and the arts are hotbeds of activity for marketing. A big part of these efforts involves promoting athletes like Sidney Crosby and artists like Avril Lavigne—who themselves create customer experiences.

No matter where they work, all marketers are real people who make decisions that affect themselves, their companies, and very often thousands if not millions of consumers or customers. At the beginning of each chapter we will introduce you to a marketing professional like Richard Hill, in a feature called "Real People, Real Decisions." We will tell you about a decision the marketer had to make and give you the options she or he considered. Think about these options as you read through the chapter so you can build an argument for selecting one of the options. At the end of the chapter we will tell you what option the decision maker made, and why. It is important to recognize that the decision maker may not have made the most appropriate decision. In fact, there are no "right answers" in business and, ultimately, consumers are the only judges of whether we, as marketers, have made good decisions. What you want to practise is making and defending your decisions based on appropriate analysis, application of marketing theory, concepts, and principles, and your judgment. Do not worry if you think that you might not have good judgment yet. That comes with experience and practice in making marketing decisions. So what decisions do marketers make?

WHAT IS MARKETING?

Marketing. Lots of people talk about it, but what is it? When you ask people to define **marketing**, you get many answers and there are many misconceptions about what marketing is. Some say, "That's what happens when a pushy salesperson tries to sell me something I don't want." Others say, "Oh, that's simple—TV commercials." Others might say "merchandising," "pricing," "packaging," or "telephone soliciting."

As you can see, the term *marketing* means different things to different people (in England, it is even used as a synonym for shopping). Each of these responses has a grain of truth to it, but they are very incomplete. The official definition of marketing adopted in 2004 by the American Marketing Association (which has many Canadian chapters) is:

> Marketing is an organizational function and a set of processes for creating, communicating, and delivering value to customers and for managing customer relationships in ways that benefit the organization and its stakeholders.[1]

marketing An organizational function and a set of processes for creating, communicating, and delivering value to customers and for managing customer relationships in ways that benefit the organization and its stakeholders.

Focus on Value Creation

The basic idea of this somewhat complicated definition of marketing is that marketing is all about creating and delivering value, and doing this for all parties involved in an exchange. It involves a decision-making process, and these decisions are typically (but not always) made by people who have official marketing roles in areas of an organization such as a marketing department, a sales department, a marketing communications department, or a new product development department.

Another definition of *marketing* is:

> Marketing is the process of achieving individual and organizational objectives by creating superior customer value for one or more target markets with a sustainable strategy.

Exhibit 1.3

Pepsi-Cola hopes that the product, price, distribution, and communication decisions it makes for Aquafina result in a value proposition preferred by customers.

customer value What the customer gets in the purchase, use, and ownership of a product relative to the costs and sacrifices incurred.

This definition suggests that "the prime directive" of marketing is to achieve objectives. We do that by creating superior customer value—creating offers that are perceived as being more valuable to customers than any other solutions (competing brands), or even more valuable than the money in their wallet. **Customer value** is what you get from buying and using a product relative to the costs and sacrifices you incur to do so. To create a transaction or an economic exchange of value, both parties need to believe that the exchange is fair—that what they get is worth more to them than what they give up. Of course each of us has our own perceptions of how to best satisfy our needs, what is valuable, and what exchanges are "worth it." One enterprising entrepreneur in England recently offered deluxe 61-step car washes for $10 000. Enough customers thought the two-week process was worth it that he has nine months' worth of business lined up.[2] The challenge to the marketer is to create, price, distribute, and communicate an attractive value proposition to the customer to get the most value in return (Exhibit 1.3).

This alternative definition also focuses on the idea of creating value for specific target markets, groups of people that have different needs, wants, or preferences from other groups of people and would seek a different value proposition (solution). Not everyone would want a $10 000 car wash, but apparently some people (sheiks and billionaires) do. This definition also suggests that we want to develop a sustainable strategy, not in the environmental sense (although as we will see later in this chapter, it often makes good business sense to make decisions that are good for the environment), but in the sense of making a set of decisions that will allow us to compete effectively until our objectives have been achieved—which for most organizations is a long-term perspective.

Marketing Is About Creating Customer Value

One important part of our definition of marketing is that it is about creating value for diverse stakeholders. The term **stakeholders** here refers to buyers, sellers, investors in a company, community residents, and even citizens of the nations where goods and services are made or sold—in other words, any person or organization that has a "stake" in the outcome of an economic **exchange**.

One important stakeholder is the consumer. A **consumer** is the ultimate user of a good or service. Consumers can be individuals or organizations (although we usually use the term "customer" when referring to an organization), whether a company, government, charity, or association. So while some like to say "the customer is king" (or queen), it's important to recognize that marketing is not just about satisfying customer needs, it is about satisfying the needs of all the parties involved in an exchange. The seller needs to make a profit to stay in business to be able to continue offering the goods and services valued by the customer. Similarly, a not-for-profit organization needs to match its supply of resources with customer demand. This is the philosophy behind the **marketing concept**. The marketing concept suggests that organizational objectives such as long-term profitability are best met by first understanding what customers need (value sought) and then determining the associated costs of satisfying those needs (creating and delivering that value)—thus creating exchanges of mutual satisfaction. Central to the philosophy reflected in the marketing concept is an understanding that organizations exist to create value for consumers where it is neither efficient nor effective for consumers to attempt to satisfy their needs themselves.[3]

A **need** is the difference between a consumer's actual state and some ideal or desired state. When the difference is big enough, the consumer is motivated to take action to satisfy the need. When you are hungry, you buy a snack. If you're not happy with your hair, you get a new look. As we will see in Chapter 5, needs are related to physical conditions, such as being cold, hungry, or scared, and psychological conditions such as being liked, communicating with others, or being fulfilled. The specific way a need is satisfied depends on an individual's history, learning experiences, and cultural environment. A **want** is a desire for a particular product used to satisfy a need in specific ways that are culturally and socially influenced. For example, two classmates' stomachs rumble during a noon-hour class, and both need food. How each of them satisfies this need may be quite different. One might crave a salad or a bag of trail mix to go. The other might buy a cheeseburger and fries. Or the want may be even more specific. I want Mountain Country Yogurt Trail Mix (Exhibit 1.4) or a McDonald's cheeseburger. Consumers are motivated by needs, but make purchase decisions based on wants.

A product delivers a **benefit** when it satisfies a need or want. For marketers to be successful, they must develop products that provide one or more benefits. The challenge is to identify what benefits people look for, develop a product that delivers those benefits, and then convince buyers that it does so better than a competitor's product. As the management expert Peter Drucker wrote, "The aim of marketing is to make selling superfluous."[4] What Drucker means is if we succeed in creating a product that meets the needs of the customer, he or she will happily buy it without any "persuasion" from a salesperson. The salesperson may still be required to make the customer aware of the product and its relative merits in meeting the customer's needs. Customers care most about benefits—what's in it for them—and typically less about the particular features or functions that deliver those benefits. You buy a cordless drill because you care about the ease of making holes (the benefit). You may buy a particular brand of cordless drill because of differences in particular features that enable some drills to deliver the core benefit better than others.

Everyone can want your product, but that doesn't ensure sales unless they have the means to obtain it. When you couple desire with the buying power or resources to satisfy

stakeholder People or organizations who influence or are influenced by marketing decisions.

exchange The process by which some transfer of value occurs between a buyer and a seller.

consumer The ultimate user of a good or service.

marketing concept A business orientation that focuses on achieving organizational objectives by understanding customer needs, and creating and delivering value in exchanges that satisfy the needs of all parties.

need The recognition of any difference between a consumer's actual state and some ideal or desired state.

want The desire to satisfy needs in specific ways that are culturally and socially influenced.

benefit The outcome sought by a customer that motivates buying behaviour (that satisfies a need or want).

Exhibit 1.4

Consumers with the same need may have very different wants.

demand Customers' desire for products coupled with the resources to obtain them.

a want, the result is **demand**. So, the potential customers for a snappy, red BMW convertible are the people who want the car minus those who can't afford to buy or lease one. A market consists of all the consumers who share a common need that can be satisfied by a product purchase and who have the resources, willingness, and authority to make the purchase.

marketplace Any location or medium used to conduct an exchange.

A **marketplace** used to be a location where buying and selling occurred face to face. The marketplace may still be a street corner or an open air market, but in today's "wired" world, buyers and sellers might not ever see each other. Increasingly the modern marketplace takes the form of a glitzy shopping mall, a mail-order catalogue, a television shopping network, an eBay auction site, or an e-commerce website. Indeed, a marketplace may not even exist in the physical world. Residents of cyberworlds like the Sims, Second Life (Exhibit 1.5), and Project Entropia buy and sell virtual real estate or character profiles—with real money. One Project Entropia player recently paid $100 000 (in real U.S. dollars) for a space resort he calls Club Neverdie. He plans to develop the station's facilities and sell condos for game dollars, which the project's developer converts into real dollars at a 10:1 exchange rate.[5]

Successful firms realize that the basic marketing concept applies to all aspects of the firm's activities. As a result, there has been a trend toward integrating marketing with other business functions instead of setting it apart as a separate function. In such organizations, marketing managers work with financial and accounting officers to figure out whether products are profitable, to set marketing budgets, and to determine prices. They work with people in manufacturing to be sure that products are produced on time, in the right quantities, and to quality specifications. Stratos Product Development, a Seattle industrial design

Exhibit 1.5

Some transactions today, like those of the online game Second Life, are virtual exchanges.

firm, uses cross-functional teams (people with different educational backgrounds) to create products that offer more value. When it set about developing a passenger video player for British Airways, Stratos (**www.stratos.com**) brought together mechanical specialists, customers, and British Airways personnel in brainstorming sessions, where everyone could propose new ideas. The system came together in four months, one-third of the time estimated for the project.[6]

Marketing Is About Exchange Relationships

At the heart of every marketing act—big or small—is something we refer to as an "exchange relationship." An exchange occurs when something is obtained for something else in return. The buyer receives an object, service, or idea that satisfies a need and the seller receives something he or she believes is of equivalent economic value. Usually this is money, but it could be other goods or services. Almost anything of value can be exchanged—including, if you remember the beginning of the chapter, you! (your time, your ideas, and the things you can do). Politicians exchange promises for votes, athletes and performers exchange performances for ticket sales and exchange their images via endorsements in exchange for product sales. Places like Canada's Wonderland or Prince Edward Island exchange experiences for customers' time and money. Not-for-profit organizations like Covenant House (Exhibit 1.6) exchange services for the time of their clients and exchange the concept of making a difference to the problem of homelessness for the money of their donators.

For an exchange to occur, at least two people or organizations must be willing to make a trade, and each must have something the other wants. Both parties must agree on the value of the exchange and how it will be carried out. Each party also must be free to accept or reject the other's terms for the exchange. Under these conditions, a gun-wielding robber's offer to "exchange" your money for your life does not constitute a valid economic exchange.

To complicate things a bit more, everyone does not always agree on the terms of the exchange. Consider, for example, music piracy, which is a huge headache for music producers. On the one hand, they claim that they lose billions of dollars a year when consumers download songs without paying for them. On the other hand, a lot of people think the producers charge way too much for new songs, and consider downloading a socially valid (albeit illegal) act.

All of these exchanges involve marketing decisions to create the value being exchanged, communicate the value proposition, and facilitate the exchange relationship. Let's look at these decisions in more detail.

THIS CHRISTMAS, HELP GIVE STREET KIDS A HOME.

COVENANT HOUSE covenanthouse.ca

Exhibit 1.6

Not-for-profit organizations like Covenant House exchange services for time, and the concept of making a difference for the money of donators.

MARKETING AS A DECISION-MAKING PROCESS

The American Marketing Association definition of marketing suggests that marketing is primarily a decision-making *process* that allows individuals and organizations to achieve objectives by creating value that satisfies stakeholder needs and wants. As such, marketing decision making involves a series of steps that entail both careful thought (planning) and action (executing). When it's done right, marketing is a strategic decision-making process in which marketing managers determine the most appropriate set of decisions for a particular

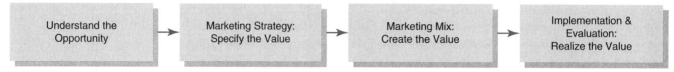

Figure 1.1 The Marketing Decision Process

organization at a particular time that will help the organization meet its long-term objectives. This decision-making process is summarized in Figure 1.1.

Understand the Opportunity

Marketing decisions start with understanding the situation, or context, in which the decisions need to be made. As depicted in Figure 1.2, and explored more fully in Chapter 2, situational analysis involves identifying opportunities to create value for the organization by creating value for customers. This first involves understanding factors relating to the markets in which an organization competes, such as understanding general trends in that market, consumer or organizational buying behaviour, industry dynamics, and the strategies and likely reactions of competitors. Then marketing decision makers need to assess factors relating to their own organization and their ability to create value and compete effectively in those markets. These internal factors include understanding the relative effectiveness of their current marketing strategy, their resources, competencies, and expertise, and the values or mission of the organization. The decision context is better understood by the application of marketing theory, concepts, and principles—which you will learn about in this text.

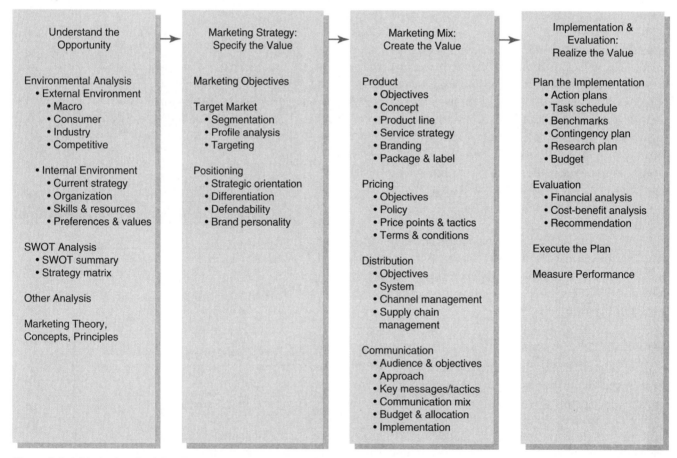

Figure 1.2 A Marketing Decision Framework

Specify the Value: Marketing Strategy

As will be discussed in more detail in Chapter 2, marketers make marketing strategy decisions to achieve the objectives of their organization, which usually include both financial objectives (such as a particular profit target) and marketing objectives (such as sales targets or market share targets). Once the marketing and other objectives are developed, the organization develops a marketing strategy aimed at achieving those objectives.

SEGMENTATION The most critical decision marketers make in developing marketing strategy is the selection of the specific group of customers on which they will focus their customer value creation efforts. A **market segment** is a distinct group of customers within a larger market who have similar needs, wants, preferences, and behaviours, who seek similar product solutions, and whose needs differ from other customers in the larger market. Parents with young children, for example, typically seek different entertainment products than teenagers and young adults.

As will be discussed in more detail in Chapter 3, **market segmentation** is a process of dividing the overall market into groups of consumers who are sufficiently similar within the group to want a similar value offer and different enough from other groups to want a different value offer than those other groups. The challenge is to identify groups with real differences in underlying needs, wants, preferences, behaviours, and opinions about value. Consequently, detailed **segment profiles** of each group must be developed that specify these differences and other characteristics of the groups that will help marketers design and present a valued offer. One way that Levi Strauss slices up the market is in terms of age segments—this makes sense, since different age groups have different clothing wants and may wear jeans for different purposes. Business-to-business markets are sometimes divided into segments using characteristics such as type of business, decision-making criteria, size, or sales volume, if these characteristics reflect differences in the needs, wants, or behaviours of organizations.

TARGETING Marketers weigh each of the segments in terms of profitability potential against a number of factors, including the organization's ability to create value and satisfy the needs of the segments, their goals and resources, and their ability to compete effectively against other offerings. On the basis of this analysis, the organization decides whether it will focus on a single segment or on several segments. The chosen market segment(s) become the organization's **target market(s)** toward which it directs its marketing efforts. For example, Hewitt (see Exhibit 1.7) is an outsourcing company that has decided to focus exclusively on the needs of the human resources (HR) professional. As the ad for Hewitt illustrates, it offers tailored solutions in HR areas such as talent, benefits, payroll, health care, and retirement.

Because different target markets have different and sometimes conflicting needs, wants, and preferences, marketers typically have to choose among alternative segments on which to focus. This is one of Richard Hill's dilemmas at Yellow Point Lodge—how to attract new consumers without turning off long-loyal consumers at the same time. Similarly, Canadian fashion

market segment A distinct group of customers within a larger market who have similar needs, wants, preferences, and behaviours, who seek similar product solutions, and whose needs differ from other customers in the larger market.

market segmentation A process of dividing the overall market into groups of consumers who are sufficiently similar within the group to want a similar value offer and different enough from other groups to want a different value offer than those other groups.

segment profiles Detailed descriptions of the characteristics, behaviours, and thinking of a market segment that help marketers design and present a valued offer.

target market(s) The market segment(s) on which an organization focuses its marketing plan and toward which it directs its marketing efforts.

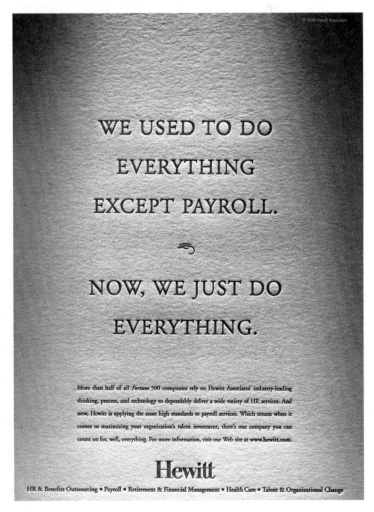

Exhibit 1.7

Hewitt targets HR professionals.

designer Linda Lundström (and her company, Linda Lundström Ltd.) doesn't make clothes for everyone. First, she designs clothing only for women. Lundström further narrows her market by focusing on the needs of women with less-than-perfect figures. She also gears her line toward working women who need clothes that can wear and travel well. Her most successful item is an extremely warm winter coat that combines comfort and function with a style based on First Nations artist Norval Morrisseau's traditional patterns.

mass market All possible customers in a market, regardless of the differences in their specific needs and wants.

Some firms choose to reach as many customers as possible by offering their products to a **mass market**, which consists of all possible customers in a market, regardless of the differences in their specific needs and wants. This strategy, however, is not tenable in the long run. Usually competitors of mass marketers, or even the mass marketers themselves, bring alternative products to market that have greater appeal to a subset of the people in the mass market, eroding the market share of the mass market product.

Many companies know that they must look for potential target markets beyond their own geographical borders to compete in today's world economy. Modern marketers are busy meeting the needs of people all around the world, especially when the demand for products at home flattens. Expanding internationally is desirable, for example, to the Mattel Corporation (**www.mattel.com**). The average North American girl owns eight Barbies, making it the best-selling toy ever. The domestic market is starting to become saturated, so Mattel is diversifying to offset the company's reliance on North American Barbie sales (Exhibit 1.8). Europe has nearly twice as many children as North America; and numbers in Mexico, South America, Japan, and Southeast Asia are even greater. Mattel now manufactures 75 percent of its toys in plants around the world, including Indonesia, Malaysia, China, Mexico, and Italy.[7]

One trend for multinational companies is to focus on selling products to developing countries, a trend some refer to as B2–4B ("business to four billion"), which refers to the approximate number of potential customers in these markets. Hewlett Packard (HP), for example, believes that much of the firm's future growth could come from developing countries. The company has begun to implement a plan to sell, lease, or donate US$1 billion in goods and services to governments, development agencies, and not-for-profit groups in these areas. In fact, to satisfy the needs of this market, HP is developing low-power or solar-powered

Exhibit 1.8

Mattel is exporting the Barbie craze to consumers around the world.

devices that will connect to the net wirelessly or via satellites. But Hewlett Packard's Third World efforts are not just philanthropic. It believes that this kind of investment will allow HP to tap into the huge potential markets that will develop in these countries.[8]

Throughout the text we will emphasize marketers' need to think globally—even if they only act locally. Smart marketers know that whether in Third World countries or developed countries, long-term success means finding customers wherever they are, from Montreal to Manila.

POSITIONING THE OFFERING After choosing the target market(s), marketers need to develop an offering that appeals to the needs, wants, and preferences of that target market better than alternatives provided by competitors. This process starts with positioning the product. **Positioning** involves developing a marketing strategy to differentiate an offering from others in the marketplace in the minds of the target customers. It establishes how the marketing organization wants its brand to be known—

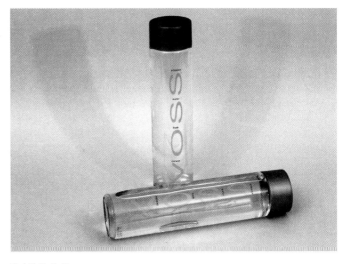

Exhibit 1.9
Brand personality is what allows Voss to sell a half-litre bottle of water for as much as $22.

what value it offers relative to competitors and why that offer is superior to others for a particular target market. Positioning also involves developing strategy to defend the image that has or will be created and specifying the unique competencies, resources, or know-how that allows a firm to sustain its superiority. The positioning of a brand often involves developing a brand personality. For example, in Norway, VOSS Water (**www.vosswater.com**) has developed a personality of sophistication (Exhibit 1.9). Its water comes from a "virgin aquifer that has been shielded for centuries under ice and rock in the untouched wilderness of Central Norway." At prices ranging up to $22.00 for a 0.5 L bottle, customers are putting a significant premium on that personality![9]

positioning Strategies to establish the unique value proposition of an offering and sustain its superiority in the eyes of target customers.

Create the Value: Marketing Mix Decisions

Once the desired positioning is established, marketers need to create the value proposition reflected in the offer. To do this, marketers make a set of decisions about the product itself, its price, the place it is available for purchase, and the activities that introduce it to consumers. These decisions, collectively called the **marketing mix** decisions, create the value promised by the product positioning and are intended to be sufficiently motivating (valuable) to create a desired exchange response among members of the target market. Just as every college student seems to have an iPod, every government official seems to have a BlackBerry. The marketing mix decisions made by Apple and RIM created a value proposition so motivating that they have had trouble keeping up with demand.

The marketing mix decisions are commonly known as *the four Ps*: product, price, promotion (communication), and place (distribution). Together, the bundle of marketing mix elements represents an offer of value to the consumer: what the customer will receive in an exchange. Sometimes marketers consider a fifth P, "people" or relationships. Others, including the authors of this book, view managing exchange relationships as being so central to what marketers do that it should be integrated into all the other marketing decisions and not treated as a separate decision.

Just as a radio DJ puts together a collection of separate songs (a musical mix) to create a certain mood, the idea of a mix in this context reminds us that no *single* marketing activity is sufficient to accomplish the organization's objectives, and that consistency among the decisions is critical to the overall marketing (or music) program. We will examine these components of the marketing mix in detail later in this book. For now, let's briefly look at each element of the marketing mix to gain some insight into its meaning and role in creating value.

marketing mix A combination of the product itself, the price of the product, the place where it is made available, and the activities that introduce it to consumers, which creates a desired response among a set of predefined consumers.

SPOTLIGHT ON REAL PEOPLE TrueCareers

People are "products" that need to be marketed, and that's especially true in the job market. After watching the hassles their friends experienced while searching for entry-level jobs after graduating, 21-year-old undergraduates Rachel Bell and Sara Sutton had an idea. They believed that the Internet was the answer to matching up student job seekers with employers. For many, blanketing companies with letters and making hours of unproductive phone calls to surly company receptionists were a real dead end. So, Bell and Sutton put their last year of school on hold, swallowed hard, and started JobDirect (now called TrueCareers, **www.truecareers. com**), an Internet-based service that is now the largest database of entry-level student jobs on the web.

The service is free to students, but companies—including IBM, Xerox, and Lotus—pay a fee to access the résumé database. These clients can search for résumés fitting specific criteria, such as students who speak French and have at least a B average.

Although all the jobs in the TrueCareers database are currently located in the United States, students from Canada and other countries around the world are able to use the database free of charge, providing they are willing and able to accept a job in the United States.

The largest Canadian site for job postings and career information is Workopolis.com, a joint venture between *The Globe and Mail* and Torstar Corporation (**www.workopolis. com**). However, Monster.ca is challenging Workopolis.com for Canadian market supremacy. Other sites include CACEE WorkWeb (**www.cacee.com**) and the Canadian government site for Human Resources and Social Development Canada (**www.hrsdc.gc.ca**).

1. What is TrueCareers' market?
2. What benefits does a service such as TrueCareers provide to these customers?
3. How does this chapter's concept of "people marketing" fit in with what TrueCareers does?
4. Compare the Workopolis.com and Monster.ca websites. What is the positioning of each site? How could each be improved to meet the needs of its target market?

product A tangible good, a service, an idea, or some combination of these that, through the exchange process, satisfies consumer or business customer needs; a bundle of attributes including features, functions, benefits, and uses.

PRODUCT The **product** is a good, service, idea, place, person—whatever is offered for exchange. Notice, therefore, that the concept of product as defined in marketing is broader than its usage in everyday language, where it primarily signifies a tangible good. Product strategy decisions begin with objectives: What do you want to achieve with your product decision? For example, Procter & Gamble (P&G) wanted to expand its market share internationally but found that many consumers could not afford its traditional brands. This prompted P&G to develop new products, such as Pampers Uni diapers, that are tailored to meet the needs of international customers, such as those in Brazil, but have a significantly lower cost structure.[10] Then you need to specify the *product concept*. What is the core value (benefits) you are offering, and how do you deliver that value through the features, functions, design, and other attributes of the product? Marketers also make *product line* decisions about how many variants or versions (models, types, sizes, colours, shapes, flavours) of a product they will offer. Honda, for example, chooses to compete with just a few models of cars, while General Motors has more than 100. *Service strategy* decisions also need to be made: What services will be provided, and what experiences offered? For service companies, like Disneyland or Walt Disney World, the strategy to create the desired customer experience is central to what they do, but even packaged goods like cereal or consumer goods like a notebook computer can have important service aspects. Dell, for example, offers free delivery, online and phone-based technical support, and a range of options for getting your computer fixed if there is a problem, including in-home repair. Product decisions also include *branding strategy*: Will a product be part of a family of products like Campbell's soups, an individual brand like BlackBerry (Exhibit 1.10), a store brand like President's Choice, or just be named for the product category, like "Spaghetti"? Finally, product decisions include packaging and labelling decisions. Be honest, how many times have you bought something because the package looked good?

PRICE The **price** is the seller's assessment of the value of a product; what they would like to receive from the buyer in exchange for the product. Pricing strategy decisions start with *pricing objectives*: What do you want to accomplish with your pricing decisions? Are you trying to support a premium position like Gucci, a competitive position like Zellers or Wal-Mart (lower prices), or are you trying to increase market share, like Procter & Gamble in Brazil? Different pricing objectives suggest different *pricing policies*. P&G used to determine its prices based on what a product actually cost to develop plus a profit, but now it prices products by what consumers in different countries can afford. Wal-Mart uses Every Day Low Prices as a policy. Marketers also have to come up with the actual price. *Price point* decisions need to take into consideration the cost of creating and delivering the product, competitors' prices, and what the customer is willing to pay, among other factors. There are also psychological considerations. Should the price of Croc shoes be $39.99, $37.54, or $40.00? Finally marketers need to decide on pricing terms and conditions: When does the price need to be paid, how can it be paid, are there any special deals or discounts?

DISTRIBUTION **Place** concerns the availability of the product to the customer at the desired time and location. *Channels of distribution* involve firms that work together to get a product from a producer to a consumer. For consumer goods like Roots clothing products, a distribution channel includes retailers such as Sears as well as their own Roots retail outlets and the Roots website. Distribution decisions begin with specifying the distribution objectives: Are you trying to make the product as widely available as possible, minimize the cost of getting the product to the customer, or make it easy for customers to compare your product with others—such as with an Auto Mall? To achieve one or another of these distribution objectives, marketers decide on a distribution system: What type of distribution system will be created, how many and what types of channel partners will be involved, and will it be a traditional approach or a non-traditional one? Channel relationship management decisions also need to be made: How will you identify, attract, motivate, and keep your channel partners working toward your common goals and how will you deal with the conflict that is inherent between the roles of channel members? Finally, *supply chain management* involves systems and processes to ensure efficient and effective value creation, from the sourcing of raw materials to the customer receiving the value. This includes *logistics*, the physical distribution of goods to the customer, or a *service blueprint* for delivering a service experience.

Exhibit 1.10

The name of a brand, like RIM's BlackBerry, is one of the product decisions marketers must make.

COMMUNICATION **Promotion** refers to the marketing communication activities undertaken to inform consumers or organizations about goods, services, or ideas, and to encourage potential customers to buy these goods, services, or ideas. Unlike the other marketing mix decisions, communication strategy decisions start with deciding the *audience*, or target of the communication, not the *communication objective*. The audience is a specific subset of a target market whose members are the receivers of the communication. A communication campaign usually has many different elements targeted at different audiences, but we design the strategy for each audience. For each audience we need to decide the communication objectives: What do you want to achieve with your communication decisions? Is the objective to create awareness about your product, develop purchase intentions, encourage trial of the

price The seller's assignment of value to a product.

place The availability of the product to the customer at the desired time and location. Also known as channels of distribution.

promotion The coordination of communication efforts by a marketer to influence consumers or organizations about goods, services, or ideas.

product, or develop trust with your customers? To achieve these or other communications objectives, marketers need to decide on an overall *approach* to the communication strategy: Will it be a push strategy where retailers are encouraged to stock products that customers can find or a pull strategy where customers are encouraged to seek products from retailers or other channel members? Will it be one-way communication or will you seek feedback from customers and try to develop a relationship with them? Once the overall approach is decided, we need to decide the *key messages*; what we want to communicate to our audience; and the *tactics* we will use to get their attention. Then we decide on the appropriate communications mix to get our message(s) to our audience: Should we develop advertising for television, radio, or print publications; create promotions like Tim Hortons' "Roll Up the Rim to Win" contest; use public relations as Raincoast Books used to gain free publicity around Harry Potter book launches; communicate using a sales force; create a website; or use viral marketing techniques such as developing entertaining video clips that customers can send their friends? We also need to decide on a *creative strategy* that will get the attention of our audience, *schedule* the timing and placement of any advertising that is used, determine a *budget* to do all this, and develop a way to *evaluate* whether our communication strategy has been effective.

For example, Mike's Hard Lemonade Company's communication strategy supports the brand image by developing and supporting the "personalities" of Mike and the lemonade. Cute stories about Mike and lemons were included on the packaging, and the product was brought to consumers' attention with print advertising, in-store displays, and on-shelf signage. After Mike's initial success, television advertising was created that showed "lemons being hurt real bad in the making of this product" and investigators trying to determine "who has been hurting the lemons." These quirky, light-hearted ads helped make Mike's the leading brand in the Canadian cooler market (Exhibit 1.11). There is also a hip Internet site (**www.mikeshardlemonade.com**) that further supports the brand's personality.

Exhibit 1.11

Mike's Hard Lemonade uses humour to support the personality of the brand.

So, this discussion and Figure 1.2 suggest that there are lots of decisions that marketers make for creating, communicating, and delivering value to customers and for managing customer relationships in ways that benefit the organization and its stakeholders. Once made, these decision need to be acted upon.

Implementation and Evaluation: Realize the Value

Before we can evaluate the relative merits of our proposed marketing decisions we need to plan for their implementation, such as identifying the key *actions* that need to be done, assigning *tasks* to people to do them, and developing a schedule of when they need to be completed. Implementation decisions also involve developing performance *benchmarks* (targets) to help us assess if our strategy is working and a *contingency* plan that outlines what we will do if things do not go as planned. Finally, we need to identify the key assumptions that we have made in developing our plan and outline how we will use *market research* to test those assumptions and ensure we are making informed decisions. We also need to specify and allocate a *budget* to make all this happen.

After planning the implementation, we then need to decide whether or not to proceed. This overall recommendation is based on an assessment of whether implementing the strategy is worth it from the organization's perspective (value to the organization). To make this decision we need to do *financial analysis* and *cost-benefit analysis*, which you will learn more about in Chapter 2. This decision is usually made in contrast to other viable alternatives, to ensure that the best strategy is being considered. The alternatives typically come from different choice of target markets, different positioning, or different ways of creating value via the marketing mix. It may seem like a lot of wasted work to end up not recommending implementation—but you can't make an informed decision without first specifying the best strategy you can think of.

If you decide to implement the strategy, the next step is *execution*—getting it done and then *measuring* performance against the plan. Throughout this text we will show you examples of measures, or "metrics," that marketers use to assess their performance.

In our final chapter, we will show you how this marketing decision process comes together in the creation of a formal *marketing plan*. Marketing planning is a process of identifying and analyzing alternative ways of competing in the marketplace. To see how much thinking and analysis goes into marketing decisions, consider some of the many factors a firm like Levi Strauss has to think about when planning and developing its marketing strategy:

- What jeans styles will our core customers of young people be looking for in three to five years?

- What are our competitors doing to attract and keep our customers? How are we positioned competitively in the mind of the consumer?

- Which customer groups that don't currently buy a lot of blue jeans might we target for Levi's products?

- How will new developments in computerized production technologies affect the denim manufacturing process?

- Will the current trend for many companies to institute "Casual Fridays," when employees can wear jeans to work, affect long-term demand for Levi's products?

- What will be the impact on our brand's image if we decide to sell our jeans through discount stores such as Wal-Mart?

- Is television advertising (an expensive marketing communications tool) the right way to communicate with our target market, or is there a better way?

- How will consumers' growing awareness about the use of child labour in Third World countries affect their attitudes toward manufacturers that locate plants overseas?

We will show you an example of a marketing plan in the appendix at the back of the book, but for now, you should recognize that the content of a marketing plan typically follows the outline of Figure 1.2 and answers the questions implicit in that Figure. This text is also organized around the decisions implicit in the Figure and the factors that are considered in making those decisions. Chapter 2 focuses on the environment of marketing decisions and introduces you to *SWOT analysis*, a useful tool for understanding the strategic implications of factors in the internal and external environment. Chapter 3 focuses on how to make target market and positioning decisions. Chapter 4 gives you an introduction to the research marketers do to make informed decisions. Chapters 5 and 6 examine key consumer and organizational buying behaviour concepts that help us develop better market segment profiles. Chapters 7 through 13 focus on the marketing mix decisions summarized in Figure 1.2. Finally, Chapter 14 pulls it all together and shows you how all the marketing decisions must support each other in the writing of a marketing plan and how the tools, concepts, and principles discussed throughout the text can be used to provide rationale for a particular course of action.

NEW ERA MARKETING: MAKE MONEY *AND* ACT ETHICALLY

social marketing concept A marketing philosophy that emphasizes that customer needs must be satisfied in ways that also benefit society.

The marketing concept talks about satisfying both consumer and organizational objectives. Many forward-thinking organizations have begun to see their commitment to value even more intensely than "just" satisfying consumers' needs during a single transaction. Instead, they have adopted a New Era orientation that focuses on developing long-term relationships with customers and adopting the **social marketing concept**, which emphasizes that customer needs must be satisfied in ways that also benefit society.

Customer Relationship Management

As will be discussed further in Chapters 5 and 6, customer relationship management (CRM) involves systematically tracking consumers' preferences and behaviours over time to tailor the value proposition as closely as possible to each individual's unique wants and needs. With the advent of the Internet, a CRM approach got a lot easier to implement and more and more firms started to rely heavily on the web to connect with customers. The Internet provides the ultimate opportunity for implementation of the marketing concept because it allows a firm to personalize its messages and products to better meet the needs of each customer.

Although dot-com companies took a beating in the marketplace, many analysts believe that this is just a preliminary shakeout—the heyday of the Internet is yet to come. More recent success stories like Google, MySpace, and Flickr seem to be proving analysts right. Indeed, some marketing analysts suggest that the Internet has created a *paradigm shift* for business, meaning that companies must adhere to a new model or pattern of how to profit in a wired world. They argue that we are moving toward an *attention economy*, one in which a company's success will be measured by its share of mind rather than share of market. This means that companies must find new and innovative ways to stand out from the crowd and become an integral part of consumers' lives rather than just being a company that makes and sells products. For example, major consumer packaged goods companies are drawing many more customers to their websites than in the past by making them "sticky"—interesting enough to keep consumers' attention and motivate them to return (Exhibit 1.12). They do this by offering games, contests, and other promotions that transform their websites into less of a store and more of a carnival. For example, the Wrigley company's Candystand.com site invites visitors to play games like Nut Vendor, where the player assumes the role of a ballpark peanut hawker. Candystand (**www.candystand.com**), like other sites, gathers customers' e-mail addresses (by permission) as they register for sweepstakes, then lures them back with offers of new recipes, games, and products.[11] This is also true of service organizations. For example, Maximum Vegas (**www.mgmgrand.com**), an interactive

Exhibit 1.12

Companies like Moosehead use "sticky" web content to keep customers on their sites longer and motivate returns to the site.

website for the MGM Grand Hotel and Casino in Las Vegas, was designed by Canadian agency Diesel in Montreal. This website was a Best of Show winner at the Digital Marketing Awards, and offers a stunningly rich media experience that lets visitors tour the hotel and experience the sights and sounds as if they were really there.

Social Marketing Concept

Large and small firms alike have adopted the practice of making decisions that benefit consumers, organizational stakeholders, and society as a whole. These efforts include satisfying society's environmental and social needs for a cleaner, safer environment by developing recyclable packaging; adding extra safety features like side-impact car air bags; voluntarily modifying a manufacturing process to reduce pollution; and sponsoring campaigns to address social problems. For example, McCain Foods Ltd., one of the world's largest makers of frozen french fries, refuses to process genetically altered potatoes.[12] Mountain Equipment Co-op (MEC) will source products only from countries that aspire to fair labour practices (Exhibit 1.13). MEC strives to sell as many Canadian-made products as possible, even reducing margins to a certain point.

An important trend right now is for companies to think of ways to design and manufacture products with a focus on environmental sustainability, which we can define as "meeting present needs without compromising the ability of future generations to meet their needs."[13] One of Mountain Equipment Co-op's brand pillars is their commitment to reducing their ecological footprint and improving the human conditions of factory workers, as is illustrated in Exhibit 1.13.

Exhibit 1.13

Mountain Equipment Co-op has adopted the social marketing concept by their commitment to reducing their ecological footprint and improving the human conditions of factory workers.

MEC has also joined 1% For The Planet, a group of businesses committed to donating 1 percent of gross sales to support environmental initiatives. Many new construction projects, including Dockside Green in Victoria (**www.docksidegreen.com**), for example, have been designed and are using materials consistent with LEED™ Platinum Standards to try to minimize the environmental impact of building construction.

Focus on Accountability

triple bottom line A business perspective that measures economic, social, and environmental value creation.

In addition to building long-term relationships and focusing on social responsibility, New Era firms place a much greater focus on *accountability*—measuring just how much value is created by marketing activities. This means that marketers at New Era firms ask hard questions about the true value of their efforts and their impact on the bottom line. Many of these organizations adopt a "**triple bottom line**" perspective that measures economic value creation (such as return on investment), social value creation, and environmental value creation.

However, assessing the value of marketing activities is not always easy. Many times marketing objectives are stated in vague phrases like "increase awareness of the product" or "encourage people to eat healthier snacks." These goals are important, but they are not specific enough to be measured. New Era marketers do their best to prove to management that they are generating measurable value by aligning marketing activities with the firm's overall objectives.[14] Throughout the text we will discuss how marketers try to measure the value they are creating. One way they do this is through scorecards—which report, in quantified terms, how the company or a brand is doing in achieving its various goals. Scorecards like the one shown in the Marketing Metrics box tend to be short and to the point, and they often use charts and graphs to summarize the information in an easy-to-read format. They might report "grades" on factors such as actual cost per sale, a comparison of website hits (the number of people who view a website), customers' satisfaction with a company's repair facilities, or even the percentage of customers who respond to direct mail pieces. New Era marketers typically adopt a *balanced scorecard* approach which, consistent with triple-bottom-line thinking, includes a variety of measures that capture economic, social, and environmental value creation.

Other Perspectives

Not all organizations have adopted a New Era orientation. Organizations that focus on the most efficient production and distribution of products, and not whether these products best

Marketing Metrics

An Example of a Customer Service Scorecard[15]

Item Text	Quarterly Scores		
	1st Qtr.	2nd Qtr.	3rd Qtr.
Satisfaction with			
C1 Employee responsiveness	60%	65%	68%
C2 Product selection	60%	62%	63%
C3 Service quality	60%	62%	55%
C4 Cleanliness of facility	75%	80%	85%
C5 Knowledge of employees	62%	62%	58%
C6 Appearance of employees	60%	62%	63%
C7 Convenience of location	60%	65%	68%

Source: Adapted from C.F. Lundby and C. Rasinowich, "The missing link," *Marketing Research*, Winter 2003, 14–19: 18.

satisfy consumers' needs, have a **product orientation**. Sales of Procter & Gamble's Ivory Soap declined because P&G viewed the brand as plain old soap, not as a cleansing product that could provide other benefits as well. Ivory Soap lost business to newer deodorant and "beauty" soaps containing cold cream that appealed to different customer needs in this market.[16] The Ivory Soap example demonstrates that firms that focus narrowly on the product learn an important lesson the hard way—customers do not buy products, they buy benefits. We will explore this concept in more detail in Chapter 7, Product Strategy.

Other firms adopt a **selling orientation**, which means that management views marketing as a selling function, or a way to move products out of warehouses so that inventories don't pile up. You have probably experienced aggressive salespeople who try to "hard sell" and get you to buy something without a lot of concern for your needs

Exhibit 1.14

By finding out what customers want and then making an exchange valued by both parties, Mega Bloks follows a consumer orientation.

and wants. This is the type of salesperson depicted in movies like *Glengarry Glen Ross* or plays like *Death of a Salesman*. Companies that still follow a selling orientation tend to be successful at making one-time sales rather than building repeat business. In the end, such companies inevitably fail because their buyers do not come back. This is particularly true in Canada where there are not as many customers as in larger countries like the United States.

Other organizations have adopted a **consumer orientation**—being proactive and responsive in identifying and satisfying customers' needs and wants. Grocery retailer Thrifty Foods enjoys a 25 percent market share on Vancouver Island by focusing on quality meats and produce, selection, value, and service. Over the past 23 years, president Alex Campbell has introduced unique services and programs for his customers, including home delivery, composting and recycling, and "kiddie-friendly" tills that offer Sesame Snaps and colouring books instead of candy.[17] Montreal-based Mega Brands Inc. is proactive in identifying consumer needs and wants with respect to building block sets that will appeal to kids, particularly boys. As seen in Exhibit 1.14, one such Mega Bloks themed set is associated with the *Pirates of the Caribbean* series of movies, which is very popular worldwide.

A consumer orientation is more progressive than a production or selling orientation, but it does not take into consideration the broader stakeholder relationship management, social marketing, and accountability considerations of New Era marketing.

product orientation A management philosophy that emphasizes the most efficient ways to produce and distribute products.

selling orientation A managerial view of marketing as a selling function, or a way to move products out of warehouses to reduce inventory.

consumer orientation A management philosophy that focuses on being proactive and responsive in identifying and satisfying consumer needs and wants.

THE MARKETING OF VALUE

So far, we've talked a lot about marketing delivering value to customers. As we noted at the beginning of this chapter, *value* refers to the benefits a customer receives from buying a good or service relative to the costs of acquiring and using it. Marketing then communicates

value proposition A marketplace offering that fairly and accurately sums up the value that will be realized if the good or service is purchased.

these benefits to the customer in the form of a **value proposition**, a marketplace offering that fairly and accurately sums up the value that the customer will realize if he or she purchases the product. The challenge to the marketer is to create an attractive value proposition. A big part of this challenge is convincing customers that this value proposition is superior to others they might choose from competitors.

How do customers (such as your potential employer) decide how much value they will get from a purchase? One way to look at value is to think of it simply as a ratio of benefits to costs—that is, customers "invest" their precious time and money to do business with a firm, and they expect a certain bundle of benefits in return. But here's the tricky part: Value is in the eye of the beholder, meaning that something (or someone) may be worth a lot to one person but not to another. Your mother may believe that you are the greatest person on the planet, but a prospective employer may form a different opinion. A big part of marketing is ensuring that the thing being exchanged is appreciated for the value it holds. Let's look at value from the different perspectives of the parties that are involved in an exchange: the customers, the sellers, and society.

Value from the Customer's Perspective

Think about something you would like to buy, say a new pair of shoes. You have narrowed the choice down to several options. Your purchase decision no doubt will be affected by the ratio of costs versus benefits for each type of shoe—that is, in buying a pair of shoes, you consider the price (and other costs) along with all the other benefits (utilities) that each competing pair of shoes provides you.

As we noted previously, the value proposition includes the whole bundle of benefits the firm promises to deliver, not just the benefits of the product itself. For example, although most people probably couldn't run faster or jump higher if they were wearing Nikes versus Reeboks, many die-hard loyalists swear by their favourite brand. These archrivals are largely marketed in terms of their images, which have been carefully crafted with the help of legions of athletes, slickly produced commercials, and millions of dollars. When you buy a Nike "swoosh," you're doing more than choosing shoes to wear to the mall—you may also be making a statement about the type of person you are or wish you were. In addition to providing comfort or letting you run faster, that statement is part of the value the product delivers to you.

You can probably think of possessions you own with which you've "bonded" in some way—that is, their value to you goes beyond their function. Marketers who understand this know that in the long run, their value proposition will be successful if they manage to build a relationship between their product and the people who buy it. The producers of *Rollergirls* (Exhibit 1.15), for example, have an interactive website where fans learn about the girls' lives outside of the rink, what it takes to be a "jammer," and what happens when skaters fight (**www.aetv.com/rollergirls**).

Exhibit 1.15

The producers of *Rollergirls* try to develop bonds with their viewers.

Value from the Seller's Perspective

We've seen that marketing transactions produce value for buyers, but how do sellers experience value, and how do they decide whether a transaction is valuable? One answer is obvious: They determine whether the exchange is profitable to them. Has it made money for the company's management, its workers, and its shareholders?

That's a very important factor, but not the only one. Just as value from the consumer's perspective can't be measured only in functional terms, value from the seller's perspective can take many forms. For example, in addition to making a buck or two, many firms measure value along other dimensions, such as prestige among rivals or pride in doing what they do well. Some firms by definition don't even care about making money, or they may not even be allowed to make money; nonprofits like Greenpeace, the Canadian Cancer Society, or CBC Radio regard value in terms of their ability to motivate, educate, or delight the public.

Because value is such a complicated but important concept, now more than ever marketers are searching for new and better ways to accurately measure just what kind of value they are delivering, how this stacks up to the competition, and—as we'll see next—in some cases even whether the relationship they have with a customer possesses enough value for them to continue it.

CALCULATING THE VALUE OF A CUSTOMER Smart companies today understand that making money from a single transaction doesn't provide the kind of value they desire. Instead, their goal is to satisfy the customer over and over again so that they can build a long-term relationship rather than just having a "one-night stand."

In recent years many firms have transformed the way they do business. They have begun to regard consumers as *partners* in the transaction rather than as passive "victims." That explains why it's becoming more common for companies to host events (sometimes called *brandfests*) to thank customers for their loyalty. For example, the Ford Motor Company sponsored "The Great American Pony Drive II" in honour of devotees of its legendary Mustang. This party included a performance of the song "Mustang Sally" by Sir Mack Rice (who recorded the original version) as well as a preview of the next-generation Mustang.[18]

Ford's decision to reward Mustang owners with a party means the car company has learned an important secret: *It often is more expensive to attract new customers than it is to retain current ones.* Although this notion has transformed the way many companies do business, in fact it doesn't always hold. In recent years, companies have been working harder to calculate the true value of their relationships with customers by asking, "How much is this customer really worth to us?" Firms recognize that it can be very costly in terms of both money and human effort to do whatever it takes to keep some customers loyal to the company. Very often these actions pay off, but there are cases in which keeping a customer is a losing proposition.

This way of thinking is similar to how we may decide which friends are "worth keeping." You may do a lot of favours for two friends, only to discover that when you need something, one of them is always there for you, while the other is nowhere to be found. Over time, you may decide that maintaining a friendship with that second person just doesn't make sense. Similarly, a company may use a lot of resources to appeal to two customers and find that one returns the favour by buying a lot of its products, while the other buys hardly anything. In the long run, the firm may decide to "fire" that second customer. Perhaps you once ordered something in a catalogue, and you get that catalogue in your mailbox every month. If you don't order anything for a certain period of time, the company will stop sending you the catalogue. In the words of Donald Trump, "You're fired!"

Companies that calculate the **lifetime value of a customer** look at how much profit they expect to make from a particular customer, including each and every purchase he or she will make from them now and in the future. To calculate lifetime value, companies estimate the amount the person will spend and then subtract what it will cost to maintain this relationship. College and university students are particularly important to banks because you represent a lifetime of value to them, and while you might not have much money now, one day you probably will.

PROVIDING VALUE TO STAKEHOLDERS BY CREATING A COMPETITIVE ADVANTAGE All things being equal, a firm creates value for stakeholders when it convinces customers that they will acquire greater value by buying its products rather than those of competitors. How are companies able to accomplish this goal? The answer is that the underlying goal of all

lifetime value of a customer How much profit companies expect to make from a particular customer, including each and every purchase he or she will make from them now and in the future. To calculate lifetime value, companies estimate the amount the person will spend and then subtract what it will cost the company to maintain this relationship.

Exhibit 1.16

Marketers like Crest communicate differential benefits as suggested by the promise of "vivid white" teeth.

competitive advantage The ability of a firm to outperform the competition, thereby providing customers with a benefit the competition can't.

distinctive competency A superior capability of a firm in comparison to its direct competitors.

differential benefit Properties of products that set them apart from competitors' products by providing unique customer benefits.

value chain A series of activities involved in designing, producing, marketing, delivering, and supporting any product. Each link in the chain has the potential to either add or remove value from the product the customer eventually buys.

marketing strategies is to create a **competitive advantage** for the firm. A firm has a competitive advantage when it is able to outperform the competition, providing customers with a benefit the competition can't. A competitive advantage gives consumers a reason to choose one product over another again and again.

How does a firm go about creating a competitive advantage? The first step is to identify what it does really well. A **distinctive competency** is a firm's capability that is superior to that of its competition. For example, Coca-Cola's success in global markets—Coke commands 50 percent of the world's soft-drink business—is related to its distinctive competencies in distribution and marketing communications. Coke's distribution system got a jump on the competition during World War II. To enable soldiers fighting overseas to enjoy a five-cent Coke, the U.S. government assisted Coca-Cola in building 64 overseas bottling plants. Coke's skilful marketing communications program, a second distinctive competency, has contributed to its global success. In addition to its television commercials, Coke blankets less-developed countries such as Tanzania with its print advertisements so that even people without televisions will think of Coke when they get thirsty.

The second step in developing a competitive advantage is to turn a distinctive competency into a **differential benefit**—one that is important to customers (Exhibit 1.16). Differential benefits set products apart from competitors' products by providing something unique that customers want. Differential benefits provide reasons for customers to pay a premium for a firm's products and exhibit a strong brand preference. For many years, loyal Apple computer users benefited from superior graphics capability compared to their PC-using counterparts. Later, when PC manufacturers caught up with this competitive advantage, Apple relied on its inventive product designers to create another differential benefit—futuristic-looking computers in a multitude of colours. This competitive advantage even caused many loyal PC users to take a bite of the Apple.

Note that a differential benefit does not necessarily mean simply offering something different. For example, Mennen marketed a deodorant with a distinctive feature: It contained vitamin D. Unfortunately, consumers did not see any reason to pay for the privilege of spraying a vitamin under their arms. Despite advertising claims, consumers saw no benefit, and the product failed. The moral: Effective product benefits must be both different from the competition and wanted by customers. A firm that delivers these desired benefits provides value to its customers and other stakeholders.

ADDING VALUE THROUGH THE VALUE CHAIN Many different players—both within and outside a firm—need to work together to create and deliver value to customers. One approach to understanding the delivery of value and satisfaction is the **value chain**. This term refers to a series of activities involved in designing, producing, marketing, delivering, and supporting any product. In addition to marketing activities, the value chain includes business functions such as human resource management and technology development.[19]

This concept reminds us that every product starts with raw materials that are of relatively limited value to the end customer. Each link in the chain has the potential to either add or remove value from the product the customer eventually buys. The successful firm is the one that can perform one or more of these activities better than other firms—this is its competitive advantage. The main activities of value-chain members include the following:

- Bringing in materials to make the product, referred to as "inbound logistics"
- Converting the materials into the final product, referred to as "operations"

Inbound Logistics	Operations	Outbound Logistics	Marketing and Sales	Service
• Planar lithium battery (Sony) • Hard drive (Toshiba) • MP3 decoder and controller chip (PortalPlayer) • Flash memory chip (Sharp Electronics Corp.) • Stereo digital-to-analog converter (Wolfson Microelectronics Ltd.) • Firewire interface controller (Texas Instruments)	• Consumer research • New-product-development team • Engineering and production	• Trucking companies • Wholesalers • Retailers	• Advertising • Sales force	• Computer technicians

Figure 1.3 A Value Chain for the Apple iPod

- Shipping out the final product, referred to as "outbound logistics"
- Marketing the final product, in which marketing and sales come into play
- Servicing the product/customer, referred to as "service"

For example, when you buy a new Apple iPod at your local Future Shop store, do you think about all the people and steps involved in designing, manufacturing, and delivering that product to the store—not to mention other people who create brand advertising, conduct consumer research to figure out what people like or dislike about their mobile music players, or even make the box it comes in or those little plastic peanuts that keep the unit from being damaged in shipment?

As Figure 1.3 shows, all these companies (and more) belong to Apple's value chain. This means that Apple must make a lot of value-chain decisions. What electronic components will go into its music players? What accessories will be included in the package? What trucking companies, wholesalers, and retailers will deliver the iPods to stores? What service will it provide to customers after the sale? And what marketing strategies will it use? In some cases, members of a value chain will work together to coordinate their activities to be more efficient and thus create a competitive advantage.

This book is organized around the sequence of steps necessary to ensure that the appropriate value exchange occurs and that both parties to the transaction are satisfied—making it more likely that they'll continue to do business in the future. Figure 1.4 shows these steps. Basically, we're going to learn about what marketers do as a product makes its way through the value chain from manufacturers into your hands. We'll start with a focus on how companies decide what to make, how and where to sell it, and whom to sell it to. Then, we'll take a look at how they decide to "position" the product in the marketplace, including choices about what it should look like, how its value should be communicated to customers, and how much to charge for it. As we reach the end of our marketing journey, we'll talk about how the product actually gets delivered to consumers.

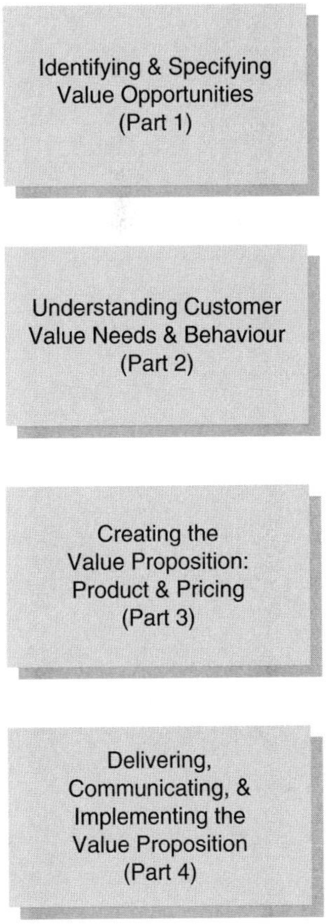

CONSUMER-GENERATED VALUE: FROM AUDIENCE TO COMMUNITY One of the most exciting new developments in the marketing world is the evolution of how consumers interact with marketers. In particular, we're seeing everyday people actually generating value instead of just buying it—consumers are becoming advertising directors, retailers, and new-product-development consultants. They are creating their own ads (some flattering, some not) for products and posting them on sites like YouTube.com. They are buying and selling merchandise ranging from Beatles memorabilia to washing machines (to body parts, but that's another story) on eBay. They are sharing ideas for new styles with fashion designers, and customizing their own unique versions of products on websites. These changes

Identifying & Specifying Value Opportunities (Part 1)

Understanding Customer Value Needs & Behaviour (Part 2)

Creating the Value Proposition: Product & Pricing (Part 3)

Delivering, Communicating, & Implementing the Value Proposition (Part 4)

Figure 1.4 Making and Delivering Value

mean that marketers need to adjust their thinking about customers. They need to stop thinking of buyers as a passive audience and start thinking of them as a community that is motivated to participate in both the production and the consumption of what companies sell. We'll talk more about this phenomenon later, but for now think about these recent examples of **consumer-generated value.**

consumer-generated value Customers functioning in marketing roles, such as participating in creating advertisements, providing input to new product development, or serving as wholesalers or retailers.

- Kao Corp., which makes Ban deodorant, invited teenage girls to make an ad that would encourage other girls their age to buy the product. The company got almost 4000 submissions from girls who were asked to submit an image and fill in the blank in the company's "Ban It" slogan. One entry shows four girls in similar jeans and tank tops, with their backs to the camera with the headline: "Ban Uniformity."[20]

- Threadless.com invites customers and other designers to submit T-shirt designs to their website. Other members vote on which designs they like best, and each week threadless produces T-shirts in the top six winning designs that the designers, members, and their friends can buy online. The appeal is unique T's—and the winning designers get $2500, tee credits, and the rights to their work. Last year Threadless shipped more than 80 000 T-shirts per month and made a profit of more than $20 million.[21]

- In 2006, the action movie *Snakes on a Plane*, which stars Samuel L. Jackson (and in which an assassin releases hundreds of venomous snakes in the hope of killing a witness), generated a huge amount of pre-release buzz—including consumer-generated websites, blogs, and even merchandise. The commotion started when a screenwriter (who had been invited to work on the script) blogged about the movie. The title inspired other bloggers to create songs, apparel, poster art, pages of fan fiction, parody films, and mock movie trailers. Now, individuals who post on Internet forums use the phrase "Snakes on a Plane" to indicate that a topic doesn't make sense—sometimes the slang form SoaP substitutes for the old phrase "sh** happens."[22]

Value from Society's Perspective

Every company's activities influence the world around it, in ways both good and bad. Therefore, we must also consider how marketing transactions add or subtract value from society. In many ways, we are at the mercy of marketers because we trust them to sell us products that are safe and perform as promised. We also trust them to price and distribute these products fairly. Conflicts often arise in business when the pressure to succeed in the marketplace provokes dishonest business practices—the collapse of energy giant Enron and the trial of its (late) former chief executive officer Ken Lay are a case in point.

The Dark Side of Marketing

Whether intentionally or not, some marketers do violate their bond of trust with consumers, and unfortunately the "dark side" of marketing often is the subject of harsh criticism.[23] In some cases, these violations are illegal, such as when a retailer adopts a "bait-and-switch" selling strategy, luring consumers into the store with promises of inexpensive products with the sole intent of getting them to switch to higher-priced goods.

In other cases, marketing practices have detrimental effects on society even though they are not actually illegal. Some alcohol and tobacco companies advertise in low-income neighbourhoods where abuse of these products is a big problem. Others sponsor commercials depicting groups of people in an unfavourable light or sell products that encourage antisocial behaviour. An online game based on the Columbine High School massacre drew criticism from some (including the father of a student who died in the 1999 attack) who say it trivializes the actions of the two teen killers.[24]

Despite the best efforts of researchers, government regulators, and concerned industry people, sometimes consumers' worst enemies are themselves (Exhibit 1.17). We tend to think of individuals as rational decision makers, calmly doing their best to obtain products and services that will maximize the health and well-being of themselves and their families and society. In reality, however, consumers' desires, choices, and actions often result in negative consequences to individuals and the society in which they live. Some of these actions are relatively harmless, but others have more onerous consequences. Some harmful consumer behaviours such as excessive drinking or cigarette smoking stem from social pressures, and the cultural value placed on money encourages activities such as shoplifting or insurance fraud. Exposure to unattainable ideals of beauty and success can create dissatisfaction with the self. Let's briefly review some dimensions of "the dark side" of consumer behaviour.

1. *Marketers create artificial needs.* The marketing system has come under fire from both ends of the political spectrum. On the one hand, some members of the religious right believe that advertising contributes to the moral breakdown of society by presenting images of sinful pleasure. On the other hand, some leftists argue that the same deceitful promises of material pleasure function to buy off people who would otherwise be revolutionaries working to change the system.[25] They argue that the system creates demand that only its products can satisfy.

   A Response: A need is a basic motive, while a want represents one way that society has taught us the need can be satisfied. For example, while thirst is biologically based, we are taught to want Coca-Cola to satisfy that thirst rather than, say, water. Thus, the need is already there; marketers simply recommend ways to satisfy it. If the basic need is not there, no amount of slick marketing communication tactics is going to convince consumers to buy.

Did you hear the one about the fat guy suing the restaurants?

It's no joke.
He claims the food was too cheap so he ate too much!

Learn more about the erosion of personal responsibility and common sense. Go to:

ConsumerFreedom.com

Exhibit 1.17
Some people feel that marketers manipulate consumers, while others argue that people should be held responsible for their own choices. This ad is critical of the current trend of lawsuits brought against fast-food companies by people who blame their health problems on the fast-food industry. What do you think?

2. *Marketing teaches us to value people for what they own rather than who they are.* Goods are arbitrarily linked to desirable qualities, so we learn that we can be popular, happy, and fulfilled only if we buy these products.

   A Response: Products meet existing needs, and advertising only helps to communicate their availability. Advertising is an important source of consumer information.[26] It is a service for which consumers are willing to pay because the information it provides reduces the time and effort needed to learn about the product.

3. *Marketers promise miracles.* Marketing leads consumers to believe that products have magical properties, that they will transform their lives. Marketers provide simplistic answers to complex problems.

   A Response: Marketers do not know enough about people to manipulate them. In testimony before the U.S. Federal Trade Commission, one executive observed that while people think that advertisers have an endless source of magical tricks and scientific techniques to manipulate people, in reality, the industry is successful when it tries to sell good products and unsuccessful when selling poor ones.[27]

4. *Marketers support addiction.* **Consumer addiction** is a physiological or psychological dependency on goods or services. These problems of course include alcoholism, drug addiction, and cigarettes—and many companies profit from addictive products or by selling solutions. Although most people equate addiction with drugs, consumers can use virtually anything to relieve (at least temporarily) some problem or satisfy some need to the point that reliance on it becomes extreme. "Shopaholics" turn to shopping much

consumer addiction A physiological or psychological dependency on goods or services.

the way addicted people turn to drugs or alcohol.[28] There is even a ChapStick addicts support group with approximately 250 active members![29]

A Response: While some customers do end up getting addicted to legal products, marketers are increasingly aware of their social responsibility in helping customers consume appropriately. For example, casinos spend considerable resources educating customers to "play within their limits" and helping customers with addiction problems.

5. *Marketers exploit people, and in particular children, in developing countries.* This charge is aimed at the procurement and manufacturing practices of some high-profile marketers like Nike and Wal-Mart that, according to rights activists, support exploitive work conditions to keep costs down for North American consumers. There are also news stories about children in China being kidnapped and put to work by companies wanting lower labour costs.[30]

A Response: Certainly there are some organizations that do not make business and marketing decisions that are consistent with the norms and expectations of North American society. There are, however, many more, like Patagonia, Ten Thousand Villages, or Alternative Grounds, that have adopted New Era thinking and explicitly compete by fair trade practices.

CAREERS IN MARKETING

Marketing was identified by *Canadian Business* as one of the "cool careers" on the Canadian business scene. This is not surprising because it is fun and challenging to work in a discipline that is directly concerned with understanding consumer needs and satisfying them for the mutual benefit of consumers, businesses, shareholders, and society.

Business schools across the country are receiving increasing numbers of inquiries from prospective students about this important discipline. Marketers are currently in great demand, both in small and large Canadian organizations, providing future marketers with some great opportunities.[31]

Many students assume that the "typical" marketing job is in a large, consumer-oriented packaged goods company like Procter & Gamble. In fact, marketers work in other types of organizations, for example:

Service organizations (e.g., Telus; Intrawest)
E-commerce organizations (e.g., Chapters Online; Amazon.ca)
Technology companies (e.g., IBM Canada; Bombardier)
Industrial equipment companies (e.g., Komatsu; Nortel)
Retailers (e.g., Shoppers Drug Mart; Sears)
Agricultural companies (e.g., B.C. Hot House; Visser Potato Ltd.)
Not-for-profit organizations (e.g., The United Way; Canadian Cancer Society)
Marketing research companies (e.g., Maritz Research; Ipsos Canada)
Consulting companies (e.g., Deloitte; CGEY)
Advertising agencies (e.g., Publicis; TAXI)

In smaller organizations, one person (perhaps the owner) may handle all the marketing responsibilities. In larger organizations, several marketing specialists may work, along with other functional experts, on different aspects of marketing strategy.

What choices do you have in the marketing field once you graduate? Take a look at Table 1.1 to discover the wide variety of exciting career choices that await you.

Table 1.1 Careers in Marketing

Marketing Field	Where Can I Work?	What Entry-Level Position Can I Get?	What Course Work Do I Need?
Advertising	**Advertising agency:** Media research and creative departments; account work **Large corporation:** Advertising department: brand/product management **Media:** Magazine, newspaper, radio, and television selling; management consulting; marketing research	Account coordinator (traffic department); assistant account executive; assistant media buyer; research assistant; assistant brand manager	Undergraduate business degree
Brand Management	**Any size corporation:** Coordinate the activities of specialists in production, sales, advertising, promotion, R&D, marketing research, purchasing, distribution, package development, and finance	Associate brand manager	M.B.A. preferred, but a few companies recruit undergraduates. Expect a sales training program in the field from one to four months and in-house classes and seminars.
Business-to-Business Marketing	**Any size corporation:** Only a few companies recruit on campus, so be prepared to search out job opportunities on your own, as well as interview on campus.	Sales representative; market research administrator; product manager; pricing administrator; product administrator; assistant marketing manager; sales administrator; assistant sales manager; sales service administrator	Undergraduate business degree. A broad background of subjects is generally better than concentrating on just one area. A technical degree may be important or even required in high-technology areas. Courses in industrial marketing and marketing strategy are very helpful.
Direct-Response Marketing	**Any size corporation:** Marketing-oriented firms, including those offering consumer goods, industrial products, financial institutions, and other types of service establishments. Entrepreneurs seeking to enter business for themselves.	Direct-response marketing is expanding rapidly and includes direct mail, print and broadcast media, telephone marketing, catalogues, in-home presentations, and door-to-door marketing. Seek counsel from officers and directors of the Direct Marketing Association and the Direct Selling Association.	Undergraduate business degree. Supplemental work in communications, psychology, and/or computer systems recommended.
Supply-Channel Management	**Any size corporation, including transportation corporations:** The analysis, planning, and control of activities concerned with the procurement and distribution of goods. The activities include transportation, warehousing, forecasting, order processing, inventory control, production planning, site selection, and customer service	Physical distribution manager; supply chain manager; inventory-control manager; traffic manager; distribution-centre manager; distribution-planning analyst; customer service manager; transportation marketing and operations manager	Undergraduate business degree and M.B.A. Broad background in the core functional areas of business, with particular emphasis in distribution-related topics such as logistics, transportation, purchasing, and negotiation.
International Marketing	**Large corporations:** Marketing department at corporate headquarters	Domestic sales position with an international firm may be the best first step toward international opportunities.	M.B.A. A broad background in marketing is recommended, with some emphasis on sales management and market research.
Marketing Models and Systems Analysis	**Large corporations:** Consult with managers who are having difficulty with marketing problems.	Undergraduate: Few positions available unless you have prior work experience. Graduate: market analyst, market research specialist, and management scientist.	M.B.A. Preparation in statistics, mathematics, and the behavioural sciences.
Marketing Research	**Any size corporation:** Provide management with information about consumers, the marketing environment, and the competition.	Assistant market analyst or assistant product analyst level	M.B.A. or an M.S. in Marketing Research, although prior experience and training may improve an undergraduate's chances.

(Continues on the next page)

Marketing Field	Where Can I Work?	What Entry-Level Position Can I Get?	What Course Work Do I Need?
New Product Planning	**Any size corporation:** Marketing of consumer products, consumer industries, advertising agencies, consulting firms, public agencies, medical agencies, retailing management	Assistant manager or director of product planning or new product development	M.B.A.
Retail Management	**Retail corporations**	Assistant buyer positions; department manager positions	Undergraduate business degree
Sales and Sales Management	**Profit and nonprofit organizations:** Financial, insurance, consulting, and government	Trade sales representative who sells to a wholesaler or retailer; missionary sales representative in manufacturing who sells to retailers or decision makers (e.g., pharmaceutical representative); technical sales representative who sells to specified accounts within a designated geographic area	Undergraduate business degree; M.B.A.; *Helpful courses:* consumer behaviour, psychology, sociology, economics, anthropology, cost accounting, computer science, statistical analysis, communications, drama, creative writing. Language courses, if you're interested in international marketing; engineering or physical science courses if you're interested in technical selling.
Services Marketing	**Any size corporation:** Banking and financial service institutions, health care organizations, leisure-oriented businesses, and various other service settings.	Assistant brand manager; assistant sales manager	Undergraduate business degree; M.B.A. Additional course work in management policy, research, advertising and promotion, quantitative analysis, consumer behaviour, and the behavioural sciences should prove useful.

Source: This information was adapted from an excellent compilation prepared by the Marketing faculty of the Marshall School of Business, University of Southern California at www.marshall.use.edu/web/marketing.cfm?doc_id=2890, accessed May 8, 2006. For recent salary figures broken down by job type and region, visit the Aquent/AMA Compensation Survey of Marketing Professionals 2006 at www.marketingsalaries.com/aquent/Home.form.

Real People, Real Decisions

▶ How It Worked Out at Yellow Point Lodge

Richard decided to implement Option 4: protect the land and decrease its value. Richard valued the land and his father's vision more than the money—which the government would take half of anyway. This option was most consistent with Richard's values and those of his father. It was also consistent with his guests' values and the value proposition they found so appealing.

Richard negotiated with The Land Conservancy and the Nanaimo Area Land Trust and signed the timber rights of the main lodge property (about 80 acres) into a conservation covenant. While Richard maintained ownership, this protected property as part of the coastal Douglas fir zone. In

making this land untouchable, Richard has ensured that neither he nor any future owner will be able to log or develop it.

There will be some tax advantage to doing this, but that was not Richard's primary motivation. He wanted the land protected. His decision also means that his children won't be faced with the increasing pressure to develop the land. By following in his father's footsteps as a "custodian" of the land instead of the "owner," Richard has been true to his and his family's values. He has also protected, to some extent, a pretty nice way of life for his children should they choose to be custodians of Yellow Point.

CHAPTER SUMMARY

1. Define the marketing concept.

Marketing is the process of planning and executing the conception, pricing, promotion, and distribution of ideas, goods, and services to create exchanges that satisfy individual and organizational objectives. Organizations that seek to ensure their long-term profitability by identifying and satisfying customers' needs and wants have adopted the marketing concept. Today, the societal marketing concept is being adopted by many firms that try to satisfy customers in a way that is also beneficial to society. Marketing activities are important to firms that provide goods and services to individual and business customers, as well as not-for-profit organizations and those that focus on sports, entertainment, places, people, and ideas.

2. Describe what tools marketers use to create value for customers: the marketing mix.

The overall objective of marketing is to achieve success (individual, organizational, and societal) by creating superior customer value, for exchange with customers in one or more target market segments, with a sustainable strategy. This objective is consistent with the marketing concept. It suggests that marketing is primarily focused on achieving objectives through value creation. Because consumers have different ideas about what they need and want, marketers focus their value creation strategy on the needs and wants of a specific group of consumers—the target market.

Value is created through marketing mix decisions, also referred to as the four *P*s of marketing: product, price, place (channel of distribution), and promotion (marketing communications). Products can be goods, services, people, places, or ideas. The price is the assigned value or amount to be exchanged for the product. The place or channel of distribution gets the product to the customer. The organization communicates the value being created for the customer through its promotional efforts.

3. Outline the basics of marketing planning.

To create a competitive advantage for themselves in the marketplace, firms need to develop superior strategies. To do this, they identify market segments, select the target market(s) they want to serve, and create value for the chosen segment(s) by tailoring the marketing mix elements. Often, firms outline their marketing strategies and tactics in a document called the marketing plan.

4. Explain the New Era orientation of marketing.

The New Era orientation of marketing takes a stakeholder value creation perspective where the needs and wants of all stakeholders are taken into consideration when creating, communicating, and delivering the offer of value. These stakeholders include society as a whole as New Era marketers adopt the social marketing concept and focus on the triple bottom line of economic, social, and environmental value. New Era marketers also put much more emphasis on accountability.

5. Explain marketing's role in creating value.

Although marketing is the only business function *directly* concerned with understanding customer needs and satisfying them, marketing decisions cannot be made in isolation from an organization's other functions. Marketing takes the lead role in creating value for key stakeholders, including customers, but marketing people must work together with people from other functional areas to achieve the organization's goals.

CHAPTER REVIEW

Marketing Concepts: Testing Your Knowledge

1. Briefly explain what marketing is.
2. What is the marketing concept? How is it different from the social marketing concept?

3. How does marketing facilitate exchange?

4. What is customer value?

5. Define these terms: consumer goods, services, and industrial products.

6. What are the elements of the marketing mix? What role do they play in creating value for the customer?

7. Explain the concept of market segmentation. Why can't a firm be successful in the long term by practising mass marketing?

8. What are target markets? How do marketers select and reach target markets?

9. Trace the evolution of the marketing concept.

10. What are some criticisms of marketing and how would you respond to them?

Marketing Concepts: Discussing Choices and Issues

1. The marketing concept focuses on the ability of marketing to satisfy customer needs. As a student, how does marketing satisfy your needs? What areas of your life are affected by marketing? What areas of your life (if any) are not affected by marketing?

2. Do you think students should study marketing even if they are not planning a career in marketing or business? Explain your reasoning.

3. In this chapter, a number of criticisms of marketing were discussed. Have you heard these criticisms before? What other criticisms of marketing have you heard? Do you agree or disagree with these criticisms, and why?

Marketing Practice: Applying What You've Learned

1. An old friend of yours has been making and selling leather handbags and bookbags to acquaintances and friends for some time and is now thinking about opening a shop in your town. But he is worried about whether he'll have enough customers who want handcrafted bags to keep a business going. Knowing that you are a marketing student, he asks you for some advice. What can you tell him about market segments, target markets, product, price, marketing communications, and distribution strategies that will help him get his business off the ground?

2. Assume that you are employed by your city's chamber of commerce. A major focus of the chamber is to get industries to move to your city. As a former marketing student, you know that there are issues involving product, price, marketing communications, and even distribution that can attract business. Next week, you have an opportunity to speak to the members of the chamber, and your topic will be "Marketing a City." Develop an outline for that presentation.

3. As a marketing professional, you have been asked to write a short piece for a local business newsletter about the state of marketing today. You think the best way to address this topic is to review how the marketing concept has evolved and to discuss the New Era orientation of marketing. Write the short article you will submit to the editor of the newsletter.

4. You and your friends sometimes discuss the various courses you are taking. One of your friends says to you, "Marketing's nothing but selling stuff. Anybody can do that without taking a course." Another friend says, "Yeah, all marketers do is write ads." As a role-playing exercise, present your arguments against these statements to your class.

Marketing Mini-Project: Learning by Doing

The purpose of this mini-project is to develop an understanding of the importance of marketing to different organizations.

1. Working as a team with two or three other students in your class, select an organization in your community that practises marketing. It may be a manufacturer, service provider, retailer, not-for-profit organization—almost any organization will do. Schedule a visit with someone in the organization who is involved in the marketing activities. Ask that person to give your group a tour of the facilities and explain the organization's marketing activities.

2. Divide the following topics among your team, and ask each person to be responsible for developing a set of questions to ask during the interview to learn about the company's program:

   - What customer segments the company targets
   - How it determines needs and wants
   - What products it offers, including features, benefits, and goals for customer satisfaction
   - What its pricing strategies are, including any discounting policies
   - What marketing communication strategies it uses, and what these emphasize to position the product(s)
   - How it distributes products, and whether it has encountered any problems
   - How marketing planning is done and who does it
   - Whether social responsibility is part of the marketing program and, if so, in what ways

3. Develop a team report of your findings. In each section of the report, share what you learned that is new or surprising to you compared to what you expected (based on your reading of Chapter 1).

4. Develop a team presentation for your class that summarizes your findings. Conclude your presentation with comments on what your team believes the company was doing well and where it could make improvements.

Real People, Real Surfers: Exploring the Web

The New Era orientation means that a firm like Mountain Equipment Co-op is devoted to excellence in sourcing and producing products that benefit customers as well as society, the organization's employees, and their members. Many firms share this on their Internet webpages. Visit the website for Mountain Equipment Co-op (**www.mec.ca**). Then visit the website for one of their competitors such as REI (**www.REI.com**) or Taiga (**www.taigaworks.ca**). Follow the links in the sites to learn as much as you can about the company. You might first check the site map to see what links are provided on the site. Look for answers to the following questions.

1. What evidence do you find on the firms' websites that each is a New Era firm?

2. Which company has the better website? What makes it better? Based on your visit to the websites, what do you think is the major purpose of each company's site? To promote their products? To sell on the web? To develop a brand image? Something else?

3. How does each company use its website for promoting its products? Is the website a unique form of marketing communications or just an extension of their normal advertising?

4. What market segments do you think each firm is targeting with its website? What features of the websites gave you this idea?

5. Do the websites provide an opportunity for the firm to gather information about customers so that it can customize contact with them?

6. Are there any features of the website that will cause consumers to come back again and again?

7. What are your major criticisms of each of the websites? What would you do to improve each site from a marketing perspective?

Chapter 1 Real Decisions at Virgin Galactic

Would you like to travel to outer space? Unless you are an astronaut or scientist conducting experiments in the weightlessness of space, is there any reason for you to undertake the risk of space travel? Sir Richard Branson, one of Britain's best-known entrepreneurs, thinks there are a lot of consumers who see outer space as the ultimate adventure holiday. In fact, up to 40 percent of people in one survey said they would like to travel to space. Branson thinks this kind of enthusiasm could lead to thousands of passengers per year hoping to go boldly where few have gone before.

Richard Branson is not new to creating successful businesses. He has created a number of companies under the "Virgin" brand name, including the Virgin Atlantic airline, Virgin Records, Virgin Megastores, and the Virgin Mobile phone service. To capitalize on the growing interest in space tourism that one day may be a multi-billion-dollar industry, Branson created Virgin Galactic after watching SpaceShipOne, the first spacecraft designed and built by a private citizen, reach space in 2004.

The product that Virgin Galactic hopes to offer to satisfy the demand for space tourism is a ride on SpaceShipTwo, a successor space vehicle to the original SpaceShipOne. The new space vehicle will be larger than the original, with seating for six passengers and two pilots, and will be launched from an airplane at an altitude of 55 000 feet. Once released from the airplane, SpaceShipTwo will fire rocket engines and the aircraft will climb, almost vertically, to the edge of space, or roughly 110 kilometres above the Earth. At this altitude, passengers can experience the effects of weightlessness and view the darkness of space and the curvature of the Earth. After spending 15 minutes at this altitude, the spaceship will descend and land like a regular airplane.

Being a space tourist will not be cheap. However, despite a fare of $200 000 per flight Virgin Galactic already has deposits of $20 000 from 38 000 people in 126 different countries. In addition, a core group of 100 tourists has paid the full $200 000 up front. Those numbers result in total revenue for the company of $780 million, a sizable amount for a start-up company to take in. And passengers won't begin flying until some time between late 2008 and 2015!

Obviously, space travel is not available from any existing airport. To satisfy the place, or distribution, element of its marketing mix, the company struck a deal with the State of New Mexico. Officials from the state agreed to build a $225 million spaceport from which Virgin Galactic can launch its space tourist flights. Virgin Galactic chose New Mexico as the site because of its steady climate, high altitude, free airspace, and overall low population density. The spaceport will be built just 25 miles south of the town Truth or Consequences, which likely will see a rise in tourism spending once the space flights begin.

A final element of the marketing mix Virgin Galactic addresses is its promotion. Aside from having a well-developed website (**virgingalactic.com**), the company has not had to engage in much promotion yet. Because the entire space tourism industry is so new, almost any development receives extensive (and free) coverage from major news outlets such as broadcast and cable TV news, newspapers, and magazines. Promotion is one element of the marketing mix that may require greater development as the space tourism business matures.

Certainly it seems that space tourism has a promising, even if somewhat uncertain, future. Still, there is no guarantee that Virgin Galactic will be a success. While there appears to be a large untapped market for space tourism, that could easily change. For instance, what might happen to the industry if an accident occurs and perhaps an entire spaceship, with its passengers and crew, is lost? Such an incident could easily lead to a drop in consumer demand and increased government regulation. And, despite the somewhat limited number of people who are willing to be space tourists and who actually can afford the price, there's growing competition. Space Adventures, Rocketplane Kistler, and PlanetSpace are companies planning to begin space flights for tourists in the near future. Space Adventures plans to price its flights at only $100 000, just half of what Virgin Galactic charges (will they serve more than a bag of peanuts?), and Rocketplane Kistler hopes to begin flights before Virgin's planned debut.

While most of Branson's Virgin businesses have been successful, there have been failures. Virgin Cola was a flop in the U.S. market. Virgin Galactic's management has made initial decisions about the four Ps—product, price, place, and promotion. But are these basic marketing decisions enough? What else is needed to ensure a smooth takeoff for Virgin Galactic?

Things to Think About

1. What is the decision facing Virgin Galactic?

2. What factors are important in understanding this decision situation?

3. What are the alternatives?

4. What decision(s) do you recommend?

5. What are some ways to implement your recommendations?

Source: Agence France Presse, "Space tourism lures a rising number of US entrepreneurs," 22 March 2006; Jane Wardell, "Virgin spaceport to be built in N.M.," *Associated Press*, 13 December 2005; and Ben Webster, "Space tourists prepare for lift-off 2008," *The Times* (London), 30 March 2006.

CHAPTER 2
Making Strategic Marketing Decisions

CHAPTER OBJECTIVES

WHEN YOU HAVE COMPLETED YOUR STUDY OF THIS CHAPTER, YOU SHOULD BE ABLE TO

1. Explain how businesses develop plans at different levels within the organization.

2. Describe the steps in the marketing planning process.

3. Explain how to conduct situational analysis and SWOT analysis to understand a decision context.

4. Explain how strategic marketing mix decisions are made in international markets.

5. Explain how firms practise ethical and socially responsible behaviour in the marketplace.

PEARSON
mymarketinglab

Visit the MyMarketingLab website at **www.pearsoned.ca/mymarketinglab**. This online homework and tutorial system puts you in control of your own learning with study and practice tools directly correlated to this chapter's content.

Real People, Real Decisions

Meet **Michel Bendayan**, a Decision Maker at Mega Bloks

Michel Bendayan is an international sales and marketing director for Mega Bloks (**www.megabloks.com**), the publicly traded, Montreal-based company that is the second largest construction toy manufacturer in the world after Lego. Mega Bloks is a worldwide organization employing over 3000 people, and selling a line of 75 to 100 Mega Bloks items in four sizes in 100 countries. Sales of Mega Bloks have grown exponentially in the past five years and Mega Bloks is now the world market-share leader in the preschool construction toy segment.

Michel has been a director of international sales and marketing since 2003, and recently took over responsibility for Asia, Australia, and Africa in addition to his previous focus on Eastern Europe and the Middle East. Before joining Mega Bloks in 1998, he worked for Hasbro Canada as assistant product manager for the Parker Brothers and Milton Bradley brands, and prior to that he completed a B.Com. degree from McGill University in 1994.

As international sales and marketing director, Michel determines international marketing strategy and product launch tactics. His role includes identifying new distributors, working on getting product listings, understanding retail and consumer preferences and trends, and working with retailers to grow the sales of Mega Bloks products.

Soon after taking over the Asia portfolio, Michel learned that Mega Bloks' sales in Japan were weak. The Japanese toy market is the second largest in the world, after the United States, and construction toys represent a much smaller proportion of that market than in either the United States or Europe, suggesting to Michel that there was an opportunity to increase Mega Bloks' sales in Japan. For the previous five years Mega Bloks had worked with three different Japanese distributors, but had only marginal sales success. Michel didn't know if the problem was with the distributors, the product line, or both.

One thing he had learned in the European market was that European consumers and distributors were quite different from those in North America. Focus group research had found that European consumers liked simple, compact box packaging (similar to that of Lego or Playmobil) that showed a picture of the product or the product in use, and had little writing. In North America, most consumers were influenced either by the flashiness of the packaging—bolder colours, graphic call-outs, and bold text that highlighted product benefits—or the size of the packaging, bigger or more interesting being better. Consequently, Mega Bloks packaged their North American products in either bulk bags or shaped theme packaging such as a set of Bloks that came in a dump truck or in a container shaped like a bear. North American consumers tend to like detailed information on the packaging that explains who the product is for and how it is used, but such detailed text makes European packaging very cluttered as it has to be presented in multiple languages. European distributors considered Mega Bloks to be a premium foreign brand while in North America it is positioned as a high quality but value brand.

Conducting similar research, Michel found that Japanese consumers were even more quality oriented than Europeans and would reject toys with the slightest scratches or dented boxes. Japanese consumers demand the use of Japanese script on the packaging, and while North American products are often considered prestigious, Japanese consumers want a Japanese look and feel to the packaging. Because Japanese households have even less space than European households, and rooms often have multiple uses, consumers demand efficient and utilitarian packaging—wanting to be able to easily put toys back in their boxes or containers and put them out of sight. Japanese consumers are also much more conscious of and involved with pop-culture characters (for example, Power Rangers). Differences were also found with Japanese retailers, who were much more varied (for example, hypermarkets, supermarkets, convenience stores), fragmented (lots of different channels), and much more relationship oriented. Although there are fewer specialty toy stores, many Japanese toy manufacturers are among the largest toy companies in the world.

With a desire to develop a strong long-term brand in the Japanese market, Michel and his colleagues considered three distribution alternatives and three product line alternatives:

Distribution alternative one (D1) *was to continue to work through small distributors.*

Even though the previous distributors did not understand the product line well and lacked focus and commitment to the product lines, Michel thought there might be some better small distributors and it might be easier to get the interest and attention of smaller distributors than the larger ones who already had strategic relationships with the large Japanese toy manufacturers. On the other hand, these small distributors were often small because they did not have access to as many channels and were not embedded in a large corporate network.

Distribution alternative two (D2) *was to sell direct.*

Michel thought that the Japanese market was potentially big enough for Mega Bloks to consider developing its own sales and distribution company in Japan. He thought that such an investment could pay off in the long run as it would be closer to the customer and would not be reliant on others. The risk, however, was that no one in the Mega Bloks organization knew a lot about Japanese business practices or Japanese consumers and it would take months, or even years, to establish the key retail relationships needed for the sales reps to be effective.

Distribution alternative three (D3) *was to partner with a large Japanese manufacturer or distributor.*

This alternative was attractive, as a strategic partner could offer local expertise, knowledge of the Japanese consumer, and access to a large distribution network. The downside was that Mega Bloks would be a much smaller organization, it might not get the attention needed, and all the "help" would come at the expense of significantly higher margins demanded by the partner organization.

With respect to the product line, Bendayan considered three alternatives.

Production line alternative one (P1) *was to sell the existing U.S. or European product lines.*

It would be easiest and fastest to sell the current lines without any customization, and the European lines had already been customized to reflect space issues. While international brands were popular in Japan, Bendayan did not know if this would be true for children's toys. He didn't know if Japanese consumer preferences would accept the brand without modification; it might be perceived as too "Western."

Production line alternative two (P2) *was to sell existing product lines but customize the packaging for the Japanese market.*

The easiest customization option was to change the packaging to portray a Japanese image, but retain the current product lines that were the most popular sellers in Europe and North America. This approach had worked well in Europe where European consumers responded well to new, cleaner package designs and packing that facilitated storage such as bags or plastic boxes.

Production line alternative three (P3) *was to develop an entirely new product line for the Japanese market.*

This option would be the most expensive and would take a year or more to implement. The key advantage would be that a new product line could be designed to specifically appeal to Japanese consumers. Such a new line would also have stronger appeal to Japanese distributors. The downside was that minimum order quantities and sales would need to be achieved to justify the production costs. If standard products were sold, it would not matter as much if sales targets were missed.

Now, join the Mega Bloks decision team. Which options would you choose, and why?

"PLAN WELL AND PROSPER"

Whether a firm is a not-for-profit organization like the United Way, a family-based retailer like Army & Navy department stores, or a major manufacturer like Mega Bloks, planning for the future is a key to prosperity. Success in the competitive world of business is not accidental; businesses that succeed do so because they are capable of developing and implementing superior strategies in the marketplace. Often, businesses that fail meet their fate because of improper planning.

All firms operate in a dynamic environment. In today's world of business, consumer interests, technologies, competition, and the economy are changing faster than ever. This makes good planning more important than ever, as planning enables a firm to meet the challenges of this dynamic environment and to control its own destiny.

In this chapter, we'll look at the different steps in creating and implementing plans within a business organization. First we'll see how managers make the decisions that guide the entire organization. Then we'll examine how marketers make the marketing decisions outlined in Chapter 1. Finally, we will discuss the global and ethical context in which marketing decisions are made.

In successful firms, both large and small, business planning is an ongoing process of making decisions that guide the firm both in the short term and for the long haul. Planning identifies and builds on a firm's strengths and helps managers at all levels make informed decisions in a changing business environment. Planning means that an organization develops objectives before it takes action. In large firms, such as IBM, Sony, and L'Oréal, which operate in many markets, planning is a complex process involving many people from different areas of the company's operations. In a small business like Mac's Diner, however, planning is quite different; Mac himself is chief cook, occasional dishwasher, and the sole company

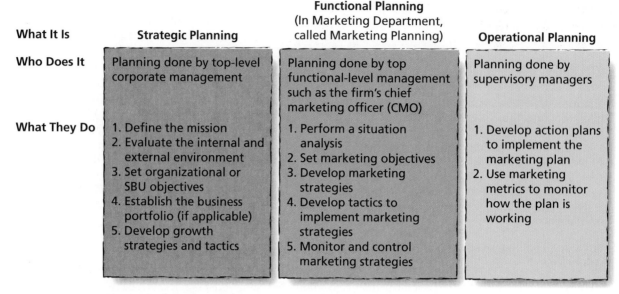

What It Is	Strategic Planning	Functional Planning (In Marketing Department, called Marketing Planning)	Operational Planning
Who Does It	Planning done by top-level corporate management	Planning done by top functional-level management such as the firm's chief marketing officer (CMO)	Planning done by supervisory managers
What They Do	1. Define the mission 2. Evaluate the internal and external environment 3. Set organizational or SBU objectives 4. Establish the business portfolio (if applicable) 5. Develop growth strategies and tactics	1. Perform a situation analysis 2. Set marketing objectives 3. Develop marketing strategies 4. Develop tactics to implement marketing strategies 5. Monitor and control marketing strategies	1. Develop action plans to implement the marketing plan 2. Use marketing metrics to monitor how the plan is working

Figure 2.1 Annual Planning at Different Levels Within a Business Organization

During planning, an organization determines its objectives and then develops courses of action to accomplish them. In larger firms, planning takes place at the strategic, functional, and operational levels.

planner. With mid-size firms, the planning process falls somewhere in between, depending on the size of the firm and the complexity of its operations.

We all know, in general, what planning is—we plan a vacation or a great Saturday night party or how we are going to get work completed. When businesses plan, the process is more complex. Business planning usually occurs on an annual basis at three levels—strategic planning, marketing planning, and operational planning. Figure 2.1 outlines this process.

strategic planning A managerial decision process that matches an organization's resources and capabilities to its market opportunities for long-term growth and survival.

Strategic planning is the managerial decision process that matches the organization's resources (for example, manufacturing facilities, financial assets, and skilled workforce) and capabilities to its market opportunities for long-term growth. These decisions focus on the firm's ability to respond to changes and opportunities in its environment. In a strategic plan, the top management team (that is, the chief executive officer, or CEO, president, and other top executives) defines the firm's purpose (mission) and specifies what the firm hopes to achieve over the next few years (organizational objectives). Increasingly this planning takes place in consultation with a cross-section of employees who bring varied perspectives and knowledge to the process. For example, a firm's strategic plan may set a goal of increasing the firm's total revenues by 10 or even 20 percent in the next five years. Strategies and tactics are then developed for achieving those objectives. **Strategies** reflect *what* a firm is going to do to achieve an objective. For example, to increase total revenues by 20 percent in the next five years, an organization like Mega Bloks may decide to enter a new market with either new or existing products. **Tactics** reflect *how* a strategy is going to be implemented. For example, Mega Bloks may decide to enter the Japanese market with a product line customized for the Japanese consumer.

strategy What a firm is going to do to achieve an objective.

tactics How a strategy is going to be implemented.

Strategic plans are usually developed for a period of three to five years and take a long-term view of the strategic health of the business. In large firms, strategic planning can actually occur at two different levels. First, there is overall corporate strategic planning, which determines the organization's different business and product pursuits. Second, the individual business units do strategic planning for their products. Strategic planning at the Walt Disney Company, for example, involves an assessment of resources and capabilities for starting new businesses. In addition to making movies and running theme parks, Disney is now in the cruise ship business and operates a number of Disney vacation resorts. Disney's corporate planning expanded its theme park business to Europe and Japan—separate business units. At Disney there are separate strategic plans for each of the different Disney businesses.

Given its high-level, long-term emphasis, a strategic plan is not a document that can be readily implemented. Therefore firms develop a one-year plan, called the marketing plan, which takes its direction from the strategic plan and develops lower-level strategies and tactics for achieving the objectives specified in the strategic plan. There are two main differences between a strategic plan and a marketing plan. The first is time horizon. While the strategic plan is developed for a period of three to five years, the marketing plan is typically developed for a period of one year. The second difference is that the marketing plan contains details regarding the marketing mix elements (product strategy, pricing strategy, channel of distribution strategy, marketing communication strategy), while the strategic plan does not contain this level of detail. What is sometimes confusing about strategies and tactics is that a tactic at the organizational (strategic plan) level becomes, or is reflected in, the strategy at the functional level, and functional level tactics become, or are reflected in, operational strategies.

For example, at the strategic planning level, Mega Bloks' strategy may be to expand internationally. Their tactic to do this may be to enter the Japanese market with a product line customized for the Japanese consumer. At the marketing planning level, this becomes the strategy to achieve more specific marketing objectives such as "have 20 percent of sales come from new markets this year" and "earn a profit of $5 million from those new market sales." At the marketing planning level, the marketing mix decisions to achieve this market entry strategy are the tactics that specify how the strategy will be implemented and the objectives achieved. In the operational (or implementation) plan, a marketing mix decision such as establishing a uniquely Japanese brand personality for Mega Bloks in Japan becomes the strategy (what you are going to do) while decisions reflecting how this will be done, such as hiring an advertising agency to create a Japanese anime cartoon character, are the tactics. So while strategies reflect what to do and tactics reflect how to do it, they are related across levels of analysis and differ in increasing levels of specificity.

Perhaps you are beginning to see the central role played by marketers in the organizational, functional, and operational planning process. The development of the marketing plan enables the business to set priorities regarding markets it wants to compete in (market segments), customers it wants to serve (target customers), and how it plans to serve those customers (marketing mix strategy). Once these priorities are set, the business develops a set of more specific plans such as a sales plan, production plan, finance plan, supply chain plan, and a human resource plan. Collectively, some businesses call these plans the operating plans or tactical plans. Based upon the requirements of each functional plan, the business is now in a position to allocate resources for the year by setting a budget. Although this process starts from the top of an organization and works its way down to specific tactical decisions, it is typically a two-way process. Marketing and other functional plans are adapted based on the specific objectives and decisions reflected in operational plans and strategic plans are adapted based on the specific objectives and decisions reflected in the functional plans.

So far, we have a general understanding of the three levels of planning. Now we'll discuss in more detail strategic planning and the important role that marketing plays in it.

STRATEGIC PLANNING: GUIDING THE BUSINESS

Marketers don't work and plan in isolation. Before we talk about the marketing planning process, therefore, we need to understand how firms develop strategic plans. In this section, we'll take a closer look at the five key stages in top-level strategic planning: defining the organization's business mission, evaluating the environment (situational analysis), setting organizational objectives, planning the business portfolio, and developing growth strategies.

Step 1: Define the Mission

Top management's first step in the strategic planning process is to answer questions such as: What business are we in? What customers should we serve? How should we develop the firm's capabilities and focus its efforts? In many organizations, the answers to questions such

Exhibit 2.1

Xerox is working to change the perception that it is a copier-only company.

as these become the lead items in the organization's strategic plan. The answers become part of the **mission statement**—a formal description of the organization's purpose and what it hopes to achieve in terms of creating value for customers with what products and resources. For example, the mission of Mothers Against Drunk Driving (MADD) is "to stop drunk driving, support the victims of this violent crime, and prevent underage drinking."[1]

The ideal mission statement is not too broad, too narrow, or too short-sighted. A mission that is too broad will not provide adequate focus for the organization. It doesn't do much good to claim: "We are in the business of making high-quality products"; yet it's hard to find a firm that doesn't make this claim. However, a mission statement that is too narrow may inhibit managers' ability to visualize possible growth opportunities. If, for example, a firm sees itself in terms of its product only, consumer trends or technology can make that product obsolete—and the firm is left with no future. If Xerox had continued to define its mission in terms of just producing copy machines instead of providing "document solutions" (Exhibit 2.1), the shift to electronic documents would have left them in the dust the way the Model T Ford replaced the horse and buggy. Similarly, imagine the disastrous consequences that would happen to McDonald's if its mission statement read: "We are in the hamburger business." It's important to remember that the need for a clear mission statement applies to virtually any type of organization, even those like Mothers Against Drunk Driving, whose objective is to serve society rather than to sell goods or services. Xerox is not alone in its efforts to

redefine itself. Philip Morris, once simply a tobacco products company, has redefined itself strategically as a consumer products company, offering many of the products we consume on a regular basis (Exhibit 2.2). Mission statements should also inspire customers and other stakeholders to want to do business with an organization. The mission of Campbell's soup, for example, is "Together we will build the world's most extraordinary food company by nourishing people's lives everywhere, every day."[2]

Step 2: Conduct an Environmental (Situational) Analysis

The second step in strategic planning is an assessment of an organization's environment, both external and internal. This process is referred to as a *situation analysis*, *environmental analysis*, or sometimes a *business review*. The **external environment** consists of those uncontrollable elements outside of the organization that may affect it either positively or negatively. While this can include everything from consumers to government regulations to competitors to the economy, there are four main categories of considerations. The first is looking for trends or issues in the *macro or general environment* that might have a positive or negative effect on your organization. These may be **p**olitical or legal, **e**conomic, **s**ocial or cultural, **t**echnological, or **o**ther (**p.e.s.t.o.**) trends or issues that might impact a particular industry and business. Mega Bloks, for example, might need to understand political or legal issues relating to foreign ownership of joint ventures before deciding how to enter the Japanese market.

mission statement A formal statement in an organization's strategic plan that describes the overall purpose of the organization and what it intends to achieve in terms of its customers, products, and resources.

external environment The uncontrollable elements outside of an organization that may affect its performance either positively or negatively. These include macro environment factors like regulatory or technology factors, consumer behaviour trends, industry factors such as industry concentration, and competitive factors such as the number and sophistication of competitors.

internal environment The controllable elements inside an organization, including its people, its facilities, and how it does things that influence the operations of the organization.

Similarly, Mega Bloks has to consider the implications of children, all around the world, being increasingly interested in electronic games. McDonald's has to consider the implications of governments imposing "fat" taxes or regulating the use of trans fats in the preparation and consumption of food and consider the social trend toward healthier lifestyles. Canadian lumber companies have to consider the relative strength of the Canadian dollar when developing export strategies. Media producers need to understand the implications of RSS (Really Simple Syndication) feed technology as teenagers and young adults increasingly seek to customize information and entertainment products accessed via the Internet.

The external environment also includes detailed *consumer analysis*. We will be examining these issues in much more detail in Chapters 5 and 6, but this is where you would look for trends, issues, or considerations with respect to changing consumer segments, segment profiles, and segment sizes. While socio-cultural trends are more general across society, consumer analysis is focused on understanding specific market segments. For example, Mega Bloks would need to understand the extent to which "North American" products are perceived positively among consumers in key Japanese market segments.

The external environment also includes *industry analysis*. Industry considerations might include factors like industry size and competitiveness, industry structure, industry dynamics (trends, norms, etc.), stage of the product life cycle (see Chapter 8), and industry key success factors. Again, we are just looking for factors that might positively or negatively impact our strategic decisions. For example, a new entrant into the computer printer industry should understand that manufacturers make little, if any, money on selling the printers, but make significant margins selling ink.

Finally we give consideration to *competitive analysis*—identifying the key competitors, understanding their strategies and strengths and weaknesses, as well as anticipating likely future strategic changes. Mega Bloks, for example, needs to understand and anticipate Lego's marketing strategy in Japan, as well as the strategies of domestic competitors, to make an informed market-entry decision.

When conducting this situational analysis, marketers focus on developing a comprehensive understanding of the environment in which they are competing. This includes a solid understanding of their own organization and its abilities to create value and compete effectively. As illustrated in Figure 2.2, the **internal environment** is all the controllable elements inside an organization that influence how well the organization operates. Marketers need to understand the current strategy of the organization and assess how well that strategy is working: How superior is the current value created by the firm's

**Philip Morris Companies Inc.
Delivering On Our Promise...**

Exhibit 2.2

Philip Morris, once simply a tobacco products company, now sees itself as a consumer products company with a variety of product offerings. Its annual report reflects that shift in strategic orientation.

**Analysis to Understand
the Decision Context (Opportunity)**

Environmental Analysis
- External Environment
  - Macro
  - Consumer analysis
  - Industry analysis
  - Competitive analysis
- Internal Environment
  - Current strategy & performance
  - Organization systems, structure, culture
  - Skills & resources
  - Preferences & values

SWOT Analysis
- SWOT summary
- Strategy matrix

Other Analysis

Marketing Theory, Concepts, Principles

Figure 2.2 Analysis to Understand the Decision Context

products? How effective is the current marketing mix? What is the relative market share of these products? What has been their financial performance? Marketers also need to understand the *resources and competencies of the organization*; its technology, intellectual capital, and other assets. For example, firms need to have appropriate technical skills to compete in their industry. Their employees need to have appropriate skills, abilities, and training to produce the firm's products. A firm's physical facilities can be an important asset for creating customer value, as can its level of financial stability, its relationships with suppliers and channel members, its corporate reputation, and its ownership of strong brands in the marketplace. Marketers also need to understand the *organization* of the firm—its structure, culture, and systems (how they get work done). Some firms, for example, have a positive work climate that encourages creativity, innovation, and teamwork. Other firms find they have a "chilly" climate, characterized by negativity, work-to-rule, and in-fighting among employees—which can seriously affect product quality and relationships with customers, suppliers, distributors, and other stakeholders. Finally the *beliefs, values, and preferences of senior management* in an organization need to be understood for marketers to consider organization-appropriate alternatives in making key marketing decisions.

Step 3: Set Organizational or SBU Objectives

After constructing a mission statement and understanding the decision environment, top management sets organizational or strategic business unit (SBU) objectives. Very large corporations are normally divided into self-contained divisions, or SBUs. Bombardier, for example, produces transportation vehicles ranging from commercial aircraft to high-speed trains, with each product class organized in an SBU. Bombardier Learjet (Exhibit 2.3) is an SBU of Bombardier. Bombardier Learjet operates as an independent business with its own mission and objectives—and its own marketing strategy. Organization and SBU objectives are a direct outgrowth of the mission statement and broadly identify what the firm hopes to accomplish within the general time frame of the firm's long-range business plan.

Exhibit 2.3

Bombardier Learjet is an SBU of Bombardier.

To be effective, objectives need to be *specific, measurable* (so firms can tell whether they've met them or not), and *attainable*. Attainability is especially important—firms that establish "pie in the sky" objectives they can't realistically obtain can create frustration for their employees (who work hard but get no satisfaction of accomplishment) and other stakeholders in the firm, such as vendors and shareholders who are affected when the firm doesn't meet its objectives.

Objectives may relate to revenue and sales, profitability, the firm's standing in the market, return on investment, productivity, product development, customer relations and satisfaction, and social responsibility. To ensure measurability, objectives are often stated in numerical terms. For example, a firm might have as an objective a 10 percent increase in profitability. It could reach this objective by increasing productivity, by reducing costs, or by selling off an unprofitable division. Or it might meet this 10 percent objective by developing new products, investing in new technologies, or entering a new market. If you are a business major, you will learn a lot more about setting and specifying objectives in your organizational behaviour and business strategy courses.

Step 4: Establish the Business Portfolio

For companies with several different SBUs, strategic planning includes making decisions about how to best allocate resources across these businesses to ensure growth for the total organization. As Figure 2.3 illustrates, each SBU has its own focus within the firm's overall strategic plan, and each has its own target market and strategies for reaching its objectives. Just like an independent business, each SBU is a separate *profit centre* within the larger

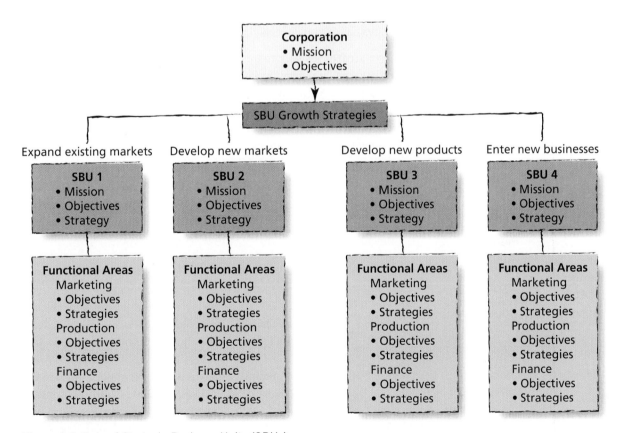

Figure 2.3 Role of Strategic Business Units (SBUs)

Very large corporations are normally divided into self-contained divisions, or SBUs. SBUs represent different major areas of the overall firm's business. For example, General Electric has a jet engine division, a lighting division, an appliance division, and numerous other divisions. At GE, as with most corporations, each SBU operates as an independent business with its own mission and objectives—and its own marketing strategy.

corporation—that is, each SBU within the firm is responsible for its own costs, revenues, and profits.

Just as the collection of different stocks an investor owns is called a portfolio, the range of different businesses that a large firm operates is called its **business portfolio**. As with the Bombardier example, these different businesses usually represent very different product lines, each of which operates with its own budget and management. Having a diversified business portfolio reduces the firm's dependence on one product line or one group of customers. For example, if travel suffers and Disney has a bad year in theme-park attendance and cruises, its managers hope that the lost sales will be made up by stay-at-homers who go to Disney movies and watch Disney's television networks. There are a variety of portfolio analysis tools available to marketers to help them decide which mix of business units makes most sense in their context, but the use of these tools is typically addressed in a marketing strategy course, and is beyond the scope of this text.

business portfolio The group of different products or brands owned by an organization and characterized by different income-generating and growth capabilities.

Step 5: Develop Growth Strategies

Although portfolio analysis tools can help managers decide which SBUs they should invest in for growth, it doesn't tell them much about *how* to make that growth happen. Should the growth of an SBU come from finding new customers, from developing new variations of the product, or from some other growth strategy? Part of the strategic planning at the SBU level entails evaluating growth strategies.

Marketers use the product market growth matrix shown in Figure 2.4 to analyze different growth strategies. The vertical axis in Figure 2.4 represents opportunities for growth, either in existing markets or in new markets. The horizontal axis considers whether the firm would be better off putting its resources into existing products or if it should acquire new products. The matrix provides four fundamental marketing strategies: market penetration, market development, product development, and diversification:

market penetration strategies Growth strategies designed to increase sales of existing products to current customers, nonusers, and users of competitive brands in served markets.

- **Market penetration strategies** seek to increase sales of existing products to existing markets such as current users, nonusers, and users of competing brands within a market. For example, Campbell's can advertise new uses for soup in lunches and dinners, encourage current customers to eat more soup, and prod nonusers to find reasons to buy soup. The firm might try to increase sales by cutting prices, improving distribution, or conducting promotions aimed at attracting users of competing soup brands.

market development strategies Growth strategies that introduce existing products to new markets.

- **Market development strategies** introduce existing products to new markets. This strategy can mean expanding into a new geographic area, or it may mean reaching new customer segments within an existing geographic market. For example, Red Bull, the "energy" drink that had its beginnings in the 1990s as a cult favourite among the emerging young club crowd, is trying to move up the generational chain to attract older users as well (Exhibit 2.4). To do this, Red Bull has recently migrated some of its marketing efforts from edgy ads to more mainstream messages. Founder and largest shareholder Dietrich Mateschitz understands the dollar power of the older generation, and to appeal to them he has broadened Red Bull's distribution into stores, restaurants, and clubs they frequent. Mateschitz is betting on the vast numbers of clubbers' parents to prop up sales, especially now that the heavyweights like

Product Emphasis

	Existing Products	New Products
Existing Markets	**Market penetration strategy** • Seek to increase sales of existing products to existing markets	**Product development strategy** • Create growth by selling new products in existing markets
New Markets	**Market development strategy** • Introduce existing products to new markets	**Diversification strategy** • Emphasize both new products and new markets to achieve growth

Market Emphasis

Figure 2.4 Market Growth Matrix

Coca-Cola, PepsiCo, and Anheuser-Busch are trying to make inroads into the market for energy drinks.[3]

- **Product development strategies** create growth by selling new products in existing markets. *Product development* may mean extending the firm's product line by developing new variations of the item, or it may mean altering or improving the product to provide enhanced performance. Take the humble mattress, for example. Lately, business-class hotels like Sheraton and Marriott have been engaged in something of a "mattress war"—that is, each one is trying to convince the traveller that its bed is softer, more comfortable, and more inviting than the competition's (and in some cases, if you fall in love with the bed you can actually buy it and take it home!). This "sleeper" strategy appears to be effective: Radisson Hotels' research with guests told it that the mere fact that a bed was "upgraded" would allow the chain to charge an additional $10 per room. These new-age beds carry their own brand names—"Heavenly Bed" at Westin, "The Revive Collection" at Marriott, and "Sweet Sleeper" at Sheraton. Radisson's "Sleep Number" beds even allow each occupant to adjust the firmness of his or her side with a remote control device.[4] A product development strategy like that is waking up the hotel industry, as the major players (and some smaller luxury hotels) are now scrambling to merchandise other room elements, such as toiletries.

- **Diversification strategies** emphasize both new products and new markets to achieve growth. After a long period of sluggish performance in the fast-food market, McDonald's has re-energized itself over the past several years through successful strategic planning. For example, feeling that it was maxing out in the hamburger business in the late 1990s, McDonald's sought to attract different customers with lines of business to diversify its portfolio of food offerings. Among those are Donatos Pizza, Boston Market, and a controlling interest in Chipotle Mexican Grills. Interestingly, now that its core business is back on track, McDonald's has begun to divest some of these other brands and

Exhibit 2.4

By appealing to older consumers, Red Bull is attempting a market development strategy.

product development strategies Growth strategies that focus on selling new products in served markets.

diversification strategies Growth strategies that emphasize both new products and new markets.

Marketing Metrics

Measuring Performance

A survey of leading marketing firms in five countries (United States, United Kingdom, France, Germany, and Japan) found that *market share* is the metric that managers are most likely to report to the company's board of directors. Other commonly used metrics include the following:

- Perceived product/service quality
- Customer loyalty/retention
- Customer/segment profitability
- Relative price

Across the five countries, German companies are the heaviest users of metrics and Japanese firms the lightest. Of the companies surveyed, 97 percent of German firms said they report their market share to their boards, compared with 79 percent of American firms and only 57 percent of Japanese firms. Overall, firms that do business in multiple countries and those that have above-average marketing budgets are more likely to rely on metrics.[5]

is shifting from diversification back to more of a product development strategy around the core McDonald's brand.[6]

THE MARKETING PLANNING PROCESS

Marketing planning uses the output of the strategic planning process as an input—that is, the strategic planning process provides the context in which marketing planning is conducted. Solid planning means that a firm has a viable product at a price consumers are willing to pay, the means to get that product to the place consumers want it, and a way to communicate (promote) the product to the right consumers. The marketing planning process culminates in the development of a formal document called the **marketing plan**. Although we will discuss the process of developing a marketing plan in great detail in Chapter 14, let us briefly examine the marketing plan template shown in Figure 2.5. You will see that it matches the marketing decision framework of Figure 1.2.

marketing plan A document that describes the marketing environment, outlines the marketing objectives and strategy, and identifies who will be responsible for carrying out each part of the marketing strategy.

Understand the Opportunity

The marketing planning process begins with a thorough analysis of the decision context facing the firm. The situational analysis conducted for the strategic plan is reviewed and updated and any constraints, assumptions, or other decision parameters that need to be taken into consideration are identified. A strategic assessment of the situation is then conducted to identify the key facts, factors, or observations in the external and internal environments that have the most important implications or bearing on the marketing planning. Some environmental considerations are more important to understand than others. For example, Mega Bloks might choose to enter the Japanese market differently if it were able to get patent protection on its building blocks. Richard Hill, at Yellow Point Lodge, needs to find a strategy consistent with the strong sense of history and tradition of his long-loyal customers. The challenge is in identifying the most important considerations on which to base your marketing strategy.

SWOT analysis An analysis of an organization's strengths and weaknesses and the opportunities and threats in its external environment.

SWOT analysis is one tool often used by marketers (and other planners) in this task. SWOT analysis seeks to identify meaningful strengths (S) and weaknesses (W) in the organization's internal environment, and opportunities (O) and threats (T) from the external environment. In conducting a SWOT analysis, marketers start with an examination of the facts or observations made in situational analysis and try to identify the implications of each of these considerations. For each fact or observation, ask yourself: Why is it important to understand this information? How does it impact a decision that I need to make? Is it a strength of my organization that will help me create superior customer value or defend my desired positioning, or is it a weakness that undermines that ability and would need to be addressed or mitigated (reduced in effect)? Is it an opportunity in the external environment that my organization could exploit or take advantage of in creating or defending value creation or is it a threat that impedes or otherwise limits my organization's ability to compete effectively?

If the implication does not have a direct bearing on a decision you have to make, it probably isn't very important and does not need to be included in the SWOT analysis. Determining the strategic implications and what is important and not important can take many years of experience—and you have to practise doing SWOT analysis to gain that experience. However, marketing and business strategy research has found that there are six basic reasons why some organizations fail.[7] These six "fatal flaws" can help you identify some of the environmental factors that are particularly important to understand and need either to be addressed or mitigated (reduce their impact) when developing your marketing strategy:

1. Failure to innovate: no differentiation. Organizations that do not create offers that are superior in some way to those already

I. Executive Summary

II. Table of Contents

III. Situation/Environment Analysis

IV. Opportunity Identification/Assessment & Assumptions

V. Objectives

VI. Marketing Strategy

VII. Marketing Mix Decisions (by Target Market)
- Product Decisions
- Pricing Decisions
- Distribution Decisions
- Communication Decisions

VIII. Implementation & Evaluation

IX. Appendices

Figure 2.5 Marketing Plan Template

available usually do not survive very long. Lack of differentiation and the inability to create and defend sustainable competitive advantage is a strategic issue that can be observed in an organization's current strategy relative to its competitive environment.

2. Failure to create value: There is not a large enough market segment that wants a particular offer. Sometimes the current strategy of an organization does not create sufficient customer value to attract customers. Insufficient value creation is a strategic issue that is sometimes observed in an analysis of an organization's current strategy relative to segment profile analysis.

3. Failure to persist over time: insufficient margins, volume, or resources. Often related to the failure to create value, but also sometimes related to the inability to communicate that value. Some organizations are not able to make sufficient margins or generate sufficient sales volume. Many startup organizations fail because they do not have the financial, technical, human, or management resources to compete effectively over time. This is particularly true of businesses with high fixed costs (those that require significant investment in buildings, equipment, people, technology, or overhead—such as software creation or car manufacturing) because it can take many months or years to recover those initial investments. More established organizations can fail because their markets change over time: competition increases, demand decreases, or they can't or don't keep up with changing technology. The inability to compete effectively is an important strategic issue that can be observed in both the internal and external environment.

4. Failure to maintain economic scarcity: Offers are imitable or substitutable. Some organizations fail to protect the value they have created and competitors are able to better satisfy customer demand with similar offers or substitutes. Organizations that are unable to limit direct competition by means of intellectual property protection; strong supplier, distributor, or customer relationships; cost structure advantages (such as economies of scale); switching costs; unique knowledge; greater customization or niche (small market) focus; strong brand name; or some other market entry barrier, may not be able to defend their positioning.

5. Failure to prevent "appropriation" of value: hold-up or slack. Some organizations get held hostage (held up) by stakeholders in strong bargaining positions, such as strong unions, single source suppliers, or key distributors. These stakeholders are able to negotiate terms that erode the profitability of the organization. Hold-up issues might be evident in an industry or competitive analysis. Other organizations are wasteful or inefficient with their resources (slack)—often because the management team does not have sufficient experience in that industry to be effective. This might be evident in an analysis of the organization structure, systems, and culture or the current strategy and performance.

6. Failure to be flexible and adapt: the ability to deal with uncertainty and ambiguity. Uncertainty is being able to anticipate events, but not their timing. For example, a chicken satay vendor could anticipate that at some point in time, despite their best food safety efforts, a customer will get food poisoning from eating the chicken. Effective organizations create risk management plans, crisis management plans, and have insurance and other "due diligence" interventions to limit the impact of potential risks—but in highly volatile, fast-changing industries (like fashion or biotechnology) this can be difficult to do. But some events cannot even be anticipated (such as terrorist attacks, currency devaluations, or stock crashes) and managers need to be capable of adapting to changing circumstances. The degree of uncertainty is often assessed in an industry analysis, and the inability of management to plan or adapt could be an issue in an assessment of an organization's management and systems.

Marketers use SWOT analysis to help them make strategic and tactical decisions. Internal strengths and external opportunities provide rationale to support a particular course of action. Internal weaknesses and external threats provide reasons why a particular course of action might not be appropriate. Weaknesses and threats, however, are not absolute; both can be addressed or mitigated through marketing strategy. Meal Exchange, for example, is a not-for-profit organization dedicated to motivating post-secondary students to increase their involvement in fighting social problems like hunger (**www.mealexchange.com**).

Ethical Decisions in Marketing

Successful marketing strategies depend on understanding a firm's environment, and that means learning as much as you can about the competition. But sometimes companies cross the ethical boundary in doing this. For example, Mark Hill, a former vice-president of strategic planning and co-founder of WestJet, used an access code from a former Air Canada employee to get information on Air Canada operations. On learning about this, Air Canada hired a private investigator to look through Hill's home garbage, seeking all documents relating to Air Canada, including reconstructing private shredded documents. This incident was reported to Hill by an observant neighbour, and the next time the private investigator came, Hill had planted false information in his garbage.

Both companies sued. Air Canada launched a $5-million lawsuit against WestJet alleging that WestJet had used information from a confidential Air Canada website. WestJet countersued for $5 million alleging that Air Canada had obtained sensitive data from Hill's garbage. Air Canada raised the stakes by increasing its claim to $220 million and WestJet launched a $30-million countersuit, claiming Air Canada was abusing the court process in WestJet's legal action of corporate espionage. After two years of legal battle, the Ontario Superior Court ruled against WestJet's claim regarding court abuse. In May of 2006 WestJet apologized to Air Canada for spying and agreed to pay $5.5 million in legal fees and contribute $10 million to children's charities.[8]

While this case was extreme, how far do you think a company should be allowed to go to learn about its competition?

The organization works with colleges and universities so that students can donate the unused money on their meal cards to local food banks, which could then purchase food for those in need. Differences in college and university policies regarding the redemption of meal cards might be a threat in the external environment of Meal Exchange that could limit expansion plans for the organization. However, this threat might be mitigated or overcome by supporters of the Meal Exchange concept lobbying college and university administrators to change their policies so that they could participate in the Meal Exchange program.

The key to SWOT analysis is not to get bogged down in analysis paralysis. Firms face hundreds, if not thousands, of internal and external environmental considerations that shape and impact their business. You will want to identify the top six to ten issues that might have the greatest implications for the marketing decisions you have to make. Ask yourself: Does this fact or piece of information have a major implication for a decision I have to make? If not, it's probably not worth documenting in a SWOT analysis. A SWOT summary is a list of the most important issues and their implications, such as those shown in Figure 2.6, which is an illustrative example of a SWOT analysis summary for the decision faced by Michel Bendayan at Mega Bloks.

Objectives

Based on the situational analysis, the business then develops a set of marketing objectives. These are more specific than the SBU objectives, and achieving the marketing objectives helps an organization achieve the overall SBU objectives. Marketing objectives normally include one or more sales objectives. After all, without sales, there are no profits, and without profits, there is no business. Some examples of sales objectives are: "To increase sales of our deluxe model toy by 15 percent during the next 12 months," "To increase our toy market share by 5 percent each year for the next three years," "To sell one million toys during the holiday season."

If a firm has decided that its growth strategy is to focus on product development—new or improved products for existing customers—it will develop product objectives. Because it is more profitable to retain customers than it is to replace them, firms often set objectives for improvements in quality or service to develop customer loyalty. In the breakfast cereal market, where consumers are more fickle than loyal, firms like Kellogg and General Mills may set objectives for developing new brands to suit the tastes of everyone—children, teens, and adults—or they may set goals for a new product to retain customers who are being lured away by a competitor's new honey-coated, fruit-and-fibre cereal. In other cases, a firm may decide to modify a product by taking advantage of trends, as when Frito-Lay developed its line of "lite" snacks.

In some instances, firms find that their best opportunities for growth are stated in the form of market objectives. These goals can involve entering new markets or increasing product usage in served markets, through using either market development strategies (existing products sold to new customers) or diversification strategies (new products for new customers).

Internal Environment:

Current Strategy & Performance
- — World market-share leader in preschool segment (**S**)
  - Ability to leverage international brand name in new markets
- — Weak sales and lack of distribution network (**W**)
  - Status quo not really an option, market may require unique strategy

Organization (structure, systems, culture)
- — Asia, Australia, and Africa are all under one international marketing director (**W**)
  - May limit ability to focus on Japan and customize Japanese lines
- — Product innovation culture (**S**)
  - Ability to compete on innovative new product development
- — Rapid growth in past five years (**S, W**)
  - Has gained significant international experience that supports its ability to enter the Japanese market
  - *But hard to maintain focus and organizational culture with such growth; high degree of Japanese customization may be difficult to implement*

Resources & Competencies
- — Second largest construction block company in the world (after Lego) (**S**)
  - Has the experience and resources needed for international expansion
- — 3000 employees, 75 to 100 product lines, in 100 countries (**S**)
  - Has the people, expertise, and resources to develop custom product lines
- — Basic product not patentable—Lego had a patent (now expired) (**W**)
  - Hard to protect markets from competitors.

Management Preferences & Values
- — Standardized products are preferable (inferred) (**?**)
  - *Mega Bloks has not previously customized products for a single country; doing so may create a precedent for a wholesale change in strategy that has significant cost implications. It might be possible to do it for one country but maybe not for all countries.*

External Environment:

Macro (General) Environment: PESTO
- — American products are often considered prestige products in Japan (**O**)
  - May be value in offering North American–style product lines
- — High quality consciousness in Japanese society (**T**)
  - *May need greater control over the supply chain*
- — Greater awareness and importance of pop culture (**T**)
  - *May need Japanese brand personality*

Consumer Analysis
- — Japanese consumers strongly nationalistic (**T**)
  - Prefer Japanese look and feel
- — Japanese houses are much smaller than those in North America or even Europe (**T**)
  - Will likely require different packaging, but also maybe different product lines that enable blocks to be used for many designs

Industry Analysis
- — Very large market (**O**)
  - Attractive market for achieving organizational goals.
- — Japanese retailers are more varied, fragmented, and relationship oriented (**T**)
  - This may require a partnership model with a strong Japanese distributor or significant investment in selling direct.
- — Many Japanese toy manufacturers, among the largest in world (**T/O**)
  - May be able to license the Mega Blok brand and utilize the distribution network of an established toy company.
  - *Threat of a domestic competitor with greater local resources.*
- — There is no patent or trademark protection on the shape & function of the blocks (**O/T**)
  - Mega Bloks can compete against Lego, anyone can compete with Mega Bloks
  - *Branding and distribution are the key sources of competitive advantage.*

Competitive Analysis
- — Lego is a strong competitor in all markets (**T**)
  - They have the resources to copy any strategy if proven effective
- — No current local competitor (**O**)
  - *By customizing the product line we reduce the threat of local competition*

Note: S: Strength; W: Weakness; O: Opportunity; T: Threat; ?: impact not clear; Italics: most significant implications for the decision faced by Michael Bendayan.

Figure 2.6 Illustrative SWOT Summary for Mega Bloks

Exhibit 2.5

The RV industry believes that baby boomers can be its next big market.

Manufacturers of recreational vehicles (motor homes and travel trailers), for example, used a market development strategy in targeting baby boomers (see Exhibit 2.5). Joining together in a "Go RVing Coalition," they spent US$15 million on advertising aimed at this under-50 market in a three-year period.[9]

Marketing Strategy: Specify the Value

Once the marketing and other objectives are developed, the organization develops a marketing strategy aimed at achieving those objectives. As was discussed briefly in Chapter 1, marketing strategy begins with identifying, profiling, and selecting market segments that will be targeted by the strategy. As will be discussed in more detail in Chapter 3, choosing the right market to compete in and the right customer to attract is a critical task for a marketer; a task that combines both art and science. Once the target market customers have been chosen, marketing strategy focuses on the positioning issues of strategic orientation, differentiation, defendability, and brand personality.

Strategic orientation is a discussion of how the organization will compete in its chosen market(s). This would include a discussion of growth strategies (as per above); customer value creation strategy (Chapter 1); or other strategy concepts that you will learn if you take another marketing course. Your SWOT analysis is another source of strategy alternatives. The SWOT Strategy Matrix in Figure 2.7 illustrates how you can develop strategy alternatives by considering how to utilize your strengths or address your weaknesses to take advantage of opportunities, and how to address or mitigate threats in the external environment.

Differentiation is how a brand will be known to its customers as being better than competitive brands. A discussion of differentiation should be specific. It is not meaningful to say that an organization will differentiate itself on quality. What does that mean in your specific context? For a car it could mean greater reliability, durability, longevity, rust protection, or more comfortable seats, among many other considerations. For a restaurant it could mean better taste, greater variety, better ingredients, faster service, or better ambiance, among other considerations. You need to be specific in identifying what your organization will do better than others.

Defendability discusses sources of sustainable competitive advantage and the systems, competencies, technology, or other resources that enable an organization to defend its chosen positioning. It is important to understand that the underlying goal of *all* marketing strategies and plans is to create a **competitive advantage** for the firm—to take what the company does really well and outperform the competition, thus providing customers with a benefit the competition cannot provide. A competitive advantage gives consumers a reason to choose one product over another again and again.

Finally, *brand personality* is a discussion of how the intended differentiation will be captured in the creation of brand meaning. Some brands, like the Apple Macintosh, have clear personalities. Imagine that Apple Macintosh was a person and he or she just walked into the room. Describe him or her in as much detail as possible. You can probably do that quite easily because Apple has spent considerable money developing the Mac Guy versus PC Guy series of advertisements (which can be found on its website: **www.apple.com**). In defining a brand personality we specify what personality we are seeking to support the overall positioning of the brand. This personality gets developed in the marketing mix decisions that we subsequently make.

competitive advantage The ability of a firm to outperform the competition, providing customers with a benefit the competition cannot.

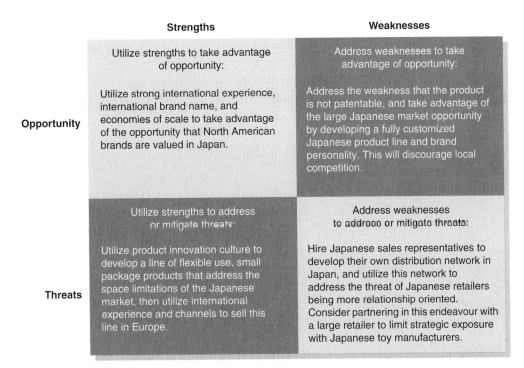

Figure 2.7 SWOT Strategy Matrix for Mega Bloks

Marketing Mix: Create the Value

As outlined in Chapter 1, a marketing plan then describes the marketing mix decisions relating to product, price, channel of distribution, and marketing communications (see Figure 1.2, on page 12). Rationale for these decisions comes from your SWOT and other analysis, your understanding of your target market profile, and the marketing theory, principles, and concepts that you will learn from reading this text and attending class.

Evaluation and Implementation

Also as outlined in Chapter 1, the collective decisions represented in a marketing plan need to be evaluated to determine if the strategy should be implemented. Throughout the writing of a marketing plan, rationale is provided for each decision made using your situational analysis, SWOT analysis, target market profile, and marketing theory, concepts, and principles. Collectively, however, the set of decisions needs to create superior customer value and achieve the organization's objectives, and marketers need to be confident that they have devised the most appropriate strategy given their circumstances. To make the overall recommendation to implement the marketing plan, financial analysis and cost-benefit analysis are required. Financial analysis involves developing projected (pro-forma) financial statements, such as a pro-forma income statement and balance sheet, and sometimes a cash flow statement or a statement of sources and uses of funds. Financial analysis might also include ratio analysis—a comparison of key figures in the financial statements. These topics are reviewed in the appendix to Chapter 9, but are the primary focus of a managerial accounting course.

Cost-benefit analysis, as the name implies, is an analysis of all the advantages and disadvantages of implementing a particular course of action. Simple cost-benefit analysis involves a judgment-based (qualitative) assessment of the net benefit (advantages relative to disadvantages) of one course of action relative to alternatives. More sophisticated cost-benefit analysis involves assigning numerical values to (quantifying) the costs and benefits and then using a decision rule or formulae to calculate the net benefit of each alternative. This more sophisticated approach allows the analyst to assign different levels of importance (weights) to different costs and benefits, but it can sometimes be very difficult to assign a numerical value to some costs and benefits. For example, how might a reasonable numeric value be assigned to the potential loss of life from a poorly designed child's toy, or the potential damage to an ecosystem from batteries that are not recycled?

Finally, if all of the above-mentioned analyses lead to a positive recommendation to implement a particular strategy, a marketing plan then outlines how the strategy will be implemented, including action plans for the marketing mix elements; responsibilities and time lines (who is going to do what, by when); the budget and how the budget will be allocated by activity; and plans to monitor and measure the results of the strategy implementation, with contingency plans if benchmarks (targets) are not met. Unless already specified as part of the marketing mix, this section of the plan would also specify how exchange relationships will be initiated and managed. This topic will be explored further in Chapters 5 and 6.

Finally, a marketing plan typically includes a set of exhibits that provide details that support the recommendations made in the body of the plan. These exhibits include the SWOT analysis, detailed market segment profiles, and a pro-forma income statement that shows the forecast sales volume and revenue and identifies the key expenses, as per the proposed marketing budget. Positioning maps (described in Chapter 3) are also often included to illustrate the relative positioning of an organization's brand(s).

Marketing Planning to Functional Plans

In more market-oriented organizations, like Apple, the marketing plan sets a common foundation for the development of functional plans such as sales, HR, and production, as illustrated in Figure 2.3. Each function develops its own plans to implement the marketing strategies outlined in the marketing plan. It should be noted, however, that some organizations, particularly government organizations (like colleges and universities), develop a financial plan first, and then make marketing and other functional decisions based on allocated budgets.

Before you read further, what do you notice about the planning process so far? What you should see is that all plans, regardless of level, dovetail into one another. In other words, if the process outlined in Figure 2.3 is working properly, all departments (functions) within an organization are following the guidelines set out by the high-level strategic plan, but at their own level of detail. It is in this way that the entire organization works together as one enterprise, each function thinking and acting toward the common good of the business by focusing on the customer.

Strategic Marketing Mix Decisions in International Markets

Marketers like Mega Bloks that operate in two or more countries have a crucial decision to make: How necessary is it to develop a customized marketing mix for each country? As the ad in Exhibit 2.6 shows, Xerox has chosen to communicate a standardized message in other countries (the ad appears in a Spanish magazine).

The choice between standardization and localization (customization) can be difficult and complex. For example, as seen in Exhibit 2.7, Wal-Mart chose standardized signs and store layout in its Japanese stores. While

Conseguir una comunicación más efectiva con 6 millones de clientes, era uno de los objetivos primordiales de "la Caixa". Para ello, confió en las soluciones Xerox de impresión de documentos personalizados con color de realce. Ahora, cada cliente recibe la información que realmente le interesa.
Hay una nueva forma de ver las cosas.

Si desea recibir más información llámenos al 900 22 00 22 o visite www.xerox.com/anuncios
➤ La Red Europea de Concesionarios de Xerox contrata a 2000 vendedores en el 2002. Contacte con nosotros en el **900 22 00 22**

THE DOCUMENT COMPANY
XEROX.

Exhibit 2.6

As this Spanish Xerox ad shows, Xerox has decided to communicate standard messages in other countries.

Japanese shoppers are confused about the term "rollback," they do understand that the sign reflects price discounts offered by the retailer.

Procter & Gamble adopted a localized strategy for Asia, packing most of the shampoos it sells in single-use sizes to adapt to consumer preferences for trying new brands.[10]

STANDARDIZATION VERSUS LOCALIZATION
Advocates of standardization argue that the world has become so small and tastes so homogeneous that basic needs and wants are the same everywhere.[11] A focus on the similarities among cultures certainly is appealing. After all, if no changes in a firm's marketing strategy had to be made to compete in foreign countries, it would realize large economies of scale, because it could spread the costs of product development and promotional materials over many markets. For example, Reebok created a new centralized product development centre to develop shoe designs that can easily cross borders.[12] Widespread, consistent exposure also helps create a global brand by forging a strong, unified image all over the world—Coca-Cola signs are visible on billboards in London and on metal roofs deep in the forests of Thailand.

Exhibit 2.7
Wal-Mart's experience in Japan highlights the role of standardization versus localization.

SPOTLIGHT ON REAL PEOPLE   Arris Design

Companies in today's global environment need to find ways to communicate ideas, strategize, plan projects, and present results in a timely and effective manner to players in multiple locations. Arris, a Toronto-based design consultancy, has developed a highly effective manner of communication that incorporates pictures and drawings into computer-based presentations and archived data. Terry Mills, an Arris partner, says that "Thinking in pictures multiplies the ability to think and provides richer, more resonant and more holistic solutions."[13]

Working with multiple clients in multiple locations, Arris realized that they needed a more effective way to communicate and, more importantly, a more innovative way to think. While watching their own strategic thinkers from account planning, urban planning, and architecture, Mills and others on the Arris team realized that the artistically based professionals drew what they were thinking about while the account planning professionals wrote down what they were thinking about. They took these two foundations and incorporated them into a "way of working that was wonderfully creative and more succinct." Arris has made this the foundation of how they work.

Instead of using visuals—photographs and drawings—only in the presentation process, they also use them in the planning process. They encourage all strategizers to "think in pictures." A sketch is simple enough to render, especially after a workshop on the process, and a digital camera can easily grasp images. Both of these "pictures" can be easily distributed online for all to share. The "pictures" are incorporated into minutes or notes for presentations to clients or to other planning professionals for strategizing and planning of the project.

Arris found that good computerized file management systems and information engines that could handle both visuals and text were extremely important for all the collaborators. And once these were in place, all the elements were readily available and reproducible for everyone. As a result of this innovative idea, every one of the collaborators, including the client, is now able to "think in pictures."

1. Is this just another example of a consulting firm trying to differentiate itself, or do you think this strategic planning approach has merit?
2. How does the use of pictures aid in the strategic planning process?
3. How might this approach help cross-functional planning teams work more effectively together?

In contrast, those in favour of localization (customization) feel that the world is not *that* small, and products and promotional messages should be tailored to local environments. These marketers feel that each culture is unique and that each country has a *national character*—a distinctive set of behavioural and personality characteristics.[14] Snapple failed in Japan because consumers there didn't like the drink's cloudy appearance. Similarly, Frito-Lay Inc. stopped selling Ruffles potato chips (too salty) and Cheetos (the Japanese didn't appreciate having their fingers turn orange after eating a handful).[15]

PRODUCT DECISIONS A firm seeking to sell a product in a foreign market has three choices. Sell the same product in the new market, modify it for the market, or develop a brand-new product for the foreign market. Let's take a closer look at each option.

- A *straight extension strategy* retains the same product for domestic and foreign markets. Coca-Cola sells the same formula in every country, and Gillette offers the same razor blades everywhere.

- A *product adaptation strategy* recognizes that in many cases people in different cultures do have strong and different product preferences. Sometimes these differences can be subtle, yet important. That explains why Kellogg's (**www.kelloggs.com**), which markets the identical version of its Corn Flakes and Rice Krispies brands in North America and Europe, had to remove the green "loops" from Froot Loops after research showed that Europeans felt they were too artificial looking.[16]

- In other cases, products must be adapted because varying living conditions or customs require different designs. When the Electrolux appliance company began selling refrigerators in Europe, it found that Northern Europeans want large refrigerators because they shop once a week in supermarkets, whereas Southern Europeans want them small because they shop daily in open-air markets. Northerners like freezers on the bottom, southerners on the top. And the British are avid purchasers of frozen foods, so they insist on a unit with 60 percent freezer space.[17]

- A *product invention strategy* means that a company develops a new product as it expands to foreign markets. Ford's "world cars," including the Focus model, are being sold around the globe. In some cases, a product invention strategy takes the form of *backward invention*. The firm may find it needs to offer a less complex product than it sells elsewhere, such as a manually operated sewing machine or a hand-powered clothes washer to people without access to a reliable source of electricity.

- In India, Coca-Cola bought a local brand called Thums Up, after finding that this Coke imitator was outselling Coke four to one. Coca-Cola abandoned the Indian market in 1977, when the government ordered the company to turn over its secret formula. By the time it returned in 1993, Thums Up had become so entrenched that Coke decided in this rare case that it was better to market a local imitator than its own brand.[18]

MARKETING COMMUNICATIONS (PROMOTION) DECISIONS The marketer must also decide whether it's necessary to change product promotions in a foreign market. Some firms endorse the idea that the same message will appeal to everyone around the world, while others feel the need to customize it. The 2006 World Cup was broadcast in 189 countries to one of the biggest global television audiences ever. This mega-event illustrates how different marketers make different decisions—even when they're creating ads to be run during the same game. MasterCard ran the same "Fever" ads in 39 countries; it featured 100-odd cheering fans from 30 countries and had no dialogue—only the words "Football fever, Priceless" under the MasterCard logo. Gillette, in contrast, customized an ad for each of the 20 countries in which it ran by digitally changing the clothing colours of the fans it featured to reflect the colours of each national team. A "one world, one message" strategy has a greater chance of success if the firm's target customers live in cosmopolitan urban areas where they regularly see images from different countries. The Swedish ad for Diesel jeans in Exhibit 2.8 includes imagery from North Korea to appeal to these "global consumers." For

Exhibit 2.8

Some marketing communications, such as this ad for Diesel jeans, are not tailored to specific foreign markets.

such a campaign to succeed, the message should focus on basic concepts, such as romance or family ties, because these are likely to be understood everywhere.

Fans of a localization strategy, on the other hand, feel that cultural differences translate into market differences, which may in turn call for different advertising strategies. When Tim Hortons moved into the U.S. market, for example, it faced a completely undeveloped "morning market" in that country for coffee and baked goods. Many U.S. customers were grabbing a cup of coffee at a local gas station on their way to work. Tim Hortons' strategy for this target market became one of creating a morning market by using an advertising tag line: "Morning people. Where do they come from?" This strategy contrasted with their focus on the target market for lunch menu items (such as sandwiches and chili) in the Canadian market.[19]

PRICE DECISIONS Costs associated with transportation, tariffs, and differences in currency exchange rates often make the product more expensive for a company to make or sell in foreign markets compared to its home country. Aside from cost factors, sometimes a higher price is charged in international markets because consumers there value the uniqueness of the product. Kokanee beer, for example, is sold for $1 more per six-pack than its American competitors, because American consumers place a higher value on a product that is Canadian.

One danger of pricing too high is that competitors will find ways to offer the product at a lower price, even if this is done illegally. A **grey market** exists when an unauthorized party imports products and then sells them for a fraction of the price. Goods such as watches, cameras, and perfumes often move through the grey market—Seiko estimates that one out of every four of its watches brought into the United States is unauthorized.[20]

A company can also run into trouble if it tries to price a product too low to establish it in a new market. Some countries outlaw a practice called **dumping**, in which a company tries to get a toehold in a foreign market by pricing its products lower than they are offered at home—often removing excess supply from home markets and keeping prices up there. In one case, Eastman Kodak accused Japanese rival Fuji Photo Film of selling colour photographic paper in the United States for as little as a quarter of what it charges in Japan.[21]

DISTRIBUTION DECISIONS Getting the product to foreign consumers is half the battle. Marketers used to dealing with a handful of large wholesalers or retailers may have to rely instead on thousands of small stores, or they may run into problems finding a way to

grey market The importing of products by an unauthorized party, who then sells them for a fraction of the price.

dumping Pricing products lower in a foreign market than they are offered in the home market.

transport, package, refrigerate, or store goods for long periods of time in less developed countries.

Even the retailing giant Wal-Mart has occasionally stumbled at going global. The company recently joined the ranks of multinationals like Nokia, Nestlé, and Google that have failed to adjust to the tastes of South Korean consumers. Wal-Mart (as well as European rival Carrefours) stuck to Western marketing strategies that concentrated on dry goods, from electronics to clothing, while its local rivals like E-Mart and Lotte emphasized food and beverages, which are more likely to attract South Koreans to large stores. Local customers also didn't take to a relatively sterile environment where products sell by the box; its competitors enticed shoppers with eye-catching displays and clerks who hawked their goods with megaphones and hand clapping. Wal-Mart bailed out of South Korea entirely in 2006 and left Germany and Argentina the same year.[22] As Mega Bloks realizes, establishing a reliable distribution system is essential if the marketer is to succeed in an international market. Establishing a reliable system might be especially difficult in developing countries where thousands of individual distributors (some who transport goods to remote rural areas on ox carts or bicycles) must be persuaded to take on the product. It's also essential in developed countries, where competition for shelf space may be fierce. With more than 60 percent of all grocery retail controlled by two large firms in Canada (the Sobey's group and the Loblaws group), it can be very difficult for new entrants to get their products listed.

ETHICAL AND SOCIALLY RESPONSIBLE BEHAVIOUR IN THE MARKETPLACE

In his 2005 bestselling book, *The World Is Flat: A Brief History of the 21st Century*, Thomas Friedman argues that in today's fiercely competitive and global marketplace, the world is indeed flat. Marketers must recognize that national borders are not as important as they once were, or risk disappearing off the face of the earth. Today, businesses like Mega Bloks must seek new and improved ways to attract customers down the street and around the globe.

In addition to adopting a global focus, marketers must meet the challenge of doing good while doing well. It is no longer enough to just make money; today we expect companies to benefit their communities at the same time. Marketing is *still* concerned with the firm's "bottom line," but now many managers also consider **social profit**, which is the net benefit both the firm and society receive from a firm's ethical practices and socially responsible behaviour. These managers recognize that the pressures to practise ethical behaviour today are part of the overall business environment in which they operate.

social profit The benefit an organization and society receive from the organization's ethical practices, community service, efforts to promote cultural diversity, and concern for the natural environment.

Creating social profit is so important to The Body Shop Canada (**www.thebodyshop.ca**) that the first line of their mission statement reads, "We dedicate our business to the pursuit of social and environmental change."[23] Evidence of this commitment to social profit can be seen in The Body Shop's long-standing environmental activism, its stand against using animals in product testing, and its community service activities, including campaigns for fair international trade and activities to fight violence against women. Mountain Equipment Co-op (Exhibit 2.9) states on its website: "Count on us to act with integrity. We are driven by passion not profit. We continue to look for ways to protect our wild spaces and reduce the ecological footprint of our business."[24] We call these efforts to do business *right* and do it *well* the *New Era of marketing*.

Doing It Right: Ethical Behaviour in the Marketplace

business ethics Rules of conduct for an organization.

Business ethics is the first step toward creating social profit. But what does ethical business behaviour mean to New Era firms and to their marketing strategies? Ethics are rules of conduct—how most people in a culture judge what is right and what is wrong. **Business ethics** are basic values that guide a firm's behaviour, and these beliefs govern the decisions managers make about what goes into their products, how they are advertised and sold, and how they are disposed of.

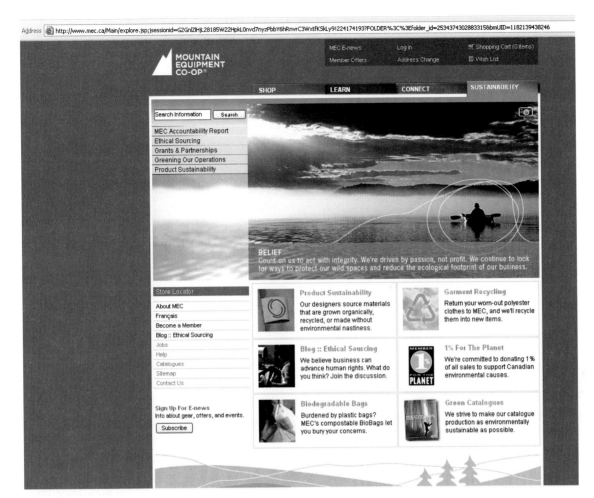

Exhibit 2.9

Mountain Equipment Co-op is a New Era firm that proudly displays its focus on "doing good" while doing well.

In the New Era of marketing, we are witnessing greater concern about business decisions based solely on short-term profits. It has been suggested that business operates in an "ethics era"—a period in which both executives and consumers are becoming concerned about the downside of "business as usual."[25] A report from the Canadian Democracy and Corporate Accountability Commission has revealed that 74 percent of Canadian shareholders believe that business executives should "embrace a broader social ethic" in their corporate responsibilities.[26]

The emphasis on ethical business practices means that sometimes firms must make decisions that hurt them in the short term. Despite robust sales of a video game called Night Trap made by Sega, executives at Toys "R" Us pulled the product from store shelves. This costly action was taken after the store chain received complaints from parents, who objected to their children playing a game in which scantily dressed sorority sisters fight off zombies who try to suck out their blood with a giant syringe.

Notions of right and wrong differ between organizations and cultures. Some businesses, for example, believe it is acceptable for salespeople to use any means to persuade customers to buy, even giving them partly true or even false information, while other firms feel that anything less than total honesty with customers is wrong. Because each culture has its own set of values, beliefs, and customs, ethical business behaviour varies in different parts of the world. Transparency International (**www.transparency.org**), an organization dedicated to fighting corruption in business around the world, created an International Corruption Perceptions Index, which highlights the differences in the perceptions of corrupt business practices around the world. Out of the 91 countries ranked in their recent Index, Finland was identified as number one, the country perceived to have the least corrupt business practices, and Canada ranked as number seven, ahead of both the United Kingdom (number 13) and the United States (number 16).

code of ethics Written standards of behaviour to which everyone in the organization must subscribe.

To reduce the confusion about what is right and wrong in international and domestic business operations, many firms develop their own **code of ethics**, or written standards of behaviour, to which everyone in the organization must subscribe. These documents eliminate confusion about what the firm considers to be ethically acceptable behaviour for employees. For example, Dow's Code of Business Conduct (available through its website in 15 different languages—**www.dow.com**) includes ethical principles and policies to deal with issues such as bribery, political contributions, equal employment opportunity, and environment, health, and safety concerns.

Regarding questionable payments, the Code states:

> It is against Dow policy to make unlawful, improper, or other kinds of questionable payments to customers, government employees, or other third parties. We sell our products on the merits of price, quality, and service. We do not seek business obtained through deviation from this principle. We will not offer expensive gifts, bribes, or any other kind of payment or benefit to representatives of customers, suppliers, competitors, government, or governmental agencies. This applies to any individual or organization at any level, whether domestic or foreign.[27]

Professional associations also often establish codes of ethics to guide the behaviour of members. For instance, to help members of the marketing profession in North America and elsewhere adhere to ethical behaviour in their marketing efforts, the American Marketing Association (AMA), the largest professional marketing association in the world, has developed its own Code of Ethics, which is shown in Figure 2.8. In Canada, the Professional Marketing Research Society (**www.pmrs-aprm.com**), the professional organization for the marketing research community, has its own set of ethical standards that all members must adhere to.

THE HIGH COSTS OF UNETHICAL MARKETPLACE BEHAVIOUR Ethical business is good business. New Era marketers understand that unethical practices can wind up costing dearly in the long run both to the firm's finances and to its reputation. Numerous examples have been front page news, such as the Enron accounting fraud, the falsified financial statements of WorldCom, Martha Stewart being convicted of insider trading, WestJet officials resigning after unethical procurement of competitive data, and Conrad Black recently being convicted of three charges of embezzlement.

CONSUMERISM: PEOPLE FIGHTING BACK

Organized activities that bring about social and political change are not new to the Canadian scene. Women's right to vote, child labour laws, universal medicare, minimum wage, and equal employment opportunities have all resulted from social movements in which citizens, public and private organizations, and business work to change society. **Consumerism** is the social movement directed at protecting consumers from harmful business practices.

consumerism A social movement that attempts to protect consumers from harmful business practices.

The modern consumerism movement in Canada began in the late 1940s, when the Consumers' Association of Canada (CAC) was established (**www.consumer.ca**). The mission of the CAC is to inform and educate consumers, and also to advocate on their behalf.[28] Since its inception, the CAC has been active in helping to establish protective legislation for consumers, related to labelling and packaging, bans on the use of certain pesticides, and improved quality standards for agricultural and manufactured goods. Recent activities of the CAC have focused on fighting the practice of negative-option marketing by the cable industry, in which consumers were automatically charged for services that they did not sign up for unless they contacted the cable company to cancel, and conducting a national consumer survey regarding Canadians' perceptions of the quality of goods and services.

Members of the American Marketing Association are committed to ethical, professional conduct. They have joined together in subscribing to this Code of Ethics embracing the following topics:

Responsibilities of the Marketer

Marketers must accept responsibility for the consequences of their activities and make every effort to ensure that their decisions, recommendations, and actions function to identify, serve, and satisfy all relevant publics: customers, organizations, and society.

Marketers' professional conduct must be guided by:

1. The basic rule of professional ethics: not knowingly to do harm;
2. The adherence to all applicable laws and regulations;
3. The accurate representation of their education, training and experience; and
4. The active support, practice, and promotion of this Code of Ethics.

Honesty and Fairness

Marketers shall uphold and advance the integrity, honor, and dignity of the marketing profession by:

1. Being honest in serving consumers, clients, employees, suppliers, distributors, and the public;
2. Not knowingly participating in conflict of interest without prior notice to all parties involved; and
3. Establishing equitable fee schedules including the payment or receipt of usual, customary, and/or legal compensation for marketing exchanges.

Rights and Duties of Parties in the Marketing Exchange Process

Participants in the marketing exchange process should be able to expect that:

1. Products and services offered are safe and fit for their intended uses;
2. Communications about offered products and services are not deceptive;
3. All parties intend to discharge their obligations, financial and otherwise, in good faith; and
4. Appropriate internal methods exist for equitable adjustment and/or redress of grievances concerning purchases.

It is understood that the above would include, but is not limited to, the following responsibilities of the marketer: In the area of product development and management,
- disclosure of all substantial risks associated with product or service usage;
- identification of any product component substitution that might materially change the product or impact on the buyer's purchase decision;
- identification of extra cost-added features.

In the area of promotions,
- avoidance of false and misleading advertising;
- rejection of high pressure manipulations, or misleading sales tactics;
- avoidance of sales promotions that use deception or manipulation.

In the area of distribution,
- not manipulating the availability of a product for purpose of exploitation;
- not using coercion in the marketing channel;
- not exerting undue influence over the reseller's choice to handle a product.

In the area of pricing,
- not engaging in price fixing;
- not practicing predatory pricing;
- disclosing the full price associated with any purchase.

In the area of marketing research,
- prohibiting selling or fundraising under the guise of conducting research;
- maintaining research integrity by avoiding misrepresentation and omission of pertinent research data;
- treating outside clients and suppliers fairly.

Organizational Relationships

Marketers should be aware of how their behavior may influence or impact on the behavior of others in organizational relationships. They should not demand, encourage, or apply coercion to obtain unethical behavior in their relationships with others, such as employees, suppliers, or customers.

1. Apply confidentiality and anonymity in professional relationships with regard to privileged information;
2. Meet their obligations and responsibilities in contracts and mutual agreements in a timely manner;
3. Avoid taking the work of others, in whole, or in part, and represent this work as their own or directly benefit from it without compensation or consent of the originator or owner;
4. Avoid manipulation to take advantage of situations to maximize personal welfare in a way that unfairly deprives or damages the organization of others.

Any AMA member found to be in violation of any provision of this Code of Ethics may have his or her Association membership suspended or revoked.

Figure 2.8 AMA Code of Ethics

The CAC outlines seven Consumer Rights, which it argues that both government legislation and ethical businesses should recognize and provide:

- *The Right to Safety:* Consumers should be confident that products are not dangerous when used as intended.

- *The Right to Be Informed:* Businesses should provide consumers with adequate information to make intelligent product choices. This right means that product information provided by advertising, packaging, and salespeople should be honest and complete.

- *The Right to Be Heard:* Consumers should have the means to complain or express their displeasure to obtain redress or retribution from companies. Government agencies and industry self-regulatory groups should respond to every customer complaint.

- *The Right to Redress:* Consumers should be provided with the opportunity to take action if their needs are not met in the marketplace.

- *The Right to Choose:* Consumers should be able to choose from a variety of products. No one business should be allowed to control the price, quality, or availability of goods and services.

- *The Right to a Healthy Environment:* Consumers have the right to expect that government and businesses will make choices that ensure a healthy environment.

- *The Right to Consumer Education:* Consumers have a right to expect that they will be provided with the skills necessary to make educated choices in the marketplace.

The Consumers Council of Canada, another consumer organization that strives to improve the marketplace for Canadian consumers, has suggested an eighth consumer right to be protected: the right to privacy, an increasingly important right in the age of information technology.[29]

Consumers continue to have a vigorous interest in consumer-related issues, and New Era marketers are responding by voluntarily making changes to prevent both consumer anger and government intervention. New Era marketers avoid both the financial losses and loss of reputation that consumerism activities may cause by having their customers' best interests in mind from the start.

Ethics in the Marketing Mix

As we've seen previously, marketing mix strategies are crucial to a firm's success in achieving its objectives. Marketing managers are responsible for determining the most ethical way to price, package, communicate, and distribute their offerings to reach profit and market share objectives. Let's examine how ethical considerations can influence marketing mix decisions.

In product strategies, a key ethical decision concerns product safety. It may be tempting to cut costs on design, safety testing, and production to be able to rush a new product to market or to beat competitors on price. However, responsible companies realize that product safety needs to be a priority. They do everything to ensure that their product meets safety standards when it goes to market, and they react swiftly if a product is found to be unsafe after it is on the market. In any month in Canada, there are several product recalls: Manufacturers recognize safety problems with their products and ask consumers to return them. You can log on to the CBC website to check out the latest product recalls (**www.cbc.ca/consumer/recalls**).

PRICING THE PRODUCT FAIRLY The potential for unethical pricing strategies is so great that many shady pricing practices are illegal. For example, firms that compete in a market in which there are only a few other firms are not allowed to decide in advance on a common price for their product. This practice, called **price fixing**, eliminates price competition, which otherwise would keep prices down. Another pricing strategy is *price discrimination*, charging lower prices to larger customers. This is acceptable only if it reflects real cost savings for the manufacturer or is necessary to meet competitors' pricing.

price fixing An illegal business practice in which firms decide in advance on a common price for their product.

A pricing strategy that is unethical but not illegal is *price gouging*—raising the price of a product to take advantage of its popularity. When Chrysler introduced its PT Cruiser, some consumers paid up to US$10 000 over the sticker price to get the car. Some Canadian consumers think oil companies are price gouging with unreasonable high gasoline prices.

New Era firms price their products fairly—and they have been known to cut their prices in times of need. During an eastern Canadian ice storm in 1998, some Ontario and Quebec businesses didn't just lower prices; they gave away products for free. St. Viateur Bagel Shop in Montreal, for example, gave away their famous bagels to people without power, and IGA stores gave away baked goods to those in need.[30]

PROMOTING THE PRODUCT ETHICALLY Marketing management's decisions on how to promote the firm's products are likely to draw the most criticism from consumers. To promote ethical behaviour on the part of advertisers and to provide consumers with a forum for expressing complaints about advertising, the Canadian advertising industry follows a process of self-regulation through Advertising Standards Canada (ASC, **www.adstandards.com**). The Canadian Code of Advertising Standards, which ASC administers, has specific guidelines regarding unfair or deceptive advertising to ensure the accuracy and appropriateness of claims. For example, ASC heard a complaint against Gone Hollywood Video, of Burnaby, British Columbia, regarding a newspaper ad that the organization had run to recruit franchisees. The ads promised "100% success rate" and claimed that franchisees could "Earn Jurassic Profits." Gone Hollywood Video was unable to substantiate the claims made in the ad, so the complaint against them was upheld.[31]

ASC also enforces guidelines with respect to appropriate gender portrayal in ads. These Gender Portrayal Guidelines state that advertising should not include sexual exploitation and should always portray women and men as equals. KIA, for example, stirred controversy with an ad that implied that a young female police officer was making out with a KIA driver she had pulled over. KIA eventually pulled the ad after significant public backlash. Although these guidelines were originally intended to fight negative portrayals of women in advertising, complaints by consumers have increasingly related to the portrayal of men. Just prior to its demise, a complaint was lodged against Eaton's, and the company agreed to stop showing an ad that ASC found to sexually objectify men. The ad depicted a glamorous woman going off to work, while her husband remained behind, shackled to the kitchen. Although Eaton's claimed that the ad was meant to fight gender myths by using humour, ASC reinforced the Gender Portrayal Guidelines, which state that the use of humour "should not serve as an excuse to stereotype women or men or portray behaviour that is not acceptable today."

GETTING THE PRODUCT WHERE IT BELONGS Channels of distribution decisions can also create ethical dilemmas. For example, because their size gives them bargaining power in the channel of distribution, many large retail chains are forcing manufacturers to pay a **slotting allowance**, a fee paid in exchange for agreeing to place the manufacturer's products on the retailer's valuable shelf space. While the retailers claim that such fees pay the cost of adding products to their inventory, many manufacturers feel slotting fees are unethical. Certainly the practice prevents smaller manufacturers that cannot afford the slotting allowances from reaching consumers.

slotting allowance A fee paid by a manufacturer to a retailer in exchange for agreeing to place products on the retailer's shelves.

DOING IT RIGHT: A FOCUS ON SOCIAL RESPONSIBILITY

We've learned how New Era firms gain social profit by practising business ethics when making marketing mix decisions. The second part of social profit is **social responsibility**, a management process in which organizations engage in activities that have a positive effect on society and promote the public good. These activities include environmental stewardship, cause marketing, and encouraging cultural diversity. Firms like Ben & Jerry's that believe in social responsibility represent a business value system that goes beyond the short-term bottom line. Instead, they consider the short- and long-term effects of decisions on the company, its employees, consumers, the community, and the world at large.

social responsibility A management practice in which organizations seek to engage in activities that have a positive effect on society and promote the public good.

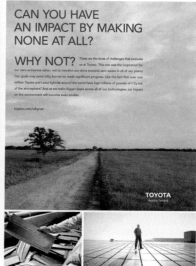

Exhibit 2.10

Toyota is conscientious about environmental stewardship.

Serving the Environment

environmental stewardship A position taken by an organization to protect or enhance the natural environment as it conducts its business activities.

When New Era firms make socially responsible business decisions that also protect the environment, they assume a position of **environmental stewardship**. The Body Shop Canada practises this through "sustainability" strategies, the development of products that use resources sparingly to sustain those resources for future generations. Toyota has developed a hybrid car, the Toyota Prius, which combines a gasoline engine with a powerful electric motor.

green marketing A marketing strategy that supports environmental stewardship by creating an environmentally founded differential benefit in the minds of consumers.

The term **green marketing** describes efforts by firms to choose packages, product designs, and other aspects of the marketing mix that are earth friendly but still profitable (see Exhibit 2.10). The Canadian government, through Environment Canada, encourages Canadian companies to practise green marketing through such programs as the EcoLogo. This program promotes stringent, environmentally friendly guidelines for industries, ranging from automotive products to office supplies. If a business meets the guidelines, it may use the EcoLogo on its product to signal its environmental soundness to consumers. Companies that have been granted the right to use the EcoLogo include Frigidaire Canada, which manufactures energy-efficient dishwashers and washing machines, and Fuji Graphics Systems, which has developed photo processing systems that are gentle to the environment.[32]

Green marketing practices can indeed be successful for a firm's bottom line. For example, Electrolux found that profits from its solar-powered lawn mowers, chain saws lubricated with vegetable oil, and water-conserving washing machines were actually 3.8 percent higher than profits from the company's conventional products.[33]

Serving Society: Cause Marketing

cause marketing A marketing strategy in which an organization serves its community by promoting and supporting a worthy cause or by allying itself with a not-for-profit organization to tackle a social problem.

Cause marketing is a strategy of joining forces with a not-for-profit organization to tackle a social problem. In the past, this practice usually meant running a short-term promotion and then donating profits to a charity. But consumers often saw these programs as gimmicky and insincere, especially when there was no apparent connection between the company and the cause. As a result, sales increased during the promotion, but there were no long-term benefits to either the sponsoring firm or the cause it was trying to help.

Today, New Era firms have abandoned this one-shot approach and instead make a long-term commitment to tackle a social problem, such as illiteracy or child abuse.[34] Avon Canada's Flame Crusade Against Breast Cancer (Exhibit 2.11) is one example of cause marketing. Since its inception in 1993, the program has raised over $5.2 million for breast cancer research through the sales of such products as the Flame pin.[35] Avon hopes that its long-term involvement with breast cancer awareness will result in both health benefits for women and increased goodwill for the company—a "win-win" situation.

Serving the Community: Promoting Cultural Diversity

In a country as culturally diverse as Canada, promotion of **cultural diversity** is not only the right thing to do, it's also important to the long-term financial health of the organization. When firms adopt cultural diversity programs, they make sure that marketing policies and hiring practices give people an equal chance to work for the company and buy its products.

Warner-Lambert Canada, manufacturer of such brands as Listerine, Trident, and Dentyne, embraces cultural diversity; as one company document states, "The more our organization reflects the consumer population, the more it will be in sync with what customers want, need, and are looking for."[36]

The diversity philosophy also extends to the disabled. Smart marketers view the disabled as both customers and valued employees. Hertz, for example, offers cars at nearly 800 rental locations that disabled people can drive and has worked to equip shuttle buses and vans with lifts to transport these customers.[37]

We've seen that New Era firms create social profit by adhering to ethical business practices. Social profit is also created when firms practise social responsibility by being concerned about the environment, promoting diversity, and serving their communities through cause marketing.

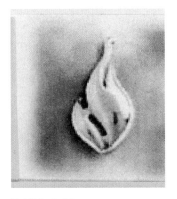

Exhibit 2.11

Avon Flame: a successful cause marketing program that female customers appreciate.

cultural diversity A management practice that actively seeks to include people of different sexes, races, ethnic groups, religions, and sexual preferences in an organization's employees, customers, suppliers, and distribution channel partners.

Real People, Real Decisions

▶ How It Worked Out at Mega Bloks

Michel Bendayan and other senior Mega Bloks managers decided to re-enter the Japanese market using a large strategic partner (alternative D3). They approached Bandai, the largest toy manufacturer in Japan and one of the top toy manufacturers worldwide. Bandai was well known for its character-licensed toys, which included lines of Power Rangers, Masked Riders, Ultraman, and Anpanman products. Bandai, however, did not make construction toys, so even though the company is much larger than Mega Bloks, the partnership held some advantages for Bandai. The Bandai-Mega Bloks partnership was the largest distribution deal Mega Bloks had ever done. Because the consumers were thought to be highly character oriented, because Bandai had experience and licences for key Japanese characters, and because there were concerns that the Western culture themes of the current Mega Bloks might not be desired by Japanese consumers, Michel and his colleagues decided to jointly develop two new product lines with Bandai (alternative P3). Using many of the same components as North American products, the preschool line featured Anpanman characters and was sold in tubs and resealable bags for ease of cleanup and storage. The other line targeted

boys five to eight with more action-oriented characters and themes, and was offered in more standard boxes. The intent was to develop a foundation of Japanese-themed products that would be the base from which top-selling world lines could be added.

The preschool line exceeded sales expectations, but the product targeted at five- to eight-year-olds did not. Michel thought this might have mostly been the result of the licensed characters being "old"—they get refreshed every year and manufacturers have to hit a much faster production cycle than in North America to keep abreast of the trends—but it might also have been because there were fewer buckets and resealable bags in the line. There were also some consumer concerns about the preschool line—Bandai had thought that the small-sized building blocks would be suitable for three- to five-year-olds, but feedback suggested the bricks were too small for this age group. Similar blocks were targeted to five- to seven-year-olds in North America. Thus, while Bandai understood the general Japanese toy market, it did not fully understand the construction toy market. This joint learning has fuelled the development of a new line of construction blocks targeting five- to eight-year-old Japanese boys.

CHAPTER SUMMARY

1. Explain how businesses develop plans at different levels within the organization.

Planning in most business organizations occurs mainly at two levels: strategic and functional. Strategic plans are high-level plans that envision where the business is going within the next three to five years. Mission statements guide the formation of strategic plans, which are developed for the entire business or for individual strategic business units (SBUs) within the organization.

Given their high-level nature, strategic plans cannot be implemented directly. For this reason, firms develop a one-year plan, which takes its direction from the strategic plan, called the marketing plan. From this, the different functions such as production, sales, finance, and human resources develop their own plans. In this way, the entire organization is working toward a common goal.

2. Describe the steps in the marketing planning process.

Marketing planning begins with an evaluation of the external and internal environments facing the business. Marketing managers then set quantitative and qualitative market objectives, such as desired levels of sales, development of new or improved products, or growth in new or existing markets. Next, marketing managers select the target market(s) the organization will go after and decide what marketing mix strategies they will use. Tactical plans are developed to implement the strategies and mechanisms to control the marketing plan are put in place. Therefore, the marketing planning process ends with the development of a formal, written document—the marketing plan.

3. Explain how to conduct situational analysis and SWOT analysis to understand a decision context.

Situational analysis is an environmental scan that identifies factors in the external and internal environment that are important to understand when making marketing decisions. SWOT analysis is a tool used to summarize a situational analysis for a particular organization. This tool helps the organization identify the strengths and weaknesses of its internal environment and the opportunities and threats of its external environment with the aim of being able to utilize strengths or address weaknesses to take advantage of opportunities or mitigate threats to create value.

4. Explain how strategic marketing mix decisions are made in international markets.

Firms competing in the international marketplace have strategic decisions they need to make regarding the deployment of the marketing mix elements. The main question they have to ask is this: Should we standardize our strategies across international markets, or should we customize? These decisions are not easy because a number of factors influence them, such as laws in foreign countries, consumer preferences, and availability of resources and channels of distribution.

5. Explain how firms practise ethical and socially responsible behaviour in the marketplace.

Many consumers today are concerned with the ethical practices of companies. As a result, astute marketers recognize that long-term profitability depends on making quality products while acting in an ethical and socially responsible manner. Marketing is *still* concerned with the firm's "bottom line," but now many managers also consider social profit, which is the net benefit both the firm and society receive from a firm's ethical practices and socially responsible behaviour.

The second part of social profit is social responsibility, a management process in which organizations engage in activities that have a positive effect on society and promote the public good. These activities include environmental stewardship, cause marketing, and encouraging cultural diversity. Firms like Ben & Jerry's that believe in social responsibility represent a business value system that goes beyond the short-term bottom line. Instead, they consider the short- and long-term effects of decisions on the company, its employees, consumers, the community, and the world at large.

CHAPTER REVIEW

Marketing Concepts: Testing Your Knowledge

1. What are the different levels of planning within a business organization?

2. What is a mission statement? Why is a mission statement important to an organization?

3. What is a SWOT analysis? What role does it play in the planning process?

4. What is a business portfolio? Why do firms develop SBUs?

5. Why is marketing planning important to a firm?

6. What are the elements of a sound marketing plan?

7. What does it mean for a firm to have a competitive advantage? What factors give a firm a competitive advantage in the marketplace?

8. What are marketing objectives? What types of marketing objectives do firms normally include in marketing planning?

9. How are marketing plans related to other functional plans within a business?

10. Explain the tradeoffs involved in marketing mix decisions when firms enter international markets. Provide concrete examples.

11. What is social profit? What are the two main components of social profit?

Marketing Concepts: Discussing Choices and Issues

1. What do you think about the different levels of planning in business organizations? What are the benefits of such an approach? Do you see any drawbacks?

2. Do you agree with the idea that marketing is a firm's most essential functional area, or do you think a firm's success depends equally on all of its functional areas? Explain your reasoning.

3. Do you think firms should concentrate on developing products that are better in some way than competitors' products, or should each firm focus on making the best product it can without regard to competing products? As a consumer, which approach is more likely to produce products that satisfy you the most?

4. Most planning, whether by businesses or by not-for-profit organizations, involves strategies for growth. But is growth always the right direction? Can you think of some organizations that should have contraction rather than expansion as their goal? Do you know of any organizations that have planned to get smaller rather than larger to be successful?

Marketing Practice: Applying What You've Learned

1. Assume that you are the marketing director for a local microbrewery and that your boss, the company president, has decided to develop a mission statement to add to this year's annual report. He's admitted that he doesn't know much about developing a mission statement and has asked you to help guide him in this process. Write a memo outlining what exactly a mission statement is, why firms develop such statements, how firms use mission statements, and your thoughts on what the firm's mission statement might be.

2. As a marketing student, you know that large firms often organize their operations into a number of strategic business units (SBUs). A college or university might develop a similar structure where different academic units are seen as separate businesses. Working with four to six classmates, consider how your college or university might divide its total academic units into separate SBUs. What would be the problems with implementing such a plan? What would be the advantages and disadvantages for students and for faculty? Present your analysis of university SBUs to your class.

3. Assume you are the new marketing assistant in a small metropolitan medical clinic whose market consists of the residents in the city district and the students and faculty of a large nearby college or university. You have been asked for ideas that the organization might use in promotional activities to draw clients who might otherwise choose a larger facility across town. Develop a list of the consumer segments in the clinic's market (for example, elderly, children, college or university athletes, international students), and for each segment, identify possible features and benefits the clinic might emphasize in its promotions to attract that segment.

4. Pick two firms that both operate in foreign markets but use different strategies to compete. In your opinion, which strategy is superior? Why? Base your answer on a thorough analysis of the marketing mix variables.

5. Do you think firms practising New Era marketing are doing it for the financial benefit? What do you think is the future of New Era marketing? What is the next big idea that will emerge from this concept?

Marketing Mini-Project: Learning by Doing

The purpose of this mini-project is to gain an understanding of marketing planning through actual experience.

1. Select one of the following for your marketing planning project:
   - Yourself (in your search for a career)
   - Your college or university
   - A specific department in your college or university

2. Next, develop the following elements of the marketing planning process:
   - A mission statement
   - A SWOT analysis
   - Objectives
   - A description of the target market(s)
   - A brief outline of the marketing mix strategies—product, pricing, distribution, and marketing communications strategies—that satisfy the objectives and address the target market

3. Prepare a formal, but brief, marketing plan using the template provided in this chapter as a guide.

Real People, Real Surfers: Exploring the Web

Visit the homepages of one or more of the firms of your choice. Follow the links to find out about the company's products, pricing, distribution, and marketing communications strategies. Do a web search for other information about the company. Based on your findings, answer the following questions.

1. What is the organization's "business"? What is the overall purpose of the organization? What does the organization hope to achieve?

2. What customers does the organization want to serve?

3. What elements of the webpage specifically reflect the business of the organization? How is the webpage designed to attract the organization's customers?

4. Do you think the marketing strategies and other activities of the organization are consistent with its mission? Why do you feel this way?

Develop a report based on your findings and conclusions about the organization. Present your report to your class.

Managers at the Seiyu supermarket chain in Japan, which is 38 percent owned by Wal-Mart Stores, start their day with a ritual just as their counterparts do in Bentonville, Arkansas, where Wal-Mart is headquartered. "Give me an S!" their Japanese manager shouts. "S!" comes the reply. The group spells "S-E-I-Y-U." Finally, the manager asks: "Who is number one?" Their reply: "Customers!"

While it may appear that Wal-Mart has simply replicated its North American strategy in Japan, nothing could be further from the truth. The Wal-Mart story in Japan is one of market entry strategy, product positioning, learning about cultural differences, and making strategic choices.

Unlike Toys "R" Us or Costco, which opened stores under the corporate name in Japan, Wal-Mart decided to buy a part of Seiyu and use its name to compete instead of the Wal-Mart name and logo. Wal-Mart felt that it could not only take advantage of Seiyu's well-known but struggling brand, but also use a local partner to navigate through Japan's complex supplier network.

Many analysts feel Wal-Mart will not succeed in Japan for several reasons. One, the Japanese market is dominated by powerful manufacturers and wholesalers, who keep prices high. How will a discounter like Wal-Mart, which relies on low prices, succeed? Two, Japanese consumers are very different from North American consumers. They are very finicky and are set in their buying habits. Three, the entire Japanese corporate culture is unlike that of North America. Many Japanese corporations are very hierarchical, with rigid boundaries between senior managers and juniors. At Wal-Mart, on the other hand, managers interact in a very informal way with colleagues, lavishing them with praise for a job well done, something that is new to the Japanese way of thinking.

At present, Wal-Mart has been concentrating its attention on managing stores based on sales information rather than managers' hunches. To do this, it has invested heavily in product scanners and databases that provide managers with accurate information about inventory, sales, and prices.

Wal-Mart has been sensitive to local cultural issues. In the process of modernizing stores, it has added small fish markets in the stores where consumers can buy fresh fish. In North America, Wal-Mart relies on consumers to know that it practises "Every Day Low Prices." However, Japanese consumers rely on weekly circulars informing them of specials. Initially, Wal-Mart refused to use these promotional materials. However, consumers complained, so Wal-Mart returned to the Japanese practice of using circulars.

Although some North American tactics do not translate well in Japan (for example, consumers did not know the meaning of the term "rollback"), others appear to be working well. Wal-Mart uses the strict training methods it uses in North America in Japan. For example, it is teaching managers to be more assertive and to be more at ease when interacting in public. Japanese managers, in a training session, had to dance in front of the class for being late or forgetting to turn off their cellphones!

Source: Adapted from Ken Belson, "Wal-Mart hopes it won't be lost in translation," *The New York Times*, 14 December 2003, Section 3: 1, 12.

Things to Think About

1. What factors do you think Wal-Mart would have taken into account to make strategic choices in the Japanese market?

2. Evaluate Wal-Mart's decision to enter the Japanese market with a partner instead of opening its own stores.

3. Do you think Wal-Mart will be successful in Japan? Why or why not?

4. If you were working for Wal-Mart in Japan, what steps would you take next to ensure successful entry into the Japanese market?

TRUE CANADIAN® TASTE
FROM CANADA'S OLDEST BREWERY.

CHAPTER 3
Market Segmentation and Positioning

Real People, Real Decisions

Meet **Michael Shekter,** Brand Director for Molson Canadian

Michael Shekter doesn't give up. Michael has worked his way through the marketing hierarchy in Canada to earn his position with Molson Canadian. Achieving a great education with a B.A. (Political Science/History) from McGill and then an M.B.A. in Marketing Strategy from York, he positioned himself well. Michael started his marketing career in 1992 as a brand manager for Procter & Gamble, managing brands like Tide, Ivory, Cascade, Vicks, and Comet. He moved to Kraft (Nabisco) as marketing director for their cookies business, and then to Maple Leaf Consumer Foods as director of innovation. As a Marketing instructor at York University and the University of Toronto, and as an independent marketing consultant for companies such as Microsoft, Unilever, Maple Leaf Foods, AIM Trimark Investments, and ACNielsen he gained further professional perspective. He was a winner of the Grocery Industry "Grand Prix" award for Innovation, Snack Food Category. In 2004 he was ready to take on the challenge of brand director for Molson Canadian.

Molson Canadian experienced decreasing market share from the early 2000s on, despite award-winning advertising with "The Rant" and subsequent campaigns promoting the "I Am. Canadian" positioning. Similar premium brands like Labatt Blue were also losing market share to both super-premium brands like Heineken and to value brands and microbrew brands. In response to cost pressures, the price of Canadian and other middle-priced brands had been slowly increasing. This eroded the differentiation between the premium brands and the super-premium brands, providing an easier decision for consumers to choose super-premium brands. The price increases had also created greater demand, in some segments, for the lower-priced "value" brands. In addition, government tax incentives for small brewers—especially in Ontario and Alberta—had made it easier for smaller breweries to make a profit with a lower price point, allowing more of these value-priced brands to enter the market and compete effectively.

This left Molson with the challenge of defining what their Canadian brand stood for. They were not a low-cost brand as there were new players and brands claiming this position. They also could not claim the import or super-premium position as this was taken by either the established older brands or the new microbrewed local brands. Canadian occupied the "mushy middle." Their reason for existing had become confusing in the consumer's mind.

Molson considered three options:

Option 1: Back to the future.

The first option the team looked at was trying to effect changes that would return the Canadian brand to its competitive position during its period of highest growth—in the late '80s and early '90s. This would involve lowering the price of the product to enhance the value proposition and focusing more strongly on the "best beer for good times" positioning, versus the more "flag waving" positioning of the "I Am" campaign.

Michael thought that the advantages of this approach were threefold: (1) This was a very successful and sustainable model for Canadian at its peak—it had worked in the past and could work now. (2) This positioning reflected what a lot of people bought Canadian for and how they thought of it—Molson Canadian would have credibility with this approach. (3) Molson still had strong associations with music and hockey, which they could activate.

Michael also saw some disadvantages. The market had changed, and consumers may have moved on—it was high risk to try to recapture the past. If Molson lowered its price, it would have a huge impact on profitability—if it couldn't recover sufficient market share, it would be a bad business decision that would leave the brand still weak, and much poorer. There was also the consideration that a price decrease could signal a warning on Molson's stock, as Marlboro's price decrease did in the 1980s. If only a small price decrease was implemented, Molson would still be more expensive than value beers, so the whole exercise could be for naught.

Option 2: Stay the course.

The second option the team looked at was to continue with the "I Am. Canadian" campaign. There is something definitive in this campaign—it is an iconic symbol. People still recognized "The Rant," the slogan, and still expected to see new creative strategies from the team that had taken the advertising world by storm. The Canadian brand team almost felt "obligated" to continue with this campaign as it had made such an emotional impact on consumers. Also, there was already a large investment in this campaign. It was more than a TV campaign. It was on bottles, cases, trucks, T-shirts, and many other brand marketing items. The campaign had the added advantage of being understood by both the company and the consumer. Although this approach had not stemmed the decline in sales, the team might be able to develop a stronger strategy with better campaign execution to be successful in converting the strong emotional connection to the brand into stronger sales of the brand.

Option 3: Clean sheet.

The third option for the team was to create a new premium positioning for the brand that would allow it to compete more effectively with the super-premium brands. This would require a stronger "emotional story" that provided consumers with a reason to believe on a personal level, not on a nationalistic level. To differentiate the brand from the value brands, the positioning would also need to tell a "product story" focused on the quality difference. Developing a new positioning and supporting this with an entirely new campaign was an expensive and risky option. It would mean a huge financial risk and a huge emotional risk, as Molson employees cared a lot about the fate of this brand. They would need to completely change the brand, the perception of the consumer, the company's perception of itself, and start over. The key advantages of this alternative were: (1) It would allow the brand to compete on a "product" basis, where it was losing credibility to super-premiums. (2) It would be an opportunity to "refresh" the brand, shake off the strong patriotic (but not beer-selling) associations of the "I Am." campaign. (3) It might provide a broader and more sustainable platform for the brand moving forward. On the other hand, Shekter wondered if consumers would accept the new positioning. A competitor might find the "patriotic" theme compelling and pick it up for their own brand. Finally, a change at this time might look like a "blink"—recognition that Molson had been wrong—and it might motivate their competitors into taking a stronger run at Molson Canadian.

Now, join Michael Shekter and the Molson Canadian marketing team: Which option would you choose and why?

THE CONCEPT OF SEGMENTATION

The goal of the marketer is to satisfy needs, but in our complex society, it is naive to assume that everyone's needs are the same. Michael Shekter and his colleagues at Molson know that different types of consumers have different priorities when it comes to buying beer. So when Molson designs and markets its beverages, it needs to consider the different needs that exist in the marketplace. Understanding these needs is especially complex today, because technological and cultural advances have created a condition of market fragmentation. **Market fragmentation** occurs when people's diverse interests and backgrounds have divided them into different groups with distinct needs and wants. Because of this diversity, the same product or service will not appeal to everyone.

Consider, for example, the effects of fragmentation in the fast-food industry. When a McDonald's hamburger was still a novelty (with under a million sold), people were happy to order just a plain hamburger, fries, and drink. Today's consumers would be very unhappy if salads, chicken, or wraps disappeared from the menu. But how many menu items do McDonald's, Harvey's, or Pizza Hut need to offer? Why is it that kids insist on a Happy Meal, whereas their parents prefer to grab a pita at Wendy's or a veggie burger at Harvey's?

At one time, it was sufficient to divide the sports shoe market into athletes and non-athletes. Today, a walk through any sporting goods store will reveal that the athlete market has fragmented in many directions, and includes shoes designed for jogging, basketball, tennis, cycling, cross-training, and skateboarding. Some manufacturers of athletic footwear geared to young boarders, such as Vans (Exhibit 3.1), Airwalk, and DC Shoes, chalked up annual sales gains of 20 to 50 percent in the past few years. Known to their peers as shredders, riders, or skaters, the youth who wear these shoes can be seen riding skateboards down the handrails and steps of city parks, and riding rails or doing jumps on snowboards, stunt bikes, or wakeboards. Over the next few years, sports marketers expect the skateboard and snowboard populations to double and wakeboarders to soar sixfold. To cash in on this trend, PepsiCo Inc.'s Mountain Dew began to feature snowboarding in its advertisements and was rewarded with a hefty increase in sales.[1]

Instead of trying to sell the same thing to all customers, marketers often select a **target marketing strategy**, in which they divide the total market into different segments based on customer characteristics, select one or more segments, and develop products to meet the needs of those specific segments. The five-step process of segmentation, targeting, and positioning is illustrated in Figure 3.1.

market fragmentation Creation of many consumer groups due to a diversity of distinct needs and wants in modern society.

target marketing strategy Dividing the total market into different segments based on customer characteristics, selecting one or more segments, and developing products to meet the needs of those specific segments.

Exhibit 3.1

Young shredders are the focus of many marketers.

1. Select Markets	2. Market Segmentation	3. Market Targeting	4. Market Positioning	5. Create and Execute Marketing Mix Programs
a. Define your market b. Understand customers: needs and wants; benefits, features, and attributes sought; and purchase and consumption behaviour	a. Identify groups: geographic, behavioural, pyschographic, and demographic segmentation b. Describe (profile) the groups: who, what, when, where, why	a. Evaluate segment attractiveness: size, growth; strategic fit, competitive or comparative advantage; level of competition, defendability b. Decide which one(s) to target	Decide how you want to compete, be differentiated, and be known for value creation in the minds of consumers	

Figure 3.1 Steps in the Target Marketing Process

Understanding customers will be discussed in Chapters 4, 5, and 6. The creation of marketing mix programs is discussed in Chapters 7 through 13. Our focus here is on segmentation, targeting, and positioning.

segmentation The process of dividing a larger market into smaller pieces, based on one or more meaningful, shared characteristics.

Segmentation is the process of dividing a larger market into subgroups, where within groups people have fairly homogeneous needs and wants and where between groups people have sufficiently different needs and wants that they would be interested in very different product solutions or marketing programs. Because consumers have different needs and wants and the same marketing program is unlikely to appeal to all consumers, marketers identify the key groups in a market, choose which group(s) to focus on (target), decide how they want their brand to compete and be known by these consumers (positioning), and design marketing programs (make marketing mix decisions) to create product offers that uniquely appeal to the chosen target groups. There are very few, if any, products with universal appeal. Even for products as popular as cola soft drinks, some consumers prefer Coca-Cola over Pepsi, some prefer Pepsi over Coke, some prefer diet colas, some prefer flavoured colas (e.g., Dr. Pepper, Vanilla Coke; Exhibit 3.2), some prefer caffeine-enhanced colas like Jolt, and others prefer non–soft drink beverages. Theresa Bergeron, president of Thermohair Inc. (Exhibit 3.3), has developed a product line of specialty socks made of kid (baby goat) mohair. Not everyone would be interested in a $25 pair of durable, warm, comfortable socks, but people involved in outdoor recreational sports like hiking and camping might be.

Exhibit 3.2

Coca-Cola developed Vanilla Coke to appeal to a flavoured-cola market segment.

Selecting and Segmenting a Market

One of the challenges in developing a marketing strategy is determining what market you are in and what market you should be segmenting. For example, should Michael Shekter at Molson be segmenting the beer market, the alcoholic beverage market, or the social beverage market? Kodak redefined itself from being in the film business to being in the imaging business—leading Kodak to venture into new markets. Deciding what "market" you are competing in has significant implications for the segments you might identify. You must also consider the geographic scope of the market—are you segmenting the beverage market in North America, Canada, or one or more provinces? The decision about how to define the markets you are competing in is typically done at the executive (strategic planning) level of an organization. As an entrepreneur or consultant, you may need to make this decision yourself—based on your experience, your understanding of the consumer, competitive, and technological environments, and your understanding of the mission, strategic directions, and competencies of your organization.

CRITERIA FOR IDENTIFYING MARKET SEGMENTS Before discussing how to segment a market, let's review the criteria for a successful segmentation scheme. There is no right or wrong way to segment a market, but some segmentation schemes are more useful than others for identifying market opportunities and being able to position products that uniquely appeal to a well-defined group of consumers or customers—the term used to describe organizational or business-to-business buyers.

A viable segmentation scheme should satisfy the requirements outlined in Figure 3.2.

1. Members of the segment must be similar to each other in their product needs and wants such that the same marketing programs (product offers) would be appealing to most members of the group.

2. At the same time, consumers in each segment should be sufficiently different from consumers in other segments that different marketing programs or product offers would be appealing to the different segments. Segment differences need to be actionable—that is, they require different product, pricing, distribution, and/or communication strategies to create a product offer that appeals to each segment. Without real differences in consumer needs and wants, firms might as well use a mass-marketing strategy. For example, it's a waste of time to develop two separate lines of skin care products for working and non-working women, if both segments have the same needs and wants with respect to skin care.

3. The segment must be large enough now and in the future to warrant targeting. What is large enough is a judgment call, and usually depends on the size of the company doing the segmentation scheme. Large organizations like Procter & Gamble may be interested only in market segments with sales potential in the millions of dollars. A smaller company may be interested in segments with sales potential in the tens or hundreds of thousands of dollars. In considering the B.C. market, for example, the Beef Information Centre evaluated the Chinese Canadian community as a possible segment. Chinese Canadians spend more money on food than any other ethnic group, and if just 25 percent of the close to 300 000 Chinese Canadians in British Columbia ate one more beef meal a month, sales of beef in British Columbia would increase by 77 000 kilograms per year. This analysis led the organization to target the Chinese Canadian segment in Vancouver through magazine ads like the one in Exhibit 3.4, recipes distributed at grocery stores, and the sponsorship of a Chinese cooking show on TV.[2]

4. The segment must represent a measurable market—that is, people in the segment have purchasing power: the authority, willingness, and ability to make a purchase decision. Children, for example, may not have the authority

Exhibit 3.3

Thermohair Inc. focuses on a narrow segment interested in warm, comfortable, durable socks that are made for cold weather (they even have a rib-free line for people with circulation problems).

- Similar Enough Within the Group
- Different Enough Between the Groups
- Large Enough
- Measurable Market
- Reachable

Figure 3.2 Criteria for Effective Segmentation Schemes

Exhibit 3.4

Chinese Canadian consumers were identified as a large segment for the Beef Information Centre of British Columbia.

to make a purchase. Religious or cultural beliefs may impact willingness to buy (such as beef-based hamburgers in India). Low-income consumers may not have the ability to buy.

5. Finally, the segment must be reachable. Marketers must be able to identify consumers or organizational customers in the segment and communicate the product offer to them in a cost-effective manner. It is easy to select television programs or magazines that will efficiently reach older consumers, consumers with specific levels of education, certain ethnic groups, or residents of major cities, because the media they prefer are easy to identify. It is unlikely, however, that marketing communications can reach only left-handed blond people with tattoos who listen to hip-hop. Therefore, it may not make sense to target that segment.

THE PROCESS OF SEGMENTATION

Segmentation is the central tenet or cornerstone of marketing strategy. Not all consumers or business market customers want the same things, and marketers have to decide which consumers or customers they are going to focus on to create an appealing product-offer. Several **segmentation variables**, or bases for segmentation, can be used to group consumers into actionable segments. For example, consider the sports shoe industry. Some sports, such as running, are more popular in some provinces than others, so marketers consider geography. Not everyone is willing or able to pay $150 for the latest running shoe, so marketers consider disposable and discretionary income. Men may be more likely to participate in some sports, such as basketball, whereas women may be more likely than men to want the latest aerobics styles, so marketers also consider gender. Not all age groups are going to be equally interested in buying specialized athletic shoes, and some kids may be more inclined to "extreme" sports than others. As this example shows, the larger consumer "pie" can be sliced into smaller pieces in a number of ways, including geographic,

segmentation variables Bases for dividing the total market into fairly homogenous groups, each with different needs and preferences.

demographic, psychological, and behavioural differences. These segmentation variables are used to identify the groups, and then create descriptions or profiles of the groups. So, just how do marketers segment a population? The process is similar for organizational (business-to-business) markets, and we will discuss some of the differences shortly.

Behavioural Segmentation

Savvy marketers realize that if the objective is to create groups that want very different product offers, it makes sense to try to group them by the similarity of their needs, wants, and preferences, the benefits they seek, the features and attributes they desire, or their purchasing or consumption behaviour. This approach to segmentation is called **behavioural segmentation**, and marketers such as Palm (Exhibit 3.5) and McDonald's have found it a useful place to start because it identifies groups that require distinct marketing programs. Recent research by Digital Consumer Projects in New York suggests that online individual behaviour matters more than the demographics of an individual, finding seven behavioural segments that include "surfers," "loiterers," and "quickies."[3]

Behavioural segmentation divides consumers on the basis of how they act toward, feel about, or use a product or service. **Benefit segmentation**, or value segmentation, is a powerful behavioural segmentation approach where consumers are grouped by the benefits they seek in a product category. For example, Peachtree Network, a company that operated online grocery stores across Canada, originally segmented its market into three benefit segments: busy people, people with mobility difficulties, and people who liked and were motivated to use the technology behind the service.[4] In many industries, consumers seek different types of benefits from products and can be grouped accordingly. For example, the following benefit-based groups might be identified (among others) as restaurant industry segments: convenience seekers, fun seekers, health-oriented, fine-dining experience seekers, novelty seekers, cost-oriented, family-oriented, image- or status-oriented, or culture seekers. Each of us may fall into more than one of these benefit-seeking categories at different times or in different contexts, but restaurant owners know that different consumers seek different benefits from a restaurant and select restaurants based on the benefits they wish to receive at a particular time. That is why restaurants are usually clearly positioned to appeal to one or more of these benefit segment groups. Think of all the restaurants you know: What benefit(s) do they primarily focus on delivering? The advantage of segmenting by benefits is that the resulting groups are usually seeking very different product solutions, which makes the segmentation scheme very actionable in terms of designing appropriate marketing programs.

Another common approach to behavioural segmentation is **product usage segmentation**. In

behavioural segmentation Technique that divides consumers into segments on the basis of how they act toward, feel about, or use a product or service.

benefit segmentation A segmentation approach that groups consumers or customers based on the benefits or value they seek in buying and using products.

product usage segmentation A segmentation approach that groups consumers or business customers based on the amount of a product purchased or consumed or how the product is used.

Exhibit 3.5

Palm and other PDA manufacturers often use behavioural segmentation to target segments that use communication devices differently.

this approach, groups are identified based on how they use a product or how much they use a product. Baking soda, for example, is marketed to a variety of end-use segments, including deodorizing fridges, sinks, or rugs; cooking; and teeth brushing. Airlines often identify consumer and business traveller segments, which is a proxy for describing the frequency of product use (light users versus heavy users) and how they use the service. Many marketers (particularly those in business-to-business markets) abide by a rule of thumb called the **80/20 rule**: 20 percent of purchasers account for 80 percent of the product's sales (this ratio is just an approximation). Therefore, it often makes more sense to focus on the smaller number of people who are heavy users of a product rather than on the larger number who are just casual users. Kraft Foods began an advertising campaign to remind its core users to not "skip the zip" after its research showed that, indeed, 20 percent of households account for 80 percent of the usage of Miracle Whip. These heavy users consume about 8 kilograms of Miracle Whip a year![5]

80/20 rule A marketing rule of thumb that 20 percent of purchasers typically account for 80 percent of a product's sales.

While the 80/20 rule still generally holds in the majority of situations, the Internet's ability to offer an unlimited choice of goods to billions of people is starting to change how marketers think about segmentation. A new approach called the **long tail** is turning traditional thinking about the virtues of selling in high volume on its head. The basic idea is that we no longer need to rely solely on the big hits (like blockbuster movies or bestselling books) to find profits. Companies can also make money by selling small amounts of items that only a few people want—if they sell enough different items. For example, Amazon.com maintains an inventory of 3.7 million books compared to the 100 000 or so you'll find at a Chapters retail store. Most of these will sell only a few thousand copies (if that), but the 3.6 million books that Chapters *doesn't* carry make up a quarter of Amazon's revenues! Similarly, about a fifth of the videos Netflix delivers to its customers are older or obscure titles that Blockbuster does not stock. Other examples of long tail include successful microbreweries and TV channels that make money on reruns of old shows.

long tail A new approach to segmentation based on the idea that companies can make money by selling small amounts of items that only a few people want, provided they sell enough different items.

Some marketers find it useful to divide the market into users and non-users of a good or service so that they can reward current users (as Air Canada does with frequent flyer miles) or try to win over new ones. However, non-users are often not clearly identifiable and reachable, thus failing to satisfy the fifth criterion for identifying market segments outlined above. And current users may not be a very homogeneous group, which is the first criterion (see Figure 3.2 on page 77), and they may not reflect the users desired by the marketing organization.

usage occasions Indicator used in one type of market segmentation based on when consumers use a product most.

Another way to segment a market based on behaviour is to look at **usage occasions**, or the context in which consumers use the product most. Many products are associated with specific occasions, including time of day and holidays, whether for a business function or casual situation. Greeting cards, for example, are a product associated with specific occasions. Carlton cards, Canada's leading greeting card marketer, experiences peak demand related to four special occasions: Christmas, Valentine's Day, Mother's Day, and Easter. In addition to meeting the demand for these occasions with specialized cards, advertising, and in-store promotions, Carlton engages in marketing efforts designed to encourage the giving of cards on other occasions, such as Earth Day. Similarly, ski resorts like Mont Tremblant, which experience heavy demand during vacation periods, might offer great bargains during the off-season to tempt vacationers who would otherwise just visit the resort during Christmas vacation.

Being strongly associated with an occasion can be a mixed blessing for a product. On the one hand, sales can be almost guaranteed at that time (think about how many people cook a whole turkey on Thanksgiving); on the other hand, a product can become locked into an occasion (few people cook whole turkeys as a standard menu item). For the past 10 years, Ocean Spray has worked hard to expand cranberry consumption beyond the holiday season, introducing new cranberry foods like Craisins® Sweetened Dried Cranberries, spritzers, and cranberry-based beverages. Now it's trying to increase consumption frequency by communicating the health benefits of its products and encouraging consumers to take the Ocean Spray® Cranberry Cocktail "One Glass A Day Challenge" (Exhibit 3.6).

Segmenting by Psychographics

Consumers and customers often make purchase decisions that reflect or support their attitudes, values, interests, opinions, emotions, personality, and lifestyles. Collectively these concepts are referred to as *psychographics*, and they will be discussed further in Chapter 5. **Psychographic segmentation** groups consumers by these and other variables related to an individual's psychology, mental state, or self and is concerned with the motivation for consumers to buy products. As we will see in Chapter 5, marketers not only seek to understand how consumers behave but also how they think and feel about products, what motivates them, how they learn, and how they make purchase decisions.

Grouping consumers by their psychological orientation to a purchase often results in a useful segmentation scheme that meets the criteria of Figure 3.2, since differences in these psychological considerations usually reflect differences in needs and wants and are precursors to purchase and consumption behaviour. For example, Covenant House, a charitable organization that helps homeless people, recognized that donors care more about the homeless than non-donors do, and believe their donations will make a difference. With this understanding, Taxi Advertising and Design of Toronto developed a series of highly effective (and award-winning) campaign elements to increase the number of people who care about the homeless, thus increasing the pool of potential donors. One showed black and white images of homeless people sitting alone on the ground in a transit shelter, replaced by images of young children in the same position, with the tag line, "How old do they have to be before you give a damn?" The Covenant House print ad in Exhibit 3.7 is another execution of the concept, enabling readers to physically take people off the street.

Lifestyles are a powerful segmentation variable because they capture a number of behavioural, psychographic, and demographic characteristics that reflect how different groups of people live, what they care about, and how they behave. Think about your high-school experience. Were there cliques or groups of students like Jocks, Nerds, Preppies, Stoners, and others who hung out together, dressed similarly, had similar attitudes and values, and behaved similarly? You could probably describe each of those groups

Exhibit 3.6
Ocean Spray wants to expand cranberry consumption beyond traditional holiday usage occasions.

psychographic segmentation A segmentation approach that groups people based on their attitudes, beliefs, values, lifestyles, or other psychological orientations.

An actual peel-off sticker was placed on this magazine ad.

When readers peeled the sticker off, a message was revealed.

Exhibit 3.7
Removable stickers of homeless children in this Covenant House public service announcement demonstrate that donations make a difference: "Your donation gets kids off the street."

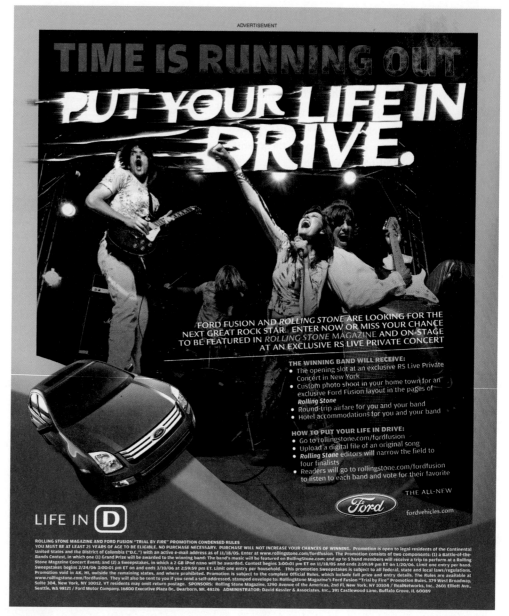

Exhibit 3.8

Ford Fusion: Car manufacturers like Ford often use lifestyle segmentation to identify groups of people interested in different types of cars.

in some detail. That's what marketers do. Some advertising agencies and manufacturers develop their own psychographic classifications of consumers, identifying lifestyle segments like Yuppies (young urban professionals), Dinks (dual income, no kids), Shredders (boarders), Granolas (earthy, environmentally concerned, peaceniks), Metrosexuals (urban heterosexual males who are sensitive, well educated, and in touch with their feminine side), and others. Products are communicated to people in these segments by showing how the brand supports or is consistent with a particular lifestyle. Beer marketers like Molson, for example, often use lifestyle advertising to demonstrate what your life (or at least social life) would be like if you adopted their particular brand. Similarly, car marketers like Toyota, Mazda, Volvo, Saturn, and Mercedes try to show you a lifestyle that they suggest could be yours if you drive their cars. The Ford Fusion ad in Exhibit 3.8 relates the Fusion brand to a young, high-energy lifestyle. Web-based services like GeoCities (**geocities.yahoo.com**) allow people to sort themselves into lifestyle communities based on specific shared interests.

Online marketers can then target these specific lifestyle groups. Apple's use of lifestyle segmentation has been particularly effective. Apple positions Macs and iPods as being for people with a young, hip, unconventional outlook on life.

Other marketers choose to subscribe to larger services that divide the population into segments and sell pieces of this information to clients for specific strategic applications. The most well known of these systems is **VALS™ (Values and Lifestyles)**, developed by SRI International. The original VALS system was based on social values and lifestyles. Today VALS2 is based on psychological traits that correlate with consumer behaviour. It divides people into eight groups based on both psychological characteristics, such as willingness to take risks, and "resources," which include such factors as income, education, energy levels, and eagerness to buy. As shown in Figure 3.3, three primary consumer motivations are key to the system: ideals, achievement, and self-expression. Consumers who are motivated primarily by ideals are guided by knowledge and principles. Consumers who are motivated primarily by achievement look for goods and services that demonstrate success to their peers. Consumers who are motivated primarily by self-expression desire social or physical activity, variety, and risk. VALS2 helps match products to particular types of people. For example, VALS2 survey data show that 12 percent of North American adults are Experiencers, who tend to be thrill seekers. VALS2 helped Isuzu market its Rodeo sport-utility vehicle by repositioning it to Experiencers, many of whom believe it is fun to break rules (in ways that do not endanger others). The company and its advertising agency repositioned the car as a vehicle that lets a driver break the rules by going off road, using images like kids jumping into mud puddles or purposefully colouring outside the lines to illustrate "rule breaking." Isuzu sales increased significantly after this campaign.[6]

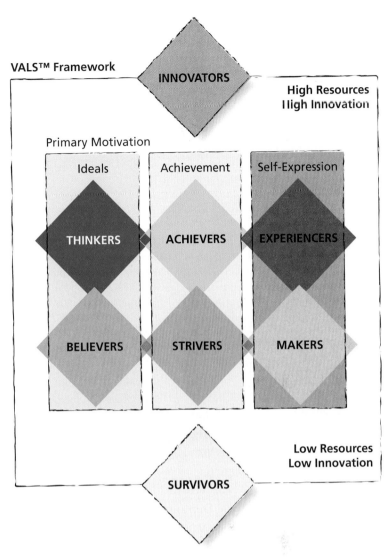

Figure 3.3 VALS

VALS uses psychological characteristics to segment the U.S. market into eight unique consumer groups.

Marketing researchers can integrate the VALS2 questionnaire into custom surveys to identify VALS2 types of respondents and to correlate their preferences and other behaviour with their type. You can find out your VALS2 type by taking their online survey at **www.sric-bi.com**.

VALS is one of the most comprehensive psychographic systems available, but because its conclusions are based on residents of the United States, many Canadian firms prefer to use Canadian psychographic systems, such as the one developed by the Environics Research Group (**www.environics.net**). Like VALS, Environics segments people on the basis of attitudes, values, and lifestyles. The 12 "tribes" identified by Environics range from the Rational Traditionalists (who are motivated by financial independence, security, and stability, and whose key values include respect for authority, duty, and delayed gratification) to the Social Hedonists (who are motivated by experience seeking, and who value hedonism, immediate gratification, and sexual permissiveness).[7] While the Rational Traditionalists may be a good target market for certain financial and insurance services, the Social Hedonists would

VALS™ (Values and Lifestyles) A psychographic system that divides people into eight segments.

Segment	Percentage	Characteristics
Traditionalists		
Day-to-Day Watchers	24	Represent the status quo; don't like the fast pace; motivated by familiarity, loyalty, and security; influenced by quality, brand name, and authority figures.
Old-Fashioned Puritans	18	Prefer simpler times; express conservative values; motivated by price and quality; influenced by value-oriented messages; motivated by sales and other forms of discounts.
Responsible Survivors	12	Frugal shoppers who look for best price; have money but do not like to spend it; motivated by price; shop at low-end stores; heavy television viewers, so it is a good medium to reach them with.
Non-traditionalists		
Joiner Activists	16	Idealists; liberal-minded; careful decision makers; willing to spend; motivated by information, therefore receptive to advertising messages; rational appeals have influence (quality, service, dependability, etc.).
Bold Achievers	15	Aggressive and confident individuals; success- and responsibility-oriented; innovators who lead in attitude and purchase decision; motivated by status, prestige, and success; products purchased reflect success; want higher-priced goods and exclusivity.
Self-indulgents	14	Resent authority; motivated by self-gratification, therefore often buy impulsively (even on major purchases); price not a factor; want easy road to success; messages should stress gratification as source of motivation.

Figure 3.4 Goldfarb Segments

probably be a prime target for *Tribe Magazine* and such leisure activities as snowboarding. Another Canadian-based lifestyle scheme is the Goldfarb segments (Figure 3.4) that identify six groups of Canadian adults: structured, discontented, fearful, resentful, assured, and caring.

Segmenting by Demographics

demographics Variables that describe objective characteristics of a population or group.

Demographics are vital for identifying the best potential customers for a product or service because objective characteristics like a person's sex or age are (usually) easy to identify, and information about the demographics of a consumer market are easily obtained from government sources like Statistics Canada (**www.statcan.ca**). Demographics are extremely useful in the development of profiles or descriptions of market segments because demographic variables help identify people in segments so that they can be reached with a marketer's communication strategy. Communications media publish demographic information about their viewers, listeners, or readers to help marketers decide which media are best for reaching which audiences.

However, with a few notable exceptions, demographic variables like age, sex, income, family structure, social class, ethnicity, and education do not usually provide a good starting point or main basis for segmentation because demographic-based segmentation schemes usually do not meet the criterion that the people within each group are similar enough that the same marketing programs (product offers) would be appealing to most members of that group (first criterion, Figure 3.2 on page 77). For example, one might be tempted to segment the music market by age, suggesting that teenagers may listen to different music than people in their twenties, forties, or sixties. While teenagers may be more likely than other age groups to listen to grunge or hip-hop music, not all teens like and listen to this style of music, and there are people in their twenties, thirties, forties, and perhaps even older, who do. By creating age segments we are suggesting that most people in a particular age category have similar needs, wants, preferences, and buying behaviour with respect to music and that they would likely purchase the same or similarly positioned artists or brands, which are different from the artists or brands that consumers in other segments would likely purchase. If you thought this were true, then age would be an appropriate basis for segmenting the music market. However, it might make more sense to segment the music market by psychographic

Exhibit 3.9

Jones Soda targets psychographic segments.

variables such as values, attitudes, interests, opinions, or lifestyles, and then use age and other demographic variables to describe each of the psychographic groups created. This is a subtle but important point for creating useful segmentation schemes—demographics are extremely useful for describing market segments and for directing communication messages, but are generally limited as the primary basis for segmentation. As Peter van Stolk, the Vancouver-based founder of Jones Soda (Exhibit 3.9, **www.jonessoda.com**), told the Beverage Forum in Manhattan, "It's not about demographics. It's psychographics. You didn't grow up with the computer and crack and AIDS. Our consumers did."[8]

There are some notable exceptions where demographic variables are related to differences in needs, wants, preferences, and purchase behaviour, and it would make sense to use these variables as the main basis for segmentation.

SEX It makes sense to segment the clothing, fashion, footwear, or fragrance industries by sex, for example, because physiological and socialization differences between men and women can result in different needs, wants, and preferences. However, men and women may also seek different benefits, features, or attributes, so, in many cases, starting with benefit segmentation would result in a similar segmentation scheme as if starting with sex. Socialization by sex starts at a very early age and markets need to be responsive to consumer preferences; even diapers come in pink for girls and blue for boys. As proof that consumers take these differences seriously, market researchers report that most parents refuse to put male infants in pink diapers.[9] Ford Canada recognizes that women and men may have different needs when it comes to purchasing and servicing cars and trucks, which is why the company is now focusing efforts on trying to better understand and serve the needs of Canadian women. Volvo has created a concept car designed by women for women.[10] Similarly, companies such as Home Depot Canada, Marriott Hotels, and Mr. Lube, which have traditionally focused on marketing to men, have started developing products and messages specifically targeting Canadian women.[11] The publishers of *What* magazine focus on a segment of co-gender lifestyles of Canadian youth, but *Fuel*, a new entry by Youth Culture (which also publishes *Verve* for girls), is focused on male teens— its research finding that boys and girls liked and wanted to learn and read about different things (Exhibit 3.10). Its biggest hurdle has been convincing advertisers that boys shop, and develop brand loyalty, but for different products than girls.[12]

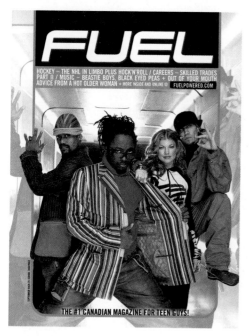

Exhibit 3.10

Fuel magazine targets a segment of young males.

baby boomers The largest age segment in Canada, it includes people who were born between 1947 and 1966.

AGE Consumers in different age groups have very different needs and wants with respect to *product categories*. Members of a generation tend to share the same outlook and spending priorities, and these outlooks and priorities change as people age (what you spend your discretionary money on is likely different from what your parents spend their discretionary money on). However, unless brands specifically reflect these differences in product category needs and wants (such as we saw with *What* and *Fuel* magazines), age is less useful for identifying differences in *brand* preferences than for identifying differences in product category preferences.

Canadian demographer David Foot has identified several segments of Canadian consumers based on age. These include members of the Baby Boom (those people born in 1947–1966), the Baby Bust (generation X; those born in 1967–1979), the Baby Boom Echo (generation Y; those born in 1980–1995), and the Millennium Busters (those born in 1996–2010).[13] While each of these groups of consumers presents needs that some marketers are interested in, the largest demographic segment in Canada, the **baby boomers**, accounts for about one-third of the Canadian population and is, therefore, a segment of prime importance to many marketers. Several companies have achieved success by monitoring the changing needs of this group of consumers. Coca-Cola, for example, can attribute part of its success in North America to the fact that boomers drank a lot of pop when they were young. Coke has now modified its marketing efforts to keep up with the changing tastes of the boomers. It changed its product line to include juice and bottled water to cater to the concerns that aging boomers have for their health.[14] One characteristic of boomers for marketers to always remember is that they invest a ton of money, time, and energy to maintain a youthful image. The TV show *Nip/Tuck* chronicles the experiences of two cosmetic surgeons in Miami who crassly market their surgical fountain of youth to a seemingly endless stream of fifty-somethings. The President's Choice private label products, sold through Loblaws and affiliated stores, also appeal to the needs of the baby boom segment (Exhibit 3.11). These products include the Decadent chocolate chip cookie, which offers indulgence, low-fat foods that are "Too Good to Be True" and help boomers stay healthy, and ready-made frozen meals that offer a meal solution for time-starved boomers.[15] Boomer women in their fifties are becoming a hot new market for "reward cars": sexy, extravagant vehicles that are a reward for all those years of driving kids around in a minivan.

The echo boom (generation Y) comprises the children of the baby boomers. The largest segment of the echo boom are now teens and young adults, who also represent a lucrative group of consumers. The youth market in Canada is estimated to be worth over $13.5 billion, and teens are the second fastest growing segment in Canada.[16]

They are the first generation to grow up online and are more ethnically diverse than earlier generations. These consumers tend to spend their money on items such as clothing, personal grooming, entertainment, sports, and eating out. Montreal-based La Senza has successfully targeted teen and tween (aged 8 to 14) girls with La Senza Girl stores (Exhibit 3.12), and banks such as the Royal Bank and CIBC have savings programs and debit cards specifically aimed at kids.[17] VanCity Credit Union recently targeted youth with a banking service "Not for the majority," offering free banking service to anyone under the age of 25. The campaign is

Exhibit 3.11

Loblaws targets baby boomers with President's Choice products.

backed with a combination of street marketing, web promotions, contests, special events, and a text messaging campaign targeting 5000 youth in Vancouver who had been given cellphones by research company Digital Youth, in exchange for volunteering to receive promotional messages and advertising. Echo boomers are hard to reach because they resist reading, increasingly turn off the TV, and, on average, spend four or more hours online a day. When they do watch TV, they tend toward alternative fare such as the late-night lineup on *Adult Swim*, which is consistently the number-one show on basic cable for this age group in the United States.[18] As a result, marketers are increasingly using online marketing techniques and guerrilla marketing techniques to reach these consumers.

The older part of the echo boom, those people born in the early- to mid-1980s, are now in colleges and universities, or have joined the workforce, and are starting to make major purchases on their own. This college-age group is an important target group for companies like DirectProtect, which sells insurance to students, and brewers such as Moosehead, Molson, and Labatt, who realize that many of the heavy users of their products can be found on campuses across Canada.

In between the baby boomers and the echo boomers are Generation Xers, sometimes labelled busters. Many of these people have a cynical attitude toward marketing, and most don't have the spending power of boomers or even echo boomers. However, because baby boomers have taken and held on to the top jobs in the country, Generation Xers have had to be much more entrepreneurial. They have been responsible for upwards of 70 percent of the new startup businesses in North America. As one industry expert observed, today's Gen Xer is both values oriented and value oriented—and this generation is really about settling down.[19]

Exhibit 3.12

La Senza Girl stores target teens and tweens.

Older consumers, most of whom are the parents of the baby boomers, are another age segment of interest to Canadian marketers. Twenty-two percent of the Canadian population is 55 years of age or older.[20] Since many people are now retiring younger than age 65, these consumers are enjoying increased leisure time, making them an ideal target for travel and other leisure products. Health is also a major concern for these consumers; some of them may be experiencing failing health, and others are simply interested in maintaining good health as they age. The Healthwatch service provided by Shoppers Drug Mart, which provides advice from pharmacists, a database of individualized health information, and a health magazine, is a good example of a service targeted to the needs of these consumers.

Teens are also an attractive segment. The 12 to 17 age group is growing nearly twice as fast as the general population, and teens and tweens spend an average of $3000 per year.[21] Much of this money goes to "feel good" products: cosmetics, posters, and fast food—with the occasional nose ring or tattoo thrown in as well. Many marketers are attracted to this group, hoping to groom them into lifelong customers. Avon, for example, has developed a new product line called mark (**www.meetmark.com**), so named in celebration of young women making their mark in the world today.

And, of course, there are subgroups within the teen market with their own musical idols, distinctive styles, and so on. For example, the emo (short for emotional) youth subculture is a label both for a musical genre and for the youthful adherents to that genre. The common thread uniting emo kids is a strong current of alienation. Emo kids tend to look like they have just shopped at a garage sale or Value Village. The emblematic hairstyle (shown in Exhibit 3.13) is short, slick, dyed-black hair with pronounced bangs.[22]

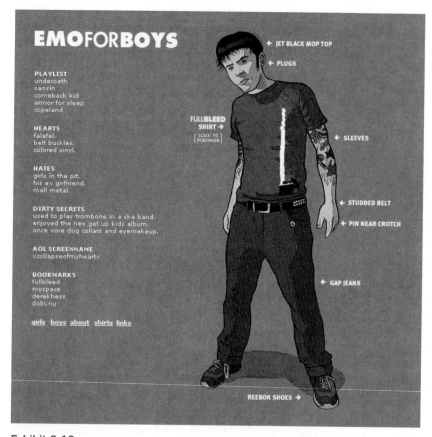

Exhibit 3.13

A guide to the EMO subculture.

FAMILY STRUCTURE Because family needs and expenditures change over time, one way to segment consumers is to consider the stage of the family life cycle they occupy (this will be discussed further in Chapter 5). Not surprisingly, consumers in different life cycle segments (such as teens, young adults, married with children, empty nesters) are unlikely to need the same products, or at least in the same quantities.[23] For example, many food companies cater to the needs of people who live alone by providing single-portion frozen and prepared foods, but also offer "jumbo" packs for those people who live in larger households.

As we age and move into new life situations, different product categories ascend and descend in importance to us. Young singles and newlyweds are the most likely to exercise, to go to bars, concerts, and movies, and to consume alcohol. Young families are heavy users of disposable diapers and toys and games for children. They are also interested in household appliances, furniture, and such vehicles as minivans. Older couples and singles are more likely to use maintenance services, and older people are a prime market for retirement communities and golf products. Condominiums that are built in Canadian cities are often designed with different family structures in mind. Some target single divorced men and women; others go after young families and include amenities such as on-site day care; and still others target vacation home buyers.[24] Canadian department stores also consider family life cycle by specifically targeting brides- and grooms-to-be with wedding registry services.

INCOME AND SOCIAL CLASS The distribution of wealth is of great interest to marketers, because it determines which groups have the greatest buying power. Many marketers are interested in capturing the hearts and wallets of high-income consumers. In Canada, the average family income is about $58 000, but 13.5 percent of the population has a household income above $100 000.[25] These high-income consumers are a good target market for such luxury products as expensive jewellery, as well as financial services of brokers and investment products. The Wealthy Boomer Inc. is a Canadian company that targets high-income baby boom consumers with its magazine, *The Wealthy Boomer*. At the same time, other marketers target average- and lower-income consumers—the majority of Canadian consumers. The Hudson's Bay Company successfully targets these income groups with its Bay and Zellers department stores.

ETHNICITY As will be discussed further in Chapter 5, many Canadian marketers are adopting a multicultural approach to their marketing activities in recognition of the ethnic diversity of the Canadian population. Ethnicity can have a strong impact on a consumer's preferences for products and services, such as magazines or television shows, foods, apparel, and choice of leisure activities.

French Canadian consumers, who account for 20 to 30 percent of Canadians, are the second largest ethnic market in Canada (after those people of British origin) and are, therefore, an important segment for marketers.[26] Most French Canadian consumers live in Quebec, but there are also large segments of French Canadian consumers in New

Brunswick and Ontario. As will be discussed further in Chapter 5, national marketers often decide to specifically target the French Canadian market through the development of different products to suit the needs of this group and the use of French language advertising. For example, MusiquePlus and MusiMax are the French language music video TV stations owned by CHUM, the same company that operates MuchMusic and MuchMoreMusic in the English Canadian market. While MusiquePlus and MusiMax show many of the same videos as do the English stations, French music and programming is featured to appeal to the music tastes of French Canadian consumers. As the vice-president of sales for CHUM Specialty Television observes, "They are not MuchMusic and MuchMoreMusic in French. They have an identity of their own with a more regional than national focus."[27] So when Procter & Gamble was looking for a French Canadian spokesperson for Cover Girl cosmetics, it chose Genevieve Borne, a MusiquePlus VJ, because of her appeal to female French Canadian teens.

Over one million people in Canada are of Aboriginal origin; they are located in various regions throughout the country, and 42 percent live off-reserve.[28] The Aboriginal population is growing at four times the rate of any other segment, with half of the Aboriginal people in Canada currently under the age of 25. The income of Aboriginal consumers is rising faster than that of other Canadians, and there are more than 20 000 Aboriginal-owned business.[29] One company that targets Aboriginal consumers is Dinawo Sportswear and Casuals, a Native-owned clothing business located on the Six Nations Reserve in Ontario that produces clothing incorporating native art and symbols.[30] The banking sector in Canada has also been proactive in targeting both Aboriginal consumers and business owners. All the major Canadian banks operate branches in Aboriginal communities with services targeted to meet their needs, as the ad for the Royal Bank in Exhibit 3.14 shows.[31] The Aboriginal Peoples Television Network (APTN) and *Spirit* magazine are examples of media targeting Aboriginal peoples. A key challenge in marketing to Aboriginal peoples is to recognize the ethnic diversity within this group: Inuit, Metis, and First Nations (such as Cree, Maliseet, Dene, Anishnabe, Mohawk, Haida) have significantly different languages, history, traditions, and environments that influence current thinking, attitudes, and behaviours. As this segment has traditionally been misunderstood and under-researched, it is particularly important to conduct research (see Chapter 4) to understand these consumers.

Other than people of British, French, and Aboriginal origins, the three largest ethnic groups in Canada are German, Italian, and Chinese. Of these three, the fastest growing is the Chinese Canadian community.[32] Tropicana Products Ltd. considers the Chinese Canadian community to be one of the most important target markets for its orange juice product. It communicates with this target with Chinese language print ads placed in Chinese Canadian newspapers and promotions such as coupons for 68 cents (both six and eight are considered to signify prosperity in the Chinese culture). The company is careful to avoid the use of the number four (which signifies death) in any of its pricing and advertising.[33]

Other large ethnic groups in Canada include the South Asian community, which accounts for

Exhibit 3.14
Aboriginal consumers are an important segment for the Royal Bank.

Ethical Decisions in Marketing

Terra Footwear, a supplier of footwear to the Canadian military, law enforcement agencies, and construction industries, recently had to pull a controversial communications campaign it had developed for workboots (Exhibit 3.15). The theme of the campaign was sexy images featuring female models in lingerie, in suggestive poses, wearing Terra workboots, with humorous tag lines. The website featured a streaming video commercial of topless dancers wearing the boots. According to Robert Worrall, Terra Footwear vice-president, the intent was to present the product in a lighthearted and humorous manner. The Manitoba Federation of Labour, which has more than 95 000 members, threatened a boycott against Terra over the ads. The women's committee of the Canadian Auto Workers, one of the largest trade unions in Canada, soon followed and union leaders began organizing demonstrations at stores where Terra products are sold. They also put pressure on Terra Footwear by calling MPs to demand that they pressure the firm to pull its ads or cancel Terra's contracts to supply boots to the Canadian military. Mark Krausewitz, marketing manager for Terra, said that the reaction was unexpected and that "essentially there was a large group of people who did not see the humour in our spots."[37] Some industry observers thought the campaign was short-sighted considering that Terra has a popular line of women's workboots. Shari Graydon, formerly head of Media Watch, an organization that monitors the depiction of women in media, argues that media images have social consequences and play a role in "normalizing sexual harassment in the workplace." However, Toronto writer David Menzies argues that it is only advertising, it works, it wasn't pornographic, and why should "a small gaggle of humorless harpies ruin things for the rest of us"? He further adds that there has been no outcry over the well-endowed "boy-toy" currently being exploited by those Calvin Klein briefs billboards.[38] What do you think? Should marketers be allowed to use highly sexual appeals? What if the appeal was specifically targeting young people—such as with many of the Calvin Klein ads?

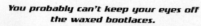

You probably can't keep your eyes off the waxed bootlaces.

See more: terrafootwear.com

Exhibit 3.15

Terra Footwear: an example of a controversial ad.

2.4 percent of the population, and the black community, which is 2 percent of the Canadian population.[34] Bell Canada provides customer service representatives who speak Hindi, Punjabi, Urdu, and Tamil to better serve its South Asian customers.[35] To reach the over 351 000 people in Canada of Jewish origin, companies such as Baskin-Robbins offer kosher food products, Hallmark offers cards and festive products targeted to Jewish holidays, and the Liquor Control Board of Ontario offers 80 different types of kosher wines.[36]

GEOGRAPHY People's preferences for products and services often depend on which region of the country they live in. For example, a recent study of how upper-income people across Canada spend their money showed significant regional differences. Compared to the average Canadian, upper-income people living in Edmonton were more likely to spend their money on skiwear and snowmobile suits, those in Saskatoon were more likely to purchase home exercise equipment, those in Montreal were more likely to purchase leather and fur coats and jackets, those in Halifax were more likely to purchase art goods and decorative ware, those in St. John's were more likely to buy snow blowers, and those in the north were more likely to purchase outboard motor boats.[39] Similarly, a study of snacking behaviour found that Maritimers consume more potato chips than consumers in other regions (almost double the national average), and Quebec consumers eat less than half of the average amount of corn chips that consumers in other regions do.[40]

Recognition of these kinds of regional differences can lead marketers to focus efforts on one or more regions, or to have different marketing strategies in different regions. When marketers want to segment regional markets even more precisely, they sometimes combine geography with demographics by using a technique called **geodemography**. A basic assumption of geodemography is that "birds of a feather flock together." People who live near one another share similar characteristics. Sophisticated statistical techniques identify geographic areas that share the same preferences for household items, magazines, and other products. This allows marketers to construct segments consisting of households with a common pattern of preferences, so that a company can home in on those customers who are most likely to be interested in its specific offerings—in some cases so precisely that families living on one block will be included in a segment whereas those on the next block will not.

One Canadian geodemographic system, PSYTE, is a large database developed by Compusearch Micromarketing Data and Systems. This system classifies Canadian consumers into 60 clusters, based on postal code and demographic information. The resulting clusters include Boomers and Teens, Conservative Homebodies, Young City Singles, Brie and Chablis, and Suburban Nesters.[41] The PSYTE system is used by Canada Post in its GeoPost Plus program, which allows marketers to target direct mail to clusters of consumers that match their target segment. For example, the Boomers and Teens segment is described as "late middle-aged consumers who are university and college educated with children over the age of six. Mostly double income families who live in their own homes." The cluster Young City Singles are "young singles and some couples who rent predominantly newer, downtown apartments and other dwellings." Using a geodemographic system like GeoPost Plus, a marketer of home improvement products like outdoor paint and fencing can identify precisely which postal codes will be the best prospects for direct mail advertising for their product, while avoiding other postal codes where residents aren't likely to be interested.

geodemography Segmentation technique that combines geography with demographics.

SEGMENTING BUSINESS MARKETS

We've reviewed the segmentation variables marketers use to divide up the consumer market, but how about all the business-to-business or industrial marketers? Segmentation also helps them to divide up business and organizational customers. Though the specific variables may differ, the underlying logic of dividing the larger market into manageable pieces that share relevant characteristics is the same.[42] Although industrial markets tend to be smaller (in numbers of customers) and more concentrated, it is still important to segment these markets because no company has unlimited resources for developing and selling products and segmentation enables these companies to focus on the best opportunities and develop products that uniquely meet the needs of their customers.

Company-Specific Behaviour or Characteristics

Just as it is fruitful to consider the behaviour of individual consumers when devising a segmentation scheme, it is fruitful to consider how businesses and other organizations behave when devising segmentation schemes for industrial or business-to-business segmentation. Organizational buying behaviour will be the focus of Chapter 6. For now, it is important to recognize that organizations, through the people within them, act and behave in ways that are both similar to and different from consumers, and that the way they behave and operate is influenced by the types of products and services they both sell and need. Consequently, one way to segment organizations is by the unique ways each operates.

Organization buying and consumption behaviour is influenced by the production technology used; the type of purchases made; the business customer's degree of technical, financial, or operations expertise; how they make purchase decisions and who is involved in those decisions; whether the prospect is a current user or non-user of the product; and the frequency or size of the transactions. These **operating variables** are all useful bases of segmentation. For example, Grand & Toy (Exhibit 3.16) recognized the differences in the buying behaviour of large and small businesses when it launched The Stockroom (**www.thestockroom.ca**), an Internet-based office supplies store that targets small businesses. While the Grand & Toy website is geared to the needs of large businesses (offering benefits like large volume discounts), The Stockroom site caters to small businesses with its products and pricing policies. The general manager of The Stockroom describes the company's approach this way: ". . . we felt it was important to take a very aggressive, focused stance, purely aimed at the small business segment."[43]

operating variables The production technology used, the business customer's degree of technical, financial, or operations expertise, and whether the prospect is a current user or non-user of the product.

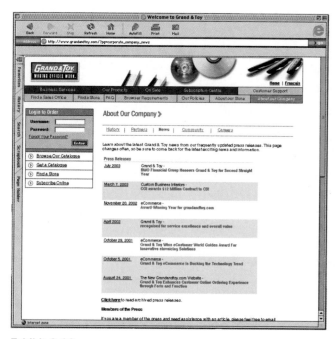

Exhibit 3.16

Grand & Toy targets behaviour-based business segments.

Business marketers also must consider how different customers will use their products or services. They must focus on identifying different end-use applications for these offerings. The personal computer industry is a good example of how firms can segment a market based on end use. Some major PC manufacturers, such as Dell, have divided the market into four segments: corporate, small business, government, and home or home office (Exhibit 3.17)—each with its own computer-use profile. IBM segments its mainframe market into user "verticals"; different applications (such as health care or manufacturing) for which the mainframe computers might be used.

Industrial Psychographics

industrial psychographics The application of psychographics to the business-to-business context.

Being concerned with psychology, thinking, feeling, and other mental states, the concept of psychographics relates only indirectly to organizations, but it does relate to the people who run and work in those organizations. **Industrial psychographics**, the application of psychographics to the business-to-business context, has mainly been applied to understanding buyers (purchasing agents or multiple people in a buying centre) to help salespeople better understand their one-on-one relationships with clients. It may also be fruitful to segment business markets by the mission, goals, and values of an organization and its management team, since purchase and consumption decisions and behaviours are likely to be consistent with those missions, goals, and values. This is the thinking of Steve Munden, director of research at the Toronto-based marketing firm Warrillow and Co. Munden is developing a psychographic profile of Generation Xers who own small- and medium-sized businesses. These entrepreneurs are people in their mid twenties to thirties who are increasingly leaving the workforce to take control of their lives and find financial independence. Munden thinks a psychographic profile of these entrepreneurs will help his clients better target these business organizations—as the beliefs, values, and orientation of these entrepreneurs are expected to play a large role in their company's purchase decisions.[44]

Exhibit 3.17

Dell Canada focuses on four main product-use segments.

ORGANIZATIONAL DEMOGRAPHICS Demographic data help business marketers understand the needs and characteristics of their potential customers. For example, a manufacturer of work uniforms needs to know which industries currently provide uniforms for employees. For each industry that uses uniforms, from chemical processing to pest control, a marketer needs to know how many companies are potential customers, the number of employees in each company, what types of uniforms are needed, and so on. That information enables the manufacturer to offer its services to the prospects that are most likely to be interested in outfitting employees in its protective clothing.

Many industries use the North American Industry Classification System (NAICS), which will be further discussed in Chapter 6, to obtain information about the size and number of companies operating in a particular industry. Other government information sources, such as Statistics Canada and Strategis (**www.strategis.gc.ca**), provide valuable business demographic information.

DEVELOPING PROFILES

Once marketers have divided a market into segments that meet the criteria of Figure 3.2, the next task is to develop a brief **segment profile**, or description of each segment, with sufficient depth to be able to understand the segment so that it can be evaluated and either be targeted or rejected. One way marketers do this is to put a name to a typical customer, then describe that customer in as much detail as possible.

One useful template for developing these profiles is illustrated in Figure 3.5. A rich profile would normally include a description of: (1) who is in the segment (using demographics, psychographics, and geographic variables); (2) what people or organizations in this segment want (benefits, features, and attributes) and why (needs, motivations); (3) when and where they expect to buy and use the product; (4) how they typically buy the product (such as purchase decision process, influences, sources of information, media preferences); and (5) how they typically use the product (consumption behaviour). In addition, marketers try to estimate the size of each segment and its expected growth rate. An example of the application of this framework can be found in Chapter 14. For the purposes of selecting market segments to target, these profiles are usually created based on experience and judgment. Sophisticated marketers, however, use market research and analytic tools such as cluster analysis to verify profile assumptions or to more scientifically identify the segments and their

segment profile A description of the "typical" customer in a segment.

Who are they?
- What are their demographic characteristics?
- What are their psychographic characteristics?
- What are the geodemographic characteristics?
- How price sensitive are they?

What do they want and why?
- What are the benefits, features, attributes, or characteristics sought by consumers in this segment?
- What do they need and want?
- What motivates the purchase and consumption decision?

When do they buy and use it?
- What triggers the purchase decision?
- What is the context in which they buy the product?
- How often do they buy the product?
- What time of day, part of the week, or month, or year is it purchased?
- What time of day, part of the week, or month, or year is it used or consumed?

Where do they buy and use it?
- What stores or other distribution channels do they use?
- Where are they when they use the product?

How do they buy and use it?
- How do they decide what to buy? (decision-making process used)
- What or who influences the purchase decision?
- What media do they use/access in making the decision?
- Is it a thinking (cognitive) or feeling (emotional) decision?
- Is it a high involvement (important or risky) decision or a low involvement (not important or risky)?
- How do they use or consume the product?
- How much of it do they use?

Segment Size
- What is the market potential?
- What is the expected growth rate of the segment?

Figure 3.5 Framework for Creating Rich Segment Profiles

characteristics. This is discussed further in Appendix 4A. The profiles of the segment(s) chosen for targeting (see below) are developed in much more detail and provide, in part, the basis for making marketing mix decisions.

To estimate the size and growth of a segment, marketers try to forecast each segment's **market potential**. This is the maximum demand expected among consumers or customers in that segment for a particular product. To determine market potential, the firm must identify the number of consumers or customers in the segment and how much they spend in the product category. Then it must determine the sales potential for its product if it targets this segment—how many consumers or customers would buy this product during the forecast period and with what frequency or quantity. This number is the total dollar potential. The firm then projects its market share—what percentage share of the market is likely to buy its particular brand(s). Multiplying total dollar potential by market share gives the likely actual dollar amount the firm might make. Forecasting is an advanced topic that you will likely learn more about in senior level courses. For the initial, brief profiles, an estimate of the relative size of each segment is expected. This would be based on experience, observation, analysis, and/or market research.

market potential The maximum demand expected among consumers in a segment for a product or service.

Market Targeting

target market A group that a marketing organization focuses on when developing marketing programs.

Once marketers have divided a market into actionable segments and developed a brief profile of each segment, they need to evaluate the attractiveness of each potential segment and decide which one or more of these groups they will target with marketing programs. The consumer or customer group(s) selected are the firm's **target market(s)**.

SoyaWorld, a Canadian soy beverage marketer, has attained 60 percent of the dairy alternative market by carefully considering specific target markets. Soy beverages make up the fastest-growing beverage category in Canada, and SoyaWorld has identified three main targets in the total market: the mainstream dairy market, the Asian market, and the organic market. For the mainstream dairy segment, SoyaWorld introduced So Good, a soy beverage with an improved taste that comes in several flavours. Since the product was being promoted as an alternative to milk, So Good was packaged to look like milk and was placed in the dairy cases of major supermarkets. Billboards, TV, and magazine ads, such as the one shown in Exhibit 3.18, were all used to reach the mainstream market. SoyaWorld targets Asian consumers with its Sunrise brand, a product that has a more traditional soy taste. For the organic target segment, it offers So Nice, a soy beverage, and Rice Choice, a fortified rice beverage. To reach the organic and Asian segments, the SoyaWorld products are distributed through specialty retailers, such as Chinese grocery stores and health food stores, in addition to selected larger grocery stores.[45] In this section, we'll review how marketers like SoyaWorld assess the customer groups in the market, and what selection strategies they use for effective targeting.

TARGET MARKET SELECTION There are three basic criteria for deciding which market segments are attractive to an organization: segment size and growth, the external decision environment, and the internal decision environment (see SWOT analysis in Chapter 2). Figure 3.6 summarizes these criteria.

So Good™ In Your Pasta.

SO GOOD™ is so delicious, you can put it in anything. Plus, it's fortified with 14 essential nutrients, including high levels of protein and calcium. So it's great to put in your body too.

For more information on SO GOOD™, call toll-free: 1-888-491-0018 or visit www.sogoodbeverage.com

❋ It's not just good. It's So Good.

Exhibit 3.18

SoyaWorld targets the mainstream dairy market with the So Good soy beverage.

1. *Segment Size and Growth.* When choosing market segments to target, one consideration is the size and growth of the segment. The segment must be "the right size"—large enough to be profitable now and in the future, but small enough that an organization can compete effectively in it. It is a lot easier to compete in a high growth segment than in a low or declining growth segment because in a high growth segment, new customers do not have to be taken away from existing competitors.

2. *External Environment.* While segment size and growth is part of the external environment, marketers tend to give that issue special attention because of its strategic importance. There are, however, other external environment considerations when choosing market segments. One is the level of competition. Large and high growth segments are highly attractive to other competitors and a smaller organization may not have the resources to compete effectively against them. It may make sense for smaller companies, with more limited resources, to focus on smaller segments (market niches) and not compete directly with larger competitors. This was the strategy of Sun Microsystems when it focused on the computer segment of engineering and scientific workstations in the early 1990s. As a small company it was able to dominate a very small, but high growth, niche and grow with that niche to become a dominant player in the overall computer market. Similarly, when Toyota introduced the Echo subcompact car into the Canadian market, the target segment was described demographically as "60/40 male/female, 40% married, median age 32, 48% university educated with an average household income $42 000." In addition, the segment displayed the following psychographic traits: idealistic, experimental, independent, educated, urban, and not brand loyal.[46] This is likely a fairly small segment, even on a national level, and it suggests that even large companies may decide to focus on small segments if they can create unique value there better than competitors can. It may be more profitable to be a "big fish in a small pond," and being that "big fish" may discourage other competitors from entering the market segment.

   Related to the extent and level of competition is the industry structure. A local monopoly (or near monopoly) like Rogers Cable may choose to focus on large, less well-defined segments because there are no direct competitors (other than satellite TV services) focusing their strategies on more narrow segments. Where there is extensive competition, different competitors will focus on increasingly narrow market segments, making it difficult for others to compete effectively in multiple segments.

   A segment with many substitute products may limit the price and hence profits in that segment. Segments where there are few buyers or buyers with otherwise strong bargaining positions might also be unattractive as these buyers can keep prices down and play one supplier off another. Segments with strong suppliers (large, concentrated, or with few competitors or substitutes) may similarly be unattractive. Finally, as we will see in Chapter 8, segment attractiveness is also related to the stage of the product life cycle—where mature and declining markets are less attractive than new and growing ones.

3. *Internal Environment.* The marketer must also be able to adequately serve the needs of the segment and have the expertise and resources to do so better than the competition. Some years ago, Exxon made the mistake of trying to enter the office products business, a growing segment. The company's expertise at selling petroleum products did not transfer to copying machines, and the effort was unsuccessful. Four Seasons Hotels, on the other hand, was recently able to transfer its expertise in exceptional accommodation services aimed at a tightly defined, luxury lifestyle audience to an entirely new market sector, residential properties.[47] The attractiveness of a segment depends on a company's ability to create value in that segment and defend their strategy in that segment. This requires an assessment of the strengths and weaknesses of the organization relative to the needs of the consumers and competition in that segment (see SWOT analysis in Chapter 2).

Figure 3.6 Criteria for Choosing Target Market Segments

TARGETING STRATEGY
Undifferentiated Marketing

A company like Wal-Mart that selects an **undifferentiated (or mass) targeting strategy** is appealing to a broad spectrum of people. If successful, this type of operation can be very efficient, especially because production, research, and promotion costs benefit from economies of scale—it's cheaper to develop one product or one advertising campaign than to choose several targets and create separate products or messages for each. But the

undifferentiated (mass) targeting strategy Appealing to a broad spectrum of people.

company must be willing to bet that people have similar needs, or that any differences among them will be so trivial that they will not matter, so that the same product and message will appeal to many customers. This is the approach Henry Ford used in offering the Model-T Ford—"in any colour, so long as it was black." Today it is difficult to create a single product or offering that has very broad appeal. Consumers expect choices, there are many distribution channels from which to purchase products, and there are many focused-communication outlets that let marketers cost-effectively communicate to increasingly narrow target markets. Companies with new-to-the-world innovations are the ones that most commonly practise undifferentiated marketing, but segments in these markets quickly develop as competitors enter these markets with differentiated products and consumers become more knowledgeable and demanding about the product category. When competitors are using a differentiated strategy it makes it difficult for the original innovator to continue using an undifferentiated strategy.

Differentiated Marketing

differentiated targeting strategy Developing one or more products for each of several distinct customer groups and making sure these offerings are kept separate in the marketplace.

A company that chooses a **differentiated targeting strategy** develops one or more products for each of several distinct customer groups and makes sure these offerings are kept separate in the marketplace. A differentiated strategy is called for when consumers are choosing among well-known brands, when each has a distinctive image in the marketplace, and when it's possible to identify one or more segments that have distinct needs for different types of products. Most large organizations follow a differentiation strategy. The cosmetics company L'Oréal uses a differentiated targeting strategy. The company has the resources to offer several product lines at a variety of prices. It targets the luxury market with such brands as Lancôme and Helena Rubinstein, whereas less expensive offerings such as Elsève and L'Oréal target large department stores and discounters.[48] Even within product lines, Procter & Gamble has multiple laundry detergent products focused on different laundry detergent segments.

concentrated targeting strategy Focusing a firm's efforts on offering one or more products to a single segment.

niche marketing A type of concentrated targeting strategy where the market segment chosen is relatively small.

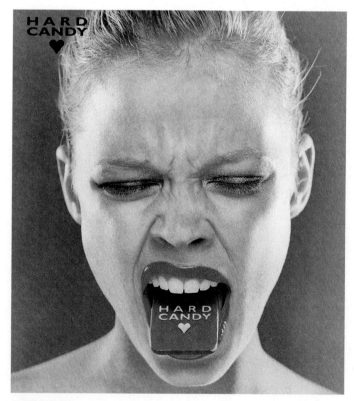

Concentrated Marketing

When a firm focuses its efforts on offering one or more products to a single segment, it is using a **concentrated targeting strategy**. A concentrated strategy is often useful for smaller firms that do not have the resources or the desire to be all things to all people. For example, the cosmetics company Hard Candy, shown in Exhibit 3.19, markets its funky line of nail polish and other products only to twentysomething women (or to those who wish they still were). **Niche marketing** is a type of concentrated targeting strategy where the market segment chosen is relatively small. Jones Soda, for example, focuses on the alternative soft drink niche by offering a series of soft drink products for people who want a premium beverage that stands out, is individualized, expresses personality, and makes a fashion statement. Niche marketing is becoming the norm in many markets as it allows many competitors to each make unique appeals and be the product of choice for some group of consumers.

Exhibit 3.19

Hard Candy uses a concentrated targeting strategy as the company targets twentysomething women.

Customized Marketing

Ideally, marketers should be able to define segments so precisely that they can offer products and services that exactly meet the needs of every individual or firm.

Custom marketing strategy, also called micro-marketing strategy, is when specific products and the messages about them are tailored to individual customers or locations. An individualized strategy is often used in business markets by companies, such as aircraft manufacturer Bombardier, to make sure the individual needs of its few customers who spend a lot of money are met. In consumer markets, this level of concentration shows up in personal or professional services, by doctors, lawyers, and hair stylists, for example. In most consumer markets, individualized marketing strategies are neither practical nor possible when products are mass-produced. However, advances in technology, coupled with the new emphasis on building solid relationships with customers, have enabled **mass customization**. Clothing manufacturers like Levi Strauss and the high-end German clothier Engelhorn, for example, use digital imaging technology to do body scans of customers that enable the creation of perfectly fitting jeans, swimwear, or other clothing products. Calgary-based Critical Mass has worked with Nike to develop NIKEiD, an interactive part of the Nike website where consumers can design and purchase their own running shoes.[49] Dell uses the Internet to provide custom-built computers; customers choose among various options and Dell makes the computer to order. Individualized communication has also been enabled by Internet and e-mail technologies. Online retailers, such as **HMV.com**, for example, are able to send customized messages to users regarding the status of their orders, upcoming promotions that may be of interest based on the products they have bought in the past, and announcements of new releases. We will return to the issue of customization in Chapter 13 when we review new advances in the management philosophy of customer relationship management.

custom marketing strategy Approach that tailors specific products and the messages about them to individual customers.

mass customization Approach that modifies a basic product or service to meet the needs of an individual.

POSITIONING

The final, crucial stage of the target marketing process is providing consumers in a targeted market segment with a product or service that meets their unique needs and expectations. **Positioning** means developing a marketing strategy that clearly differentiates a firm from its competitors along key dimensions of value that are important to target consumers or customers. When describing a positioning strategy, marketers often focus on four elements: differentiation, strategic orientation, defendability, and brand personality.

Differentiation relates to how your offer will be different from, and better than, competitive offerings, at least in the minds of your target customers. A **brand concept** is how a firm wants to be differentiated. WestJet, for example, wants to be known as the airline brand that provides the best value—low prices and good service from friendly, personable staff (Exhibit 3.20a). BC Ethic, the apparel manufacturer known for repopularizing the retro, button-down bowling shirt style worn by *Seinfeld*'s Kramer,[50] positions its shirts as being "cool" and supports that differentiation by offering customized embroidered shirts free to music artists like the Barenaked Ladies and Cypress Hill (Exhibit 3.20b). Most successful organizations are able to differentiate themselves on more than one dimension of value to customers. Starbucks, for example, competes on quality (an affordable luxury), selection and customization (you can have it your way), convenience (many locations), and atmosphere (replacing bars as a place to socialize with friends). While much of marketing communication strategy involves establishing a brand's differentiation in the minds of its customers, sometimes the intended result is not achieved. **Brand image** is the perceived positioning of a product by consumers. Canadian consumers, for example, perceived Knorr soups, sauces, and marinades as being "refined, polished, and sophisticated"—but Unilever wanted its Knorr brand to be more accessible and work as an everyday solution. The company developed its "A Little Bit More" campaign to reinforce the idea that Knorr products have more interesting ingredients than competitors' brands and offer numerous opportunities for everyday culinary creativity. The phrase "a little bit more" in Knorr's communication strategy is its slogan or tag line—which usually communicates the unique selling proposition or key point of differentiation underlying a brand's positioning. We will see other examples of this shortly.

positioning Developing a marketing strategy aimed at influencing how a particular market segment perceives a product or service as being differentiated in comparison to the competition.

brand concept How the marketer wants the brand to be positioned.

brand image How consumers perceive the positioning of the brand.

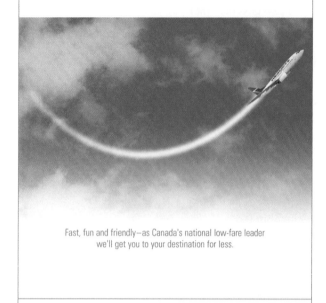

Smiles from coast to coast.

Fast, fun and friendly—as Canada's national low-fare leader
we'll get you to your destination for less.

westjet.com

CALL YOUR TRAVEL AGENT, BOOK ONLINE
OR CALL 1.800.538.5696

WESTJET

Value in Canada's skies

Skull & Bones PROVIDED BY Cypress Hill

BC ETHIC

CLOTHING

WWW.BCETHIC.COM

Exhibit 3.20

WestJet competes with a value positioning while BC Ethic wants to be "cool."

SPOTLIGHT ON REAL PEOPLE   Pita Boys

Understanding their consumer segment's characteristics and the practice of target marketing have led to success for two young entrepreneurs, Stephen Vail and David Fullerton, founders of the Pita Boys restaurants in Halifax. Although the four Pita Boys restaurants attract 18- to 45-year-old consumers, the focus of marketing efforts has been on the younger end of that range, namely university and college students. While the older customers are professionals, who view the meat and vegetable pita offerings at Pita Boys as a healthy lunch alternative, the younger customers are students, who not only like the food but also respond to the Pita Boys advertisements that appear in student and entertainment newspapers. The ads are simple (black and white) but feature creative, memorable slogans such as "We serve drunks," "Crazy, Dancin' Pita Rollin' Machines," and "Because Size Does Matter." Sponsorship of movie premieres and concerts has also been effective in reaching the student market. As Fullerton says, "The student market is easy. I know people that age, and I know what it feels like to be them."

The success of the targeting activities of the Pita Boys restaurants has grabbed the attention of much larger, more experienced marketers. Coca-Cola, for example, pays for ads on a local Halifax radio station that feature both Coke and the Pita Boys, simply because it wants to be associated with the popular restaurants. Two beer companies are also involved in marketing activities with the Pita Boys to enhance their own profiles among students, even though the restaurants do not serve beer.[51]

1. What dimensions, in addition to age, can be used to segment the market for Pita Boys restaurants?
2. The Pita Boys restaurants currently use a concentrated targeting strategy. Evaluate the pros and cons of the company switching to a differentiated targeting strategy.

STRATEGIC ORIENTATION

Strategic orientation is the marketing strategy behind the desired differentiation. It is the overall approach to how you plan to compete and create value for your customers. There are numerous frameworks or typologies that summarize key marketing and positioning strategies, and they all have different perspectives on how products can be differentiated. One of these suggests that firms can focus on one or more of the following strategies: product leadership, customer intimacy, or operational excellence.[52] Product leadership is a strategy of competing by continually bringing innovative and useful new products or technologies to market. Adopted by companies such as 3M, Apple, and Nike, it is concerned with product innovation, quality, performance superiority, and other forms of functional value (see Chapter 1). Positioning consistent with a product leadership strategy focuses on dimensions such as the following:

- Quality (e.g., Ford: "Quality is Job 1"; Gillette: "The best a man can get")
- Reliability or durability (e.g., Timex: "It takes a lick'n and keeps on tick'n")
- Key features or attributes (e.g., Honda Civic: "Better gas mileage. A Civic responsibility")
- Innovation (e.g., Lexus: "The relentless pursuit of excellence"; GE: "Progress is our most important product")
- Performance (e.g., BMW: "The ultimate driving machine"; Apple: "The power to do your best")
- Outcomes (e.g., Buckley's: "It tastes awful. And it works"; Exhibit 3.21)

Customer intimacy, or micro-marketing, is a strategy concerned with creating tailored solutions for narrowly defined market segments. Companies such as Kraft, Nordstrom, Marriott, and Levi Strauss aim to excel at providing superior customer experiences and/or personalized or customized interactions through outstanding service quality, customer support, flexibility, and customization. Concerned with the creation of experiential or emotional value, customer intimacy positioning strategies focus on dimensions such as the following:

- Sensory experience (e.g., KFC: "Finger lick'n good"; A&W: "That frosty mug sensation")
- Excitement, adventure (e.g., Nike: "Just do it"; Pontiac: "We drive excitement"; Club Med: "Do it now, do it fast, and do everything at the same time")
- Fun or pleasure (e.g., McDonald's: "I'm lovin' it"; Lay's: "Betcha can't eat just one")
- Emotion (e.g., Harlequin: "Live the emotion"; Hallmark: "When you care enough to send the very best")
- Social value (e.g., De Beers: "Diamonds are forever"; AT&T: "Reach out and touch someone")
- Responsiveness, customized, personalized (e.g., Burger King: "Have it your way"; Speedy Muffler: "At Speedy you're a somebody")
- Safety or security (e.g., Allstate: "You're in good hands with Allstate"; Michelin: "Because so much is riding on your tires")
- Novelty, knowledge, or fantasy (e.g., Disney Online: "Where the magic comes to you"; Microsoft: "Where do you want to go today?")

Operational excellence is a strategy focused on cost effectiveness, efficiency, and customer convenience. Companies such as Zellers, WestJet Airlines, Dell, and Ikea (Exhibit 3.22) are tenacious at lowering costs and customer prices while making it more convenient to do business with them. Concerned with the creation of cost-sacrifice value, operational

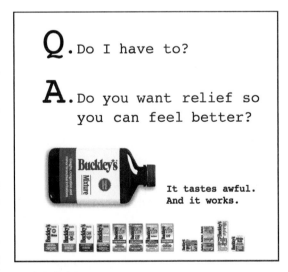

Exhibit 3.21

Buckley's cough syrup is positioned on the outcome "it works," consistent with a product leadership strategy.

Exhibit 3.22

Ikea promotes a value positioning, consistent with an operational excellence strategy.

excellence positioning strategies focus on dimensions such as the following:

- Price (e.g., Zellers: "The lowest price is the law"; Buy.com: "Canada's low price Internet superstore")
- Value (e.g., Ikea: "Swedish for common sense")
- Convenience (e.g., 7-Eleven: "Oh thank heaven"; American Express: "Don't leave home without it")
- Personal investment of time, effort, or energy (e.g., Yellow Pages: "Let your fingers do the walking")
- Risk (e.g., Levi's Jeans: "Have you ever had a bad time in Levi's?"; Listerine mouthwash: "Even your best friends won't tell you")

Another common positioning strategy is concerned with symbolic-expressive value—differentiating your brand by the psychological meaning associated with it. Some products (luxury goods for example) appeal to consumers' self-concepts and self-worth—that is, they make us feel good about ourselves. Other products (such as music or comfort foods, among many others) have personal meaning—associations with people or events that only have meaning to a particular consumer (such as an association with Tide because Mom used it). Products can also provide a means of self-expression. Products such as Calvin Klein fragrances, Roots clothes, a Volkswagen Beetle, or Body Shop lotions allow consumers to reflect or express their personalities, tastes, and values. Still other products focus on social meaning—how others see us. Products such as BMW cars, Birks jewellery, and Lee Valley Tools are purchased because of their prestige, status, or image. Brands can also be positioned on one or more of these four symbolic meaning dimensions. For example:

- Self identity/concept/worth (e.g., L'Oréal: "Because I'm worth it")
- Personal meaning: (e.g., Kodak: "Share moments. Share life")
- Self-expression (e.g., Canon: "Express yourself")
- Social meaning (e.g., Grey Poupon: "Pardon me. Do you have any Grey Poupon?"; Rolls-Royce: "Trusted to deliver excellence")

There are many other marketing strategy frameworks or typologies that you will learn about in a marketing strategy course. However, there are some other ways to differentiate products and establish a brand's position in the marketplace. These include strategies that emphasize:

- Product class leadership: The Mazda Miata is a sporty convertible.
- Relative positioning: The Pepsi Challenge claims "More people prefer the taste of Pepsi over Coke." (This is an example of head-to-head competitive positioning, where other organizations try to *associate* their brand with the market leader.)
- Use occasions: Wrigley's gum is an alternative at times when smoking is not permitted.
- Users: Sunny Delight is the "Goodness kids go for."

Defendability

The choice of strategic orientation and the basis of differentiation is dependent on an organization's ability to defend that positioning. Analysis of your ability to defend a particular positioning requires an assessment of the strengths and weaknesses of your own organization and your ability to create sustainable competitive advantage, and the opportunities and threats in the external environment, in particular consumer behaviour and your assessment of the strategies and capabilities of your competitors (recall SWOT analysis from Chapter 2).

ANALYZE COMPETITORS' POSITIONS

Marketers typically start by understanding how their competitors are perceived by the target market. Aside from direct competitors in the product category, marketers consider whether there are other products or services that provide the same benefits that people in the segment are seeking. For example, when a company such as Coca-Cola develops a new drink, it must consider not only archrival Pepsi, but also how to compete against many alternative soft drinks and other beverages. The surprise success of Jolt Cola, which is fortified with caffeine, led Coca-Cola to develop Surge to target students, athletes, and people who don't like the taste of coffee but who need to "Feed the Rush."[53] By understanding the positioning of your competitors, and the strength of that positioning (their ability to defend their positioning), you can begin to assess whether there is room in the marketplace for the positioning of your offer. This is what Michael Shekter is doing when he examines the positioning of the super-premium beers and the value beers relative to Molson Canadian.

How do marketers determine where competitors' products (and their own) actually stand in the minds of consumers? One solution is to ask consumers what characteristics are important and how competing offers would rate on these attributes. Marketers use this information to construct a **perceptual map**, a picture of where products or brands are "located" in consumers' minds.

perceptual map A picture of where products or brands are "located" in consumers' minds.

For example, suppose you want to construct a perceptual map of women's magazines as perceived by Canadian women to give you some guidance while developing an idea for a new magazine. After interviewing a sample of female readers, you determine questions women ask when selecting a magazine: Is it "service oriented," emphasizing family, home, and personal issues, or is it "fashion forward," oriented toward personal appearance and fashion? Is it for "upscale" women, who are older and established in their careers, or for relatively "downscale" women, who are younger and just starting out in their careers?

The perceptual map in Figure 3.7 illustrates how these ratings might look for certain major women's magazines. It depicts the aggregate or average perception of how brands are

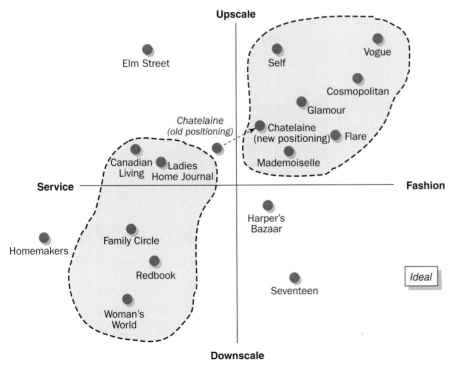

Figure 3.7 Perceptual Map

perceived by multiple consumers on the dimensions of upscale/downscale and service/fashion, and it should be recognized that no individual consumer may hold these average perceptions. The shaded areas in Figure 3.7 represent two segments of consumers who seek the benefits and attributes offered by the set of magazines encircled. These are only two of many dimensions on which consumers compare magazines; marketers typically produce a series of positioning maps to understand how their and other brands are perceived by consumers. Other dimensions on which to position magazines might include cost (high/low), age appropriateness (young/old), sex appropriateness (mainly for men/mainly for women), and content (serious/frivolous)—among other possible dimensions.

The map also provides some guidance as to where your new women's magazine might be positioned. You might decide to compete directly with either the cluster of "service magazines" in the middle left or the fashion magazines in the upper right. In this case, you would have to determine what benefits your new magazine might offer that these existing magazines do not. *Chatelaine*, for example, repositioned itself in 1999 from a service-type magazine to a more urban, contemporary, youth- and fashion-oriented publication. This repositioning moved *Chatelaine* further away from its nearest Canadian competitor, *Canadian Living*.

blue ocean strategy A positioning strategy where you create a new market and get to define the playing field before competitors enter.

To introduce a new magazine, you might try to locate an unserved area in this perceptual map. A **blue ocean strategy** is where you create a new market and get to define the playing field before competitors enter. *Elm Street*, a relatively new entrant to the Canadian women's magazine scene, has tried to position itself for the upscale woman who is interested in articles on a broad range of topics, a part of the market that it felt was unserved. An unserved area of the map represents either an unserved segment and hence a potential opportunity for marketers, or a positioning that is not in demand by a segment of consumers. According to Figure 3.7 (see "ideal"), there may be room for a magazine targeted to downscale "cutting-edge" fashion, perhaps for younger women.

Positioning maps are similar to perceptual maps, except that they may include factual as well as perceptual information. By including factual information in the map, marketers can illustrate how brands compete in a marketplace. Figures 3.8 and 3.9 illustrate multiple

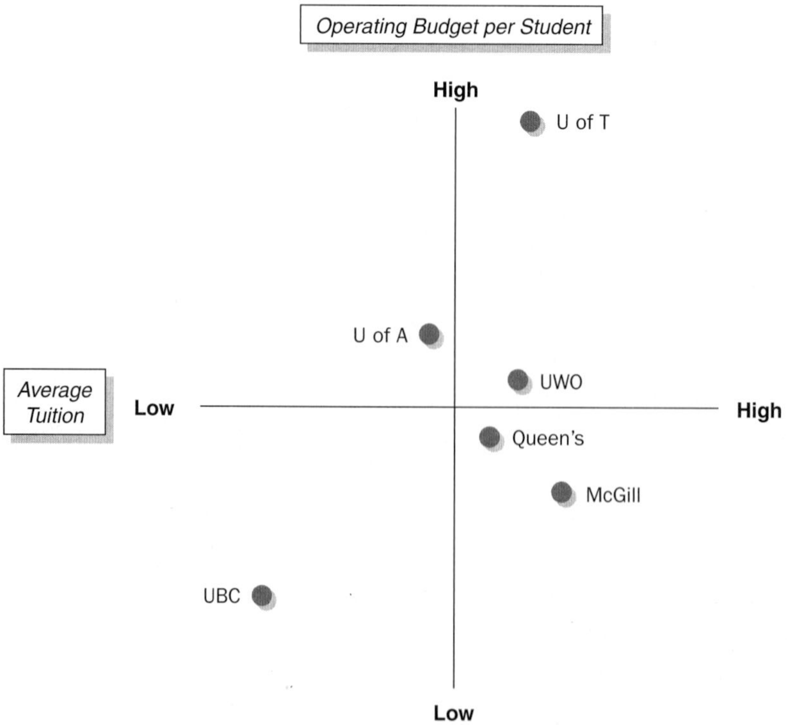

Figure 3.8 A Factual Positioning Map

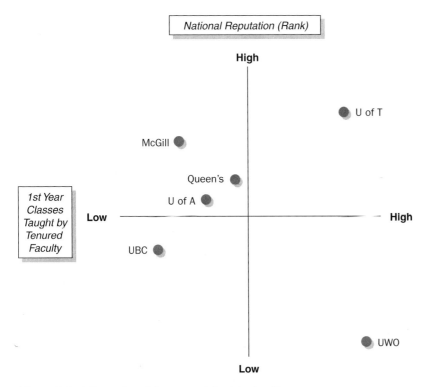

Figure 3.9 A Factual and Perceptual Positioning Map

Table 3.1 *Maclean's* Rating of Universities with Medical/Doctoral Programs (2002)

	U of T	Queen's	McGill	UWO	UBC	U of A
Average Entering Grade (%)	85.7	87.3	86.1	85.1	86.6	84.0
1st Yr Classes by Tenured Faculty	70.9	53.2	42.9	72.6	38.7	46.9
% of Classes Sized 51–100	44.7	34.1	35.8	17.6	39.8	33.4
Operating Budget per Student	9884	7861	7529	8246	6981	8669
National Reputation (Rank)	2	4	3	10	7	5
Average Tuition	4875	4828	5156	4870	2883	4491

Source: Reprinted with permission from *Maclean's* magazine.

positioning maps for a subset of Canadian universities with medical or doctoral programs, based on research conducted by *Maclean's* magazine (Table 3.1).[54] National reputation, a perceptual dimension included in the *Maclean's* ratings, is assessed by guidance counsellors, recruiters, and university officials from across the country. The other information collected is factual.

VALUE CREATION AND SUSTAINABLE COMPETITIVE ADVANTAGE

The second aspect of an assessment of defendability is to assess your ability to create the value proposition and basis of differentiation that you intend in your brand concept, and your ability to sustain your strategic orientation in the face of competitive reaction. Different

Table 3.2 Positioning Strategy Implementation

	Product Leadership	Customer Intimacy	Operational Excellence	Symbolism/Meaning
Strategy	Innovate, bring new products to market quickly that have superior features, functions, performance or outcomes	Develop exceptional customer experiences and tailored, customized solutions	Provide the best value by reducing costs, lowering prices, and by making it easy to do business with you	Develop superior symbolism or meaning for your product that creates psychological attachment to your brand
Structure	Flat, organic, flexible	Decentralized, empowerment close to customer contact	Strong centralized decisions focused on process or system improvements	Centralized decision making to control corporate and brand image, strong brand management structure
Culture	Entrepreneurial, creative, rewards innovation	Customer oriented, flexible, rewards customer satisfaction and loyalty	Bureaucratic, run by accountants, cost savings are rewarded.	Culture reflects and supports brand positioning. Brand management is rewarded.
Resource	Research & development	Customer research	Procurement	Marketing communications
Focus	New product development, Production, Distribution	Service quality, Customer support, Flexible manufacturing	Distribution, Scale efficiencies, Manufacturing efficiencies	Product quality, Brand management, Customer research

strategic orientations require different organizational strengths (capabilities), focus, and resource allocation, and they are often associated with different organizational cultures (Table 3.2). This makes it difficult to be the industry leader in more than one of these areas. At issue is whether an organization has the skills, abilities, resources, organizational structure, and culture to create the intended offer such that it will be perceived as superior by members of the target market on the differentiation dimensions reflected in the positioning strategy; whether the organization can communicate this effectively to the target market; and whether it can continue to do this until its goals are met as an organization. Marketers need to explain how they are going to be able to sustain the basis for value creating differentiation in the minds of its target customers.

There are three main ways to defend a positioning strategy. The first is to continuously innovate to keep ahead of competitors. This is the approach typically followed by organizations adopting a product leadership strategy. The second approach is to hide in a small enough niche market that competitors are not likely to enter—either because the market is not big enough to warrant attention, or because there are significant first-mover advantages in that market, such that followers into the market are at serious disadvantage. The third is to protect current source(s) of competitive advantage by erecting barriers to competition. Some of these barriers include:

- Marketing expertise: companies that are market oriented and customer driven can protect a customer intimacy positioning by being closer to and more understanding of customer needs, wants, and behaviours; by being more flexible; and by being more responsive to customers.
- Customer loyalty: competitors find it difficult to get loyal customers to switch brands. Companies who have developed loyal customers can protect their positioning by maintaining high levels of customer satisfaction. Some strategy experts argue that relationships are the only true source of sustainable competitive advantage as other barriers can eventually be eroded.

SPOTLIGHT ON REAL PEOPLE   Girl Guides Go Groovy

The world is ever changing. Businesses are constantly predicting and reacting, and sometimes a call for change must be turned into complete repositioning for company survival. This predicament is exactly what the Girl Guides of Canada encountered in 2002 after experiencing a steady decline in membership. The organization was formed in 1910 and remains the largest organization for girls and women in Canada, but its concepts and activities had been stuck in the '90s. The Guides hired Tony Ritchie, principal strategist at Ritchie-Bridges Strategy who admitted, "It's as simple and complex as saying we need a complete brand transformation." The Guides also hired Cossette Communications Marketing to handle its creative, media, and public relations, and Youthography out of Toronto to redesign the Girl Guides website. The Guides replaced the old brown uniforms with brightly coloured cargo pants and fleeces, "You go girl" was incorporated as the theme in promotional materials, and the rebranding strategy that Girl Guides were "fun, bold, energetic, popular, and real" was pushed as well. To keep up with technology the website was revamped to be used not just as a corporate information mechanism but also as a communication tool, and as a fun place for current and potential guides and volunteers to surf. The world-famous cookies were changed too. The cookie boxes have a fresh up-to-date look that reinforces the fun, bold, energetic, and "you go girl" themes. The focus of all of this change and energy is ultimately a revived and healthier organization. There is still a long way to go but the Girl Guides know that the organization and its overall concepts must change and adapt to the outside environment to survive and prosper.

Source: Sarah Dobson, "The Girl Guides go GROOVY," *Marketing Magazine Online*, 28 April 2003.

1. What obstacles will the Girl Guides and other companies face in the midst of repositioning? What can companies do to deal with these challenges?
2. How do you think an organization as geographically spread out as the Girl Guides of Canada could best unite its efforts to change? What would be the best way to communicate within the organization?

- Monopolization of a scarce resource: retailers restrict competition by gaining exclusive access to retail locations. Other organizations secure exclusive supply or distribution contracts to limit the ability of competitors to enter markets.

- Proprietary technology: patents, copyrights, and other mechanisms that protect intellectual property can help protect current sources of competitive advantage.

- Culture-based expertise: companies that develop core competencies or specialized knowledge in applications, manufacturing, new product development, or other value-creating activities within organizations can protect a positioning strategy based on that expertise if it permeates an organization's culture in a way that is difficult to emulate. Cultures take a long time to develop and it is very difficult for competitors to emulate culture-based expertise.

- Legislation or regulatory approval: cellphone companies and cable companies are partially protected from competition by the Canadian Radio-television and Telecommunications Commission and the need for regulatory approval to set up cell networks or cable networks.

- Capital requirements: high market-entry costs, such as the cost of specialized equipment, technology, or setting up a sales force or distribution channel, can be a barrier to competitors, particularly in small market niches that may support only one or two competitors.

BRINGING A PRODUCT TO LIFE: THE BRAND PERSONALITY

The final element of a positioning strategy is creating a brand personality. Brands, like people, can be described in terms of personality traits. These descriptions might include words like cheap, elegant, sexy, bold, or wimpy. A positioning strategy often tries to create a **brand personality** for a product or service—a distinctive image that captures its character, soul, and benefits. An advertisement for *Elle* magazine once said, "She is not a reply card.

brand personality A distinctive image that captures a product or service's character and benefits.

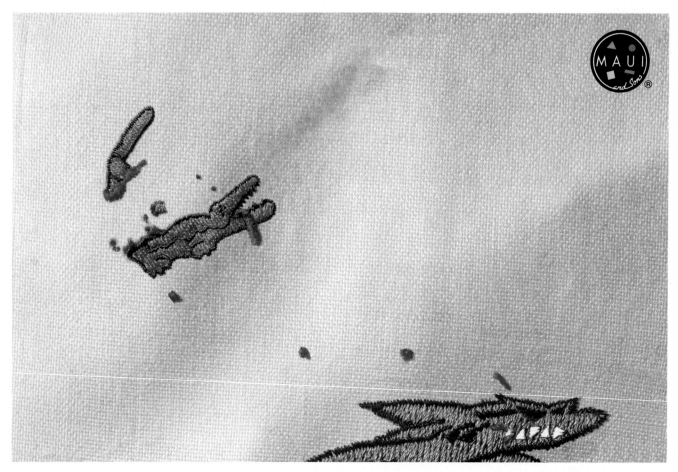

Exhibit 3.23

Brand personalities are often reflected in logos.

She is not a category. She is not shrink-wrapped. *Elle* is not a magazine. She is a woman." When the Mark Anthony Group was developing a name for its lemonade-based alcohol product, it did research with consumers to determine what name would communicate the right brand personality. The "person" it chose for its hard lemonade, "Mike," is described as a "fun, party, happy-go-lucky guy who is infatuated with lemons."[55] Other organizations use mascots or characters to help create brand personality. Pillsbury personifies its products through the Pillsbury Doughboy—a sufficiently iconic symbol that a giant-sized "Doughboy" (the Stay Puft Marshmallow Man) was featured as one of the possessed characters in the *Ghost Busters* movie. Energizer has the Energizer Bunny. Cellphone companies have focused on various animals to promote brand personality, from lizards to fish to beavers. Brand personalities are often reflected in logos. The clothing ad from Chile in Exhibit 3.23 pits a shark against the more familiar crocodile—with bloody results.

Marketing researchers find that most consumers have no trouble describing what a product would be like "if it came to life." People tend to anthropomorphize (ascribe human attributes) to many things around us: pets, cars, and brands. Try it. If Air Canada walked into the room would Air Canada be male or female? How old would she or he be? Thin or overweight? Is Air Canada married or unmarried? Is s/he friendly or cold and aloof? Service oriented or self-serving? What does s/he do with her spare time? What does s/he care about? What kind of house does s/he live in and what kind of car does s/he drive? People often give clear, detailed descriptions of what brands would be like if they were people, including what colour hair the product would have![56] What colour is Air Canada's hair?

After 124 years of positioning itself as the brand that "kills the germs that cause bad breath," Listerine lost market leadership in the 1980s to Scope and private label brands, in part because the brand was perceived as being cold, old-fashioned, authoritarian, serious, and stuffy—much like Margaret Thatcher, the British prime minister at the time.[57] In the 1990s Listerine tried many times to reposition its brand, but it could not shake its authoritarian brand personality and consumers closed their ears to bad-breath lectures. In the late 1990s Listerine research identified that consumers were now much more aware of plaque, tartar, and gingivitis and that a shift to healthier gums positioning could be compelling and ownable; research also found that the use of Listerine reduces gingivitis better than brushing and flossing alone. The challenge was then to develop a new brand personality that was both lighthearted and powerful. By developing a parody of a comic book action hero that fights the evil gingivitis, Listerine was able to transform its image and is now perceived by consumers as powerful, larger than life, immortal, and unfailing (Exhibit 3.24). Listerine's dollar share went from 38 percent in 1999 to 45 percent in early 2002, strong growth for a mature brand in a mature market.

One of the most effective marketing campaigns to establish brand personality as been Apple's Mac–PC campaign that depicts PC as an overweight, middle-aged accountant-type person and Mac as a personable, creative, and sophisticated young adult. In a series of interactions between Mac and PC, the audience learns the key basis of differentiation between Macs

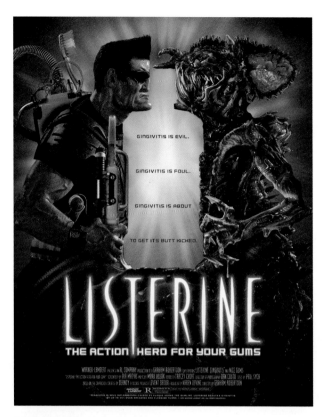

Exhibit 3.24

Listerine was able to change its brand personality using its action-hero campaign and significantly regained market share.

Marketing Metrics

How do you measure the personality of a brand? Professor David Aaker offers the Aaker Brand Personality Scale, where 42 questions relate to five dimensions of brand personality: sincerity, excitement, competence, sophistication, and ruggedness. This scale was used in a "Measuring the Value of Product Placement" study conducted by CTV Market Research and Group M (a unit of marketing giant WPP Group, comprising its media networks Mediaedge:cia and MindShare). The objective of the study was to determine what impact placement/integration has on a brand's personality. The study used CTV's nightly entertainment show *e-Talk Daily* as a test vehicle. A total of 300 people aged 18 to 54, who are viewers of *e-Talk Daily* or similar programs, participated in the study.

They were divided into groups and shown one of four test tapes in which the marketers' involvement ranged from no ad exposure to a 30-second commercial, to a 30-second commercial augmented by either product placement or product integration. Product placement and integration was found to have a discernible impact on brand personality, product recall, and purchase intent. One of the brand participants, LG, found that their ranking in the excitement category of Aaker's Brand Personality Scale grew 32 percent following the integration. Mark Husak, managing partner of MindShare Canada in Toronto, calls this "one of the most important findings" of the study. "It allows us to relate back to some specific marketing strategies to understand how that dimension works," he says.[58]

and all the PC brands. You can see the ads on Apple's website (**www.apple.com**), and on YouTube you will find many parodies of these ads—evidence of their resonance with their target audience.

IMPLEMENTING THE POSITIONING STRATEGY

The success of a target marketing strategy hinges on a marketer's ability to identify and select an appropriate market segment or market segments. Then the marketer must devise a positioning that will set apart their offer from their competitors', that will be highly appealing to the target market, and that can be defended. The marketing mix decisions relating to product, pricing, distribution, and communication are then made in a way that supports the desired positioning. In effect, the marketing mix is the way that positioning gets implemented. Because everything else depends on segmentation and positioning decisions, segmentation and positioning, together, are the two most important concepts in marketing.

Montreal-based G.I. Energy Drinks developed the following strategy when it introduced the Guru energy drink. The company segmented the market in terms of age and psychographics, and then targeted a segment of 16- to 24-year-olds, whose profiles indicated they were into "new-age" beverages that would give them a feeling of energy without unhealthy additives. The company reached these consumers by selling its drinks at raves in Montreal and Toronto (see Exhibit 3.25), advertising in club culture magazines, and sponsoring events like snowboarding demonstrations. A company spokesperson describes the Guru positioning strategy this way: "We really feel the best way to reach people is through trial and onsite promotions. . . . We want to provide the consumer with a drink that will enhance the activity they are already participating in."[59]

We previously discussed some of the challenges in segmentation. The four main positioning challenges are: (1) vague positioning, where companies do not clearly articulate their main point(s) of differentiation; (2) confused positioning, where the positioning strategy keeps changing (like McDonald's), making it difficult for consumers or customers to understand what the brand is supposed to mean to them; (3) off-target positioning, where

Exhibit 3.25
Many Canadian energy drinks, such as Generator and Guru, reach target segments by being sold at raves.

companies do not differentiate themselves on dimensions important to consumers or customers; and (4) over positioning, where companies position themselves too narrowly, either appealing to too small a market segment or being unable to change or adapt their positioning with changing market conditions.

EVALUATE THE TARGET MARKET'S RESPONSES AND MODIFY THE STRATEGY The target marketing process is ongoing. Over time an organization like Molson may find that it needs to change the segments it targets, and the needs or wants of people in these chosen segments may change as well. Marketers need to monitor these changes and adjust their positioning strategies when necessary. Sometimes marketers redo a product's position to respond to marketplace changes.

Real People, Real Decisions

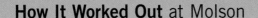

How It Worked Out at Molson

Michael Shekter and the Molson Canadian marketing team chose Option 3: Clean Sheet.

Going back was not a viable option. The cost of decreasing the price of a case of Canadian and then increasing its market share to cover the loss was prohibitive. Also, the market had changed—so they really couldn't go back, even if they wanted to.

The "I Am. Canadian" campaign was a great piece of theatre. Consumers took away Canadian pride from the campaign—"I love Canada"—but they did not take away "I love your beer." Molson realized that a great ad does not necessarily make a great campaign. The company had good reason to believe that it did not resonate for beer.

A huge emotional, strategic, and financial investment had been made in this campaign. To abandon the campaign meant that the brand's marketing team was admitting defeat and saying that the last five years was a waste of time. They took this risk and abandoned the devil they knew and switched to an all-new campaign.

The first "new" campaign was "It Starts Here"—a brand positioning campaign that focused heavily on the consumer insight that "Sometimes the best part of the night is the anticipation of the great things to come." This campaign was followed for the next two years. However, while it was emotionally focused on the beer consumer instead of national pride, it lacked a product story. Other companies were talking about their product. The value companies were saying their product was "pretty good" and the premium companies were saying it was "excellent." The lack of a product focus made it hard for Canadian to compete. Consequently the campaign provided no real increase in product share.

The next and current campaign is the "True Canadian Taste" campaign. This campaign provides both an "emotional story" and a "product story." It provides the consumer with a "reason to believe." The emotional story speaks to Canadian as a sociable brand. We Canadians "cheer with beer" and that beer is Canadian. The product story speaks to what is inside the bottle, and that is Canadian as the definitive Canadian lager. It provides the credentials to back up this claim: Molson, brewing beer for the last 221 years, is the oldest brewing company in Canada. It is also the only truly national brand available in all ten provinces and three territories. These credentials provide legitimacy as the true Canadian beer.

The keys to the campaign are the extent to which it:

1. Resonates with their core target consumer (Legal Drinking Age [LDA] to 24 years old) in a meaningful way.
2. Allows ample opportunity to execute within the campaign—patriotism can be somewhat limiting when it comes to promotion, but a "Let's all cheer with beer" emotional positioning is rich territory for developing promotional ideas.
3. Ties in a product and an emotional story in a symbiotic way. Canadian is "the perfect beer for those great Canadian beer occasions."

The revised campaign has had a strong impact on the Molson Canadian brand, strengthening its brand franchise and steadying its footprint in English Canada compared to the previous two years. The campaign won a "Cassie" in the "Off to a Good Start" category last year, and the current campaign was voted "Best Beer Campaign of the Summer" by *Strategy Magazine*. The "True Canadian Taste" campaign has been a success. Canadian has stabilized its market share in every region, while Labatt's Blue continues to decline at an accelerating rate. Canadian continues to maintain an enormous footprint in the Canadian market, and remains an iconic symbol of great Canadian beer and of Canada itself. Maintaining the price bracket has also allowed Canadian to remain an extremely profitable brand, which has allowed it to continue to support the programming and develop a stronger, more value added brand positioning.

repositioning Redoing a product's position to respond to marketplace changes.

An example of such a makeover, a strategy called **repositioning**, was undertaken by Adults Only Video, a Canadian video chain that specializes in the sale and rental of pornographic movies. The company decided to reposition itself to appeal to couples aged 25 to 54. The company's traditional target market was males 18 to 25, but increased competition for this segment from Internet providers caused the company to reassess its position. The management at Adults Only Video described its repositioning as a move from a "sleazy" image to a "softer" one. The repositioning was accomplished by changing the product mix in the stores (to include products like candles, books, and magazines) and changing its advertising strategy to include female voiceovers in its radio ads and the placement of print ads in mainstream newspapers. The company also ran a large promotion, the "Millionaire Kiss-off," in which couples could win $1 million by breaking the world's record for the longest kiss.[60]

The Campbell Company of Canada is trying to reposition itself from being a soup company to being a food company. Its Power2Cook campaign (**www.power2cook.ca**) uses traditional advertising, direct marketing, and a re-tooled website to teach young and busy cooks, male and female, how to prepare tasty meals using Campbell products.

CHAPTER SUMMARY

Key Terms

- 80/20 rule, p. 80
- baby boomers, p. 86
- behavioural segmentation, p. 79
- benefit segmentation, p. 79
- blue ocean strategy, p. 102
- brand concept, p. 97
- brand image, p. 97
- brand personality, p. 105
- concentrated targeting strategy, p. 96
- custom marketing strategy, p. 97
- demographics, p. 84
- differentiated targeting strategy, p. 96
- geodemography, p. 91
- long tail, p. 80
- industrial psychographics, p. 92
- market fragmentation, p. 75
- market potential, p. 94
- mass customization, p. 97
- niche marketing, p. 96
- operating variables, p. 91
- perceptual map, p. 101
- positioning, p. 97
- product usage segmentation, p. 79
- psychographic segmentation, p. 81

1. Understand the five steps of developing a target marketing strategy.

The first step, select and understand markets, involves specifying the market that you are going to segment, including its geographic scope. Then you need to sufficiently understand consumers or customers in this market to be able to identify groups. The second step, market segmentation, involves dividing a large market into a set of smaller markets that share important actionable characteristics, and developing profiles of the segments that describe them in sufficient detail to be able to choose among them. The third step is targeting, in which marketers select one or more of these groups to serve as their target market. The fourth step, called positioning, is developing a clear image to communicate to members of the target market of how a brand is different and better than its competitors. The fifth step is developing marketing mix recommendations that create the offer for consumers or customers in the chosen segment(s) with the desired positioning.

2. Define the terms *segmentation*, *target marketing*, and *positioning*.

Segmentation is the process of dividing a larger market into smaller pieces, based on one or more meaningful, shared characteristics. Target marketing is dividing the total market into different segments based on customer characteristics, selecting one or more segments, and developing products to meet the needs of those specific segments. Positioning is how a particular market segment perceives a product or service as being differentiated in comparison to the competition.

3. Segment consumer and business-to-business markets.

Marketers frequently find it useful to segment consumer markets based on how consumers behave toward the product, for example, benefits or value sought, their brand loyalty, usage rates (heavy, moderate, or light), usage occasions, and product type purchased. A second dimension, psychographics, uses measures of psychological and social characteristics to identify people with shared preferences or traits. Demographic characteristics including age, gender, family life cycle, social class, ethnic identity, and place of residence may be a viable basis for segmentation but are critical elements in developing profiles of the segments. Categories similar to those in the consumer market are used for segmenting business markets. Business demographics include industry or company size, North American Industry Classification (NAICS) codes, and geographic location. Business markets may also be segmented based on operating variables and end-use applications. The recommended process is to start with a behavioural basis to see if groups can be identified by "what they want" or "how they use" a product. The other bases can then be used to develop the segment profiles more fully.

4. Explain how marketers evaluate and select potential market segments.

An effective segmentation scheme is one that meets the following criteria: groups are similar enough within that members would want similar product solutions; different enough between that they would want different product solutions; large enough to warrant targeting; measurable; and reachable. To choose one or more segments to target, marketers examine each segment and evaluate its potential for success as a target market based on an assessment of its size and growth, other external environment factors like level of competition, and internal environment factors like the organization's ability to create unique value for the segment. The firm may choose an undifferentiated, differentiated, concentrated, or custom strategy, based on the company's characteristics and the nature of the market.

5. Understand how a firm develops and implements a positioning strategy.

After they have selected the target market(s) and overall strategy, marketers must determine how they wish the brand to be perceived by consumers relative to the competition: Should the brand be positioned like, against, or away from the competition? Brand concept is how the marketer wants its brand to be positioned; brand image is how consumers perceive the positioning of the brand. Through positioning, a brand personality is developed. Brand positions can be compared using such research techniques as perceptual mapping. In developing and implementing the positioning strategy, firms analyze the competitors' positions, determine the competitive advantage offered by their product, tailor the marketing mix in accordance with the positioning strategy, and evaluate responses to the marketing mix selected. Marketers must continually monitor changes in the market that might indicate a need to reposition the product.

6. Describe how a positioning strategy can be defended.

There are three main ways to defend a positioning strategy. The first is to continuously innovate to keep ahead of competitors. The second approach is to hide in a small enough niche market that competitors are not likely to enter—either because the market is not big enough to warrant their attention, or because there are significant first mover advantages in that market, such that followers into the market are at serious disadvantage. The third is to protect current source(s) of competitive advantage by erecting barriers to competition, such as marketing expertise (closer to the customer or more responsive); customer loyalty; control of a scarce resource; or proprietary technology.

CHAPTER REVIEW

Marketing Concepts: Testing Your Knowledge

1. What is market segmentation and why is it an important strategy in today's marketplace?
2. Explain consumer psychographic segmentation.
3. How can consumer behaviour be used for segmenting consumer markets?
4. List and explain the major demographic characteristics frequently used in segmenting markets.
5. What are the major dimensions used for segmenting business markets?
6. List the criteria used for determining whether a segment may be a good candidate for targeting.
7. Explain undifferentiated, differentiated, concentrated, customized, and mass-customization marketing strategies.
8. What is product positioning? Describe the process marketers use to create product positions.
9. Describe the various ways positioning strategies may be defended.
10. What are positioning and perceptual maps and how are they used by marketers?

Marketing Concepts: Discussing Choices and Issues

1. Some critics of marketing have suggested that market segmentation and target marketing lead to an unnecessary proliferation of product choices, which wastes valuable resources. These

critics suggest that if marketers didn't create so many different product choices, there would be more resources to feed the hungry, house the homeless, and provide for the needs of people around the globe. Are the results of segmentation and target marketing harmful or beneficial to society as a whole? Should these criticisms be of concern to firms? How should New Era firms respond to these criticisms?

2. Retailers like Canada Safeway and Zellers have membership programs that ask customers to provide personal and sometimes financial information. The purchases the customer makes are then captured by the checkout scanner when the membership or loyalty card is presented. Explain how this data could be used to identify market segments and develop detailed segment profiles.

3. Some firms have been criticized for targeting unwholesome products to certain segments of the market—the elderly, ethnic subcultures, and the disabled. What other groups deserve special concern? Should a firm use different criteria in targeting such groups? Should the government oversee and control such marketing activities?

4. What are some ways in which a small business could defend its positioning against larger competitors?

Marketing Practice: Applying What You've Learned

1. Assume that you have been hired to develop a marketing plan for a small regional brewery. In the past, the brewery produced and sold a single beer to the entire market—a mass marketing strategy. As you begin your work for the firm, you feel that the firm could be more successful if it developed a target marketing strategy. The owner of the firm, however, is not convinced. Write a memo to the owner outlining:

   a. the basic reasons for target marketing.

   b. the specific advantages of a target marketing strategy for the brewery.

2. Assume that you are the director of marketing for a company that markets personal computers to business and organizational customers. You feel that if your market is segmented, you will be able to satisfy your customers' needs more efficiently and effectively. You must first decide what bases to use for segmenting the market.

   a. Develop a list of the potential segmentation variables you might use.

   b. Include your thoughts on how useful each might be to your marketing strategy.

   c. Develop a segmentation scheme for this market and develop a rich profile of at least one segment.

3. As the marketing director for a company that is planning to enter the business market for photocopy machines, you are attempting to develop an overall marketing strategy. You have considered the possibility of using mass marketing, concentrated marketing, differentiated marketing, and custom marketing strategies.

   a. Write a report explaining what each type of strategy would mean for your marketing plan in terms of product, price, promotion, and distribution channel.

   b. Evaluate the desirability of each type of strategy.

   c. What are your final recommendations for the best type of strategy?

4. You are an account executive for a marketing consulting firm, and your newest client is an educational institution—the one you are currently attending. With a group of classmates, develop an outline of your ideas for positioning the institution, including the following:

   a. Who are your competitors?

   b. What are the competitors' positions?

   c. What target markets are most attractive for your client?

   d. How will you position your client for those segments relative to the competition?

   Present your results to your class.

Marketing Mini-Project: Learning by Doing

This mini-project will help you develop a better understanding of how target-marketing decisions are made. The project focuses on the market for automobiles.

1. Gather ideas about different dimensions useful for segmenting the automobile market. You may use your own ideas or talk to your friends and family. You probably will also want to examine advertising and other marketing communications developed by different automobile manufacturers; read articles in newspapers and magazines; look at Internet automobile sellers; and talk with salespeople at local automobile dealerships about different types of consumers and the cars they buy.

2. Based on the dimensions for market segmentation you have identified, develop a questionnaire and conduct a survey of consumers. You will have to decide which questions should be asked and which consumers should be surveyed.

3. Analyze the data from your research and identify the different potential segments.

4. Develop segment profiles that describe each potential segment.

5. Generate several ideas for how the marketing strategy might be different for each segment based on the profiles.

6. Develop a presentation (or write a report) outlining your ideas, your research, your findings, and your marketing strategy recommendations.

Real People, Real Surfers: Exploring the Web

In this chapter, you learned about psychographic segmentation systems, such as VALS and the Environics "tribes." To learn more about these systems, visit the SRI (the creators of VALS) website (**www.sric-bi.com**) and the Environics website (**www.environics.net**). When you follow the VALS links, you will discover that SRI has also developed other segmentation systems, such as Geo-VALS and Japan-VALS.

1. Based on the Environics site, describe all of the Environics tribes. For each tribe, identify what companies might be interested in targeting them. What tribe do you identify with?

2. From the information on the SRI website, describe Geo-VALS, Japan-VALS, and iVALS. What are some ways these segmentation systems might be used by organizations?

3. You can determine your own VALS type by taking the survey on the SRI website. Although the segments are based on people who live in the United States, the questions are also relevant for Canadians. When taking the survey, simply omit the zip code question. After you determine which segment you belong to, assess whether you think this VALS type accurately portrays you.

4. What is your opinion of the SRI and Environics websites? Whom do you think the companies are targeting with the sites? Do you think the sites are an effective way to promote products to potential customers? What suggestions do you have for improving the websites?

   Write a report of your findings.

Chapter 3 Spitz International

Spitz International Inc. is the new name for Alberta Sunflower Seeds Limited, but we all know them as Canada's number one sunflower seed company—"Spitz." The company was started in 1982 by Tom and Emmy Droog as a sunflower seed supplier for the bird seed market. The Droogs arrived in Canada from Holland in 1972, speaking no English and with only $125 in their pocket. Today sales have grown to more than $30 million a year.

In 1990 the Droogs introduced Spitz, a line of roasted confection sunflower seed snacks for humans. Sales success was immediate. Yearly sales increases of 300 and 400 percent between 1990 and 1995 still did not meet the demand for this new snack. The company increased its market share by eliminating its competition— buying out Sid's Sunflower Seeds in Regina in 1993 and Tasty Seeds in Winkler, Manitoba, in 2005.

Today, this privately held company commands a 75 percent market share in the Canadian confectionary sunflower and pumpkin seed category and is the third-largest-selling sunflower seed brand in the United States.

Myles Hamilton was appointed vice-president in 2006, and has taken over the day-to-day operations from Tom and Emmy. Hamilton has been tasked with doubling the total company sales over the next three years with a goal of making Spitz North America's leading sunflower and pumpkin seed brand. He brings expertise to the position with a background that includes 6 years at P&G in sales and marketing roles and 15 years with Frito-Lay, a large U.S. snack food company, during which time he served most of his tenure as vice-president of Frito-Lay Western Canada. To expand Spitz's sales and bring them to the top of the sunflower seed snack food market, Hamilton is considering either targeting current markets with new products, finding new markets for existing products, or both.

Innovation has always been the name of the game for Spitz. The company was the first in the North American sunflower industry to come up with flavours and resealable bags. North American competitors have matched these innovations and have now developed some of their own, enhancing the product to increase sales. One option would be to follow the U.S. trend toward coated kernels—chocolate, honey roasted, or candy. Another option would be to follow the lead of Sunseeds in South Dakota, which infuses their seeds with popular energy boosters such as caffeine, ginseng, taurine, and lysine—similar to those found in energy drinks. Sunflower seeds could be made even healthier by infusing the product with vitamins and minerals. Another option would be to more actively pursue the baking or salad markets. Health-oriented consumers are finding new ways to use seed kernels in baking or as salad, and coated and/or infused seeds might expand the possibilities—maybe even replacing chocolate chips!

There may also be opportunities to enter new markets. The company recently entered the Quebec market, changing their packaging and working the French translation into their new logo and new look. They are also planning on expanding current distribution from 41 states in the United States to full distribution across all states. There is potential to expand beyond North America and into China, where they already process pumpkin seeds.

Hamilton knew that the place to start was to segment the seed consumption market and then choose which segments to focus on, and with what positioning.

Source: This case was written by Bev Duthie and Brock Smith, drawing on the following sources: Gina Teel, "Sunflower power," *Times Colonist*, 22 May 2007: B1; www.spitz.ca.

Things to Think About

1. If you were Myles Hamilton and the Spitz company, what would you do and why?

2. How might the seed consumption market be segmented?

3. Which segment(s) should the Spitz company be targeting?

The Vault Helmet

For three years Morgan Matthews and Charlie Smith have been helping big-name hockey equipment companies design and test pads, skates, gloves, and sticks. Now this design team has its own special product, the Vault Helmet—specially designed to reduce the risk of head injuries. A series of concussions forced Smith out of the game, so he's excited about being involved in a radical product that can make a real difference to improve safety and career longevity. The problem is that it might be too radical. The design is very futuristic and they risk losing current clients if the design is perceived as too extreme.

Matthews and Smith don't have the $500 000 it will take to bring the product to market, so they've headed to Boston to try to score a partnership at the largest hockey equipment tradeshow in the world. Nike Bauer won't even look at the helmet without a legal agreement in place that protects their own R&D activities. Smaller companies, however, love the helmet and like the aggressive price point—$300, which is $100 more than the most expensive helmet currently on the market.

After three days at the trade show Matthews and Smith still have not found a partner interested enough to help them bring their product to market, so they take the Vault Helmet to Pat Leahy, an old college friend of Smith's who plays for the NHL Boston Bruins. Leahy is taken aback by the futuristic design but says he is more concerned about safety than looks. Not discouraged, Matthews and Smith regroup. They are getting closer and hope to secure a partnership deal soon so they can get their helmet to market.

Questions

1. Describe the current marketing strategy of the Vault Helmet. Given your understanding of the decision environment, what changes would you recommend to this strategy and why?
2. What adoption barriers do you perceive and how might these barriers be addressed or reduced?
3. What type of partner should they be looking for? What would be some of the key characteristics of a good partner for Matthews and Smith?

The Business of God

The barriers between business and religion are being broken down to bring religion into the workplace. Since 9/11, more and more people are calling themselves Christians and turning to faith. In Minnesota, the first Christian bank, Riverview Community Bank, has had miraculous growth since it opened. Employees and customers do not have to be religious to join; however, the employees who are religious are expected to pray for the bank and customers can come in and pray with their banker if they are having financial troubles. Once a week Christian businessmen gather and network: they pray together for their businesses, their customers, and their bosses.

In Dallas, Gil Stricklin convinces other businesses to bring chaplains into the workplace because he believes it makes employees happier and more productive. He has had quite a bit of success too, now placing more than 1600 chaplains in twenty years of business and making more than $7 million per year. Companies such as Northwood Golf Club and Encore Wire both use Gil's company. Employee participation is completely voluntary, but at Encore Wire, turnover has been reduced by 40 percent. If an employee wishes to take part, they are responsible for using the service themselves. Despite the great financial success Gil has had, he says it is not about the money, it is about the ability to reach out and help someone.

Religion and business has not taken off in Canada the same way it has in the United States. However, Cloud Ten Productions, a Canadian film company, has been experiencing huge success making movies about the end of the world for Christians. Making apocalyptic films starring "B" actors from Hollywood has made Cloud Ten the most profitable independent film company on the continent. Harlequin Enterprises, a publisher known for racy love stories, has created a line of Christian books under a different label, Steeple Hill, which is highly profitable. Harlequin is targeting the 30 million women in the United States and Canada who want to read books with no swearing, no drinking, and no sex. This market is easily reachable and the growth is in double digits.

For Christian entrepreneurs these are booming times when barriers between religion and business are being broken down.

Questions

1. Religion and business has not taken off in Canada the same way it has in the United States. Why? How is the business and cultural environment different in the two countries?

2. Harlequin suggests that the target market for its Steeple Hill books is easily reachable. In what ways might this target market be reached?

3. Church attendance has been in decline in Canada for many years. Evaluate the positioning and marketing mix strategies of a church you are familiar with. How might these strategies be adapted to achieve what you think are the main objectives of the church?

Source: This case was prepared by Brock Smith and Michael Rawluk and is based on "The Business of God," *Venture* #943, 2005.

PART II

Understanding Customer Value Needs and Behaviour

You learned in Part I that successful businesses accurately understand customers' needs. Perhaps two questions were left unanswered in your mind: How do customers behave to satisfy those needs; and What tools do firms use to understand customer needs? In this part you will learn all about marketing research tools used to understand customer needs. You will also learn about the buying behaviour of customers and consumers: fundamental concepts, without which a firm cannot develop superior marketing strategies.

CHAPTER 4
Marketing Research

CHAPTER OBJECTIVES

WHEN YOU HAVE COMPLETED YOUR STUDY OF THIS CHAPTER, YOU SHOULD BE ABLE TO

1. Explain the role of the marketing information system and the marketing decision support system in marketing decision making.

2. Describe methods to measure customer satisfaction.

3. List and explain the marketing research process.

4. Understand the differences among exploratory, descriptive, and causal research,

and describe some research techniques available to marketers.

5. Describe the different types of data collection methods and types of samples that researchers use.

6. Understand the impact of the growing use of online research.

Real People, Real Decisions

Meet **Fred Wall,** a Decision Maker at Farm Credit Canada

Fred Wall is director of research at Farm Credit Canada (FCC), the leading provider of agricultural business and financial services in Canada. With almost 100 offices across rural Canada, FCC provides more than $12 billion in farm and agribusiness credit as well as management consulting, field management, and accounting service solutions. FCC is rated as one of Canada's top companies to work for and agribusiness is one of Canada's most important industries. As director of research, Fred is responsible for developing FCC's research strategy, and managing a 10-person staff and a million dollar–plus budget for implementing that strategy.

Fred grew up in rural Ontario, where he developed a strong appreciation for the rewards and risks of the agri-food industry. He studied in arts programs at the University of Guelph, followed by a master's degree in Political Science at the University of Calgary. Fred became particularly passionate about game theory and research in his studies and sought fields in which he could make what he was passionate about become his career. Market research seemed a perfect fit.

He interned at the Angus Reid Group (now Ipsos-Reid), then became a research manager in the Global area, eventually moving on to become vice-president of research at COMPAS. To make the mark he wanted to make in the industry, Fred knew he had to switch from the vendor side to the client side, where he could set his sights on building long-term infrastructure. He took the newly created director of research position with FCC in 2002 and has been there ever since, loving his work. For Fred, a core value is loving what he works at; life is too short to do something you don't like. Finding and developing customer insights is his passion. He loves representing the voice of the marketplace in his company.

Upon joining FCC in 2002, Fred observed that farm operations in Canada are consolidating: There are increasingly fewer, bigger, wealthier, and more sophisticated agribusiness organizations and busier people running them. Consequently, this market is increasingly attractive to financial service providers, equipment suppliers, chemical companies, and many other goods and services providers. One implication of this increased competition for fewer, bigger customers is that there is much greater focus on customer retention and developing strong customer relationships through added-value services and customer responsiveness strategies. All of these marketers want to understand their customers, and the customers are being inundated with market research requests—to the point where response rates have plummeted, and it is increasingly difficult to get the attention and time of respondents.

Fred found that the traditional "interruption" survey market research approaches that he'd learned at Ipsos and COMPAS just weren't doing the job anymore, particularly for survey-fatigued audiences. Fred used the term "interruption"

research to refer to phone surveys that interrupted customers from what they were doing, research that happened at the convenience of the research company rather than at the convenience of the respondent. At FCC, this type of research was done periodically (once every year, at most), sampling different regions of the country. Fewer and fewer customers were responding to this approach, raising the question of non-response bias while increasing significantly the length and the cost of a typical study. Moreover, as fewer respondents agreed to participate, those who did participate were being given ever-longer questionnaires. Fred also wondered about validity—being increasingly busy, were the respondents giving sufficient thought to their answers? FCC did not have as large a budget as some of the other players in the industry, such as agrichemical companies and other financial institutions, and Fred wondered whether his more limited resources could be spent more appropriately.

A further weakness of this approach was that cost and time kept the view of the customer at a very high level, typically with provincial-level insights at most. FCC's markets are differentiated at the local level. The most effective research for FCC had to produce information that could be actionable at the local level.

The strength of FCC's dependence on interruption research was that trackable measures had already been developed. The company had grown used to bi-annual reporting on the status of its customer relationships in a standard format that had been established. Any departure from the old approach would also mean a departure from the established measures.

In thinking about this he considered four options:

Option 1: Enhanced interruption research.

The key limitation of the current interruption research was that respondents were increasingly protective of their time and resented being interrupted for what they considered to be relatively unimportant questions. The other critical limitations were cost and time. Although interruption research studies were relatively quick to launch, declining response rates meant that they were taking much longer to complete. Option 1 involved a greater investment of time and money, using the same techniques as before. FCC would simply adjust its expectations for cost and time and spend what was required to get a full sample, using the previous techniques on the phone. Fred also considered breaking out the larger, infrequent surveys into smaller, more frequent soundings. This approach had the advantage of maintaining the existing measures and methods of collection, so continuity could be ensured and accumulated knowledge could be preserved. Unfortunately, it carried many of the same drawbacks: time, cost, reliability, and level of analysis. Fred wondered if more detailed results by office location might better identify marketing issues or opportunities.

Option 2: Agribusiness panel program.

Another option was to stop doing interruption surveys and develop a large panel of agribusiness customers who have opted in to do research and could be randomly selected by mail or e-mail to give feedback on specific research questions. Panel members would be recruited from a variety of sources, so that a wide array of customers, non-customers, and key influencers could be included as part of the sample universe. All panellists would be provided incentives (cash and gift cards) to complete an online profile that indicated their interests in different topics, as well as demographic, geographic, and psychographic details that could be searched when a panel needed to be created. With fewer, larger, wealthier customers becoming the norm, the challenge of finding niche samples had become even more challenging. The panel, with profiles completed, would allow for rapid targeting of respondents for focus groups or surveys. In all cases, the panel members would be paid for their participation in each project they were involved in, whether online or offline. Fred thought that the panel approach might give FCC better insight into how customers think about issues and why, in a more engaging and cost-effective manner. The most obvious disadvantage was time: it would take considerable time to establish the panel database, but the resulting cost of providing the incentives would be less than the money now spent on interruption research. Having opted-in in advance to participate in research, rather than at the moment of a phone call, respondents would be more involved and interested in the research and would likely give more thought to their answers. On the other hand, the time required to produce an opt-in panel that could represent the entire universe of agribusiness stakeholders would be significant, thus limiting the generalizability of results in the formative stages of panel construction. Once recruited, however, the panel would be available any time for testing new product concepts, advertising campaigns, or other issues or initiatives that FCC wanted customer feedback on.

Option 3: Continuous feedback scoreboards.

Rather than continuing to implement discrete market research projects, Fred wondered if FCC might be better served by a continuous market research in the form of ongoing customer satisfaction surveys, linked to the typical life cycle of a customer at FCC. This approach would take three forms: a post-loan survey, an annual report card survey, and an exit survey. After receiving a loan from FCC, customers could be given an opportunity to provide feedback on their loan experience (post-loan), an annual survey could be distributed to all customers by mail or e-mail (report card), and an exit survey could be given to customers who terminate their involvement with FCC products and services.

When a customer received a loan, that would automatically trigger the post-loan survey and put them on the schedule for an annual customer survey. Similarly, when customers no longer had FCC products, the exit survey could be automatically sent to them. The key advantages of this approach would be much more detailed information by customer type and location, much more current data (continuous updating), and easy access to this information throughout the FCC organization. With the right methodology, FCC could ensure a consistent stream of actionable data at the local, regional, and national levels. It would require an upfront investment of between $150 000 and $200 000 to create the system and buy the hardware and software to support it, but the ongoing maintenance costs would be relatively low.

The disadvantages of this approach were logistical. Continuous surveys are much more difficult to administer than a typical discrete survey, and FCC had no experience in this area. The initial costs for a program outside of the established practices were prohibitive. Changing the questions once a survey was up and running would be much more difficult with this approach, and the number of questions that could be asked would be limited, as customers would likely be willing to give only a couple of minutes of their time. Finally, adopting a different approach to customer research would mean that new measures would likely need be established.

Selecting the right methodology would also be a challenge. Given the mixed nature of Internet access in rural Canada, Internet-only options could not be the complete solution for FCC. Telephone surveys suffered from the interruption research issues discussed above. Were this option to be pursued, the most viable approach was to offer customers a choice between mail and Internet completion for each survey. The logistical challenge of this approach would be daunting: FCC would have to allow for multiple completion options with each survey and would have to capture every response in the same central reporting facility.

Option 4: Refocus on data mining.

Rather than seeking primary data solutions, Fred considered refocusing his attention on secondary data within FCC and "mining" the customer data already collected as part of the loan application process. Fred had learned that many companies were abandoning or downplaying survey research, substituting effective data mining from internal and publicly available sources. There were a number of impressive case studies of companies that had had success by following this path. A focus on data mining would reduce FCC's research costs considerably and would provide basic information about customer profiles that could be used for "profile matching," where new services could be targeted to customers that match a particular profile. When combined with external data sources (Statistics Canada, purchased data from Equifax, and other sources), solid profiles of key customer segments could be constructed. The data could be acquired quickly, at low cost, and would not be subject to the difficulties of survey research in a shrinking market. This secondary data by itself, however, would not enable Fred to explore how customers think, why they think the way they do, and what new services they might want from FCC.

Now put yourself in Fred Wall's shoes. Which option or options would you implement and why?

KNOWLEDGE IS POWER

In Chapter 1 we talked about how marketing is a decision process in which marketing managers determine the strategies that will help the organization meet its long-term objectives. In Chapter 2 we said that successful planning means that managers make good decisions for guiding the organization. But how do marketers make good decisions? How do they go about developing marketing objectives, selecting a target market, positioning—or repositioning—their product, and developing product, price, promotion, and place strategies? The answer is information. To make good decisions, marketers must have information that is accurate, up to date, and relevant. As described above, Fred Wall at Farm Credit Canada needs timely and accurate information on his customers to make sound marketing decisions. Canadian Tire, the 84-year-old Canadian retailing icon, recently used marketing research to guide an extensive brand rejuvenation effort. Based on insights into its consumers garnered from this research, Canadian Tire initiated the Concept 20/20 store model, which meant launching stores with 20 percent more floor space than a traditional store. Canadian Tire used to be the place to go for auto parts and bikes—not anymore! Research uncovered that today Canadians go to Canadian Tire for four reasons: "driving, living, playing, and fixing." The Concept 20/20 model means that consumers will find more of what they are looking for at Canadian Tire. The plan is working—retail earnings and store sales were both up as a result of Canadian Tire's new strategy.[1] In this chapter we will talk about some of the tools that marketers use to get the information they need.

The Marketing Information System

marketing information system (MIS) Procedure developed by a firm to continuously gather, sort, analyze, store, and distribute relevant and timely marketing information to its managers.

Firms develop a **marketing information system (MIS)** to meet the information needs of marketing managers. The MIS is a process that first determines what information managers need and then gathers, sorts, analyzes, stores, and distributes relevant and timely marketing information to system users. The MIS system includes three important components: (1) four types of data, (2) computer hardware and software to analyze the data and create reports, and (3) MIS experts who actually manage the process to generate and distribute the needed information.

Where does the data come from? Information to feed the system comes from four major sources: internal company data, marketing intelligence data on competition and other elements in the firm's business environment, information gathered through marketing research, and acquired databases.

These data are stored and accessed through computer hardware and software. Based on an understanding of managers' needs, MIS personnel generate a series of regular reports for various decision makers. Frito-Lay's MIS, for example, generates daily sales data by product line and by region that its managers use to evaluate the market share of different Frito-Lay products compared to each other and to competing snack foods in each region.[2] Imperial Tobacco Canada's MIS includes asking 2000 adult smokers a month to provide information on their brand usage, brand switching, reasons for brand switching, new product awareness, and purchase location. Each year the company measures awareness, consumption behaviour, and loyalty for every brand in the Canadian market, converting this to brand and benefit segmentation. Figure 4.1 shows the elements of an MIS.

INTERNAL DATA SYSTEM The internal data system uses a variety of information from within the company to produce reports on the results of sales and marketing activities. Internal data include a firm's internal records of

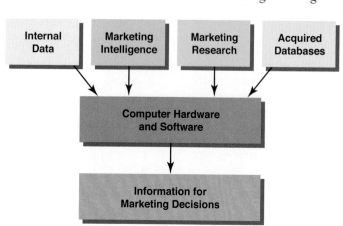

Figure 4.1 The Marketing Information System

A firm's marketing information system (MIS) stores and analyzes data from a variety of sources and turns the data into information useful for marketing decision making.

sales—information such as which customers buy which products in what quantities and at what intervals, what items are in stock, and which ones are back-ordered because they are out of stock, when items were shipped to the customer, and what items have been returned because they are defective.

A firm's marketing information system (MIS) stores and analyzes data from a variety of sources and turns the data into information useful for marketing decision making.

Often an MIS allows salespeople and sales managers in the field to access the internal records using laptop computers through a company **intranet**. An intranet is an internal corporate communication network that uses Internet technology to link company departments, employees, and databases. Intranets are secured so that only authorized employees have access. When the MIS is made available to salespeople and sales managers, they can serve their customers better by having immediate access to information on pricing, inventory levels, production schedules, shipping dates, and the customers' sales history. But, equally important because salespeople and sales managers are the ones in daily direct contact with customers, their reports (which are entered directly into the system via the company intranet) can provide a significant source of information on changes in sales patterns or new sales opportunities.

From the internal data, marketing managers can get daily or weekly sales data by brand or product line. They can also get monthly sales reports to measure progress toward sales goals and market share objectives. Marketing managers of retailers like Wal-Mart and Zellers, for example, use up-to-the-minute sales information obtained from store cash registers around the country so that they can detect problems with products, promotions, and even the firm's distribution system (Exhibit 4.1).

MARKETING INTELLIGENCE As we discussed in Chapter 2, to make good decisions marketers need to have information about the marketing environment. Thus, a second important element of the MIS is the **marketing intelligence** system, a method by which marketers get information about everyday happenings in the marketing environment. Although the name *intelligence* may suggest cloak-and-dagger spy activities, in reality nearly all the information companies need about their environment, including the competitive environment, is available by monitoring everyday sources: newspapers, trade

intranet An internal corporate communication network that uses Internet technology to link company departments, employees, and databases.

marketing intelligence A method by which marketers get information about everyday happenings in the marketing environment.

Exhibit 4.1

Retailers like Zellers and Wal-Mart use scanner data to help make marketing decisions.

Exhibit 4.2

Industry Canada's Strategis website offers data and tools for market intelligence.

scenarios Possible future situations that futurists use to assess the likely impact of alternative marketing strategies.

publications, or simple observations of the marketplace. Marketing intelligence is an ongoing process that allows firms to monitor conditions that affect demand for existing products or create demand for new products. TD Canada Trust regularly undertakes polls to better understand the travel habits of Canadians. A recent poll uncovered some interesting insights into Canadians and their travel preferences. While most Canadians chose Europe as their favourite destination, almost 1 percent of respondents chose Antarctica as their dream destination! The survey, which was conducted online, also uncovered interesting regional differences in travel habits and perceptions. Albertans and Manitobans have the highest incidence of leisure travellers, while travellers from Alberta are the biggest spenders—spending more than the national average for their travel plans. Ongoing marketing intelligence such as this allows marketers at TD Visa to tailor their product and promotion strategy to better meet the needs of their customers.[3]

One of the most effective marketing intelligence tools is the company's own salespeople. Because salespeople are the ones "in the trenches" every day, talking with customers, distributors, and prospective customers, they can often be an invaluable source of marketing intelligence.

The web has become a major source of marketing intelligence. Tremendous amounts of information are available on company webpages (including those of competitors), through news sources from around the globe, through government reports, and on trade association sites. The ease of accessing and searching the web and individual sites makes the Internet an even more attractive source of marketing intelligence. Industry Canada, for example, offers a variety of online tools and resources to help Canadian businesses be more effective in market intelligence (Exhibit 4.2).

Sometimes companies engage in specific activities to gain intelligence. For example, retailers often hire "mystery shoppers" (see Spotlight on Real People, page 138) to visit their stores (and those of their competitors) posing as customers to see how people are treated—imagine being paid to shop for a living! Other information may come from purchasing competitors' products and from attending trade shows.

Marketing managers may use marketing intelligence data to forecast the future so that they will be on top of developing trends. Indeed, some marketing researchers, known as *futurists*, specialize in predicting consumer trends to come. They try to forecast changes in lifestyles that will affect the wants and needs of customers in the coming years. Futurists try to imagine different **scenarios**, or possible future situations, that might occur and assign a level of probability to each. A scenario can be shaped by a number of key outcomes. For example, deregulation laws could shape the future of the Canadian banking, airline, energy, or dairy industries. In those cases the futurist might develop different scenarios for different levels of deregulation, including forecasts assuming no deregulation, moderate deregulation, and complete deregulation. Each scenario allows marketers to consider the impact of different marketing strategies and come up with plans based on which outcomes it considers most likely to happen. No one can predict the future—especially sudden, momentous events that change our lives like large-scale terrorist attacks—but it's better to make an educated guess than no guess at all and be caught totally unprepared. Most large organizations are involved in scenario planning. At Siemens, for example, a multidisciplinary team called FutureScape is spread all over the world, and its members work on FutureScape scenarios alongside their normal work, interacting mostly on the company's intranet, although members occasionally meet in person for workshops.[4] At Nokia, hundreds of people throughout the organization focus on building scenarios and investigating the link between business concepts and possible futures in which they will work.[5] Of course, collecting marketing intelligence is just the beginning. An effective MIS must include procedures to ensure that the intelligence data are translated and combined with internal data and other marketing information to create useful reports for marketing managers.

One prominent futurist company, BrainReserve, tracks themes that show up in movies and other mass media. BrainReserve has predicted such recent trends as "99 lives" (too fast a pace, too little time, causes societal schizophrenia and forces us to assume multiple roles), "Atmosfear" (polluted air, contaminated water, and tainted food stir up a storm of consumer doubt and uncertainty), "Cashing Out" (working women and men, questioning personal/career satisfaction and goals, opt for simpler living), and the surge of demand for such products as organic food and hybrid cars.[6] Although many marketers disagree with these predictions, others eagerly retain the services of these futurists to help them prepare for the years ahead.

MARKETING RESEARCH A third type of information that is part of a company MIS is data gathered through marketing research. Whether their business is selling cool stuff to teens or coolant to factories, firms succeed by knowing what customers want, when they want it, where they want it—and what competing firms are doing about it. In other words, the better a firm is at obtaining valid marketing information, the more successful it will be. The process of collecting, analyzing, and interpreting data about customers, competitors, and the business environment to make a specific marketing decision is called **marketing research**. Although marketing intelligence information is collected continuously to keep managers abreast of happenings in the marketplace, marketing research is called for when unique information is needed for specific decisions. Virtually all companies rely on some form of marketing research, though the amount and type of research vary dramatically (Exhibit 4.3).

In general, marketing research data available in an MIS includes **secondary research**, syndicated research reports, and primary research (custom research) reports. Secondary research is research produced by another organization or individual, for another purpose than the problem at hand, which may also address some information needs of an MIS. One type of secondary data is published material. This includes general business sources such as guides, directories, indexes, and statistical data, and articles and reports published by the popular and business press, such as the *Globe and Mail Report on Business*, the *Financial Post*, and *Marketing* magazine (Exhibit 4.4). Much of this information is now available on the Internet. Some useful secondary data sources are found in Table 4.1.

Published material also includes government sources, such as reports generated by Statistics Canada or reports produced by Industry Canada. One data source used by many Canadian marketers is Statistics Canada's *Market Research Handbook*, which contains such demographic information as population size, average household income, and family structure for all provinces and 45 major cities across the country.[7] Because this information is available in many libraries across the country, it is an especially cost-effective resource for small businesses that are trying to better understand their markets. Industry Canada's Strategis website is a valuable source of

marketing research The process of collecting, analyzing, and interpreting data about customers, competitors, and the business environment to make a specific marketing decision.

secondary research Research collected for a purpose other than the decision at hand.

Exhibit 4.3

Companies like Léger Marketing provide customized market research for businesses.

Exhibit 4.4

Marketing magazine is a useful source of information about Canadian marketing and communications practices, campaigns, and people.

Canadian industry information. Trade associations also conduct research on behalf of their members and produce industry reports, such as the *Directory of Chains* published by *Canadian Grocer*.

Another type of secondary data is computerized databases. Your college or university library likely has online directories, full-text databases, and special-purpose databases that allow you to access information produced from a variety of information sources. These may include:

- Lexis/Nexis: A very large database containing the full text of over 200 newspapers and many other materials such as newsletters, trade journals, legal cases, reference works, and a few academic journals. Covers topics in all areas but is strongest in the areas of business, management, government, political science, law, current events, patents, and medicine.

- Hoover's Company Profiles: Corporate profiles and financial information on publicly traded companies.

- Standard & Poor's NetAdvantage: Lists public and private companies trading on U.S. stock exchanges. Includes company name, location, address, executive biographies, SIC codes, and sales information.

- ABI Inform/ProQuest: Full-text article search capability covering more than 6000 academic and popular press business journals worldwide.

- Canadian Newsstand: Full-text article search covering major Canadian newspapers and magazines.

- Predicasts PROMT: Summary and full-text information about products and markets from nearly 1000 business and trade journals, industry newsletters, newspapers, market research studies, news releases, and investment and brokerage firm reports.

Syndicated research firms collect fairly general data on a regular basis and sell the information to many firms. Nielsen Media Research, for example, tracks television viewership and program ratings across Canada. D-code (**www.d-code.com**) is a syndicated research firm that focuses on understanding the Nexus generation (18- to 34-year-olds) in Canada. Other firms focus on tracking sales and brand attitude information in specific industries. As

Table 4.1 Some Useful Secondary Data Sources

The Blue Book of Canadian Business (**www.cbr.ca**) includes profiles of Canada's top-performing companies (public, private, crown, and cooperatives), including executive biographies, sales, assets, net income, and stock trading volume, and can be a very useful resource for business-to-business marketing activities.

CompuServe (**www.compuserve.com**) provides full-text articles from more than 450 business and trade publications.

Dun & Bradstreet Canada (**www.dnb.ca**) provides customized market information to businesses by combining their database of market information with the information their customers have already collected.

SEDAR (**www.sedar.com**) provides company profiles, financial filing information, and annual reports for Canadian public companies.

TradeMap (**www.exportsource.ca**) is an online database of trade statistics that provides detailed export and import profiles and trends for more than 5300 products in 200 countries and territories.

Strategy Magazine Online (**www.strategymag.com**) contains articles on marketing in Canada and has a search engine that searches the archives of the magazine.

Marketing Magazine Online (**www.marketingmag.ca**) contains articles on marketing practices, campaigns, and people in Canada and has a search engine that searches the archives of the magazine.

Canoe (**www.canoe.ca**) contains Canadian news and information.

valuable as it may be, **syndicated research** doesn't provide all the answers to marketing questions because the information collected typically is broad but shallow; it gives good insights about general trends such as who is watching what TV shows or what brand of perfume is hot this year. Often firms need to undertake custom marketing research, especially when they need to know more about *why* these trends have surfaced.

Primary research is research conducted for a single firm to provide answers to specific questions. Sometimes marketing managers need more specific information, such as immediate feedback on a proposed change in pricing strategy or consumers' perceptions of a new advertising campaign. Marketers might also use specific information to identify opportunities for new products or to provide data about the quality of their existing products, who uses them, and how (Exhibit 4.5). Most of the research conducted by market research companies such as SurveySite is customized research that provides this type of specific information. For example, SurveySite helped Hewlett-Packard determine a name for their new scanning product by performing an online survey with over 4000 respondents.[8]

Marketers may use marketing research to identify opportunities for new products, to promote existing ones, or to provide data about the quality of their products, who uses them, and how. Sometimes a company will even do research to counter a competitor's claim. For example, Procter & Gamble (P&G) challenged rival Revlon's claim that its ColorStay line of cosmetics won't rub off. P&G researchers wanted to answer a specific question: Was ColorStay's claim true? That kind of question can't be answered by buying a syndicated report, so Procter & Gamble

Exhibit 4.5
Automakers such as Ford conduct extensive market research on consumers' car preferences.

commissioned 270 women to provide the specific information needed to support its case against Revlon. The women rubbed their cheeks against their shirts while wearing ColorStay and reported that, in fact, most of the shirts did get stained. But Revlon countered that P&G's test was flawed because the women may have been encouraged to rub too hard. Revlon did their own test on 293 women who were told to use "the pressure they use when caressing someone else's face." This time the women found few stains. To avoid further controversy, Revlon now says that ColorStay won't rub off under "normal circumstances."[9] Aren't you relieved?

ACQUIRED DATABASES A large amount of information that can be useful in marketing decision making is available in the form of external databases. Firms may acquire databases from any number of sources. For example, some companies are willing to sell their customer database to non-competing firms. Privacy legislation in Canada will restrict this particular practice, however, as information provided to an organization can be used by that organization only for the expressed purpose for which respondents have given consent.

Marketing Decision Support Systems

As we have discussed, a firm's MIS generates regular reports to decision makers on what is going on in the internal and external environment. But sometimes these reports are inadequate. Different managers may want different information and in some cases the problem that must be addressed is too vague or unusual to be easily answered by the MIS process. As a result many firms beef up their MIS with a **marketing decision support system (MDSS)**. An MDSS includes analysis and interactive software that allows managers, even

syndicated research Research by firms that collect data on a regular basis and sell the reports to multiple firms.

primary research Research conducted by or for a single firm to provide information for a specific marketing decision.

marketing decision support system (MDSS) The data, analysis software, and interactive software that allow managers to conduct analyses and find the information they need.

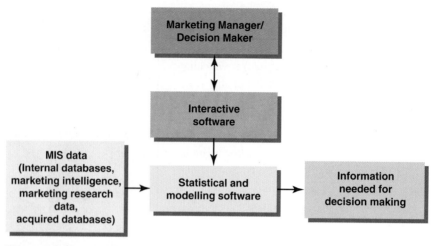

Figure 4.2 The Marketing Decision Support System

Although an MIS provides many reports managers need for decision making, it doesn't answer all their information needs. The marketing decision support system (MDSS) is an enhancement to the MIS that makes it easy for marketing managers to access the MIS system and find answers to their questions.

those who are not computer experts, to access MIS data and conduct their own analyses, often over the company intranet. Figure 4.2 shows the elements of an MDSS.

Typically an MDSS includes both basic and sophisticated statistical software and modelling tools. Such software allows managers to examine complex relationships among factors in the marketplace and to examine possible or preconceived ideas about relationships in the data—by asking "what-if" questions. For example, media modelling software allows marketers to see what would happen if they made certain decisions about where to place their advertising versus other possibilities. Manager may be able to use sales data and a model to find out how many consumers stay with their brand and how many switch, thus developing projections of brand share over time. Table 4.2 presents some examples of the different questions that might be considered by an MIS versus an MDSS. Appendix 4A provides an introduction to the basic and advanced analytic tools used by marketers. These are just some of the analytic tools available to marketers, and they should suggest to you that there can be significant "science" behind making marketing decisions.

Searching for Gold: Data Mining

data mining Sophisticated analysis techniques to take advantage of the massive amount of transaction information now available.

As we have discussed, most MIS systems include internal customer transaction databases and many include acquired databases. Often these databases are extremely large. To take advantage of the massive amount of data now available, sophisticated analysis techniques called **data mining** are now a priority for many firms. Data mining is a process in which analysts sift

Table 4.2 Examples of Questions That Might Be Answered by an MIS and an MDSS

Questions Answered with an MIS	Questions Answered with an MDSS
What were our company sales of each product during the last month and the last year?	Have our sales declines simply reflected changes in overall industry sales or is there some portion of the decline that cannot be explained by industry changes?
What changes are happening in sales in our industry and what are the demographic characteristics of consumers whose purchase patterns are changing the most?	Are the same trends seen in our different product categories? Are the changes in consumer trends very similar among all of our products? What are the demographic characteristics of consumers who seem to be the most and the least loyal?
What are the best media for reaching a large proportion of heavy, medium, or light users of our product?	If we change our media schedule by adding or deleting certain media buys, will we reach fewer users of our product?

Marketing Metrics

Bigelow Tea

Bigelow Tea, makers of Constant Comment and over 50 other tea flavours, was struggling to develop a planning system that would let sales and marketing executives access data about the company's performance to make decisions about which products to promote, how to help a retailer with low sales, and to identify just what kinds of consumers were buying which varieties of tea Bigelow sold. The IT (Information Technology) department chose a business intelligence program called BusinessObjects Enterprise 6 to better understand the firm's performance.

This software allows Bigelow Tea to analyze factory sales, forecast sales based on shipment levels, and compare consumer and market trends up to five years old. Metrics such as these help the company determine which products are no longer profitable and where opportunities exist for new tea varieties. One lump or two with your data?[10]

through massive amounts of data (often measured in terabytes—much larger than kilobytes or even gigabytes) to identify unique patterns of behaviour among different customer groups.

Financial institutions, such as Scotiabank, use data mining to customize their offers to customers based on their website-usage patterns. For example, data mining could be used to identify customers that visited the company website to research mortgage rates. These customers could then receive a special offer from the bank on mortgages.[11]

Data mining uses supercomputers that run sophisticated programs that allow different databases to be combined to understand relationships among buying decisions, exposure to marketing messages, and in-store promotions. These operations are so complex that often companies need to build a *data warehouse* (sometimes costing more than $10 million!) simply to store the data and process it.[12]

Data mining has four important applications for marketers.[13]

- *Customer acquisition:* Many firms work hard to include demographic and other information about customers in their database. For example, a number of supermarkets like Canada Safeway offer weekly special price discounts for store "members." And, of course, the membership application form requires that customers indicate their age, family size, address, and so on. With this information the firm can determine which of its current customers respond best to specific offers and then send the same offers to non-members who share the same characteristics.

- *Customer retention:* The firm can identify big-spending customers and then target them for special offers and inducements other customers won't receive. Cellphone companies, such as Bell Mobility, can use data mining to identify customers with contracts that are going to expire soon and then target these customers with special offers if they renew their contract before it expires.

- *Customer abandonment:* Strange as it may sound, sometimes a firm wants customers to take their business elsewhere because they actually cost the firm too much to service them. A bank may use data mining to identify unprofitable customers—those who keep minimal balances but require a lot of attention and service. For example, data mining has allowed Federal Express to identify customers as "the good, the bad, and the ugly."[14] As a result, FedEx's strategy is to keep the "good" consumers as profitable customers and make "bad" customers (those who cost the company more than they generate in revenues) more profitable by charging them higher shipping rates. For the "ugly" customers who spend very little, FedEx is saving money by no longer trying to attract their business.

- *Market basket analysis:* The firm can develop focused promotional strategies based on its records of which customers have bought certain products. DVD rental companies like Blockbuster can analyze their database to determine the types of movies rented by customers to target offers. For example, customers that often rent children's movies can be sent a special promotional offer for the latest children's DVD release.

TOOLS TO MEASURE CUSTOMER SATISFACTION

The importance of customer loyalty and customer satisfaction was discussed earlier in Chapter 1 and will be revisited in Chapter 14. While all companies use marketing research to help them understand and attract new customers, most companies see that the key to long-term profitability and success is understanding your current customers.

As outlined in Table 4.3, there are different ways to measure customer satisfaction. Most customer-oriented businesses use at least one of the methods outlined in the table. However, there are certain cautions to heed in measuring customer satisfaction.[15] When customers rate their satisfaction with an element of the company's performance (e.g., delivery), the company needs to recognize that customers vary in their definition of this factor. To some customers, delivery may mean on-time delivery, while to others it may mean delivery accuracy. Yet, if the company detailed these terms, the customer satisfaction questionnaire would get very lengthy.

The company should also recognize that two customers could report being "very satisfied" with the product for different reasons. Customer A could have had a very satisfactory experience with the product (e.g., a hotel stay) on this occasion, while Customer B could be basing her answer on a totality of past experiences, both good and not so good.

The timing of customer satisfaction surveys is key. Surveys should not be sent to customers immediately after the company has done something nice for them. Customers should not be bothered with questionnaires during busy time periods, for example beginning-of-year planning periods. Finally, customer satisfaction measurement should be consistent from one period to the next so that meaningful comparisons can be made.

WHY IS MONITORING CUSTOMER SATISFACTION NOT ENOUGH?

While measuring customer satisfaction using one of the methods described above is important, simply monitoring customer satisfaction is not enough. In Table 4.4, and in many customer satisfaction surveys, a five-point scale is used to measure satisfaction, with "Very Dissatisfied" and "Very Satisfied" being the two end points. On this scale, a score of 4 would

Table 4.3 Tools to Measure Customer Satisfaction

Customer Satisfaction Surveys
Most customer satisfaction surveys have three sections:
(1) a global satisfaction index with the good, service, or firm (typically measured on a 5-point scale, with "Very Dissatisfied" and "Very Satisfied" being the two end points),
(2) a detailed evaluation of the goods and services offered by the firm,
(3) intentions to repurchase the firm's offerings.
A customer satisfaction survey for a fictitious business, Widget Co., is shown in Table 4.4.

Mystery Shopping
A form of marketing research, mystery shopping involves a researcher buying the firm's goods and services and assessing the purchase experience vis-à-vis the firm's competitors.

Customer Complaint Analysis
Analyzing customer complaints is another way to understand customer satisfaction.

Lost Customer Analysis
Some business organizations contact customers who have stopped being repeat purchasers to assess what went wrong. This provides a good assessment of customer satisfaction levels and what needs to be done to retain customers.

Table 4.4 Customer Satisfaction Survey, Widget Co.

Dear Customer:
We want your satisfaction level with the Widget Co. to be the highest at all times. Our goal is to ensure your complete satisfaction and earn your loyalty. Only YOU can tell us if we have met your expectations. Your candid comments will help us constantly improve our services.

Please take a few minutes and fill out this satisfaction questionnaire. You may mail it or, if you prefer, you can e-mail your comments to us.

Thank you for your business. We look forward to hearing from you and having the opportunity to serve your needs.

Sincerely,

Bella Adams, General Manager
Widget Co.

Your Overall Widget Co. Experience
Please rate your overall satisfaction with Widget Co.:

Very Satisfied	Satisfied	Neutral	Dissatisfied	Very Dissatisfied
5	4	3	2	1

Please indicate the overall reason(s) for your score above:

_____

_____

_____

Performance Ratings
Please rate your level of satisfaction with the following services using the 5-point scale below:

Very Satisfied	Satisfied	Neutral	Dissatisfied	Very Dissatisfied
5	4	3	2	1

Widget Co. employees (overall)	5	4	3	2	1
Availability	5	4	3	2	1
Competence	5	4	3	2	1
Responsiveness	5	4	3	2	1
Professionalism	5	4	3	2	1
Product performance	5	4	3	2	1
Price-value ratio	5	4	3	2	1
Delivery	5	4	3	2	1
Technical assistance	5	4	3	2	1
Website	5	4	3	2	1
Other _____					
_____	5	4	3	2	1

Please indicate your level of agreement or disagreement with the following statements using the 5-point scale below:

Strongly Agree	Agree	Neither Agree Nor Disagree	Disagree	Strongly Disagree
5	4	3	2	1

I plan to repurchase from Widget Co.	5	4	3	2	1
I would recommend Widget Co. to another person looking for a similar product	5	4	3	2	1

Please indicate any additional comments you may have that will help us meet your needs better:

_____

_____

_____

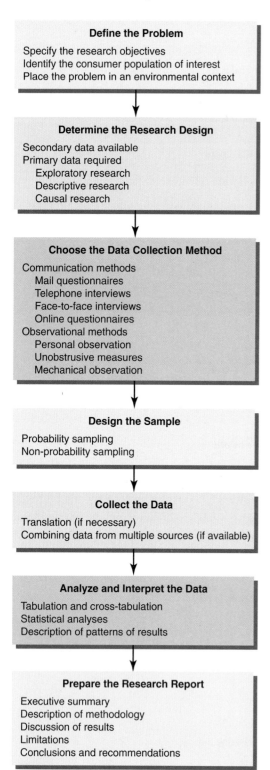

Figure 4.3 Steps in the Marketing Research Process

The marketing research process includes a series of steps that begins with defining the problem or the information needed and ends with the finished research report for managers.

mean the customer is "Satisfied." Many business organizations falsely believe that it is enough to obtain a score of 4 from a majority of customers. After all, they argue, how many customers actually give a score of 5?

This belief is false because *complete* customer satisfaction is the key to customer retention. Research conducted by Xerox found that a customer who gives a score of 5 is six times more likely to be a repeat buyer than a customer who gives a score of 4. This is the reason why firms strive to *totally* satisfy their customers and why there is so much emphasis on customer retention as the end goal, with customer satisfaction as the antecedent variable.

So far, we have looked at the MIS and the MDSS, the overall systems that provide the information marketers need to make good decisions. We've seen how the data included in the MIS and MDSS include internal records, marketing intelligence data gathered by monitoring everyday sources, acquired databases, and information gathered to address specific marketing decisions through the marketing research process. We have also examined customer satisfaction research and its importance. In the rest of the chapter we'll look at the steps that marketers must take when they conduct marketing research.

THE STEPS IN THE MARKETING RESEARCH PROCESS

The collection and interpretation of strategic information is hardly a one-shot deal that managers engage in "just out of curiosity." Ideally, marketing research is an ongoing *process*, a series of steps marketers take to learn about the marketplace. Whether a company conducts the research itself or hires another firm to do it, the goal is the same—to help managers make informed marketing decisions. Figure 4.3 shows the steps in the research process, and we'll review each of these now.

Define the Problem

Defining the research problem as precisely as possible allows marketers to search for the right answers to the right questions. Sometimes marketers cannot determine exactly what the problem is because they're focusing on symptoms, such as declining sales, and not on the underlying problem that's causing sales to drop. For example, a drop in sales of a sunscreen may be due to a new competitor, lack of cooperation from distributors, or even a fashion trend promoting a deep tan.

Defining the problem has four components:

1. Specify the management decision.

   The most important stage of the research process is figuring out what marketing (or other) decisions need to be made with the information being sought. For example, is the key decision "What market segments should I target?" or is the key decision "How should I price this product?" The research needed for making the first decision won't be useful for making the second decision or vice versa—and generally, you can only focus on one key decision in any given piece of research because different decisions require different research questions, samples, and methods. Specifying the relative importance of the decision is also useful as it helps guide the scope of the research activity and how much time, effort, and resources should be allocated to the project.

2. Specify the research objectives or research questions.

What questions will the research attempt to answer? Once the key decision is identified, you need to ask yourself "What general questions do I need to answer to make that decision?" For example, if the key decision is "What market segments should I target?" some key questions (among others) that need to be answered are:

What are the key alternative market segments?
What are the profiles and size of these segments?
What brands are currently targeted at each segment?
How is our brand positioned (or how might it be positioned) relative to competitors?
What are sources of competitive advantage that will allow us to defend our desired positioning?

Often the importance of a research question surfaces during exploratory research. For example, Mercedes-Benz regularly monitors drivers' perceptions of its cars, partly through feedback from dealers. When the company started getting reports from its dealers that people were viewing the cars as being deserved only after they become "successful," it developed the "ice cream" television ad shown in Exhibit 4.6. It attempts to dispel the attitude that consumers should wait until their big promotion to indulge themselves.[16] Often marketers want to know how much of a product they are likely to sell. There are many approaches to developing a sales forecast. Some of the common approaches are described in Appendix 4B at the end of this chapter.

3. Identify the information needs.

Once researchers specify the research questions or objectives, they need to specify what needs to be learned or known, and from whom—indicating the population or group of interest. For example, to answer the research question "What are the profiles of each segment?" we would want to know specific information like:

What are the benefits sought by each identified segment?
What are the demographic characteristics of each segment? (e.g., sex, age, income)
What are the psychographic characteristics of each segment? (e.g., lifestyle, interests, values)
What are the media use behaviours for each segment? (e.g., magazines and newspapers read, radio stations listened to, TV programs watched)

Exhibit 4.6

Mercedes-Benz tried to project a more "everyday" image by running ads such as this one featuring Raymond, a man who put off trying ice cream until his big promotion.

These information needs are not the questions you would see in a questionnaire or interview guide, but they inform those questions and give a researcher rationale for including or not including specific questions on a questionnaire. If the question does not address an information need, it is not required on the questionnaire. Information needs also inform methodology, or the research technique, as different types of information can be gathered from different sources or by using different techniques.

4. Place the problem in an environmental context.

The problem definition should also specify the factors in the firm's internal and external business environment that might be causing or influencing the situation. Placing the problem in the context of the firm's environment helps researchers structure the research, determine the specific types of questions to ask, and identify factors they will need to take into account when interpreting results. Environmental conditions also provide a valuable perspective. For example, when the economy is tight and sales of luxury cars are generally declining, the population to be studied might be narrowed down to a select group of consumers who are still willing and able to indulge in a luxury vehicle. Alternatively, consumers may be moving away from glitzy status-conscious materialism, so that the research question comes down to how promotional strategies can convey honest and basic values that go beyond "snob appeal."

Determine the Research Design

research design A plan that specifies what information marketers will collect and what type of study they will do.

Once marketers have isolated specific problems, the second step of the research process is to decide on a "plan of attack." This plan is the **research design**, which specifies what information marketers will collect and what type of study they will do. All marketing problems do not call for the same techniques, even though marketers can solve some problems effectively with a number of alternative techniques, and diversity in approaches can often provide greater insight and greater confidence in the results. Figure 4.4 summarizes many of the techniques used by market researchers.

SECONDARY VERSUS PRIMARY RESEARCH The very first question to ask in determining the research design is whether or not the information required for making a decision already exists—either inside the organization or from external secondary sources. For example, a coffee producer who needs to know the differences in coffee consumption among different demographic and geographic segments of the market may find that the information needed is available from a study conducted by the Canadian Coffee Association for its members or even from Agriculture and Agri-Food Canada. Data that are collected for some purpose other than the problem at hand are called *secondary data*. The use of

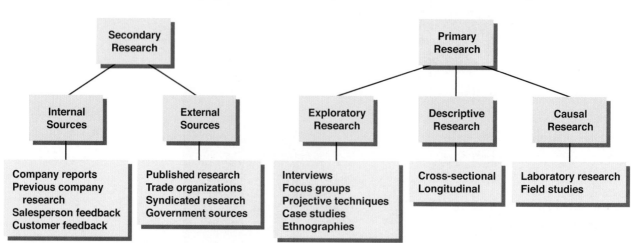

Figure 4.4 Marketing Research Design Techniques

For some research problems, the secondary research may provide the information needed. At other times, one of the primary research methods may be needed.

secondary data can save time and money because the expense of designing and implementing a study has already been paid. However, secondary data, having been created for another purpose, may not be current enough or relevant enough for a particular marketing decision. Another key limitation of secondary data is that the methodology used to collect it is often not reported and users do not know whether there were any flaws or limitations in the research design.

Sometimes secondary research is not enough. When a company needs to make a specific decision, it often needs to conduct research to collect *primary data*—that is, information collected directly from respondents to specifically address the question at hand. The advantage of primary data is that it is designed specifically to meet the needs of the organization. However, collecting primary data can be a difficult, expensive, and time-consuming process.

EXPLORATORY (QUALITATIVE) RESEARCH Marketers use **exploratory research** to generate topics for future, more rigorous studies; ideas for new strategies and opportunities; or just to get a better handle on a problem they are experiencing with a product. Because the studies are usually small in scale and less costly to conduct than other techniques, marketers can use exploratory research to test their hunches about what's going on without too much risk. Exploratory studies often involve in-depth probing of a few consumers who fit the profile of the "typical" customer. Researchers may interview consumers, salespeople, or other employees about products, services, ads, or stores. They may simply "hang out" and watch what people do when choosing among competing brands in a store aisle. Or they may locate places where the consumers of interest hang out and ask questions in these settings. As Exhibit 4.7 shows, some researchers find that many young people are too suspicious or skeptical in traditional research settings, so they may interview young people waiting in lines to buy concert tickets or in clubs.[17] Pantene and Sony, for example, have reached over 500 000 Canadian teens by sponsoring high school video dance parties and then providing incentives for the teens to visit the company websites to provide product feedback and answer buying behaviour questions.[18] Corby Distilleries discovered that its focus groups were more effective when carried out in its consumers' natural environment—their local bar on a Friday night.[19]

> **exploratory research** Technique that marketers use to generate insights for future, more rigorous studies.

> **consumer interviews** One-on-one discussions between a consumer and a researcher.

Most exploratory research provides *qualitative data*, detailed verbal or visual information (for example, videotapes of people preparing dinner at home) about consumers' attitudes, feelings, and buying behaviours that is summarized in words rather than numbers. Researchers for a manufacturer of Swiss chocolate, for example, interviewed consumers and found that many chocolate lovers hide secret stashes around their home. The company used the results of this exploratory research to develop an advertising campaign built around the theme: "The True Confessions of Chocaholics."[20]

Exploratory research can take many forms. **Consumer interviews** are one-on-one discussions in which an individual shares his or her thoughts in person with a researcher.

Exhibit 4.7

Video dance parties help marketers collect data from young people on their own turf.

Exhibit 4.8

Direct Energy used focus group results to develop these ads aimed at repositioning the company as a source of energy ideas.

focus group A product-oriented discussion among a small group of consumers led by a trained moderator.

projective techniques Tests that marketers use to explore people's underlying feelings about a product, especially appropriate when consumers are unable or unwilling to express their true reactions.

In addition to interviewing actual users of their product, some marketers find it useful to interview people who may not themselves be consumers, but who may know a lot about the consumers. One Canadian ad agency working on an ad campaign for scotch interviewed bartenders to gain additional insight into scotch drinkers. Another agency in England, working on an ad for a shoe company, talked to people who shined shoes and to prostitutes who had clients with foot fetishes.[21]

The **focus group** is the technique marketing researchers most often use for collecting exploratory data. Focus groups usually consist of eight to twelve recruited consumers, who sit together to discuss a product, ad, or some other marketing topic introduced by a discussion leader or moderator. Ontario energy and energy service provider Direct Energy, for example, used focus groups in a repositioning process that resulted in the company wanting to be known for its people and ideas rather than just for its products, technology, or dependability. The ad depicted in Exhibit 4.8 used talking appliances to encourage consumers to pay more attention to the needs of their home that would save them money, time, and inconvenience.[22] Typically, the moderator tapes these group discussions, which may be held at special interviewing facilities that allow for observation ("spying") by the client, who watches from behind a one-way mirror. Focus groups don't *always* run smoothly, particularly if one or two opinionated members dominate the session or if "professional" focus group participants get by screening criteria intended to ensure that the participants fit the intended participant profile (Exhibit 4.9).

Researchers screen focus group participants in advance to meet criteria that will make their opinions relevant. For example, participants may be recruited, not because they use the company's brand, but because they use a competitor's product. Prior to undertaking an extensive re-branding effort in an attempt to reposition themselves as more contemporary, Country Style conducted focus groups. In addition to talking to their own customers, they spoke to non-customers so that they could better understand what people thought of Country Style compared to competitors such as Tim Hortons.[23]

As will be discussed in more detail later in this chapter, web-based research companies like SurveySite are able to conduct focus groups with people around the country or around the world by setting up interactive sessions online.

Many researchers use **projective techniques** to get at people's underlying feelings, especially when they feel that people will be unable or unwilling to express their true reactions. A projective test asks the participant to respond to some ambiguous object, often by telling a story about it. For example, Georgia-Pacific—the manufacturer of Brawny paper towels—was locked in a struggle with Scott Towels for the number-two market position behind Bounty. The company decided to re-examine its brand identity, personified by a character named the Brawny Man, a giant man holding a peavey, a heavy wooden lever used by lumbermen to

Exhibit 4.9

Focus groups are typically run with six to ten participants.

handle logs (Exhibit 4.10). Managers believed Brawny was a bit old-fashioned. Women in focus groups were asked questions such as, "What kind of woman would he go out with?" and "What is his home life like?" Then they were asked to imagine how he would act in different situations. Responses were reassuring—the women saw Brawny as a knight in shining armour who would get them out of difficult situations—a good spokesperson for a product that's supposed to be reliable and able to get the job done. Brawny Man kept his job.[24]

The **case study** is a comprehensive examination of a particular firm or organization. In business-to-business marketing research in which the customers are other firms, for example, researchers may try to learn how one company makes its purchases. Their goal is to identify the key decision makers, to learn what criteria they emphasize when choosing between suppliers, and perhaps to learn something about any conflicts and rivalries among these decision makers that may influence their choices.

An **ethnography** is a detailed report on observations of people in their own homes or communities. Although a true ethnography, as conducted by anthropologists, can involve living with a group for months or years, marketing researchers usually devise shortcuts to get the information they need. True North Communications, for example, has devised an ethnographic research technique called "Mind and Mood," in which consumer interviews are conducted in a few hours in the respondent's home. As one advertising professional who uses the technique says, "You actually go into people's homes to talk to them. You meet them where they're most comfortable, see what they've got on their walls, what kind of furnishings they have, and you can get a sense of what's important to them."[25]

When the Ontario Ministry of Health was creating an anti-smoking campaign, ethnographic interviews were conducted with teenagers to understand their motivations for smoking as well as what was important to them. The researchers determined that a health message (such as the traditional "If you smoke, you will get cancer") was not going to convince teens to give up smoking. Instead the ads needed to touch on important issues for that age group. The final ads used messages such as "Smoking cigarettes will make you ugly" and showed images like a girl aging as she smoked.[26]

DESCRIPTIVE RESEARCH We've seen that marketers have many tools at their disposal, including focus groups and ethnographic techniques, to help them better define a problem or opportunity. These are usually modest studies involving a small number of people. In some situations, this information is all that the marketer needs to make decisions; but very often, the next step after exploratory research is to conduct **descriptive research**, which probes more systematically into the problem and bases its conclusions on larger numbers of observations. These observations typically are quantitative data that take the form of averages, percentages, or other statistics summarizing results from a large set of measurements. Quantitative data can be as simple as the number of large-screen TVs sold in a month in Future Shop locations in different regions of the country, or as complex as statistical analyses of responses to a survey mailed to thousands of consumers. In each case, analyses are conducted to answer a specific question in contrast to the "fishing expedition" that may occur in exploratory research.

The most common descriptive technique is **cross-sectional design**. This involves the systematic collection of quantitative information, such as responses to a survey or data from store register receipts, from one or more samples of respondents at one point in time. The data may be collected on more than one occasion but generally not from the same pool of respondents. Lever Pond's did a cross-sectional survey of dermatologists to determine which soap they recommend to their patients for mildness. Since 87 percent of the

Exhibit 4.10

Projective techniques help consumers express their image of the Brawny Man—the personification of Brawny paper towels.

case study A comprehensive examination of a particular firm or organization.

ethnography A detailed report on observations of people in their own homes or communities.

descriptive research Tool that probes more systematically into the problem and bases its conclusions on large numbers of observations.

cross-sectional design Type of descriptive technique that involves the systematic collection of quantitative information at one point in time.

SPOTLIGHT ON REAL PEOPLE Gateway to Excellence

Marketers have many sophisticated research tools at their disposal, and one of the most effective is a form of observation that's about as low-tech as you can get: Go shopping. Many businesses hire "mystery shoppers" to visit stores, hotels, and restaurants. Posing as regular customers, they report back on how they were treated, how employees described products to them, the cleanliness of the facilities, or even what other shoppers say in casual conversation about the choices available. This "customer viewpoint" information is invaluable to managers who want to improve service levels and sales. Colleen Stech, manager of the

Greater Nanaimo Chamber of Commerce's Gateway to Excellence program, has sent out a team of secret shoppers to Nanaimo businesses to find out how well they look after their customers. The Gateway team has been able to pass on valuable information to businesses, from a neutral, outside source, about just how these businesses are doing. The Chamber has rewarded those that have demonstrated excellent customer service. Stech notes that one of the leading causes of poor employee morale is lack of training and offers an optional training program for the Nanaimo businesses that need to work on customer service.[27]

1. This chapter describes several ways to conduct marketing research. How would you classify the research technique used by mystery shoppers?
2. What are the advantages of mystery shoppers over other forms of marketing research?
3. What are the disadvantages or limitations of making decisions based on reports of mystery shoppers?

respondents recommended the Lever Pond's brand Dove, and only 13 percent recommended the competitive brand, the company turned the results of its survey directly into an advertising campaign. Outdoor billboards that showed the results of the survey were used in major centres across Canada.[28]

longitudinal design Technique that tracks the responses of the same sample of respondents over time.

In contrast to the one-shot study, a **longitudinal design** tracks the responses of the same sample of respondents over time. Market researchers often create *consumer panels* to gather this kind of information; a sample of respondents representative of a larger market agrees to provide information about purchases on a weekly or monthly basis. To help determine what product assortment to offer in each of their stores, Wal-Mart uses data gathered by ACNielsen through consumer panels. These panels track things like what consumers buy, where they buy it, how they use it, and their attitudes toward the product.[29]

CAUSAL RESEARCH It's a fact that purchases of both diapers and beer peak between 5:00 p.m. and 7:00 p.m. Can we say that purchasing one of these products caused shoppers to purchase the other as well—and, if so, which caused which? Or is the answer simply that this happens to be the time that young fathers stop at the store on their way home from work for brew and Pampers?[30]

The descriptive techniques we've examined do a good job of providing valuable information about *what* is happening in the marketplace, but they can't tell us *why*. Sometimes marketers need to know if something they've done has brought about some change in behaviour. For example, does the layout and design of a store affect the amount people buy? This question can't be answered through simple observation.

For example, managers at a grocery chain notice from their sales data across a number of stores that purchases of produce are higher in those stores that are designed to resemble farmers' markets, with free-flowing layouts and "stalls" where produce is displayed. Can we say that design of these stores caused the increased sales, or is the answer simply that these stores happen to be located in areas where people buy more produce no matter what the store looks like?

causal research Techniques that attempt to understand cause-and-effect relationships.

Causal research refers to techniques that attempt to understand cause-and-effect relationships. In causal research, marketers want to know if a change in something (for example, layout used in a store) is responsible for a change in something else (for example, an increase in produce sales). They call the factors that might cause such a change *independent variables* and the outcomes *dependent variables*. In this example, the layout of the store is an independent variable and sales data for produce are a dependent variable.

To rule out alternative explanations, researchers must carefully design **experiments** that test specified relationships among variables in a controlled environment. Because this approach tries to eliminate competing explanations for the outcome, respondents may be brought to a *laboratory* where the researcher can be sure that they are reacting to precisely what they should be and nothing else. For example, a study testing whether the layout in a grocery store influences the likelihood that shoppers will buy more produce might bring a group of people into a testing facility, where they are shown a "virtual store" on a computer screen and asked to fill a grocery cart as they click through the "aisles" (Exhibit 4.11). The experiment might vary the interior of the store as a market style layout or a more typical grid layout to see if this affects whether people put more produce into their carts.

Although a laboratory allows researchers to exert careful control over what test subjects see and do, marketers don't always have the luxury of conducting this kind of "pure" research. It is possible to conduct *field studies* in the real world, as long as care is taken to be sure that the variables are carefully controlled.

For example, the grocery chain could choose two grocery stores for which the demographics of the people who shop there are known to be the same. Then the company could vary the layouts in the stores, using the market-style design in one store and the traditional design in the other, and record produce purchases made over a six-month period. If a lot more produce was bought in the first store than in the second (and the company was sure that nothing else was different between the two stores, such as discounted prices on produce offered by a competitor of one of the stores during the same time), the company might conclude that the presence of a market-style layout in the store does indeed result in increased produce sales.

> **experiments** Techniques that test prespecified relationships among variables in a controlled environment.

Exhibit 4.11

Some marketing research firms such as Decision Insight are developing sophisticated in-store simulations that allow respondents to navigate around a "virtual store" to select merchandise. Clients can use this technique to conduct marketing research on such issues as package designs, pricing changes, and optimal placement of merchandise.

Ethical Decisions in Marketing

Sometimes telemarketers portray themselves as marketing re-searchers to get consumers to listen to their sales pitches. They ask consumers to answer a "survey" and then follow up with a sales offer. This practice, called *sugging*, is a concern of legiti-mate market researchers, who often find their own information gathering affected by the negative consumer reaction to this practice. The Canadian Marketing Association has taken a strong stance in its Code of Ethics against sugging, but many telemarketers continue using this technique, presumably be-cause it is so effective. Do you think it is appropriate for tele-marketers to engage in sugging?[31]

Choose the Method for Collecting Data

When the researcher decides to conduct de-scriptive research, the next step in the market-ing research process is to figure out just how to collect it. The two main primary data collection methods can be broadly described as interactive and passive.

INTERACTIVE METHODS Interactive meth-ods involve some kind of interview or other direct contact with respondents who answer questions. These responses are then combined with those of other respondents to arrive at some general conclusions. The most common interactive instrument is a **survey**, a questionnaire asking participants about their beliefs or behaviours. For example, when Virgin Mobile wanted to find a theme for its new promotional campaign, it conducted a survey of Canadian cellphone users to find out what it would take for consumers to switch from their current cellphone provider. The survey found that 40 percent of Canadian respondents indicated that if they could retain the cellphone numbers, they would switch. Virgin used this insight to develop a new cam-paign centred around the "you can switch" concept.[32] Surveys can be administered on the phone, in person, through the mail, by fax, or over the Internet.

Surveys or questionnaires differ in their degree of structure. With a totally unstructured questionnaire, the researcher loosely determines the questions in advance. Questions may evolve from what the respondent says to previous questions. At the other extreme the re-searcher uses a completely structured questionnaire. She asks every respondent the exact same questions and each participant responds to the same set of fixed choices. You have probably experienced this kind of questionnaire, where you might have had to respond to a statement by saying if you "strongly agree," "somewhat agree," and so on. Moderately struc-tured questionnaires ask each respondent the same questions, but the respondent is allowed to answer the questions in his own words.

Surveys can be administered in a variety of ways, each of which has its pros and cons. These are summarized in Table 4.5.

Mail Surveys *Mail surveys* are easy to administer and offer a high degree of anonymity to respondents. On the downside, because the questionnaire is printed and mailed, researchers have little flexibility in the types of questions they can ask and little control over the circum-stances under which the respondent is answering them. Mail surveys also take a long time to get back to the company and are likely to have a much lower response rate than other types of surveys because people tend to ignore them.

Telephone Surveys *Telephone surveys* usually consist of a brief phone conversation in which an interviewer reads a short list of questions to the respondent. One problem with this ap-proach is that the growth of *telemarketing*, the sale of products and services over the phone, has eroded the willingness of many consumers to participate in phone surveys—especially when those telemarketers have pretended to be conducting marketing research (see Ethical Decisions in Marketing). Another drawback of telephone surveys is that the respondent may not feel comfortable speaking directly to an interviewer, especially if the survey is about a sensitive subject. Finally, increasing numbers of people use answering machines and caller identification to screen calls, further reducing the response rate.

Face-to-Face Surveys *Face-to-face surveys*, in which a live interviewer asks questions of a re-spondent by, for example, going door to door, used to be a common way to collect data. However, this practice has declined markedly in recent years due to escalating costs and security concerns—people just aren't willing to open their doors to strangers anymore.

survey A questionnaire that asks participants about their beliefs or behaviours.

Table 4.5 Advantages and Disadvantages of Data Collection Methods

Date Collection Method	Advantages	Disadvantages
Mail Questionnaires	Respondents feel anonymous Low cost Good for ongoing research	May take a long time for questionnaires to be returned Low rate of response and many may not return questionnaires Inflexible questionnaire Length of questionnaire limited by respondent interest in the topic Unclear if respondents understand the questions
Telephone Interviews	Fast High flexibility in questioning Low cost Limited interviewer bias	Decreasing levels of respondent cooperation Limited questionnaire length High likelihood of respondent misunderstanding Respondents cannot view materials Cannot survey households without phones Consumers screen calls with answering machines and caller ID
Face-to-Face Interviews	Flexibility of questioning Can use long questionnaires Can determine if respondents have trouble understanding questions Can use visuals or other materials	High cost Interviewer bias a problem Take a lot of time
Online Questionnaires	Instantaneous data collection and analysis Questioning very flexible Low cost No interviewer bias Lack of geographic restrictions	Unclear who is responding No assurance respondents are being honest Limited questionnaire length Unable to determine respondent understanding of question Self-selected samples

More typically, today's face-to-face interviews occur in a "mall-intercept" study (Exhibit 4.12) in which researchers recruit shoppers in malls or other public areas. Mall-intercepts offer good opportunities to get feedback about marketing issues like new package designs or styles or even reactions to new foods or fragrances. However, because only certain groups of the population frequently shop at malls, a mall-intercept study does not provide the researcher with a representative sample of the population unless the population of interest is mall shoppers. In addition to the mall-intercept being more expensive than mail or phone surveys, respondents may be reluctant to answer questions of a personal nature in a face-to-face context. Rather than relying on face-to-face surveys, Staples Business Depot Canada decided to use automated kiosks in its stores to survey consumers about their satisfaction with the company. Because of the anonymity that the kiosk affords respondents, the company estimates that two out of three people take part in the kiosk surveys, compared with one out of three who are asked to do a face-to-face survey.[33] BC Ferries used kiosks aboard its ferries to ask consumers about their onboard experience. The survey found that visitors wanted a wider variety of snacks than the coffee, tea, doughnuts, and pastries currently offered onboard. As a result of the survey, BC Ferries broadened their offerings to include juices, cheese, and crackers. The fact that the survey was administered right on board meant that the turnaround time for information was very quick

Exhibit 4.12

Mall intercepts are a common way to collect data from shoppers.

and the response rate was higher than would have been achieved with more traditional survey methods.[34]

Online Surveys *Online surveys* are growing in popularity. The Carrier Corporation, which makes air conditioners, found respondents more willing to answer questions about its products via computer, perhaps because it's more interesting to take a survey this way.[35] Companies are making it even easier for consumers to respond to surveys by administering surveys on handheld devices like Palms and Pocket PCs. Online surveys are a quick and cost-effective way to collect data. Unlike mail and phone surveys, online surveys can generate a large number of responses very quickly. However, it must be remembered that, like the people who visit malls, people who use the Internet are not representative of the total population. Online surveys are, therefore, useful only for those companies whose population of interest is people who are online. An additional concern about online surveys relates to the quality of responses the firm will receive—particularly because no one can be really sure who is typing in the responses.[36] Online research is discussed in more detail later in this chapter.

All these interactive techniques require a response from the consumer, whether in the form of a verbal response to an interview question, a checkmark placed on a piece of paper, or a mouse click on a computer screen.

PASSIVE METHODS Other forms of data collection use a *passive instrument* in which the consumer's behaviours are simply recorded—often without his or her knowledge. Researchers do this through personal observation, unobtrusive measures, and mechanical observation.

Personal Observation With *personal observation*, consumers in public settings are watched to understand how they react to marketing activities (Exhibit 4.13). After Frito-Lay spent some time in grocery stores, it found that shoppers spend a lot less time in the grocery store, and spend little time in the aisles. This meant that it had to get its product displays on the perimeter of the store whenever possible.[37] Researchers for Rocky Mountaineer rail tours observed its customers' behaviour as they were travelling through the Canadian Rockies by train. They noticed that these travellers seemed to like the experience of the train trip itself as much as the beautiful scenery they were seeing. This led the company to change the theme of its advertising from just talking about the mountain scenery to talking about the train service experience. One of the ads claimed: "No one ever wrote a folk song about a minivan," and the overall slogan for the new ads was "The only way to see the Canadian Rockies." The company saw a 23 percent increase in its bookings as a result of the ads.[38]

Some companies have successfully used observation in combination with other methods, such as consumer interviews, in an effort to improve the quality of information gathered. To examine how consumers make milk brand decisions, researchers in Atlantic Canada observed over 200 consumers in 12 stores and followed up with brief interviews. In the interviews, consumers claimed that they bought a certain brand, even though the researcher knew from observation that they had bought a different one. Similarly, in interviews most consumers claimed that they checked the expiry date on the milk cartons, whereas observation showed that hardly anyone did so. All of this information allowed the researchers to conclude that milk is a low-involvement purchasing decision with weak loyalty levels.

Exhibit 4.13

Producers of children's toys use observation to test new toy designs.

The consumers were not deliberately lying in the interviews; they simply did not pay that much attention to their milk buying behaviour.[39] As this example shows, sometimes it is wise to use multiple research methods when performing marketing research.

Unobtrusive Measures Researchers also use *unobtrusive measures* to check traces of physical evidence that remain after some action has been taken, when they suspect that people will probably alter their behaviour if they know they are being observed. For example, instead of asking a person to report on the alcohol products currently in his or her home, the researcher might go to the house and perform a "pantry check," recording the bottles found there. The Vancouver Police Department (VPD) developed a campaign called "Bait Cars" (Exhibit 4.14) that included radio ads targeted to a younger listening audience. These ads air throughout the day to serve as deterrents to thieves who were thinking about stealing cars. The VPD started running more ads on the radio station the BEAT when anecdotal testaments from police and evidence from the stolen Bait Cars indicated that many thieves regularly tuned into the BEAT. Another measure taken by the VPD included placing transit shelter ads in areas where significant numbers of stolen cars were abandoned, the rationale being that thieves steal cars from all over town, but abandon them closer to where they live.[40]

Some companies and their research firms sift through garbage, searching for clues about family consumption habits (Exhibit 4.15). The "garbologists" can tell, for example, which soft drink accompanied what kind of food. As one garbologist noted, "The people in this study don't know that we are studying their garbage so the information is totally objective."[41] Garbology is also conducted in business Dumpsters to find competitive information—although many marketers question the ethics of doing so.

Mechanical Observation *Mechanical observation* relies on non-human devices to record behaviour. For example, some grocery stores use GPS units on their grocery carts to track shoppers' movement through their stores to determine shopping patterns and hot spots.[42] Another application of mechanical observation is people meters, operated by such companies as Nielsen Media Research and BBM Bureau of Measurement. These boxes are attached to the television sets of selected viewers to record patterns of television watching. These "television ratings" are how the networks determine how much to charge advertisers for commercials and which shows to cancel or renew. Nielsen also uses observation on the Internet to determine which websites are most popular on a daily and weekly basis. The Nielsen web usage data can be viewed at the Nielsen NetRatings site.

Exhibit 4.14

The Vancouver Police Department used unobtrusive measures to find out what radio stations car thieves listen to in the Bait Car campaign.

Exhibit 4.15

"Garbologists" search for clues about consumption activities, an unobtrusive measure.

Data Quality: Garbage In, Garbage Out

A firm can gather data in many ways, including focus groups, ethnographies, observational studies, and controlled experiments. But how much faith should it place in what it finds?

A research project is only as good as the information it collects. All too often, marketers who have commissioned a study assume that because they have a massive report full of impressive-looking numbers and tables, they must have the "truth." Unfortunately, there are times when this "truth" is really just one person's interpretation of the facts. At other times, the data used to generate recommendations are flawed. As the expression goes, "Garbage in, garbage out."[43] Typically, three factors influence the quality of research results—validity, reliability, and representativeness.

VALIDITY **Validity** is the extent to which the research actually measures what it was intended to measure. This was part of the problem underlying the famous New Coke fiasco in the 1980s, in which Coca-Cola underestimated people's loyalty to its flagship soft drink after it replaced "Old Coke" with a new, sweeter formula. The company assumed that blind taste testers' preferences for one anonymous cola over another were a valid measure of consumers' preferences for a cola brand. Coke found out the hard way that only measuring taste is not the same as measuring people's deep allegiances to their favourite soft drink, and sales eventually recovered after the company brought back the old version as "Coca-Cola Classic."[44]

RELIABILITY **Reliability** is the extent to which the research measurement techniques are free of errors. Sometimes, for example, the way a researcher asks a question creates an error by biasing people's responses. Imagine that an interviewer working for Trojans condoms stopped male college students on campus and asked them if they used contraceptive products. Do you think their answers might change if they were asked the same questions on an anonymous survey they received in the mail? Most likely they would be different, because people are reluctant to disclose what they actually do when their responses are not anonymous. Researchers try to maximize reliability by thinking of several different ways to ask the same questions, by asking these questions on several occasions, or by using several analysts to interpret the responses.

Reliability is a problem when the researchers can't be sure the consumer population they're studying even understands what is being asked. For example, children are difficult subjects for market researchers, because they tend to be undependable reporters of their own behaviour, have poor recall, and often do not understand abstract questions.[45] In many cases, the children cannot explain why they prefer one item over another (or they're not willing to share these secrets with grown-ups).[46] For these reasons, researchers have had to be especially creative in designing studies involving younger consumers. In the example shown in Figure 4.5 (called a *completion test*), boys are told to write in the empty balloon what they think the boy in the drawing will answer when the girl asks, "What program do you want to watch next?" Reliability is increased because the children can respond to pictures depicting a familiar situation in their own words.

REPRESENTATIVENESS **Representativeness** is the extent to which consumers in the study are similar to a larger group in which the organization has an interest. This criterion for evaluating research underscores the importance of **sampling**, the process of selecting respondents for a study. The issue then becomes how large or small the sample should be and how these people are chosen. We'll talk more about sampling in the next section.

Design the Sample

Once the researcher has defined the problem, decided on a research design, and determined how to collect the data, the next step is to decide from whom to obtain the needed data. Of course, the researcher *could* collect the information from every single customer or prospective customer, but this would be extremely expensive and time consuming, if possible at all. Instead, researchers collect most of their data from a small proportion or *sample* of the population of interest. Based on the answers of this

validity The extent to which research actually measures what it was intended to measure.

reliability The extent to which research measurement techniques are free of errors.

representativeness The extent to which consumers in a study are similar to a larger group in which the organization has an interest.

sampling The process of selecting respondents who statistically represent a larger population of interest.

Figure 4.5 A Completion Test Designed for Children

It can be especially difficult to get accurate information from children. Researchers often use visuals such as this completion test to encourage children to express their feelings.

Source: James McNeal, "Child's play," *Marketing Tools*, January–February 1998: 20.

sample, researchers hope to generalize to the larger population. Whether such inferences are accurate or inaccurate depends on the type and quality of the study sample. There are two main types of samples: probability and non-probability samples.

PROBABILITY SAMPLING With a **probability sample**, each member of the population has some known chance of being included in the sample. Using a probability sample ensures researchers that the sample is representative of the population and that inferences about the population made from the sample are justified. For example, if a larger percentage of males than females in a probability sample say they prefer action movies to "chick flicks," one can infer with confidence that a larger percentage of males than females in the general population also would rather see a character get sliced and diced.

The most basic type of probability sample is a *simple random sample* in which every member of a population has a known and equal chance of being included in the study. For example, if we simply take the names of all 40 students in your class and put them in a hat and draw one out, each member of your class has a 1 in 40 chance of being included in the sample. In most studies the population from which the sample will be drawn is too large for a hat, so marketers use a computer program to generate a random sample from a list of members of the population.

Sometimes researchers use a *systematic sampling procedure* in which they select the *n*th member of a population after a random start. For example, if we want a sample of 10 members of your class, we might begin with the second person on the roll and select every fourth name after that; that is, the second, the sixth, the tenth, the fourteenth, and so on. Researchers know that studies that use systematic samples are just as accurate as simple random samples. Unless a list of members of the population of interest is already in a computer data file, it's a lot simpler to create a systematic sample.

Another type of probability sample is a *stratified sample* in which a researcher divides the population into segments that are related to the study's topic. For example, imagine that you are interested in studying what movies are most liked by members of a population. You know from previous studies that men and women in the population differ in their attitudes toward different types of movies—men like action flicks and women like romances. To create a stratified sample, you would first divide the population into male and female segments. Then respondents from each of the two segments would be selected randomly in proportion to their percentage of the population. In this way, you have created a sample that is proportionate to the population on a characteristic that you know will make a difference in the study results.

Cluster sampling also divides a population into groups, but in this approach the groups are representative microcosms of a population, in that each reflects the characteristics of the population as a whole. In cluster sampling the population is divided into mutually exclusive and collectively exhaustive subpopulations and then a subset of the groups is chosen using a probability sampling technique like a simple random sample. Respondents are then chosen within the groups using another probability sampling technique. Cluster sampling is quite cost effective because you only have to create a sampling frame (list of potential respondents) for the cluster groups chosen. Political pollsters use cluster sampling to make national assessments of party popularity based on the responses of a few hundred voters.

NON-PROBABILITY SAMPLING Sometimes researchers do not feel that the time and effort required to develop a probability sample are justified, perhaps because they need an answer quickly or they just want to get a general sense of how people feel about a topic. They may choose a **non-probability sample**, which entails the use of personal judgment in selecting respondents—in some cases just asking whomever they can find! With a non-probability sample, some members of the population have no chance at all of being included in the sample. Thus, there is no way to ensure that the sample is representative of the population. Results from non-probability studies can be generally suggestive of what is going on in the real world but not necessarily definitive.

probability sample A sample in which each member of the population has some known chance of being included in the sample.

non-probability sample A sample in which personal judgment is used in selecting respondents.

Exhibit 4.16

Gap Inc. used a convenience sample of its own employees to help develop Old Navy's merchandising strategy.

A *convenience sample* is a non-probability sample composed of individuals who just happen to be available when and where the data are being collected. For example, if you simply stand in front of the student union and ask students who walk by to complete your questionnaire, that would be a convenience sample.

In some cases firms even use their own employees as a convenience sample or as "guinea pigs." When Gap Inc. was developing the concept for its chain of Old Navy stores, the company gave employees who fit the desired Old Navy customer profile $200 apiece and set them loose on a shopping spree (Exhibit 4.16). The employees were then interviewed about what they had bought so that these products would be on Old Navy's shelves when the stores opened (nice work if you can get it!).[47]

A *quota sample* is the division of the total population into categories by age, income, marital status, or other demographic. The researcher draws a portion (quota) of names from those categories relevant to the study, ignoring those who belong to other categories, until a predetermined quota of potential respondents is met. A quota sample is much like the stratified sample except that with a quota sample, individual members of the sample are selected through personal judgment as they are in a convenience sample.

Collect the Data

At this point the researcher has determined the nature of the problem that needs to be addressed. He or she has decided on a research design that will specify how to investigate the problem and what kinds of information (data) will be needed to do so. Once these decisions have been made, the next task is to actually collect the data.

Although collecting data may seem like a simple process, researchers are well aware of its critical importance to the accuracy of research. When interviewers are involved, researchers know that the quality of research results is only as good as the poorest interviewer collecting the data. Careless interviewers may not read questions exactly as written or they may not record respondent answers correctly. So marketers must train and supervise interviewers to make sure they follow the research procedures exactly as outlined. In this section we'll talk about some of the problems in gathering data and some solutions.

Many people are concerned about potential violations of privacy, as firms continue to gather detailed data about their personal lives. The Blockbuster Entertainment Corp., for example, encountered a firestorm of criticism when it was accused of trying to sell information detailing customers' video rental habits.[48] Critics charged that people's movie preferences (whether for action movies, pornography, or cartoons) were their own business. Data gatherers need to ensure that the information collected will be used only for the stated purpose and that respondents are aware of their right to refuse to provide information.

On January 1, 2004, the Canadian government enacted a new privacy law (the Personal Information Protection and Electronic Documents Act, or PIPEDA) intended to balance consumer rights against business needs. The key underlying principles of the act are outlined in Table 4.6.[49] Complicating matters, however, is that the provinces of Alberta and British Columbia have their own consumer privacy laws that have not been deemed "substantially similar" to the PIPEDA—making it unclear as to which law organizations those provinces should adhere. Since the law has been on the books, the privacy commissioner has conducted over 350 investigations into apparent breaches. Critics of the law are calling for tougher

Table 4.6 Canada's Privacy Law

Accountability: All organizations must have a privacy officer or representative who will ensure that the organization is compliant with the new law.

Expressed Purpose: Information may only be used for the expressed purpose for which consumers have given their consent. New consent must be acquired if you want to use the information for another purpose.

Consent: Information can only be used after gaining informed consent from consumers. For sensitive information (e.g., financial information) consumers must actively express consent (opt in) while for non-sensitive information (e.g., phone numbers or addresses) consumers must be able to easily opt out of providing consent for its use.

Third Party Use: You can only make customer information available to others if you have consent of the customer and you keep a record of having received that consent.

Accuracy: Organizations are required to keep personal information on consumers as accurate, complete, and up-to-date as possible.

Need: Information collected can only be retained if it is being used for the purpose collected. Information collected from people who are no longer customers must be destroyed.

Safeguards: Reasonable safeguards must be in place to ensure against unauthorized access or alteration of records.

Openness: Organizations must be prepared to publicize their information-handling practices through all points of contact with customers. Organizations should have privacy policies and their staff must be trained in these policies.

Individual Access: Consumers have the right to know what information has been collected about them, their records must be made available upon request, and they may request erroneous information be corrected.

Compliance: Organizations must have a formal inquiry and complaint-handling mechanism to investigate if a consumer challenges an organization's compliance with the new law. Consumers may also challenge compliance with Federal privacy commission.

regulations and the Canadian Parliament is in the process of reviewing the legislation to see if it goes far enough to protect the privacy of Canadians.[50]

GATHERING DATA INTERNATIONALLY Conducting market research in other countries is important for Canadian firms operating in international markets. However, market conditions and consumer preferences vary widely in different parts of the world, and there are big differences in the sophistication of market research operations and the amount of data available to global marketers.

For these reasons, choosing an appropriate data collection method is difficult. In some countries, many people do not have phones, or low literacy rates may interfere with mail surveys. Local customs can be a problem as well. Offering money for interviews, a common practice in Canada, is considered rude in Latin American countries.[51] Focus groups are virtually impossible in Saudi Arabia, where gatherings of four or more people except for family or religious events are banned. Interviews are also difficult there since it is illegal to stop strangers on the street or knock on the door of someone's house.[52] Cultural differences also affect responses to survey items. Both Danish and British consumers, for example, agree that it is important to eat breakfast, but the Danish sample may be thinking of fruit and yoghurt, whereas the British sample is thinking of toast and tea. And in Mexico, for instance, because there are still large areas where native Indian tribes speak languages other than Spanish, researchers end up bypassing these groups in surveys.[53] Sometimes these problems can be overcome by involving local researchers in decisions about the research design, but, even so, care must be taken to ensure that they fully understand the study's objectives and can relate what they find to the culture of the sponsoring company.

Language differences can also pose challenges for international marketing research. When SurveySite conducted an online survey for Microsoft across 13 countries, for example, the study had to be translated into seven different languages.[54] To ensure that surveys using many languages are translated properly, researchers often use a process called *back-translation*, which requires two steps. First, a questionnaire is translated into the second language by a native speaker of that language. Second, this new version is translated back into the original language to ensure that the correct meanings survive the process. Even with precautions such as these, however, researchers must interpret data obtained from other cultures with care.

SINGLE-SOURCE DATA One research issue that marketers have been trying to solve for years is knowing what impact each piece of their marketing mix is having on their total marketing strategy. Short of moving in with a family for a few months, marketers had no way to determine the effect of multiple promotional activities. Today, though, sophisticated technology allows researchers to gather data from actual store transactions that they can then trace to different components of the marketing mix.

single-source data Information that is integrated from multiple sources in order to monitor the impact of marketing communications on a particular customer group over time.

The term **single-source data** refers to information that is integrated from multiple sources. In single-source systems, data on purchasing behaviour and advertising exposure are measured for members of a consumer panel using electronic television meters, retail scanners, and split-cable technology in which different customers on a television cable system can be exposed to different ads. Because single-source systems can measure the impact of a number of different marketing activities in combination, they allow marketers to monitor the impact of many marketing communications on a particular customer group over time. For example, a firm that sells laundry detergent might use single-source systems to answer the following questions:

- Which consumer segments are more likely to be brand loyal and what segments frequently switch brands of laundry detergent?
- Are coupons or price-off packs more likely to increase sales?
- Does increased advertising exposure influence brand switching?
- What is the total effect of increased advertising and the use of coupons?

A great deal of single-source data comes from checkout scanners in stores. In addition to speeding up your checkout time, scanners store a record of just how many bags of munchies you bought and what brands you chose. Combined with records from the store's other customers (and buyers at other locations), this is a potential pot of gold for firms willing to invest in the research needed to track all those millions of transactions.

For retailers who can specifically identify individual consumers, perhaps because they have a loyalty card that links their purchases with demographic information, the data from scanners are especially useful. For example, Shoppers Drug Mart tracks the purchases of regular customers who show an Optimum card when they get to the register (Exhibit 4.17). Using this information, Shoppers Drug Mart can more effectively make merchandising decisions and tailor special offers, including coupons, to these customers. So heavy consumers of diapers, for example, might be sent cents-off coupons for baby food or children's Tylenol.

Purchases made online are also continuously recorded, and the identity (username) of the consumer (as well as their virtual address) is always recorded along with their purchases. Thus, companies such as Chapters.indigo.ca can track the purchase habits of each consumer and use that information to tailor communication messages to individuals. If a consumer has ordered several gardening books, for example, they could be sent an e-mail when a new gardening book comes out and offered a special deal if they purchase the book.

Exhibit 4.17

Shoppers Drug Mart's Optimum card allows the company to match demographic and financial data of consumers with their shopping behaviour.

Analyze and Interpret the Data

Once marketing researchers have collected the data, what's next? It's like a spin on the old "if a tree falls in the woods" question: "If results exist but there's no one to interpret them, do they have a meaning?" Well, let's leave the philosophers out of it and just say that marketers would answer "no." Data need analysis for them to have meaning.

To understand the important role of data analysis, let's take a look at a hypothetical research example. In our example, a company that

Table 4.7 Examples of Data Tabulation and Cross-Tabulation Tables

Fat Content Preference
(Number and percentages of responses)

Questionnaire Response	Number of Responses	Percentage of Responses
Do you prefer a meal with high fat content, medium fat content, or low fat content?		
High fat	21	6
Medium fat	179	51
Low fat	150	43
Total	350	100

Fat Content Preference by Gender
(Number and percentages of responses)

Questionnaire Response	Number Females	Percentage of Females	Number Males	Percentage of Males	Total Number	Total Percentage
Do you prefer a meal with high fat content, medium fat content, or low fat content?						
High fat	4	2	17	10	21	6
Medium fat	68	39	111	64	179	51
Low fat	103	59	47	27	150	43
Total	175	100	175	100	350	100

markets frozen foods wishes to better understand consumers' preference for varying levels of fat content in their diets. They have conducted a descriptive research study in which they collected primary data via telephone interviews. Because they recognize that gender is related to dietary preferences, they have used a stratified sample that includes 175 males and 175 females.

Typically, marketers first tabulate the data as shown in Table 4.7—that is, they arrange the data in a table or other summary form so they can get a broad picture of the overall responses. The data in this table show that 43 percent of the sample prefers a low-fat meal. There may also be a desire to cross-classify or cross-tabulate the answers to questions by other variables. *Cross-tabulation* means that the data are examined by subgroups, in this case males and females separately, to see how results vary between categories. The cross-tabulation in Table 4.7 shows that 59 percent of females versus only 27 percent of males prefer a meal with low fat content. In addition, researchers may wish to apply additional statistical tests (such as those described in Appendix 4A), which you'll learn more about in subsequent courses.

Based on the analysis, the researcher must then interpret or draw conclusions from the results and make recommendations. For example, the study results shown in Table 4.7 may lead to the conclusion that females are more likely than males to be concerned about a low-fat diet. The researcher might then make a recommendation to a firm that it should target females in the introduction of a new line of low-fat foods.

Prepare the Research Report

The final step in the marketing research process is to prepare a report of the research results. In general, a research report must clearly and concisely tell the readers—top management, clients, creative departments, and many others—what they need to know in a way that they can easily understand. In general, a research report will include these sections:

- An executive summary of the report that covers the high points of the total report
- An understandable description of the research methodology
- A complete discussion of the results of the study, including the tabulations, cross-tabulations, and additional statistical analyses

ONLINE RESEARCH

The growth of the Internet is rewriting some of the rules of the marketing research process. As more and more people have access to the web, many companies are using services like those provided by SurveySite (**www.surveysite.com**)—it's fast, it's relatively cheap, and it lends itself well to forms of research from simple questionnaires to online focus groups.

The web is revolutionizing the way many companies collect data and use them to guide their strategic decisions. There are two major types of online research. One type is information gathered by tracking consumers while they are surfing. The second type is information gathered through questionnaires on websites, through e-mail, or from moderated focus groups conducted in chat rooms—such as the one illustrated in Exhibit 4.18. Online research accounts for more than 25 percent of all marketing research.[55]

Online Tracking

The Internet offers an unprecedented ability to track consumers as they search for information—we'll talk more about this process in the next chapter. Marketers can better understand where people go to look when they want to learn about products and services—and which advertisements they stop to browse along the way. How can marketers do this? One way is by the use of "cookies." **Cookies** are text files inserted by a website sponsor into a user's hard drive when the user connects with the site. Cookies remember details of a visit to a website, typically tracking which pages the user visits. Some sites request or require that visitors "register" on the site by answering questions about themselves and their likes and dislikes. In such cases, cookies also allow the site to access these details about the customer.

This technology allows websites to customize services, such as when Amazon.ca or Chapters.indigo.ca recommends new books to users based on what books they have ordered in the past (Exhibit 4.19). Most consumers have no idea that cookies allow websites to gather and store all this information. You can block cookies or curb them, although this can make life difficult if you are trying to log on to many sites such as online newspapers or travel agencies that require this information to admit you.

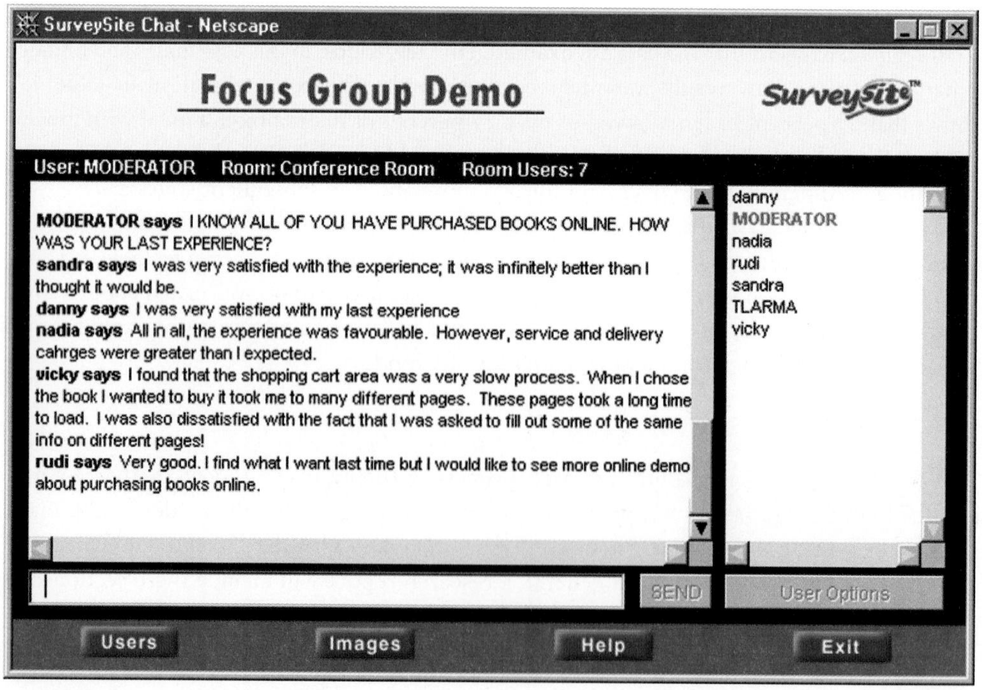

cookies Text files inserted by a website sponsor into a web surfer's hard drive that allow the site to track the surfer's moves.

Exhibit 4.18

SurveySite online focus groups help clients understand consumers' buying behaviour.

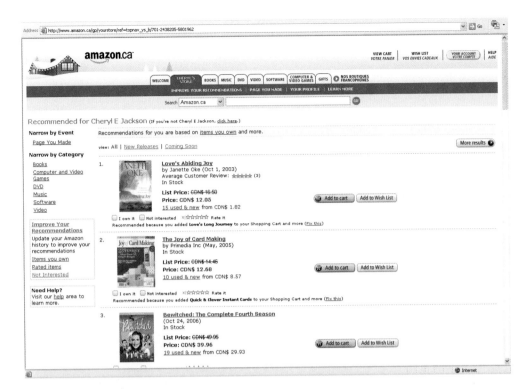

Exhibit 4.19

Amazon.ca uses sophisticated software called "collaborative filtering" to keep track of shoppers' book choices and recommend new books based on past patterns.

Who owns your cookies? This information generated from tracking consumers' online journeys has become a product as well—companies sell this consumer data to other companies that are trying to target prospects. But consumers have become increasingly concerned about the sharing of these data. In a study of 10 000 web users, 84 percent objected to the reselling of their information to other companies. Although Internet users can delete cookie files manually or install anti-cookie software on their computers, there are many people who feel there is a need for privacy regulation and for cookie regulation to limit potential abuses.

Online Testing, Questionnaires, and Focus Groups

The Internet offers a faster, less expensive alternative to traditional communication data collection methods. Websites like **surveymonkey.com** make it inexpensive and easy for anyone to create and administer online surveys. Companies use the Internet to get feedback from consumers when conducting new-product development research, estimating market response, and in many other types of exploratory research.

NEW-PRODUCT DEVELOPMENT Procter & Gamble spent more than five years testing products such as Febreze, Dryel, and Fit Fruit & Vegetable Wash the old-fashioned way before launching nationally. Using online tests, the Crest MultiCare Flex & Clean toothbrush was launched in less than a year. General Motors and Nissan are two automakers that now gather online consumer reactions to upcoming products. Such research allows manufacturers to learn what consumers want in future vehicles.[56]

ESTIMATING MARKET RESPONSE Both Mercury Records and Virgin Records have used online research to test music for performers, including Bon Jovi and the Spice Girls.[57] In a typical test, respondents listen to the songs and then click on buttons to indicate how much they like or dislike the music.

EXPLORATORY RESEARCH Conducting focus groups online has mushroomed in popularity in recent years. For example, Procter & Gamble's website includes a Try & Buy New Products section that sells P&G products still being test-marketed and directs consumers to virtual, real-time focus groups.[58] Of course, with online groups it is impossible to observe body language, facial expressions, and vocal inflection. But marketers continue to develop new ways to talk to consumers in virtual space, including software that allows online focus group participants to indicate nonverbal responses. For example, an online participant can register an expression of disgust by clicking on the command to "roll eyes."[59]

Many marketing research companies are running, not walking, to the web to conduct studies for clients. Why? For one thing, replacing traditional mail consumer panels with Internet panels allows marketers to collect the same amount of data in a weekend that used to take six to eight weeks. And consumers can complete surveys when it is convenient—even at 3 a.m. There are other advantages: Even large studies can be conducted at low costs. International borders are not a problem either, as Internet use is very high in many countries and it's easy to recruit respondents. Web-based interviews eliminate interviewer bias or errors in data entry.[60]

However, no data collection method is perfect, and online research is no exception—though many of the criticisms of online techniques also apply to offline techniques. One potential problem is the representativeness of the respondents. Although the number of Internet users continues to grow, many segments of the consumer population, mainly the

Real People, Real Decisions

How It Worked Out at FCC

Fred Wall decided to implement both Option 2 (panel program) and Option 3 (scoreboards) as complementary systems. The two major initiatives work in conjunction to answer most of the major research questions at FCC. The scoreboards tell FCC how they are doing (at the most local level) and why they are performing as they are. The Vision Panel tells them what they should be doing next, and why.

The scoreboards approach allowed FCC to cover all of its critical customer satisfaction and loyalty research in one major project. The initial time and cost to set up the program were a challenge, but the eventual benefits—continuous feedback, cost savings, and higher response rates—outweighed the disadvantages. The logistical complexity of the program remains a challenge, though one well worth facing.

Each of the three surveys—Post-Loan, Report Card, and Exit—contains a common core of seven questions that are combined to form the Customer Experience Index, a critical balanced scorecard measure at FCC. The scope of the program, with between 12 000 and 15 000 completed surveys per year, allows FCC to determine the strengths and weaknesses of each of its almost 100 offices and to reward local areas according to their performance.

In an environment where customers were becoming fewer, smarter, and wealthier, Fred decided that it was critical to move first in establishing the Vision panel and accustoming the market to FCC's new approach to research. Fred wanted the concept established in the agriculture space and owned by FCC before others also turned to similar concepts. More and more of FCC's research also required specific niche samples, and Fred realized that to reach those samples effectively

and efficiently, he'd need to recruit as many of them in advance as possible.

The Vision panel now drives much of the primary research agenda at FCC. Vision panellists are asked to evaluate everything from new products, advertisements, and product names to the state of agriculture in Canada. Panellists participate in face-to-face research, mail research, online research (quantitative and qualitative), and sometimes a combination of all of the above. Panellists have responded extremely positively to the initiative, often noting their appreciation for the different approach FCC is taking to getting and using their feedback.

The scoreboards produce FCC's Customer Experience Index, which is based on seven criteria that align with FCC's core values: transactional satisfaction, loyalty, advocacy, problem resolution, value received, ease of doing business, and care for customer success.

Response rates for the scoreboards have more than tripled relative to the prior interruption approaches and the cost per complete has been cut by two-thirds. The data are captured at a volume that allows for every one of FCC's offices to determine its strengths and weaknesses on a continuous basis.

The Vision panel has grown to over 8000 participants (as of summer 2007), with excellent coverage of every major market segment across the country, including customers, prospects, and market influencers. More than half of the panel is active online, allowing FCC to do overnight polling on issues requiring immediate attention.

By implementing this strategy, the FCC research team is able to deliver more and better information, on a more timely basis, for less money than was possible before.

poor and elderly, do not have equal access to the Internet. Also, in many studies (just as with mail surveys or mall intercepts) there is a *self-selection bias* in the sample: Respondents have agreed to receive invitations to take part in online studies, which means they tend to be the kind of people who like to participate in surveys. As with other kinds of research such as live focus groups, it's not unusual to encounter "professional respondents"—people who just enjoy taking part in studies (and getting paid for it). Online firms such as Harris Interactive address this problem by monitoring their participants and regulating how often they are allowed to participate in different studies over a period of time.

There are other disadvantages of online research. Hackers can actually try to influence research results. Even more dangerous may be competitors who can learn about a firm's marketing plans, products, advertising, and so forth by intercepting information used in research. One company, E-Poll, uses a methodology to prevent some of these problems.[61] To preview TV pilots, commercials, and ad campaigns, E-Poll sends respondents a CD-ROM.

CHAPTER SUMMARY

Key Terms

1. **Explain the role of the marketing information system and the marketing decision support system in marketing decision making.**

   A marketing information system (MIS) is composed of internal data, marketing intelligence, marketing research data, acquired databases, and computer hardware and software. Firms use an MIS to gather, sort, analyze, store, and distribute information needed by managers for marketing decision making. The marketing decision support system (MDSS) allows managers to use analysis software and interactive software to access MIS data and to conduct analyses and find the information they need.

2. **Describe methods to measure customer satisfaction.**

   There are four main methods used to measure customer satisfaction.

   1. Customer Satisfaction Surveys. Most customer satisfaction surveys have three sections: a global satisfaction index with the good, service, or firm (typically measured on a five-point scale, with "very dissatisfied" and "very satisfied" being the two end points); a detailed evaluation of the goods and services offered by the firm; and intentions to repurchase the firm's offerings.
   2. Mystery Shopping. A form of marketing research, mystery shopping involves a researcher buying the firm's goods or services and assessing the purchase experience against the firm's competitors.
   3. Customer Complaint Analysis. Analyzing customer complaints is another way to understand customer satisfaction.
   4. Lost Customer Analysis. Some business organizations contact customers who have stopped being repeat purchasers to assess what went wrong. This provides a good assessment of customer satisfaction levels and what needs to be done to retain customers.

3. **List and explain the marketing research process.**

   The research process begins by defining the problem and determining the research design or type of study. Next, researchers choose the data collection method; that is, whether there is secondary data available or if primary research with a communication study or through observation is necessary. Then researchers determine what type of sample is to be used for the study and then collect the data. The final steps in the research are to analyze and interpret the data and prepare a research report.

4. **Understand the differences among exploratory, descriptive, and causal research, and describe some research techniques available to marketers.**

   Exploratory research typically uses qualitative data collected by individual interviews, focus groups, or observational methods such as ethnography. Descriptive research includes cross-sectional and longitudinal studies. Causal research goes a step further by designing controlled

- case study, p. 137
- causal research, p. 138
- consumer interviews, p. 135
- cookies, p. 150
- cross-sectional design, p. 137
- data mining, p. 128
- descriptive research, p. 137
- ethnography, p. 137
- experiments, p. 139
- exploratory research, p. 135
- focus group, p. 136
- intranet, p. 123
- longitudinal design, p. 138
- marketing decision support system (MDSS), p. 127
- marketing information system (MIS), p. 122
- marketing intelligence, p. 123
- marketing research, p. 125
- non-probability sample, p. 145
- primary research, p. 127
- probability sample, p. 145
- projective techniques, p. 136
- reliability, p. 144
- representativeness, p. 144
- research design, p. 134
- sampling, p. 144
- scenarios, p. 124

experiments in order to understand cause-and-effect relationships between marketing independent variables, such as price changes; and dependent variables, such as sales.

5. **Describe the different types of data collection methods and types of samples that researchers use.**

Researchers may choose to collect data using mail questionnaires, telephone interviews, face-to-face interviews, or online questionnaires. A study may utilize a probability sample, such as a simple random or stratified sample in which inferences can be made about a population based on the sample results. Non-probability sampling methods include a convenience sample and a quota sample. The research tries to ensure that the data are valid, reliable, and representative. Validity is the extent to which the research actually measures what it was intended to measure. Reliability is the extent to which the research measurement techniques are free of errors. Representativeness is the extent to which consumers in the study are similar to a larger group in which the organization has an interest.

6. **Understand the impact of the growing use of online research.**

Online research accounts for more than 25 percent of all marketing research. Online tracking uses cookies to record where consumers go on a website. Consumers have become increasingly concerned about privacy and how this information is used and made available to other Internet companies. The Internet also provides an attractive alternative to traditional communication data collection methods because of its speed and low cost. Many firms use the Internet to conduct online focus groups.

CHAPTER REVIEW

Marketing Concepts: Testing Your Knowledge

1. What is a marketing information system (MIS)? What types of information are included in a marketing information system? How does a marketing decision support system (MDSS) allow marketers to easily get the information they need?
2. What are the steps in the marketing research process? Why is defining the problem to be researched so important?
3. What is the goal of exploratory research? What techniques are used to gather data in exploratory research?
4. What is descriptive research? What techniques are used in descriptive research?
5. What is causal research?
6. What are some advantages and disadvantages of telephone interviews, mail questionnaires, face-to-face interviews, and online interviews? What unique data collection problems exist in foreign markets?
7. What are some ways in which we can measure customer satisfaction? Describe the pros and cons of each.
8. How do probability and non-probability samples differ? What are some types of probability samples? What are some types of non-probability samples?
9. What are single-source data? What are some ways that marketers use single-source data?
10. What is meant by reliability, validity, and representativeness of research results?
11. What are online tracking studies? What are some strengths and weaknesses of Internet focus groups?

Marketing Concepts: Discussing Choices and Issues

1. Do you think marketers should be allowed to conduct market research with young children? Why or why not?
2. Some marketers attempt to disguise themselves as marketing researchers when their real intent is to sell something to the consumer. What is the impact of this practice on legitimate researchers? What do you think might be done about this practice?
3. Are you willing to divulge personal information to marketing researchers? How much are you willing to tell, or where would you draw the line?

4. What is your overall attitude toward marketing research? Do you think it is a beneficial activity from a consumer's perspective? Or do you think it merely gives marketers new insights on how to convince consumers to buy something they really don't want or need?

5. Can you design a method to measure customer satisfaction that we have not discussed in this chapter?

6. Sometimes firms use data mining to identify and abandon customers who are not profitable because they don't spend enough to justify the service needed or because they return a large proportion of the items they buy. What do you think of such practices? Is it ethical for firms to prune out these customers?

7. Many consumers are concerned about online tracking studies and their privacy. Do consumers have the right to "own" data about themselves? Should governments limit the use of the Internet for data collection?

8. One unobtrusive measure mentioned in the chapter involved going through consumers' or competitors' garbage. Do you think marketers should have the right to do this? Is it ethical?

9. Consider the approach to tracking consumers' exposure to promotions via portable people meters, or PPMs. How would you feel about participating in a study that required the use of a PPM? What would be the advantage of a PPM approach versus keeping a written diary of television shows you watched and ads you saw?

Marketing Practice: Applying What You've Learned

1. Your firm is planning to begin marketing a consumer product in several global markets. You have been given the responsibility of developing plans for marketing research to be conducted in Eastern Europe, Western Europe, and China. In a role-playing situation, present the difficulties you expect to encounter, if any, in conducting research in each of these areas.

2. As an account executive with a marketing research firm, you are responsible for deciding on the type of research to be used in various studies conducted for your clients. For each of the following client questions, list your choices.

   a. What do consumers like and dislike about shampoo?

   b. What are the best media vehicles for a local insurance broker to use for its advertising?

   c. How much label information on cereal boxes do consumers read before they make a purchase?

   d. Are consumers more likely to buy brands that are labelled as environmentally friendly?

   e. How do women determine if a particular perfume is right for them?

   f. What types of people read the local newspaper?

   g. How frequently do consumers switch brands of soft drinks?

   h. How will an increase in the price of a brand of laundry detergent affect sales?

   i. How do the different members of a family participate in the purchase of a new car?

3. Your marketing research firm is planning to conduct surveys to gather information for a number of clients. Your boss has asked you and a few other new employees to do some preliminary work. He has asked each of you to choose three of the topics that will be included in the project and to prepare an analysis of the advantages and disadvantages of mail surveys, telephone surveys, face-to-face surveys, or observation for each.

   a. the amount of alcoholic beverages consumed in a city

   b. young adults' use of illegal drugs

   c. why a local convenience store has been losing customers

   d. how heavily the company should invest in manufacturing and marketing home fax machines

   e. the amount of money people spend on lottery tickets

   f. reader recall of magazine advertisements

   g. what local doctors would like to see changed in the hospitals in the city

   h. consumers' attitudes toward several sports celebrities

Marketing Mini-Project: Learning by Doing

The purpose of this mini-project is to familiarize you with research techniques used by marketers and to help you apply these techniques to managerial decision making.

1. With a group of three other students in your class, select a small retail business or fast-food restaurant to use as a "client" for your project. Be sure to get the manager's permission before conducting your research. Then choose a topic from among the following possibilities to develop a study problem:

   - Employee–customer interactions
   - The busiest periods of customer activity
   - Customer perceptions of service
   - Customer likes and dislikes about offerings
   - Customer likes and dislikes about the environment in the place of business
   - The benefits customers perceive to be important
   - The age groups that frequent the place of business
   - The buying habits of a particular age group
   - How customer complaints are handled

2. Develop a plan for the research:

   a. Define the problem as you will study it.

   b. Choose the type of research you will use.

   c. Select the techniques you will use to gather data.

   d. Develop the mode and format for data collection.

3. Conduct the research.

4. Write a report or develop a class presentation that includes four parts.

   a. Introduction: a brief overview of the business and the problem studied.

   b. Methodology: the type of research used, the techniques used to gather data (and why they were chosen), the instruments and procedures used, the number of respondents, duration of the study, and other details that would allow someone to replicate your study.

   c. Results: a compilation of the results (perhaps in table form) and the conclusions drawn.

   d. Recommendations: a list of recommendations for actions management might take based on the conclusions drawn from the study.

Real People, Real Surfers: Exploring the Web

Monitoring changes in demographics and other consumer trends is an important part of the marketing intelligence included in an MIS. Today, much of this information is gathered by government research and is available on the Internet.

Statistics Canada provides tabled data for Canadian cities at its site, **www.statcan.ca**. Using both Statistics Canada data and any other data you can find on the Internet, develop a report on a Canadian city of your choice that answers the following questions.

1. What is the total population of the city?

2. Describe the population of the area in terms of age, income, education, ethnic background, marital status, occupation, and housing.

3. How does the city compare to the demographic characteristics of the entire Canadian population?

4. What is your opinion of the different websites you used? How useful are they to marketers? How easy were they to navigate? Was there information you wanted that was not available? Was there more or less information from the sites than you had anticipated? Explain.

Entrepreneur Robert Deluce turned heads in February 2006 when he announced that his new airline, Porter Airlines Inc., would soon be flying out of Toronto's Island Airport. The airline offers consumers a convenient downtown alternative to Lester B. Pearson International Airport. The airline started with daily flights to Ottawa and Montreal, adding Halifax to its list of destinations in June 2007.

Porter Airlines is branded as the refined, upscale alternative to the bare-bones service offered by other carriers, such as Air Canada. Porter's waiting lounge at the Toronto Island Airport is designed to make every Porter passenger feel like he's flying first class. With its comfortable grey leather chairs, wood flooring, and wireless Internet connection, passengers feel like they are in the lobby of a first-class hotel.

The experience continues once passengers board the plane, where they enjoy comfortable and spacious leather seats and a free meal including wine, beer, and even Porter-branded water. Consistent with the Porter brand image, flight attendants are dressed in posh designer uniforms.

Although they are still a small player in the air travel market, Porter has had considerable success attracting flyers to its new airline. The one market that Porter would like to tap into further is the lucrative business travel market. The Toronto-Montreal-Ottawa business travel market (often referred to as the "Golden Triangle") is very lucrative and is still dominated by Porter's rival, Air Canada. Porter knows that time-starved business travellers demand scheduling flexibility and frequent flights. The airline is also aware that another competitor, WestJet, is trying to make inroads into this market. Porter needs to formulate a strategy soon—or it will be squeezed out of this market.

To understand the business travel market better, Porter Airlines may want to consider conducting some market research. An online survey of business passengers who have flown with their airline recently is one way to gather the information that they are looking for. The following questionnaire lists questions that Porter may ask in its marketing research.

1. Overall, how satisfied were you with your recent flight on Porter airlines?
   a. Completely satisfied
   b. Somewhat satisfied
   c. Neither satisfied nor dissatisfied
   d. Somewhat dissatisfied
   e. Completely dissatisfied
2. What, if anything, could Porter have done to make your experience better?
3. What things are important to you when you take a business flight?
4. How satisfied were you with the check-in process when you recently flew with Porter?
   a. Completely satisfied
   b. Somewhat satisfied
   c. Neither satisfied nor dissatisfied
   d. Somewhat dissatisfied
   e. Completely dissatisfied
5. If you used the facilities in the waiting lounge at the Toronto Island Airport, how satisfied were you with them? (If you did not use the waiting lounge, proceed to the next question.)
   a. Completely satisfied
   b. Somewhat satisfied
   c. Neither satisfied nor dissatisfied
   d. Somewhat dissatisfied
   e. Completely dissatisfied
6. What do you need/want in an airport waiting lounge to make your time there more efficient or enjoyable?

7. Approximately how many times in total have you flown with Porter Airlines?
   a. Once
   b. 2 times
   c. 3–5 times
   d. 6–10 times
   e. 11 or more times

8. Considering all airlines, approximately how many times within the past year have you taken a business flight?
   a. Once
   b. 2–5 times
   c. 6–10 times
   d. 11–20 times
   e. 21 or more times

9. Would you fly with Porter Airlines again?
   a. Yes
   b. No

10. If you answered "no" to question 9, why would you not fly with Porter again?

11. If you answered "yes" to question 9, why would you fly with Porter again?

Sources: Chris Sorenson, "Upstart is flying under the radar," *Toronto Star*, 9 June 2007: B1, B4; Barry Avrich, "Buckle up for a bumpy ride," *Marketing*, 12 March 2007: 33; Erin Pooley, "Flight Time," *Canadian Business*, 9 October 2006: 11.

Things to Think About

1. Evaluate Porter's proposed research technique (Internet survey). Develop a more comprehensive research plan based on the first two stages of the marketing research process.

2. What changes would you make to the questionnaire?

3. What other sources of information would be useful to Porter as it develops its strategy to tap into the business travel market?

DESCRIPTIVE STATISTICS

As the name suggests, descriptive statistics are statistical tools used to describe data. Many marketing reports use only descriptive statistics, as these are the easiest to interpret and they answer many marketing questions.

Frequency distributions are used when marketers need to answer questions about a single variable, such as what percentage of visitors comes to Victoria, B.C., to attend a convention or conference; or how much money visitors spend on accommodation. A frequency distribution is a count of the different values associated with a variable (a question in a questionnaire). Table 4A.1 is an example of a frequency distribution. It reports information collected by Tourism Victoria, the destination marketing organization responsible for attracting tourists to Victoria. Frequency distributions could also be represented in chart form, such as a bar chart.

In this frequency distribution, the frequency of answers to each response category is reported, as is the percent—the ratio of the frequency versus total observations or cases, including missing values. The valid percent is what marketers usually interpret as the frequency divided by the valid number of cases (the ones without missing values). Cumulative percent adds the valid percentages of each successive category.

Marketers report measures of *central tendency*, or the midpoint of a frequency distribution, in order to understand and make comparisons of how respondents typically answered a question. Common measures of central tendency include the mean, median, and mode. The mean, the arithmetic average, is the most common measure of the midpoint of a frequency distribution and is appropriate when data are interval or ratio scaled. The mode is the value that occurs most frequently—representing the highest peak in the frequency distribution—and is used when data are categorical. The median is the middle value when data are arranged in ascending or descending order—it is the value where 50 percent of cases are below that value and 50 percent are above. It is the best measure of central tendency for ordinal data or when there are extreme values (outliers) in interval or ratio data that would make the mean too high or low to be a good indicator of the midpoint of a frequency distribution.

BIVARIATE STATISTICS

Bivariate statistics compare the distributions of two variables to see if they are related in some way. A *cross-tabulation* reports the joint frequency distribution of two categorical variables in a single contingency table, as in Table 4A.2. It helps us to understand how one variable, such as tourist expenditure, relates to another variable, such as country of origin.

Some researchers prefer contingency tables that only include the percentage of cases in each cell, for ease of interpretation, while others prefer to see the frequencies or both the frequencies and percentages. The question of whether or not there is a relationship between the two variables in a cross-tab analysis can be assessed using statistics such as the *chi-square statistic*, which tests the null hypothesis that there is no relationship between the two variables. Hypothesis testing would be discussed further in a market research course. Cross-tabulation is widely used in marketing research because managers find it easy to interpret, and understanding how two variables relate

Table 4A.1 Reasons for Visiting Victoria

		Frequency	Percent	Valid Percent	Cumulative Percent
Valid	Vacation/Pleasure	263	51.9	52.2	52.2
	Visiting Friends/Family	86	17.0	17.1	69.2
	Business & Pleasure	48	9.5	9.5	78.8
	Business Only	57	11.2	11.3	90.1
	Convention/Conference	13	2.6	2.6	92.7
	Sporting Event	9	1.8	1.8	94.4
	Other	28	5.5	5.6	100.0
	Total	504	99.4	100.0	
Missing	System	3	0.6		
Total		507	100.0		

Table 4A.2 Tourist Expenditure by Country of Origin

		Country			
		Canada	International	U.S.A.	Total
Categorical	$0–$100	377	33	162	572
expenditure	$101–$200	257	41	160	458
per party	$201–$500	218	28	222	468
	More than $500	60	3	54	117
Total		912	105	598	1615

can provide useful insight to inform marketing decisions. For example, it might be very helpful for Tourism Victoria to know that U.S. visitors spend more, proportionately, than other visitors when it is deciding where to target its advertising dollars.

A second common bivariate statistic is the *Pearson correlation coefficient* (also called simple correlation, or just correlation). Correlation is the strength of the linear association between two interval- or ratio-scaled variables—that is, as the values of one variable increase, what happens to the values of the other variable? Correlation does not imply causation—it just indicates, on a range from −1 to +1, the strength of the association between the two variables, where zero is no relationship at all. Marketers find correlation analysis useful because it helps them to understand whether relationships exist between variables of interest, such as whether sales increase as more money is spent on advertising, or whether spending on a customer loyalty program, like Air Miles, is correlated with an increase in customer loyalty. In Table 4A.3, Tourism Victoria learns that there is a small, positive correlation of 0.12 between the variables "Overall Visitor Satisfaction" and "Total Number of Activities" the respondent participated in. We do not know if greater activity results in greater satisfaction or whether greater satisfaction results in greater activity, but we do know that there is a relationship between these variables (the significant value, "Sig," is less than 0.05, indicating that the

likelihood of there being no relationship between these variables is very low). This might be useful to help Tourism Victoria decide whether or not to encourage the development of more attractions or other things to do in Victoria, or whether or not to develop information sources on what there is to do in Victoria.

There are many other statistical tools used by marketers. A *t-test* is a bivariate tool used to assess whether the mean of a variable is equal or different for two groups. Cereal marketers, for example, might like to know whether boys under the age of 13 eat more of their cereal than girls under the age of 13 when making packaging decisions and promotion decisions.

MULTIVARIATE STATISTICS

Multivariate statistics refers to analytic tools that involve more than two variables. Each of these tools has different data requirements (the type of scale used to capture the data). The common types of scales and the statistics or analysis that are permissible with each type of data are summarized in Table 4A.4. This is an issue that would be addressed in detail in a course on market research. For now, you should be aware that most of the tools require at least interval scale data. Interval scale data is where the response categories to a question on a questionnaire represent equal increments, such as with the Celsius temperature scale (10°C is 5°C colder than 15°C and 5°C warmer than

Table 4A.3 Correlation Between Satisfaction and Number of Activities

Correlations

		Overall Visitor Satisfaction	Total Number of Activities
Overall Visitor Satisfaction	Pearson Correlation	1	0.120**
	Sig. (2-tailed)	.	0.000
	N	1871	1698
Number of Activities	Pearson Correlation	0.120**	1
	Sig. (2-tailed)	0.000	.
	N	1698	1871

**Correlation is significant at the 0.01 level (2-tailed).

Table 4A.4 Common Scales

Scale	Basic Characteristics	Common Examples	Marketing Examples	Permissible Statistics	
				Descriptive	**Inferential**
Nominal	Numbers identify and classify objects	Social Security numbers, numbering of football players	Brand numbers, store types, sex classification	Percentages, mode	Chi-square binomial test
Ordinal	Numbers indicate the relative positions of the objects but not the magnitude of differences between them	Quality rankings, rankings of teams in a tournament	Preference rankings, market position, social class	Percentile, median	Rank-order correlation, Friedman ANOVA
Internal	Differences between objects can be compared; zero point is arbitrary	Temperature (Fahrenheit, Celsius)	Attitudes, opinions, index numbers	Range, mean, standard deviation	Product-moment correlations, t-test, ANOVA, regression, factor analysis
Ratio	Zero point is fixed; ratios of scale values can be computed	Length, weight	Age, income, costs, sales, market shares	Geometric mean, harmonic mean	Coefficient of variation

Source: Naresh Malhotra, *Marketing Research: An Applied Orientation,* 4th Edition, © 2004. Reprinted by permission of Pearson Education Inc. Upper Saddle River, NJ.

5°C), or where equality is assumed, such as in a Likert scale (e.g., Strongly Agree, 1, 2, 3, 4, 5, Strongly Disagree).

One-way analysis of variance determines whether the mean (average) response to a question is statistically different in three or more groups. Tourism Victoria, for example, finds it useful to know that people who come to Victoria via the Victoria Clipper catamaran passenger service spend more money while visiting Victoria than visitors who come by air or come in their cars via BC Ferries. The null hypothesis being tested with one-way ANOVA is that the mean values of the groups with respect to a variable of interest are equal. This is usually rejected, and the alternative hypothesis that at least two of the groups differ is accepted, if the significant value is less than 0.05 (corresponding to a 95 percent confidence interval). The data on transit methods, for example, demonstrate that at least two of the BC Ferries, Clipper Navigation, and air travel visitor groups to Victoria differ in expenditure per party. Something called a post-hoc test is required to determine which of the groups differ from each other.

Discriminant analysis determines which variables are the most important for differentiating (determining the differences between) two or more groups. One-way analysis of variance tells us if the means of the groups differ with respect to a variable, but discriminant analysis tells us which of these differences are the most important. If marketers knew, for example, what are the most important differences in the profiles of different market segments, they could use that information to target those segments more effectively.

Cluster analysis is an analytic tool that groups respondents by the commonality or consistency of their answers to questions. Cluster analysis identifies groups where the people in the group are of maximum similarity to each other, based on their answers to the questions, and of maximum difference from people in other groups—two of the criteria for effective segmentation schemes discussed in Chapter 3. If questions have been asked about benefits and features sought, purchase and consumption behaviour, and response to marketing mix variables (like price sensitivity), then cluster analysis will identify actionable, behaviour-based market segments—another objective of a good segmentation scheme. To help develop a rich profile of these clusters or segments, marketers capture demographic and psychographic information from respondents; describe the segments using frequency distributions, means, correlations, and cross-tab analysis; and determine how the segments are similar or different using one-way analysis of variance and discriminant analysis.

Regression analysis is a powerful tool for analyzing relationships between a metric (interval or ratio scale) variable and one or more other variables (called independent variables), when the focal variable of interest is considered dependent on the others. It is used to determine whether a relationship exists between the dependent variable and one or more of the independent variables. Marketers, for example, might want to know if there is a relationship between sales and advertising expenditure, pricing, or distribution intensity. It can also be used to determine the strength of this relationship and the structure or form of the relationship—in the way of an equation. It is most often used to predict values of the dependent variable. Marketers, for example, would like to predict sales volumes or market share (see the discussion on forecasting in Appendix 4B). It can also be used to determine the unique effects or impact of one variable (such as price) when others (such as level of competitor advertising) are taken into account.

Multidimensional scaling (MDS) is a sophisticated analytic tool that creates perceptual maps like the ones illustrated in Chapter 3. It takes data related to consumer preferences or their perceptions of the similarity of brands or other stimuli and represents the geometric relationships among the brands in a multidimensional space. Market researchers infer the underlying dimensions respondents use to form their similarity perceptions or preferences by interpreting groupings of brands on the map—identifying what those brands have in common that would cause respondents to consider them similar. MDS is used to determine (1) the number and nature of the dimensions used by consumers in comparing brands, (2) the positioning of current brands on these dimensions, and (3) the positioning of consumers' ideal brands on these dimensions.

Sales forecasting is one of the most important and difficult challenges for marketers. It is important because key decisions, such as the amount of product to produce, the size of plant to build, the number of employees to hire, and the amount of financing required, are based on a sales forecast. It is difficult because a lot of factors influence demand for a product. In some industries, like fashion, computers, and consumer electronics, these factors are either highly dynamic or difficult to identify. In these contexts, forecast accuracy of plus or minus 70 percent might be considered good. In stable, mature industries, past demand is often a good indication of future demand and forecast accuracy in the plus or minus 5 percent range might be achievable. While forecasts can be for any future time period, most organizations try to predict sales one to three years into the future. There are numerous approaches to sales forecasting, and these can generally be grouped into subjective (qualitative) and objective (quantitative) approaches. Sophisticated sales organizations use multiple approaches to make their forecasts, and some of these are described below.

Subjective methods are based on perceptions or opinions.

- Users' Expectations: Asking customers how much of a product they expect to buy in the forecast period. This approach works well in stable industries where there are not a lot of customers.

- Sales Rep Composite: Sales reps are asked to estimate demand in their territory based on their understanding of customer buying intentions, and then the individual estimates are added together to generate the forecast. This approach requires an established sales force but can be quite accurate, as an overestimate by one sales rep is often made up for by an underestimate of another. Most sales organizations, however, find that their sales reps tend to be overly optimistic, and based on experience with their sales force, discount their composite forecast between 5 and 15 percent.

- Executive Opinion: Senior managers are asked their opinion about future sales. This approach can be effective if the executives are close to their customers, and have a strong understanding of industry dynamics and market factors.

- Goal Based: Some marketers set their forecast at the level needed to achieve their marketing goals or objectives. This approach is often used by small start-up organizations that simply want to achieve some level of profitability. The problems with this approach are that the goal may be too optimistic and may not be reflective of actual demand, or the goal may be set too low, inviting competitors to meet the excess demand.

Objective methods are based on some sort of modelling approach and the use of quantitative analytic tools or statistics.

- Time Series: In this approach the sales data from previous years are used to predict sales in future years (trend analysis). A moving average takes the average sales of the previous five years as the forecast for each successive year. Exponential smoothing gives greater weight to the most recent years. These approaches can be effective in stable industries if future sales are expected to be a lot like prior sales.

- Market Factor: A common and simple approach is to forecast derivation sales based on an understanding of the factors that influence demand. A market-build-up approach would use market research to find out the typical demand per person in a target market, and this figure would be multiplied by the size of the target market to establish the forecast. For example, the demand for Gatorade in Canada might be determined by multiplying the average beverage consumption of Canadians (available from Statistics Canada) by the number of Canadians who are physically active (also available from Statistics Canada) by the number of Canadians who fit the profile of Gatorade consumers (determined by primary research). As discussed in Appendix 4A, regression analysis is an analytic tool that allows market researchers to predict sales as a dependent variable using a set of independent variables (demand factors) thought to be determinants of sales.

- Test Markets: Test market data can also be used to develop a sales forecast. Test market locations are chosen to be representative of the overall population of interest. By changing levels of price, advertising, shelf location, and other marketing mix decisions for different, equivalent groups, marketers can develop models that will optimize those decisions to maximize sales.

- Conjoint Analysis: Conjoint analysis is an analytic tool that uses consumer preference and attribute rating data of a relatively small subset of product concepts or brands to estimate demand for any combination of the attributes. It is appropriate only for those product categories, like computers, where consumers make purchase decisions by making trade-offs among levels of key attributes (e.g., processor speed, memory, hard drive capacity).

- Base Modelling: Base modelling techniques estimate demand for new-to-the-world innovations by comparing key attributes of the innovation to previous innovations and basing the forecast on the known demand curves of those prior innovations.

CHAPTER 5
Consumer Buying Behaviour

PEARSON
mymarketinglab

Real People, Real Decisions

Meet **Ron Outerbridge,** President of Coast Tire

Ron Outerbridge is the president of Coast Tire, an automotive service business with 25 locations across New Brunswick, Nova Scotia, and Prince Edward Island. Ron lives in Quispamsis, New Brunswick, with his wife, Carol, and their two children. Raised in Bermuda, Ron received his Bachelor of Commerce degree from Mount Allison University. He then completed his Chartered Accountant designation with Touche Ross in 1990. Ron joined Baxter Foods Ltd. in 1995, and Coast Tire was at that time owned by Baxter Foods. As director of strategic planning for Baxter Foods, Ron's responsibilities included Coast Tire. Before buying Coast Tire from Baxter Foods in 2002, Ron served as director of finance and assistant general manager, and then vice-president and general manager of Coast Tire.

Tires and automotive services are "grudge" purchases. Customers don't want to spend money on new tires, new brakes, or to fix other parts of their car. Also, having little knowledge of the problems and what is involved in fixing them, they typically do not trust the service provider. The industry has also changed in the past 15 years. As Ron says, "Cars don't need to be fixed very often anymore, they need to be maintained." Today's cars are built much better than they used to be and customers really shouldn't see major problems in the first five years of its life. The challenge is that most customers don't see the value in regular maintenance. They are used to bringing their cars in when they are broken—and they don't think about automotive service until they need a repair. Then they look into where it might best be repaired. Coast Tire wants to change that mentality and develop ongoing relationships with customers, such that customers see Coast Tire as a partner in keeping their vehicle running and avoiding the inconvenience of downtime. It doesn't want to compete on price; it wants to compete on service and relationships. Finally, Coast Tire was fully engaged in April and May, and then again in October and November during the change of seasons when most customers replace their summer and winter tires and often have service work done on their cars while they're in for tire changes. Ron wanted to increase his business in the shoulder seasons, particularly in December through March when very few customers think about car maintenance. With this goal in mind he considered four alternatives:

Option 1: Target Air Miles program members.

Coast Tire was already an Air Miles sponsor, but one option would be to target Air Miles program members with special promotions to entice them into one of the Coast Tire stores. This option had a few benefits. Goodyear is a national sponsor and Coast Tire is a Goodyear distributor, so there was already a fit there. About 40 percent of Coast Tire customers already were Air Mile subscribers. Air Miles also has detailed customer information that Coast Tire could get access to. However, the Air Miles program has become diluted. There are lots of Air Miles sponsors, including credit card

companies. Therefore there was not a lot of competitive advantage, but Coast Tire realized that it might not want to be the only one without it. This option also provided a broad customer profile. Lots of different kinds of people have Air Miles cards, and not necessarily those that fit the profile of a strong Coast Tire customer. These customers may be less loyal than others, as their loyalty is to the Air Miles program, not necessarily to Coast Tire.

Option 2: Targeted relationship with Canadian Automobile Association members.

Coast Tire had developed targeted campaigns for Welcome Wagon participants, thinking that incentives might entice people who are new to town to come into a Coast Tire store. Once there, Ron hoped that the service experience would bring them back. This program had limited success, but Coast Tire thought that a more targeted program with the Canadian Automobile Association could help it build a repeat business. Coast Tire would provide a $10 off per tire discount for CAA members, and CAA would coordinate communicating this to their members. Coast Tire could then develop a direct mail campaign with an auto service special and then measure its success by tracking the pickup rate and ongoing loyalty of CAA members by tracking their average spend, frequency of spend, and customer satisfaction.

The key advantage of this option is that the program would be more targeted—CAA members have automobiles; have already demonstrated greater involvement in automobile issues; and have demonstrated membership loyalty that might be transferable to Coast Tire. Coast Tire would also be able to target particular profiles of CAA members and track the success of promotions aimed at each profile. It could also focus on promotions during shoulder seasons. However, this option would mean giving up margin to CAA members, including current customers who are CAA members—potentially giving discounts to already loyal customers. This campaign would also require using a mail distribution list, which would make the cost of promotional campaigns higher than if the distribution list was e-mail based. However, once they came into a store, e-mail addresses could be collected.

Option 3: Develop a new database and scheduling system.

Coast Tire also wondered about developing an internal information system that would enable it to better maintain customer relationships. The automobile service industry is known for being later adopters of technology, and few of Coast Tire's competitors had customer databases that would track manufacturer-recommended scheduled maintenance. Ideally, a new computer system would keep track of what scheduled maintenance needed to be done for each customer and would automatically e-mail that customer to remind her it was time for a particular maintenance task—such as oil changes or belt replacement. Ron knew that customers didn't want to be inundated with e-mails, but that ones they found helpful would be acceptable. For example, the computer system could remind customers that it was time for their government-mandated Motor Vehicle Inspection. If a customer's auto failed this inspection he would be given a rejection sticker and would have 10 days to complete the work necessary to pass the inspection. If he did not have this work completed he could potentially be fined $200. The system could also track "share of wallet." Coast Tire knew what customers, on average, spend per year on automobile maintenance, and a new system could track expenditures per customer against that average to provide Coast Tire a measure of how much of each customer's business it was likely getting. This would be useful for building sales with customers who do only some of their work at Coast Tire—perhaps thinking that they need to go back to their dealer to maintain the warranty on their newer car purchase. The cost of developing such a system was not much of a barrier; the key challenge was finding the time to get it done, and it would realistically take six months to do it. With the busy fall period coming, Ron didn't know if this was going to be feasible.

Option 4: Introduce a new tire storage service.

Coast Tire also considered developing new services to encourage customers to return periodically. One of these new services might be tire storage. Most of Coast Tire's customers had winter tires for the hard Maritime driving conditions, and many found it annoying to have to store their summer tires during the winter and their winter tires during the summer. They took up a lot of space and were messy to handle. For a nominal fee, Coast Tire could store the set of tires the customer was not using, keep them well maintained, and then change the tires semi-annually. This concept seemed to be working in Quebec, and Ron thought customers would get other work done if they brought their cars in for the tire changes. Ron also thought customers would be more loyal to Coast Tire if it had the customers' tires. They might also be more willing to open e-mail or read postcards from Coast Tire, as it might relate to their stored tires. The only downside to doing this was the cost of renting a storage facility and the cost of taking the tires back and forth. Ron was not sure how much customers would be willing to pay for this service, and whether that price would cover the storage costs.

UNDERSTANDING CUSTOMERS

Compelling new products, clever packaging, and creative advertising surround us, clamouring for our attention—and our money. But consumers don't all respond in the same way to marketing activities. Each consumer is a unique person, with unique reasons for choosing one product over another. As Ron Outerbridge of Coast Tire knows, the first step in building long-term relationships is understanding your customer. Recall that the focus of the marketing concept is to satisfy consumers' wants and needs. These wants and needs can be satisfied only to the extent that marketers understand why and how people buy products. D-Code, for example, is a Canadian research firm that helps Canadian marketers understand 18- to 34-year-old "Nexus" consumers by answering such questions as, What are the attitudes and lifestyles of Nexus consumers, why do they prefer certain products, which ads do they respond to, and how do they purchase products? Uthink, another Canadian marketing research and strategy firm, offers similar services to help marketers understand 13- to 29-year-olds. **Consumer behaviour** is the process individuals or groups go through to select, purchase, and use goods, services, ideas, or experiences. Marketers recognize that consumer behaviour is an ongoing process—it is more than what happens at the moment a consumer hands over money and, in turn, receives a good or service.

consumer behaviour The process individuals or groups go through to select, purchase, and use goods, services, ideas, or experiences to satisfy their needs and desires.

Although it seems as if some purchases are made spontaneously (and we may regret our rashness later), in reality we make most buying decisions only after we have undergone a series of steps—problem recognition, information search, evaluation of alternatives, product choice, and post-purchase evaluation—summarized in Figure 5.1.

Let's look at an example of a consumer purchase—one you yourself probably make on a regular basis: dry cereal. While this may seem like a simple purchase, in reality there are quite a few steps in the process that cereal marketers need to understand. The first decision in the process is where to buy your cereal. If you eat a lot of cereal, you may choose to make a special trip to a warehouse-type retailer, such as Costco, that sells very large boxes of

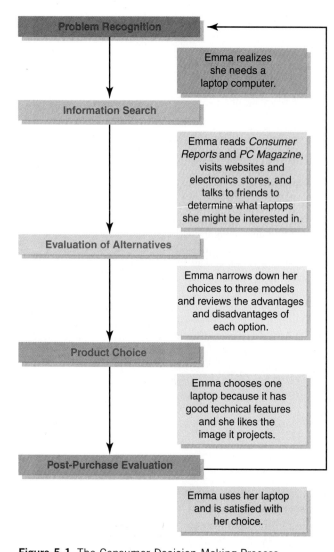

Figure 5.1 The Consumer Decision-Making Process

The consumer decision-making process involves the series of steps summarized here.

involvement The relative importance of perceived consequences of the purchase to a consumer.

perceived risk The belief that use of a product has potentially negative consequences, either financial, physical, or social.

cereal. Of course, if you get a yearning for cereal in the middle of the night, you may dash to the local convenience store. Then there is the decision of the type of cereal. Do you eat only low-fat, high-fibre bran cereals, or do you go for sugar-coated varieties with marshmallows? As you can see, the purchase decision for something as simple as cereal can actually be quite complicated.

Traditionally, researchers have tried to understand how consumers make decisions by assuming that people carefully collect information about competing products, determine which products possess the characteristics or product attributes important to their needs, weigh the pluses and minuses of each alternative, and arrive at a satisfactory decision. But how accurate is this picture of the decision-making process?

Although it does seem that people undergo these steps when making an important purchase, is it realistic to assume that they do this for everything they buy? Researchers now realize that consumers actually possess a set of decision approaches, ranging from painstaking analysis to pure whim, depending on the importance of what is being bought and how much effort the person is willing to put into the decision.[1] Researchers have found it convenient to think in terms of an "effort" continuum, which is anchored on one end by *habitual (or routine) decision making* (such as deciding to purchase a can of pop) and at the other end by *extended problem solving* (such as deciding to purchase a computer). Many decisions fall somewhere in the middle and are characterized by *limited problem solving*, which means that consumers do work to make a decision, but most likely rely on simple rules of thumb instead of learning about and considering all the ins and outs of every product alternative. For most of us, the dry cereal purchase decision described above falls into the limited problem solving category. Some Internet marketers believe that the Internet can reduce the effort needed to make product decisions by offering so many products and services in one place. We will discuss the role of the Internet in consumer decision making in more detail later in this chapter.

Involvement determines the extent of effort a person puts into deciding what to buy. **Involvement** is the importance of the perceived consequences of the purchase to the person. As a rule, we are more involved in the decision-making process for products that we perceive as being important, pleasurable, or risky in some way. **Perceived risk** may be present if the product is expensive, complex, and hard to understand, or if the purchase of the wrong product could result in embarrassment or social rejection. For instance, some people perceive clothing purchases as risky because they feel a wrong choice could lead to negative social consequences. Perceived risk can also be a factor in the buying process for certain products. A study of condom buying among Canadian university students, for example, found that 66 percent of men and 60 percent of women reported being embarrassed when buying condoms and, therefore, do not buy them. As one researcher put it, "Approaching the cashier is the moment of truth. There is also the worry that a 'price check on a 12-pack of Durex condoms' will be announced to the entire store."[2] Marketers will sometimes refer to high- or low-involvement products, but this is misleading. Products are not high or low involvement—decisions are. What is a high-involvement decision for one consumer may be a low-involvement decision for another (Exhibit 5.1). Bill Gates, for example, probably doesn't spend a lot of time thinking about what type of television to buy.

When marketers say that a car is a high-involvement product, they really mean it is a high-involvement decision for most consumers.

When perceived risk is low, as in buying a pack of gum, the consumer feels *low involvement* in the decision-making process—the consumer is not overly concerned about which option he or she chooses because it is not especially important or risky. In low-involvement situations, the consumer's decision is often a response to environmental cues, such as deciding to try a new type of chewing gum because it is prominently displayed at a store checkout counter. Under these circumstances, managers must concentrate on how products are displayed at the time of purchase to influence the decision maker. For example, a chewing gum marketer may decide to spend more money to be sure its gum stands out at a checkout display or to change the colour of the gum wrapper to a bright pink to be sure it gets noticed among the other gums.

For other purchase decisions, such as for a house, car, computer, or interview suit, the consumer is more likely to carefully process all the available information and to have thought about the decision well before buying the item. The consequences of the purchase are important and risky, especially because a bad decision can result in significant financial losses, aggravation, decreased performance, or embarrassment. These types of purchase decisions are *high-involvement* decisions. Products are not inherently high or low involvement, but the level of involvement engaged by a consumer is often associated with the price, importance, and perceived risk of the purchase decision. So for products purchased with a high-involvement decision process,

Exhibit 5.1

Soft drink purchase decisions are low involvement for most consumers. By linking its brand to hockey, Coke® is trying to make it more involving to Canadian consumers.

managers must start to reduce perceived risk by educating the consumer about why their product is the best choice well in advance of the time that the consumer is ready to make a decision. To understand what goes on during each of the steps in the decision-making process, in the next section we'll follow the fortunes of one consumer, a student named Emma, who is in the market for a new notebook computer. This is a high-involvement purchase decision for her because of the cost of the product and because the performance of the computer will have an important impact on her own performance in courses and, perhaps, in future jobs.

problem recognition The process that occurs whenever the consumer sees a significant difference between his or her current state of affairs and some desired or ideal state. This recognition initiates the decision-making process.

Problem Recognition

Problem recognition occurs whenever the consumer sees a significant difference between their current state of affairs and some desired or ideal state. The consumer needs to solve a *problem*, which may be small or large, simple or complex (Exhibit 5.2). Emma has a problem. She needs to have a computer for writing papers, doing research on the Internet, and sending e-mail, but the computers provided on campus are always busy when she needs a computer the most, such as at the end of term. Emma also wants her computer to be portable so that she can use it to take notes in classes and take it to the library while she researches her assignments. Thinking about the future, Emma realizes that, in her job, she will probably have a lot of work to do after hours. Having a notebook computer will allow her to do the work in the comfort of her own apartment.

Exhibit 5.2

Marketers like Pfizer Canada help consumers recognize needs and wants. Launching Viagra with the "Good Morning" campaign got consumers to wonder why this fellow was so happy.

Stage in the Decision Process	Marketing Strategy	Example
Problem Recognition	Encourage consumers to see that existing state does not equal desired state	TV commercials showing the excitement of owning a new car
Information Search	Provide information when and where consumers are likely to search	Targeted advertising on TV programs with high target market viewership
		Sales training that ensures knowledgeable salespeople
		Make new car brochures available in dealer showrooms
		Design exciting, easy to navigate, and informative websites
Evaluation of Alternatives	Understand the criteria consumers use in comparing brands and communicate own brand superiority	Conduct research to identify most important evaluative criteria
		Create advertising that includes reliable data on superiority of a brand (e.g., kilometres per litre, safety, comfort)
Product Choice	Understand choice heuristics used by consumers and provide communication that encourages brand decision	Advertise "Made in Canada" (country of origin)
		Stress long history of the brand (brand loyalty)
Post-Purchase Evaluation	Encourage accurate consumer expectations	Provide honest advertising and sales presentations

Figure 5.2 Marketers' Responses to Decision Process Stages

When they understand the stages of the consumer decision process, marketers can develop strategies to lead consumers to a choice that pleases both the consumer and the marketer.

Do marketing decisions have a role in buyers' problem recognition? Although most problem recognition occurs spontaneously, marketers can develop creative advertising messages that stimulate consumers to recognize that their current state—that old car—just doesn't equal a shiny, new convertible. Figure 5.2 provides examples of marketing activities for problem recognition and the other stages of the consumer decision process.

Information Search

information search The process whereby a consumer searches for appropriate information needed to make a reasonable decision.

Once Emma recognizes her computer problem, she needs adequate information to resolve it. During the **information search** part of the decision-making process, consumers check their memory and survey the environment to identify what options exist to solve the problem. Marketing communication helps consumers in this task, and many advertisements are focused on generating awareness about brands. When Virgin Mobile launched its new Virgin brand cellphone service in Canada, it kicked off its campaign with an innovative publicity stunt to create immediate awareness for its brand. Attached to a wire and dressed as Captain Canada, Richard Branson, the chair and founder of Virgin Group, jumped from a 15-storey media tower in Toronto's Dundas Square, and then proceeded to ride a monster truck over three cars representing his company's wireless competition. For her information search, Emma might rely on ads she has seen for notebook computers, recommendations from friends, and additional research she might do by reading *Consumer Reports* and *PC Magazine*, or by signing onto websites for companies, such as Dell Canada and Apple Canada. She also might visit some electronics stores, like Future Shop, where she can discuss her purchase with salespeople and try out some computers.

Increasingly, consumers are using Internet search engines, portals, or "shopping bots" for information search. Search engines are sites such as Google, AltaVista, and Webcrawler that find information on the web by searching sites for keywords (Exhibit 5.3). Other sites such as Expedia simplify searches because they organize information from a lot of separate websites according to common themes. Consider the purchase of a new car. The car dealer was once the key source of information during the information search stage of a new car purchase. Now, most new car purchasers visit a car dealership only after extensive research on the Internet.

When they understand the stages of the consumer decision process, marketers can develop strategies to lead consumers to a choice that pleases both the consumer and the marketer.

Some portals, such as Yahoo Kids (**http://kids.yahoo.com**), focus on specific customer segments. This unique portal makes it easy for kids to access information relevant to them, such as homework tips, games, and music. The site includes a feature called "Ask Earl," where kids can type in any question, such as "What is plagiarism?" and receive an answer back, written in language that is easy for them to understand. Yahoo Canada recently launched a new site aimed at women aged 24 to 54. The site (**http://lifestyle.yahoo.ca**) includes content from Canadian sources such as *Chatelaine* and *Today's Parent*, as well as U.S. sources such as Martha Stewart and Rachael Ray. The site also includes blogs from personalities like athlete Gabby Reece, plus a question and answer feature.[3]

Robots, also called "shopbots" or "intelligent agents," are software programs used by some websites that find Internet retailers selling a particular product. The programs troll the web for information and then "report" it back to the host site. Some of these sites also provide information on competitors' prices, and may even ask customers to rate the various retailers they have listed to provide recommendations for other consumers on which sellers are good and which are less than desirable. We should note, however, that some sites do not wish to compete on price and don't give bots access. Emma, in her search for a personal computer, could visit **ComputersCanada.com** to quickly search computer prices across Canada. The role of marketers during the information search phase of the decision process is to make sure that information about their brand is available when and where consumers look. Most computer manufacturers make sure information about their newest models is on the web, is advertised frequently in dealer flyers and magazines, and, of course, is available in dealer showrooms.

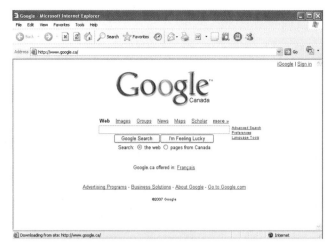

Exhibit 5.3

Google is a popular search engine for web surfers.

Marketing Metrics

Clickstream Analysis

Conventional Internet metrics have relied on counting the number of eyeballs viewing a website. Research shows, however, that conversion rates and average order value are better measures for a website's success. A new method allows companies to conduct funnel-based analysis of where revenue is lost when consumers drop off. One such method is **clickstream analysis**, which helps companies analyze where customers enter their websites and where they exit. The managers at **Playboy.com** are using clickstream data to increase site subscription and convert free visitors into paying members. Playboy.com can now examine exactly where it converts customers on the website and where it loses them by specifically tracking each user's movements around the site. The company receives reports from the clickstream provider about how traffic comes in from other websites, how the site compares with those of competitors, and where conversions are specifically failing.[4]

clickstream analysis A means of measuring a website's success by tracking customers' movement around the company website.

Information search is often an ongoing process, and this stage may be more extensive and intensive for some consumers than others. It ends with the identification of alternatives for consideration, called the **consideration set**.

Evaluation of Alternatives

consideration set   The set of alternative brands the consumer is considering for the decision process.

Once consumers have identified the set of products they are interested in, they narrow down their choices by deciding which of all the possibilities are feasible and evaluating the remaining alternatives. Emma might want a top-of-the-line notebook, like a Dell XPS, but she realizes that her student budget doesn't allow for such a purchase. As she looks around, she decides that the notebooks she likes in her price range are the Apple MacBook, the Compaq Presario, and the Gateway Solo. She has narrowed down her options by considering only affordable notebooks.

evaluative criteria   The dimensions that consumers use to compare competing product alternatives.

heuristics   A mental rule of thumb that leads to a speedy decision by simplifying the process.

Now, Emma has to choose. It's time for her to look more systematically at each of the three possibilities and identify the important characteristics, or **evaluative criteria**, she will use to decide among them. These may be the power of the computer, its weight, the size of the monitor, the battery life, the warranty offered, or even the computer's design or colour options. During her evaluation, Emma learns that the Apple product, the MacBook, seems to her to have a lot of the features she is looking for. Judging from the ad in Exhibit 5.4, it appears that it has all the great features of other notebooks, but with much greater speed.

brand loyalty   A pattern of repeat product purchases, accompanied by an underlying positive attitude toward the brand, which is based on the belief that the brand makes products superior to its competition.

Marketers often play a role in educating consumers about *which* product characteristics should be used as evaluative criteria—usually, they emphasize the dimensions in which their product excels. Where Compaq Presario might focus on price because it is one of the least expensive notebook computers available, Apple is educating consumers about the value of their new operating system.

Product Choice

But how do consumers like Emma actually apply their evaluative criteria? Some consumers use **heuristics** (mental shortcuts) to simplify the evaluation process—taking the advice of someone else, buying the cheapest brand or the most expensive brand (assuming that price reflects quality), or buying the one that "feels" right (has the greatest emotional appeal). Perhaps the most common heuristic is just buying the brand a consumer always buys—either through habit or through brand loyalty. Consumers are brand loyal when they make repeat brand purchases because they believe that brand is superior, have such strong preferences that they will pay more or search harder to find that brand, and feel that it's not worth the effort to consider competing options. The creation of **brand loyalty** is a prized goal for marketers. People form preferences for a favourite brand and then may literally never change their minds in the course of a lifetime, making it extremely difficult for rivals to persuade them to switch. Loyal customers are very valuable—as loyalty increases, consumers will buy at least twice as much as those who are just slightly less attached to the brand, and often three to four times more. The most loyal customers can be worth up to 20 times more than other consumers. Some people take the concept of brand loyalty even further. At a recent lecture, Saatchi & Saatchi Worldwide CEO Kevin Roberts

Exhibit 5.4

One role of marketing communication is to make consumers aware of evaluative criteria.

stressed his belief that the job of marketers is to "create loyalty beyond reason," to move their products and services "from being irreplaceable to irresistible." The success of the iPod illustrates this concept clearly—despite being critically viewed as not being the best MP3 available, the iPod continues to dominate the market.[5]

Many companies are now employing customer relationship management (CRM) strategies to help them organize and manage their relationship with their customers. CRM helps companies target their best customers and form ongoing relationships with them in the hope of increasing loyalty and improving customer satisfaction. CRM will be discussed in more detail in subsequent chapters.

Another heuristic that is often used by consumers is based on country of origin. We assume that a product has certain characteristics if it comes from a certain country. In the car category, many people associate German cars with fine engineering and Swedish cars with safety.

Other consumers put more thought into their purchase decision and have key criteria that absolutely have to be met. Emma, for example, is considering only laptop or notebook computers and is not willing to consider a desktop model. In doing so, she is applying a non-compensatory evaluation strategy—where a consumer is unwilling to make trade-offs on product attributes such as getting a faster processor, more memory, and a larger hard drive for a lower price on a desktop computer. A compensatory strategy is where consumers are willing to make trade-offs to get the best overall deal (value) for their needs. There are different types of compensatory and non-compensatory strategies and many consumers use a mix of these strategies, even within the same decision process. These are summarized in Figure 5.3.

Emma has spent several weeks thinking about the alternatives, and she's finally ready to take the plunge and buy! After agonizing over her choice, she decides that, even though the Gateway and Dell laptops were rated highly by *Consumer Reports*, the Apple MacBook just feels right. It meets all the basic technical criteria and it appeals to her sense of individuality. The MacBook is the lightest of all the options and will easily fit in her backpack. She signs onto the Apple Canada website and buys her notebook computer. A few days later the computer arrives at her door. In the end, Emma used a mix of decision strategies (lexigraphic, conjunctive, and heuristics) to make her purchase decision.

Post-Purchase Evaluation

In the last stage of decision making, the consumer evaluates the quality of the decision made. After mulling over the alternatives and picking one, they evaluate just how good a choice it was. Everyone has experienced **cognitive dissonance** (regret, or buyer's remorse) after making a purchase, and (hopefully) we have all been pleased with something we've bought. Marketers pay particular attention to cognitive dissonance, as they want consumers to have enduring positive attitudes toward the brands they have purchased so they become loyal consumers—reducing the cost of marketing in the future and reducing the likelihood of the consumer switching to another brand. Cognitive dissonance is greatest when decisions are important and there are other viable brands in the consideration set. Through marketing communication strategies that reaffirm consumers in what a good decision they made, marketers try to reduce or minimize cognitive dissonance.

cognitive dissonance The regret or remorse buyers may feel after making a purchase.

The evaluation of the product results in a level of **consumer satisfaction/ dissatisfaction**, which is determined by the overall feelings, or attitude, a person has about a product after purchasing it. In this case, fortunately, Emma's feelings couldn't be better. Her computer is reliable and easy to use, and its light weight means that she can easily carry it to her classes.

consumer satisfaction/dissatisfaction The overall feelings or attitude a person has about a product after purchasing it.

Just how do consumers decide if they are satisfied with their purchases? One answer would be, "That's easy. The product is either wonderful, or it isn't." However, it's a little more complicated than that. When consumers buy a product, they have some *expectations* of product quality. How well a product or service meets or exceeds these expectations determines customer satisfaction. In other words, consumers assess product quality by

	Decision Rule	**Marketing Implications**
Compensatory	Simple Additive: Sum the scores of each brand rating on each attribute, choose the brand with the highest overall score.	Develop brands with strong overall value. Help consumers compare brands to make the overall value choice.
	Weighted Additive: Give weights to each criteria, for each brand multiply the rating and the weight, sum the scores and choose the brand with the highest overall score.	Understand the criteria weights and design products that excel on those criteria. Position your product on the key criteria. Try to change the weights of criteria to make them more or less important in the minds of customers—such as Intel did with the Intel Inside campaign.
Non-Compensatory	Lexicographic: Rank the decision criteria; evaluate the brands on the most important criteria. Choose the brand with the highest rating on the most important criteria. If there is a tie, go on to the next most important criteria until a brand is chosen.	Understand the top three or four most important criteria for your target market and continuously innovate to lead on those criteria. If you are not the leader, try to change consumer attitudes about the importance of the criteria or try to get them to adopt a different evaluative strategy.
	Elimination by Aspects: Rank the decision criteria, and determine minimal acceptable levels for each criterion. Keep in the evoked set brands that meet the minimum level of the most important criteria. Go on to the next most important criteria until there is only one brand in the consideration set and choose that brand.	Understand the most important criteria for your target market and continuously innovate to be close to the leaders on the top criterion. Try to establish a criterion in the minds of consumers where your competitors are not able to compete effectively. Demonstrate that your brand exceeds typical minimum standards on key criteria.
	Conjunctive: Determine minimal acceptable levels for each criterion. Keep in your evoked set brands that meet or exceed the minimal level on all criteria. If there is a tie, add criteria or raise the minimum standards.	Understand the criteria and minimum levels. Continuously innovate to meet minimum levels on all criteria. Innovate to develop features or functions not provided by competitors. Try to establish these features or functions as criteria in the evaluation process.
Heuristics (Illustrative Examples)	Habit: Buy the brand you bought last time.	Make your brand available; develop strong brand recognition; remind consumers that this is their brand.
	Price: Buy the cheapest or most expensive brand.	Innovate to keep a low cost structure and position your brand as the value leader—or position your brand as a premium brand and support the quality inference through marketing communications.
	Affect: Buy the brand that "feels" right.	Develop strong emotional connections to your brand through packaging and marketing communications.
	Recommendation: Buy the brand that someone says is best.	Market to the opinion leaders and market mavens (see page 191). Provide incentives or recognition for referrals.

Figure 5.3 Product Decision Strategies

Consumers use a mix of strategies to simplify the evaluation process of decision making. These strategies are summarized here.

comparing what they have bought to a *performance standard* created by a mixture of information from marketing communications, informal information sources such as friends and family, and their own experience with the product category.

So, even though Emma's new MacBook is not as powerful as some of the other options she considered, she's happy with her purchase because it meets or exceeds her expectations. Emma has completed the consumer decision-making process by recognizing a problem, conducting an information search to resolve it, identifying the feasible alternatives, making a product choice, and then evaluating the quality of her decision.

OTHER DECISION PROCESSES

Emma's computer purchase was an example of a high-involvement, extended problem-solving decision that typically follows the process outlined in Figure 5.1. But marketers know that not all consumer decisions are well researched and thought through. Some people make emotional or affective (feeling-based) decisions like buying a car because it looks good, or buying a new dress because it's cute. For example, Mazda Canada has recently tried to differentiate the company based on emotion—remaking their image from boring high-quality cars to fun, hip, and sporty high-quality cars—with "Zoom-Zoom." Other people make impulse decisions, acting without giving a lot of thought to the decision—grabbing a chocolate bar at a grocery checkout counter or deciding to play a video game after walking past an arcade.

A framework developed by the Foote, Cone, and Belding advertising agency offers a useful way of looking at these different consumer decision processes.[6] The FCB grid (Figure 5.4) identifies thinking (cognition) and feeling (affect) as two primary approaches to consumer decision making, for both high- and low-involvement decisions. The four quadrants of the resulting 2×2 matrix represent four common decision approaches: informative decisions, affective decisions, habitual or responsive decisions, and self-satisfaction or impulse decisions. These approaches differ in the order in which consumers learn about brands (evaluate brands

	Thinking		Feeling	
High Involvement	Informative		Affective	
	Extended Problem Solving	Evaluation–Belief (learn)	Emotional Decision Making	Feeling
	Examples: Cars, Computers, High-End Bikes	Feeling	Examples: Jewellery, Cosmetics, Fashion, Apparel, Motorcycles	Evaluation–Belief
		Action		Action
	Quadrant 1		**Quadrant 2**	
Low Involvement	Habitual		Self-Satisfaction (Reaction)	
	Routine Problem Solving	Evaluation–Belief	Impulse Decisions	Action
		Action		Feeling
	Examples: Food, Household Items, Beverages	Feeling	Examples: Candy, Snacks, Liquor, Cigarettes	Evaluation–Belief
	Quadrant 3		**Quadrant 4**	

Figure 5.4 The FCB Grid

Marketers understand that not all decisions are researched and thought out in the same way. The FCB grid offers a useful way of looking at different decision processes followed by consumers.

and establish beliefs), feel about brands (emotional response or attachment), and act to purchase brands. The extended problem-solving model of Figure 5.1 is represented in Quadrant 1. Decisions in this quadrant are made using rational thinking and extensive evaluation of alternatives using information and data. The purchase of a new car or house would fall into this quadrant for most people. In Quadrant 2, consumers have emotional responses or attachments to brands and then learn enough about them to decide whether or not to buy them. Purchases in this quadrant are often made based on emotion rather than information. For many people the purchase of jewellery or other high-fashion apparel might fall into this quadrant. In Quadrants 3 and 4, consumers act first, then evaluate or interpret (feelings) the outcomes. While the FCB model has been criticized for being simplistic, not accounting for consumer experience, and not accounting well for negative emotions, many marketers find it useful to include in segment profiles because of its strategy implications. Informative decisions (Quadrant 1), for example, are aided by marketers: providing specific and detailed information; providing product demonstrations; and making direct comparisons to alternatives. Other communication strategy implications will be discussed in Chapter 12.

WHAT INFLUENCES CONSUMER DECISIONS?

As well as understanding the mechanics of the consumer decision-making process, marketers try to ascertain what influences in consumers' lives affect this process. There are three main categories: internal, situational, and social influences. In Emma's case, for example, the evaluative criteria she used to compare notebook computers and her feelings about each computer may have been influenced by such internal factors as her desire to be unique, such situational factors as her satisfaction with the information and service provided on the Apple Canada website, and such social influences as her prediction that her friends would be impressed when they saw her taking notes in class on a new notebook computer. Figure 5.5 shows the influences in the decision-making process and emphasizes that all of these factors work together to affect the ultimate choice each person makes. Let's consider how each of these three types of influence works, starting with internal factors.

Internal Influences on Consumer Decisions

perception The process by which people select, organize, and interpret information from the outside world.

People associate the textures of fabrics and other surfaces with product qualities, and some marketers are exploring how touch can be used in packaging to arouse consumer interest. Some new plastic containers for household beauty items incorporate "soft touch" resins that provide a soft, friction-like resistance when held. Focus group members who tested one such package for Clairol's new Daily Defense shampoo described the sensations as "almost sexy" and were actually reluctant to let go of the containers![7] That's a powerful impact for a piece of plastic. Now we will examine how internal factors relating to the way people absorb and interpret information influence the decision-making process.

PERCEPTION **Perception** is the process by which people select, organize, and interpret information from the outside world. We receive information in the form of *sensations*, the immediate response of our sensory receptors—eyes, ears, nose, mouth, and fingers—to such basic stimuli as light, colour, and sound. Our impressions about products often are based on their physical qualities. We try to make sense of the sensations we receive by interpreting them in light of our past experiences. For example, Emma chose the Apple notebook computer

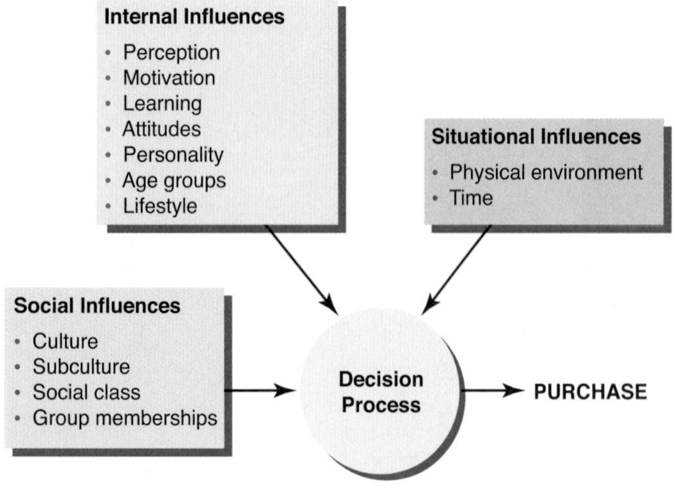

Figure 5.5 Influences on Consumer Decision Making

A number of different factors in consumers' lives influence the consumer decision-making process. Marketers need to understand these influences and which ones are important in the purchase process to make effective marketing decisions.

partly because of its distinctive design, which she associates with style and individuality.

The perception process has important implications for marketers because, as consumers absorb and make sense of the vast quantities of information competing for their attention, it is likely that they won't notice any one marketing message. And, if they do notice it, there's no guarantee that the meaning they give it will be quite the same one the marketer intended. The issues that marketers need to understand during this process include exposure, perceptual selection, and interpretation.

Exposure The stimulus must be within range of people's sensory receptors to be noticed. For example, the lettering on a billboard must be big enough for a passing motorist to read easily, or the message will be lost. Many people believe (falsely) that even messages they can't see will persuade them to buy advertised products. Claims about subliminal advertising involving messages hidden in ice cubes, among other places, have been surfacing since the 1950s. Although many consumers believe in subliminal advertising and are convinced this technique can get them to buy things they do not really want, there is little evidence of its use or even evidence that this technique would work even if it were used. Images that can be perceived are so effective that marketers really do not even consider subliminal effects. The Pepsi ad shown in Exhibit 5.5 is effective because the characters in the ice cubes are clearly visible.

Perceptual Selection Consumers choose to pay attention to some stimuli but not to others. Consumers are more likely to be aware of messages that speak to their current needs. A newspaper ad for a fast-food restaurant that would go unnoticed after lunch may grab your attention if you sneak a glance at the paper during a class that ends at lunchtime.

Interpretation Meaning is assigned to the stimulus. This meaning is influenced by prior associations the person has learned. The Benetton ad shown in Exhibit 5.6 is a great example of how these assumptions alter our interpretations. Although the ad shows two men handcuffed to each other, some people assumed that the black man was cuffed to the white man, and the company was the target of many complaints about racism after the ad appeared.

MOTIVATION **Motivation** is an internal state that drives us to satisfy needs. Once we activate a need, a state of tension exists that *drives* the consumer toward some *goal* that will reduce this tension by eliminating the need. For example, Emma began to experience a gap between her present state—having to rely on the computers on campus—and a desired state—having a computer that allows her to work at home and on campus. The need for a new notebook computer was activated, which motivated Emma to test and learn about different models, to talk with friends about their experiences with notebook computers, and finally to buy a new notebook computer.

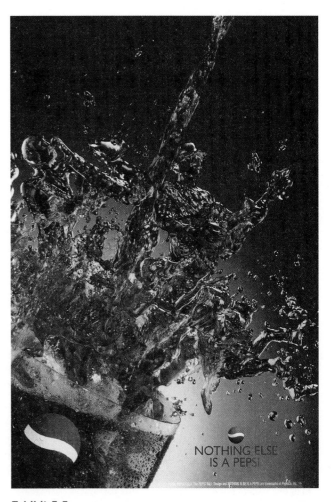

Exhibit 5.5

This Pepsi ad pokes fun at the idea of subliminal advertising—the images in the ice and splashes are not subliminal at all.

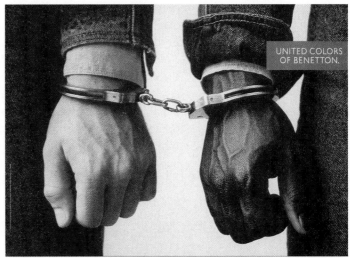

Exhibit 5.6

People's prior assumptions coloured their interpretations of this controversial ad.

motivation An internal state that drives us to satisfy needs by activating goal-oriented behaviour.

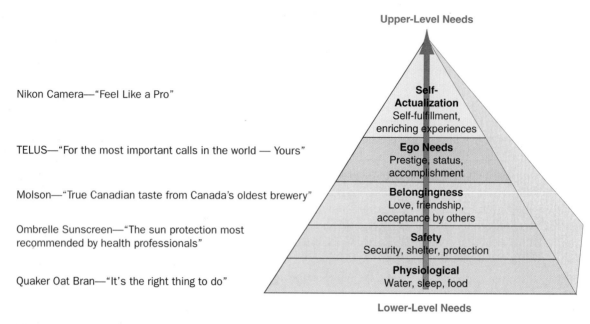

Figure 5.6 Maslow's Hierarchy of Needs and Related Advertising Slogans

Abraham Maslow proposed a hierarchy of needs that categorizes motives. Savvy marketers know they need to understand the level of needs that motivates a consumer to buy a particular product or brand.

hierarchy of needs An approach that categorizes motives according to five levels of importance, the more basic needs being on the bottom of the hierarchy and the higher needs at the top.

Psychologist Abraham Maslow developed an influential approach to motivation.[8] Maslow formulated a **hierarchy of needs**, which categorizes motives according to five levels of importance, the more basic needs being on the bottom of the hierarchy and the higher needs at the top. The hierarchy suggests that before a person can meet needs in a given level, they must first (at least partially) meet the needs in the levels below. As illustrated in Figure 5.6, this approach shows individuals starting at the lowest level with basic needs for food, clothing, and shelter and then progressing to higher levels to satisfy more complex needs, such as the need to be accepted by others or to feel good about themselves. Ultimately, people can reach the highest-level needs and they will be motivated to attain such goals as spiritual fulfillment. As the figure shows, if marketers understand the particular level of needs that is relevant to consumers in their target market, they can tailor their products and messages to point out how these needs can be satisfied. In 1969 Clayton Alderfer proposed a revision to Maslow's need hierarchy based on empirical evidence that the middle levels of Maslow's hierarchy overlap. Alderfer proposed three levels: Existence (concern with basic material existence requirements), Relatedness (desire we have for maintaining interpersonal relationships), and Growth (intrinsic desire for personal development). He also recognized that more than one need may be motivational at the same time and that if higher order needs are not satisfied, people will compensate with satisfying more lower order needs.[9]

learning A relatively permanent change in behaviour caused by acquired information or experience.

behavioural learning theories Theories of learning that focus on how consumer behaviour is changed by external events or stimuli.

classical conditioning Learning that occurs when a stimulus eliciting a response is paired with another stimulus that initially does not elicit a response on its own but will cause a similar response over time because of its association with the first stimulus.

LEARNING **Learning** is a change in behaviour after gaining information or experience. Learning about products can occur deliberately, as when we set out to gather information about different MP3 players before buying one brand. We also learn even when we are not trying. Consumers recognize many brand names and can hum many product jingles, for example, even for products they do not use. Psychologists who study learning have advanced several theories to explain the learning process, and because a major goal for marketers is to "teach" consumers to prefer their products, these perspectives are important. In this section, we'll briefly review the most important perspectives on how people learn.

Behavioural Learning **Behavioural learning theories** assume that learning takes place as the result of connections that form between events perceived by the individual. In one type of behavioural learning, **classical conditioning**, a person perceives two stimuli at about the same time. After a while, the person transfers his or her response from one stimulus to the other. For example, an ad shows a product and a breathtakingly beautiful scene, so that (the marketer hopes) you will transfer the positive feelings you get from looking at the scene to the advertised product. Another common form of behavioural learning is called **operant conditioning**, which occurs when people learn that their actions result in rewards or punishments. This feedback influences how they will respond in similar situations in the future. Just as a rat in a maze learns the route to a piece of cheese, consumers who receive a reward, such as a prize in the bottom of a box of cereal, will be more likely to buy that brand again. The feedback acts as a *reinforcement* for the behaviour. Behaviour modification is similar to operant conditioning, only the reward is offered up front to encourage the desired behaviour, such as the *Time* magazine incentive in Exhibit 5.7.

The learned associations in classical and operant conditioning also have a tendency to transfer to other similar stimuli in a process called **stimulus generalization**. This means that the good or bad feelings associated with a product will "rub off" on other products that resemble it. For example, some marketers create *product line extensions*, in which new products share the name of an established brand so that people's good feelings about the current product will transfer to the new one. Dole, which is associated with fruit, was able to introduce refrigerated juices and juice bars; Sun Maid branched out from raisins to raisin bread.

Cognitive Learning In contrast to behavioural theories of learning, **cognitive learning theory** views people as problem solvers who do more than passively react to associations between stimuli. Supporters of this viewpoint stress the role of creativity and insight during the learning process. One type of cognitive learning theory is *observational learning* (also called vicarious learning), which occurs when people watch the actions of others and note what happens to them as a result. They store these observations in memory and, at some later point, use the information to guide their own behaviour, especially when they admire or identify with these people in some way. Many promotional strategies, such as the ad in Exhibit 5.8, centre on endorsements by movie stars, athletes, and music idols whose fans have observed their successes.

ATTITUDES An **attitude** is a lasting evaluation of a person, object, or issue.[10] Consumers have attitudes toward very product-specific behaviours, such as using Crest toothpaste rather than Colgate, as well as toward more general consumption-related behaviours, such as how often to brush one's teeth.

A person's attitude has three components: affect, cognition, and behaviour. In a marketing context, *affect* is the overall feeling a person has about a product. *Cognition* is the beliefs and knowledge the person has about the product. *Behaviour* is what happens when the person takes action by buying or using the product.

Depending on the nature of the product, one of these three components—feeling, knowing, or doing—will be the dominant influence in creating an attitude toward a product. Affect is usually dominant for expressive products that we use to say something about ourselves (such as perfume), in which the way the product makes us feel determines our attitude toward it. Cognition may be more important for complex products, such as computers, which require us to process technical information. Behaviour often determines attitudes for commonly purchased, low-involvement items, such as chewing gum, for which we often form an attitude based simply on how the product tastes or performs.

PERSONALITY **Personality** is the set of unique psychological characteristics that consistently influences the way a person responds to situations in the environment. One

Exhibit 5.7

Premiums such as this one provide consumers with another reason to choose one brand over the other.

operant conditioning Learning that occurs as the result of rewards or punishments.

stimulus generalization Behaviour caused by a reaction to one stimulus that occurs in the presence of other similar stimuli.

cognitive learning theory A theory of learning that stresses the importance of internal mental processes and that views people as problem solvers, who actively use information from the world around them to master their environment.

attitude A learned predisposition to respond favourably or unfavourably to stimuli based on relatively enduring evaluations of people, objects, and issues.

personality The psychological characteristics that consistently influence the way a person responds to situations in the environment.

Exhibit 5.8

Observational learning means we learn by observing the behaviour or the experiences of others. In this ad, a guitar company wants to encourage observational learning by associating the Alvarez guitar with singer Ani DiFranco.

Exhibit 5.9

Personality and style can influence product choice.

adventure-seeking consumer may always be on the lookout for new experiences and cutting-edge products, while another is happiest in familiar surroundings, using the same brands repeatedly. To appeal to thrill seekers who like to break the rules, Isuzu positioned its Rodeo sport utility vehicle as a car that lets a driver break the rules. Advertising was created to support this idea by showing kids jumping in mud puddles, running with scissors, and colouring out of the lines.[11] For marketers, identifying differences in personality contribute value to crafting marketing strategies. Some specific characteristics, called personality traits, that are relevant to marketing strategies include innovativeness, self-confidence, and sociability.

Innovativeness Innovativeness is the degree to which a person likes to try new things. Cutting-edge products, such as radical new hairstyles and fashions, might appeal to innovative people.

Self-Confidence Self-confidence is the degree to which a person has a positive evaluation of his or her abilities, including the ability to make good product decisions. People who don't have much self-confidence are good candidates for the services of image consultants, who assist in making the right choices.

Sociability Sociability is the degree to which a person enjoys social interaction. A sociable person might, for example, respond to entertainment-related products that claim to bring people together or make parties more fun.[12]

The notion that consumers buy products that are extensions of their personality traits makes sense. Marketers try to create *brand personalities* to appeal to different types of consumers. The ad for Benjamin Moore paints in Exhibit 5.9, for example, positions its brand of paint as a way of expressing personality and style.

How we feel about our own personalities strongly influences our purchasing decisions. We may buy a certain type of clothing or drink a particular brand of beer because we think it makes a statement about who we are. A person's **self-concept** is his or her attitude about the self. The self-concept is composed of a mixture of beliefs about one's abilities, observations of one's own behaviour, and feelings (usually both positive and negative) about one's personal attributes, such as body type or facial features. The extent to which a person's self-concept is positive or negative can influence the products he or she buys.

In developing a new line of snack cakes, Sara Lee found that consumers who had a negative self-concept preferred portioned snack items because they felt they lacked the self-control to regulate how much they ate.[13] On the more positive side, *self-esteem advertising* attempts to stimulate positive feelings about the self.[14] This technique is used by Kellogg's to position Special K cereal as a lifestyle choice. Kellogg's attempts to counter negative self-esteem by making consumers feel good about themselves and feel good about the product, while promoting a healthy lifestyle. This message has recently been adapted to position Special K as part of a low-carb lifestyle (Exhibit 5.10). Dove's "Campaign for Real Beauty" centred around the belief that beauty could be reflected in different shapes, sizes, and ages. The brand's mission statement is "to make more women feel beautiful every day, by widening today's stereotypical view of beauty and inspiring women to take great care of themselves." The campaign was very successful and changed the way women defined beauty.

AGE GROUPS As we discussed in Chapter 3, a person's age is an important determinant of the product categories he or she wants. Many of us feel we have more in common with those of our own age because we share a common set of experiences and memories about cultural events, whether these involve World War II or Edgefest. Indeed, marketers of products from cookies to cars are banking on *nostalgia* to draw in customers, as people are attracted to products and services that remind them of past experiences. Winnipeg-based K-Tel International has successfully introduced several products that appeal to consumer nostalgia. Its online music store offers 1970s music classics from K.C. and the Sunshine Band and ABBA. Because of numerous calls from nostalgic consumers, the company also recently re-introduced one of its most successful products from the 1970s: the Patty Stacker, a plastic tube that helps consumers make perfect hamburger patties.[15] Many marketing strategies appeal to a specific age group, such as children, Nexus consumers, the middle-aged, or the elderly. As we age, our needs change. The young adult, who spends a lot of time in bars, clothing stores, or perhaps backpacking across Europe, grows into the newlywed, who focuses on setting up house—and perhaps anticipates the time when a baby's diapers and toys will fill it up. Canadian demographer David Foot has a series of books that look at the marketing and business implications of past and future demographic changes in North America—look for the most recent one in your school's library (Exhibit 5.11).

Exhibit 5.10

Promotion of healthy living and lifestyles is one way Kellogg's links positive consumer attitudes about themselves with positive attitudes toward the Special K brand.

Young people are among the most enthusiastic users of the Internet, and Canadians are among the highest Internet users in the world. According to one study, 37.4 percent of teens are spending at least three hours online daily outside of school settings. Additionally, 40 percent of teens say they're also text messaging or talking on their mobile phones while online.[16] For many teenagers, this activity has replaced "old-fashioned fun" such as watching the tube or hanging out at the mall. Age is a key factor in the amount of time that teens spend online. A recent study by the Solutions Research Group reports that although tweens (kids ages 7 to 12) are spending 14 percent of their media time on the Internet, teens aged 12 to 19 spend 25 percent of their media time on the Internet.[17]

North American teens spend over $1 billion online each year, so many firms are working hard to develop websites to capture their interest. What do teens do online? Approximately three out of four do research and nearly two out of three use it for e-mail, while far fewer use the Internet for finding or buying products. The Internet is now seen by teens as the top source of information on music artists and bands. For marketers, this means that the Internet may be a great way to get information about their goods and services to teens but not so good for sales. Etailers are expecting teens to buy more online as they get older and have more discretionary income.

And so the process goes, until a person reaches old age, at which time his or her priorities may shift from saving for the kids' education to buying a retirement home. Therefore, our purchase preferences depend on our current position in the **family life cycle**—the life stages people typically pass through as they grow older. Marketers who understand the

self-concept An individual's self-image that is composed of a mixture of beliefs, observations, and feelings about personal attributes.

family life cycle A means of characterizing consumers based on the different family stages they pass through as they grow older.

The #1 National Bestseller

BOOM BUST & ECHO

PROFITING FROM THE DEMOGRAPHIC SHIFT IN THE 21st CENTURY

David K. Foot
with Daniel Stoffman

Exhibit 5.11

The popular series of books inspired by *Boom, Bust, and Echo* examines the marketing and business implications of demographic changes.

family life cycle can anticipate product needs. Campbell's soup, for example, understands that parents of tweens are very busy taking their kids to soccer, ballet, swimming, skating, and other lessons, often while working full time. Campbell's recently launched a new product aimed at mothers on the go. It is important to note that dramatic cultural changes affecting people's living arrangements have forced marketers to change their concept of the traditional family life cycle. This updated view takes into account single-parent families, childless couples, and homosexual relationships and considers the unique needs of each living situation when developing new products and communicating with these consumers.

PSYCHOGRAPHICS As discussed in Chapter 3, psychographics describe the activities, attitudes, interests, opinions, and lifestyles of consumers, and these can have a great bearing on purchase decisions. A **lifestyle** is a pattern of tastes as expressed in a person's preferences for activities such as sports, interests such as music, and opinions on politics and religion. *Lifestyle marketing* is a strategy that recognizes that people can be grouped into common market segments based on similarities in lifestyle preferences.[18] Consumers often choose products, services, and activities that are associated with a certain lifestyle. As the D-Code researchers found out, there are some unique lifestyles that characterize Nexus consumers and lead to product preferences. Beer and car marketers often use lifestyle advertising to show consumers how particular brands fit with the way you live (or might like to live). Unilever Canada is now promoting its Becel margarine brand as part of a healthy lifestyle. Television, print, and in-store advertising, sales promotions, mini-magazines, and a healthy-living website all focus on how Canadian consumers can improve their health.

Situational Influences on Consumer Decisions

lifestyle The pattern of living that determines how people choose to spend their time, money, and energy that reflects their values, tastes, and preferences.

We've seen that such internal factors as how people perceive marketing messages, their motivation to acquire products, and their unique personalities influence the decisions they will make. In addition, when and where consumers shop influences their purchase choices. Important cues include people's physical surroundings, as well as the number and type of other consumers present in that situation. Dimensions of the physical environment, such as decor, smells, the "feel" of natural fabrics like wool versus synthetic ones like polyester, and even temperature, can significantly influence consumption. One study found that pumping certain odours into a casino actually increased the amount of money patrons fed into slot machines.[19]

THE PHYSICAL ENVIRONMENT It's no secret that people's moods and behaviours are strongly influenced by their physical surroundings. Despite all their efforts to pre-sell consumers through advertising, marketers know that the store environment influences many purchases. For example, consumers decide on about two out of every three supermarket product purchases in the aisles. Therefore, the messages they receive at the time and their feelings about being in the store are important influences on their decisions.[20] Two dimensions, *arousal* and *pleasure*, determine if a shopper will react positively or negatively to a store environment. In other words, the person's surroundings can be either dull or exciting (arousing), and either pleasant or not. Just because the environment is arousing doesn't

Exhibit 5.12

The Rainforest Cafe is a themed environment that integrates shopping and eating.

necessarily mean it will be pleasant—we've all been in crowded, hot stores that are anything but. Maintaining an upbeat feeling in a pleasant context is one factor behind the success of theme parks such as Walt Disney World, which try to provide consistent doses of carefully calculated stimulation to patrons.[21]

The importance of these surroundings explains why many retailers are combining two favourite consumer activities, shopping and eating, into elaborate *themed environments*. Eating out is an important form of out-of-home entertainment for many consumers, and innovative firms are scrambling to offer customers a chance to eat, buy, and be entertained all at once. The West Edmonton Mall, the largest shopping and entertainment complex in the world, provides its customers with a themed environment including over 800 stores, 110 restaurants, 26 movie theatres, a casino, and a large indoor amusement park. A lot of the appeal of these themed environments is that there are plenty of interesting things to look at while eating a meal or shopping. In addition to visual stimuli, other sensory cues can influence consumers—one reason why the Rainforest Cafes in Vancouver and Toronto offer simulated thunder and lightning storms in addition to rainforest scenery in their restaurants (Exhibit 5.12). Research supports the assertion that sounds and music can affect eating behaviour—one study found that diners who listened to loud, fast music ate more and faster than those who listened to classical music.[22]

Indeed, a growing recognition of the important role that is played by a store or restaurant's audio environment has created a new market niche; some companies are selling musical collections tailored to different activities. These include RCA Victor's "Classical Music for Home Improvements" and Sony Classics' "Cyber Classics," which are billed as music specifically for computer hackers to listen to while programming. Sony's "Extreme Classics," packaged just for bungee jumpers, is claimed to be the "loudest and most dangerous music ever written."[23]

Retail brands must differentiate themselves based on the "experience" they provide for shoppers. For consumers, the in-store experience (the sights, sounds, and smells) must match the expectations they have for the brand. Best Buy, for example, approaches its in-store experience as a "toy store for adults." Customers have plenty of opportunities to try new gadgets and to "play" with the merchandise.[24]

In-store displays are a commonly used device to attract attention in the store environment. Although most displays consist of simple racks that dispense the product or related coupons, some include elaborate performances and scenery.[25] For example:

- Sunlight Detergent: A plastic mud puddle on the floor of the aisle next to the Sunlight product, with the message "go ahead, get dirty." Consumers stop to look at and avoid stepping in what looks like brown liquid and are directed to the Sunlight product display.

- Quebec Frozen Food Association: A cardboard display showing a man peering around the corner plays the following message when a consumer is in front of it: "Psst! Yes, you. You've got to taste our frozen foods. They're so good. They're so fresh. And they're really practical."[26]

- Timex: A still-ticking watch sits in the bottom of a filled aquarium.

- Kellogg's Corn Flakes: A button with a picture of Cornelius the Rooster is placed within the reach of children near the Corn Flakes. When a child presses the button, they hear the rooster cock-a-doodle-do.

Advertisers also are being more aggressive about hitting consumers with their messages, wherever they may be. *Place-based media* is a growing specialized medium that targets consumers in airports, doctors' offices, campuses, or health clubs. Montreal-based Zoom Media targets the 18 to 34 age group with washroom ads, including ones that "speak" a taped message when someone stands in front of the ad.[27]

TIME Another important situational factor is how much time one has to make a decision. Time is one of consumers' most limited resources. We talk about "making time" or "spending time," and we are frequently reminded that "time is money." Many consumers believe they are more pressed for time than ever before.[28] This sense of time poverty makes consumers responsive to marketing innovations that allow them to save time, including such services as one-hour photo processing, bagged salads and other prepared foods in supermarkets, and ordering products on the Internet.[29] CDPlus is a Canadian company that sells music over the Internet. The company has been successful because consumers can log on to the CDPlus webpage, browse through thousands of titles, listen to selections from many of them, and order and pay for them—all without setting foot inside a store. This saves the customer time and the "store" is always open. Emma, our decision maker buying a notebook computer, appreciated the fact that she was able to save time by searching the Internet for product information and buying her computer online.

Social Influences on Consumer Decisions

Our discussion of consumers so far has focused on factors that influence us as individuals, such as the way we learn about products. Although we are all individuals, we are also members of many groups that, whether we realize it or not, influence our buying decisions. Families, friends, and classmates often influence our decisions, as do larger groups with which we identify, such as ethnic groups and political parties. Now let's consider how social influences such as culture, social class, and influential friends and acquaintances affect the consumer decision-making process.

culture The values, beliefs, customs, and tastes that a group of people value.

CULTURE Culture is a society's personality. It is the values, beliefs, customs, and tastes, as well as the products and services produced or valued by a group of people. Cultural values are deeply held beliefs about right and wrong ways to live.[30] Canadian values include freedom and autonomy, mixed with a strong sense of community that is expressed through social institutions, such as our medical system.[31] Canadians also value education, and the bilingual and multicultural nature of Canada has made Canadians respectful of people's differences.

A consumer's culture influences his or her buying decisions, and a renewed sense of nationalism has led many marketers to recognize the value of identifying their products specifically with Canada and Canadian cultural symbols.[32] For example, when Zellers introduced Martha Stewart products in Canada for the first time, ads showed Martha with a Mountie saying, "I think I'm going to like Canada." Post used a Canadian flag with a Shreddie in the middle instead of a maple leaf when the company introduced Maple Crunch Shreddies, and Molson used a moose in its ads to introduce Miller Lite beer to the Canadian market.[33] Another Molson product, Canadian, not only builds on national pride with its brand name, but also has consistently been promoted with culturally based, patriotic images and ads. Molson recently capitalized on the "Canadian" name by launching the True Taste of Canada Day campaign. Leading up to the Canada Day holiday, Canadian cellphone users were encouraged to be part of the biggest group of "cheers" in Canadian history by texting the word "Canada" to a specified number before July 1 and by texting "Cheers" on Canada Day. On the **molsoncanadian.ca** site, viewers could find information on Canada Day and "Official Beer of Canada Day" merchandise[34] (Exhibit 5.13). American retail giant Wal-Mart uses real Canadians in its Canadian ads. The company has taken this strategy one step further in recent years and reached out to ethnic Canadians by featuring members of various ethnic communities speaking in their native languages about their experiences shopping at Wal-Mart.[35] The ad for Canoe.ca in Exhibit 5.14 also tries to appeal to the Canadian identity.

As the Canoe.ca ad shows, identifying and understanding differences between Canadian and American consumers is often an important issue for Canadian marketers, especially those working in U.S.-owned companies. U.S. management may favour using a U.S. marketing strategy in Canada, assuming that cultural differences are small and that Canadian consumers will respond the same way that American consumers do. In many ways, Canadian and American consumers are similar. However, as Lever Pond's found out in marketing its Degree deodorant product, Canadian consumers can sometimes be quite different from their U.S. counterparts—its successful, humorous U.S. advertising campaign was not

Exhibit 5.13

Molson Canadian links its brand to Canadian culture.

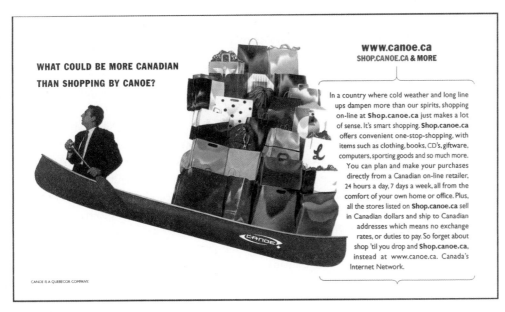

Exhibit 5.14

The use of cultural symbols can be an effective way to connect with consumers.

seen as funny by Canadian consumers and had to be adapted to a more Canadian style of humour—self-deprecating and low-key. The "Stress" campaign that eventually ran in Canada showed stressful situations and a meter on the screen registering the stress levels. One ad showed a man in a bar being approached by a number of people who ask, "Remember me?": When a pregnant woman asks the question, the stress meter gives a maximum reading.[36]

Having spent considerable time in both cultures, author Elliott Ettenberg observes that Canadians are fort people and Americans are homesteaders. The Hudson's Bay Company helped settle Canada and the country was populated by people who wanted the security and safety of living in a fort. The British North America Act promised Canadians laws for peace, order, and good government—the essentials for a fort society to grow. Canadians strive to fit in, and prize collaboration, consensus, and compromise—also important virtues in a fort society. Ettenberg suggests that this has resulted in Canadian management being more fearful of change and being more controlling of expenditures. In contrast, entrepreneurial homesteaders settled the United States—exploring, staking a claim to land, building a home, defending it by force, and then inviting friends and relatives to build nearby. The American constitution promises life, liberty, and the pursuit of happiness—the essentials for an entrepreneurial homesteader to succeed. Americans live to stand out and value leadership, insight, and action, resulting in management styles that are aggressive, focused on competitive advantage, and where quick decisions are made with little collaboration, committing full resources to experimental projects. You may not agree with Ettenberg, but it is one perspective that suggests why Canadian and American cultures differ in perspectives that could have implications for consumer decision making.[37]

Many American multinational companies operating in Canada have chosen to create separate Canadian websites despite the fact that the Internet is a global medium. The reasons why companies such as Microsoft, Nabisco, Kellogg's, Kraft, and Pepsi-Cola have Canadian websites include a need to serve consumers in both English and French; the existence of different products or models (as in the case of the Ford Motor Company); and the desire to cater to the unique needs of Canadian consumers. The manager of Microsoft's Canadian website argues that "to properly service this environment, we feel it necessary to have a website representative of Canada's uniqueness."[38]

Canadian marketers also need to understand differences in culture between French Canadians and English Canadians and how these differences should impact marketing strategies. For instance, Bell Mobility found out that there were differences between French and English consumers with respect to their cellphone behaviour. English Canadians liked certain practical aspects of the cellphones while French Canadian consumers were much more interested in being able to use the phones in minor emergency situations. Bell had originally used the same campaign in both French and English Canada, with the only difference being language. But after the English campaign did poorly in Quebec, it hired a Quebec ad agency to do a uniquely French ad, and consumers responded well to it.[39] Similarly, Wampole Canada launched maple-flavoured vitamin C tablets in Quebec only. The company has found that Quebec consumers prefer sweeter products and are more willing to try something new.[40] When Krispy Kreme entered the Quebec market it consulted with the provincial language office to ensure that it used the correct term—*beignet* (doughnut) instead of the less formal *beigne* (donut)—to be consistent with their English use of the term *doughnut*.[41] General Motors recently discovered the importance of understanding the French Canadian culture when it learned from Quebec focus group participants that the name "Lacrosse," which it was considering for the Canadian version of a Buick sedan, was slang among Quebec youth for masturbation.[42]

SUBCULTURES A **subculture** is a group, coexisting with other groups in a larger culture, whose members share a distinctive set of beliefs or characteristics. Each of us belongs to many subcultures, including religious groups, ethnic groups, and regional groups, as well as those that form around media creations such as Trekkies (fans of *Star Trek*).

subculture A group within a society whose members share a distinctive set of beliefs, characteristics, or common experiences.

For Canadian marketers, some of the most important subcultures to consider are racial and ethnic groups, because Canada is such a diverse society. Many Canadian consumers identify strongly with their heritage and are influenced by products that appeal to this aspect of their identities. Additionally, the actual needs and wants of consumers in different subcultures may be very different. For example, research has found that 87 percent of Chinese Canadian homes have an automobile, compared to 72 percent of other Canadians. Seventy-one percent of Chinese Canadians prefer to buy new cars over used, and 81 percent pay with cash when purchasing a car.[43] These are some of the reasons why automakers, such as Ford Canada, have recognized the importance of the Chinese Canadian market. Several Canadian firms are now practising **multicultural marketing** by successfully targeting consumers in several subcultures. Nearly 3 out of 10 Canadians are of neither French nor British descent. The Chinese community represents the largest visible minority, but the South Asian and Korean communities are both growing quickly and capturing the attention of marketers due to their size.[44]

For example, Burger King Canada has successfully targeted marketing efforts to Italian Canadians and Chinese Canadian consumers.[45] TELUS is targeting the Indian community in Canada (more than 900 000 people) by developing ads in "Hinglish," a colloquial mix of Hindi and English (Exhibit 5.15). The ads celebrate key religious festivals and use creative concepts that straddle the Indian and Canadian cultures (commonly observed behaviour within the targeted audience of people under 35).[46]

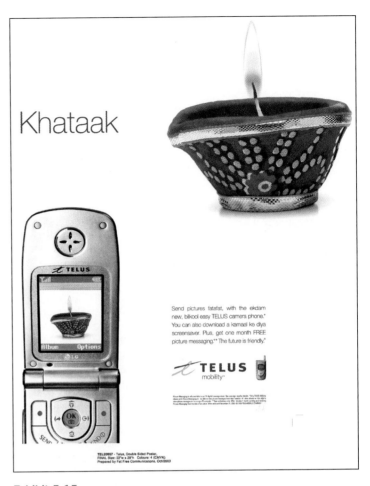

Exhibit 5.15

TELUS developed ads such as this one to appeal to the multicultural nature of its customers.

multicultural marketing The practice of recognizing and targeting the distinctive needs and wants of one or more ethnic subcultures.

As briefly described in Chapter 3, marketers are only just beginning to recognize that men and women have different needs, beliefs, values, and approaches to purchase decisions. Female crash-test dummies, for example, only became standard in 2002 and life jackets designed for female physiology only became mass-produced in 2001. A study by the Television Bureau of Canada recently found that 70 percent of advertisements directed at women are virtually ignored, yet more women than men said advertising was important to them.

Women make 80 percent of all consumer goods decisions, and according to research, the female economy makes up more than 40 percent of GDP. Yet over 50 percent of women don't think that manufacturers understand them and 68 percent of women can't identify with the women used in advertising at all.[47] The reason why women feel so misunderstood is that in many cases, marketers fail to recognize that men and women are very different in their needs, wants, and ultimately, their behaviour. Women are driven by the desire to create a harmonious, safe, and happy environment in which they and their dependants can thrive. They care about the aesthetics of their environment and are driven to create harmony and communities. Men, by contrast, survive through self-interest, hierarchy, power, and competition. Given these fundamental differences, messages that resonate with men often have no impact on women, and sometimes even have a negative effect. Brands that understand what drives females, such as Dove, develop messages that resonate with female consumers.

When men complain about organizations, it is about inferior products or uninformed salespeople. When women complain, it is about bad treatment because of gender—being

Ethical Decisions in Marketing

Marketers play an important role in helping consumers understand and act on their wants, but they can also influence expectations and demonstrate attitudes and beliefs that not only reflect but also help shape cultures and subcultures. Media and advertising, in particular, have been at the heart of arguments and discussions concerning the cause and influencers of eating disorders. Female models such as Kate Moss look emaciated and are underweight while male models are overly muscular and hairless (Exhibit 5.16). A recent American Psychological Association study into the sexualization of girls in television, music videos, and ads sounds alarm bells over how sexy images are damaging the mental and physical health of women. A culture bombarding young girls and women with images of over-sexed females is leading them to develop eating disorders, depression, and low self-esteem, the report warns.[51] In addition, we have recently seen an alarming trend of male teenagers struggling with adolescent identity issues turning to anabolic steroids in an effort to live up to the unreasonable standards set by the media.[52] Can marketers and advertising campaigns be blamed for eating disorders and falsified body perceptions? Should marketers have greater responsibility for promoting a positive body image? Why or why not?

Exhibit 5.16

Calvin Klein, like many other fashion and clothing companies, uses provocative imagery to promote its products. Many people believe that media and advertising have been major influences on cultural and subcultural beliefs.

ignored or talked down to. Joanne Thomas Yaccato, author of *The 80% Minority: Reaching the Real World of Women Consumers*, suggests that corporate Canada does not understand the multi-dimensional nature of women's lives and has a disconnect around the importance corporate soul plays in their decision-making process. In the late 1990s, RBC Financial Group embarked on creating a "gender intelligent sales force," taking four years to train 1500 account managers on how to meet the financial needs of women. RBC saw a 10 percent increase in marketing share and a 29 percent increase in customer satisfaction with female entrepreneur clients.[48] International insurance company AXA developed a highly successful women-focused insurance brand in Quebec called Assurelle that included car insurance with free roadside assistance 24/7 anywhere in Canada or the United States—a program launched in a campaign with the platform "We treat you right."[49] Marketers are also focusing more on men. New men's magazines such as *Toro*, *Razor*, *Rev*, *Menz*, and *Umm* provide male-oriented content and enable marketers to specifically target men.[50]

In a country as large as Canada, regional subcultures also exist and influence consumer behaviour. For Tim Hortons, regional differences can be important in deciding what products to offer in its restaurants. Sugar pies, baked beans, and toast are available only in Quebec; Ontarians love fritters; and in some communities in British Columbia, chocolate croissants are a popular menu item.[53]

GREEN MARKETING Once the domain of hardcore environmentalists, concern for our environment has become mainstream and is shaping consumer buying behaviour significantly. A recent poll by *Marketing Magazine* and Ipsos Reid shows that over 70 percent of Canadians are buying more environmentally friendly products than they did a year ago, almost 60 percent of consumers are willing to pay *more* for environ-

social class The overall rank or social standing of groups of people within a society according to the value assigned to such factors as family background, education, occupation, and income.

status symbols Products that consumers purchase to signal membership in a desirable social class.

mentally friendly products, and over 60 percent of consumers say that information about a company's environmental behaviour affects their purchase decision significantly.[54] This has forced marketers to scramble to develop "green marketing plans" in an effort to not be left out in the cold by environmentally concerned consumers. Wal-Mart is putting every part of its business under the "green microscope"—including the products it sells, the suppliers it deals with, and the design and operation of its stores.[55] Meanwhile, Loblaws recently introduced "Canada's greenest shopping bag," a reusable bag made with 85 percent post-consumer recycled plastic, mostly from water bottles. The bags are available in-store for 99 cents (which consumers get back via 10-cent discounts each time they use the bags) and can

SPOTLIGHT ON REAL PEOPLE   Universityparty.ca

As a recent university graduate, Daniel Warner knew two things—that university students needed to connect with each other and party and that he could find a way to make money by tapping into this need. Warner was recently named one of two Ontario Student Entrepreneur Competition Champions by the national charitable organization Advancing Canadian Entrepreneurship (ACE).

Always highly involved in campus activities, Daniel saw great potential in the market to simultaneously connect businesses to students and students to each other. With the incredibly popular website **UniversityParty.ca**, Daniel's company has created an interactive online community of Canadian students from across the country. Billing itself as "the No. 1 Party Site in Canada," UniversityParty.ca predominantly boasts photos of partying students across Ontario.

The website also promotes events at clubs, provides information on selected club DJs, and includes a daily top five iTunes list. One of the major features is the identification of the "Hottest" male and female members, as well as "Best Partier," as selected by website visitors. As well, online forums allow members to chat live. The site's motto is, "We remember what happened last night, so you don't have to."

Warner has built a database of 50 000-plus students who signed up to receive e-mail promotions and other info from UniversityParty.ca. In addition, the site has attracted some mainstream advertisers such as Rogers and Trojan—looking to tap into this lucrative market.

Source: Shauna Rempel, "Good time for the planner," *Toronto Star*, 1 May 2007.

1. Describe how the UniversityParty.ca concept might help subcultures develop.
2. What decision-making process might consumers use in deciding whether to be a member of the UniversityParty.ca online community? What internal and social influences might influence this decision?
3. What other communities do you think could benefit from having an online forum for interaction?

---

be brought back to Loblaws stores to be recycled again when they wear out.[56] Marketers are convinced that consumer concern for the environment is not a passing fad, but here to stay. As seen in Exhibit 5.17, companies like Bosch Home Appliances are focusing on the environmentally friendly nature of their products and their company to attract consumers.

SOCIAL CLASS Social class is the overall rank of people in a society. People within the same social class work in similar occupations, have similar income levels, and usually share common tastes in clothing, decorating styles, and leisure activities. These people also share many political and religious beliefs, as well as ideas about valued activities and goals.[57]

Many products and stores are designed to appeal to people in a specific social class.[58] Working-class consumers tend to evaluate products in more utilitarian terms, such as sturdiness or comfort, rather than in style or fashionability. They are less likely to experiment with new products or styles, such as modern furniture or coloured appliances, because they tend to prefer predictability to novelty.[59]

Luxury goods often serve as **status symbols**, visible markers that provide a way for people to flaunt their membership in higher social classes (or at least to make others believe they belong). Although ostentatious products fell out of favour in the 1990s, we are witnessing a resurgence of consumer interest in luxury goods. Companies such as Hermès International, LVMH Moët Hennessy-Louis Vuitton, and Baccarat are enjoying

Saving the planet.
One drop at a time.

BOSCH
Invented for life

Exhibit 5.17

Bosch Home Appliances, like many companies, uses "green marketing" to differentiate itself from the competition.

Exhibit 5.18

Louis Vuitton products are status symbols among affluent young women.

sales gains of 13 to 16 percent, as affluent consumers are once again indulging their desires for the finer things in life (Exhibit 5.18).[60]

GROUP BEHAVIOUR

Anyone who has ever "gone along with the crowd" knows that people act differently in groups than they do on their own. There are several reasons for this. With more people in a group, it becomes less likely that any one member will be singled out for attention, and normal restraints on behaviour may be reduced. Decisions made by groups differ from those made by each individual. In many cases, group members show a greater willingness to consider riskier alternatives following group discussion than they would if each member made his or her own decision with no discussion.[61]

Even shopping behaviour changes when people do it in groups. For example, people who shop with at least one other person tend to make more unplanned purchases, buy more, and cover more areas of a store than those who go alone.[62] Group members may be convinced to buy something to gain the approval of the others, or they may simply be exposed to more products and stores by pooling information with the group. For these reasons, retailers are well advised to encourage group-shopping activities.

Most of us enjoy belonging to groups, and we may even derive comfort from knowing what others are thinking or doing as we try to make up our own minds. Group membership has entered cyberspace, as netizens around the world are rapidly forming virtual communities.[63] Communities such as Facebook, Tripod, and Geocities allow people to chat about their mutual interests, help one another with inquiries and suggestions, gain purchasing power, and, perhaps most importantly from a marketer's perspective, get suggestions for new products and services. We will delve further into the impact of technology on consumer behaviour later in the chapter.

Reference Groups

reference group An actual or imaginary individual or group that has a significant effect on an individual's evaluations, aspirations, or behaviour.

A **reference group** is a set of people a consumer wants to please or imitate. Unlike a larger culture, the "group" can be composed of one person, such as your spouse, or someone you've never met, such as a rock singer like Sarah McLachlan. The group can be small, such as your immediate family, or it could be a large organization, such as Greenpeace. The idea that reference groups can have a strong influence on consumer purchase decisions was the motivation behind a recent promotion by Coors. The beer company partnered with *Maxim* magazine (a magazine that targets males 19 to 24 years old) and invited the magazine's "Maxim Girls" to a Coors event. Marketers at Coors were capitalizing on their belief that *Maxim* and the "Maxim Girls" were a reference group for consumers of Coors beer.

conformity A change in beliefs or actions as a reaction to real or imagined group pressure.

Consumers often change their behaviour to gain acceptance into a particular reference group. **Conformity** is at work when a person changes as a reaction to real or imagined group pressure. For example, someone preparing to go out to a club with a new group of friends may choose to wear clothing similar to what they think the others will be wearing to be sure of acceptance.

Home shopping parties, epitomized by the Tupperware party, capitalize on group pressures to boost sales.[64] A company representative makes a sales presentation to a group of people, who have gathered in the home of a friend or acquaintance. Participants model the behaviour of others who can provide them with information about how to use certain products, especially since the home party is likely to be attended by a relatively homogeneous group (for example, neighbours or co-workers). Pressures to conform may be particularly intense and may escalate as more and more group members "cave in" (a process sometimes termed the *bandwagon effect*). Canadian companies such as The Pampered Chef and Weekenders have no doubt benefited from the bandwagon effect by using home shopping parties to distribute their products.

Some of the strongest pressures to conform come from our **sex roles**: society's expectations of the appropriate attitudes, behaviours, and appearance for men and women. These assumptions about the proper roles of women and men, flattering or not, are deeply ingrained in marketing communications.[65] Many products take on masculine or feminine attributes, and consumers often associate them with one sex or the other.[66] For example, for many years, hardware stores were seen as "masculine," so much so that Home Hardware, based in St. Jacobs, Ontario, had the advertising slogan, "Home of the Handyman." But at the end of the 1990s, Home Hardware replaced its slogan of 25 years when it was realized that the company had equal numbers of male and female customers in their stores. Their new slogan, "Help is close to home," avoided any sex role references.[67]

sex roles Society's expectations about the appropriate attitudes, behaviours, and appearance for men and women.

Opinion Leaders

Some individuals are particularly likely to influence others' product decisions. An **opinion leader** is a person who influences others' attitudes or behaviours.[68] Opinion leaders are valuable information sources, because they are usually knowledgeable about a product category and, unlike commercial endorsers who are paid to represent the interests of just one company, they have no "axe to grind." In addition, opinion leaders often are among the first to buy new products, so they absorb much of the risk. This experience reduces uncertainty for others who are not as courageous. And, although company-sponsored communications tend to focus exclusively on the positive aspects of a product, this hands-on experience makes opinion leaders more likely to impart *both* positive and negative information about product performance.

opinion leader A person who is frequently able to influence others' attitudes or behaviours by virtue of his or her active interest and expertise in one or more product categories.

Opinion leaders can create "buzz" for a brand by talking it up to others. Research shows that the most influential consumers, called "conversation catalysts," generate more than one-third of brand conversations, even though they represent only 15 percent of the population.[69]

Think about the people you know on campus who may be opinion leaders when it comes to setting trends in fashion or being the first to get a new CD. One study identified a group of male students who were opinion leaders for fashion products on campus. These men shared some important characteristics:[70]

- They were socially active.
- They appeared self-conscious and narcissistic.
- They were involved in rock culture.
- They were heavy readers of magazines, including *Playboy* and *Sports Illustrated*.
- They were likely to own more clothing in a broader range of styles than other students.

Related to the concept of opinion leaders are market mavens—people who are very knowledgeable about a product category such as cars, computers, or fashion and are sought by others for advice—they have been referred to as "super recommenders."[71] They may not have direct experience with a particular brand, but provide general buying advice to those who ask them. In his book *The Tipping Point: Little Things Can Make a Big Difference*, Malcolm Gladwell talks about how some people have the power to initiate change or "social epidemics." The focus on the environment or the "green" movement is an example of a social epidemic. Gladwell discusses three types of people who initiate social epidemics: "mavens," "connectors," and "salesmen." Market mavens are people who are especially involved with or fascinated by a particular product category, and actively seek out new ideas, trends, and innovations. With today's technology, ideas can now be spread faster and more credibly by mavens through interpersonal networks via the Internet. Mavens use "connectors" to help them spread their message about products and brands. Connectors are people who usually acquire their information from mavens, but are well connected and use their connections to spread the message. "Salesmen" are charismatic people with powerful negotiation skills. They exert "soft" influence on others, rather than forceful power.[72]

Marketers agree on the value of mavens, salesmen, and connectors; the challenge is trying to identify who these key influencers are.

PEER-TO-PEER E-COMMERCE

consumer-to-consumer (C2C) e-commerce Communications and purchases that occur among individuals without directly involving the manufacturer or retailer.

One of the most exciting aspects of the new digital world is that consumers can interact directly with other people who live around the block or around the world. Peer-to-peer, or as it is more commonly known, **consumer-to-consumer (C2C) e-commerce**, refers to online communications and purchases that occur among individuals without directly involving the manufacturer or retailer. Picture a small group of local collectors who meet once a month at a local diner to discuss their shared interests over coffee. Now multiply that group by thousands, and include people from all over the world who are united through the Internet by a shared passion for sports memorabilia, Harley-Davidson motorcycles, or refrigerator magnets—all are participating in C2C e-commerce.

Yes, group membership has entered cyberspace in a big way, as netizens around the world are forming virtual communities of consumption. These are groups of people who meet online and share their enthusiasm for a product, recording artist, art form, celebrity, and so on. These groups allow consumers to remain anonymous while they form around an incredibly diverse set of interests—everything from Barbie dolls to fine wine. Marketers who target these online communities know that members are more likely to buy products that other group members find of value.

It has been estimated that over 40 million people worldwide participate in virtual communities. These loyal consumers help one another evaluate the quality of choices in the marketplace.

Companies such as Warner Bros. also are actively promoting virtual communities related to their products. The company noticed that many fans of Bugs Bunny, Batman, and the Tasmanian Devil were including images and sound clips on their personal webpages and then selling ad space on those pages. Instead of suing its fans, Warner created an online community called ACME City that builds homepages for registered members.[73] Let's look at some specific types of brand communities that are shaking up the ways businesses operate.

Virtual Communities

Virtual communities come in different forms, including multi-user dungeons; rooms, rings, and lists; boards; auction sites; product rating sites; protest sites; and blogs.

MULTI-USER DUNGEONS Originally, these communities were environments where players of fantasy games met. Now they refer to any cyber environment in which people socially interact through role and game playing. In a game called EverQuest, more than 50 000 people around the globe pay to roam around a fantasy land in cyberspace. This game combines the stunning graphics of advanced gaming with the social scene of a chat room. Players create a character as a virtual alter ego, which may be a wise elf or a backstabbing rogue. If a character is powerful enough, it can sell on eBay for $1000 or more! Players can travel around this cyberworld in groups of six. In many cases they settle into a regular group and spend two to three hours each night online with the same people. One couple even held a virtual wedding while playing. The bride reported, "We only had one death, a guest who was killed by the guards. It was a lot of fun."[74]

Realizing that the average online player logs 17 hours per week, firms such as Sony, Microsoft, and Sega are building virtual worlds to get a piece of the action. As one game company executive put it, "This is not a genre of game but a breakthrough new medium. It provides a completely new social, collaborative, shared experience. We're basically in the Internet community business."[75] This new medium opens up many possibilities for marketers, since participants often render judgments on a variety of topics such as hot new bands or movies that can influence the opinions of other participants.

ROOMS, RINGS, AND LISTS These virtual communities include Internet relay chat (IRC), otherwise known as chat rooms. Rings are organizations of related homepages and lists are groups of people on a single e-mail list who share information. For example, ICQ maintains rings devoted to many topics such as music, electronics, and genealogy. **Clubzone.com** is a Vancouver-based online community targeting club goers. **Ryze.com** is a North American networking community of professionals.

BOARDS Boards are online communities organized around interest-specific electronic bulletin boards. Active members read and post messages sorted by date and subject. There are boards devoted to musical groups, movies, wine, cigars, cars, comic strips, and even fast-food restaurants. Ponder the case of Widespread Panic. The band has never had a music video on MTV or cracked the Billboard Top 200. But it's one of the top 40 touring bands in the United States. How did it get to be so successful? Simple—the group built a virtual community of fans. Fans send messages to its recording studio and hardcore followers can find out vital information, such as what band members ate for lunch.[76] Frugal Shopper Canada (**www.frugalshopper.ca**) is a virtual community of Canadians dedicated to saving money, with discussion forums on how to win contests, collect coupons, and save money.

AUCTION SITES Auction sites let consumers buy, sell, and barter with each other. The best-known auction site is eBay, where you can buy anything from a rare Beatles poster to an antique iron. At one point, an eBay member even tried to sell a human kidney ("You can choose either kidney. . . . Of course, only one is for sale, as I need the other one to live"). Bidding went to over $5.7 million before the company ended the auction.[77]

PRODUCT RATING SITES Sites such as Mountain Bike Review (**www.mtbr.com**) give people a forum for their opinions and let them rate products.[78] One product-rating site called **Epinions.com** even rates and rewards product reviewers. Anyone can sign up to give advice on products that fit into the site's 12 categories, and shoppers can rate the reviews on a scale from not useful to very useful. Reviewers earn royalties of between $1 and $3 for every 10 times their review is read. When recommendations result in a sale, the company earns a referral fee from merchants. One of the site's founders observes that the site relies on a "web of trust," and he claims, "It mimics the way word of mouth works in the real world."[79]

PROTEST SITES Protest sites let consumers "vent" by sharing negative experiences they have had with companies. In some cases these protest sites pose a public relations problem for companies, so companies try to eliminate them. Dunkin' Donuts bought a site from a disgruntled customer who created the webpage to complain after he could not get skim milk for his coffee.[80] And sometimes these sites spread untrue information about corporations. For example, rumours began spreading on newsgroups that Procter & Gamble's Febreze cleaning product killed dogs. In a pre-emptive move to minimize problems before they started, P&G registered numerous website names so that no one else could—including febrezekillspet.com, febrezesucks.com, and ihateprocterandgamble.com. P&G now maintains a page on its website dedicated to fighting rumours.[81]

BLOGS The newest and fastest-growing form of online community is the weblog, or blog. These online personal journals are building an avid following among Internet users, who like to dash off a few random thoughts, post them on a website, and read similar musings by others. Although these sites are similar to webpages offered by Geocities and other free services, blogs use a different technology that lets people upload a few sentences without going through the process of updating a website built with conventional homepage software. Bloggers can fire off thoughts on a whim, click a button, and quickly have them appear on a site. Weblogs frequently look like online diaries, with brief musings about the day's events and perhaps a link or two of interest. This burgeoning blogosphere (the universe of active weblogs) is indeed a force to be reckoned with.

Yamaha Canada recently launched its "Yamaha Sled Talk Blog" to support the release of its newest snowmobile models. The blog targets men aged 18 to 34, the key demographic for Yamaha. The blog was designed as a resource for and a means to engage "sled heads" to create interest in Yamaha's snowmobiles. The strategy worked—the blog received posts from across Canada and as far away as India.[82]

consumer-generated media (CGM)
Posts (including video, audio, and multimedia posts) created by consumers in support or against products, brands, and corporate institutions.

The emergence of blogs and other virtual communities has led to a relatively new term, **consumer-generated media (CGM)**, also referred to as consumer-generated content or user-generated content. CGM are the various types of media generated by end users. Perhaps the most widely known example of CGM is the video posted by a juggler and a trial lawyer in Buckfield, Maine. The two decided to test out the geyser effect caused by dropping Mentos candies into bottles of Diet Coke. They set up their experiment in such a way that the bottles would erupt somewhat like the famous Bellagio fountains in

Real People, Real Decisions

▶ ## How It Worked Out at Coast Tire

Coast Tire decided to implement Option 2: targeted relationships with CAA members. The clientele was pre-qualified—they had automobiles, and membership loyalty to CAA might be transferable to Coast Tire. Coast Tire therefore had the ability to focus on select profiles of CAA members. It also had the ability to focus on promotions during shoulder seasons. The prospect of giving existing customers a discount for CAA membership was not too much of an issue, as it gave those customers more reasons to come back to Coast Tire for all their work and only about 5 percent of current customers were CAA members at the start of the program.

Although at least 40 percent of Coast Tire's customers were Air Miles customers, the CAA participants were more loyal than Air Miles customers. They were also less price sensitive than other customers. The return rate was higher with the CAA members compared to the non-CAA members. The relationship with Coast Tire, the service provider, was more important to the client than shopping around for a small price benefit. With the added loyalty Coast Tire was better able to offer new services to ongoing customers. One such service Ron is going to look at more carefully is the feasibility of the tire storage concept mentioned previously, as it might be a relatively easy way to ensure that customers return to Coast Tire at least twice a year. The customers in the Maritimes change their tires every spring and every fall. Coast Tire would store the tires not in use. The benefits of this service are customer loyalty (as Coast Tire is keeping

something of theirs) and an opportunity to have an ongoing relationship with those clients.

Coast Tire also decided to implement Option 3, the new database and scheduling system, but not for another year. It would take time to either hire someone to create a custom solution or to research off-the-shelf scheduling products. This work would best be done in the winter slow season. The data collection focuses on the customer's vehicle, what they do with it, and where they live. Coast Tire has kept away from the household demographic information, as there are privacy issues with this type of information. The scheduling portion focuses on scheduling appointments in advance and then, about 10 days before the appointment, informing the customer of any specials that are coming up. This system would also inform the customer of regular maintenance their vehicle should be scheduled for. It would also inform customers when their vehicle is due for Vehicle Inspections. As technology has become more accessible and broader, options like this one have become available to many smaller businesses in Canada.

Observable measures of loyalty as well as customer satisfaction have already been collected. Coast Tire has looked at average spent each visit, average spent per year, and the frequency of visits. It has also measured customers' satisfaction, with the ultimate measurement being "Would you recommend Coast Tire to a friend?" This information is used to increase customer satisfaction and to help focus customer service training for its employees.

Las Vegas. They posted the video online, and the rest is history. Within hours, the video received thousands of hits. The video generated an enormous amount of buzz and free publicity for both brands—even though neither had anything to do with it. Although marketers enjoy free publicity when CGM appears for their brand, they also lose control of the message. This is a frightening prospect for some marketers, although many have come to realize that this level of consumer interaction with brands is inevitable with today's technology. Mark Tutssel, Leo Burnett's worldwide chief creative officer, recently said that "Marketers must learn to let go of the control they think they have over their brand. . . . Once consumers have interacted with brands, they will not go back to being shouted at by marketers."[83]

Another technology, RSS (Really Simple Syndication), has emerged through blogs. RSS is a content feed that users can subscribe to. When a website is updated, subscribers can be automatically notified of those updates. Princess Cruises uses RSS to simplify its communication with a key target audience: travel agents. When they log onto the Princess website, agents can access real-time RSS feeds containing travel information and updates on sales and specials based on their personal profiles—all without opening an e-mail. RSS lets marketers speak more often to those customers who really want to hear from them.[84]

In the last part of this chapter, we've seen how other people, such as friends or even casual acquaintances, influence our purchase decisions. We've considered how our preferences are shaped by our group memberships, by our desire to please or be accepted by others, even by the way we think we're "supposed" to act as men or women. We've explored why some people are more influential than others in affecting our product preferences. In addition to the influences exerted on each of us by virtue of being members of a culture, a social class, and several subcultures, it's easy to see that group affiliations exert a powerful pull on us as we make marketplace decisions. It's clear that people truly are "social animals," and to understand consumer behaviour we need to consider internal factors such as personality, situational factors such as the amount of time available to decide, and social factors such as group identity to get a handle on what we thought was the relatively simple business of making a decision.

CHAPTER SUMMARY

1. Explain why understanding consumer behaviour is important to organizations.

The marketing concept focuses on satisfying consumers' wants and needs. For organizations to succeed at this, they need to understand the processes that occur before, during, and after the selection of goods or services.

2. Explain the process (pre-purchase, purchase, and post-purchase) consumers engage in when making decisions.

Consumer decisions differ greatly, ranging from habitual, almost mindless, repeat (low-involvement) purchases to complex, extended problem-solving activities for important, risky (high-involvement) decisions. First, consumers recognize that there is a problem to be solved. The search for information in memory and in the marketplace reduces the risk of making a wrong choice. The set of alternatives, those that will be actively considered, are judged based on various dimensions or evaluative criteria. Consumers may simplify the process by using mental shortcuts or heuristics. Following the purchase, consumer perceptions of product quality lead to satisfaction or dissatisfaction.

3. Describe how internal factors influence consumers' decision-making processes.

A number of internal factors influence consumer decisions. Perception is how consumers select, organize, and interpret stimuli. Consumers must first be exposed to the marketing communications. To prevent sensory overload, consumers practise perceptual selectivity; that is, they are selective in their attention by focusing on stimuli. Consumers differ in interpretation of stimuli, because the meaning assigned is based on individuals' prior experiences or beliefs. Marketers should understand that consumers act because they are motivated to achieve goals, which may depend on which level of needs is currently satisfied. Learning is a change in behaviour that results from information or experience. Behavioural learning results from external events such as rewards, punishments, or the previous pairing of stimuli. Behavioural learning may result in stimulus generalization in which attitudes toward a brand or company may be transferred to other products, such as product line extensions. Cognitive learning refers to internal mental activity and includes observational learning in which behaviour results from imitation of the observed behaviour of socially attractive others.

An attitude is a lasting evaluation of a person, object, or issue. There are three components to attitudes: affective, cognitive, and behavioural. Marketers design products consistent with consumer attitudes or seek to change attitudes, frequently focusing on one of the three components.

Marketing strategy should also consider consumers' psychological makeup or personality. Personality traits, such as innovativeness, self-confidence, and sociability, may be used to develop market segments. Marketers seek to understand a consumer's self-concept to develop product attributes that match some aspect of the consumer's self.

Both the age of consumers and their family life cycle classification are strongly related to consumption preferences. Consumer behaviour may also differ based on lifestyles, thus creating different marketing segmentation opportunities. Similarly, the use of psychographics in which people are grouped according to activities, interests, and opinions may explain reasons for purchasing products.

4. **Describe how situational factors at the time and place of purchase may influence consumer behaviour.**

The physical and social environments at the time of purchase create differences in consumer behaviour. Retailers often create themed environments and in-store displays to influence customers to make purchases. Time (or the lack of it) influences which products are selected and characteristics of the decision process.

5. **Describe how consumers' relationships with other people influence their decision-making processes.**

Consumers' overall priorities for products and activities are determined by the culture of the society in which they live. Consumer decisions may be influenced by cultural values, or the enduring beliefs of the culture. In Canada, differences between French Canadian and English Canadian consumers often influence marketing strategies. Consumers within the same culture may also be members of different religious, ethnic, or regional subcultures. Many Canadian companies practise multicultural marketing by targeting their marketing strategies to consumers from various ethnic subcultures.

Social class and reference groups are other types of social influence that have an impact on product and store choices. One way social influences are felt is in the expectations of society regarding the proper roles for men and women, which have led to many sex-typed products. Consumers are motivated to please or imitate people they know or whom they respect. Purchases often result from conformity to real or imagined group pressure. Opinion leaders are especially influential people.

6. **Understand how the Internet offers consumers opportunities for peer-to-peer marketing.**

Peer-to-peer or consumer-to-consumer (C2C) e-commerce includes marketing communication and purchases between individuals. C2C activities include virtual brand communities, auction sites, product rating sites, and protest sites.

CHAPTER REVIEW

Marketing Concepts: Testing Your Knowledge

1. What is consumer behaviour? Why is it important for marketers to understand consumer behaviour?

2. How does the decision process differ under conditions of high involvement and low involvement? What are the steps in the decision process and what activities occur in each?

3. What is perception? For marketers, what are the implications of each component of the perceptual process?

4. How are consumers motivated to buy certain products over others? How has Maslow's hierarchy of needs contributed to an understanding of consumer behaviour?

5. What behavioural and cognitive learning theories are important to marketers? How do these perspectives differ when applied to consumer behaviour?

6. How do the three components of attitudes account for consumer decision making and purchasing behaviour?

7. What is personality? How is consumer behaviour influenced by an individual's personality and self-concept?

8. Why is self-concept such an important personal influence on purchasing behaviour? How do age and the family life cycle influence consumers? What is the significance of lifestyles in understanding consumer behaviour and purchasing decisions?

9. Why is an understanding of social influences such as culture and subculture important to marketers? What is the significance of social class to marketers? What are reference groups, and how do they influence consumers? What are opinion leaders?

10. What are the situational influences on consumer purchasing behaviour? How does each affect purchasing decisions?

11. What is peer-to-peer e-commerce? What are virtual communities, gaming, chat rooms, boards, and blogs, and how are they related to consumer behaviour?

Marketing Concepts: Discussing Choices and Issues

1. Some consumer advocates have criticized marketing messages that link products to idealized people and situations and encourage the belief that the products will change consumers' lives in the portrayed direction. Do you agree or disagree? Explain your reasoning.

2. This chapter raised the question, "Do we buy what we are?" What answer would you give based on your experience? Provide examples that support your opinion.

3. A number of current demographic or cultural trends are important to marketers. What are some important trends that may affect marketing of the following products?
   a. housing
   b. home health care
   c. newspapers
   d. education
   e. travel and tourism

4. Affect, cognition, and behaviour are three components that can be used by marketers to shape people's attitudes about products. Identify the product categories you think are most likely to be influenced by each component and discuss the merits of trying to change people's attitudes.

5. Culture is not static. What values, beliefs, and customs of Canadian culture do you see changing? How are these changes affecting marketing? What products will be affected by these changes?

6. Consumers often buy products because they feel pressure from reference groups to conform. Does conformity exert a positive or negative influence on consumers? How do consumer demographics, psychographics, and lifestyles affect their readiness to conform? With what types of products is conformity more likely to occur?

7. Many Canadians and consumers around the globe use C2C e-commerce to supplement their incomes or as their primary source of income. What do you think of the future of sites such as eBay? What opportunities does eBay provide for twenty-first-century entrepreneurs?

Marketing Practice: Applying What You've Learned

1. Assume that you are the director of marketing for a chain of camping and outdoor gear stores. Your firm is expanding and it is your job to develop general recommendations for store design. Prepare a summary of your recommendations for store design elements that you believe will provide the best shopping environment for your customers.

2. Assume that you are an account executive with an advertising agency. Your current client is a firm that makes swimwear. You know that swimwear purchases are often influenced by a variety of social or "other people" factors. Write a report that lists these social influences, explain why each is important, and outline how you might use these influences in developing an advertising campaign.

3. This chapter indicated that consumers go through a series of steps (from problem recognition to post-purchase evaluation) as they make purchases. Write a detailed report describing what you would do in each of these steps when deciding to purchase one of the following products:

   a. an automobile

   b. a suit

   c. a vacation

4. Sometimes advertising or other marketing activities cause problem recognition to occur by showing consumers how much better off they would be with a new product or by pointing out problems with products they already own. For the following product categories, what are some ways in which marketers might try to stimulate problem recognition?

   a. cellphone

   b. toothpaste

   c. vitamins

   d. fast food

5. You work for a firm that markets frozen foods and are concerned about the effects of current consumer trends, including the increasingly diverse ethnic makeup of the population, changing roles of men and women, increased concern for time and for the environment, and decreased emphasis on owning status goods. Others in your firm do not understand or care about these changes. They believe that the firm should continue to do business just as it always has. Develop a role-playing exercise with a classmate to discuss these two different points of view for your class. Each of you should include the importance of each of these trends to your firm and your suggestions for marketing strategies to address these trends.

Marketing Mini-Project: Learning by Doing

The purpose of this mini-project is to increase your understanding of the roles of personal, social, and situational factors in consumer behaviour.

1. With several other members of your class, select one of the following product categories (or some other product of your choice):

   a. perfume

   b. computers

   c. women's or men's shoes

   d. automobiles

2. Visit three stores or locations where the product may be purchased. (Try to select three that are very different from each other.) Observe and make notes on all the elements of each retail environment.

3. At each of the three locations, observe people purchasing the product. Make notes about their characteristics (e.g., age and sex) and their actions in the store in relation to the product.

4. Prepare a report for your class describing the situational variables and individual consumer differences you discovered and how they relate to the purchase of the product.

5. Present your findings to your class.

Real People, Real Surfers: Exploring the Web

Visit the website for D-Code (**www.d-code.com**). Answer the following questions about the information at the site.

1. What research methods that D-Code uses to understand Nexus consumers are described on the site? What do you think are the advantages and disadvantages of using these methods to understand consumer behaviour?

2. What information about Nexus consumer behaviour is described on the site?

3. Identify five Canadian companies that you think would be interested in information on Nexus consumers. How might these companies use information about Nexus consumers in designing their marketing strategies?

When was the last time you were on Facebook? If you are a typical college or university student, it probably was sometime within the last 24 hours. In fact, so many people check their Facebook profile regularly that the company claims that 65 percent of all undergraduate students in colleges and universities across the country are members of the Facebook community. Traffic on the site has increased by over 270 percent in the last year alone. With growth numbers like that, Facebook is meeting the needs of its users.

Mark Zuckerberg, a 21-year-old Harvard University dropout, started Facebook.com in 2004. Zuckerberg got the idea after he and a few friends realized that Harvard did not have a face book, in other words a directory, with student ID pictures that classmates could use to look each other up. Within two weeks of building the initial Facebook site, two-thirds of Harvard students had uploaded a picture and added some information about themselves. After experiencing such instant popularity among Harvard students, Zuckerberg and his buddies expanded Facebook to include more schools and students. This time, roughly 150 000 students from 30 schools established profiles for themselves. Shortly thereafter, Zuckerberg moved to California and formed the company that exists today.

Why did Facebook become such a huge success in such a brief time frame? In short, Facebook is satisfying an unmet desire on the part of students to connect with and stay connected to other students in an electronic, easy-to-use, and fun format. The success also is related to influencers to whom students are exposed when deciding to participate in a social networking website. For example, reference groups are huge influencers when it comes to consumers deciding on which movies to see, what jeans to wear, or any number of other consumption decisions. As a result, if someone establishes a profile on Facebook and invites his or her friends to also develop a profile, the desire to be "part of the group" almost guarantees that those friends will use Facebook. In addition, self-concept is a very powerful motivator for some people. Since Facebook is an electronic networking site, it is possible for an individual to develop an online persona that is different from his or her in-person identity. Consequently, student users have the opportunity to develop a profile that transforms their in-person identity into the type of person they wish to portray. In some cases, they even develop more than one persona to appeal to different reference groups.

A third reason for Facebook's success is personality. Some people by nature are more sociable than others. As a result, growing numbers of social networking sites on the Internet provide an opportunity for these socialites to interact with others who are similar to them. Finally, Maslow's hierarchy of needs specifies two elements of motivation that consumers can fulfill by participating in Facebook: belongingness and self-actualization needs. Facebook allows members to gain acceptance by others and to engage in self-fulfilling, enriching experiences by sharing those experiences with a community of friends they establish on the site.

Despite Facebook's success in the early stages of its existence, there are still many questions and concerns that could limit its long-term future. Parents and school administrators are advising participants to be very careful about the type of information they post. In addition, many participants themselves are becoming more guarded in the type of information they make available on their profiles. School administrators have used information and pictures students post on Facebook to expel and suspend students from school. Many companies now routinely check out a job applicant's Facebook posting and ding him or her if they find unacceptable material there. Furthermore, information on Facebook is available for viewing by sexual predators.

Also calling into question the long-term potential of Facebook is the negative effect of increased commercialization. Advertisers are lining up to appeal to the lucrative but fickle group of consumers making up the Facebook community. But, for Mark Zuckerberg to make more money on this venture, he will have to figure out how to expose Facebook members to advertisers without alienating posters. Determining the degree of exposure to ads that Facebook members will tolerate will be a difficult balancing act.

In summary, Mark Zuckerberg's ability to keep the Facebook phenomenon going is tied to his ability to plan for the company's long-term future given privacy concerns and increased usage by authority figures to enforce school policies. How can Facebook address these privacy concerns? How much advertising can Facebook expose to its members without turning them off? And how does Facebook keep the site "cool" and one that its target audience will want to visit over and over?

Things to Think About

1. What is the decision facing Facebook.com?

2. What factors are important in understanding this decision situation?

3. What are the alternatives?

4. What decision(s) do you recommend?

5. What are some ways to implement your recommendation?

Sources: Matthew Creamer and Abbey Klaassen, "Social climbers: Irrational exuberance 2.0? Media moguls risk overpaying for fickle fans of Facebook, MySpace," *Advertising Age*, 1 May 2006: 3; Olga Kharif, "Big Brother is reading your blog," *BusinessWeek Online*, 28 February 2006; Erik Brady and Daniel Libit, "Alarms sound over Facebook time," *USA Today*, 9 March 2006: 1C, 2C; Janet Kornblum and Mary Beth Marklein, "Online truths & consequences: What you say online could haunt you," *USA Today*, 9 March 2006: 1A, 4A.

CHAPTER 6
Organizational Buying Behaviour

CHAPTER OBJECTIVES

WHEN YOU HAVE COMPLETED YOUR STUDY OF THIS CHAPTER, YOU SHOULD BE ABLE TO

1. Describe the general characteristics of the external environment, business-to-business markets, and business buying practices.

2. Explain how marketers classify trends, business, and organizational markets.

3. Explain the business buying situation, understand the business nature of an industry, and describe business buyers.

4. Summarize the main stages in the business buying decision process and appreciate the competitive environment.

5. Explain how e-commerce is dramatically changing business-to-business marketing.

6. Explain the importance of Customer Relationship Management (CRM) and describe how it works.

Real People, Real Decisions

Meet **Deborah McKenzie**, IBM Global Marketing Manager

Deborah McKenzie is passionate about marketing. She has worked for IBM for her entire career and has always received personal job satisfaction working for a company that continually encouraged employee skills development and job movement throughout all areas of the business. Deborah started off her career teaching Office Systems, which then led her to a variety of sales positions. In the early 1990s she attended an IBM career counselling seminar, which helped her explore her own strengths and discover a focus for the next step in her career path. The tests indicated that she would be good in marketing. Deborah then transitioned to a new career in marketing at IBM Canada.

Marketing courses, books, and trade publications helped her learn more about her new career. IBM also supported her attendance at a two-year correspondence program sponsored by the Chartered Institute of Marketing and the University of Manchester in England. This gave her the additional training to continue to grow into more senior marketing roles. She received an Advanced Certificate in Marketing Management Practice in 2002 and is currently a global marketing manager for IBM Corporation.

Deborah has taken this career to an even higher level by becoming very connected to the marketing community outside IBM. She joined the Toronto chapter of the American Marketing Association in 2003, became vice-president of the Programming Committee, and then president of the Toronto Chapter for the year 2005–2006. She sits on the executive committee of the Marketing Hall of Legends, which was created to honour Canadians who have dedicated their lives to the pursuit of excellence in the field of marketing. She is an active fundraiser for the National Advertising Benevolent Society, the only charitable organization in Canada that provides assistance to advertising, media, and related industry professionals who may need help due to illness, injury, or unemployment. She is also a part-time faculty member teaching marketing at York University and Seneca College in Toronto. Deborah McKenzie has embraced the field of marketing, both globally and locally.

Background.

Early in 2001, the IBM Canadian Marketing Council (consisting of Canadian, North American, and global marketing managers living in Canada) identified five key priorities that could help accelerate IBM's revenue growth in Canada. IBM Canada individual business units had been working as separate entities under the larger IBM corporate umbrella. The company consisted of a hardware division, a software division, and a services division. Even though it was a global company, each division was focused on its own development and its own results. There was the added difficulty that, as a Canada-wide and global company, each geographic area often worked independently from the others. Consequently, marketing, within this large company, was not consistent and, in some cases, either contradicted or duplicated various

individual business-unit marketing activities. The Canadian marketing team realized that they needed to change the perception that IBM only sold hardware and software. They needed to communicate an integrated message to the Canadian market that IBM was a service and solution provider first. IBM needed to be perceived as one brand—IBM.

However, the budget for the current year was already in place. Also, the market knew IBM as it had been marketed in the past. To change this perception would require a lot of work, and it was questionable whether it would be worth it. The external business partners, the inside sales representatives, and all of IBM were comfortable with working in individual business units and the "silo" organization structure. Would integrating the message accelerate sales and broaden existing customers' use of IBM products and services? Could a plan even be executed without additional funding from the corporation? The IBM Canadian Marketing Council looked at the following three options:

Option 1: Canadian integration.

The first option the team looked at was to completely integrate the marketing messages of all the different business units within the company. To do this they would need to provide an immediate, cohesive, and focused marketing plan to the players within the company and to the external business partners. They would need to present this combined focus to the customer in a series of tight and centred events. However, there were many difficulties with this choice. First of all, the budget was already in place for the following year. There was no budget for a complete change in marketing strategy. Secondly, it would be very difficult to move the different areas out of their "silos" and into a country-wide, focused, cohesive "face" of IBM to the marketplace. The team questioned both the possibility of switching this focus and the cost involved. It was spring, and they needed to roll out the events in the fall. The time to build the theme, the message, and the structure of the events, with enough time to ensure that invitations were delivered four to six weeks prior to the first event, would be tight.

Option 2: Give themselves some time.

The second option the team looked at was to go forward but to give themselves a year to plan and get funding in place for the project. IBM, like all large companies, plans at least a year ahead for its marketing budget. With IBM, this budgeting was global. Also, if they gave themselves a year they would have the time to present the changes to the different areas of the company in stages. They thought that this communication style might have greater buy-in from the IBM marketing managers who were used to running their own show. They also questioned whether by waiting a year they would forfeit the opportunity to gain business right then. How much would waiting a year hurt them? Would they lose their competitive advantage?

Option 3: Informal coordination.

The last option they looked at, considering the difficulties that had presented themselves in the above two options, was to retain the status quo and just encourage more integration between the different geographic areas and departments by helping to communicate the current messages used by the different IBM divisions and suggest ways that these might be adapted to improve coordination and consistency. This option meant that each area could continue their own development, follow the budget that was already in place, and stay with what they knew. Selling and delivering a service that would solve a customer's problem was a lot different from selling a computer or software application. Perhaps focusing on a more integrated approach over the long term would be better.

Now, join Deborah McKenzie and the IBM Canada marketing team: Which option would you choose and why?

BUSINESS MARKETS: BUYING AND SELLING WHEN STAKES ARE HIGH

You might think most marketers spend their days dreaming up the best way to promote cutting-edge web browsers or funky shoes. Not so. Many marketers know that the "real action" is more likely to be found in lead pipes, office supplies, safety shoes, meat lockers, or machine tools. In fact, some of the most interesting and most lucrative jobs for young marketers are in industries you probably have never heard of.

An individual consumer may decide to buy two or three T-shirts at one time, each emblazoned with a different design. Large companies such as Canadian Tire, Petro-Canada, Air Canada, and Cirque du Soleil buy hundreds, even thousands, of employee uniforms embroidered with their corporate logos in a single order. Like an end consumer, a business buyer makes decisions—with an important difference. The purchase may be worth millions of dollars, and both the buyer and seller have a lot at stake in making a wise decision. In 2007, Streetsville, Ontario–based Menu Foods learned the importance of "business-to-business" relationships the hard way. Menu Foods is one of the largest pet-food makers in North America, and it had to recall 60 million containers of food feared to cause sickness or even death of household pets across North America. The contamination was traced to a Chinese supplier that had laced wheat gluten with melamine to bulk it up. Because of the pressures of globalization and hypercompetition, relationships between businesses are increasingly becoming important to marketers.[1]

Exhibit 6.1

Moosehead Breweries does not sell beer directly to consumers but rather to retailers and distributors.

In this chapter, we'll look at the big picture of the business marketplace, in which the fortunes of business buyers and sellers can hang in the balance of a single transaction. Then we'll examine how marketers categorize businesses and organizations to develop effective business marketing strategies. Finally, we'll look at business buying behaviour and the business buying decision process.

To begin, consider these transactions: Moosehead Breweries, Canada's oldest independent brewery, sells its beer (such as Moosehead Lager, as shown in Exhibit 6.1) directly to food and beverage retailers and distributors. Procter & Gamble sells cases of Tide to RC Distributors, a Northern Ontario wholesaler. The Stratford Festival buys costumes, sets, and programs. Merck Frosst plans to purchase 1000 Dell computer systems for employee home use. BC Gas buys advice from Anderson Consulting. The Winnipeg Public Library buys a Canon copier. Rona buys drywall from the Canadian Gypsum Company.

Characteristics That Make a Difference in Business Markets

business-to-business marketing
The marketing of goods and services that business and organizational customers need in order to produce other goods and services for resale or to support their operations.

All of these market activities have one thing in common—they are part of **business-to-business marketing**. This is the marketing of goods and services that businesses and other organizational customers buy for some purpose other than personal consumption. Firms may resell these goods and services or may use them to produce still other goods and services to sell to other businesses or to support their own operations. Business-to-business customers include manufacturers, wholesalers, retailers, and a variety of other organizations such as hospitals, colleges and universities, and government agencies. Another name for business-to-business markets is organizational markets.

Business customers create vast opportunities for marketers. When measured in dollars, the market for business and organizational goods and services is *four* times larger than the consumer market.[2]

To put the size and complexity of business markets into perspective, let's consider a single product—a pair of jeans. A consumer may browse through several racks of jeans and ultimately purchase a single pair, but the store at which the consumer shops has purchased many pairs of jeans in different sizes, styles, and brands from different manufacturers. Each of these manufacturers purchases fabrics, zippers, buttons, and thread from other manufacturers that, in turn, purchase the raw materials to make these components. In addition, all the firms in this chain need to purchase equipment, electricity, labour, computer systems, office supplies, packing materials, and countless other goods and services. So, even a single purchase of the latest style of Diesel jeans is the culmination of a series of buying and selling activities among many organizations—many people have been keeping busy while you're out shopping.

In theory, the same basic marketing principles hold in both consumer and business markets—firms identify customer needs and develop a marketing mix to satisfy those needs. For example, imagine the company that made the desks and chairs in your classroom. Just like a firm that markets consumer goods, the classroom furniture company first must create an important competitive advantage for its target market of colleges and universities. Next the firm develops a marketing mix strategy beginning with a product—classroom furniture that will withstand years of use by thousands of students while providing a level of comfort required of a good learning environment (and you thought those hard-backed chairs were intended just to keep you awake during class). The firm must offer the furniture at prices the schools will pay and must develop a sales force or other marketing communication strategy to make sure your school (and hundreds of others) consider—and hopefully choose—its products when furnishing classrooms. Although marketing to business customers does have a lot in common with consumer marketing, there are differences that make this basic process more complex.[3] Figure 6.1 looks at some of these differences and they are reviewed in the following sections.

MULTIPLE BUYERS In business markets, products often have to do more than satisfy an individual's needs. They must meet the requirements of everyone involved in the company's purchase decision. If you decide to buy a new chair for your room or apartment, you are the only one who has to be satisfied. For your classroom, the furniture must satisfy students, faculty members, administrators, campus planners, and the purchasing department. Instead of simply deciding on an appropriate price for the product, business-to-business marketers frequently must submit written quotes stating their prices and then hope a competitor doesn't submit a lower quote.

NUMBER OF CUSTOMERS Compared to consumers, organizational customers are few and far between. In Canada, there are about 10 million consumer households but fewer than 50 000 businesses and organizations. Unless your name is Bronfman or Gates, each organizational buyer has more to spend than you do as an individual consumer. Business marketers have a narrow customer base and a small number of buyers. Kodak's business division, which markets sophisticated medical products to hospitals and other medical

Organizational Markets	Consumer Markets
• Purchases made for some purpose other than personal consumption	• Purchases for individual or household consumption
• Purchases made by someone other than the user of the product	• Purchases usually made by ultimate user of the product
• Decisions frequently made by several people	• Decisions usually made by individuals
• Purchases made according to precise technical specifications based on product expertise	• Purchases often made based on brand reputation or personal recommendations with little or no product expertise
• Purchases made after careful weighing of alternatives	• Purchases frequently made on impulse
• Purchases made based on rational criteria	• Purchases made based on emotional responses to products or promotions
• Purchasers often engage in lengthy decision process	• Individual purchasers often make quick decisions
• Interdependencies between buyers and sellers; long-term relationships	• Buyers engage in limited-term or one-time-only relationships with many different sellers
• Purchases may involve competitive bidding, price negotiations, and complex financial arrangements	• Most purchases made at "list price' with cash or credit cards
• Products frequently purchased directly from producer	• Products usually purchased from someone other than producer of the product
• Purchases frequently involve high risk and high cost	• Most purchases are low risk and low cost
• Limited number of large buyers	• Many individual or household customers
• Buyers often geographically concentrated in certain areas	• Buyers generally dispersed throughout total population
• Products: often complex; classified based on how organizational customers use them	• Products: consumer goods and services for individual use
• Demand derived from demand for other goods and services, generally inelastic in the short run, subject to fluctuations, and may be joined to the demand for other goods and services	• Demand based on consumer needs and preferences, is generally price elastic, steady over time, and independent of demand for other products
• Promotion emphasizes personal selling	• Promotion emphasizes advertising

Figure 6.1 Differences Between Organizational and Consumer Markets

groups, has a limited number of potential customers compared with its consumer film division.

SIZE OF PURCHASES Business-to-business products can dwarf consumer purchases, both in the quantity of items ordered and in the price of individual purchases. A company that supplies uniforms to other businesses, for example, buys hundreds of large drums of laundry detergent each year in contrast to a consumer household that buys one box of detergent every few weeks. Organizations purchase some products (e.g., highly sophisticated pieces of manufacturing equipment, computer-based marketing information systems) that can cost into the millions of dollars. For example, DALSA, which specializes in the design and manufacture of sophisticated electronic cameras, sells charge-coupled devices as shown in Exhibit 6.2 for $50 000. Recognizing such differences in the size of purchases allows marketers to meet business customers' needs. Although it makes perfect sense to use mass-media advertising to sell laundry detergent to consumers, selling thousands of dollars worth of laundry detergent or a million-dollar computer is best handled by a strong personal sales force.

GEOGRAPHIC CONCENTRATION Another difference between business markets and consumer markets is geographic concentration—many business customers are located in a small geographic area rather than spread out across the country. Consumers buy and use products like toothpaste and televisions whether they live in the heart of Toronto or in a small

Exhibit 6.2

DALSA charge-coupled devices are usually considered large purchases by organizations.

Exhibit 6.3

Customers for Caterpillar heavy equipment are geographically concentrated.

fishing village on Prince Edward Island. This is not true for business-to-business customers, who may be exclusively located in a single region of the country (Exhibit 6.3). In Canada, much of the industrial buying power is concentrated in Toronto, Montreal, and Calgary, where major Canadian corporations have their head offices.

Business-to-Business Demand

Demand in business markets differs from consumer demand. Most demand for business-to-business products is derived, inelastic, fluctuating, and joint. Understanding these differences in business-to-business demand is important for marketers in forecasting sales and in planning effective marketing strategies.

DERIVED DEMAND Consumer demand is a direct connection between a need and the satisfaction of that need. Business customers don't purchase goods and services to satisfy their own needs. Business-to-business demand is **derived demand**, because a business's demand for goods and services comes either directly or indirectly from consumers' demand. For example, the demand for building products such as Canadian Gypsum's drywall or a Sony home entertainment centre is derived from the demand for new homes and luxury goods. Retailers buy goods to resell in response to consumer demand while other organizations and firms buy products that are used to produce still more goods and services that consumer markets demand.

derived demand The demand for business or organizational products that is derived from demand for consumer goods or services.

inelastic demand The demand for products does not change because of increases or decreases in price.

Consider Figure 6.2. Demand for forestry products comes from the demand for pulp to make paper used to make textbooks. The demand for textbooks comes from the demand for education. As a result of derived demand, the success of one company may depend on another company in a different industry. The derived nature of business demand means that marketers must be constantly alert to changes in consumer trends that ultimately will have an effect on business-to-business sales.

INELASTIC DEMAND The demand for business or organizational products is generally *inelastic*. **Inelastic demand** means that, regardless of whether the price of a business-to-business product goes up or down, customers will still buy the same quantity. (The notion of price elasticity in discussed further in Chapter 9.) We see inelastic demand in business-to-business markets because an individual business product is usually one of the many parts and materials that go into producing the consumer product. It is not unusual for a large increase in price for a single business product to have little effect on the price of the final consumer product. For example, the BMW in Exhibit 6.4 sells for about $75 000. To produce the car, BMW purchases thousands of different parts. If the price of tires, batteries, or stereos goes up—or down—BMW will still buy enough to meet consumer demand for its cars. As you might imagine, increasing the price of a $75 000 car by $30 or $40 or even $1000 won't change consumer demand.

Business-to-business demand isn't always inelastic. Sometimes producing a consumer good or service relies on only one or a few materials or component parts. If the price of the part increases, demand may become elastic if the manufacturer of the consumer good passes the increase on to the consumer. Steel, for example, is a large component of automobiles. If the price of steel goes up, automobile manufacturers will pay a

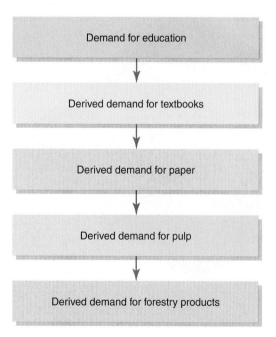

Figure 6.2 Derived Demand

Exhibit 6.4

The final sticker price of the BMW convertible depends on the price BMW has to pay for thousands of parts.

lot more for a necessary component of their product. An increase in the price of steel can drive up the price of automobiles so much that consumer demand for them drops, decreasing the demand for steel.

FLUCTUATING DEMAND Considering that demand comes from the end consumer, even small changes can create large increases or decreases in business demand. The **acceleration principle** (also called the multiplier effect) explains how a small percentage change in consumer demand can create a large percentage change in total industrial or business demand. Consider, for example, a 5 percent increase in consumer demand for air travel. If the airlines are already filling their flights, they may decide to buy new planes to meet the increased consumer demand. For Boeing or Bombardier Aerospace, the orders for new planes may double or even triple the normal demand.

A product's *life expectancy* is another reason for fluctuating demand. Business customers tend to purchase certain products (e.g., large machinery) infrequently, perhaps only every 10 or 20 years. Thus, demand for such products fluctuates; it may be very high one year when customers' machines are wearing out but low the following year because the old machinery is working fine.

Changes in a company's inventory policies can also create demand fluctuations. Consider a firm that has historically kept a 30-day supply of parts. Operations managers may decide to keep a 14-day supply of parts to reduce costs. Demand for the part will first go down because the manager will be placing a smaller order (for 14 days) and then level off at that 14-day quantity.

JOINT DEMAND **Joint demand** is the result of two or more goods being necessary to create a product. For example, General Motors requires tires, batteries, and spark plugs. If the supply of one of these products decreases, General Motors will be unable to manufacture as many automobiles and will not buy as many of the other items. Therefore, the sale of B.F. Goodrich tires to General Motors partly depends on the availability of batteries and spark plugs, even though the tire manufacturer has nothing to do with these products.

acceleration principle (multiplier effect) A marketing phenomenon in which a small percentage change in consumer demand can create a large percentage change in business-to-business demand.

joint demand The demand for two or more goods that are used together to create a product.

CLASSIFYING BUSINESS-TO-BUSINESS MARKETS

Many firms buy products in business markets so that they can produce other goods in turn. Many of the Canadian Gypsum Company's customers are contractors who build homes and offices and sell them to families and organizations. Other business-to-business customers

North American Industry Classification System (NAICS) The numerical coding system that the United States, Canada, and Mexico use to classify firms into detailed categories according to their business activities and shared characteristics.

resell, rent, or lease goods and services. Still others, such as the Red Cross, provincial governments, and local churches, serve the public in some way. As Figure 6.3 shows, these distinctions lead to broad categories: producers, resellers, and organizations. For business marketers, the classification of firms is significant because it identifies firms that purchase similar products and that have similar buying practices. This identification helps marketers develop strategies that effectively target different organizational customers.

One tool that firms use is the **North American Industry Classification System (NAICS)**. This is a numerical coding system for classifying industries, and was developed

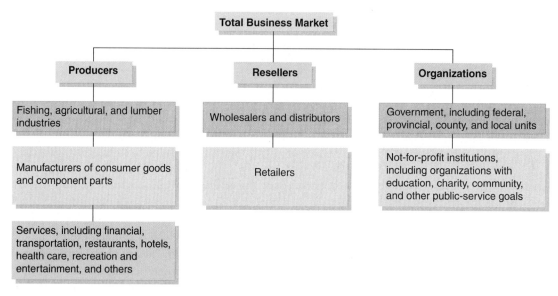

Figure 6.3 The Business Marketplace

SPOTLIGHT ON REAL PEOPLE   AdFarm Marketing

Agriculture is big business. Kim McConnell is CEO of Ad-Farm, a Canada-based North American advertising firm specializing in agricultural products. AdFarm has taken the idea of understanding customers and target markets to the next level. Where "other agencies speak to agriculture," says creative director Glenn Dawes, "we embody it." The AdFarm office is decorated in farm decor. The reception hall is rimmed with steel walls, making it resemble a grain silo. Papier mâché cows poke their heads over imitation "stalls." In the centre of the room, a scarecrow overlooks a mini grain field and, in a corner, there are dancing papier mâché pigs. The "creative room" is a Winnipeg designer's airy metallic take on a collapsing Prairie barn. AdFarm staff blend into the decor wearing wool shirts, workboots, and jeans.

Employees at AdFarm take turns overlooking company-rented farms in Calgary and Fargo (North Dakota) to help

them understand their market and their customers' customers even better. AdFarm recognizes that farmers have a minimal "bullshit" meter and that agri-chemical and product companies appreciate it when they can work with an agency that understands their industry. AdFarm is reaping the benefits: It's the largest agency in North America focusing solely on agriculture, with billings topping $70 million, and it has set its sights on the global market. The secret to AdFarm's success? McConnell admits, "In agriculture, clients need more than good creativity. They need knowledge in business and that's our advantage."

Source: Based on Norma Ramage, "Crazy about Ag Marketing," *Marketing Magazine Online*, 25 August 2003.

1. What can other marketers learn from AdFarm in terms of understanding their customers?
2. Is AdFarm's competitive advantage sustainable? How easy would it be for others to copy it?
3. What challenges may AdFarm encounter as it tries to spread its market reach globally?

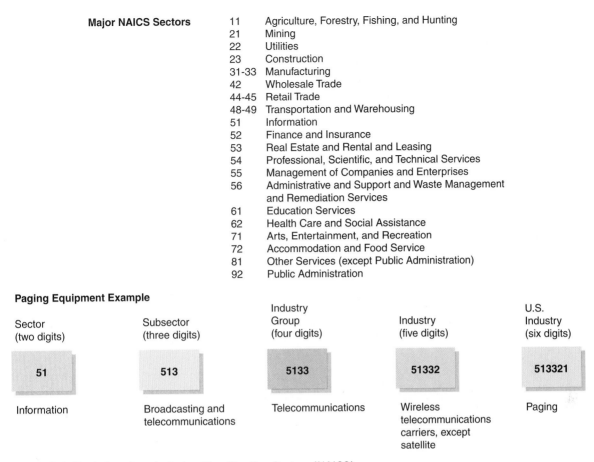

Major NAICS Sectors

11	Agriculture, Forestry, Fishing, and Hunting
21	Mining
22	Utilities
23	Construction
31-33	Manufacturing
42	Wholesale Trade
44-45	Retail Trade
48-49	Transportation and Warehousing
51	Information
52	Finance and Insurance
53	Real Estate and Rental and Leasing
54	Professional, Scientific, and Technical Services
55	Management of Companies and Enterprises
56	Administrative and Support and Waste Management and Remediation Services
61	Education Services
62	Health Care and Social Assistance
71	Arts, Entertainment, and Recreation
72	Accommodation and Food Service
81	Other Services (except Public Administration)
92	Public Administration

Paging Equipment Example

Sector (two digits)	Subsector (three digits)	Industry Group (four digits)	Industry (five digits)	U.S. Industry (six digits)
51	513	5133	51332	513321
Information	Broadcasting and telecommunications	Telecommunications	Wireless telecommunications carriers, except satellite	Paging

Figure 6.4 North American Industry Classification System (NAICS)

jointly by the United States, Canada, and Mexico. NAICS replaced the U.S. Standard Industrial Classification (SIC) system in 2002 so that the North American Free Trade Agreement (NAFTA) member nations could compare economic and financial statistics.[4] Like the SIC system, the NAICS is used to collect and report data on business activity such as the number of firms, the total dollar amount of sales, the number of employees, and the growth rate for industries—broken down by geographic region. These reports have become an essential tool for classifying business-to-business customers. Many firms use them to assess potential markets and to determine how well they are doing compared to their industry group as a whole.

The NAICS uses a different six-digit numerical code for each industry. At its inception, the system included 20 major sectors identified by two-digit numbers, shown in Figure 6.4. The major sectors are further broken down into subsectors (third digit), industry groups (fourth digit), industries common to Canada, the United States, and Mexico (fifth digit), and data related to the industry in a specific country (sixth digit—"0" for Canada). The system is updated every five years to allow classifications to keep up with changes in the economy.

To use the NAICS to find new customers, a marketer might first determine the NAICS groups of current customers and then evaluate the sales potential of the overall NAICS groups or particular segments based on the number of employees of firms in the groups. For example, a firm that supplies employee uniforms could evaluate the sales potential of firms having 150 and 1000 employees in an NAICS category and set its sights on attractive firms in that category. In other cases, a firm might choose to target firms in a cross-section of categories, as Sprint did in its "Real Solutions" campaign which was aimed at all companies that employed 100 to 500 people.[5] Now we will take a closer look at the four major categories into which organizations fall.

Exhibit 6.5

Allstream, a division of Manitoba Telecom Services Inc., offers business communication solutions for its clients. This ad was part of a campaign to help differentiate the company in the minds of business customers.

Exhibit 6.6

Governments are the only customers for certain products.

Producers

Producers purchase goods for use in the production of other goods and services that are, in turn, sold to make a profit (Exhibit 6.5). Producers are customers for a vast number of products, from raw materials to goods manufactured by other producers. For example, DuPont buys resins and uses them to manufacture insulation material for sleeping bags. Ontario mould maker Protoplast buys aluminum ingots, which it turns into industrial moulds. Auto manufacturers, such as Honda or Ford, buy a variety of component parts—from transmissions to carpet—for use in the cars they ship to consumers. Service producers buy linens, furniture, and food to create the quality accommodations and meals their guests expect.

Resellers

Resellers buy finished goods for the purpose of reselling, renting, or leasing to other businesses. Resellers include retailers and wholesalers. Bestfoods, for example, sells its food products to the distribution arms of giant resellers such as Loblaws, Sobeys, A&P, and Safeway, who then distribute the food to their retail stores. Although resellers do not produce goods, they do provide their customers with the time, place, and possession utility we talked about in Chapter 1 by making the goods available to consumers when and where they want them.

Governments

Government markets make up the largest single business or organizational market in Canada. The Canadian government market includes more than 6000 government agencies and organizations, more than 740 municipal and local governments, 10 provincial governments, 3 territorial governments, and a federal government that collectively spent more than $515 billion in 2006.[6] The federal government alone has more than 225 separate institutions[7] that typically procure (through a tendering process) $5 to $6 billion worth of goods and services each year.[8]

Governments are just about the only customers for certain products such as snowplows, garbage trucks, transit buses, and light rapid trains like the one illustrated in Exhibit 6.6. Many government expenditures are for more familiar and less expensive items, such as printer toner, pens, and Post-it Notes. The Vancouver–Whistler 2010 Olympic organizing committee, for example, will be spending more than $20 million to set up offices and the athletes village—buying products ranging from office equipment to beds and pillows.

For business marketers, selling goods and services to governments is different from selling to producer or reseller markets. Taking a prospective buyer to lunch may be standard practice in the corporate world, but in government markets, this practice may be in conflict with ethical (and legal) standards for government personnel. Because governments make purchases with taxpayer money, laws require them to adhere to strict regulations. Generally, government buyers must develop detailed specifications and obtain **competitive bids** for even the simplest purchases. With competitive bids, potential suppliers must submit detailed proposals including price and associated data for a proposed purchase. The firm making the best offer gets the bid. Government agencies are often required by law to accept the lowest bid from a qualified vendor.

Governments regularly publish information on upcoming bidding opportunities to let possible vendors know about purchases they are about to make. In Canada, the federal government's tendering process is managed by a private company called MERX, which offers a website for searching and submitting tenders for government procurement opportunities with a value of $25 000 or more (**www.merx.com**). MERX also gives companies access to thousands of other procurement opportunities from provincial and municipal governments as well as hundreds of colleges, universities, hospitals, and school boards across Canada.

Not-for-Profit Institutions

Not-for-profit institutions are organizations (for example, hospitals, churches, colleges, universities, museums, nursing homes) that operate for charitable, educational, community, and other public service goals and buy goods and services to support these functions. The institutional market also includes charitable and cause-related organizations, such as the Salvation Army and the Red Cross. Not-for-profit institutions tend to operate on low budgets and, in all but the largest ones, non-professional part-time buyers who have other duties—or are volunteers—normally make the purchases. These customers often rely on marketers to provide more advice and assistance before and after the sale than professional business buyers require.

THE NATURE OF BUSINESS BUYING

So far we've talked about how business-to-business markets are different from consumer markets and about the different types of customers that make up business markets. In this section, we'll discuss some of the important characteristics of business buying.

To be successful in business-to-business markets means developing marketing strategies that meet the needs of organizational customers better than the competition. To do this, marketers must understand business buying behaviour. Armed with this knowledge, marketers are able to participate in the buyer's decision process from the start. Take a firm that sells equipment to hospitals. Understanding that physicians (rather than buyers) who practise at the hospital often initiate decisions to purchase new equipment means that the firm's salespeople will make sure the physicians know about new technologies and improved equipment. In this section, we'll first look at the different types of buying situations found in business markets. Then we'll examine the role of professional purchasers and buying centres in business buying.

The Buying Situation

Like end consumers, business buyers spend more time and effort on certain purchases than on others. Devoting such effort to a purchase decision often depends on the complexity of the product and how often the decision has to be made. A **buy class** identifies the degree

producers The individuals or organizations that purchase products for use in the production of other goods and services.

resellers The individuals or organizations that buy finished goods for the purpose of reselling, renting, or leasing to others to make a profit and to maintain their business operations.

government markets Federal, provincial, and local governments that buy goods and services to carry out public objectives and to support their operations.

competitive bids A business buying process in which two or more suppliers submit proposals (including price and associated data) for a proposed purchase and the firm providing the better offer gets the bid.

not-for-profit institutions Organizations with charitable, educational, community, and other public service goals that buy goods and services to support their functions and to attract and serve their members.

buy class One of three classifications of business buying situations that characterize the degree of time and effort required to make a decision in a buying situation.

of effort required of the firm's personnel to collect information and make a purchase decision. These classes are straight rebuys, modified rebuys, and new-task buys.

STRAIGHT REBUY Buyers, when a purchase has low risk, often rely on strategies to simplify the process, such as using a fixed set of trusted suppliers for routine purchases.[9] Products like computer paper, shipping cartons, and cleaning compounds are low risk. Being successful in such markets means keeping prices down and developing selling policies to keep the buying process as simple as possible. A **straight rebuy** is the purchase of items that a business-to-business customer regularly needs. The buyer has purchased the same items many times before and routinely reorders them when supplies are low, often from the same suppliers. Reordering takes little time. Buyers typically maintain a list of approved vendors that have demonstrated their ability to meet the firm's criteria for pricing, quality, service, and delivery (Exhibit 6.7).

Because straight rebuys can mean steady income for a firm, many business marketers go to great lengths to cultivate and maintain relationships with customers that will lead to straight rebuys. Salespeople, for example, regularly call on these customers to personally handle orders and to see if there are additional products the customer needs; they may also attempt to obtain long-term contracts. Rebuys keep a supplier's sales volume up and selling costs down.

MODIFIED REBUY Straight rebuy situations do not last forever. A **modified rebuy** occurs when a firm wants to shop around for suppliers with better prices, quality, or delivery times. A modified rebuy can also occur when an organization has new needs for products it already buys. A buyer who has purchased many copying machines in the past, for example, may have to evaluate several lines of equipment, such as the document centre in Exhibit 6.8, if the firm has a new need for digitized office equipment.

NEW-TASK BUYING A first-time purchase is a **new-task buy**, often characterized by uncertainty and risk. New-task buys require the most effort because the buyer has no previous experience on which to base a decision. Companies like Vancouver-based FatPort are selling Wi-Fi network hubs to pubs, laundromats, independent hotels, and other small businesses, helping them become wireless Internet service providers. This technology allows different devices and people to communicate with each other through radio frequencies. Most small business owners have little experience with wireless communication technology, making this a new-task purchase decision that comes with some risk and a lot of uncertainty. In new-task buying situations, buyers not only lack experience with the product, but are also unfamiliar with firms that supply the product. Supplier choice is therefore critical and buyers will gather much information about quality, pricing, delivery, and service from several potential suppliers.

For suppliers, new-task buying represents both a challenge and an opportunity. Although a new-task buy can be significant in itself, many times the chosen supplier gains the added advantage of becoming an "in" supplier for more routine purchases that will follow. A growing business that needs an advertising agency for the first time, for example, may seek exhaustive information from several firms before selecting one and will continue to use the chosen agency's services for future projects

straight rebuy A buying situation in which business buyers make routine purchases that require minimal decision making.

modified rebuy A buying situation classification that business buyers use to categorize a previously made purchase that involves some change and that requires limited decision making.

new-task buy A new business-to-business purchase that is complex or risky and that requires extensive decision making.

Exhibit 6.7

Delivery and shipping services are a straight rebuy decision for most businesses.

without exploring other alternatives. Marketers know that to get the order in a new-task buy situation, they must develop a close working relationship with the business buyer. Such relationships mean that buyers can count on business marketers to help develop product specifications and terms for the purchase that are in the best interests of the customer's organization and its needs.

The Professional Buyer

Just as it is important for marketers of consumer goods and services to understand their customers, it is essential that business-to-business marketers understand who handles the buying for business customers. Trained professional buyers typically carry out buying in business-to-business markets and are often called *purchasing agents*, *procurement officers*, or *directors of materials management*. Unlike consumers who may spend only a few hours a month making purchase decisions, professional purchasers do it all day, every day.

Professional buyers have a lot of responsibility. They spend the company's money and buy the products that keep it running. These buyers tend to focus on economic factors beyond the initial price of the product, including transportation and delivery charges, accessory products or supplies, maintenance, and other ongoing costs. They select suppliers, negotiate for the lowest prices, and are responsible for selecting quality products and ensuring their timely delivery. Their purchases can range in price and significance from paper clips to multimillion-dollar computer systems.

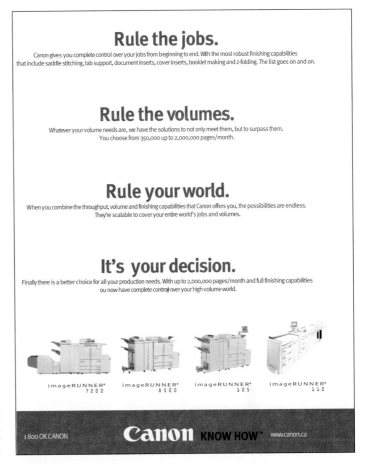

Exhibit 6.8

Changing technology makes purchasing for the digitized office a modified rebuy.

Sometimes business buyers, like consumers, make decisions based on emotions, brand loyalty, long-term relationships established with particular salespeople, or aesthetic concerns. Even age, income, education, personality, and attitudes can affect a buyer's decisions. Marketing communications play a crucial role in the buyer's decision process. For example, most buyers depend on vendors' salespeople to keep them informed of new products.

A key factor in many purchase decisions is whether the buyer perceives the purchase to be risky.[10] Some buyers are more risk averse than others. Successful business marketers try to develop strategies that help the buyer avoid risk. These include providing samples of a new product for a business customer or placing a new piece of equipment in the customer's facility to try for a few weeks.

Big firms with many facilities in different locations often practise **centralized purchasing**. This means that, even when others in the organization participate in the decision of what to buy, one department does all the buying for the company.[11] With centralized purchasing, a firm has more buying power and can get the best prices. Wal-Mart Canada can offer its customers lower prices than other stores (see Exhibit 6.9), because its centralized purchasing department buys large quantities of items and can demand volume discounts from suppliers. For sellers such as Kraft Foods, centralized purchasing means they only need to make a single sale to have their peanut butter in Sobeys/IGA locations across the country.

The professional buyers who work in centralized purchasing offices often become experts at the ins and outs of certain types of products, and each may have a specialized role in the

centralized purchasing A business buying practice in which an organization's purchasing department does all the buying for the company.

Exhibit 6.9

Centralized purchasing is one way Wal-Mart keeps "dropping" prices for its customers.

purchasing function. In the buying departments of retail chains, for example, an individual buyer (and several assistant buyers) may be responsible for buying only women's sleepwear or junior tops or children's sizes 2 to 6X. This specializing leads to greater expertise in the buyer's specific area.

The Buying Centre

Whether or not a firm's buying is a centralized process and whether or not the purchase situation calls for a modified or new-task buying situation, several people may need to work together to reach a decision. Depending on what they need to purchase, these participants may be production workers, supervisors, engineers, secretaries, shipping clerks, or financial officers. In a small organization, everyone may have a voice in the decision. The group of people in the organization who participate in the decision-making process is the **buying centre**.

buying centre The group of people in an organization who influence and participate in purchasing decisions.

THE FLUID NATURE OF THE BUYING CENTRE Although the term *buying centre* may conjure up an image of offices buzzing with purchasing activity, it usually is a cross-functional team of decision makers. Generally, the members of a buying centre have some expertise or interest in the particular decision and they are able, as a group, to make the best decision.

Hospitals, for example, frequently make purchase decisions through a large buying centre. When making a decision to purchase disposable oxygen masks, for example, one or more physicians, the director of nurses, and purchasing agents may work together to determine quantities and select the best products and suppliers. A separate decision regarding the types of pharmaceutical supplies to stock might need a different group to advise the purchasing agent. This means that marketers must continually identify which employees are involved in every purchase and develop relationships with them all.

ROLES IN THE BUYING CENTRE Buying centre participants have unique roles in the decision process. In some cases, the purchasing agent or professional buyer who makes the purchase may also make the decision. In other cases, the buyer's chief role is to gather information for users of the product or a top manager who will ultimately make the decision.

Role	Potential Player	Responsibility
• Initiator	• Production employees, sales manager, almost anyone	• Recognizes that a purchase needs to be made
• User	• Production employees, secretaries, almost anyone	• Individual(s) who will ultimately use the product
• Gatekeeper	• Buyer/purchasing agent	• Controls flow of information to others in the organization
• Influencer	• Engineers, quality control experts, technical specialists, outside consultants	• Affects decision by giving advice and sharing expertise
• Decider	• Purchasing agent, managers, CEO	• Makes the final purchase decision
• Buyer	• Purchasing agent	• Executes the purchase decision

Figure 6.5 Roles in the Buying Centre

For suppliers, the buying centre concept complicates the marketing process. A salesperson, for example, may have to provide different types of information to satisfy the interests of all participants. For example, a customer's engineers may want to know about the technical specifications of the product, whereas managers who will oversee the use of the product are interested in the safety of the product or in what types of in-service training the supplier is willing to provide. The salesperson also has to determine who has the most influence on the decision, who plays the key role of decision maker, and who actually makes the purchase. Consider again the hospital purchase of oxygen masks. The purchasing department's major concerns likely centre on price and delivery schedules, the nursing staff may be interested in packaging that is easy to open, and the physicians may be concerned with product design and that there will be few, if any, faulty masks. The salesperson must convince everyone that his or her product will satisfy their needs better than that of the competition.

Depending on the complexity of the purchase and the size of the buying centre, a participant may assume one, several, or all of the six roles shown in Figure 6.5. Let's review them.

The *initiator* begins the buying process by first recognizing that the firm needs to make a purchase. A production employee, for example, may notice that a piece of equipment is not working properly and notify a supervisor. At other times, the initiator may suggest purchasing a new product because it will improve the firm's operations. Depending on the initiator's position in the organization and the type of purchase, the initiator may or may not influence the actual purchase decision. For marketers, it is important to make sure individuals who might initiate a purchase are aware of improved products they offer.

The *user* is the member of the buying centre who needs the purchased product. The user's role in the buying centre varies. For example, an administrative assistant may give his or her input on the features needed in a new copier that the assistant will be "chained to" for several hours a day. Marketers need to inform users of their products about ease of use and other user benefits their products provide over those of competitors.

The *gatekeeper* is the member who controls the flow of information to other members. Typically, the gatekeeper is the purchasing agent who gathers information and materials from salespeople, schedules sales presentations, and controls suppliers' access to other participants in the buying process. For salespeople, developing and maintaining strong personal relationships with gatekeepers is critical to being able to offer their products to the buying centre.

An *influencer* affects the buying decision by dispensing advice or sharing expertise. By virtue of their expertise, engineers, quality control specialists, and other technical experts in the firm generally have a great deal of influence in purchasing equipment, materials, and component parts used in production. The influencers may or may not wind up using the product. Marketers need to identify key influencers in the buying centre and work to convince them of their product's superiority.

The *decider* is the member of the buying centre who makes the final decision. This person usually has the greatest power within the buying centre and often has power within the organization to authorize spending the company's money. For a routine purchase, the decider may be the purchasing agent. If the purchase is complex, a manager or CEO may be the decider. The decider is key to a marketer's success and deserves a great deal of attention in the selling process.

The *buyer* is the person who has responsibility for executing the purchase. Although the buyer often has a role in identifying and evaluating alternative suppliers, this person's primary function is handling the details of the purchase. The buyer obtains competing bids, negotiates contracts, and arranges delivery dates and payment plans. Once a firm makes the purchase decision, marketers turn their attention to negotiating the details of the purchase with the buyer. Successful marketers are well aware that providing exemplary service in this stage of the purchase can be key to future sales.

THE BUSINESS BUYING DECISION PROCESS

We have seen a number of players in the business buying process, beginning with an initiator and ending with a buyer. To make matters more challenging to marketers, members of the buying team go through several stages in the decision-making process. The business buying decision process, as Figure 6.6 shows, is a series of steps similar to those in the consumer decision process (discussed in Chapter 5). The business buying process is more complex than the consumer decision-making process, however, and each step can mushroom into several additional steps.

Problem Recognition

As in consumer buying, the first step in the business buying decision process occurs when someone sees that a purchase can solve a problem. For straight rebuy purchases, this step may be a result of the firm running out of paper, pens, or garbage bags. In these cases, the buyer places the order and the decision-making process ends. Recognition of the need for modified rebuy purchases often comes from wanting to replace outdated equipment, from changes in technology, or from an ad, brochure, or other form of marketing communication that offers the customer a better product at a lower price. The need for new-task purchases often arises because the firm wants to enhance its operations in some way or a smart salesperson tells the business customer about a new product that will increase the efficiency of the firm's operations.

INFORMATION SEARCH In the second step of the decision process for purchases other than straight rebuys, the buying centre searches for information about products and suppliers. Members of the buying centre may individually or collectively refer to reports in trade magazines and journals, seek advice from outside consultants, and pay close attention to marketing communication from different manufacturers and other suppliers. As in consumer marketing, marketers ensure that information is available when and where business customers want it—by placing ads in trade magazines, mailing brochures and other printed material to prospects, and having a well-trained, enthusiastic sales force regularly calling on customers.

DEVELOPING PRODUCT SPECIFICATIONS Business buyers often develop product specifications, written descriptions laying out their exact product requirements—quality, size, weight, colour, features, quantities, warranty, service terms, and delivery and training requirements for the purchase. When the product needs are complex or technical, engineers and other experts are key players in identifying specific product characteristics and determining whether standardized, off-the-shelf or customized, made-to-order goods and services will do.

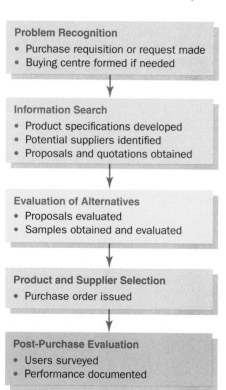

Problem Recognition
- Purchase requisition or request made
- Buying centre formed if needed

Information Search
- Product specifications developed
- Potential suppliers identified
- Proposals and quotations obtained

Evaluation of Alternatives
- Proposals evaluated
- Samples obtained and evaluated

Product and Supplier Selection
- Purchase order issued

Post-Purchase Evaluation
- Users surveyed
- Performance documented

Figure 6.6 Steps in the Business Buying Decision Process

OBTAINING PROPOSALS Once the product specifications are in hand, the buyer's next step is to obtain written or verbal proposals, or *bids,* from one or more potential suppliers. For standardized or branded products in which there are few, if any, differences in the products of different suppliers, this may be as simple as an informal request for pricing information, including discounts, shipping charges, and confirmation of delivery dates. At other times, the request is a formal written *request for proposal* or *request for quotation*, which requires suppliers to develop detailed proposals or price quotations for supplying the product.

Evaluation of Alternatives

When evaluating alternatives, the buying centre assesses the proposals. Total spending for goods and services can have a major impact on the firm's profitability, so all other things being equal, price is the primary consideration. Pricing evaluations take into account discount policies for certain quantities, returned goods policies, the cost of repair and maintenance services, terms of payment, and the cost of financing large purchases. For capital equipment, cost criteria also include the life expectancy of the purchase, the expected resale value, and disposal costs for old equipment. In some cases, the buying centre may negotiate with the preferred supplier to match the lowest bidder. Although a bidder often is selected because it offers the lowest price, the buying decision may be based on other factors. For example, American Express wins bids for its travel agency business by offering extra services such as a corporate credit card and monthly reports that detail the company's total travel expenses.

The more complex and costly the purchase, the more time spent searching for the best supplier—and the more marketers must do to win the order. For example, marketers often make formal presentations and product demonstrations to the buying centre group. In the case of installations and large equipment, marketers sometimes arrange for buyers to speak with or even visit other customers to see for themselves how the product performs.

Product and Supplier Selection

Once buyers have assessed all proposals, they make a purchase decision—the selection of the best product and supplier to meet the firm's needs. Although price is usually a factor, in firms that have adopted a total quality management approach (discussed in Chapter 2), the quality, reliability, and durability of materials and component parts are paramount. Reliability and durability rank high for equipment and systems that keep the firm's operations running smoothly without interruption. For some purchases, warranties, repair service, and regular maintenance after the sale are important.

A supplier's ability to make on-time deliveries is the critical factor in the selection process for firms that have adopted an inventory management system called **just in time (JIT)**. JIT systems reduce inventory and stock to very low levels (or even zero) and ensure a constant supply through precisely timed deliveries just when needed (Exhibit 6.10). For both manufacturers and resellers, the choice of supplier may come down to one whose location is nearest. To win a large customer, a supplier organization may even have to be willing to set up production facilities close to the customer to guarantee JIT delivery.[12]

One of the most important functions of a buyer is deciding how many suppliers can best serve the firm's needs. Sometimes one supplier is more beneficial to the organization than multiple suppliers. **Single sourcing**, in which a buyer and seller work quite closely, is particularly important for a firm that needs frequent deliveries

just in time (JIT) Inventory management and purchasing processes that manufacturers and resellers use to reduce inventory to very low levels and ensure that deliveries from suppliers arrive only when needed.

single sourcing The business practice of buying a particular product from only one supplier.

Exhibit 6.10

Toyota publicized and was an early adopter of the JIT system, as space is at a premium in Japan and operations are constantly being challenged to run more smoothly.

multiple sourcing The business practice of buying a particular product from many suppliers.

reciprocity A trading partnership in which two firms agree to buy from one another.

outsourcing The business buying process of obtaining outside vendors to provide goods or services that otherwise might be supplied in-house.

reverse marketing A business practice in which a buyer firm attempts to identify suppliers who will produce products according to the buyer firm's specifications.

or specialized products. But reliance on a single source means that the firm is at the mercy of the chosen supplier to deliver the needed goods or services without interruption. **Multiple sourcing** is buying a product from several suppliers. With multiple sourcing, suppliers are more likely to remain price competitive. And if one supplier has problems with delivery, the firm has others to fall back on.

Using one (or a few) suppliers rather than many has advantages. A firm that buys from a single supplier becomes a large customer with a lot of clout when it comes to negotiating prices and contract terms. Having one (or a few) suppliers also lowers the firm's administrative costs because it has fewer invoices to pay, fewer purchase orders to put into the system, and fewer salespeople to see.

Sometimes supplier selection is based on **reciprocity**, which means that a buyer and seller agree to be each other's customers by saying essentially, "I'll buy from you and you buy from me." For example, a firm that supplies parts to a company that manufactures trucks would agree to buy trucks from only that firm. Consumer and Corporate Affairs Canada frowns on reciprocal agreements and often determines that such agreements between large firms are illegal because they limit free competition—new suppliers simply don't have a chance against the preferred suppliers. In other countries, reciprocity is a common and, often, expected practice in business-to-business marketing.

With **outsourcing**, firms obtain outside vendors to provide goods or services that might otherwise be supplied in-house. For example, the federal government could have managed its own electronic tendering system but found it more cost effective and efficient to outsource this service to MERX. Outsourcing has undoubtedly become a growing trend in recent years as highly trained services providers in China, India, and other parts of the world are able to do increasingly sophisticated work—including preparing Canadian corporate tax and personal tax returns!

Another type of buyer-seller partnership is **reverse marketing**. Instead of sellers trying to identify potential customers and then "pitching" their products, buyers try to find suppliers capable of producing specific products they need and then attempt to "sell" the idea to the suppliers. The seller works to satisfy the buying firm's needs while assuring themselves of product quality, sufficient supply, and reasonable terms.

Ethical Decisions in Marketing

In the past decade, Canadian schools have been in a quandary.[13] Funding cutbacks have crippled school budgets, forcing many to seek corporate sponsorships and exclusive contracts for vending machine rights. Marketers want to establish brand loyalty and teens are both a coveted and, when in schools, a captive audience. The Peel District School Board in Ontario received $5.5 million for three years of an exclusive 10-year contract with Coca-Cola. The York Region District received $3.5 million plus to put toward scholarships for a five-year contract with Pepsi products. The Calgary Board of Education announced that public schools, classrooms, and programs can now be named for corporate donors.

Concerned parents claim that, while schools are preaching nutrition in the classroom, they are pushing junk food in the hallways. Advocates argue that kids are going to buy junk food anyway, so some of the money may as well go to support education. This issue has been heating up. The principal of Pitt River Middle School in Coquitlam, B.C., tried to replace the fast-food mall in her school with fresh sandwiches, bagels, fruit, and milk, but the school district insisted that the school return to selling fast foods in order to "maintain buying efficiencies."

A number of marketers, however, are taking it upon themselves to be more socially responsible. Kraft Foods recently announced it would stop all in-school marketing and promotions for a range of products including Oscar Mayer meats, Oreos, and Kool-Aid. The soft drink industry announced it would voluntarily withdraw its carbonated drinks from Canadian elementary and middle schools by the beginning of the next school year. Concerned consumers see this as a token gesture because many elementary schools don't allow soft drink vending machines on their premises and the big money is in high schools.

Do you think schools or school boards should be seeking corporate sponsorships or distribution contracts? Should the fast-food industry be allowed to self-regulate on this issue or should a provincial or national policy be set? Do you think Kraft Foods' strategy will be effective in the long run if others do not follow its lead?

Post-Purchase Evaluation

Just as consumers evaluate purchases, an organizational buyer assesses whether the performance of the product and the supplier is living up to expectations. The buyer surveys the users to determine their satisfaction with the product as well as with the installation, delivery, and service provided by the supplier. By reviewing supplier performance, a firm decides whether to keep or drop the supplier. Many suppliers recognize the importance of conducting their own performance reviews on a regular basis. Measuring up to a customer's expectations can mean winning or losing a big account.

ELECTRONIC BUSINESS-TO-BUSINESS COMMERCE

The Internet has brought about the most important changes in organizational buying behaviour in recent years. Electronic commerce, or e-commerce, is the buying and selling of products electronically via the Internet. We see e-commerce in consumer markets—sites such as Chapters.Indigo.ca or Futureshop.ca that sell consumer goods (to be discussed further in Chapter 11). In this chapter we are concerned with e-commerce in business markets. **Business-to-business (B2B) e-commerce** refers to the Internet exchanges between two or more businesses or organizations. B2B e-commerce includes exchanges of information, products, services, and payments (Exhibit 6.11). It's not as glitzy as consumer e-commerce, but it has changed the way businesses operate.

business-to-business (B2B) e-commerce Internet exchanges between two or more businesses or organizations.

For several decades, firms have used electronic data interchange (EDI) systems to communicate with business partners. Despite the growing popularity of technologies such as XML services (Extensible Markup Language, which support a wide variety of applications that allow businesses to communicate with each other), EDI is still the most used data format by e-commerce transactions around the world. EDI allows for limited communication through the exchange of computer data between two companies. But EDI is expensive and transmits only rigidly formatted electronic documents such as purchase orders and invoices.

Today, firms with limited resources or with unlimited financial capacity have replaced their EDI systems with Internet tools that allow electronic transfer of all kinds of data—even engineering drawings—as well as EDI-type exchanges. General Electric, for example, is one of the world's most innovative companies. A partnership between Beazer Homes, GE's appliance business, and software vendor Hyphen Solutions produced a system in which Beazer's GE appliance orders get processed through Hyphen's BuildPro and SupplyPro interfaces and SupplyPro Connect servers. Think of SupplyPro Connect as a messaging system that takes converted XML or spreadsheet documents and feeds the orders into GE's back-office system. Now, orders between businesses are processed in seconds.[14] For sellers, too, e-commerce provides remarkable advantages. Boeing, for example, received orders for $100 million in spare parts in the first year that its website was in operation.[15] The Internet also allows businesses to reach new markets. Ottawa-based **Agdealer.com**, for example, is able to coordinate the sale of used farming equipment that would otherwise have been discarded because of the cost to an individual seller of finding a buyer for their specialized equipment.[16]

Using the Internet for e-commerce allows business marketers to link directly to suppliers, factories, distributors, and customers, radically reducing the time necessary for order and delivery of goods, tracking sales, and getting feedback from customers. One implication of this is that all firms, big and small, will need to have an international orientation as well as a source of competitive advantage to compete successfully. This is what Victoria-based **WorldBid.com** hopes to facilitate. Worldbid.com is the largest source of international trade leads, requests for quotation, and tender opportunities from companies and government organizations around the world. Over 430 000 businesses have registered to help increase sales, reduce supplier costs, and find new business contacts.[17]

Exhibit 6.11

While Future Shop mainly focuses on business-to-consumer marketing, this ad shows that it also caters to B2B customers.

In the simplest form of B2B e-commerce, the Internet provides an online catalogue of products and services that businesses need. Companies find that their Internet site is important for delivering online technical support,

Exhibit 6.12

Companies such as Staples Business Depot have made a consistent effort to increase their business-to-business sales in recent years.

product information, order status information, and customer service to corporate customers (Exhibit 6.12).

Intranets, Extranets, Private Exchanges, and Buying Groups

Although the Internet is the primary means of e-commerce, some companies have used similar computer technology to develop more secure means of conducting business. **Intranets** are in-house computer connections an organization creates to distribute information internally. City workers in Mississauga, Ontario, for example, use the intranet "WebBoard" to communicate all official announcements, new policies, technology implementations, staff appointments, and most recently, smog alerts.[18] Intranets are more secure than Internet connections, because they are protected by electronic firewalls that prevent access by unauthorized users.

When the intranet is opened to authorized external users, it is called an *extranet*. With extranets, marketers allow suppliers, distributors, and other authorized users to access data that the company makes available. Toronto-based 3Com Canada Inc., for example, uses extranet technology as a way to connect to branch offices, keep in touch with partners, and offer employees better ways of getting their jobs done.[19]

In addition to saving companies money, extranets allow business partners to collaborate on projects (such as product design) and to build better relationships. Hewlett-Packard and Procter & Gamble, for example, swap marketing plans and review ad campaigns with their advertising agencies through extranets. Extranets are also used by public service organizations to coordinate their resources and ability to serve the public. Ontario hospitals, for example, have an emergency patient referral system called CritiCall that allows admitting clerks, hospital administrators, and even physicians to track beds, emergency department status, and other medical resources. This allows the direction of patients to facilities that can help them quickly.[20]

Some of the most interesting online activity in the B2B world is taking place on **private exchanges**. These are systems that link a specially invited group of suppliers and partners over the web. A private exchange allows companies to collaborate with suppliers they trust—without sharing sensitive information with others.

Wal-Mart, IBM, and Hewlett-Packard are among the giant firms already operating private exchanges. IBM Canada, for example, created Airweb—a B2B e-market that allows IBM's 20 000 employees to book corporate travel online 24/7. Airweb was created in partnership with American Express and is supported by Air Canada, Hertz, Delta Hotels, and 17 other American Express partners.[21] Many other companies are getting on board as well. For example, the director of inventory control for Ace Hardware can click his mouse and instantly get an up-to-the minute listing of the screwdrivers, hammers, and other products his suppliers have in stock. In addition, suppliers he has invited to participate in his private exchange (and only those suppliers) can submit bids when he sees that Ace stores are running low on hammers. In the "old days" before this process, it would take 7 to 10 days to purchase more hammers, and Ace's suppliers could only guess how many they should have on hand to supply the chain at any given time. The system benefits everyone because Ace keeps tighter controls on its inventories and its suppliers have a more accurate picture of the store's needs so that they can get rid of unneeded inventory and streamline their costs.

Buying groups reflect a cooperative purchasing effort among organizations that individually may be too small to command volume discounts or enjoy other economies of scale. By pooling their purchases with other companies, buying group members can cut overall procurement costs by as much as 10 percent.[22]

intranet An internal corporate communication network that uses Internet technology to link company departments, employees, and databases.

private exchanges Systems that link an invited group of suppliers and partners over the web.

buying group The coordination of purchasing among member organizations to realize economies of scale and other efficiencies.

Gold Leaf Office Products Ltd. is a Canadian buying group that has 11 member companies, with combined annual sales of about $180 million. In addition to handling their bulk buying, the staff at Gold Leaf's office publishes catalogues for members, prints advertising flyers, and runs a group-wide private brand of supplies—all of better quality and at a lower cost to the firms than they could manage on their own. Onvia, Inc., founded in Vancouver in 1996 and now operating out of Seattle (**www.onvia.com**), combines the purchasing power of more than 400 000 small business owners and gives them access to the goods and services of about 700 manufacturers and 25 wholesale distributors at reduced prices.[23]

Security Issues

There are several security issues with B2B e-commerce. The Internet is a cheap and relatively easy way for fraudsters to con consumers out of money (Exhibit 6.13). You may be concerned about someone obtaining your credit card number and charging even more to your account than you do, but companies have even greater worries. When hackers break into company sites, they can destroy company records and steal trade secrets. Both B2C and B2B e-commerce companies worry about *authentication* and ensuring that transactions are secure. Authentication means making sure that only authorized individuals are allowed to access a site and place an order. Maintaining security also requires firms to keep the information transferred as part of a transaction, such as a credit card number, out of criminals' hands.

Well-meaning but careless employees can create security problems as well. They can give out unauthorized access to company computer systems by not keeping their passwords into the system a secret. For example, hackers guess at passwords that are easy—nicknames, birth dates, hobbies, a spouse's name. To increase security of their Internet sites and transactions, most companies now have safeguards in place—firewalls and encryption devices, to name the most common two.

Exhibit 6.13

Internet security is a major problem for B2B marketers.

CUSTOMER RELATIONSHIP MANAGEMENT: A TOOL TO RETAIN CUSTOMERS

In the last section we discussed how business-to-business commerce and e-commerce are important parts of our economy. Experts advocate that, to retain customers, we should build a learning relationship with each of them.[24] In other words, technology enables us to build meaningful relationships with our customers by understanding their needs accurately, satisfying those needs in a superior fashion to our competitors, and adjusting our offerings as customer needs change. **Customer Relationship Management (CRM)** is a tool that enables a firm to do just that.

The CRM trend has also been referred to as one-to-one (1:1) marketing and relationship marketing.[25] Don Peppers, a leading writer and consultant in this area, defines CRM as ". . . managing customer relationships. If I'm managing customer relationships, it means I'm treating different customers differently, across all enterprises. . . . The relationship develops a context over time, it drives a change in behaviour . . . [this] means that I have to change my behaviour as an enterprise based on a customer."[26] A CRM strategy allows a company to

Customer Relationship Management (CRM) A strategy and process used by companies to identify their best customers, stay on top of their needs, and increase their satisfaction.

Table 6.1 How to Use Customer Satisfaction Information

	Bulk of Responses	Strategic Response
Stage 1	2 – 3 (dissatisfied)	Deliver the basic product or service elements as expected of anyone in the industry.
Stage 2	3 – 4 (neutral)	Provide an appropriate range of supporting services. Develop proactive service recovery to make amends when something goes wrong.
Stage 3	4 – 5 (satisfied)	Understand and achieve results in customers' terms.

Source: Based on Thomas O. Jones and W. Earl Sasser, Jr., "Why satisfied customers defect," *Harvard Business Review,* November–December 1995: 88.

identify its best customers, stay on top of their needs, and increase their satisfaction. In Chapter 4 you learned a little bit about customer satisfaction research. Table 6.1 outlines how customer satisfaction information can be used in CRM strategies.

Is CRM for all companies? Of course, CRM seems to make more sense for business-to-business companies and consumer products companies that have a limited number of customers. But, as we'll see in the next section, even soft drink and auto companies have used CRM to build customer relationships and brand loyalty.

CRM: A New Perspective on an Old Problem

CRM is about communicating with customers and customers being able to communicate with a company one-to-one. CRM systems are applications that automate interactions between customers and companies, through computers, CRM computer software, databases, and often the Internet. They include everything from websites that let you check on the status of a bill or package to *call centres* that solicit your business. The Federal Express website uses a CRM system to let customers track lost packages (Exhibit 6.14). When you get a phone message from the dentist reminding you about that filling appointment tomorrow, that's a CRM system. Car dealers use CRM when they call to ask how you like your new vehicle.

To appreciate the value of a CRM strategy, consider the experience of financial services firms such as Salomon Smith Barney and Fidelity Investments, both of which have adopted this new perspective. In general, an investment banker needs to manage accounts as well as open new ones—often 30 to 50 per month. The process of opening the account can take 45 minutes, not a satisfying process for the banker or for the customer. But with an automated CRM system the banker can open an account, issue a welcome letter, and produce an arbitration agreement in 10 minutes.

She can create a unique marketing communications campaign for each client based on that person's life cycle—including such variables as when a person opened an account, their annual income, family situation, and desired retirement age. The marketer can generate a happy

Exhibit 6.14

FedEx uses Internet technology to communicate with customers worldwide. From Chile to China, customers can track their packages and know where they are and when they will arrive.

anniversary letter to clients (to commemorate when they joined the firm, not when they got married) and include an invitation to update their investment objectives.

These firms have found that this level of individualized attention results in a much higher rate of customer satisfaction and retention, so CRM creates a win-win situation.[27] This success helps to explain why CRM is hot: Industry sources estimate that, in 2007, companies, small and large, spent US$20 billion to purchase sophisticated software that will let them build these electronic bridges.[28]

In addition to mollifying angry customers, marketers can use CRM systems to keep better track of enthusiastic ones. For example, marketers of youth products are integrating CRM technology into their efforts in the following ways:[29]

- Sprite staged a "Rocket Cash" sweepstakes promotion by sending out legions of marketing representatives with handheld touch-screen devices. They hung out at concerts and on street corners and enticed young people to enter the sweepstakes by tapping their names, e-mail addresses, and birthdays into the devices on the spot. Every evening, data were uploaded to Sprite's website and entrants were kept informed by e-mail of their status in the sweepstakes. Needless to say, in return Sprite wound up with a great list of consumers with whom it could continue to communicate in the future.

- Bacardi held a similar sweepstakes, but in this case the rum marketer also took digital photos of drivers' licences to verify consumers' ages.

- Ford sponsored a concert tour called Area One on behalf of its youth-oriented Focus model. At each of the tour's 17 stops, attendees could have their pictures taken next to a souped-up version of the Focus. If you wanted to see your photo, you registered your e-mail address with Ford and went to a special website where you could download your picture in a special frame (branded with Focus information) and e-mail the picture to your friends. Successful? Ford reported that 87 percent of the people who had their picture taken went to the website to retrieve them. And Ford was able to use the e-mail addresses to build relationships with these prospective customers.

Perhaps the most important aspect of CRM is that it presents a new way of looking at how to compete effectively in the marketplace. This begins with looking at customers as partners. CRM proponents suggest that the traditional relationship between customers and marketers is an adversarial one, where marketers try to sell their products and customers seek ways to avoid buying.[30] The customer relationship perspective sees customers as partners, with each partner learning from the other every time they interact. Successful firms compete by establishing relationships with individual customers on a one-to-one basis through dialogue and feedback. Business-to-business relationships can be maintained by calling to check on orders and assess future needs (Exhibit 6.15). What does *this* customer really want?

And, of course, when we say customers we don't just mean end consumers—CRM is widely used to strengthen business-to-business relationships as well. To understand the importance of this kind of thinking, consider the experience of Dow, a giant corporation that sells US$60 billion worth of chemicals, plastics, and agricultural products each year in more than 170 countries. Although Dow uses cutting-edge manufacturing technology every day, it had literally no centralized mechanism to keep track of its many customers.

Eventually, Dow launched a major effort to install a company-wide CRM system that would be a central repository for customer information and would allow its customers to interact with Dow more

Exhibit 6.15

To personalize its approach to customers, a business often calls current customers to monitor orders, future trends and needs, or even assess new opportunities.

efficiently—letting them access information automatically without having to deal with a large corporate bureaucracy. The result? A web-based interface called MyAccount@Dow that lets customers log on (with a secure password, of course), enter new orders, check on the status of old orders, pay invoices electronically, and collaborate with others throughout the system. As a result, Dow lowered its customer support costs by US$15 million and is taking electronic orders of US$100 million per month.[31]

Characteristics of CRM

In addition to having a different mindset, companies that successfully practise CRM have different goals, use different measures of success, and look at customers in some different ways. So, CRM marketers look at their share of the customer, at the lifetime value of a customer, at customer equity, and at focusing on high-value customers.

SHARE OF CUSTOMER Historically, marketers have measured success in a product category by their share of market. For example, if there are 100 million pairs of athletic shoes sold each year, a firm that sells 10 million of them has a 10 percent market share. If the shoemaker's marketing objective is to increase market share, it may lower the price of its shoes, increase its advertising, or offer customers a free basketball with every pair of shoes purchased. Such tactics may increase sales in the short run but, unfortunately, they may not do much for the long-term success of the shoemaker. In fact, such tactics may actually *decrease* the value of the brand by cheapening its image with giveaways.

Because it is always easier and less expensive to keep an existing customer than to get a new customer, CRM firms focus on increasing their **share of customer**, not share of market. Let's say that a consumer buys six pairs of shoes a year—two pairs from each of three different manufacturers. Let's assume one shoemaker has a CRM system that allows it to send letters to its current customers inviting them to receive a special price discount or gift if they buy more of the firm's shoes during the year. Or, the CRM system could alert the consumer when the firm receives the consumer's favourite styles in stock. If the firm can get the consumer to buy three or four or perhaps all six pairs from it, it has increased its share of customer. And that may not be too difficult because the customer already buys and supposedly likes the firm's shoes.

Without the CRM system, the shoe company would probably use traditional advertising to increase sales, which would be far more costly than the customer-only direct-mail campaign. So, the company can increase sales and profits at a much lower cost than it would spend to get one, two, or three new customers.

LIFETIME VALUE OF THE CUSTOMER With CRM, a **customer's lifetime value** is identified and is the true goal, not an individual transaction. It just makes sense that a firm's profitability and long-term success are going to be far greater if it develops long-term relationships with its customers so that those customers buy from it again and again. Costs will be far higher and profits lower if each customer purchase is a first-time sale.

How do marketers calculate the lifetime value of customer? They first estimate a customer's future purchases across all products from the firm over the next 20 or 30 years. The goal is to try to figure out what profit the company could make from the customer in the future. For example, an auto dealer might calculate the lifetime value of a single customer by first calculating the total revenue that could be generated by the customer over his lifetime: the number of automobiles he would buy times the average price, plus the service the dealership would provide over the years, and even possibly the income from auto loan financing. The lifetime value of the customer would be the total profit generated from the revenue stream.

CUSTOMER EQUITY Today, an increasing number of companies are considering their relationships with customers as financial assets. Such firms measure their success by calculating the value of their **customer equity**—the financial value of customer relationships throughout the lifetime of the relationships.[32] To do this, firms compare the investments they make in acquiring customers, retaining customers, and relationship enhancement with the

share of customer The percentage of an individual customer's purchase of a product that is a single brand.

customer's lifetime value The potential profit generated by a single customer's purchase of a firm's products over the customer's lifetime.

customer equity The financial value of a customer relationship throughout the lifetime of the relationship.

financial return on those investments. The goal is to reap a high return on the investments made in customer relationships and maximize the value of a firm's customer equity.

A GREATER FOCUS ON HIGH-VALUE CUSTOMERS Using a CRM approach, customers must be prioritized and communication customized accordingly. For example, any banker will tell you that not all customers are equal when it comes to profitability. Some banks now use CRM systems to generate a profile of each customer based on factors such as value, risk, attrition, and interest in buying new financial products. This automated system helps the bank decide which current or potential customers it will target with certain communications or how much effort to expend on retaining a person's account—all while cutting its costs by as much as a third.

It just makes sense to use different types of communication contacts based on the value of each individual customer. For example, personal selling may constitute 75 percent of all contacts with high-volume customers, while direct mail or telemarketing is more often the best way to contact low-volume customers.

Steps in CRM Marketing

There are four steps in CRM marketing.[33] The first step is to identify customers and get to know them in as much detail as possible. In step two, marketers need to differentiate these customers in terms of both their needs and value to the company. For step three, CRM marketers must interact with customers and find ways to improve cost efficiency and the effectiveness of the interaction. In step four, marketers need to customize some aspect of the goods or services they offer to each customer. This means treating each customer differently based on what has been learned through customer interactions. Table 6.2 suggests some activities for implementing these four steps.

Table 6.2 Customer Relationship Management Allows for Better Understanding of an Industry and Competitive Environment

Step	Suggested Activities
Identify	Collect and enter names and additional information about your customers.
	Verify and update, deleting outdated information.
Differentiate	Identify top customers.
	Determine which customers cost the company money.
	Find higher-value customers who have complained about your product or service more than once.
	Find customers who buy only one or two products from your company but a lot from other companies.
	Rank customers into A, B, and C categories based on their value to your company.
Interact	Call the top three people in the top 5 percent of dealers, distributors, and retailers that carry your product and make sure they're happy.
	Call your own company and ask questions; see how hard it is to get through and get answers.
	Call your competitors and compare their customer service with yours.
	Use incoming calls as selling opportunities.
	Initiate more dialogue with valuable customers.
	Improve complaint handling.
Customize	Find out what your customers want.
	Personalize your direct mail.
	Ask customers how and how often they want to hear from you.
	Ask your top 10 customers what you can do differently to improve your product or service.
	Involve top management in customer relations.

Source: Adapted from Don Peppers, Martha Rogers, and Bob Dorf, "Is your company ready for one-to-one marketing?" *Harvard Business Review*, January–February 1999, reprint #99107.

Real People, Real Decisions

How It Worked Out at IBM Canada

Deborah McKenzie and the IBM Canadian marketing team chose Option 1: Canadian integration by launching the IBM e-Business Breakaway Tour event. This mega event provided an opportunity for IBM to consolidate multiple events put on by individualized business units and to gain efficiencies from both a cost and a resource perspective. The centralization of the event development and execution would ensure that a comprehensive marketing discipline was applied—including a formal, closed-loop lead development process that would ensure a focused message. A corresponding follow-up on initiatives would be required. Although six months was pushing it, they decided that they had just enough time to organize a cross-Canada tour.

The team faced many challenges in this execution. They had permission from corporate headquarters to move in this direction, but had no budget. They approached all areas, from corporate headquarters to the Canadian brand sectors and their participating business partners, for small amounts of additional funding, and received resources from all the brands. They also moved a large portion of their funding for the year into this series of events. The next step was to convince all participants to remove themselves from the "silo structure" and to think of IBM as one brand. Surprisingly, this did not prove to be a difficult task. Although switching to a services focus would require changes in "internal" management's mindset, culture, and area control, all the brand and business units were supportive and buy-in went quite smoothly, as the marketing participants quickly saw the customer and business advantages to this approach.

The marketing for the event used an integrated marketing communication mix. Budget was spent on advertising, inter-active (web), and e-mail messaging. There were major press releases, and individual customers and potential customers were invited to the event in their area through direct mail, telemarketing, and by sales reps and IBM business partners. Follow-up programs were in place before the start of the events.

The main event included a "main tent" featuring keynote speakers. There were also six breakout sessions. IBM also demonstrated a showcase of solutions—24 pedestals demonstrating solutions from both IBM and its business partners. At each event it also hosted a CEO breakfast meeting to allow relationship marketing between senior IBM executives and current and potential customers.

This series of events was effective in getting the IBM message out. There was a higher than anticipated response and the attendance rates were exceptional, with more than 2400 customers and business partners attending the five events—more than twice as many as originally forecast. Results indicated that 65 percent of the attendees were new to IBM and 75 percent were from companies with fewer than 1000 employees. The events demonstrated that IBM not only had all the pieces to provide solutions to the marketplace, but also could pull the pieces together. A headline in *eWeek* supported this new positioning, proclaiming that IBM now sells services first and boxes second. IBM's strategy continues to focus on the total solutions and it has won many multi-year service contracts with this approach. It has gained strong market awareness of its products in the small- and medium-sized-business space, which has resulted in revenue growth. This marketing strategy has proven successful!

Key Terms

- **acceleration principle (multiplier effect)**, p. 209

- **business-to-business (B2B) E-commerce**, p. 221

- **business-to-business marketing**, p. 206

- **buy class**, p. 213

- **buying centre**, p. 216

- **buying group**, p. 222

- **centralized purchasing**, p. 215

- **competitive bids**, p. 213

- **customer equity**, p. 226

CHAPTER SUMMARY

1. Describe the general characteristics of business-to-business markets and business buying practices.

Business-to-business markets include business and organizational customers that buy goods and services for purposes other than personal consumption. Business and organizational customers are usually few in number, may be geographically concentrated, and often purchase higher-priced products in larger quantities. Business demand is derived from the demand for another good or service, is generally not affected by price increases or decreases, is subject to great fluctuations, and may be tied to the demand and availability of some other good.

2. Explain how marketers classify business and organizational markets.

Business customers include producers, resellers, governments, and not-for-profit organizations. Producers purchase materials, parts, and various goods and services needed to produce other goods and services to be sold at a profit. Resellers purchase finished goods to resell at a profit, as well as other goods and services to maintain their operations. Governments and other not-for-profit organizations purchase the goods and services necessary to fulfill their objectives. The North American Industry Classification System (NAICS), a numerical coding system developed by NAFTA countries, is the most widely used classification system for business and organizational markets.

3. Explain the business buying situation and describe business buyers.

The business buy class identifies the degree and effort required to make a business buying decision. Purchase situations can be straight rebuy, modified rebuy, and new-task buying. Business buying is usually handled by trained professional buyers. A buying centre is a group of people who work together to make a buying decision. The roles in the buying centre are initiator, user, gatekeeper, influencer, decider, and buyer. The most important recent change in business buying is the growth of e-commerce, in which firms buy and sell products using the Internet, intranets, or extranets.

4. Summarize the main stages in the business buying decision process.

The stages in the business buying decision process are similar to, but more complex than, the steps in consumer decision making. These steps include problem recognition, information search during which buyers develop product specifications and obtain proposals from prospective sellers, proposal evaluation, supplier selection, and formal evaluation of the performance of the product and the supplier. A firm's purchasing options include single or multiple sourcing. In outsourcing, firms obtain outside vendors to provide goods or services that otherwise might be supplied in-house. Other business buying activities are reciprocity and reverse marketing.

5. Explain how e-commerce is dramatically changing business-to-business marketing.

Every company, large or small, can now become a global competitor and supplier. This means that all firms need to have an international orientation and some source of competitive advantage. The Internet allows business marketers to link directly to suppliers, factories, distributors, and customers, radically reducing the time necessary for the order and delivery of goods, for tracking sales, and for getting feedback from customers. It also means companies can get access to a worldwide supply of goods and services, putting pressure on both pricing and quality.

6. Explain the importance of Customer Relationship Management (CRM) and describe how it works.

CRM is important because it presents organizations with a new way of looking at how to compete effectively in the marketplace. This begins with looking at customers as partners. CRM proponents suggest that the traditional relationship between customers and marketers is an adversarial one, where marketers try to sell their products and customers seek ways to avoid buying. Instead, CRM's goal is to establish a learning relationship with each customer, with the business organization changing its offering of goods and services in response to (or even ahead of) changing customer needs.

A four-step process is involved in implementing CRM:
1. Identify. This step involves collecting and storing information about customers, such as their buying patterns and needs.
2. Differentiate. This step involves differentiating among customers to identify the most attractive customers the organization should be serving.
3. Interact. This step involves initiating more dialogue with the organization's best customers. For example, in this step marketers may develop a better way to handle customer complaints.
4. Customize. This step involves personalizing the elements of the marketing mix (product, price, channel of distribution, and marketing communications) to develop a one-to-one relationship with customers.

CHAPTER REVIEW

Marketing Concepts: Testing Your Knowledge

1. What are some general characteristics of business-to-business markets? What is one primary difference between business customers and consumers?
2. How is business-to-business demand different from consumer demand? What are some of the factors that cause business demand to fluctuate?

3. How are business-to-business markets generally classified? What types of purchases do the major types of organizations make?

4. What is the NAICS? What purpose does it serve? Of what use is it to business marketers?

5. Describe the three buy class situations.

6. What is the role of electronic commerce in business-to-business marketing?

7. What are the characteristics of business buyers?

8. What is a buying centre? What are the roles of the various people in a buying centre?

9. What are buying groups, and how is the Internet facilitating rapid growth in these groups?

10. What are the stages in the business buying decision process? What happens in each stage?

11. What is single sourcing? Multiple sourcing? Outsourcing? Explain how reciprocity and reverse marketing operate in business-to-business markets.

12. What is CRM and why is it important?

13. Describe steps in implementing a CRM system.

Marketing Concepts: Discussing Choices and Issues

1. Do you agree with the idea that business-to-business marketing is more important to a country's economy than consumer marketing? Which one do you think provides better career opportunities for new college and university graduates? Explain your answers.

2. A number of business buying practices may be criticized as being unfair to one or more suppliers. What are the benefits of reciprocity to business firms? Is anyone hurt by reciprocity?

3. The practice of buying business products based on sealed competitive bids is popular among all types of business buyers. What are the advantages and disadvantages of this practice to buyers? What are the advantages and disadvantages to sellers? Should companies always give the business to the lowest bidder? Why or why not?

4. When firms engage in outsourcing, they relinquish control over how goods and services are produced. What are the advantages of outsourcing to a firm? What are some of the hazards of outsourcing? What can firms do to make sure that outsourcing is beneficial to both them and the outsourcing firm?

Marketing Practice: Applying What You've Learned

1. You are looking for a part-time job and being considered by a small, weekly newspaper. Knowing that you are a marketing student, the editor has asked you to provide a sample article that explains business demand in a way that will be interesting to the owners of small local shops and other businesses. Write that article and circulate it among three classmates, asking each to provide brief written comments and suggestions.

2. You've just been hired by a small consulting company that services small- to medium-sized firms. One of the company's clients produces custom-imprinted T-shirts for local sports teams and other groups and is thinking about switching to a JIT inventory control system. The client, who has 10 employees, currently buys the T-shirts in bulk and keeps large quantities of stock imprints and other supplies on hand. Your boss has asked you to prepare a list of issues the owner has to consider. Prepare the list and discuss each point with a classmate who assumes the client's role.

3. As a new director of materials management for a textile firm that manufactures sheets and towels, you are hoping to simplify the buying process where possible, thus reducing costs for the firm. You have first examined each purchase and classified it as a straight rebuy, a modified rebuy, or a new-task purchase. Your next job is to outline the procedures or steps in the purchasing process for each type of purchase. Indicate the type of purchase and outline the steps that must be taken in the purchase of each of the following items.

   a. computer paper

   b. textile dyes for this year's fashion colours

   c. new sewing robotics

   d. new software to control the weaving processes

4. Go to your library and search for business organizations that have installed a CRM system. Provide a report on their experiences, both good and bad. What recommendations do you have for successfully implementing a CRM strategy?

Marketing Mini-Project: Learning by Doing

The purpose of this mini-project is to gain knowledge about one business-to-business market using the NAICS codes and other government information.

1. Select an industry of interest to you and use the NAICS information found on the Internet (**www.statcan.ca/english/Subjects/Standard/naics/2007/naics07-menu.htm**) or in your library.

   a. What are the codes for each of the following classifications?
   - NAICS Sector (two digits)
   - NAICS Subsector (three digits)
   - NAICS Industry Group (four digits)
   - NAICS Industry (five digits)
   - Canadian Industry (six digits)

   b. What types of products are or are not included in this industry?

2. Find out what information Industry Canada has on your industry. Go to the Strategis website (**http://strategis.ic.gc.ca/sc_mrkti/tdst/engdoc/tr_homep.html**) to review Canadian industry statistics.

   Statistics Canada is the country's national statistical agency with a mandate to collect, compile, analyze, abstract, and publish statistical information on virtually every aspect of the nation's society and economy. Go to the Statistics Canada website (**www.statcan.ca**) and enter the name of your industry into the search engine. What information does Statistics Canada have on your industry?

3. *Canadian Industry Norms & Key Business Ratios,* a CD-ROM resource available in many libraries, has data useful for analyzing trends and assessing the strengths and weaknesses of the agriculture, mining, construction, transportation, wholesaling, utilities, retailing, finance, insurance, real estate, and services industries. Information on specific companies is also available. See what information is available on one of these industries.

4. *The Blue Book of Canadian Business* provides detailed profiles of leading Canadian companies (public, private, crown, and cooperatives) in terms of sales, assets, net income, and stock trading volume. The *Canadian Key Business Directory* profiles the top 20 000 public and private companies. Look up one of the companies in your industry and find its net sales, gross profits, and income before tax.

Real People, Real Surfers: Exploring the Web

Mega Bloks (see Chapter 2) isn't the only company that makes construction toy products. Visit Mega Bloks' website (**www.megabloks.com**) and that of its main competitor, Lego (**www.lego.com**), and other specialty toy producers such as Rokenbok (**www.rokenbok.com**) or K'nex (**www.knex.com**).

Based on your experience, answer the following questions.

1. In general, how do the websites compare? Which are easier to navigate, and why? Which are more innovative and attractive, and why?

2. Evaluate each site from the perspective of a toy store buyer. What features in each site would be useful? What information is available that a buyer might need? Which site would be most useful for a buyer? Why?

3. Evaluate each site from the perspective of a parent. What features in each site would be useful? What information is available that a parent might need? Which site would be most useful for a parent? Why?

Chapter 6 **Venture 4th**

Venture 4th provides office space, secretarial services, technology services, and marketing, accounting, and other business expertise for start-up ventures in Halifax, Nova Scotia. The brain trust of four commerce graduates (Sean O'Connor, Sarah Brown, Rick Styles, and Paul Rainer), Venture 4th currently has six clients, ranging from a fledgling e-tail business to a profitable specialty food importer.

Ever since Venture 4th opened its doors two years ago, office technology has been a major headache. The four partners started their service business on a shoestring budget—using their own computers and desktop printers, purchasing an inexpensive fax machine and scanner, and renting a low-end photocopier for general use. (Clients with special computer and high-speed Internet access needs provided those resources for themselves.) Unable to afford a more elegant Ethernet solution, the company ran a "sneaker net" system, where users brought disks to a central computer to use the laser printer, colour inkjet printer, and scanner. This system was adequate for the first year, when there were only two clients. With greater demand on the resources, however, and differences in computer speeds, software versions, and printer drivers, the system was driving everyone crazy—particularly Rick Styles, who was responsible for keeping this hodgepodge of equipment operating. The issue came to a head when the e-tail client said he couldn't continue to run his business out of the Venture 4th office space without more reasonable office technology support.

When this was discussed at the weekly partners' meeting, Sarah Brown, the partner primarily responsible for new business development, indicated that she thought she could land two more clients and another $40 000 a year revenue if the company had more modern and higher-capacity office equipment linked in a network solution. With this to motivate them, the Venture 4th team began to investigate the purchase of an Ethernet office network linked to high-speed Internet access and a digital imaging system comprising an integrated network printer, copier, scanner, and fax machine.

It took Styles three weeks to do a preliminary investigation of the options. He called Copies Plus, from which Venture 4th was renting its Rocket copier, and Iain Carver, their small business representative, came the following day to do a needs analysis. Based on current and projected printing and copying volume, Carver recommended a digital imaging system that could make at least 10 000 copies a month. This ruled out the "all in one" desktop solutions Styles had been looking at the last time he was in Future Shop. Carver recommended the Rocket 3000E system, left a brochure, and promised to follow up with a price quote. During the visit, Carver "tuned up" the rental unit and left some samples of a new brand of laser printer paper that Copies Plus was carrying.

The next day, a Xena representative called, asked for Styles, and made an appointment for the following week to discuss Xena document solutions. The rep, Peter Smith, having overheard Sarah Brown talking about their need for a new copier one evening at a downtown bar, had approached her with a funny "pick-up" line, engaged her in polite conversation, and then returned (to her relief) to his friends. Later he approached one of Brown's friends and found out where she worked. When he met with Styles, he marvelled at his ability to keep the current system running and promised to return with a system recommendation and prices.

About a week after Styles had received a faxed Rocket quote and a couriered envelope with Smith's recommendation and pricing for a Xena 33DT system, Sean O'Connor mentioned that he had seen a Cambon digital imaging system in the law firm used by Venture 4th. O'Connor had been quite impressed with the system and had talked with one of the secretaries about it while waiting to see the firm's lawyer. The secretary said that the system had been in place for about a year and had made a big difference in the law firm's ability to produce and manage the receipt of thousands of documents. This recommendation prompted Styles to call a Cambon distributor, who faxed him the specifications of the Cambon DC330.

At Venture 4th, strategic decisions and those involving more than $10 000 had to have unanimous approval by the partners. Therefore, Styles invited Carver, Smith, and a representative from the Cambon distributor to the partners' meeting to present the merits of their systems. At the end of each presentation, Styles asked the reps whether the presented price was the best they could do. In a "Regis" parody, Paul Rainer followed this with, "Is that your final answer?" Only the rep from the Cambon distributor responded with a last-minute price reduction, taking $200 off the price of the system.

The Rocket system had the fastest copying—35 pages per minute versus 33 for the Cambon and 32 for the Xena—and it was rated for the greatest volume—20 000 to 60 000 copies per month versus 10 000 for the other two. While the Rocket system was the least expensive at $14 500, its printing technology was not PostScript compatible without adding an optional $1500 feature. PostScript compatibility is important for desktop publishing applications—which some of Venture 4th's clients might want.

The Xena system, priced at $19 200, came with a PostScript printing capability but did not have a stapling feature. Xena had a strong reputation for product quality and support, and its history of copying innovation impressed the partners.

The rep from the Cambon distributor arrived late but did a credible job explaining the benefits of his system. The Cambon system, priced at $18 100 (after the $200 reduction) had been awarded a "recommended buy" by the U.S.-based Buyers Laboratory, a product testing and rating organization. Although the Cambon product took longer to warm up than the others, it had the highest printing resolution at 1200 × 600 dpi (dots per inch) versus 600 × 600 for the other two, and the greatest paper capacity at 3500 sheets compared to 2000 sheets for the others. The Xena rep, presenting before the Cambon rep, had explained that there were more important factors than dpi for print quality and that the Xena system had the crispest image.

At the end of the partners' meeting, Styles summarized the advantages and disadvantages of each system. The partners agreed that they should purchase one of the systems. O'Connor liked the Cambon solution best, having been impressed on his visit to the law firm, and noted that the Cambon distributor had lowered his price once and might do so again if pressed. Brown liked the idea of saving some money by buying the Rocket, then upgrading later if anyone wanted to get the PostScript option. Styles and Rainer leaned toward the Xena solution, considering company's reputation; they also noted that the rep from the Cambon distributor came late and questioned what kind of support they might get from him. The partners decided that they should all go to see each of the systems in action.

The next day, Styles called the reps and arranged a visit to one of their installations. When they visited the company with a Rocket system, the paper had just jammed on the system and a technician had to be called. The staff that used the system said that this didn't happen very often and that they were generally happy with the system. Both the Xena and Cambon solutions were working when the Venture 4th partners came to see them, and the staff who used the systems raved about the products.

A few days later, Styles called the three reps to say that he and his partners were going to make a purchase decision at 4:00 that afternoon. He told them that if they wanted to reconsider their pricing and submit a lower quote, they could do so before 3:00. At 1:00, the Rocket rep faxed in a new price of $14 000 and a one-year option to buy the PostScript upgrade at $1300. At 2:00, the Cambon rep faxed in a new price of $17 900 and offered free installation and three hours of staff training. Styles called the Rocket rep back, confirmed that his price included installation, and got a verbal commitment to three hours of staff training. At 2:45, Styles called Smith at Xena and was told that the original price of $19 200 was the best he could do and that the price included installation and three hours of training. At 4:15, during the partner deliberations, the Xena rep called back. He told Styles that Xena was going to announce a price reduction on the 332DC system the next day and that his manager had authorized a $500 price reduction for Venture 4th. Armed with this new information, Styles went back into the partner meeting to get a consensus decision.

Source: This case was written by Professor Brock Smith of the University of Victoria.

Things to Think About

1. If you were a partner at Venture 4th, which system would you vote to purchase, and why?

2. How does this purchase process compare with the model illustrated in Figure 6.6?

3. Where was the most time spent in this purchase process? Why?

4. Assuming that this decision process is typical, what are the implications for sales and marketing organizations?

Advertising in Crisis

Arlene Dickinson, a Calgary-based marketing consultant, suggests that the advertising industry—or at least part of it—is in crisis. Digital Video Recorders (DVRs) are changing the way consumers watch television. Josh Bernoff of Forrester Research suggests that people with DVRs record 60 percent of programs while skipping 92 percent of the ads. With DVR sales on the rise and the recent introduction of popular U.S. brands like TIVO, this technology has traditional advertisers worried. Bernoff suggests that TV advertising cannot stay the same, and the conventional 30-second TV spot will likely be a victim of this new technology.

Marketers are now turning to alternative ways of reaching customers. While online media offers a range of choices, television programming development requires television advertising revenue. Product placement is an alternative that enables products to be shown in use by actors in the television shows, but there are limits on how many products can be woven into show plots. American Express is developing video CDs to distribute to business travellers at airports to view on their laptops. Edutainment content (entertaining education) encourages the viewer to watch the programming long enough to receive the key messages of the advertiser.

Mark Sherman of Media Experts promotes etc.tv, an advertising-on-demand network concept. The idea is for advertisers to develop interesting program content that takes advantage of DVR capabilities. Campbell's soup, for example, might develop a cooking show that uses Campbell's products. Viewers would be encouraged to record the show and then follow along making the meal or snack item in their own kitchens, pausing the DVR whenever they needed to perform a task. Interactive features would allow the viewer to find out more about specific products used during the show, and even order them online.

Bret Mitchell of the Forzani consulting firm suggests that organizations need to reach further and do different things to reach customers with messaging; including advertising in movie theatres. Expect to see advertising in all sorts of new locations.

For Arlene Dickinson, the shift means a need for accountability. The old adage in advertising was that we know half our advertising expenditure is wasted, but we don't know which half. That's not good enough any more. Market research is needed to establish benchmarks on key performance indicators and track the effectiveness of every dollar spent. She says, "You've got to know what you are doing . . . and to do that you need to measure everything." By putting more interactive elements into television programming and advertising, advertisers will be able to track what works and what doesn't.

Questions

1. What kinds of performance measures should marketers track to determine the effectiveness of advertising?
2. What would be the central elements of a market research methodology to determine the needed benchmarks and track performance?
3. As more young people turn to the Internet as a source of news and entertainment, how should the television industry react? How does its marketing strategy need to change? How might specific marketing mix elements need to change?
4. Is all this benchmarking and performance measurement going to take the creativity out of marketing communications and make it formulaic?

Source: This case was prepared by Brock Smith and is based on "Advertising in Crisis," *Venture* #923, 2004.

The Brand Man

Bernard Hadley-Beauregard, or Bernie for short, knows that for most products branding is critical for sales success. Bernie recently quit his job with a popular Vancouver marketing company to launch his own image and branding consulting venture. A branding expert, he has just taken on the most challenging project of his career—to turn the badly named "A' Very Fine Winery" of Abbotsford into a hip, cool new brand.

But Bernie has his work cut out for him with this struggling and broke winery, and his own brand reputation is on the line. David and Liz Avery, the owners of the struggling three-hectare winery (hence the name "A' Very Fine Winery") are over one million dollars in debt and will face bankruptcy in months if sales don't take a turn for the better. The Averys have been scraping by for the past few years selling their wine through buffet restaurants and independent beer and wine stores. Lately sales have been very disappointing and bottles of wine have started to pile up on the Averys' property, and this isn't planned "aging." The Averys know that they need a fast and effective change if they want their dream business and life investment to survive. So they have hired "Brand Man" Bernie to revitalize their brand and get sales rolling again.

Bernie needs his newly launched company to start off on the right foot and has his sights set on selling the Averys' wine to some of Vancouver's finest restaurants and wine stores. Bernie has the challenge of turning the Avery winery's product into a stylish, appealing, and profitable wine before the Christmas season. A successful and complete re-branding is in the wings for the Averys and this 180-degree change will determine whether the winery makes it through the New Year, and whether Bernie will see a paycheque and a profitable company. A few obstacles, however, stand in the way, like getting more financing, and the need to focus on making the wine while the grapes are at their peak.

Bernie's concept is the brand "Lotusland"—a term used by many Canadians to refer to British Columbia's Lower Mainland. Bernie wants to put images of Vancouver celebrities on the label with recognizable Vancouver landmarks. The idea is to create a Vancouver brand for Vancouver consumers. A year and a half after launch, Lotusland is being sold in 30 Vancouver restaurants, and the Averys are almost out of debt. They have been asked to start an organic vineyard as the central feature for a subdivision of luxury homes. They have asked Bernie to join the project but he's hesitant—working with the Averys wasn't easy.

Questions

1. Although there can be many beneficial aspects to re-branding, what are some potential dangers associated with a complete brand transformation?
2. Why do you think that this winery was struggling in the first place? Do you think that the Averys could have turned their business around themselves? Why or why not?
3. What considerations should go into choosing a brand name? Is "Lotusland" a good brand name for a wine?
4. How might Bernie support the Lotusland brand identity through other marketing mix decisions?

Source: This case was prepared by Brock Smith and is based on "Avery Wines, The Brand Man Update," *Venture* #943, 2005.

PART III

Creating the Value Proposition

You learned in Part I that the process of market segmentation enables an organization to choose the target markets it wants to serve, and that positioning describes the type of value that will be created and how that organization will compete effectively. Positioning strategies are executed using a combination of product, pricing, channels of distribution (place), and marketing communications (promotion), strategies. In this part you will learn how marketers make product and pricing decisions—which are the heart of the value proposition.

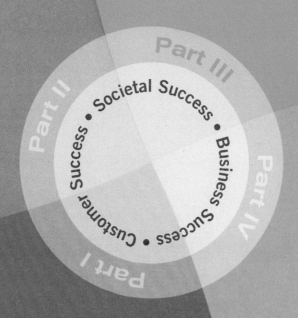

OPTION 1   OPTION 2   OPTION 3

CHAPTER 7
Product Strategy

CHAPTER OBJECTIVES

WHEN YOU HAVE COMPLETED YOUR STUDY OF THIS CHAPTER, YOU SHOULD BE ABLE TO

1. Explain the different product objectives and strategies a firm may choose.

2. Explain how the layers of a product or a product line lead to competitive advantage.

3. Explain the good–service continuum and its importance.

4. Explain the key differences between goods and services.

5. Describe how firms develop new products.

6. Discuss the importance of innovations.

7. Explain the process of product adoption and the diffusion of innovations.

Visit the MyMarketingLab website at **www.pearsoned.ca/mymarketinglab**. This online homework and tutorial system puts you in control of your own learning with study and practice tools directly correlated to this chapter's content.

Real People, Real Decisions

Meet **Dee Dee Gordon,** a Decision Maker at Lambesis

Dee Dee Gordon is co-president of Look-Look, Inc., a youth culture research and marketing solutions company. Prior to this, she was the head of research at Lambesis advertising agency, at which she and colleague Sharon Lee developed the *L Report*, a document to track youth trends.

A few years ago, the Cosmar division of Renaissance Cosmetics, Inc. launched a product called Nail Fetish, a small collection of artificial nails and decals targeted to teenage girls. To build on this product, the company's Dana fragrance division decided to market a perfume called Fetish to the same audience. Dana's goal was to sell $8 million of the fragrance in its first year. Reaching this goal would not be easy—the women's mass fragrance market had been experiencing steadily declining sales, and the category was dominated by heavyweights like Coty and Revlon. The company retained Lambesis advertising agency to help it research the best way to capture the hearts and pocketbooks of this young audience.

Lambesis started by asking teenage girls what they wanted in a fragrance. Although respondents said they preferred expensive boutique brands like MAC, a different picture emerged when the girls were asked to empty their handbags—in reality, they were buying mostly cheap drugstore brands. Feedback compiled via the *L Report* underscored the importance of status symbols for this group and emphasized the importance these girls attach to displaying valued possessions on their dressers. They valued objects that were so cool that they could be used to hold things or be reused in some way.

Dee Dee Gordon saw an opportunity to create a new mass-market fragrance, targeted to teenage girls, that would be prestigious and cool enough to motivate the girls to keep the bottle and show it off to their friends. The product positioning strategy became "Fetish is cool, hip, and fun; it's the only beauty brand that really understands me." Research showed that girls in this age group were fascinated by futuristic bottle designs and interesting packaging such as the Orbitz beverage bottle or the CK One perfume holder.

The company focused on creating a design that would express this new attitude. As inspiration, its designers used findings from the initial research that asked girls to empty their purses. It modelled the bottle after other items found in these bags, such as beepers and pagers, toys like Hello Kitty, and accessories like hair barrettes. A set of eight package concepts was developed, and a series of focus groups among girls aged 14 to 17 was conducted to get reactions. Based on the responses, the company narrowed its package choice down to three options (shown at the beginning of this chapter).

Option 1

The girls liked this concept because it could be clipped to their clothing or bags. The girls also said they would enjoy collecting the different-coloured fragrance bottles.

Option 2

Overall, the girls disliked the vial, but they did like the stand because it could also be used to hold pens and pencils.

Option 3

The girls liked the functionality of this design. Many said they would wear the cap as a hair accessory. Others said they were concerned the elastic band would break when worn in their hair. Some girls had concerns about the perfume spilling once the cap was removed.

Now, put yourself in Dee Dee's shoes: Which option would you choose and why? To get a handle on this product problem, it may be helpful to try to understand the mindset of teenage girls. If possible, interview some 12- to 15-year-old girls about what they look for in a perfume. Ask them how they display their bottles and other personal care products. How do they carry these around, or do they? What kinds of statements are these girls trying to make through their fragrance choices?

BUILD A BETTER MOUSETRAP . . .

"Build a better mousetrap and the world will beat a path to your door." Although we've all heard that adage, the truth is: Just because a product is better, there is no guarantee it will succeed. For decades, the Woodstream Company built wood mousetraps. Then the company decided to build a better one. Woodstream's product development people researched mouse eating, crawling, and resting habits; built prototypes of different mousetraps to come up with the best possible design; and tested them in homes. Finally, the company unveiled the sleek-looking "Little Champ," a black plastic miniature inverted bathtub with a hole. When the mouse went in and ate the bait, a spring snapped upward, and the mouse was history.[1]

Sounds like a great new product (if you're not a mouse), but the "Little Champ" failed. Woodstream studied mouse habits, *not* consumer preferences. The company later discovered that husbands set the trap at night, but wives were left to dispose of the trap holding the dead mouse in the morning. Unfortunately, wives thought the "Little Champ" looked too expensive to throw away, so they felt they should empty the trap for reuse. This was a task most women weren't willing to do—they wanted a trap they could happily throw away.

Another example of product development failures for marketers is Coca-Cola. In an attempt to revitalize its brand in the '80s, Coca-Cola introduced the New Coke. It has become a classic case in marketing. The introduction of the new product almost destroyed the company (Exhibit 7.1). Reputable firms like McDonald's (Exhibit 7.2), Levi's, and Fruit of the Loom all failed at one point. What's behind these marketing failures? What can we learn from them? It just demonstrates that **new product failure** is rarely a black-and-white issue and that the final result often takes a long time to manifest itself. Woodstream's and Coke's failures underscore the importance of creating products that provide benefits people seek.

CREATING AND NURTURING PRODUCTS

What makes one product fail and another enjoy great success? What is the difference between a product and a brand? Do all products enjoy brand status? It's worth repeating what we said in Chapter 2: Firms that plan well succeed. Product planning plays a big role in the firm's *marketing plans*. The strategies outlined in the product plan tell how the firm expects to develop a product that will meet marketing objectives. The next two chapters are intrinsically related. We will introduce the product decision process (Figure 7.1). In Chapter 7, we will discuss what a product really is and how new products are developed and introduced into the marketplace. This will include developing product objectives and the strategies required to successfully market products as they evolve over time. In Chapter 8, we'll finish the product part of the story by discussing how companies manage products and examine the steps in product planning. We'll also discuss branding, one of the most important decisions product planners make, and examine how firms organize for effective product and brand management.

Exhibit 7.1

The New Coke, which was introduced by Coca-Cola in the '80s, became a classic case of new product failure.

new product failure A new product that does not reach expectations for success, failing to reach sales objectives set.

PRODUCT OBJECTIVES

When marketers develop product strategies, they are making decisions about product benefits, features, styling, branding, labelling, logos, and packaging. But what do they want to accomplish? Clearly stated product objectives provide focus and direction. Product objectives should support the broader marketing objectives of the business unit in addition to supporting the overall mission of the firm. For example, if the objectives of the firm focus on a certain return on investment, its marketing objectives may then focus on market share and/or unit or dollar sales volume necessary for the firm to attain that return on investment. Product objectives need to specify how product decisions will support or contribute to reaching a desired market share or level of sales. (You will find more on the relationship between marketing objectives and marketing strategies in Chapter 14 on developing and implementing marketing plans.)

Exhibit 7.2

In 1992, McDonald's unsuccessfully introduced pizzas in many restaurants across North America. Many customers felt that not only were the pizzas overpriced, but that McDonald's was not the proper place to eat pizza.

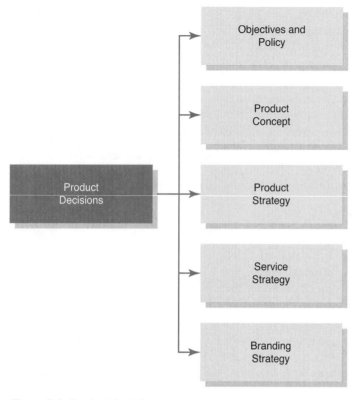

Figure 7.1 Product Decisions

To be effective, product-related objectives must be measurable, clear and unambiguous, and feasible, and must specify a time frame. Consider, for example, how a frozen-entrée manufacturer might state its product objectives:

- "In the upcoming fiscal year, modify the product's fat content to reflect the trend toward low-fat foods."
- "Introduce three new items to the product line to take advantage of increased consumer interest in ethnic foods."
- "During the coming fiscal year, improve the chicken entrées to the extent that consumers will rate them as better tasting than the competition's."

The frozen entrée manufacturer might use a matrix, like the one shown in Figure 7.2, to guide product objectives.

As shown in Figure 7.2, the firm can follow one of four strategies, depending on whether the products or markets are current or new. A good way for a firm to use the grid is to ensure it has a good balance between the four quadrants. A focus on only one or two quadrants suggests that the firm may be vulnerable to marketplace forces.

Planners must keep in touch with consumers or business customers so that their objectives accurately respond to customer needs. Equally important in developing product objectives is an up-to-date knowledge of competitive product innovations. Above all, product objectives should consider the *long-term implications* of product decisions. Planners who sacrifice the long-term health of the organization to reach short-term sales or financial goals are being irresponsible. Product planners may focus on one or more individual products at a time, or they may look at a group of product offerings as a whole. In this section, we examine these different strategies.

THE PRODUCT CONCEPT

As defined in Chapter 1, a product is anything tangible or intangible that, through the exchange process, satisfies consumer or business customer needs. Products can be physical goods, services, ideas, people, or places. A good may be a sweatshirt, pack of cookies, digital camera, house, tractor, or pair of jeans. A **good** is a tangible product, something that we

goods Tangible products we can see, touch, smell, hear, or taste.

	Current Markets	New Markets
Current Products	**Market Penetration** The frozen entrée manufacturer may entice consumers to buy more of its products	**Market Development** The frozen entrée manufacturer may expand internationally
New Products	**Product Development** The frozen entrée manufacturer may develop a new line of fat-free products aimed at current consumers	**Diversification** The frozen entrée manufacturer may introduce a new line of products aimed at a new market: the ethnic consumer

Figure 7.2 A Product–Market Grid to Guide Product Decisions

can see, touch, smell, hear, taste, or possess. In contrast, intangible products—services, ideas, people, places—are products that we can't always see, touch, taste, smell, or possess. Banking services, a concert, convincing people to recycle or vote for a particular political candidate, and getting people to visit a particular province on their next vacation are all examples of intangible products.

Marketers think of the product as more than just a *thing* that comes in a package. They view a product as a *bundle* of attributes, including packaging, brand name, benefits, and supporting features, in addition to a physical good. In this chapter, we'll first examine what a product is, and how thinking about the different layers of a product helps a marketer build an edge in the marketplace. Then we'll look at the differences between goods and services and the implications this has for marketing strategy. Finally, we will examine new products—how marketers develop new products, and how markets accept them.

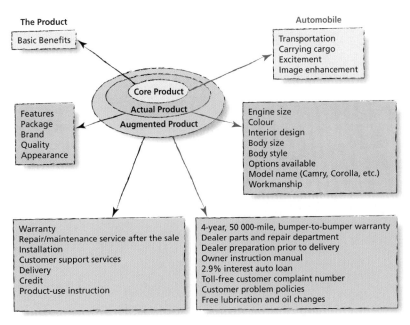

Figure 7.3 Layers of the Product

A product is everything a customer receives—the basic benefits, the physical product and its packaging, and the "extras" that come with the product.

Layers of the Product Concept

A product is *everything* that a customer receives in an exchange. As Figure 7.3 shows, the product has three distinct layers—the core, actual, and augmented product. These layers are very useful because they teach us how to build a competitive edge in the marketplace. Let us see how.

The **core product** refers to product features or attributes: Dove soap has moisturizing cream. The **actual product** refers to how the product actually looks and performs: How easy it is to use Dove, how foamy it is, etc. The **augmented product** refers to the augmentations (that is, the additions) the marketer attaches to the basic product: Dove's packaging, logo, brand name, customer satisfaction guarantees, etc.

How does this knowledge of product layers build a competitive advantage? The answer is simple—consumers do not buy product features, they buy the benefits offered by the product. So, Dove should not focus on the fact that its soap contains moisturizing cream; instead, it should focus its marketing communications efforts on the benefits the brand provides to consumers. It is this potential product that consumers can relate to and that can build a relationship with the brand. Also, the potential product is difficult for competitors to successfully imitate because Dove has claimed it first.

core product All the benefits the product will provide for consumers or business customers.

actual product The physical good or the delivered service that supplies the desired benefit.

augmented product The actual product plus other supporting features such as a warranty, credit, delivery, installation, and repair service after the sale.

Product Line Decisions

After deciding on concepts for their products, marketers need to decide how many different types of products and how many variants of each type they are going to offer.

STRATEGIES FOR INDIVIDUAL PRODUCTS The Volkswagen Beetle is an interesting story of a product that triumphed over great obstacles. When the product was first introduced in North America in the 1960s, dealers complained that the car was too ugly to sell. Many of those dealers were soon kicking themselves; dealers who did accept the challenge sold over 21 million Beetles to true believers who adored the car's simple engineering and funky image. The Beetle was a tremendously successful product in the 1960s and 1970s despite its poor image. In the late 1990s, Volkswagen decided to capitalize on baby boomers' warm memories of the Beetle by introducing a "concept car" model reminiscent of the original (Exhibit 7.3).

Exhibit 7.3

Volkswagen capitalized on baby boomers and nostalgia to successfully introduce the new Beetle.

Some product strategies, including those used in introducing the new VW Beetle, focus on a single new product. However, strategies for individual products may be quite different for new products, for regional products, and for mature products.

For new products, the objectives relate to successful *introduction*. Warner-Lambert Canada worked hard to introduce Dentyne Ice gum to youth across Canada.[2] After a firm has experienced considerable success with a product in a local or regional market, however, it may consider it time to grow the business by introducing the product nationally. Big Rock Brewery, a Calgary microbrewery, used its success in the Alberta beer market to introduce its beer into Ontario and British Columbia.[3]

For mature products, product objectives may focus on breathing new life into a product long taken for granted while holding onto the traditional brand personality. In the case of Cracker Jack, for instance, this means keeping consumer perceptions of the product positive. The images of Sailor Jack and his dog Bingo have been updated at least four times since the original design of 1893.[4]

STRATEGIES FOR MULTIPLE PRODUCTS Although a small firm might focus on one product, a larger company usually markets a mix of related products. This means that some strategic decisions affect two or more products at once. Thus, the firm must think in terms of its entire *portfolio* of products. Product planning means developing *product line* and *product mix* strategies that encompass multiple offerings. Figure 7.4 illustrates these concepts, using some Procter & Gamble products as examples.

product line A firm's total product offering designed to satisfy a single need or desire of target customers.

Product Line Strategies A **product line** is a firm's total product offering designed to satisfy a single need or desire of a group of target customers. For example, Procter & Gamble's line of fabric and home-care products includes four different types of laundry soap: Tide, Cheer, Gain, and Ivory Snow. To do an even better job of meeting varying consumer needs, each of the brands comes in several different formulations. For example, in addition to

		Width of Product Mix		
Paper Products	**Fabric and Home-Care Products**	**Health Care Products**	**Beauty Care Products**	**Food and Beverage Products**
Pampers	Bounce	Metamucil	Cover Girl	Crisco
Always	Cascade	Pepto Bismol	Max Factor	Folgers
Tampax	Ivory Liquid	Crest	Old Spice	Pringles
Bounty	Downy	Scope	Secret	Sunny Delight
Royale	Swiffer	Vicks	Head & Shoulders	
	Mr. Clean		Pantene	
	COMET		Pert	
	Spic and Span		Vidal Sassoon	
	Tide		Camay	
	Cheer		Clearasil	
	Gain		Noxema	
	Ivory Snow		Coast	
	Dryel		Ivory soap	
	Febreze		Zest	
			Oil of Olay	

Length of Product Line

Figure 7.4 Product Line Length and Product Mix Width

regular Tide, there is Tide with bleach and Ultra Tide. The number of separate items offered within the same category determines the length of the product line.

When a firm has a large number of variations in its product line, it is said to carry a *full line*. With a full-line strategy, it is possible to please many customer segments, thus increasing total sales potential. A company that adopts a *limited-line strategy* markets a smaller number of product variations. Sometimes, having a limited product line can improve the image of a firm, because it is perceived to be a specialist and has a clear, specific position in the market. Rolls-Royce, for example, makes only expensive, custom-built automobiles and, for years, has maintained a unique position in the automobile industry.

In developing product strategies, organizations may decide to extend their product lines by adding more brands or models. Bombardier Inc., the manufacturer of Sea-Doos and Ski-Doos, extended its recreational product line with the introduction of its Traxter ATV (Exhibit 7.4).

Exhibit 7.4

Bombardier added the Traxter ATV to its recreational product line, which already included Ski-Doo and Sea-Doo.

When a company stretches its product line, it must decide on the best direction in which to go. If a firm's current product line includes middle- and lower-end items, an *upward line stretch* would add new items—those with a higher price, better quality, or more features. Folgers and Maxwell House took this route by adding such new coffee varieties as Gourmet Supreme, Colombian Supreme, French Roast, and Italian Espresso Roast.

Conversely, a *downward line stretch* completes a line by adding items at the lower end. Here the firm must be careful that the lower-end items don't blur the images of higher-priced, upper-end offerings. A firm like Godiva may not want to run the risk of cheapening its image, for example, by creating a new, less expensive chocolate bar to compete with products like Mr. Big and Sweet Marie.

In some cases, a firm may decide that its existing product line is meeting the needs of only a small portion of the market and that there is more than one opportunity for growth. Then the product strategy may call for a *two-way stretch*, that is, adding items at both the upper and lower ends. Marriott Hotels, for example, has added Fairfield Inns and Courtyard at the lower end and Marriott Marquis Hotels and the Ritz Carlton at the upper end.

A *filling-out* strategy may mean adding sizes or styles not previously available in a product category. Quebec's Lassonde did this when it was the first juice company in North America to use aseptic plastic bottles for its Fruité drinks. It also introduced the first refrigerated vegetable juice in North America, Vegetable Delight.[5] Sometimes the best strategy may be to *contract a product line*, particularly when some of the items are not profitable. For example, when sales for the once-popular Oldsmobile brand slowed, GM dropped the brand from its line.

As we have seen, there are many ways a firm can modify its product line to meet the competition or take advantage of new opportunities in the marketplace. To further explore these strategic decisions, we return to Procter & Gamble. What does P&G do if the objective is to increase market share in the fabric-care market? One possibility would be to expand its line of laundry detergents. If the line extension meets a perceived consumer need not being addressed currently, this would be a good strategic move. But, whenever a product line or a product family is extended, there is the danger of **cannibalization**, which occurs when sales of an existing brand are eaten up by the new item, as the firm's

cannibalization The loss of sales of an existing product when a new item in a product line or product family is introduced.

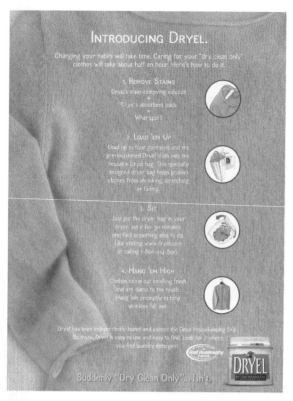

Exhibit 7.5

By introducing a new product line with Dryel, Procter & Gamble was able to meet new customer demands and avoid cannibalizing laundry detergent brands.

Exhibit 7.6

Victorinox has extended its product into apparel and watches.

product mix The total set of all products a firm offers for sale.

current customers switch to the new product. This explains why P&G has created a whole new product line with its Dryel product to achieve growth in fabric care. The Dryel product (Exhibit 7.5) is not cannibalizing sales from detergents such as Tide and Ivory Snow.[6]

Product Mix Strategies Product planning can go beyond a single product item or a product line to entire groups of products. A firm's **product mix** is its entire range of products. For example, in addition to a deep line of shaving products, Gillette makes toiletries such as Dry Idea and Right Guard deodorant, Paper Mate and Flair writing instruments, Oral B toothbrushes, Braun small appliances, and Duracell batteries.

In developing a product mix strategy, planners usually consider the *width of the product mix*, the number of product lines produced by the firm. By developing several different product lines, firms can reduce the risk associated with "putting all their eggs in one basket." Normally, firms develop a mix of product lines that have some similarities, for example, products that can share distribution channels or manufacturing facilities. Sometimes, firms expand into new product lines to take advantage of a strong brand reputation with an existing target market. As you can see in Exhibit 7.6, Victorinox, the makers of the popular Swiss Army knife, has extended its product lines into apparel and watches.

Service Strategy Whether it is customer support, training, delivery, gift-wrapping, helpful advice, or a customized experience, "service" is associated with most products and some products, like getting a haircut, are mostly about the service offered. Marketing decision makers need to decide what type of service they are going to provide, at what level of quality. In the section that follows we are going to examine key differences between goods and services and discuss the marketing implications of these differences. In more advanced marketing courses you will learn that service strategy decisions also involve service recovery systems and approaches for measuring service quality.

The Goods–Services Continuum

In reality, most products are a *combination* of goods and services. The purchase of a "pure good" like a car still has service components, such as bringing it to the dealer for maintenance work. The purchase of a "pure service" like a makeover at a department store has product components, for example, lotions, powders, and lipsticks the cosmetologist uses to create the "new you."

The goods–services continuum in Figure 7.5 shows that some products are dominated by either tangible or intangible characteristics—for instance, salt versus teaching—whereas others tend to include a mixture of goods and services—such as flying in an airplane. A product's placement on this continuum gives some guidance as to which marketing issues are likely to be most relevant. As the product approaches the tangible pole of this continuum, there is fairly little emphasis on service; the physical product itself is the focal point, and people will choose one over others based on the product's function or image. To compete, the marketer will try to differentiate based on services. So, car manufacturers may

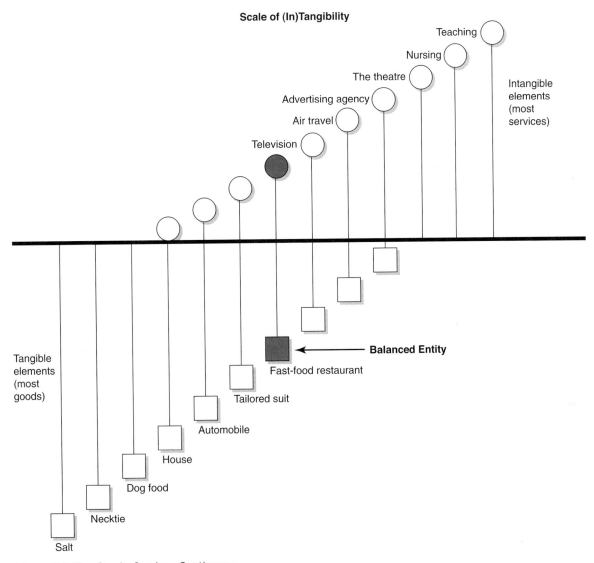

Figure 7.5 The Goods–Services Continuum

try to differentiate goods by providing a unique service dimension (e.g., the dealership experience).

As the product gets near the intangible pole, the physical product shrinks in importance, and the service encounter plays a key role in shaping the service experience. Marketers of these products try to make their offerings more tangible. Scarborough General Hospital, for example, provides all patients with a chart explaining precisely when and exactly what is going to happen to them during their stay in the hospital. This minimizes patient frustration by shaping their expectations (we discuss this further in the next chapter).

In the middle of the continuum, however, both goods and services contribute substantially to the quality of the product, because these products rely on people to satisfactorily operate equipment that will deliver quality service. Let's consider each of these three positions as we move from products dominated by tangibles to those dominated by intangibles.

GOOD-DOMINATED PRODUCTS Many tangible products are accompanied by supporting services, even if this means only that the company maintains a toll-free telephone line or website for questions or provides a 30-day warranty against defects. Including a service with the purchase of a physical good is termed **embodying**.[7] This is a popular option in the computer industry, especially for companies that are trying to break into international markets saturated with cheap products but with insufficient guidance in their use. As millions

embodying The inclusion of a service with a purchase of a physical good.

of people buy computers and other hardware, they are apt to find it difficult to navigate the maze of set-up instructions, and next to impossible to cope with machines that unexpectedly crash. Indeed, one survey by *PC Magazine* found that 28 percent of its readers needed technical support in the first year of owning a personal computer. What's more, in grading manufacturers' service performance, they gave two-thirds of them Cs and Ds. Companies with the resources to do so find that embodying follow-up service is a potent marketing tool when competing with "clone" manufacturers. As an executive at Compaq (now owned by Hewlett Packard) observed, "The bad guys give us an opportunity to differentiate."[8]

EQUIPMENT- OR FACILITY-DRIVEN SERVICES As Figure 7.5 shows, some products require a mixture of tangible and intangible elements. Many hospitals and restaurants fall in the middle of the continuum because they rely on expensive equipment or facilities and skilled personnel to deliver a product.

Facility-driven services, such as automatic car washes, amusement parks, museums, movie theatres, health clubs, and zoos, must be concerned with these three important factors:[9]

- *Operational factors:* Technologies must move customers smoothly through the service. Clear signs and other guidelines must show customers how to use the service. In particular, firms need to minimize waiting times. Marketers have developed a number of tricks to give impatient customers the illusion that they aren't waiting too long. One hotel chain, responding to complaints about the long wait for elevators, installed mirrors in the lobby: People's tendency to examine their appearance occupied them until the elevators arrived, and protests declined.[10] Burger King's research showed that multiple lines create stress in customers—especially if one moves faster than the others—so it shifted to single lines in which customers at the head of the line order at the next available register.[11]

- *Location factors:* These are especially important for frequently purchased services, such as dry cleaning, that are obtained at a fixed location. Fast food restaurants, such as Subway, try to have several restaurants, all in convenient locations, to satisfy customers' need for convenience.

- *Environmental factors:* Service managers who operate a storefront service requiring people to come to their location realize they must create an attractive environment to lure customers. That's why sports venues such as the Saddledome in Calgary offer plush luxury suites, where wealthy patrons can watch sports events in style. The Calgary Flames, like many Canadian sports franchises, tries to provide all fans with a fun, exciting environment when they attend their games by including such features as between-period contests, promotions, and other fun events.[12]

One trend is for services to adopt a more retail-like philosophy, borrowing techniques from clothing stores or restaurants to create a pleasant environment. Banks, for example, are creating signature looks for branches through the use of lighting, colour, and art. When ING Direct, a Netherlands-based bank, opened in Canada, it didn't open any traditional bank branches. The company, which specializes in web- and telephone-based banking transactions, decided to open cafés instead of branches, where banking services were sold along with Starbucks and other brands of coffee.[13]

PEOPLE-BASED SERVICES At the intangible end of the continuum are people-based services. In the Great American Backrub store, for instance, customers sit in a specially designed chair and, for $7.95, get a massage that lasts exactly eight minutes (no appointment necessary). The owner of the store explained, "To get Americans to buy massages, I realized you had to solve three problems. You had to come up with something that was quick, inexpensive, and most important, you had to find a way to do it without asking people to take their clothes off."[14]

Because people have less and less time to perform various tasks, the importance of people-based services is increasing. Personal concierge services, such as Toronto-based Orderly Lives, is a growing industry, because they help consumers meet obligations despite time pressures by doing almost anything for them, from organizing a party to doing the grocery shopping to planning a vacation.[15] Self-improvement services such as those offered by personal shoppers, wardrobe consultants, and personal trainers are also popular and, in some cities, even professional dog walkers do a brisk business.

What Are the Key Differences Between Services and Goods?

Exhibit 7.7

The airline industry, one of Canada's major service sectors, makes a significant contribution to the Canadian economy. It generates over $10 billion in operating revenues and employs 53 000 people.

Services are acts, efforts, or performances exchanged from producer to user without ownership rights. Like other intangibles, a service satisfies needs by providing pleasure, information, or convenience. About 75 percent of the Canadian population is employed in the services sector in such industries as banking, insurance, professional services, hospitality, transportation (see Exhibit 7.7), education, health care, hotels, restaurants, and recreational services.[16]

> **services** Intangible products that are exchanged directly from the producer to the customer.

Services come in many forms, from those done *to* you, such as a massage or a teeth cleaning, to those done *for* you, such as having your CD player repaired, getting a new paint job on your car, or having an organization like Charity.ca ensure that your money gets to the charity of your choice. Regardless of whether they affect our bodies or our possessions, *all* services share four characteristics that make them distinct from goods: intangibility, perishability, variability, and inseparability.

INTANGIBILITY Service intangibility means that customers can't see, touch, or smell good service. Unlike the purchase of a good, they cannot inspect or handle services before they purchase them. Because they're buying something that isn't there, consumers look for reassuring signs before purchasing, and marketers must ensure that these signs are available when consumers look for them. That's why the service provider's appearance and the "look" of the facility can make or break a service business. When we talk about how customers decide if a service is giving them what they want, marketers overcome the problem of intangibility by providing physical cues to reassure the buyer. These cues include uniforms, brand logos, and carefully designed websites.

PERISHABILITY Service perishability means that a firm can't store its services—it's a case of use it or lose it. When rooms go unoccupied at a ski resort, there is no way to make up for the lost opportunity to exchange a product for money. Marketers try to avoid these problems by using the marketing mix to encourage demand for the service during times when it would otherwise be low. **Capacity management** is the process by which organizations adjust their services in an attempt to match demand. In the summer, for example, Whistler combats its perishability problem by opening its lifts to mountain bikers, who tear down the sunny slopes.

> **capacity management** The process by which organizations adjust their offerings in an attempt to match demand.

VARIABILITY Service variability is the inevitable differences in a service provider's performances from one day to the next: An NHL goalie may be "hot" one game and ice cold the next. Even the same service performed by the same individual for the same customer can vary. It's rare that you get exactly the same cut from a hair stylist.

It is difficult to standardize services, because service providers and customers vary. Your experience in courses is an example. A university or college can standardize its offerings to some degree—course calendars, course content, and classrooms are fairly controllable. Professors, however, vary in their training, life experiences, and personalities, so there is little hope of being able to make teaching uniform. And because students with different backgrounds and interests vary in their needs, the lecture that one finds fascinating might put another to sleep.

Firms handle this aspect of services by standardizing their processes as much as possible. McDonald's, for example, has a Hamburger University outside Chicago where managers and franchisees are taught different aspects of the restaurant process, including the correct arm motion to use when salting french fries!

INSEPARABILITY Although a firm can manufacture goods before sale, a service can take place only at the time the service provider performs an act on either the customer or the customer's possession. In some cases, the service can be sold before delivery, such as a ticket to a concert months before the event.

> **service encounter** The actual interaction between the customer and the service provider.

Still, the expertise, skill, and personality of a provider, or the quality of a firm's facilities and equipment, cannot be detached from the offering itself. The central role played by employees in making or breaking a service underscores the importance of the **service encounter**, or the interaction between the customer and the service provider.[17] The most expertly cooked meal is ruined if a surly or incompetent waiter brings it to the table. Our interactions with service providers can range from the most superficial, such as buying a movie ticket, to telling a psychiatrist (or bartender) our most intimate secrets. In each case, though, the quality of the service encounter can play a big role in determining how we feel about the service we receive.

> **disintermediation** The process of eliminating interaction between customers and service providers.

To minimize the potentially negative effects of bad service encounters and to save on labour costs, some service businesses are experimenting with **disintermediation**, which eliminates the need for customers to interact with people. Examples are self-service gas stations, Internet banking, and ABM machines. Even salad and dessert bars reduce reliance on a server. A recent *Economist* article suggested that pilots eventually will be made redundant as advances in aviation technology become incorporated into new products.[18]

DEVELOPING NEW PRODUCTS

Building on our knowledge of the nature of a product, we'll now examine how firms go about developing new products. Product development doesn't simply mean creating totally new products never before on the market. Many companies do that; but for many other firms, product development is a continuous process of looking for ways to make an existing product better or finding just the right shade of green for this year's bath fashions.

Not all new products are important. Consider what happened when a man named Lonnie Johnson walked into the slick conference room of Larami Corporation. He smiled mischievously at the assembled executives. Then he opened his pink, battered Samsonite suitcase and took out a gizmo that looked a bit like a phaser from *Star Trek*. Holding out this combination of a hand-held pump apparatus, PVC tubing, Plexiglas, and plastic pop bottles, Johnson aimed and fired. A giant stream of water shot across the room. Within a year, the Super Soaker (see Exhibit 7.8) had become one of the most successful water toys in retail history.[19]

The successful introduction of new products is getting tougher for entrepreneurs to accomplish. Even for large corporations, successful new product introductions are becoming more and more difficult. First, the costs of research and development are often so huge that firms must limit the number of new products in development. The fast pace of technological change means that products are outdated faster than ever, giving firms less time to recover their research and development costs. And, with so many products competing for limited shelf space, retailers often charge manufacturers exorbitant fees to stock a new product, increasing manufacturers' costs even more.[20] Firms must reduce the time it takes to get good products to market and increase the speed of adoption to quickly recover these costs.

Exhibit 7.8

Lonnie Johnson, a nuclear and mechanical engineer, invented the Super Soaker, which is one of the most commercially successful summertime toys in recent years.

Phase of Development	Outcome
Visionary	
• Idea generation	Identify product ideas that will provide important customer benefits compatible with company mission.
• Product concept screening	Estimate potential technical and commercial success of product ideas.
• Perform business analysis	Estimate potential for profit. What is the potential demand, what expenditures will be required, and what is the cost of marketing the product?
Planning and Development	
• Begin commercial development	Develop a marketing plan.
• Begin technical development	Design the product and the manufacturing and production process.
Test and Improve	
• Test complete marketing plan	Develop evidence of potential success in the real market.
• Marketing mix adjustments	Make improvements in marketing mix as needed.
• Launch product	Implement full-scale marketing plan.

Figure 7.6 Phases in New Product Development

New product development occurs in three phases, as Figure 7.6 shows. In the *visionary phase*, a firm generates and screens ideas to identify those that will work best for it. The *planning and development phase* means turning those ideas into a product. The *test and improve phase* means trying out marketing strategies in test markets to improve the marketing plan and product, if needed, before full commercial launch.

The Visionary Phase

In the visionary phase of product development, marketers generate new product ideas, screen new product concepts, and complete a business analysis. Marketers use a variety of sources to come up with great new product ideas that provide important customer benefits and are compatible with the company's mission. Ideas can come from employees, customers, as well as salespeople, service providers, and others who have direct customer contact. Often firms use such marketing research activities as focus groups for new product *idea generation*. For example, a company like CanWest Global Communications that operates TV stations might hold focus group discussions to get ideas about types of programs not currently available.

Although ideas for products initially come from a variety of sources, it is up to marketers to expand these ideas into more complete product concepts. Product concepts describe what features the product should have and the benefits those features will provide for consumers. The second step in developing new products is screening product concepts. In *screening*, marketers and researchers examine the chances that the product concept might achieve technical and commercial success, thereby weeding out concepts that have little chance of success. Estimating *technical success* is assessing whether the new product is technologically feasible—is it possible to build this product? Estimating *commercial success* is deciding whether anyone is likely to buy the product. The marketing graveyard is littered with products that sounded interesting but that failed to catch on, including jalapeño pop, aerosol mustard, microwavable ice cream, aerosol toothpaste, and edible deodorant.[21]

The marketers of Fit (see Exhibit 7.9) had to first determine that producing a fruit and vegetable wash product would be possible—technical success. Researchers then had to interview consumers to see if they thought a fruit and vegetable cleaning product was something they would purchase.

Exhibit 7.9

Marketers must make sure that consumers will buy unique product concepts such as Fit, or risk heavy losses.

Once a product concept passes the screening stage, marketers conduct a *business analysis*. Even if they have evidence that there is a market for the product, they still must find out if the product can be a profitable contribution to the organization's product mix. How much potential demand is there for the product? Does the firm have the resources that will be required for successful development and introduction of the product?

The business analysis for a new product begins with assessing how the new product will fit into the firm's total product mix. Will the new product increase sales, or will it cannibalize sales of existing products? Are there possible synergies between the new product and the company's existing offerings that may improve visibility and the image of both? What is the probable customer demand for the new product? An equally important part of the business analysis is estimating the marketing costs necessary to stimulate demand and achieve desired distribution levels. This estimation may include the costs of training a sales force, recruiting distributors, advertising, conducting sales promotions, and communicating through press releases and direct mail.

Planning and Development

If it survives the scrutiny of a business analysis, a new product concept then undergoes commercial and technical development. *Commercial development* means putting together a marketing plan that builds on the initial projections made during product screening and business analysis. Forecasts are adjusted to fit more precise information about the market and how customers will respond to the product. Marketers also plan pricing, advertising, and distribution strategies. Prospective customers are again involved in the planning and development process—the better a firm understands how customers will react to a new product, the better its chances of commercial success.

In *technical development*, a firm's engineers work with marketers to refine the design and production process. Those involved in the technical development process must, for example, determine which parts of a finished good the company will make and which ones will be bought from other suppliers. If goods are to be manufactured, the company may have to buy new production equipment or modify existing machinery. Someone has to develop work instructions for employees and train them to produce the product. In developing service processes, technical development includes such decisions as which activities will occur within sight of customers and whether parts of the service can be automated to make delivery more efficient.

Technical development sometimes requires applying for a patent. Because patents legally prevent competitors from producing or selling the invention, a patent can reduce or eliminate competition in a market for many years, allowing a firm "breathing room" to recoup investments in technical development. For example, for many years, G.D. Searle Pharmaceuticals (makers of Metamucil and Celebrex, now owned by Monsanto) held the patent for its NutraSweet brand of artificial sweetener. This exclusive right to make and sell the product allowed the company to reap huge profits, because no other company had a similar product. Now that the patent has expired, there will be competition in this market.

Testing and Improving the Product

test marketing Testing the complete marketing plan in a small geographic area that is similar to the larger market the firm hopes to enter.

The final phase of new product development includes test marketing, making final adjustments to the marketing mix, and commercial launch. In **test marketing**, the firm tries out the complete marketing plan—the distribution, advertising, sales promotion—but in a

SPOTLIGHT ON REAL PEOPLE   1-800-GOT-JUNK?

1-800-GOT-JUNK?, headquartered in Vancouver, British Columbia, is now the world's largest full-service junk removal company. Even though the name is not that original and the idea of collecting junk was anything but novel, Brian Scudamore was able to grow his business by way of franchising. His choice of franchising as a business model allowed him rapid growth without having to turn to outside investors or other funding sources. Scudamore was able to turn a low-tech business into a sophisticated central dispatching system that covers the entire continent.[22]

1. What do you believe is the most innovative aspect of 1-800-GOT-JUNK?'s business model? Why?
2. Could 1-800-GOT-JUNK? have grown faster otherwise? In your opinion, is instinct or intuition the most important tool in innovation?

small geographic area that is similar to the larger market it hopes to enter. Test marketing can be conducted in an area as small as one city or as large as a country. For example, Vancouver has become a popular test market for innovative products, because Vancouverites have a reputation for being interested in new and unconventional things.

Kera Vision, a U.S. optical company, chose Vancouver as a test market for Intacs, a product that attaches to the eye to reshape the cornea and improve vision.[23] LG Electronics, a Korean appliance manufacturer, used all of Canada as a test market for the North American launch of its "smart" appliances, including an Internet fridge, which allows users to surf the web, send e-mail, or watch TV on a monitor built into the fridge, and a washing machine that automatically measures the detergent, determines water level, and sets the speed.[24]

There are pluses and minuses to test marketing. On the negative side, test marketing is extremely expensive. It can cost over a million dollars to conduct a test market even in a single city. A test market also gives the competition a free look at the new product, its introductory price, and the intended marketing communications strategy—and an opportunity to foil the test market by increasing their own promotion or get to the market first with a competitive product.

Because of the problems with test marketing, marketers sometimes conduct *simulated test markets*. Simulated test markets imitate the introduction of a product into the marketplace using computer software. These simulations allow the company to test the impact of price cuts, new packaging, or even where on store shelves to feature the product. The process entails gathering basic research data on consumer perceptions of the product concept, the physical product, the advertising, and other promotional activity. The test market simulation model uses that information to predict the product's success much less expensively (and more discreetly) than a traditional test market. As this simulated test market technology improves, traditional test markets may become a thing of the past.

On the positive side, by offering a new product in a limited area of the market, marketers can evaluate and improve the marketing program. Sometimes, test marketing uncovers a need to improve the product itself; sometimes, it indicates product failure, allowing the firm to save millions of dollars by "pulling the plug."[25]

The last step in new product development is the *product launch*. Launching a new product requires full-scale production, distribution, advertising, sales promotion—the works. For this reason, full-scale introduction of a new product cannot happen overnight. A launch requires planning and careful preparation. Marketers must implement trade promotion plans, which offer special incentives to encourage dealers, retailers, or other members of the channel to stock the new product so that customers will find it on store shelves the very first time they look. They must also develop consumer promotions, such as coupons. Marketers may arrange to have point-of-purchase displays designed, built, and delivered to retail outlets. If the new product is especially complex, customer service employees must receive extensive training and preparation.

As launch time nears, preparations gain a sense of urgency. Sales managers explain special incentive programs to salespeople. Soon, the media announce to prospective customers why they should buy and where they can find the new product. All elements of the marketing program—ideally—come into play like a well-tuned orchestra.

Table 7.1 Classification of Products

Marketers classify products as a means of better understanding how consumers make purchase decisions.

Consumer Products

Classified by how long they last
Durable: products that provide a benefit over a long period
• Example: Refrigerator

Nondurable: products that provide a benefit over a short time
• Example: Toothpaste

Classified by how consumers buy them
Convenience Products: products that are frequently purchased with little effort
• Examples: Staples (milk)
        Impulse products (candy bars)
        Emergency products (drain opener)

Shopping Products: products that are selected with considerable time and effort
• Examples: Attribute-based (shoes)
        Price-based (water heater)

Specialty Products: products that have unique characteristics to the buyer
• Examples: Favourite restaurant, Rolex watch

Unsought Products: products that consumers have little interest in until need arises
• Example: Retirement plans

Business-to-Business Products

Classified by how organizational customers use them
Equipment
• Examples: Capital equipment (buildings)
        Accessory equipment (computer terminals)

Maintenance, Repair, and Operating (MRO) Products
• Examples: Maintenance products (light bulbs, mops)
        Repair products (nuts, bolts)
        Operating supplies (paper, oil)

Raw Materials
• Example: Iron ore

Processed Materials
• Example: Sheets of steel

Specialized Services
• Example: Legal services

Component Parts
• Example: Car water pump

CLASSIFYING PRODUCTS

Classifying a product can be challenging. A product can be a tangible good or an intangible service or idea, and different layers of a product exist. Marketers classify products into different categories since they want to cater to different customers and products are perceived differently by customers as well. Classifying products assists marketers in understanding what marketing mix should apply for certain products and certain markets.

Usually, products are consumer-oriented products, or simply designed to develop the business-to-business market, although businesses and consumers may be attracted to the same product, such as toilet paper, vacuum cleaners, and light bulbs. In these cases, though, businesses tend to buy a lot more of them at once. Of course, as we saw in earlier chapters, customers differ in how they decide on a purchase, depending on whether the decision maker is a consumer or a business purchaser. Let's first consider differences in consumer products based on how long the product will last and on how the consumer shops for the products. Then we will discuss the general types of business-to-business products.

Classifying Goods: How Long Does the Product Last?

Marketers classify consumer goods as durable or nondurable depending on how long the product lasts. You expect refrigerators to last many years, but a litre of milk will last only a week until it turns into a science project. **Durable goods** are consumer products that provide benefits over a period of months, years, or even decades, such as cars, furniture, and appliances. In contrast, we consume **nondurable goods**, such as newspapers and food, in the short term.

We are more likely to purchase durable goods under conditions of high involvement, while nondurable goods are more likely to be low-involvement decisions. When consumers buy a computer or a house, they will spend a lot of time and energy on the decision process. When they offer these products, marketers need to understand consumers' desires for different product benefits and the importance of warranties, service, and customer support. So they must be sure that consumers can find the information they need to make a sound decision. Blogs and a section called "Frequently asked questions" on the company's website can serve that purpose. When a company itself sponsors such forums, odds are the content will be much more favourable and the firm can police peripheral postings.

In contrast, consumers usually don't look for details so much when choosing among nondurable goods. There is little if any search for information or deliberation. Sometimes this means that consumers buy whatever brand is available and reasonably priced. In other instances, they base their decisions largely on past experience, or even habit. For example, some consumers buy that familiar orange box of Tide laundry detergent again and again. In such cases, marketers can probably be less concerned with developing new product features to attract customers; they should focus more on pricing and distribution strategies.

Classifying Goods: How Do Consumers Buy the Product?

Marketers classify products based on where and how consumers buy the product. We can think of both goods and services as convenience products, shopping products, specialty products, or unsought products. In earlier chapters, we talked about how consumer decisions differ in terms of effort, from habitual decision making to limited problem solving to extended problem solving. We can tie these differences in consumer decision making to the classification of products in terms of how consumers buy them. By understanding how consumers buy products, marketers have a clearer vision of the buying process that will help them develop effective marketing strategies based on the category into which their product falls.

CONVENIENCE PRODUCTS A **convenience product** typically is a nondurable good or service that consumers purchase frequently with a minimum of comparison and effort. As the name implies, consumers expect these products to be handy and will buy whatever

durable goods Consumer products that provide benefits over a long period of time, such as cars, furniture, and appliances.

nondurable goods Consumer products that provide benefits for a short time because they are consumed (such as food) or are no longer useful (such as newspapers).

convenience product A consumer good or service that is usually low-priced, widely available, and purchased frequently with a minimum of comparison and effort.

brands are easy to obtain. In general, convenience products are low-priced and widely available. You can buy butter or a loaf of bread at grocery stores, at convenience stores, and even at many service stations. Consumers know all they will need or want to know about a convenience product, devote little effort to purchases, and willingly accept alternative brands if their preferred brand is not available in a convenient location. Most convenient product purchases are the result of habitual consumer decision making. Accessibility and availability are essential for this type of product. Marketers classify convenience products as staples, impulse products, and emergency products.

staples Basic or necessary items that are available almost everywhere.

Staples such as eggs, toothbrushes, and bottled water are basic or necessary items that are available almost everywhere. Most consumers don't perceive big differences among brands. When selling staples, marketers must offer customers a product that consistently meets their expectations for quality and make sure it is available at a price comparable to the competition's prices.

impulse product A product people often buy on the spur of the moment.

Consider this situation: You are standing in the checkout line at the supermarket and notice a copy of *Canadian Business* magazine featuring a photo of Mike Weir, a famous Canadian professional golfer. If you enjoy golfing, you will check out that article! This magazine is an **impulse product**, something people often buy on the spur of the moment. With an impulse product, marketers have two challenges: to create a product or package design that is enticing, that "reaches out and grabs the customers," and to make sure their product is highly visible; for example, by securing prime end-aisle or checkout-lane space.

emergency products Products we purchase when we're in dire need.

Emergency products are products we purchase when we're in dire need. Bandages, umbrellas, and something to unclog the bathroom sink are examples of emergency products. Because we need the product badly and immediately, price and sometimes product quality may be irrelevant to our decision to purchase. If you're caught out in a sudden downpour, any umbrella at any price may do. To be successful, an emergency product should be reliable, and should be offered in the sizes customers want.

fast-moving consumer goods (FMCG) Products that exhibit consistently high velocity of sales in the consumer marketplace.

Fast-moving consumer goods (FMCG) are any products that exhibit consistently high velocity of sales in the consumer marketplace, and represent an important part of our economy. Soap, diapers, and shampoo are considered FMCGs. Major consumer packaged goods companies such as Procter & Gamble, Colgate-Palmolive, and Unilever, each of which has an extensive line of products sold for various aspects of convenience, refer to the majority of their products as FMCG.

shopping product A good or service for which consumers spend considerable time and effort gathering information and comparing alternatives before making a purchase.

SHOPPING PRODUCTS In contrast to convenience products, **shopping products** are goods or services for which consumers will spend time and effort gathering information on price, product attributes, and product quality. They are likely to compare alternatives before making a purchase. Often consumers have little prior knowledge about these products. Because they gather new information for each purchase occasion, consumers are only moderately brand-loyal and will switch whenever a different brand offers new or better benefits. They may visit several stores and devote considerable effort to comparing products. Laptop computers and digital cameras are good examples of shopping products because they offer an ever-expanding array of new features and functions. There are trade-offs and decisions to make about the price, speed, screen size, accuracy, weight, and battery life. Some shopping products have different characteristics. When people shop for *attribute-based shopping products*, such as a new party dress or a pair of designer shoes, they spend time and energy finding the best possible product selection. At other times, when choices available in the marketplace are just about the same, we consider these to be shopping products because of differences in price. For these *price-based shopping products*, determined shoppers will visit numerous stores in hopes of saving an additional $10 or $20.

specialty products A good or service with unique characteristics that are important to the buyer and for which the buyer will devote significant effort to acquire.

SPECIALTY PRODUCTS Consumers can buy a mop at Canadian Tire for well under $10, but sales of industrial carpet cleaners are brisk. Industrial carpet cleaners are good examples of **specialty products**. Specialty products have unique characteristics that are important to buyers at almost any price. Consumers usually know a good deal about specialty products, and they tend to be loyal to specific brands. Generally, a specialty product is an extended problem-solving purchase that requires a lot of effort to choose. That means that firms selling these kinds of products need to create marketing strategies that make their products stand apart from the rest. For example, advertising for a specialty product such as a flat-screen plasma TV may talk about plasma's unique and superior characteristics, attempting to convince prospective customers that savvy shoppers won't accept a substitute such as a mere LCD screen.

UNSOUGHT PRODUCTS **Unsought products** are goods or services (other than convenience products) for which a consumer has little awareness or interest until a need arises. For university graduates with their first "real" job, retirement plans and disability insurance are unsought products. It requires a good deal of advertising or personal selling to interest people in these kinds of products. It is a real challenge to find convincing ways to interest consumers in unsought products. One solution may be to make pricing more attractive; for example, reluctant consumers may be more willing to buy an unsought product for "only pennies a day" than if they have to think about their yearly or lifetime cash outlay.

unsought products Goods or services for which a consumer has little awareness or interest until the product or a need for the product is brought to his or her attention.

Business-to-Business Products

Although consumers purchase products for their own use, as we saw in Chapter 6 organizational customers purchase items to use in the production of other goods and services or to facilitate the organization's operation. Marketers classify business-to-business products based on how organizational customers use them. As with consumer products, when marketers know how their business customers use a product, they are better able to design products and craft the entire marketing mix. Let's briefly review the five different types of business-to-business products.

EQUIPMENT **Equipment** refers to the products an organization uses in its daily operations. Heavy equipment, sometimes called installations or capital equipment, includes items such as buildings and robotics used to assemble automobiles. Installations are big-ticket items and last for a number of years. Computers, photocopy machines, and water fountains are examples of light or accessory equipment; they are portable, cost less, and have a shorter lifespan than capital equipment. Marketing strategies for equipment usually emphasize personal selling and may mean custom-designing products to meet an industrial customer's specific needs.

equipment Expensive goods that an organization uses in its daily operations that last for a long time.

MRO PRODUCTS **Maintenance, repair, and operating (MRO) products** are goods that a business customer consumes in a relatively short time. *Maintenance products* include light bulbs, mops, cleaning supplies, printing paper, and the like. *Repair products* are items such as nuts, bolts, washers, and small tools. *Operating supplies* include computer paper and oil to keep machinery running smoothly. Although some firms use a sales force to promote MRO products, others rely on catalogue sales, the Internet, and telemarketing to keep prices as low as possible.

maintenance, repair, and operating (MRO) products Goods that a business customer consumes in a relatively short time.

RAW MATERIALS **Raw materials** are products of the fishing, lumber, agricultural, and mining industries that organizational customers purchase to use in their finished products. For example, a food company may transform soybeans into tofu, and a steel manufacturer changes iron ore into large sheets of steel used by other firms to build automobiles, washing machines, and lawn mowers.

raw materials Products of the fishing, lumber, agricultural, and mining industries that organizational customers purchase to use in their finished products.

PROCESSED MATERIALS AND SPECIAL SERVICES **Processed materials** are purchased by organizations that use them as part of the product they make. A builder uses treated lumber to add a deck onto a house, and the company that creates aluminum cans for Red Bull buys aluminum ingots for this purpose.

processed materials Products created when firms transform raw materials from their original state.

In addition to tangible materials, some business customers purchase specialized services from outside suppliers. Specialized services may be equipment-based, such as repairing a copy machine or fixing an assembly line malfunction, or non-equipment-based, such as market research and legal services. These services are essential to the operation of an organization but are not part of the production of a product.

COMPONENT PARTS **Component parts** are manufactured goods or subassemblies of finished items that organizations need to complete their own products. For example, a

component parts Manufactured goods or subassemblies of finished items that organizations need to complete their own products.

computer manufacturer needs silicon chips to make a computer, and an automobile manufacturer needs batteries, tires, and fuel injectors. As with processed materials, marketing strategies for component parts usually involve nurturing relationships with customer firms and on-time delivery of a product that meets the buyer's specifications.

To review, we now understand what a product is. We also know how marketers classify consumer products based on how long they last and how they are purchased, and we've seen how they classify business-to-business products according to how they are used. In the next section we'll learn about the marketing of new products, or *innovations*.

IT'S "NEW AND IMPROVED!": UNDERSTANDING THE IMPORTANCE OF INNOVATIONS

innovation A product that consumers perceive to be new and different from existing products.

"New and improved!" What exactly do we mean when we use the term *new product*? From a marketing standpoint, a new product or an **innovation** is anything that customers *perceive* as new and different. Innovations may be a cutting-edge style such as body piercing, a fad such as Beanie Babies, a new communications technology such as wireless communication, or a new product such as MP3 players. It may be a completely new product that provides benefits never available before, or it may simply be an existing product with a new style, in a different colour, or with some new feature. If an innovation is successful, it spreads through the population. First, it is bought and used by only a few people, and then more and more consumers adopt it.

Not all innovations are successful. Windows Millennium Edition was one of those products that failed. As a matter of fact, Windows Me frequently makes the list of most disappointing products in history. The Millennium Edition came out between the highly successful Windows 98 and Windows 2000. It had few real features beyond Windows 98 and even rolled back a few options. It was considered unreliable by most and it was released along with the much more reliable Windows 2000. Still today, nobody knows if anything good came out of Windows Me. Microsoft certainly learned from that dreadful experience.

Understanding innovations can be critical to the success of firms for at least two reasons. First, technology is advancing at a dizzying pace. Products are introduced and become obsolete faster than ever before. In many industries, firms are busy developing another new-and-better product before the last new-and-better product even hits store shelves. Nowhere is this more obvious than with personal computers, where a steady change in technology makes consumers want a better, faster machine before the dust even settles on the old one. One company, Gateway, offers consumers a purchase plan that gives them the option of trading the machine in for a newer model every two years to make sure customers have what they want—and that they get it from Gateway.

Another reason why understanding new products is important is the high cost of developing them and the even higher cost of new products that fail. In the pharmaceutical industry, the cost of bringing each new drug to market is between $200 and $500 million.[26] Even the most successful firms can't afford many product failures with that kind of price tag.

Marketers must understand what it takes to develop a new product successfully; they must do their homework and learn what it is about existing products consumers find less than satisfactory and what exactly it will take to do a better job satisfying customer needs. Savvy marketers know they'll waste a lot of investment money if they don't.

Finally, new product development is an important contribution to society. We would never suggest that *everything* new is good, but many new products allow us to live longer, happier lives of better quality than before (see Table 7.2). Although there are some who disagree, most of us feel that our lives are better because of telephones, televisions, CD players, microwave ovens, and computers—except when these items break down. We're not saying that firms create new products because they want to make our lives better—businesses create new products that make our lives better because that's how they make profits and keep their shareholders happy.

Table 7.2 Innovations That Have Changed Our Lives

Products that have changed how we play		*Products that have changed our homes*	
1900	Kodak Brownie camera	1907	Vacuum cleaner
1948	Polaroid camera	1918	Frigidaire refrigerator
1976	JVC videorecorder	1928	Home air conditioner
1982	Philips/Sony CD player	1942	Permacel duct tape
Products that have changed how we work		1946	Tupperware
1900	Paper clip	1967	Amana microwave oven
1959	Xerox photocopier	*Products that have changed the way we communicate*	
1966	Xerox fax machine		
1971	Intel microprocessor	1921	RCA radio
1980	3M Post-it Notes	1935	RCA television
1984	Apple Macintosh	1939	The paperback book
Products that have changed how we travel		1991	World Wide Web
1903	Harley-Davidson motorcycle	*Products that have changed our clothing*	
1908	Ford Model T	1913	Zipper
1936	DC-3	1914	Bra
1950s	Skateboard	1936	Bass penny loafer
1957	Boeing 707	1939	Nylons
Products that have changed our health and grooming		1954	Velcro
1903	Safety razors	1959	Lycra
1921	Johnson & Johnson Band-Aid	1961	P&G Pampers
1928	Penicillin		
1931	Tampax tampon		
1960	Searle birth control pill		
1988	Eli Lilly Prozac		

Source: Adapted from Christine Chen and Tim Carvell, "Products of the century," *Fortune*, 22 November 1999: 133–136.

Types of Innovations

Innovations differ in their degree of newness, and this helps to determine how quickly the products will be adopted by many members of a target market. Because innovations that are more novel require greater effort and more changes in behaviour, they are slower to spread throughout a population than new products that are similar to what is already available.

Marketers classify innovations into three categories based on their degree of newness; however, it is better to think of these three types as ranges along a continuum. The three types of innovations are based on the amount of disruption or change they bring to people's lives. For example, when the first automobiles were produced, they caused tremendous changes in the lives of their owners, far greater changes than when auto manufacturers introduced "new and improved" autos with automatic transmissions, air conditioning, and driving directions provided via satellite.

CONTINUOUS INNOVATIONS A **continuous innovation** is a modification to an existing product, such as MasterCard's ability to handle business expenses (Exhibit 7.10). This type of modification can set one brand apart from its competitors. Roots has used continuous innovation in many of its product lines, adding a new style of leather jacket or a new neckline for a shirt. Most product innovations are continuous innovations. The term *continuous* tells us that the changes are evolutionary rather than revolutionary. Small changes reposition the product or allow a manufacturer to offer new product options.

With a continuous innovation, the consumer doesn't have to learn anything new to use the innovation. From a marketing perspective, this means that it is far easier to convince consumers to adopt the innovation. A typewriter company, for example, many years ago modified the shape of its product to make it more "user friendly" to secretaries. One simple change was curving the tops of the keys, as we see on today's computer keyboards, because secretaries complained that flat surfaces were hard to use with long fingernails. Today,

continuous innovation A modification of an existing product that sets one brand apart from its competitors.

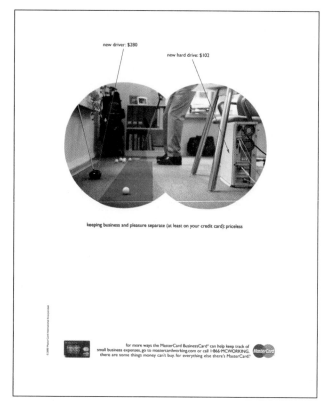

new driver: $280

new hard drive: $102

keeping business and pleasure separate (at least on your credit card): priceless

for more ways the MasterCard BusinessCard® can help keep track of
small business expenses, go to mastercardworking.com or call 1-866-MCWORKING.
there are some things money can't buy. for everything else there's MasterCard®

Exhibit 7.10

The introduction of the ability to keep track of small business
expenses is an example of continuous innovation.

knock-off A new product that
copies with slight modification the
design of an original product.

dynamically continuous innovation
A change in an existing product
that requires a moderate amount
of learning or behaviour change.

discontinuous innovation A totally new product that creates
major changes in the way we live.

computer manufacturers have gone a step further by building
ergonomic keyboards that are less likely to cause painful wrist
ailments.

How different does a new product have to be from existing
products? It is said that "imitation is the sincerest form of flattery," and decisions regarding how much (if at all) one's product should resemble those of competitors often are at the
centre of marketing strategy development. Sometimes, marketers feel that the best strategy is to follow the competition.
For example, the packaging of "me-too" or look-alike products,
such as store-brand versions of national brands, can create instant market success, because consumers assume that similar
packaging means similar products.

A **knock-off** is a new product that copies, with slight modification, the design of an original product. Firms deliberately
create knock-offs of clothing, jewellery, or other items, often
with the intent to sell to a larger or different market. For example, companies may copy the haute couture clothing styles
of top designers and sell them at lower prices to the mass market. It is difficult to legally protect a design (as opposed to a
technological invention), because it can be argued that even a
very slight change—different buttons or a slightly wider collar
on a dress or shirt—means the knock-off is not an exact copy.
However, industry pressure is building for legal protection of
designs. Manufacturers argue that a design element—say, a distinctive curve on a car bumper—is as important to the integrity of the car as a mechanical innovation.[27]

DYNAMICALLY CONTINUOUS INNOVATIONS A **dynamically continuous innovation**
is a pronounced modification to an existing product that requires a modest amount of learning or change in behaviour to use it. The history of audio equipment is a series of dynamically continuous innovations. For many years, consumers enjoyed listening to their favourite
songs on record players. Then in the 1960s, that same music became available on a continu-
ous-play eight-track tape, requiring the purchase of an eight-track tape player. Then came
cassette tapes, requiring a cassette player. In the 1980s, consumers could hear songs digitally
mastered on compact disks; that required the purchase of a new CD player. In the 1990s,
recording technology moved one more step forward with digital video disk (DVD) technology. Now, consumers download music into MP3 players and take their custom mix of music
everywhere. Even though each of these changes required learning how to operate new
equipment, consumers were willing to buy the new products because of the improvements
in music reproduction, the core product benefit.

DISCONTINUOUS INNOVATIONS A **discontinuous innovation** creates major changes
in the way we live. To use a discontinuous innovation, consumers must engage in a great
amount of learning, because no similar product has ever been on the market. Such major
inventions as the airplane, car, and television have radically changed lifestyles. Another discontinuous innovation, the personal computer, is changing the way we shop and is allowing
more and more firms' employees to work from their homes.

Recognizing the degree of newness of innovations is important in developing marketing
strategies. For example, if marketers know that consumers may resist adopting a new and
radically different product, they may offer consumers free product trial or place heavier emphasis on a personal selling strategy to convince consumers that the new product offers benefits worth the hassle. Business-to-business marketers of technology products such as
software, for instance, often provide in-service training for employees of their customers
who invest in new products.

ADOPTION AND DIFFUSION PROCESSES

We've presented the steps marketers take to develop new products, from generating ideas to launch, and we have examined the importance of understanding innovations. Now, we'll look at what happens after that new product hits the market—how an innovation spreads throughout a population.

New products do not satisfy customer needs until the customer uses them. **Product adoption** is the process by which a consumer or business customer begins to buy and use a new good, service, or idea. The term **diffusion** describes how the use of a product spreads throughout a population. Once a product is bought by a small group of consumers, it may reach the moment of critical mass. This moment of truth in marketing is known as the **tipping point**. To reach that critical point, a marketer should understand the product adoption process.

After months or even years spent developing a new product, a firm faces the challenge of getting consumers to buy and use the product—and to do so quickly—so that it can recover the costs of product development and launch. To accomplish this, marketers must understand the product adoption process. In this section, we'll discuss the stages in this process. We'll also see how consumers and businesses differ in their eagerness to adopt new products and how the characteristics of a product affect its adoption rate—an important consideration for the introduction of new products.

product adoption The process by which a consumer or business customer begins to buy and use a new good, service, or idea.

diffusion The process by which the use of a product spreads throughout a population.

tipping point In the context of product diffusion, the point when a product's sales spike from a slow climb to an unprecedented new level, often accompanied by a steep price decline.

Stages in a Customer's Adoption of a New Product

Whether the innovation is a new type of retail store or a better mousetrap, individuals and organizations pass through six stages in the adoption process. Figure 7.7 shows how a person goes from being unaware of an innovation through the stages of awareness, interest, evaluation, trial, adoption, and confirmation. At every stage, people drop out of the process, so the proportion of consumers who wind up using the innovation on a consistent basis is a fraction of those who are exposed to it.

AWARENESS Learning that the innovation exists is the first step in the adoption process. To make consumers *aware* of a new product, marketers often conduct a massive advertising campaign, or media blitz. Car companies use this approach to communicate to consumers that a new model has been introduced. This strategy works for new products when consumers see a new product as something they want and need and just can't live without.

INTEREST For some of the people who become aware of a new product, a second stage in the adoption process is *interest*—a prospective adopter begins to see how a new product could satisfy an existing or newly realized need. Interest also means that consumers look for and are open to information about the innovation. Marketers often design teaser advertisements to give prospective customers just enough information about the new product to make them curious and to stimulate their interest. A recent ad for the telecommunications company Telus had billboards across Canadian cities featuring a very adorable pig. The billboards created a buzz, with people wondering whom the ads were for and what product it represented. It turned out that the ads were for new camera cellphones by Telus. Despite the marketers' best efforts, though, some consumers drop out of the process at this point.

The concept of different layers of a product discussed at the beginning of this chapter provides an excellent guide for marketers at this stage. Recall that consumers do not buy product features (attributes), they buy product benefits. Therefore, smart marketers stress the product's benefits at this stage to generate interest. For example,

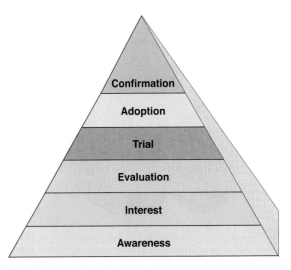

Figure 7.7 Adoption Pyramid

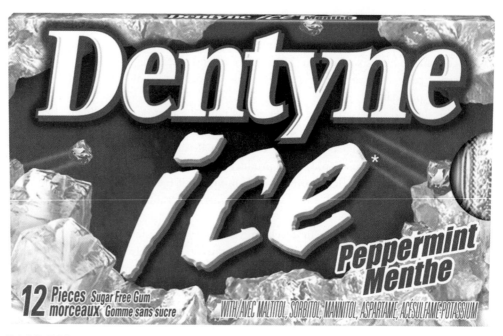

Exhibit 7.11

Consumers aren't likely to spend much time evaluating new impulse products like chewing gum before buying them.

when Goodyear introduced a new tire, the Aquatread, it stressed the fact that the tire would help drivers with superior traction in wet conditions.

EVALUATION In the *evaluation* stage, a prospect weighs the costs and benefits of the new product. For complex, risky, or expensive products, people think about the innovation a great deal before trying it. For instance, a firm will carefully evaluate buying a $6000 video conferencing system before purchase.[28] Marketers for such products help prospective customers see how such products can benefit them—holding video conferences means a company doesn't have to pay travel costs for employees to attend central-location meetings.

However, little evaluation may occur with an impulse purchase. For example, consumers may do very little thinking before buying a chewing gum such as Dentyne Peppermint, shown in Exhibit 7.11. For these products, marketers design the product and packaging to be eye-catching and appealing to get consumers to notice the product quickly.

Some potential adopters will evaluate an innovation positively enough to move on to the trial stage. Those who do not think the new product will provide adequate benefits drop out.

TRIAL The next stage in the adoption process is *trial*—the potential adopters will actually experience or use the product for the first time. Often marketers stimulate trial by providing opportunities for consumers to sample the product. For example, when Barq's Root Beer (Exhibit 7.12) was introduced into the Canadian market, the company used a sampling team, the Barq's Brigades, to give consumers free samples in stores and at sporting events to ensure that people tried the product.[29] Based on the trial experience, some potential buyers move on to adoption of the new product.

ADOPTION At the *adoption* stage, a prospect chooses a product. If the product is a consumer or business-to-business good, this means buying the product and learning how to use and maintain it. If the product is an idea, this means that the individual agrees with the new idea. For example, consumers who have adopted the idea that recycling helps protect our natural resources will carefully sort and recycle their glass, aluminum, plastic, and paper products.

Exhibit 7.12

When Barq's was introduced in Canada, sampling teams (the Barq's Brigades) conducted product sampling events to drive product trial.

This does not mean that all individuals or organizations that first choose an innovation are permanent customers, although many firms make this mistaken assumption. Some potential customers, even after initial adoption, do not go on to the final stage of confirmation. Marketers need to provide follow-up contacts and communications with adopters to ensure that they are satisfied and remain loyal to the new product over time.

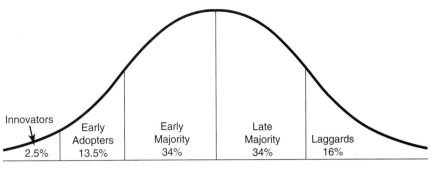

Figure 7.8 Categories of Adopters

CONFIRMATION With initial adoption of an innovation, a customer weighs expected versus actual benefits and costs. Favourable experiences contribute to new customers becoming loyal adopters, as their initially positive opinions result in *confirmation*. Nothing lasts forever, however. Even loyal customers may decide that a new product is not meeting expectations and reject it. Some marketers feel that *reselling* the customer in the confirmation stage is important. They provide advertisements, sales presentations, and other communications to reinforce a customer's choice.

The Diffusion of Innovations

Diffusion describes how the use of a product spreads throughout a population. Marketers would prefer that their entire target market immediately adopt a new product; but this does not happen. Consumers and business customers differ in how eager or willing they are to try something new, lengthening the diffusion process by months or even years. Based on adopters' roles in the diffusion process, experts have classified them into five different categories.

ADOPTER CATEGORIES Some people like to try new products. Others are so reluctant, you'd think they're afraid of anything new. As Figure 7.8 shows, there are five categories of adopters: innovators, early adopters, early majority, late majority, and laggards.[30] To understand how these differ, we'll study the adoption of one product—the microwave oven.

Innovators are roughly the first 2.5 percent of adopters. This segment is extremely adventurous and willing to take risks with new products. Innovators are typically well educated, younger, better off financially than others in the population, and worldly. Innovators who were into new technology knew all about microwave ovens before other people were aware they existed. Because innovators pride themselves on trying new products, they probably purchased microwaves when they were first introduced to the market in the mid-1970s.

Early adopters, approximately 13.5 percent of adopters, buy product innovations early in the diffusion process, but not as early as innovators. After reading articles in *Consumer Reports* and other sources of information on new products, early adopters of the microwave made their first purchase in the late 1970s. Unlike innovators, early adopters have greater concern for social acceptance. Typically, they are heavy media users and often are heavy users of a new product category. Others in the population often look to early adopters for their opinions on various topics, making them key to a new product's success. For this reason, marketers often target early adopters in developing advertising and other

innovators The first segment (roughly 2.5 percent) of a population to adopt a new product.

early adopters Those who adopt an innovation early in the diffusion process but later than the innovators.

Ethical Decisions in Marketing

When a new product is hot, it's hot—but the burning desire to get hold of it can make it too hot to handle. Athletic shoe manufacturers compete fiercely to produce dynamically continuous innovations that kids want. For example, Nike, Adidas, Reebok, and other manufacturers introduce new models every year, and with each new version, the products become more and more desirable to young kids. News of one new model's arrival date in stores sometimes causes a frenzy. Students go so far as to skip school—with permission from their parents—to be the first in line to buy the latest shoe. Do you think marketers should feel good or bad about kids being so anxious to buy their new products?

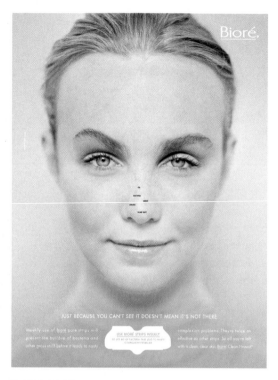

Exhibit 7.13
Bioré targeted young 18- to 37-year-olds by giving out free samples at Lilith Fair.

early majority Those whose adoption of a new product signals a general acceptance of the innovation.

late majority The adopters who are willing to try new products when there is little or no risk associated with the purchase, when the purchase becomes an economic necessity, or when there is social pressure to purchase.

laggards The last consumers to adopt an innovation.

communications efforts. For example, early adopters of the Bioré pore-cleaning strips (see Exhibit 7.13) were young, 18- to 34-year-old women who were heavy readers of fashion magazines. Bioré targeted this group with heavy advertising for the strips in fashion magazines and by giving out free samples at the Lilith Fair tour.[31]

The **early majority**, about 34 percent of adopters, avoid being either first or last to try an innovation. They are typically middle-class consumers and are deliberate and cautious. Early majority consumers have slightly above-average education and income levels. When the early majority adopts a product, it is no longer considered new or different—it is, in essence, already established. Early majority microwave owners made their purchase in the early and mid-1980s, by which time there were 10 to 15 brands of microwaves sold by a wide variety of retailers.

Late majority adopters, about 34 percent of the population, are older, more conservative, and typically have lower-than-average levels of education and income. The late majority adopters avoid trying a new product until it is no longer risky. By that time, the product has become an economic necessity, or there is pressure from peer groups to adopt. Late majority homes did not have a microwave until their friends began asking, "How can you survive without a microwave?" By that time, the price of the ovens had gone down, and the innovators, early adopters, and even many of the early majority were purchasing a second or even a third microwave. To attract late majority buyers, marketers may offer lower-priced models of a product.

Laggards, about 16 percent of adopters, are the last in a population to adopt a new product. Laggards are typically lower in social class than other adopter categories and are bound by tradition. By the time laggards adopt a product, it may already be superseded by other innovations.

By understanding these adopter categories, marketers are better able to develop strategies to speed the diffusion or widespread use of their products. For example, early in the diffusion process, marketers may put greater emphasis on advertising in special-interest magazines to attract innovators and early adopters. Later they may lower the product's price or come out with lower-priced models with fewer features to attract the late majority. We'll discuss the strategies for new and existing products in the next chapter.

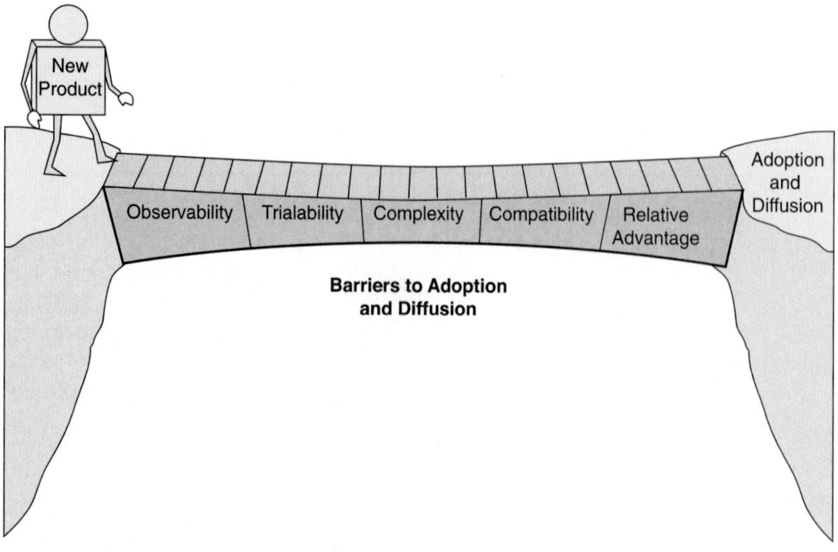

PRODUCT FACTORS AFFECTING THE RATE OF ADOPTION If you could predict which new products will succeed and which will fail, you'd quickly be in high demand as a consultant by companies worldwide. That's because companies make large investments in new products; but failures are all too frequent. Estimates of new product success rates range from 46 to 65 percent.[32] Much research is devoted to making us smarter about new product successes and failures.

Researchers have identified five characteristics of innovations that affect the rate of adoption. Figure 7.9 summarizes these factors: relative advantage, compatibility, complexity, trialability, and observability.[33] Whether a new product has each of these

Figure 7.9 Adoption Rate Factors

characteristics affects the speed of diffusion. As we've discussed, it took many years for the microwave to diffuse or spread throughout the Canadian population—from the mid-1970s to the early 1990s.[34] Examining these five factors helps us understand both why the new product was not adopted during its early years and why adoption sped up later.

Relative advantage is the degree to which a consumer perceives that a new product provides superior benefits. In the case of the microwave oven, consumers in the 1960s and early 1970s did not feel that the product provided important benefits that would improve their lives. But by the late 1970s, that perception had changed, primarily because more women had entered the workforce. The 1960s' woman had all day to prepare the evening meal—she didn't have a need for the microwave. But in the late 1970s, when many women left home for work at 8:00 a.m. and returned home at 6:00 p.m., an appliance that would "magically" defrost a frozen chicken and cook it for dinner in 30 minutes provided a genuine advantage.

Compatibility is the extent to which a new product is consistent with existing cultural values, customs, and practices. Did consumers see the microwave oven as being compatible with existing ways of doing things? No. Cooking on paper plates? If you put a paper plate in a conventional oven, you'd likely get a visit from the fire department. By anticipating compatibility issues early in the new product development stage, marketing strategies can address such problems in planning communications programs, or there may be opportunities for altering product designs to overcome some consumer objections.

Complexity is the degree to which consumers find a new product or its use difficult to understand. Many microwave users today haven't a clue about how a microwave oven cooks food. But when the product was introduced, consumers asked and marketers answered—microwaves cause molecules to move and rub together, creating friction, which produces heat—cooked pot roast. But that explanation was complex and confusing for consumers of the 1960s.

Trialability is the ease of sampling a new product and its benefits. Marketers took a very important step in the 1970s to speed up adoption of the microwave oven—product trial. Just about every store that sold microwaves invited shoppers to visit the store and see and sample an entire meal cooked in the microwave.

Observability is how visible a new product and its benefits are to others who might adopt it. The ideal innovation is easy to see. For example, in-line skates gained instant attention, because walkers, runners, and bikers saw bladers (see Exhibit 7.14) zip by them on bike and jogging paths. The microwave was moderately observable. Only close friends and acquaintances who visited someone's home could see whether the household had a microwave. Although marketers can't do much about the observability of new products—consumers are likely to keep their mattresses away from public viewing no matter what marketers do—they do recognize that marketing strategies for new products that are not observable face difficult challenges. They must develop a marketing mix that convinces consumers to invest in the product, even though no one else will know.

Organizational Differences Affect Adoption

Just as there are differences among consumers in their eagerness to adopt new products, businesses and other organizations are not alike in their willingness to buy and use new industrial products.[35] Firms that

Exhibit 7.14

The observability of in-line skating helped to increase the rate of adoption of in-line skates.

SAIC's Formula for Sourcing Success

OUTSOURCING 101

INNOVATION + EXPERIENCE
× TECHNICAL DEPTH =
REAL BUSINESS VALUE

SAIC has a long history of finding solutions to the kinds of problems that keep you from focusing on what's most important to you… your business. For more than thirty years we've been providing technology-based answers to the difficult questions our customers face.

SAIC
An Employee-Owned Company
saic.com

THE EXPERTS OF CHOICE IN THE SCIENCE OF BUSINESS

Exhibit 7.15

SAIC positions itself as the sourcing expert.

welcome product innovations are likely to be younger companies, in highly technical industries, with younger managers and entrepreneurial corporate cultures. Early adopter firms are likely to be market-share leaders that adopt new innovations and try new ways of doing things to maintain their leadership. Firms that adopt new products only when they recognize they must innovate to keep up are in the early majority. Late majority firms tend to be oriented toward the status quo and often have large financial investments in existing production technology. Laggard firms are probably already losing money.

Business-to-business products, like consumer products, can possess characteristics that will increase their likelihood of adoption. Organizations are likely to adopt an innovation that helps them increase gross margins and profits. It is unlikely that firms would have adopted new products like voice mail unless they provided a way to increase profits by reducing labour costs. Organizational innovations are attractive when they are consistent with a firm's ways of doing business. Cost is also a factor in the new products firms will adopt. Firms are more likely to accept a new product if they perceive the improvement to be large in relation to the investment they will have to make.

For example, SAIC (see Exhibit 7.15) positions itself as the outsourcing expert for technical solutions. It tells customers that they can focus on running their business while SAIC focuses on other issues, such as back-office functions. This enables businesses to save money in the long run by not having to do all functions in-house.

Real People, Real Decisions

▶ How It Worked Out at Lambesis

Dee Dee and her colleagues decided to merge the strongest features of Options 1 and 2. The final design appears in the advertisement developed for the fragrance (shown here in Exhibit 7.16). In the first month following the Fetish product launch, the fragrance sold 500 percent faster than any other product in Dana's history. Based on this promising early start, the company increased its sales goals by 50 percent.

The option chosen by Dee Dee fits with her motto: "Don't be afraid to innovate." No wonder she has chosen this motto—she considers Mary Kay Ash and her mother her heroes. Mary Kay Ash started with $5000 and built Mary Kay Inc., a billion-dollar cosmetics company. She famously said, "If your mind can conceive it, and if you can believe it, you can achieve it." Dee Dee regrets not finishing college, and makes up for this by reading biographies (so she can learn from other people's experiences) and continuing her "can do" attitude.

Exhibit 7.16

This ad for Fetish shows the design option that was selected by Lambesis for the new perfume.

CHAPTER SUMMARY

1. Explain the different product objectives and strategies a firm may choose.

Objectives for individual products may be related to introducing a new product, expanding the market of a regional product, or rejuvenating a mature product. For multiple products, firms may decide on a full- or a limited-line strategy. Companies often decide to extend their product line with an upward, downward, or two-way stretch, with a filling-out strategy, or they may decide to contract a product line. Firms that have multiple product lines may choose a wide product mix with many different lines or a narrow one with few.

2. Explain how the layers of a product lead to competitive advantage.

A product may be anything tangible or intangible that satisfies consumer or business-to-business customer needs. Products include goods, services, ideas, people, and places. The *core product* refers to product features or attributes. The *functional product* refers to how the product functions or performs. The *augmented product* refers to the augmentations (additions) the marketer does to the basic product (e.g., packaging or customer warranties). Finally, the *potential product* refers to the solution the customer seeks from the product.

The layers of a product enable a firm to build competitive advantage in this way—firms recognize (sometimes reluctantly) that customers do not buy product features; they buy product benefits. By emphasizing benefits instead of features, the firm is in a position to differentiate itself from its competitors.

3. Explain the good–service continuum and its importance.

Although some products are pure goods (e.g., salt) and others are pure services (e.g., a haircut), most products fall along a continuum of goods and services. That is, most products have characteristics of goods and services. This is important to remember because a marketer with a product that has a higher percentage of tangibility (a good) will try to differentiate the offering by including services. On the other hand, a marketer with a product that has a higher percentage of intangibility (a service) will try to "tangibilize" the offering as much as possible.

4. Explain the key differences between goods and services.

All services share four characteristics that make them distinct from goods: intangibility, perishability, inseparability, and variability. Services are intangible (they cannot be touched). Therefore, marketers must use other means such as marketing communications to communicate the service experience to the customer (for example, an ad can show the pleasure one may experience spending a week soaking in the sun on an island). Services, unlike goods, cannot be stored. Therefore, marketers must utilize their capacity wisely, or else the service (such as an unsold hotel room) is gone forever.

Services cannot be separated from their point of production (unlike a good, which may be manufactured thousands of kilometres away from its point of consumption). This means that the service encounter between customer and service provider is crucial to measure and manage. Finally, services are variable because they rely on human "production." Therefore, such firms as McDonald's leave nothing to chance—all elements of the service delivery are standardized.

5. Describe how firms develop new products.

New product development includes a visionary phase and a planning and development phase followed by testing and improvement. In the visionary phase, marketers generate new product ideas, assess their potential technical and commercial success, and conduct a business analysis to estimate the profitability of the new product. Planning and development includes developing a marketing program, planning how the product will be manufactured (if it is a good), and possibly obtaining a patent. The effectiveness of the new product may then be assessed in an actual or a simulated test market. Finally, the product is launched, and the entire marketing plan is implemented.

6. Discuss the importance of innovations.

Innovations are anything consumers perceive to be new. Understanding new products is important to companies because of the fast pace of technological advancement, the high cost of developing new products, and the contributions to society that new products can make. Marketers classify innovations by their degree of newness. A *continuous innovation* is a modification of an existing product, a *dynamically continuous innovation* provides a greater change in a product, and a *discontinuous innovation* is a new product that creates major changes in people's lives.

7. Explain the process of product adoption and the diffusion of innovations.

Product adoption is the process by which an individual begins to buy and use a new product, whereas the diffusion of innovations is how a new product spreads throughout a population. The stages in the adoption process are awareness, interest, trial, adoption, and confirmation. To better understand the diffusion process, marketers classify consumers according to their readiness to adopt new products: as innovators, early adopters, early majority, late majority, and laggards.

Five product characteristics that have an important effect on how quickly (or if) a new product will be adopted by consumers are relative advantage, compatibility, product complexity, trialability, and observability. Similar to individual consumers, organizations differ in their readiness to adopt new products based on characteristics of the organization, its management, and characteristics of the innovation.

CHAPTER REVIEW

Marketing Concepts: Testing Your Knowledge

1. List and explain some popular objectives and strategies used for individual and multiple products.

2. What is a product? (Hint: the term *product* is used differently in marketing than in everyday language.)

3. What is meant by the core product, the functional product, the augmented product, and the potential product?

4. Explain how understanding the layers of a product leads a marketer to build competitive advantage.

5. Explain the good–service continuum and its importance.

6. What are some key characteristics of services that distinguish them from goods? Why is this understanding important?

7. What is a new product? Why is understanding new products so important to marketers?

8. List and explain the steps in developing new products.

9. Explain the different types of innovations based on their degree of newness.

10. List and explain the stages in an individual's adoption of an innovation.

11. List and explain the categories of adopters.

12. Describe the product factors that affect the speed of adoption for (a) consumers and (b) business organizations.

Marketing Concepts: Discussing Choices and Issues

1. This chapter discussed the core product, functional product, augmented product, and potential product. Does this mean that marketers are simply trying to make products that are really the same seem different? When marketers understand these four layers of the product and develop products with this concept in mind, what are the benefits to consumers? What are the benefits to marketers?

2. Can you provide examples of core versus potential products? How easy or hard was it for you to come up with these examples? Do you find your thinking about product strategy

(and building competitive advantage, in general) has changed as a result of learning these concepts?

3. Some people argue that there is no such a thing as a tangible good; everything is a service (that is, an experience). What do you think? What are some advantages and disadvantages of such thinking?

4. The phrase "new and improved" has been used so many times that, for many people, it is meaningless. Why has this occurred? What challenge does this present to marketers?

5. Discontinuous innovations are totally new products—something seldom seen in the market-place. What are some examples of discontinuous innovations introduced in the past 50 years? What do you think the future holds for new products: Will they be continuous or discontinuous innovations?

6. This chapter explained that knock-offs are slightly modified copies of original product designs. Should knock-offs be illegal? Who is hurt by knock-offs? Is the marketing of knock-offs good or bad for consumers in the short run? In the long run?

7. It is not necessarily true that all new products benefit consumers or society. What are some new products that have made our lives better? What are some new products that have actually been harmful to consumers or to society? Should there be a way to monitor new products that are introduced to the marketplace?

Marketing Practice: Applying What You've Learned

1. Assume that a firm marketing a new low-calorie, fat-free chocolate candy bar has recently hired you. Because of your knowledge of new product adoption, you know that consumers go through a series of stages in adopting a new product—awareness, interest, and so on. You also realize that it is important for marketers to "help" customers move from one stage to the next. Develop your recommendations for marketing activities that would be appropriate for each stage in the adoption process.

2. As a member of a new product team with your company, you are working with engineers in developing the world's first practical, battery-powered automobile. You know that different product characteristics (relative advantage, compatibility, and so on) influence the speed of adoption of the product. Considering such product characteristics, make a list of suggestions for the engineers (or for the marketing department) that will speed the adoption of the new product when it is introduced.

3. Assume that you are employed in the marketing department of the firm in the preceding example. How would you use your knowledge of goods and services to communicate the benefits of this car? Can you think in terms of core versus potential products when you provide your answer?

4. Firms go to great lengths to develop new product ideas. Sometimes new ideas come from brainstorming, in which groups of individuals get together and try to think of as many different, novel, creative—and hopefully profitable—ideas for a new product as possible. With a group of other students, participate in brainstorming for new product ideas for one of the following (or some other product of your choice).

   a. an exercise machine

   b. computer software

   c. a new type of college or university

   Then, with your class, screen one or more of the ideas for possible further product development.

Marketing Mini-Project: Learning by Doing

What product characteristics do consumers think are important in a new product? What types of service components do they demand? And most important, how do marketers know how to develop successful new products? This mini-project is designed to let you experience making some of these decisions.

1. Create (in your mind) a new product item (a good or service) that might be of interest to students like you. Develop a written description and possibly a drawing of this new product.

2. Show this new product description to a number of your fellow students who might be potential users of the product. Ask them to tell you what they think of the product. Some of the questions you might ask them are:

   a. What is your overall opinion of the new product?

   b. What basic benefits would you expect to receive from the product?

   c. What about the physical characteristics of the product? What do you like? Dislike? What would you add? Delete? Change?

   d. What do you like (or would you like) in the way of product packaging? (If the product is a service, think how you would communicate its existence and benefits.)

   e. What sort of services would you expect to receive with the product?

   f. Do you think you would try the product? How could marketers influence you to buy the product?

3. Develop a report based on what you found. Include your recommendations for changes in the product and your feelings about the potential success of the new product.

Real People, Real Surfers: Exploring the Web

Visit the websites for three fashion retailers: Roots (**www.roots.com**), the Gap (**www.gap.com**), and Le Château (**www.lechateau.ca**). After you have visited the company websites, explore the Internet for additional information on each firm. Based on your experience on the Internet, answer the following questions:

1. Describe the number and variety of consumer and business-to-business products each company produces.

2. Is an emphasis on product development evident in the description of the companies from their websites?

3. Does the website provide opportunities for consumers to purchase products? To provide input about existing products? To offer new product ideas?

4. What can you find out about each firm's new product development process? How does the process lead to extraordinary new products?

5. What is your evaluation of each website? Does the website focus more on the company's products or on some other aspect of the company? Does it provide easy access to important information about the company's products? What visitors would be attracted to the website? Is the website designed in such a way as to encourage visitors to return to the site?

Throughout its history, Boeing has been a very successful company. When it introduced its first product, the 707, it did not even know if a market existed for it. It went ahead anyway, and the bold gamble paid off. The 707 became wildly popular, enabling Boeing to focus on new product innovations.

The 737, initially developed for the U.S. Armed Forces, was targeted at the commercial market. Boeing's timing was just right. During the 1970s air travel was becoming a reality for many people. Before then, travelling by air was reserved only for the privileged few. The Boeing 737 was a boon for airlines. It enabled them to pack many passengers on one flight, thus apportioning costs such as landing fees, salaries, and fuel over a broader range of passengers.

For decades Boeing has enjoyed a near monopoly in commercial aviation. But that has changed. Airbus, a European maker of commercial and defence airplanes, has overtaken Boeing in sales numbers. Airbus has also introduced a slate of new models over the years, but perhaps nothing will come close to the ultimate battle shaping up between these two corporations.

The difference lies in product strategy and assumptions about the future. Airbus has bet that, in the future, airlines are going to succeed by packing as many passengers as possible into an aircraft. In response, it is building the A380, a monster airplane that will fly 555 passengers at one time. Even with many production setbacks, Airbus has already secured several concrete orders for this plane.

Boeing, on the other hand, has bet on the opposite, claiming that airlines will succeed by moving people faster between two airports. In response, it is introducing the 7E7, an airplane that will move passengers from point to point faster than ever.

But this is not the end of the story. Boeing has made several missteps. It totally underestimated Airbus's resolve to build the A380. Boeing also toyed with other new product ideas, none of which got under way. For example, Boeing thought about developing the Sonic Cruiser, capable of travelling near the speed of sound. While Boeing dithered, Airbus made strategic gains by making a commitment to the A380.

In the meantime, Boeing has tried to diversify its product line by entering the defence market and buying McDonnell Douglas. However, Boeing has been embroiled in scandals involving defence contracts. In response, Boeing's CEO at the time resigned.

Source: Adapted from articles in *Business Week* and *The New Yorker*.

Things to Think About

1. Describe the core, actual, and augmented products for Boeing and Airbus.

2. What type of innovation (continuous, dynamically continuous, or discontinuous) is the A380? What implications does this have for the future marketing of the A380?

3. Why do you think Boeing has suffered the missteps listed in the case? Why do successful companies suffer this fate?

4. Whose strategy for commercial aviation do you think is superior? Why?

5. If you were a member of Boeing's board of directors, what questions would you have asked the former CEO? What questions would you want to ask the new CEO?

CHAPTER 8
Product Management

Real People, Real Decisions

Meet **Julie Desrosier**, a Decision Maker at One of Canada's Largest Mutual Fund Companies

You will see at the end of this profile why we have kept the company identity a secret!

Julie Desrosier is an advertising manager within the marketing department at one of Canada's largest mutual fund companies. After graduating with a Bachelor of Arts degree from McGill University (with a major in Anthropology), Julie joined a company called AIM Funds Management Inc. as a bilingual client relations representative. After a year on the phones she felt comfortable enough in her knowledge of the industry and of clients to apply internally for an analyst position in the marketing research group. After two and a half years of conducting research and gaining in-depth knowledge and insights into the minds of her clients, competitors, and the industry in general, the opportunity arose to apply that knowledge to the position of advertising manager within the marketing department.

Julie was motivated to choose this career path mainly because of constantly evolving interests and a thirst for knowledge. She loves a good challenge, and her career progression within the company has been based on her desire to keep learning and growing as both an employee and as a person in general. Coming from a social sciences background, the jump to working for a mutual fund company may not be obvious, as are her shifts from client relations to marketing research to advertising. As Julie says, "The truth is, I didn't plan for it to turn out that way. I simply kept an open mind to new opportunities and was able to leverage and build upon the knowledge and experience I gained in each role."

A few years ago, Trimark Investments (a long-established, homegrown mutual funds company) was purchased by AIM Funds Management Inc., a fund company from the United States and a recent entrant to the Canadian mutual fund scene. As often happens when two companies (and brands) come together, the question "What should we call ourselves?" came up almost immediately.

With the joining of the two companies, Julie and her colleagues were faced with a case of "opposites attract." Trimark was a large, well-known, and well-established Canadian company that promoted a traditional, family-style environment for its employees. Its product offerings (mutual funds) were based on a "value" style of investing. AIM Funds was a small, youthful, ambitious firm that had only been in Canada a short while, and its product offerings were based on a "growth" style of investing.

From a product standpoint, it was a perfect match in terms of creating a well-rounded product offering. From a cultural standpoint, the match was a bit more awkward (e.g., large versus small, established versus youthful). To gain and maintain the confidence and trust of the financial advisers who sold the funds (and the investors who bought them), a decision needed to be made on how these two companies could be successfully integrated under a name that would not only fulfill both external and internal expectations, but would be representative of both brands.

The team considered three options.

Option 1: Keep AIM Funds Management as the company name.

The advantage of this option was the fact that AIM was a larger, more established player in the mutual funds industry. The disadvantage was that AIM was not a well-established brand name in Canada.

Option 2: Keep Trimark Investments as the company name.

Keeping the Trimark name would ensure that the brand resonated with Canadian clients and consumers. The disadvantage with this option was that the merged company name would not reflect AIM's youthful sense of energy (an important consideration in financial services).

Option 3: Choose a new name.

The challenge in brand decisions is choosing a name that will provide the firm with a competitive advantage in the marketplace.

Now, join Julie and her colleagues. Which option would you choose and why?

THE PRODUCT LIFE CYCLE AND THE DECISION-MAKING PROCESS

Product life cycle management is an all-encompassing vision for managing all data linked to design, production, support, and ultimate disposal of manufactured goods. In marketing, the product life cycle concept was first used where safety and control were extremely critical, notably in the military and aerospace industry. Product life cycle management is part of the process of competitive positioning and finding market opportunities. Proper decisions related to the product life cycle will maximize the return at every stage by adapting or retiring unprofitable products and introducing new ones.

MARKETING THROUGHOUT THE PRODUCT LIFE CYCLE

The zipper, redesigned by Swedish-American Gideon Sundback in 1913, is an example of a humble, low-tech product that has managed to live an exceptionally long life (Exhibit 8.1). Although the zipper was invented in the 1800s, it was not used in men's clothing until the 1930s. These "hookless fasteners," as they were once called, were originally intended for use on high-buttoned shoes. It took time for them to be used in men's trousers, because competitors argued that this "newfangled gadget" could result in serious injuries. In 1936, the Prince of Wales adopted the zipper and was the first monarch to "sit on a throne bezippered."

Like the zipper, many products have very long lives. The **product life cycle** is a useful way to look at how product features change over the life of a product. In Chapter 7, we discussed objectives of product decisions, the product concept, and how marketers introduce new products; but launching a product is only the beginning. Product marketing strategies must evolve as they continue through the product life cycle.

The concept of the product life cycle does not relate to a single brand but to the generic product *category*. Thus, we talk about the life cycle of personal computers, not Compaq computers, of automobiles, not the Focus. Some individual brands have short life expectancies: Who remembers the Bricklin car or Evening in Paris perfume? Others seem almost immortal: Think of such brands as Campbell's soup, Ivory Soap, or American Express.

> **product life cycle** Concept that explains how products go through four distinct stages from birth to death: introduction, growth, maturity, and decline.

> **introduction** The first stage of the product life cycle, in which slow growth follows the introduction of a new product in the marketplace.

The Introduction Stage

We can divide the life of a product into four separate stages. The first stage of the product life cycle, shown in Figure 8.1, is **introduction**—customers get their first chance to purchase the good or service. During this early stage, a single company usually produces the product. If the product is accepted and profitable, competitors will follow with their own versions.

During the introduction stage, the goal is to get first-time buyers to try the product. Sales (hopefully) increase at a steady but slow pace. As shown in Figure 8.2, the company does not make a profit during this stage, due to research and development (R&D) costs and heavy spending for advertising and other promotion.

Pricing may be high to recover the R&D costs (demand permitting) or low to attract large numbers of consumers. The Hitachi advertisement in Exhibit 8.2 is designed to appeal to consumers who are willing to pay for the latest technological advances.

Exhibit 8.1

The zipper has stood the test of time. Even though it was invented in 1913, it is now universally used around the world.

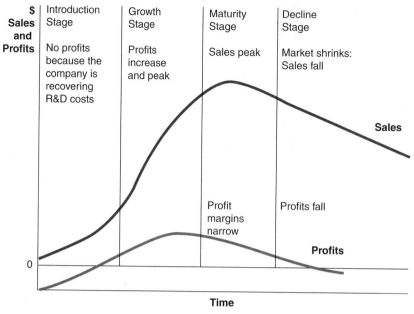

Figure 8.1 The Product Life Cycle

The product life cycle helps marketers understand how a product changes over its lifetime and suggests how marketing strategies should be modified accordingly.

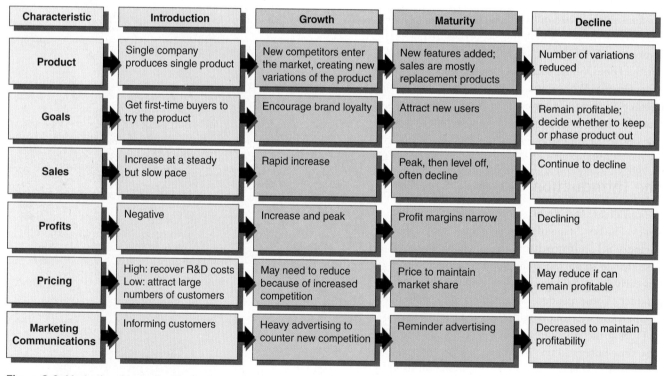

Figure 8.2 Marketing Strategies Through the Product Life Cycle

Marketing mix strategies—the four Ps—change as a product moves through the life cycle.

For a new product to be successful, consumers must first know about it and believe that it is something they need. Thus, marketing during the introduction stage often focuses on informing consumers about the product, how to use it, and its benefits.

How long does the introduction stage last? For the microwave oven, it was several years. How long the introduction stage lasts depends on a number of factors, including marketplace acceptance and producer willingness to support the product during its startup. In the case of the microwave, sales in countries such as Japan were much stronger, because the companies supported the product through its long introduction stage.

Not all products make it past the introduction stage. In fact, the failure rate for new products has been cited to be as high as 90 percent.[1] One of the most noted examples of products that never got past the introduction stage is the Ford Edsel automobile. Introduced in 1957 and named after the only son of Ford's founder, the Edsel was designed to compete with such cars as the Chrysler New Yorker. It boasted high horsepower, tail fins, three-tone paint jobs, wraparound windshields, a "horse-collar" grille, and a push-button gearshift. The problem was that consumers didn't like the Edsel. Only 110 847 Edsels were made before Ford abandoned the car, making the word *Edsel* synonymous with product failure.[2]

The Growth Stage

The second stage in the product life cycle, the **growth stage**, sees a rapid increase in sales while profits increase and peak. Marketing's goal here is to encourage brand loyalty by convincing the market that this brand is superior to others in the category. In this stage, marketing strategies may include the introduction of product variations to attract market segments and grow market share. When competitors appear, marketers must use heavy advertising and other types of promotion. Price competition may develop, driving profits down. Some firms may seek to capture a particular segment of the market by positioning their product to appeal to a certain group.

It's nice to know your loved ones are safe at home. Wherever you are, you can monitor your home – even remotely control home appliances, temperatures and security devices. And in the ubiquitous networked society of the near future, you'll be connected to everyone and everything, anytime and anyplace. Even your cat. From broadband access networks, data storage solutions and hard disk drive technologies, to information devices like plasma displays and PDAs, Hitachi's technological expertise and services are making this a reality. Just one more example of technology not for its own sake but for the benefit of all. As an innovative global solutions company, Hitachi touches your life in many ways. Visit us on the Web and see technology in action.

Exhibit 8.2
This Hitachi ad is targeted at a business-to-business audience, using consumer techniques to bring attention to the company's latest innovations.

growth stage The second stage in the product life cycle, during which the product is accepted and sales rapidly increase.

The Maturity Stage

The **maturity stage** of the product life cycle is usually the longest. Sales peak and then begin to level off and even decline while profit margins narrow. Competition grows intense when remaining competitors fight for a piece of a shrinking pie. Because most customers have already accepted the product, sales are often to replace a worn-out item or to take advantage of product improvements. For example, almost everyone owns a television, so companies typically sell new TVs to consumers whose sets have broken down. During the maturity stage, firms try to sell their product through all suitable retailers, because product availability is crucial in a very competitive market. Consumers will not go far to find one brand when others are closer at hand.

maturity stage The third and longest stage in the product life cycle, in which sales peak and profit margins narrow.

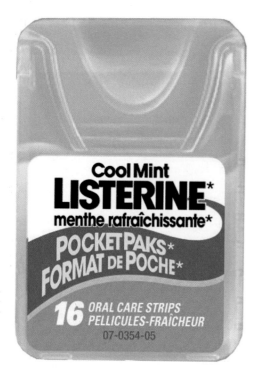

Exhibit 8.3

By introducing Listerine in a new format to meet customer needs for convenience, Warner-Lambert Canada gave a mature product new life.

decline stage The final stage in the product life cycle, in which sales decrease as customer needs change.

To remain competitive and maintain market share during the maturity stage, firms may tinker with the marketing mix, coming out with new versions of the product that include new features. For example, television manufacturers try to invigorate sales with flat-screen TVs. Warner-Lambert Canada introduced Listerine oral care strips, the first product extension of Listerine mouthwash (Exhibit 8.3). The strips offer the same breath freshening benefit of the original Listerine, but are small and dissolve in the mouth, thereby making the Listerine product portable and offering consumers a new benefit.[3]

Attracting new users of the product is another strategy used in the maturity stage. As we saw in Chapter 7, market development means introducing an existing product to a market that doesn't currently use it. Many Canadian firms are finding new markets for their products in countries around the world. To find new users for their products, firms in the Canadian wine industry, for example, have been actively pursuing markets in Pacific Rim countries such as Korea and China.

The Decline Stage

The **decline stage** of the product life cycle is characterized by a decrease in product category sales. This is often because new technology has made the product obsolete, as when computers caused the decline of the typewriter. Although a single firm may still be profitable, the market as a whole begins to shrink, profits decline, and suppliers pull out. In this stage, there are usually many competitors with no one having a distinct advantage.

A firm's major product decision in the decline stage is whether to keep the product. Once the product is no longer profitable, it drains resources from the firm—resources that could help develop newer products. If the decision is to drop the product, elimination can be handled in two ways: Phase it out by cutting production in stages and letting existing stocks run out, or drop the product immediately. If the established market leader anticipates that there will be some residual demand for the product for a long time, it may make sense to keep the product on the market. The idea is to sell a limited quantity of the product with little or no support from sales, merchandising, advertising, and distribution, and let it "wither on the vine." Some classic products have been able to hang on with little or no marketing support. For example, the Hilti launched its powder-actuated fastening system program in 1948. Despite sleeker and less costly competitors, the Hilti "shotgun" maintains its reputation as *the* heavy-duty tool.[4]

SERVICE STRATEGY

Once a product strategy is established, it is important to recognize that any product needs to be supported by a sound service strategy. To offer good-quality service, any firm should recognize that the main parameter in a service strategy is time, dealing with the "before," "during," and "after" phases of a product delivery (Figure 8.3). For the "before" phase, to obtain full value firms need to provide relevant information about the product offered, ranging from schedules to operating instructions, user warning instructions, and price. In addition, a dialogue with customers is essential to meet customer requirements and develop a tailored solution. Soon after, the firm should make it easy for customers to place orders. This might sound obvious, but many firms forget that the choice of communication channels, time, and location should be convenient for customers to place an order. For example, servers in many restaurants are now taking orders with a handheld wireless device to provide better and faster service (Exhibit 8.4).

For the "during" phase, the delivery, installation, and guarantees offered are key elements in the service offered by the firm. This step includes proper billing and payment requirement

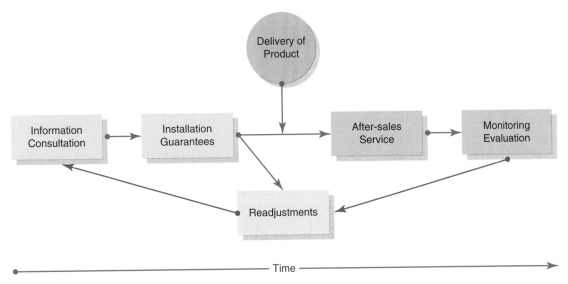

Figure 8.3 The Elements of a Service Strategy

Exhibit 8.4

Firms should make order taking more convenient for customers. For example, more restaurants are now using handheld point-of-sale wireless technology to take orders at tableside. Using such a technology makes order changing easier, and patrons often get their meal more quickly.

practices. Finally, in the "after" phase, firms should provide after-sales service that includes maintenance and repair support. This phase is critical in that firms need to allow customers to give feedback on the quality of the service. In turn, that feedback can be used to make future readjustments.

A firm's capacity to manage exceptions is also an important asset to a service strategy. Exceptions fall outside the routine of normal product or service delivery. They may include special requests, problem solving, handling of complaints, suggestions, or even restitution (compensating customers for bad product or service). Special requests are fairly common nowadays, and firms need to adapt service processes and monitor and evaluate feedback.

Exhibit 8.5

Kool-Aid has used its long-standing popularity with kids to make new iced tea products aimed at adults who drank Kool-Aid as kids.

brand A name, term, symbol, or any other unique element of a product that identifies one firm's product(s) and sets it apart from the competition.

trademark The legal term for a brand name, brand mark, or trade character; a trademark legally registered by a government obtains protection for exclusive use in that country.

CREATING PRODUCT IDENTITY: BRANDING DECISIONS

Knowing the stage of their product in the product life cycle helps marketers successfully manage the product. Equally important is giving that product an identity: Branding is an extremely important element of product strategies. In this section, we examine what a brand is, the importance of branding, and how firms make branding decisions.

What's in a Name (Or a Symbol)?

How do you identify your favourite brand? By its name? By the logo (how the name appears)? By the packaging? By some graphic image or symbol, such as Canadian Tire's red triangle and green maple leaf? A **brand** is a name, term, symbol, or any other unique element of a product that identifies one firm's product(s) and sets it apart from the competition. Consumers easily recognize the Coca-Cola logo, the pink Energizer bunny (a *trade character*), and the triangular blue Nabisco logo (a *brand mark*) in the corner of the box. Branding provides the recognition factor products need to succeed in regional, national, or international markets.

CHOOSING A BRAND NAME, MARK, OR CHARACTER There are several important considerations in selecting a brand name, brand mark, or trade character. It must have a positive connotation and be memorable. Consider Toro's experience when it introduced a lightweight snow thrower called the "Snow Pup." Sales were disappointing, because "pup" conveyed a small, cuddly animal, not a desirable image for a snow thrower. Renamed the "Snow Master," its sales went up markedly.[5]

A brand name is probably the most used and most recognized form of branding. Kool-Aid, a word that most kids know, has been used to maintain a long-term relationship with consumers. Kool-Aid now markets iced tea versions of its beverages to appeal to adult tastes (Exhibit 8.5).

Exhibit 8.6

Clarica used this humorous ad to help make its brand name more memorable.

A good brand name can position a product by conveying a certain image or personality (Molson Canadian) or describing how it works (Drano), or else it may be ambiguous, such as Exxon, Ajax, and Lotus. Brand names sometimes need to change over time. For example, Kentucky Fried Chicken became KFC when "fried" went out of style, the Canadian Imperial Bank of Commerce became CIBC to avoid the use of "imperial," and for similar reasons the Hudson's Bay Company became HBC.[6]

How does a firm select a good brand name? Good brand designers say there are four "easy" tests: *easy to say, easy to spell, easy to read,* and *easy to remember.* Consider P&G's Tide, Cheer, Gain, Downy, and Ivory Snow. And the name should also "fit" four ways: *fit the target market, fit the product's benefits, fit the customer's culture,* and *fit legal requirements.* When the Mutual Life Assurance Company of Canada decided to change its brand name, it chose a very non-traditional name for the insurance market: Clarica. A multimillion-dollar advertising campaign supported the name change, but the name was criticized by many marketers for, among other things, sounding more like a skin cleanser than an insurance company. Clarica responded with the humorous ad in Exhibit 8.6, which it hoped would further increase the awareness of its brand name.

When it comes to graphics for a brand symbol, name, or logo, the rule is: It must be recognizable and memorable. No matter how small or how large, the triangular Nabisco logo in the corner of the box is a familiar sight. And it should have

SPOTLIGHT ON REAL PEOPLE   AirSprint Inc.

When University of Alberta law school graduates Judson Macor and Phil Dewsnap put aside promising careers to kick-start a fractional-ownership aircraft company, the two partners never imagined their idea would "take off" so quickly, literally. In just six years, AirSprint Inc. has grown from a two-man operation to a growing business with 70 employees, 50 pilots, 15 aircraft, 70 clients, and annual revenues that have doubled over the past year to reach the $50-million mark.

The concept behind AirSprint is quite simple. A sort of time-share for frequent flyers, fractional ownership allows several people to split the cost of buying and operating a private jet. AirSprint charges a management fee for operating a fleet of aircraft, performing maintenance, and hiring pilots. In return, owners are guaranteed a certain number of hours of flying time, provided they give four to eight hours' notice. Although a relatively new concept in Canada, fractional ownership has already found its fair share of enthusiasts in the United States through providers such as Netjets, Bombardier Flexjet, and Flight Options. In fact, according to the Aviation Data Service, the number of U.S. fractional owners surged to 4910 in September 2005, up 75 percent from five years ago. Now, AirSprint is cashing in on the growing number of Canadian executives eager to forfeit commercial cattle cars for catered meals and designer cabin interiors.

But hassle-free travel doesn't come cheap. A minimum one-eighth fraction of ownership, which includes 100 hours of flying time annually in a Pilatus PC12, costs US$435 000 plus a monthly management fee of $4350 and an hourly direct operating charge of $850. At any time, owners may sell their interest in the aircraft back to AirSprint, which will then remarket the share at its current value. Half-a-million dollars for a slice of a luxury aircraft nonetheless compares rather favourably to the $7-million-to-$40-million price tag that accompanies today's business jets.[7]

1. In what stage of the product life cycle is aircraft fractional ownership?
2. Visit the AirSprint website (**www.airsprint.com**). Would you say that the entrepreneurs are creating a unique brand identity for their product on the site? What suggestions would you make for the development of an even stronger brand identity?
3. What are some other potential product line and product mix expansion strategies for AirSprint?

visual impact. This means that from across a store or when you are quickly flipping the pages in a magazine, the brand will catch your attention. One product that made the wrong kind of visual impact with its brand name was a snack product called HITS. It was on the shelves for only a short time, because the manufacturer realized that when the packages were put end to end on store shelves, the logos produced an unintended effect: HitsHitsHitsHitsHits.[8]

Some marketers enhance brand recognition by creating a *trade character*, such as the Pillsbury Dough Boy, the Jolly Green Giant, or Mr. Clean. A&W uses the Root Bear to strengthen brand recognition (Exhibit 8.7).

TRADEMARKS The legal term for a brand name, brand mark, or trade character is **trademark**. Marketers can legally register brands as trademarks to make their use by competitors illegal in Canada. However, it is possible for a firm to have protection for a brand even if it has not legally registered it. Common-law protection exists if the firm has used the name and established it over a period of time. Although a registered trademark prevents others from using it on a similar product, it may not bar its use for a product in a completely different type of business.

The Importance of Branding

Marketers spend vast amounts of money on new product development, advertising, and promotions to develop strong brands.

Exhibit 8.7

The A&W Root Bear is an example of a trade character.

brand equity The value of a brand to an organization.

If successful, the investment creates **brand equity**, which is a brand's value to its organization. Brand equity means that a brand has high customer loyalty, perceived quality, and brand name awareness. For a firm, brand equity provides a competitive advantage, because it gives the brand the power to capture and hold onto a larger share of the market and to sell at prices with higher profit margins. Some of the most valuable brands in the world are BMW, Nike, Nokia, and Ikea.[9]

Research shows that the following factors make a brand successful:[10]

- The brand excels at delivering the benefits customers truly desire.
- The brand stays relevant.
- The pricing strategy is based on consumers' perceptions of value.
- The brand is properly positioned.
- The brand is consistent.
- The brand portfolio and hierarchy make sense.
- The brand makes use of and coordinates a full range of marketing activities to build equity.
- The brand's managers understand what the brand means to customers.
- The brand is given proper support, and that support is sustained over the long run.
- The company monitors sources of brand equity.

brand extension A new product sold with the same brand name as a strong existing brand.

When brands possess strong brand equity, they provide important opportunities for a firm. A firm may leverage a brand's equity with **brand extensions**, new products sold with the same brand name, such as the Listerine oral care strips and Dentyne Ice mentioned earlier. If existing brand equity is high, the firm is able to sell the brand extension at a higher price than if it had given it a new brand, and the brand extension will attract new customers immediately. However, if the brand extension does not live up to the quality or attractiveness of the original brand, brand equity will suffer, reducing brand loyalty and sales.

Branding Strategies

As marketing strategists know, brands are important to a marketing program's success, so decisions about branding strategies are a major part of product decision making. Marketers have to determine whether to create individual or family brands, national or private-label brands, or to co-brand.

family brand A brand that a group of individual products or individual brands share.

INDIVIDUAL BRANDS VERSUS FAMILY BRANDS Part of developing a branding strategy is deciding whether to use a separate, unique brand for each product item—*an individual brand strategy*—or to market multiple items under the same brand name—a **family brand**—an umbrella brand strategy. Individual brands may do a better job of communicating clearly and concisely what the consumer can expect from the product, whereas family brands allow a firm to develop a brand for an entire product line. Thus, the decision to use an individual or family branding strategy often depends on characteristics of the product and whether the company's overall product strategy calls for introduction of a single, unique product or for the development of a group of similar products. Pillsbury Canada uses family branding with its Green Giant, Pillsbury, Old El Paso, Underwood, and Accent family brands. Under the Old El Paso name are such Mexican foods as salsa and Nachips; under its Green Giant name are frozen and canned vegetables and other frozen products; and under the Pillsbury name are Pizza Pops, Toaster Strudel, and refrigerated baked goods.[11]

national or manufacturer brands Brands that the manufacturer of the product owns.

store or private-label brands Brands that are owned and sold by a specific retailer or distributor.

NATIONAL AND STORE BRANDS Retailers today are often in the driver's seat when it comes to deciding what brands to sell. In addition to choosing from producers' brands like those from Pillsbury Canada, called **national or manufacturer brands**, retailers decide whether to offer their own versions. **Store brands**, also called **private-label brands**, are the retail store's or chain's exclusive trade name. Loblaws, for example, sells its President's Choice private-label brand along with national brands.

Marketing Metrics

Measuring Value

Brand equity is the value of a product with a particular brand name compared to the value of a product without the brand name. Many corporations, marketing research firms, and ad agencies have devised various measures of brand equity because this is an important way to assess whether a branding strategy has been successful. If consumers have strong, positive feelings about a brand and are willing to pay extra to choose it over others, you are in marketing heaven. Each of the following approaches to measuring brand equity has some good points and some bad points.

1. *Customer mindset metrics* focus on consumer awareness, attitudes, and loyalty toward a brand. However, these metrics are based on consumer surveys and don't usually provide a single objective measure that can be used to assign a financial value to the brand.

2. *Product-market outcomes metrics* focus on the ability of a brand to charge a higher price than the one charged by an unbranded equivalent. This usually involves asking consumers how much more they would be willing to pay for a certain brand compared to others. These measures often rely on hypothetical judgments and can be complicated to use.

3. *Financial market metrics* consider the purchase price of a brand if it is sold or acquired. They may also include subjective judgments about the future stock price of the brand.

4. A team of marketing professors has proposed a simpler measure that they claim reliably tracks the value of a brand over time. Their *revenue premium metric* compares the revenue a brand generates with the revenue generated by a similar private-label product (that doesn't have any brand identification). In this case, brand equity is just the difference in revenue (net price times volume) between a branded good and a corresponding private label.[12]

Retailers choose a private-label branding strategy because they generally make a larger profit than on national brands. Private-label strategies are also important when retailers seek to maintain a consistent store image; for example, clothing retailers such as the Gap and Holt Renfrew protect their image by offering store brands.[13] The British Columbia company Private Reserve Water produces private-label water for such companies as Holiday Inn Express, and several golf clubs, restaurants, and catering companies across North America.

LICENSING Some firms choose to use **licensing** to brand their products. A licensing agreement typically means that one firm sells another firm the right to use a brand name for a specific purpose and for a specific period of time. Firms choose a licensing strategy for a variety of reasons: Sometimes it provides instant recognition and consumer interest in a new product; at other times licensing is important in positioning a product for a certain target market. For example, bourbon maker Jack Daniels licensed its name to T. Marzetti for producing Jack Daniels bourbon-flavoured mustard. Much better known, however, is the licensing of entertainment names. Movie producers license their properties to manufacturers of a seemingly infinite number of products: When Disney movies hit the screens, such licensed merchandise as figures, toys, and clothing are sold through stores and distributed through other retail outlets such as McDonald's.

licensing An agreement in which one firm sells another firm the right to use a brand name for a specific purpose and for a specific period of time.

CO-BRANDING Starbucks cafés in Chapters stores and McDonald's outlets in Wal-Mart stores are both examples of **co-branding**. Co-branding, which some call one of the "preeminent marketing strategies" today, joins two brands in partnership to market new or existing products.[14] Co-branding ideally benefits both partners—in combination, the two brands can enjoy more recognition power than either would alone. Starbucks and Chapters products, for example, are complementary and appeal to the same target group, so by co-branding, both brands are strengthened (Exhibit 8.8).[15]

co-branding An agreement between two brands to work together in marketing new or existing products.

Exhibit 8.8

You can find a Starbucks coffee shop in many Chapters bookstores across Canada.

Ethical Decisions in Marketing

Nestlé, a multinational packaged food company founded and headquartered in Switzerland, sells many branded products to Canadians, such as Perrier water, Nescafé, and Smarties. And with over 305 000 employees, Nestlé is one of the world's biggest companies. However, some of Nestlé's business practices have been considered controversial, especially the manner in which baby milk has been marketed in developing countries, which led to the Nestlé boycott by many consumers. In 2006, Nestlé applied to the Fairtrade Foundation for its first FAIR-TRADE Mark. Fairtrade certification (usually simply Fairtrade or Fair Trade Certified™ in Canada) is a product certification system designed to allow people to identify products that meet agreed environmental, labour, and developmental standards. The application was for one of Nestlé's coffee products. If the organization refused to award the FAIRTRADE Mark to Nestlé's product, Nestlé threatened to create its own self-certification scheme, which could undermine the work of the foundation. Because of Nestlé's alleged questionable track record on transparency and disrespect toward farmers, some fair trade advocates claim that awarding Nestlé the FAIRTRADE Mark would send a confusing message to consumers about fair trade and what it means. Should Nestlé certify its own fair trade products to support its brands? Do you think Canadian legislators should intervene for Canadian-bound products made by Nestlé?[16]

ORGANIZING FOR EFFECTIVE PRODUCT MANAGEMENT

Firms don't create great brands, people do. Like all elements of the marketing mix, the effectiveness of product strategies depends on marketing managers and the decisions they make. In this section, we discuss how firms organize for the management of existing products and for the development of new products.

Management of Existing Products

In small firms such as The Body Blocker Group, the marketing function may be handled by a single marketing manager, who is responsible for new product planning, advertising, making website decisions, marketing research, and just about everything else. The Body Blocker simply is not big enough—and doesn't need—a large marketing management team.

In larger firms with many products, a number of managers are responsible for different brands, product categories, or markets.

Depending on the organization, product management may include brand managers, product category managers, and market managers.

BRAND MANAGERS Sometimes a firm has different brands within a single product category. For example, General Foods produces several brands of coffee, including Brim, Maxim, Maxwell House, International Coffees, Sanka, and Yuban. In such cases, a separate **brand manager** may be responsible for each brand.

Procter & Gamble brand managers once acted independently and were responsible for coordinating all marketing activities for a brand: positioning, identifying target markets, research, distribution, sales promotion, packaging, and evaluating the success of these decisions. Today, P&G's brand managers are more like team leaders. They are still responsible for positioning brands and developing brand equity, but they are likely to work with sales, finance, and logistics staff members as a part of customer business teams working with major retail accounts.[17]

The brand management system has its problems. Acting independently, brand managers may fight for increases in short-term sales for their own brand. They may push too hard with coupons, cents-off packages, or other price incentives to a point where customers will refuse to buy the product without them. That can hurt long-term brand equity and profitability.

PRODUCT CATEGORY MANAGERS Some larger firms have such diverse product offerings that there is a need for extensive coordination. Eastman Kodak is best known for its cameras, film, and other photography supplies; however, it also markets printers, optical disks, and photocopiers. In such cases, organizing for product management may include **product category managers**, who coordinate the mix of product lines within the more general product category and who consider the addition of new product lines. In recent years, both Procter & Gamble and Lever Brothers have consolidated brands under product category managers, who are responsible for profit and losses within the category.[18]

MARKET MANAGERS Some firms have developed a **market manager** structure, in which different managers focus on specific customer groups rather than on the products the company makes. This type of organization can be useful for firms that offer a variety of products serving the needs of a wide range of customers. For example, Raytheon (Exhibit 8.9), which specializes in consumer electronics products, special-mission aircraft, and business aviation, sells some products directly to consumer markets, others to manufacturers, and still others to government.[19]

Organizing for New Product Development

In Chapter 7, we discussed the importance of new products to the long-term health of an organization. Because launching new products is so important, the management of launching them is too. In some instances, one person handles new product development. However, in larger organizations, new product development almost always needs many people working under the new product manager.

The challenge in large companies is to get specialists in different areas to work together in **venture teams**, in which members focus exclusively on the new product development effort. The venture team may be located away from traditional

brand manager A manager who is responsible for developing and implementing the marketing plan for a single brand.

product category manager A manager who is responsible for developing and implementing the marketing plan for all the brands and products within a product category.

market manager A manager who is responsible for developing and implementing the marketing plans for products sold to a specific customer group.

venture teams Groups of people within an organization who focus exclusively on the development of a new product.

Exhibit 8.9

Firms such as Raytheon, that offer products to a wide variety of customers, need marketing managers to focus on different markets.

Real People, Real Decisions

▶ **How It Worked Out** at Julie's Company

In the end, Option 3 was the winner and a new name was chosen: AIM Trimark Investments. As Julie says, "Decisions around branding are usually not made lightly or quickly. It took almost two years of research and consultation with both employees and clients to understand the meaning and value of both brands."

On the one hand, the Trimark brand had over 20 years of equity built into it. On the other hand, the AIM name represented something new, something "bigger" from a global perspective, and (although it was relatively new to Canada) it had managed to build a solid reputation among financial advisers. Both names resonated with clients and employees in different but complementary ways. Keeping both names seemed to be the best solution.

The result? AIM Trimark Investments has successfully positioned itself as a leader within the Canadian mutual funds industry. It currently has over $40 billion in assets under management and an almost 100 percent awareness level among clients (financial advisers). Regular surveys of both external and internal stakeholders (such as employees and financial advisers) reveal a strong corporate brand that invokes pride in its employees and an image as an industry leader among its clients.

Julie loves the challenge of working in a fast-paced, competitive (and often unpredictable) industry. "What I love most about my job—in addition to the people I work with—is that it allows me to be creative and strategic at the same time. It's also pretty neat to see an ad you worked on in a magazine you're reading or on TV during a commercial break," she says.

The most important thing Julie has learned is never underestimating the importance of communication. She believes that communicating your knowledge and ideas is 49 percent content and 51 percent presentation. "The absolutely brilliant report that you spent six months preparing won't break through to key stakeholders if your presentation or communication skills are lacking. Worst case scenario is that your ideas will be dismissed because people simply did not 'get it.'"

What advice does Julie have for students in preparing for a productive career?

The importance of keeping it BRIEF. Right from primary school, students are taught to write essays with the goal of achieving a minimum number of words. That is, we are taught to add a lot of filler to the things we write and the truth is, in the "real world," if you hand a 50-page report to an executive, you can pretty much bet on it being tossed into the recycling bin or into the back of a filing cabinet. The majority of executives expect an "executive summary" of any and all reports. If you can't summarize your main message or idea into one phrase, it could get missed (or worse, dismissed).

Keep an open mind. There are a ton of interesting opportunities out there you simply don't know about while you're in school. As you go through college/university, you often feel pressured to choose a particular career direction before graduating. If you allow yourself some room to explore you might be pleasantly surprised as to where you may end up.

Never underestimate the power of "people skills." Your ability (or inability) to interact in an appropriate way with the people you work with—and for—can make or break a successful career.

company offices, perhaps in a separate building, called a *skunk works*. This odd term suggests that the group avoids opponents of change within the firm who might stop a project that challenges the status quo. Often having team members with different areas of knowledge, for example, design, engineering, and marketing, contributes to creativity and breakthrough ideas.

Whirlpool, the appliance company, can thank its venture team for winning $30 million in a nationwide save-energy refrigerator design contest sponsored by a group of electric utilities. The seven-person Whirlpool team developed a refrigerator that was 25 percent more energy efficient and did not use ozone-depleting chlorofluorocarbons.[20] Runner-up Frigidaire also used a team approach and discovered that the time it needed for new product development was cut in half.[21]

Key Terms

- brand, p. 280
- brand equity, p. 282
- brand extension, p. 282

CHAPTER SUMMARY

1. Explain how firms manage products throughout the product life cycle.

The product life cycle explains how product categories go through four stages from birth to death. During the introduction stage, marketers seek to get buyers to try the product and may use high prices to recover research and development costs. During the growth stage, characterized by rapidly increasing sales, marketers may introduce new product variations. In the maturity stage, sales peak and level off. Marketers respond by adding desirable new product features or with market development strategies. During the decline stage, firms must decide whether to phase a product out slowly, to drop it immediately, or, if there is residual demand, to keep the product.

2. Explain some of the concepts related to service decisions and product management.

It is important to recognize that any product needs to be supported by a sound service strategy. To offer good quality service, any firm should recognize that the main parameter in a service strategy is time, dealing with the "before," "during," and "after" phases of a product delivery. For the "before" phase, to obtain full value firms need to provide relevant information about the product offered, ranging from schedules to operating instructions, user warning instructions, and price. For the "during" phase, the delivery, installation and guarantees offered are key elements in the service offered by the firm. Finally, in the "after" phase, firms should provide after-sales services that includes maintenance and repair support. A firm's capacity to manage exceptions is also an important asset to a service strategy.

3. Discuss how branding creates product identity and describe different types of branding strategies.

A brand is a name, term, symbol, or other unique element of a product used to identify a firm's product. A brand should have a positive connotation and be recognizable and memorable. Brand names need to be easy to say, spell, read, and remember, and should fit the target market, the product's benefits, the customer's culture, and legal requirements. To protect a brand legally, marketers obtain trademark protection. Brands are important, because they help maintain customer loyalty and because brand equity or value means a firm is able to attract new customers. Firms may develop individual brand strategies or market multiple items with a family or umbrella brand strategy. National or manufacturer brands are owned and sold by producers, whereas private-label or store brands carry the retail or chain store's trade name. Licensing means a firm sells another firm the right to use its brand name. In co-branding strategies, two brands form a partnership in marketing a new or existing product.

4. Describe how organizations are structured for new and existing product management.

To successfully manage existing products, the marketing organization may include brand managers, product category managers, and market managers. Large firms, however, often give new product responsibilities to new product managers or to venture teams, groups of specialists from different areas who work together for a single new product.

CHAPTER REVIEW

Marketing Concepts: Testing Your Knowledge

1. Explain what is meant by a full-line strategy and a limited-line strategy. How might a firm stretch or expand its product line?
2. What is a product mix? What is meant by the width of a product mix?
3. How are products managed during the different phases of the product life cycle?
4. What is a brand? What are the characteristics of a good brand name? How do firms protect their brands?
5. List and explain some of the different branding strategies.
6. Describe some ways firms organize the marketing function to manage existing products. What are the ways firms organize for the development of new products?

Marketing Concepts: Discussing Choices and Issues

1. Firms often take advantage of a popular, well-known brand by developing brand extensions, because they know that the brand equity of the original or parent brand will be transferred to the new product. However, the transfer can go the other way. If a new product is of poor quality, it can damage the reputation of the parent brand. A new product that is of superior quality can enhance the parent brand's reputation. What are some brand extensions that have either damaged or enhanced the parent brand equity?

Marketing Practice: Applying What You've Learned

1. Assume you are the vice-president of marketing for a firm that markets a large number of specialty food items, such as gourmet sauces, marinades, and relishes.

   a. Your firm is interested in improving its marketing management structure. You are considering several alternatives: a brand manager structure, having product line managers, or focusing on market managers. Outline the advantages and disadvantages of each type of organization. What is your recommendation?

   b. Your firm is also interested in aggressively pursuing the development of a number of new products. You have been asked to develop recommendations for organizing this new product development. Prepare a report that outlines your recommendations.

2. Assume you are working in the marketing department of a major manufacturer of athletic shoes. Your firm is introducing a new product, a line of disposable sports clothing. You wonder if it would be better to market the line of clothing with a new brand name or use the family brand name, which has already gained popularity with your existing products. Make a list of the advantages and disadvantages of each strategy. Develop your recommendation.

Marketing Mini-Project: Learning by Doing

In any supermarket, you will find examples of all the different types of brands discussed in this chapter: individual brands, family brands, national brands, store brands, and co-branded and licensed products. This mini-project is designed to give you a better understanding of branding as it exists in the marketplace.

1. Go to a supermarket in your community.

2. Select two product categories of interest to you, for example, ice cream, cereal, laundry detergent, soup, or paper products.

3. Make a list of the brands available in each product category. Identify what type of brand each is. Count the number of shelf facings (the number of product items at the front of each shelf) for each brand.

4. Arrange to talk with the store manager at a time that is convenient for him/her. Ask the manager to discuss:

   a. how the store decides which brands to carry.

   b. whether the store is more likely to carry a new individual brand or a new family brand.

   c. what causes a store to drop a brand.

   d. the profitability of store or private-label brands versus national brands.

   e. other aspects of branding that the store manager sees as important from a retail perspective.

5. Present a report to your class on what you learned about the brands in your two product categories.

Real People, Real Surfers: Exploring the Web

As we discussed in this chapter, companies protect their products by obtaining patents, copyrights, and legal protection for their brands with trademarks. The Canadian Intellectual Property Office oversees all these forms of protection. Visit the Intellectual Property Office website at

http://strategis.ic.gc.ca/sc_mrksv/cipo/welcome/welcom-e.html. Use the site to answer the following questions.

1. What is a patent? What can be patented?

2. Who may apply for a patent? Can foreign individuals or companies obtain a Canadian patent? Explain.

3. What happens if someone infringes on a patent?

4. What is a copyright? Who owns a copyright?

5. What is copyright infringement? Give some examples.

6. What is a trademark?

7. Who may file a trademark application? Do firms have to register a trademark? Explain.

8. What are the benefits of trademark registration?

9. Can a person's name be registered as a trademark?

10. How long do trademarks, patents, and copyrights last?

11. How would you evaluate the Canadian Intellectual Property Office website? Was it easy to navigate? Was it useful? What recommendations do you have for improving the site?

Visit the MyMarketingLab website at **www.pearsoned.ca/mymarketinglab**. This online homework and tutorial system puts you in control of your own learning with study and practice tools directly correlated to this chapter's content.

Niall FitzGerald, the co-chairman of Unilever, the global consumer products giant, knows the importance of product mix. He constantly examines his product lines to ensure they are current. During the past five years he has bought such brands as Ben & Jerry's ice cream, SlimFast diet products, Bestfoods (maker of Hellmann's mayonnaise), and Knorr soups and sauces, while getting rid of Elizabeth Arden cosmetics.

To become more focused, lean, and competitive, Unilever has sold or eliminated 1200 brands, leaving it with 400. Under Niall's watch, Unilever has transformed itself from a conglomerate that once owned shipping lines and ad agencies to a consumer products company.

Niall believes that a company's portfolio can never reach a point of stability because the business environment is changing all the time. To keep his people motivated during times of change, he makes it very clear to them that change is no criticism of the past, but an absolute must for the future. To keep current, he spends time with retailers and young managers on his own, without their bosses present, asking about the company and how it can do better.

In spite of all the focused effort, Unilever has made mistakes. For example, as the Atkins diet craze took off in the United States, SlimFast marketers thought it was a fad. Even though SlimFast launched its own line of low-carbohydrate products, its sales fell 22 percent in 2003. To protect against such incidents and to keep brand managers current, at Unilever each manager has to earn their "marketer's licence" and demonstrate that they have spent 200 hours talking with consumers, before they can talk about any marketing issue. Further, Niall insists that the language used inside the company is relevant to the consumer. Take "edible fats." "There's no consumer who wakes up in the morning and says, 'I think I have run out of edible fats.' It's margarine or it's spreads," says Niall.

Niall feels that to be a successful marketer you have to be prepared to fail and live with failure. His golden advice is to use the 40–70 rule: If you try to make a decision with 40 percent of what you need (information), you are in trouble. However, if you wait until you've got 70 percent, it's too late. "So be brave enough to take your decisions in the 40 percent to 70 percent zone," he says.

He himself is a living, breathing example of someone who has taken risks and failed spectacularly. In 1994, in an effort to win the laundry battle against Procter & Gamble, Unilever came up with a breakthrough called the Persil accelerator, which cleaned clothes. The problem was that if used improperly by the consumer, the product not only washed away dirt, but the clothes themselves. A competitor placed ads in newspapers with pictures of knickers with holes in them that had been washed with the Persil accelerator.

Scientifically, the product was superior, but it had not been marketed right. Now, after a turnaround, the Persil business is healthier than it was before. Niall wasn't fired for his mistake, he was made chairman. This incident showcased to junior managers that it is okay to fail, as long as the failure is about taking risks based on creating more value for the consumer.

Five lessons from Niall about managing during change:

1. There are no tired brands, only tired brand managers.
2. Make sure the language used inside the company is relevant to the consumer.
3. When leading managers by example on the front lines, don't forget to step back and survey the big picture.
4. Be prepared to fail, and to live with failure.
5. When moving in a new direction, don't keep people who no longer fit the bill.

Source: Adapted from Deborah Ball, "Stocking a global pantry," *The Wall Street Journal*, 24 May 2004: B1.

Things to Think About

1. Why do you think Niall FitzGerald cast out Elizabeth Arden cosmetics from his brand stable? Provide your rationale based on concepts you have learned both in this chapter and throughout the book.

2. If you were a brand manager at Unilever, you would not want to make the same mistake SlimFast did with underestimating the Atkins diet craze. Develop a model that will help you distinguish between a fad and a trend.

3. Compare two Unilever brands in two different product categories with a major competitor's brands. How are the brands positioned? What recommendations do you have for making the Unilever brands even stronger?

CHAPTER 9
Pricing Strategy

CHAPTER OBJECTIVES

WHEN YOU HAVE COMPLETED YOUR STUDY OF THIS CHAPTER, YOU SHOULD BE ABLE TO

1. Explain the importance of pricing and how prices can take both monetary and non-monetary forms.

2. Understand the pricing objectives that marketers typically have in planning pricing strategies.

3. Understand the pricing policies used to achieve different pricing objectives.

4. Apply pricing tactics to set price points.

5. Understand key implementation and legal issues with respect to pricing.

6. Understand some of the environmental factors that affect pricing strategies, including the Internet.

Real People, Real Decisions

Meet **Leonard Hendricks,** a Decision Maker at TELUS

Leonard Hendricks is the director of product and customer marketing at TELUS Communications, a large Canadian telecommunications corporation. After a joint B.Sc. degree from the faculty of Business and the faculty of Agricultural Economics at the University of Alberta, Leonard joined the Agriculture division of Dow Chemicals doing inbound call answer for farmers and channel of distribution dealers.

From Dow, he moved to Andersen Consulting (now Accenture), where he worked on a consulting project for TELUS. He learned that TELUS was starting a data and IP company in Calgary. Excited by this opportunity, he joined other Andersen colleagues who had already left to work for the new TELUS company.

Leonard was motivated to choose this career path because he enjoyed business decisions and wanted to see the long-term impact of his work. While he felt consulting was a great way to learn, he did not experience the impact of his work as he moved from client to client. He says, "To me, the marketing department makes the main business decisions. Marketing generally decides where to invest scarce resources and priorities for a company to maximize benefits."

The achievement of which Leonard is most proud is when he was a core team member that performed the analysis for TELUS to expand nationally. "There was a lot of work on the new market opportunities, best approaches, etc., that enabled TELUS to invest substantial sums in this initiative," says Leonard. "Today, this non-traditional business generates over $800 million per year in revenue for TELUS, which is about 18 percent of the total TELUS Communications revenue."

The non-traditional markets to which Leonard is referring are the geographic markets of Ontario and Quebec. Traditionally, TELUS had operated only in the British Columbia and Alberta marketplace. TELUS decided to expand operations in the East by initially offering Dial VPOP. Dial VPOP are centrally managed dial-up Internet modems that are sold to internet service providers (ISPs). The ISPs use the service to provide dial-up Internet service to end customers. While TELUS was a large provider of this service in the British Columbia and Alberta marketplace, with the largest market share in that territory, the company was virtually unheard of in the Ontario and Quebec markets.

Leonard was faced with a classic pricing problem from a product management point of view. TELUS did not have a track record in the new markets of Ontario and Quebec but was known to most ISPs because it is the second largest telecommunications carrier in Canada. Most ISPs have either dealt with or have heard about the company. The new markets provided a challenge because TELUS would have to deal

with a new set of competitors, different pricing structures, different discount plans, and different geographic needs.

Leonard considered three pricing alternatives in the new markets.

Option 1: Cost plus margin pricing.

TELUS would calculate costs based on the investment required to provide a managed modem to an ISP. Costs would include all incremental costs to provide the service and a portion of the costs spent to get the network in place. The advantage of this option is that TELUS would certainly cover the cost of providing the service to ISPs. It would have a predictable margin in line with company expectations. The main disadvantage of using a cost-plus-pricing model is that TELUS could charge less than the going market price and, therefore, leave money on the table. Alternatively, the cost-plus-pricing could be higher than the market price and TELUS would not sell enough.

Option 2: Market pricing.

Other companies, including Bell Canada, the incumbent in the market, provided a very similar service. Pricing would be based on selling at the same rate as competitors. So, depending upon the price it charged, TELUS's margin would change. The advantage with market pricing is that you are aware of your competitors' pricing and can set your price accordingly. In this market, TELUS would have to decide where its pricing should be to attract business from competitors. "Market pricing is a great strategy to consider if gaining market share is a priority," says Leonard. The disadvantage of the market pricing approach is that market pricing is not always easy to determine. If the prices are not readily available, or the product is new and there are no major competitors, price benchmarks are difficult to attain. Another disadvantage of this option is that, if the market price were lower than your costs, you would have to sell the product at a loss. Finally, the market price could be greater than the price for substitute products, and so you may be missing a large portion of the market for the product.

Option 3: Substitute based pricing.

The alternative for the ISPs was to build the service themselves, rather than buying a centrally managed service. This would entail having the right technical staff to install and manage the service and buying the components from suppliers. By determining what the costs of the customers' alternatives were, TELUS would be able to justify its price based on substitute pricing.

"YES, BUT WHAT DOES IT COST?"

As Leonard Hendricks and the management team at Telus understand, the question of what to charge for a product is a central part of marketing decision making. What to charge for a product, whether it is a good, service, or idea, is a key strategic decision. In this chapter, we'll examine the set of decisions associated with the price element of the marketing mix, how those decisions are made, and the role of demand, costs, revenues, and the environment in the pricing decision process. We will start by discussing what price is, why pricing decisions are important, and the context in which pricing decisions are made. Then, we will examine pricing objectives, pricing policy (or strategy), price points and tactics, and implementation terms and conditions—which collectively are the key pricing decisions. These key decisions are illustrated in Figure 9.1. The chapter concludes with a discussion of environmental influences on pricing decisions.

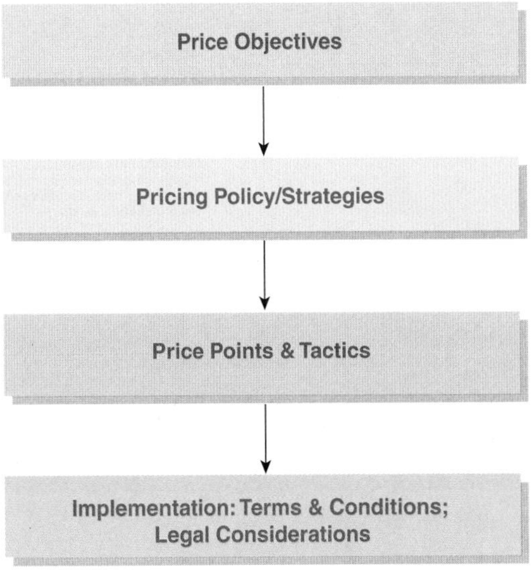

Price Objectives

↓

Pricing Policy/Strategies

↓

Price Points & Tactics

↓

Implementation: Terms & Conditions; Legal Considerations

Figure 9.1 Key Pricing Strategy Decisions

Monetary and Non-Monetary Prices

"If you have to ask how much it is, you can't afford it!" We have all heard that, but how often do you buy something without asking the price? If we weren't concerned about price, we'd all drive dream cars, take trips to exotic places, and live like royalty. Most of us, however, need to consider a product's price before buying. **Price** is the value that customers give up, or exchange, to obtain a desired product. Payment may be in the form of money, goods, services, favours, votes, or anything else that has *value* to the other party.

price The value that customers give up, or exchange, to obtain a desired product.

As Chapter 1 explained, marketing is the process that creates exchanges of things of value. We usually think of this exchange as people trading money for a good or a service. Often, the monetary value of a product is called something other than price, sometimes to hide the idea that you are being charged a price or perhaps to assume an air of greater respectability. For example, colleges and universities charge *tuition* for an education, a lawyer or accountant charges a *professional fee*, and students who join a chapter of the American Marketing Association pay *dues*. No matter what it is called, it's still a price.

But in some marketplace practices, price can mean exchanges of non-monetary value. Long before societies minted coins, people exchanged one good or service for another. This practice of **bartering** was the basis for the economic development of Canada, with the Hudson's Bay Company trading goods to Northwest trappers for furs. Bartering still occurs today, and with advances in Internet technology, it's increasing at more than 20 percent per year.[1] An estimated 450 000 North American businesses barter $10 billion worth of goods and services each year. That is in addition to the thousands more people who informally exchange everything from spaghetti sauce to music lessons.[2] Canadian organizations such as the Barter Network (based in Toronto) and the Community Exchange System (based in Quebec) have established large barter networks, where organizations can exchange goods and services for barter credits. Someone who owns a home at a mountain ski resort, for example, may exchange a weekend for barter credits to spend in a restaurant or for car repairs. In fact, in 2006, a Vancouver-based blogger named Kyle MacDonald managed to use multiple barters to trade a paper clip for a rural house in Saskatchewan.[3] No money changes hands, but as the Canada Revenue Agency understands well, there is an exchange of value: Taxpayers are supposed to report as income the value of goods or services received in exchange for other goods or services.

bartering The practice of exchanging a good or service for another good or service of like value.

Organizations that follow an operational excellence strategy (Chapter 3) or another cost-based differentiation strategy focus on making the cost to the customer as low as possible. These also include non-monetary costs. When evaluating purchase alternatives, consumers take into account other economic costs such as **operating costs**, **switching costs**, and **opportunity costs**. Operating costs are those involved in using the product, such as toner

operating costs Costs involved in using a product.

switching costs Costs involved in moving from one brand to another.

opportunity cost The value of something that is given up to obtain something else.

Exhibit 9.1

Health Canada tries to increase the perceived psychological cost of smoking.

in a printer. Switching costs are involved in moving from one brand to another, such as getting new cheques printed if you switch banks. Opportunity costs are the benefits and value you give up, or miss out on, by engaging in one activity or buying one product and not another, such as the income you forgo while in school.

Sometimes the lowest-priced product isn't the lowest-cost product over time. The personal investment consumers make in buying and using products is also a cost. Convenience-store operators, such as Mac's or 7-Eleven, and Internet companies, such as Chapters.ca, among other marketers, focus on minimizing the time, energy, and effort consumers have to expend to satisfy their needs and wants. As discussed in Chapter 5, consumers also experience psychological costs—such as stress, hassle, cognitive difficulty, and cognitive dissonance—when trying to buy and use products. (Have you ever tried to assemble a bike or gas barbecue?) Many marketers, auto-malls, and courier companies, for example, focus on making it as easy as possible to buy and use their products. Psychological costs are particularly challenging when marketing ideas, such as not smoking. Health Canada uses shocking or disturbing images such as the one in Exhibit 9.1 to increase the perceived psychological cost of smoking. As one author put it, it's a lot more difficult to sell "brotherhood than soap."[4]

The Importance of Pricing Decisions

How important are good pricing decisions? Pricing is probably the least understood and least appreciated element of the marketing mix. Marketers like to talk about advertising and other communication elements. It's fun to think about changing technology and how firms invest in new-product development. Even decisions about channels of distribution seem to be more exciting than setting the right price. Yet price has a major strategic impact on the firm—it determines the net value received by the customer in an exchange (benefits minus costs) versus the net value (profit) received by the firm.

The plight of U.S. airlines is a good example of how bad pricing decisions can hurt an entire industry. During the decade before 1992, companies in the airline industry engaged in a fierce price war. The per-mile fare was lowered nearly 25 percent (accounting for inflation of the dollar), while costs such as labour and fuel more than doubled.[5] As a result, from 1990 to 1992, the airlines lost over $10 billion, more than had been earned since the start of commercial air travel. Sometimes it's not advantageous for a firm to cut its prices. The industry rebounded in 2006 with strong ticket sales, and industry experts expected 2007 to be even stronger—as more people travel. Despite this rebound, airlines are still not making much money and industry experts predict that if the economy slows down, more airlines may have to file for bankruptcy. The industry is still feeling the impact of the pricing decisions of the early 1990s.[6]

Good pricing decisions are critical to a firm's success in the marketplace. For most organizations, the only source of profit is through the price charged for products. If customers are not willing to pay the price asked for a firm's product, the firm will not make a profit and will have failed its shareholders.

Even during the best economic times, most consumers rank "reasonable price" as the most important consideration in a purchase. In addition, reasonable prices count most when consumers decide where to shop.[7] Price is even more important during recessions, when consumers have less to spend and count their pennies carefully. Marketers try to come as close to reasonable as possible when deciding on a price.

Individual consumers aren't the only buyers who focus on price. As we saw in Chapter 6, purchasing agents for firms often put a high priority on getting the best price. At least one study has found that price may be second only to quality in these decisions. Buying professionals know that when all else is equal, getting a low price keeps costs down and helps make their firm's product competitive.[8]

DEVELOPING PRICING OBJECTIVES

Pricing objectives must support the broader objectives of the firm, such as maximizing shareholder value, as well as its overall marketing objectives, such as increasing market share. Consider, for example, the different pricing decisions of the three major rivals in the breakfast cereal market.

In the 1980s, major cereal producers increased net prices more than 6 percent per year for a total of 30 percent over a five-year period. Then came the low-priced supermarket brands, which, by the mid 1990s, had captured 9 percent of the market. In response, the top two makers of ready-to-eat cereals announced very different pricing strategies. General Mills *cut* prices on three of its major brands in the large sizes in an effort to increase its market share. Kellogg's response, however, was a 2.6 percent price *increase* on its cereals; it planned to soften the impact with discount coupons, the idea being to hold customers and to increase profits with frequent price-oriented promotions.[9] Three years later, in 1996, Post announced it was "changing the way the entire cereal category works" with an across-the-board price rollback, and, at the same time, initiating a new advertising campaign.[10] Each of these pricing strategies had an objective: General Mills sought to increase market share, Kellogg tried to increase profits, and Post hoped to increase consumers' total consumption of cereal. Table 9.1 provides examples of different types of pricing objectives.

Profit Objectives

There are three main **profit objectives**: maximizing profits, achieving a target level of profit growth, and achieving a desired net profit margin (or a target return on investment). A profit objective is important to firms that believe that profit motivates shareholders and bankers to invest in a company. Coca-Cola recently announced a change in its North American pricing strategy—to a premium pricing strategy designed to increase profits and create a premium brand image, instead of a market share strategy that had achieved 8 percent annual sales growth but declining profits.[11]

profit objective Pricing products with a focus on a target level of profit growth or a desired net profit margin.

Table 9.1 Pricing Objectives

Type of Objective	Example
Profit	During the first six months, set a price to yield a target profit of $200 000. Or Set prices to allow for an 8 percent profit margin on all goods sold.
Sales or Market Share	Institute pricing strategy changes to support a 5 percent increase in sales.
Competitive Effect	Alter pricing strategy during the first quarter of the year to increase sales during introduction of a new product. Or Maintain low-end pricing policies to discourage new competitors from entering the market.
Customer Satisfaction	Simplify the pricing structure to simplify the decision process for customers. Or Alter price levels to match customer expectations.
Image Enhancement	Alter pricing policies to reflect the increased emphasis on the product's quality image.

Although profits are an important consideration in pricing all goods and services, they are critical when the product is assumed to be a fad. Fad products can expect a rather short market life, making a profit objective essential to allow the firm to recover its investment in a short period of time. In such cases, the firm must harvest profits before customers lose interest and move on to the next electronic pet, troll doll, or cartoon idol.

sales or market share objective Pricing products to maximize sales or to attain a desired level of sales or market share.

Sales or Market Share Objectives

A **sales or market share objective** involves setting prices at a level that will maximize sales, in either dollars or units, or will attain a desired level of sales or market share. Does setting a price to increase unit sales or market share (*sales objectives*) simply mean pricing the product lower than the competition? Sometimes this is the case. The telephone industry provides a good example: Suppliers such as Telus, Sprint, and AT&T constantly make rate adjustments to keep them ahead in the "telephone wars." Lowering prices is not always necessary to increase market share. If a company's product has an important competitive advantage over competitors' offerings, keeping the price at the same level as other firms do may satisfy sales objectives.

competitive effect objective Pricing that is intended to have an effect on the marketing efforts of the competition.

customer satisfaction objective Pricing that is intended to maximize customer satisfaction and retention.

Competitive Effect Objectives

A pricing plan with a **competitive effect objective** is intended to have a certain effect on the marketing efforts of the competition. Sometimes a firm deliberately seeks to pre-empt or reduce the effectiveness of one or more competitors. Recently, Toys "R" Us sought to cut into the Christmas toy sales of Wal-Mart. It launched an early-November program offering nearly $500 worth of price-off coupons. The move gave Wal-Mart too little time to react. This "Christmas surprise" enabled Toys "R" Us to generate a significant portion of its holiday-time sales from one single price-off coupon program.[12] Price stability is another competitive effect objective. Retail gasoline companies like Shell, Esso, and Petro-Canada want to avoid price wars and closely match competitor pricing.

Customer Satisfaction Objectives

Many customer-oriented firms believe that profits result from making customer satisfaction the primary objective. Firms that have **customer satisfaction (and retention) objectives** set prices to maximize the value to the customer, believing that by focusing solely on short-term profits, a company loses sight of keeping customers for the long term. Travelocity.com, one of the leading online travel providers, is one company that focuses on customer satisfaction. As Exhibit 9.2 shows, the "Travelocity Service Guarantee" is a promise to stand behind customers and support them always, even when they are on

The Travelocity Guarantee

Exhibit 9.2

The Travelocity Service Guarantee is a promise to stand behind customers and support them always, even when they're on the road.

the road. If something goes wrong with travel arrangements made through Travelocity, it will do everything in its power to make things right by working with its travel partners on behalf of the customer.

Image Enhancement (Positioning) Objectives

Organizations that make pricing decisions based on **image enhancement (or positioning) objectives** recognize that consumers often use price to make inferences about the quality of a product. In fact, marketers know that price is often an important means of communicating not only quality but also image to prospective customers.

The image enhancement function of pricing is particularly important for prestige or luxury products like diamonds. While the high price tag on a Rolex watch or a Rolls-Royce car reflects the higher production costs, it is also vital to shaping an image of an extraordinary product with ownership limited to wealthy consumers. The Burton Snowboard Company, like many other boarding companies, sets high prices on its products to communicate an elite image and uniqueness in the boarding subculture (Exhibit 9.3).

Another example of image pricing comes from Calgary-based Nevada Bob's Golf Inc., the world's largest chain of golf specialty retail stores. Backed by cross-Canada market research, it has begun moving its image upmarket—starting by taking "discount" out of the store brand name (it was "Nevada Bob's Discount Golf"). It now offers a broader and more upscale range of golf products, a more comfortable, customer-friendly storefront, and improved customer service, while still offering a best-price guarantee.[13]

A low price is just as important in communicating a different image. Zellers uses price to position the company as a value leader with its slogan "The lowest price is the law." In other cases, such as for Timex watches, the desire is to communicate the image of a good-quality product that is reasonably priced.

Flexibility of Price Objectives

It is important that pricing objectives be *flexible*. Often, it is necessary to develop pricing objectives (and strategies) tailored to different geographic areas and time periods. There may be varying levels of competition in different parts of the country, making it necessary to lower prices in the areas with the heaviest competition. Some geographic regions may have greater sales potential, making it wise for firms to develop pricing objectives aimed at obtaining a larger market share in those areas. Mortgage lenders may do this by offering lower rates in areas where new housing starts are booming.

Market conditions can change during the year, requiring price adjustments for seasonal and other reasons. Accommodation rental rates in Whistler, British Columbia, are much higher during the winter than during the summer; rates in Summerside, Prince Edward Island, or Grand Bend, Ontario, are higher during the summer vacation months.

Pricing objectives are only one part of price planning. Before any prices can be set, marketers must understand the alternative pricing strategies available to achieve those objectives.

PRICING STRATEGIES/POLICIES

An old Russian proverb says: "There are two kinds of fools in any market. One doesn't charge enough. The other charges too much."[14] This underscores the strategic decision behind pricing—how much value to offer the customer versus how much value to retain in terms of profit for the firm. Today's marketers may ponder the message. In modern business there is seldom a one-and-only, now-and-forever, best pricing strategy; pricing today has more of the continuous decision-making character of a chess game. The organization must think two or three moves ahead. And no pricing decision is set in stone. Costs increase. Sales

Exhibit 9.3

Pricing of Burton snowboards and clothing is consistent with a positioning objective.

image enhancement objective Pricing intended to establish a desired image or positioning to prospective customers

Profit Objectives
   Cost-Based
      Cost-Plus Pricing
      Price-Floor Pricing
   Demand Based
      Target Cost Pricing
      Yield Management
      Variable (Custom) Pricing
      Skimming (New products)
   Experience Based
      Experimental Pricing
      Judgment
Sales or Market Share Objectives
   Value Pricing (Everyday low pricing)
   Frequent Discounting
   Penetration Pricing (New products)
   Trial Pricing (New products)
Competitive Effect Objectives (Stability)
   Price Leadership or Follower
   Premium Pricing
   Umbrella pricing (Pricing below the competition)
   Price Bundling
Customer Satisfaction Objectives
   Variable (Custom) Pricing
   Cost of Ownership Pricing
   Value Pricing (Everyday low pricing)
   Price Bundling
Image Enhancement / Positioning Objectives
   Premium Pricing
   Prestige/Image Pricing
Everyday Low Pricing

Figure 9.2 Price Objectives and Strategies

decline. The competition changes its prices. Price reductions can discourage new competitors or at least sabotage competitors' product introductions. Toyota is using strategic pricing to increase its market share of the lucrative pickup truck market—once dominated by the big-three North American manufacturers. Features such as side curtain air bags and traction control are standard in the Toyota Tundra—options that GM and Ford charge customers extra for. The option-loaded Toyota Tundra is priced comparably to the base price for other North American trucks. The strategy allows Toyota to appear not to be massively undercutting prices in the market—while at the same time being priced very competitively when consumers compare similarly equipped trucks. Some fear that Toyota's pricing strategy could lead to the re-emergence of profit-eroding incentives by North American manufacturers to compete, driving prices in the market down.[15]

Marketers whose responsibility it is to develop pricing strategies will consider a number of alternative strategies and try to anticipate the outcomes. Below we discuss some of the more common pricing strategies associated with each price objective—these are summarized in Figure 9.2. You will notice in some cases that the same strategy can be used to achieve different objectives. In the discussion that follows we present each strategy only once, in the order they appear in Figure 9.2.

Pricing Strategies to Achieve Profit Objectives

There are many pricing strategies consistent with profit-oriented price objectives. The three main sets of strategies are based on cost, demand, and experience.

COST-BASED PRICING STRATEGIES Cost-based strategies are typically associated with a target profit or return objectives. By understanding a product's cost structure, marketers can set prices to achieve a desired profit. Marketers use *cost-based strategies* because they are simple to calculate and are relatively safe, in that they ensure that the price will cover the costs the company incurs in producing and marketing the product.

Cost-based pricing methods, however, have drawbacks. They do not consider such factors as the nature of the target market, demand, competition, the product life cycle, and the product's image. In addition, although the calculations for setting the price may be simple and straightforward, it may be difficult to estimate costs accurately. Think about such firms as Nortel, Bombardier, and McCain, which produce many products. How do they allocate the costs for the plant, equipment, design engineers, maintenance, and marketing personnel so that the pricing plan accurately reflects the cost of production for any particular product? For example, how do you allocate the salary of a marketing executive who deals with many different products? Should the cost be divided equally among all products? Should costs be based on the actual number of hours spent working on each product? Or should costs be assigned based on the revenues generated by each product? There is no one right answer. However, even with these limitations, cost-based pricing strategies are often a marketer's best choice.

cost-plus pricing A method of setting prices in which the seller totals all the unit costs for the product and then adds the desired profit per unit.

Cost-Plus Pricing The most common cost-based approach to pricing a product is **cost-plus pricing**, in which a marketer totals the unit costs for the product and then adds an amount to cover desired profit. Many marketers, especially retailers and wholesalers, use cost-plus pricing because of its simplicity—users need only estimate the unit cost and add the markup. To calculate cost-plus pricing, marketers usually calculate either a markup on cost or a markup on selling price. With both methods, you calculate the price by adding a predetermined percentage to the cost, but as the names of the methods imply, for one the calculation uses a percentage of the costs and for the other a percentage of the selling price. Which of the two methods is used seems often to be little more than a matter of "the way our company has always done it." You'll find more information about cost-plus pricing and how to calculate markup on cost and markup on selling price in Appendix 9A—Marketing Math—at the end of this chapter.

Price-Floor Pricing These cost-based pricing methods do not take into account any factors except costs and profits. But there are times when firms need to consider other factors, such as the advantage of having a plant operating at its peak capacity, which keeps a skilled workforce fully employed. **Price-floor pricing** is a method for calculating price that considers both costs and what can be done to ensure that a plant can operate at its capacity.

Price-floor pricing is sometimes used when the state of the economy or other temporary market conditions make it impossible for a firm to sell enough units of its product at a price that covers **fixed costs** (those that do not change with the number of units produced), **variable costs** (the additional cost to make one more unit of a product), and profit goals to keep its plants operating at full capacity (for a full explanation of these terms, see the Appendix to this chapter). In such circumstances, it may be possible to sell part of the units produced at a lower price, one that covers only the variable costs of production. If the price-floor price can be set above the marginal costs, then the firm can use the difference to increase profits or to help cover its fixed costs.

For example, assume that a jeans firm, operating at full capacity, can produce 400 000 pairs of jeans a year. The average variable costs per unit are $20; the price that covers fixed costs, variable costs, and a desired level of profits is $30 per pair. Due to a downturn in the economy, the firm finds that it can sell only 350 000 units at this price. Using price-floor pricing, the firm can sell the additional 50 000 pairs of jeans at a price as low as $20 and maintain full-capacity operations.

If it adopts this approach, the firm will not make anything on the additional units, but it will not lose anything either. If it sells the additional 50 000 pairs at $25, then it will not only cover the variable costs but will also increase its total profits—50 000 × $5 or $250 000—not a bad deal. But several risks accompany price-floor pricing. Selling the additional 50 000 pairs of jeans at a lower cost might cannibalize full-price sales, and if the lower price is offered to some retailers and not others, it might anger those not included and undermine customer loyalty.

Firms that produce their own national brands as well as manufacture private-label brands sold through various retailers and distributors may use price-floor pricing for the private-label end of the business. Thus, Frigidaire may sell 70 percent of its refrigerators under the Frigidaire name and the rest to Sears for sale under its own Kenmore brand name. The consumers in Exhibit 9.4 look at specifications to compare models of different prices.

Cost-based strategies are quite popular because they ensure that prices take into account

price-floor pricing A method for calculating price in which, to maintain full plant operating capacity, a portion of a firm's output may be sold at a price that covers only marginal costs of production.

fixed costs Costs of production that do not change with the number of units produced.

variable costs The costs of production (raw and processed materials, parts, and labour) that are tied to, and vary depending on, the number of units produced.

Exhibit 9.4

Price-floor pricing is a method for calculating price that considers both costs and what can be done to ensure that a plant can operate at its capacity.

demand-based pricing A price-setting method based on estimates of demand at different prices.

an organization's costs. However, when firms base price strategies on cost, they are operating under the old production orientation and not a marketing orientation.

DEMAND-BASED PRICING **Demand-based pricing** is basing the selling price on an estimate of volume or quantity that a firm can sell at different prices. To use any of the pricing strategies based on demand, firms must research demand—they must learn what quantities of a product different target markets are willing to buy at different prices. Used pickup trucks in Alberta, for example, are in greater demand than in British Columbia, causing prices to be significantly higher in Alberta.

Often marketers use customer surveys in which consumers reveal whether they would buy a certain product and how much of it they would buy at various prices. More accurate estimates can be obtained by some type of field experiment. For instance, a firm might actually offer the product at different price levels in different test markets and map the results onto a demand curve.

demand curve A plot of the quantity of a product that customers will buy in a market during a period of time at various prices if all other factors remain the same.

The **demand curve**, which can be a curved or straight line, shows the quantity of a product that customers will buy in a market during a period of time at various prices if all other factors remain the same. Figure 9.3 shows demand curves for normal and prestige products. For most goods, the demand curve slopes downward and to the right (Normal Products, Figure 9.3). If prices decrease, customers will buy more. This is known as the *law of demand*. For example, if the price of bananas in the grocery store goes up, a customer will probably buy fewer of them. If the price increases too much, the customer will eat his or her cereal without bananas.

There are situations, however, in which otherwise rational people desire a product more as it *increases* in price. For *prestige products*, such as luxury cars or jewellery or even some business diplomas and degrees, an increase in price may actually result in an *increase* in the quantity demanded, because consumers see the products as more valuable. The higher-price–higher-demand relationship has its limits, however. At some point price increases will make the product unattainable, and demand will begin to decrease, as shown by the backward direction taken by the top portion of the backward-bending curve under Prestige Products in Figure 9.3.

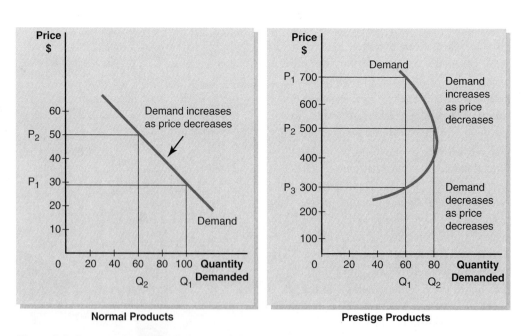

Normal Products

Prestige Products

Figure 9.3 Demand Curves for Normal and Prestige Products

For normal products there is an inverse relationship between price and demand. For prestige products, demand will increase—to a point—as price increases or will decrease as price decreases.

A strength of demand-based pricing strategies is that their use assures a firm that it will be able to sell what it produces at the determined price, because the price is based on research findings about customer demand rather than on the seller's costs. A major disadvantage is the difficulty of estimating demand accurately. Although sales forecasting is a topic covered in advanced marketing courses, it is important to know that estimating demand can be difficult. This is because the size of markets is often not known and needs to be estimated, the market share a firm might expect to capture needs to be estimated, and these projections need to take into consideration other factors that can affect demand, such as new competitors entering the market, the state of the economy, and changing consumer tastes. Dell is one company that uses demand pricing (Exhibit 9.5).[16] Dell revises the price of its computers when necessary to offset decreasing sales. The computer company reviews its prices frequently (often a few times a month) in an attempt to keep tabs on customer thinking and give customers the value they want. Marginal analysis, as discussed briefly in the Appendix to this chapter, is a technique that enables marketers to look at demand and costs at the same time; to assess profit under different forecasts.

Four specific demand-based pricing strategies are target cost pricing, yield management pricing, variable (custom) pricing, and skimming pricing. We'll talk about those next.

Target Cost Pricing Today firms are finding that they can be more successful if they match price with demand using a process called **target costing**. With target cost-

Exhibit 9.5

Dell uses a demand-based pricing strategy. The company regularly reviews sales performance and adjusts its prices accordingly.

ing, a firm first determines the price at which customers would be willing to buy the product and then it works backward to design the product in such a way that it can produce and sell the product at a profit. With target costing, a product's cost, and thus its price, is strongly tied to its design—70 to 80 percent of a product's costs are determined by its final design.

With target costing, firms first use marketing research to identify the quality and functionality needed to satisfy attractive market segments and what price they are willing to pay *before the product is designed*. As Table 9.2 shows, the next step is to determine what margins retailers and dealers require, as well as the profit margin the company requires. Based on this information, managers can calculate the target cost—the maximum it can cost the firm to manufacture the product. In addition, the company may break down this total target cost

target costing A process in which firms identify the quality and functionality needed to satisfy customers and what price they are willing to pay before the product is designed; the product is manufactured only if the firm can control costs to meet the required price.

Table 9.2 Target Costing Using a Jeans Example

Step 1: Determine the price customers are willing to pay for the jeans. $39.99

Step 2: Determine the markup required by the retailer. 40% = 0.40

Step 3: Calculate the maximum price the retailer will pay, the markup amount.
  Price to the Retailer = Selling price × (1.00 − markup percentage)
  Price to the Retailer = $39.99 × 0.60 = $23.99

Step 4: Determine the profit required by the firm. 15% = 0.15

Step 5: Calculate the target cost, the maximum cost of producing the jeans.
  Target Cost = Price to the Retailer × (1.00 − profit percentage)
  Target Cost = $23.99 × 0.85 = $20.39

into different product functions or components, allocating more of the cost to product features consumers consider critical. If the firm can meet customer quality and functionality requirements, and control costs to meet the required price, it will manufacture the product. If not, it abandons the product.

One reason that target costing is practised more today is the global economy—competitor firms can bring "me too" products to market so quickly, usually within months, that there is little time to recover development costs, much less create brand loyalty. Success is tied to designing costs out of a product.

Camera maker Olympus Optical Company has adopted target costing. When Olympus began losing money in the mid 1980s, it first tried to introduce new products. A second initiative was to improve product quality. Its third initiative was to examine production costs. Olympus managers realized that success depended on their ability to manufacture products at a cost that would meet customers' requirements. Olympus determined that a baseline price for a compact camera in the Canadian market was $140. Considering import fees and the margins dealers required, Olympus determined a target cost for any new product. Initially only about 20 percent of proposed new models would meet the target costs on the first pass. But those that did quickly became the most popular—and profitable—compact cameras in the Canadian market.

yield-management pricing A practice of charging different prices to different customers to manage capacity while maximizing revenues.

Yield-Management Pricing **Yield-management pricing** is another type of demand-based pricing strategy most commonly used by airlines, hotels, and cruise lines (Exhibit 9.6). With yield-management pricing, firms charge different prices to different customers to manage capacity while maximizing revenues. Many service firms practise yield-management pricing because they recognize that different customers have different sensitivities to price—some customers will pay top dollar for an airline ticket while others will travel only if there is a discount fare. The goal of yield-management pricing is to accurately predict the proportion of customers who fall into each category and allocate the percentages of the airline's or hotel's capacity accordingly so that no product goes unsold.

For example, an airline may have two prices for seats: the full fare ($899) and the discount fare ($299). The airline must predict how many seats it can fill at full fare and how many can be sold at only the discounted fare. The airline begins months ahead of the date of the flight with a basic allocation of seats—perhaps it will place 25 percent in the full fare "bucket" and 75 percent in the discount fare "bucket." While the seats in the full fare bucket cannot be sold at the discounted price, the seats allocated for the discounted price can be sold at the full fare.

As flight time gets closer, the airline might make a series of adjustments to the allocation of seats in the hope of selling every seat on the plane at the highest price possible. If the Toronto Maple Leafs need to book the flight, chances are some of the discount seats will be sold at full fare, decreasing the number available at the discounted price. If, as the flight date nears, the number of full-fare ticket sales falls below the forecast, some of those seats will be moved to the discount bucket. This process continues until the day of the flight as the airline attempts to have every seat filled when the plane takes off. This is why you may be able to get a fantastic price on an airline ticket through discount travel agencies like Skyauction.com or Cheapticketscanada.com if you wait until the last minute to buy your ticket.

Exhibit 9.6

Hotels like Quebec City's Fairmont Le Château Frontenac use a yield-management pricing strategy to maximize revenues.

This strategy is similar to a price discrimination strategy where different segments are targeted for different pricing levels—such as the price difference between men's and women's haircuts and men's and women's dry-cleaning.

Variable Pricing **Variable pricing**, or custom pricing, is a strategy of tailoring the price of a product to reflect variability in market demand and what different customers are willing to pay. The price of gasoline, for example, is often set higher during periods of peak demand—like long weekends. Variable pricing is common in business-to-business marketing contexts where prices are typically negotiated in new buy or modified re-buy situations like the digital imaging system purchase described in the Venture 4th case at the end of Chapter 6, or submitted as sealed bids (typical of government purchases). Coca-Cola has been experimenting with the concept of variable pricing in vending machines—with the price determined by the ambient temperature outside the machine—and a rationale that consumers may be willing to pay more for a cold Coke when it is hot outside.[17] Variable pricing could be considered a profit-oriented strategy as it ensures that products are sold at the highest price each customer is willing to pay. However, it could also be considered a customer satisfaction–based strategy as it also ensures that customers get the best "deal" they are able to negotiate.

variable pricing A flexible pricing strategy that reflects what individual customers are willing to pay.

Skimming Pricing Skimming means taking the top or best part of something—like the cream that separates and rises to the top of non-homogenized milk, used for making ice cream and whipped cream. In pricing new products, one strategy is to set a **skimming price**, which means that the firm charges a high, premium price for its new product, expecting demand from the top spending, least price sensitive, target market. For example, when Top-Flite introduced its new Strata golf balls with a new dimple design and more solid core for better flight with metal clubs, the price was three times that of regular balls. Pro shops still couldn't keep them in stock.[18]

skimming price Charging a very high, premium price for a new product.

If a product is highly desirable and offers unique benefits, and early adopters are not price sensitive during the introductory stage of the product life cycle, a skimming pricing strategy allows a firm to quickly recover research, development, and promotion costs, resulting in earlier profitability than under other pricing strategies (Exhibit 9.7). For skimming pricing to be successful, however, there should be little chance that competitors can get into the market quickly. With highly complex, technical products, it may be quite a while before competitors can develop and test new products and get them into production. This is the case for patented pharmaceutical products that have a lock on the market for 25 years.

A skimming pricing strategy is most successful when the market consists of several customer segments with different levels of price sensitivity. There must be a substantial num-ber of initial product customers who have very low price sensitivity. After a period of time, the price can go down, and a second segment of the market with a slightly higher level of price sensitivity will purchase, and so on. For example, hand calculators that once commanded $200 can now be bought for less than $2—accessible to almost everyone.

experimental pricing A strategy of experimenting with prices until the price that generates the highest profitability is found.

EXPERIENCE-BASED PRICING STRATEGIES Because of the difficulty in forecasting demand for products at different prices, many marketers, and in particular retailers, use their own experience to set prices. **Experimental pricing** is when a marketer tries different levels of pricing to see what the demand is. Experimental pricing is often used in market pre-tests where different prices are used in different geographic markets to generate the data to create a demand curve at different price levels. It is also used, less formally, by retailers who try one price for a product, then make adjustments to the price to see what price level seems

Exhibit 9.7

Manufacturers of new-to-the-world, high-technology products like Blu-ray DVD players often use a skimming pricing strategy to recover research and development costs quickly.

Exhibit 9.8

Zellers is known for its everyday low pricing strategy.

judgment A pricing strategy that draws on past experience of the marketer in setting appropriate prices.

value pricing or everyday low pricing (EDLP) A pricing strategy in which a firm sets prices that provide ultimate value to customers.

frequent discounting A strategy of frequently using sale prices to increase sales volume.

penetration pricing A pricing strategy in which a firm introduces a new product at a very low price to encourage more customers to purchase it.

to generate the greatest profitability. This is also called trial-and-error pricing. Marketers also use **judgment** in setting prices—drawing on past experience with similar products or their understanding of the market segment to set prices.

Market Share Pricing Strategies

While variable pricing can result in maximized profit and satisfied customers, the negotiation process can be time consuming, and consumers have different levels of negotiating skills. This leaves some customers with cognitive dissonance, wondering if they got the best price.

VALUE PRICING To address this issue, car manufacturers like Saturn, and retailers such as Zellers and Wal-Mart, practise **value pricing, or everyday low pricing (EDLP)**, which promises ultimate value to consumers—without having to negotiate or bargain for it (Exhibit 9.8). As discussed in Chapter 1, customer *value* is the benefits received by a customer relative to the costs and sacrifices necessary to obtain those benefits. This means that, in the customers' eyes, the product's price is justified by what they receive.[19]

Value-based pricing begins with customers, then considers the competition, and then determines the best pricing strategy. Smart marketers know that the firm that wins is not necessarily the one with the lowest prices but rather the one that delivers the most value.

This has been the strategy behind the success of WestJet Airlines. Modelled after Southwest Airlines, WestJet focuses on everyday low fares, short distances, and good customer service to attract budget-conscious leisure travellers throughout Canada. It started with understanding the target market—what it would take to get people out of their cars for short-haul trips—then the company made marketing mix decisions to deliver the value bundle sought by those customers: no-frills, direct flights, at rock-bottom prices, to and from under-utilized airports, using standard aircraft, serviced by personable staff, offering fun and lighthearted (perhaps even irreverent) customer interactions.

In practice, when marketers use EDLP strategies, consumers feel they get more for their money. Marketers hope that will make them see the price as reasonable and encourage them to remain loyal rather than snapping up whatever happens to be on sale. Deal-oriented consumers, however, have been conditioned to choose products because they are "on special" rather than because they are superior to others. The problem with "deals" or frequent price promotions is that consumers learn to wait for sales or stock up on products when they are on sale, thus making it difficult for companies to maintain "regular" margins and production volumes. Procter & Gamble tried to establish an EDLP strategy in the early 1990s for such products as Tide and Pampers, but abandoned this strategy in the face of competitors continuing to offer sales, coupons, and other price promotions.[20]

FREQUENT DISCOUNTING The approach of using sales, coupons, and other discounts to stimulate sales is a **frequent discounting** strategy. Retailers like Future Shop that have weekly sale extravaganzas use this strategy to entice consumers into their stores where they may purchase both sale and non-sale items. The problem with frequent discounting is that it conditions consumers to wait for the sale price. If they can wait, consumers will not pay the "regular" price for a two-litre bottle of Coca-Cola, knowing that it goes on sale for 99 cents periodically and is in the $1.79 range regularly.

PENETRATION PRICING Another market share–based strategy is **penetration pricing**. Penetration pricing, the opposite of skimming pricing, is when a new product is introduced at a very low price, as Intel did with its first Pentium processor chip.[21] Because rivals were way behind in developing competitive chips, Intel had used a skimming strategy for the 486 processor. However, when the Pentium 1 was introduced, Intel knew that Motorola was working with IBM and Apple to develop comparable chips, and it set a low price for the

Pentium 1 to sell more in a short period of time and derail Motorola's debut.[22] This strategy worked well for Intel. The low price encouraged demand and sales in the early stages of the product life cycle. If the marketing objective is to beef up market share, penetration pricing makes sense.

Another reason marketers use penetration pricing is to discourage competitors from entering the market. The firm first out with a new product has an important advantage. Experience has shown that a *pioneering brand* often is able to maintain dominant market share for the life of the product. Competitors looking at the market may feel that the potential for developing a profitable alternative is not good. Bayer aspirin and Hoover vacuum cleaners are examples of brands that were first to market, kept their leads for decades, and still dominate their fields. These pioneering brands don't need to do much talking to tell consumers who they are. Keeping prices low may even act as a *barrier to entry* to potential competitors, because the cost of developing and manufacturing a new similar product prevents a satisfactory return.

TRIAL PRICING With **trial pricing**, a new product carries a low price for a limited period of time to lower the risk for a customer, then the price is increased to "regular" levels.[23] In trial pricing, the idea is to win customer acceptance first and make profits later. A low-enough introductory price may be a preferred alternative to giving out free samples, as the trial price will bring some positive contribution to the organization. Via Rail recently launched its "Miss Mom's Cooking Campaign" targeting university students. The campaign is based on the assumption that many first-year students are missing Mom's home cooking and clean laundry. Ads feature empty fridges and piles of dirty laundry. Flyers were distributed to university residences encouraging students to visit a special website where they would receive a special reduced fare on a train ticket "home to Mom." According to Via Rail executives, the objective of this reduced fare was to encourage trial, so that later on when students start their careers they would be aware of Via Rail.[24]

In another example, Telus is conducting a $65 million experiment to bring digital TV, movies on demand, Internet, e-mail, and phone service into homes for one monthly bill. After the trial offer, Telus will decide how widely the services will be offered and whether there is an opportunity to increase prices.[25] Trial pricing also works for services. Health clubs and other service providers frequently offer trial memberships or special introductory prices. They hope that customers will try the service at a low price and be converted to a regular-price customer.

> **trial pricing** Pricing a new product low for a limited period of time to lower the risk for a customer.

Competitive Effect Pricing Strategies

Competitive-effect pricing strategies are those that are competitor focused. To achieve competitive effect objectives, a firm can adopt a price-leader–follower strategy, a premium pricing strategy, an umbrella pricing strategy, or a price bundling strategy.

PRICE LEADERSHIP (FOLLOWER) Before Wal-Mart came to Canada, Zellers was clearly the price leader in discount stores. Other discount stores would price their products similarly to Zellers.[26] A firm that chooses a **price leadership** strategy is either the industry leader or it follows the industry leader by setting the same or similar prices. Usually, firms practise a price leadership strategy when they're in an oligopoly with relatively few producers—such as the Canadian petroleum industry or cellphone industry. In such an industry, it is in the best interest of all firms to minimize price competition for everyone to make a profit. Price leadership strategies are popular, because they provide an acceptable and legal way for firms to agree on prices without ever talking with each other.

> **price leadership (follower)** The firm that sets prices first in an industry; other major firms in the industry follow the leader by staying in line.

Even when there isn't a single industry price leader, firms may adopt a parity pricing strategy—they try to keep their price about equal to key competitors' prices. Gasoline retailers attempt to maintain a parity pricing structure by responding quickly to competitive price moves; consumers often view this rapid response as *price fixing*. Numerous national and provincial investigations of gasoline prices have found no evidence of price fixing, and the petroleum companies are spending millions of dollars educating consumers about the cost structure of gasoline.[27]

PREMIUM PRICING Sometimes firms choose to price their products higher than competitive offerings. While this strategy helps to portray a premium or quality positioning, it also helps firms achieve the competitive effect of market leadership and price stability. IBM computers, for example, are priced 10 percent to 15 percent higher than competitive offerings, in part because IBM's industry leadership allows them to, and it protects the pricing in the industry and enables competitors to compete on price without entering a price war. For similar reasons, Microsoft computer peripherals, such as optical mice, are priced 10 percent to 20 percent higher than competitive products. Coca-Cola is counting on its market leadership position, brand equity, and customer loyalty to support a new premium pricing strategy, pricing Coke products above the competition in an attempt to increase margins and profits.[28]

UMBRELLA PRICING The opposite of premium pricing is umbrella pricing, or pricing below the competition. By using rock-bottom prices on popular CDs, electronics stores such as Future Shop have been able to get shoppers into their stores, where many will buy the high-profit electronics equipment sold by the retailer. **Umbrella pricing** is a strategy of ducking under the competition's price by a standard percentage. Corel Corp., for example, consistently prices its office software suite at least 20 percent below that of Microsoft.

PRICE BUNDLING **Price bundling**, selling two or more goods or services as a single package for one price, can be a pricing strategy or tactic. As a strategy, it is an attempt to pre-empt competition and prevent consumers or customers from entering a discrete purchase decision for the product included with the one intended for purchase. Hewlett Packard bundles computer systems, for example, to include a system unit, a monitor, and a printer. By receiving the monitor or printer "free" with the system unit purchase, Hewlett Packard ends up not competing with Lexmark, Canon, or other computer peripheral manufacturers. Price bundling could also be used to achieve customer satisfaction objectives by including another product of value to customers with their intended purchase. Malaysia Airlines, for example, bundles flights within Malaysia at a discount when international flights are purchased to Kuala Lumpur (Exhibit 9.9). We will discuss the tactical use of price bundling shortly.

umbrella pricing A strategy of ducking under a competitor's price by a fixed percentage.

price bundling Selling two or more goods or services as a single package for one price.

cost of ownership A pricing strategy that considers the lifetime cost of using the product.

Pricing Strategies to Achieve Customer Satisfaction Objectives

When firms develop pricing strategies that cater to the needs of customers, they are less concerned with short-term successes than with keeping customers for the long term. Firms truly dedicated to customer satisfaction look at the wants and needs of customers in developing pricing strategies. Three pricing strategies we have already discussed can be used to achieve customer satisfaction objectives: variable pricing, value pricing, and price bundling. Another strategy to achieve customer satisfaction objectives is to consider total **cost of ownership**. The cost of ownership is the price consumers pay for a product, plus the cost of maintaining and using the product, less its resale (or salvage) value. Sanyo, for example, bases the price of its rechargeable batteries on customer cost-of-ownership—comparing the

Exhibit 9.9

Price bundling often entices customers to spend more initially than if they bought only one product. This strategy is even used by airlines.

cost of using regular batteries to the use of Sanyo's rechargeable ones and setting a price lower than the cost of multiple regular batteries. Kodak recently introduced an inkjet printer, with ink cartridges priced far lower than its competitors—almost 50 percent per page less than the competition (Exhibit 9.10). Other printer manufacturers have sold printers at a low price, making little or no profit—making most of their profits from ink, which is priced at more per ounce than perfume or caviar. Instead, Kodak's pricing strategy is to make a higher profit on the printer, accepting lower profits from the ink. Kodak is hoping that consumers will be willing to pay slightly more for a printer that will cost less in the long run to use.[29]

Pricing Strategies to Achieve Image Enhancement/ Positioning Objectives

There are three common pricing strategies for achieving image enhancement (positioning) objectives. We have already discussed value pricing (everyday low pricing), which is used to support a value positioning strategy, in addition to being a way of increasing market share. We have also already discussed premium pricing as a competitive-effect based strategy, but premium pricing could also be used to support a premium positioning strategy where higher-than-competition pricing is intended to support inferences of higher quality or another basis of superiority. Related to premium pricing is **prestige pricing**, which is pricing products significantly higher than competitive brands to make them status symbols (Exhibit 9.11). Rolex, for example, uses a prestige pricing strategy for its watches, which retail for $5000 to $10 000 (or more!). Prestige pricing is part of an exclusive positioning strategy, where only the very wealthy or privileged can purchase the brand.

PRICE POINTS AND TACTICS

Once marketers have developed pricing strategies, the next step in price planning is to actually set prices by applying pricing tactics and to set the terms and conditions associated with that price. In practice, prices are set in the range determined by the product's costs, what customers are willing to pay, and the price of competitive or substitute products. However as seen in Figure 9.4, there are a number of considerations for setting prices within this range.

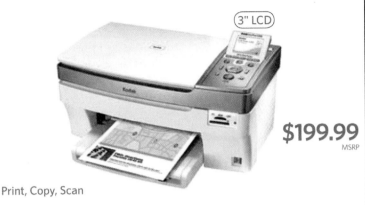

PRINT MORE. PAY LESS.

3" LCD

$199.99
MSRP

Print, Copy, Scan

Kodak EasyShare **5300**
All-in-One Printer

$9.99 MSRP
Black Ink Cartridge

- Save up to 50% on everything you print*
- Uses ultra low-cost ink
- KODAK Quality Photos and Documents

$14.99 MSRP
5-ink Color Cartridge

* Actual results may vary. See kodak.com/go/inkdata for details.
© Kodak, 2007. KODAK, EASYSHARE and KODACOLOR are trademarks of Kodak.

Exhibit 9.10
Kodak bases its pricing on customer needs using a cost-of-ownership strategy.

prestige pricing A strategy where prices are set significantly higher than competing brands.

Exhibit 9.11
Lee Valley Tools uses prestige pricing to support a prestige image among woodworking and gardening hobbyists.

Pricing for individual products
• Two-part pricing
• Payment pricing

Pricing for multiple products
• Price bundling
• Captive pricing

Geographic pricing
• F.O.B. pricing
• Zone pricing
• Uniform delivered pricing
• Freight absorption pricing

Price discounts
• Trade or functional discounts
• Quantity discounts
• Cash discounts
• Seasonal discounts

Psychological pricing
• Odd (even) number pricing
• Price lining

Figure 9.4 Pricing Tactics

Exhibit 9.12

Auto manufacturers know that a per-month price for a new car makes people less sensitive to the total price of the car.

Pricing for Individual Products

How marketers present a product's price to the market can make a big difference in the attractiveness of the offering. Here are two tactics:

• With *two-part pricing*, two separate types of payments are required to purchase the product. For example, golf and tennis clubs charge yearly or monthly fees plus fees for each round of golf or tennis. Cellular phone and Internet service providers offer customers a set number of minutes usage for a monthly fee plus a per-minute rate for extra usage.

• *Payment pricing* makes products appear more attainable by breaking up the total price into smaller amounts payable over time. For example, many customers now opt to lease rather than buy a car. The monthly lease amount is an example of payment pricing, which tends to make people less sensitive to the total price of the car (Exhibit 9.12).[30]

Pricing for Multiple Products

A firm may sell several products that consumers typically buy together. When people buy a burger, pizza, or taco for lunch, they often purchase a drink, fries, or salad as well. Similarly, when someone buys a personal computer, a box of CDs is usually not far behind. We have previously discussed price bundling as a pricing strategy. As a price tactic, price bundling is enhancing the perceived value of a purchase by combining two or more goods or services into a single offer, at a lower price than the individual items. A music buff, for example, can buy tickets to an entire concert series for a lower price than buying tickets to each concert separately. A movie ticket may include a drink and popcorn. Even an all-you-can-eat special at the local diner is an example of price bundling. Price bundling is an increasingly popular pricing tactic for consumer electronics, small and large appliances, and even automobiles, where the tangible product is bundled with an extended warranty package. The tangible product is priced near cost while more significant margins are made on the extended warranty. The thinking behind price bundling as a tactic is that whatever revenue a seller loses from the reduced prices, it makes up in increased total purchases.

CAPTIVE PRICING **Captive pricing** is a tactic a firm uses when it has two products that work only when used together. The firm sells one item at a very low price and then makes its profit on the second high-margin item. Gillette uses captive pricing to sell its shaving products. The Mach3 razor is sold for a relatively low price but the disposable blades sell for $1.50 or more per blade—and the typical user buys 30 blades a year. Although the blade and razor business generates only a third of corporate revenues for Gillette, the company's use of captive pricing tactics in this category delivers two-thirds of its profits (Exhibit 9.13).

Geographic Pricing

Geographic pricing is a tactic that establishes how firms handle the cost of shipping products to customers near, far, and wide. Characteristics of the product, customers, and competition may make it advisable to charge all customers the same price, or it may make better sense to vary the prices charged to customers in different locations, regardless of the overall pricing strategy selected.

F.O.B. PRICING Often, pricing is stated as f.o.b. factory or f.o.b. delivered—f.o.b. stands for *free on board*, which means the supplier will pay to have the product loaded onto a truck or some other carrier. Also—and this is important—title passes to the buyer at the f.o.b. location. Thus, *f.o.b. factory* or **f.o.b. origin** means that the cost of transporting the product from the factory to the customer's location is the responsibility of the customer; **f.o.b. delivered** means that the seller pays both the cost of loading and transporting to the customer, which is included in the selling price.

The f.o.b. origin pricing creates many different prices, because the purchase price for each customer changes with shipping costs. But with f.o.b. delivered pricing, every customer pays the same price. Another option combines f.o.b. origin and f.o.b. delivered—sometimes, a seller's terms indicate that title to the product is transferred at the seller's location, but the seller will pay the freight. This plan is called *f.o.b. factory, freight prepaid*.

Sellers often prefer *f.o.b. factory* pricing because of its simplicity. The marketer doesn't have to take into account the costs of shipping to different customers at varying distances from the factory. It also allows flexibility in how a product gets shipped, because pricing does not depend on a particular shipping method. In addition, the fact that the title is transferred before shipping shifts the risk of damage to the transit company and the customer.

ZONE PRICING Another geographic pricing tactic is **zone pricing**. Like f.o.b. factory pricing, zone pricing means that distant customers pay more than customers who are close to the factory. However, in zone pricing, there are a limited number of different prices charged, based on geographic zones established by the seller. All customers located in each zone pay the same transportation charge.

Zone pricing simplifies geographic cost differences, which is important in certain markets. It would be nearly impossible for Canada Post's Express courier service to charge one price if a package shipped from Winnipeg went to Toronto, a different price if it went to Mississauga, and another if it went to Don Mills, Ontario. Therefore, Express Post charges different rates for shipping packages from any single location to different zones across the country.

UNIFORM DELIVERED PRICING With **uniform delivered pricing**, an average shipping cost is added to the price, no matter what the buyer's location or distance from the manufacturer's plant—within reason. Catalogue sales, home television shopping, e-commerce, and other types of non-store retail sales usually use uniform delivered pricing.

FREIGHT ABSORPTION PRICING **Freight absorption pricing** means the seller takes on part or all of the cost of shipping. This strategy is good for high-ticket items, when the cost of shipping is a negligible part of the sales price and the profit margin. Marketers are most likely to use freight absorption pricing in highly competitive markets or when such pricing allows them to enter new markets.

IT'S NEW. IT'S COOL. IT'S BLUE.

Gillette MACH3
COOL BLUE™

Great close shave. Cool new look.

Gillette
The Best a Man Can Get™

www.MACH3.com   ©2001 The Gillette Company

Exhibit 9.13

Gillette practises captive pricing with its razors. Once customers buy the handles, they are "captive" to the company's blade prices.

captive pricing A pricing tactic for two items that must be used together; one item is priced very low and the firm makes its profit on another, high-margin item essential to the operation of the first item.

f.o.b. origin pricing A pricing tactic in which the cost of transporting the product from the factory to the customer's location is the responsibility of the customer.

f.o.b. delivered pricing A pricing tactic in which the cost of loading and transporting the product to the customer is included in the selling price, paid by the manufacturer.

zone pricing A pricing tactic in which customers in different geographic zones pay different transportation rates.

uniform delivered pricing A pricing tactic in which a firm adds a standard shipping charge to the price for all customers regardless of location.

freight absorption pricing A pricing tactic in which the seller absorbs the total cost of transportation.

Psychological Tactics

Marketers need to take into consideration consumer behaviour when making pricing decisions, and this will be discussed further later in the chapter. As we saw in Chapter 5, part of understanding consumer behaviour is understanding consumer psychology. Two pricing tactics that draw on consumer psychology are odd (even) number pricing, and price lining.

ODD (EVEN) NUMBER PRICING We usually see prices reported in dollars and cents—$1.99, $5.98, $23.67, or even $599.99. Exhibit 9.14 shows this common practice. We see prices in even dollar amounts—$2, $10, or $600—far less often. The reason? Marketers have assumed that there is a psychological response to odd prices that differs from the responses to even prices. Research on the difference in perceptions of odd versus even prices has been inconclusive and has produced no substantive evidence that the use of odd prices is superior to even prices. But that doesn't mean that marketers should change this practice.

At the same time, there are some instances in which even prices are the norm or perhaps even necessary. Theatre and concert tickets, admission to sporting events, and lottery tickets tend to be priced in even amounts, so that ticket sellers don't have to make change. Professional fees are normally expressed as even dollars. If a lawyer charged $99.99 per hour, the client might wonder why he or she has a "bargain-priced" fee and may think less of the quality of the legal advice. Many luxury items such as jewellery, golf course fees, and resort accommodations use even dollar prices to set them apart from less costly substitutes.

PRICE LINING Marketers often apply their understanding of the psychological aspects of pricing in a practice called **price lining**. This means that similar items in a product line sell at different prices, called price points. If you want to buy a personal computer, you will find that most manufacturers have one "stripped-down" model for about $650. Other desktop systems are offered at prices around $999, $1199, $1499, $1799, $1999, and $2500. While consumers can spend much more than $2500 on a desktop computer system, computer manufacturers have found that most consumers are prepared to pay $1500 to $2500 for a system. Rather than competing on price, these manufacturers compete on the features offered at each price point.

Why is price lining a good practice? From the marketer's standpoint, price lining is a way to maximize profits. In theory, a firm would charge each individual customer the highest price that customer was willing to pay. If the most one specific person would be willing to pay is $1499 for a personal computer, then that would be their price. If another person would be willing to pay $1999, that would be their price. But charging each consumer a different price is really not possible. Having a limited number of prices that generally fall at the top of the range customers find acceptable is a more workable alternative. Firms that use price lining assume that demand is inelastic within certain ranges, but that if prices go above that range, demand will become elastic and customers will balk. Figure 9.5 shows an assumed demand curve for a product for

price lining The practice of setting a limited number of different specific prices, called price points, for items in a product line.

list price The price the end customer is expected to pay as determined by the manufacturer.

Exhibit 9.14

Most companies offer prices in odd dollar amounts because they think customers will be more apt to buy.

which price lining is a good strategy. This figure shows price points within price bands for different computers in a manufacturer's product line.

Price Discounts, Terms, and Conditions

Marketers also use price discounts as a tactic in setting prices—both with customers and channel intermediaries—and for customers or distributors to get these discounts, they have to meet certain terms and conditions.

TRADE OR FUNCTIONAL DISCOUNTS Whether a firm sells to businesses or directly to consumers, most pricing structures are built around list prices. A **list price** is set by the manufacturer for the end customer to pay. In pricing for members of the channel, marketers recognize that pricing must ensure that retailers and wholesalers can cover their costs of doing business and make a profit (Exhibit 9.15).

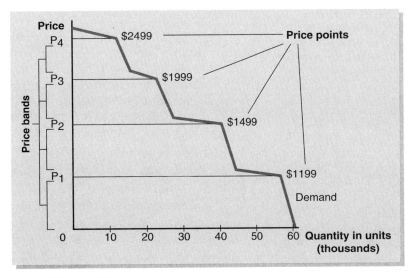

Figure 9.5 Price Lining

Sometimes firms will offer products at standard price levels to match customer expectations.

When manufacturers develop pricing tactics for channel intermediaries, they often use **trade or functional discounts**, because the channel members perform selling, credit, storage, and transportation services that the manufacturer would otherwise have to provide. Often, setting functional discounts is simplified when a firm uses set percentage discounts off the list price for each channel level.

Let's look at an example of a channel of distribution that includes a manufacturer that sells to wholesalers that in turn sell to smaller retailers. The manufacturer may state trade discounts as list price less 40/20. The first number means that 40 percent of the list price is to cover the overhead and profit requirements for the retailer—the manufacturer is suggesting that the wholesalers sell to their retail customers at list less 40 percent. If the list price of a product were $200, the price to the retailers would be:

$$\$200 - (40\% \times 200) = \$200 - \$80 = \$120$$

The second number, the 20, is the discount percentage allowed for wholesalers to cover their costs of doing business and profit. Thus, the manufacturer's selling price to the wholesaler is discounted from the retailer's price and would be:

$$\$120 - (20\% \times 120) = \$120 - \$24 = \$96$$

Note that although we talk about trade discounts being determined by manufacturers, in reality the manufacturer has little if any control over the percentage discounts. In most industries, these are standard percentages based on the margins retailers and wholesalers require to cover their overhead and profits.

QUANTITY DISCOUNTS Firms that sell to distribution channel members or end-user business customers often offer **quantity discounts**, or reduced prices, for purchases of larger quantities. Marketers commonly use quantity discounts as a way to encourage larger purchases from distribution channel partners.

trade or functional discounts Discounts off the list price of products to members of the channel of distribution that perform various marketing functions.

quantity discounts A pricing tactic of charging reduced prices for larger quantities of a product.

Exhibit 9.15

In pricing to retailers, bicycle manufacturers have to consider the amount retailers must have to operate their business and make a profit.

cumulative quantity discounts Discounts based on the total quantity bought within a specified time period.

Sometimes marketers offer buyers **cumulative quantity discounts**, which are based on a total quantity bought within a specified time period, such as a year. Cumulative quantity discounts encourage a buyer to stick with a single seller instead of moving from one supplier to another.

Cumulative quantity discounts may be rebates, in which case the firm sends the buyer a rebate cheque at the end of the discount period. In other cases, the discount is a credit against future orders. In either case, the buyer must wait until the end of the discount period to receive the discount. This delay makes cumulative quantity discounts less attractive, because the buyer must pay the non-discounted price for the goods all year long and not realize the discount until the end of the period. For businesses that operate with low gross margins, this can create some financial hardships.

non-cumulative quantity discounts Discounts based only on the quantity purchased in individual orders.

Non-cumulative quantity discounts are based only on the quantity purchased with each individual order. Non-cumulative discounts encourage larger single orders, but do little to tie the buyer and the seller together. When a competitor makes a better discount offer, the buyer may switch. In most cases, non-cumulative quantity discounts mean that the buyer pays a reduced price for the goods purchased—there is a simple cash discount. In other cases the discount offer is made in terms of free goods. For example, a grocer who buys 10 cases of peanut butter may get one case free.

Sometimes, offering quantity discounts can create problems for the manufacturer. For example, one Canadian publisher developed a four-volume set of encyclopedias, for which it established a pricing structure with steep quantity discounts and a list price of $175 per set. Small, independent bookstores bought the encyclopedias priced at $125 per set, whereas large chain stores purchased in larger quantities at $75 or $80 a set. When the chain stores decided to give up some of their margin to increase sales and sold the sets at $99, below what the small independents paid the publisher, the manufacturer faced some very unhappy "former" customers.

CASH DISCOUNTS Using money costs money, as anyone who's ever taken out a mortgage or a college loan understands. When a firm borrows money, it must pay interest for every day it has the use of the money. Conversely, if a firm has excess cash, it is able to invest that cash and make money from its money. Thus, having cash is an advantage. For this reason many firms try to entice their customers to pay their bills quickly by offering *cash discounts*. For example, a firm selling to a retailer may state that the terms of the sale are "2 percent 10 days, net 30 days." This means that if the retailer pays the producer for the goods within 10 days, the amount due is cut by 2 percent. The total amount is due within 30 days, and after 30 days, the payment is late.

SEASONAL DISCOUNTS Seasonal discounts are price reductions offered during certain times of the year. Products such as snow blowers, lawn mowers, and water skiing equipment are priced in this way. If such products are sold only during a few months of the year, then the manufacturer must either build a large plant that has to be shut down during the off-season or build a large warehouse to store inventory until the season comes around again. Both of these options are unattractive; so to entice retailers and wholesalers to buy off-season and store the product at their locations until the right time of the year, a firm may offer seasonal discounts. Seasonal discounting is also used extensively by tourist attractions and destinations—enticing visitors in slower seasons (Exhibit 9.16).

OTHER TERMS AND CONDITIONS In setting prices, marketers also have to set other terms and conditions. One of these is whether they are going to accept cash only, or also accept credit card, debit card, or other forms of payment. Credit and debit card acceptance makes it more convenient for customers to pay for products, but the credit card companies and banks charge the seller a commission ranging from 1 percent to 4 percent for processing the transaction and

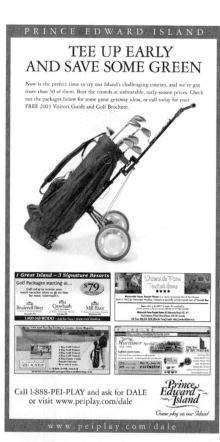

Exhibit 9.16

Tourism PEI, like other destination marketing organizations, promotes seasonal discounts to attract visitors.

guaranteeing payment. Marketers also have to decide what currencies they are willing to accept. Canadian retailers that target tourists, for example, are often willing to accept U.S. dollars, but few are equipped or willing to provide change in U.S. dollars—because of the hassle of keeping two sets of cash registers and currencies stocked and the exchange rate risk of dealing in multiple currencies. Businesses that have a larger international trade find it advantageous to make it as easy as possible for customers to buy and do business in their own currency.

LEGAL AND ETHICAL CONSIDERATIONS IN PRICING

The free enterprise system is founded on the idea that the marketplace will regulate itself. Supplies of goods and services will be made available if there is an adequate profit incentive and prices will rise or fall according to demand. Unfortunately, some business people are greedy and/or unscrupulous. The federal and provincial governments have found it necessary to enact legislation to protect consumers and to protect businesses from predatory rivals.

The Competition Bureau, a unit of Industry Canada, is responsible for ensuring that Canadian businesses (including foreign businesses that operate in Canada) adhere to federal laws that are designed to maintain and encourage fair competition. Most of these laws are found within statutes of the Competition Act, but others are found in the Consumer Packaging and Labelling Act, the Textile Labelling Act, and the Precious Metals Marking Act. The Competition Act was recently amended to enable civil (as well as criminal) action to more quickly and effectively stop unfair, deceptive, or otherwise anti-competitive behaviour. In the next section, we will discuss these behaviours and some of the more important regulations to combat them. A more detailed discussion is available on the Competition Bureau website (**www.competitionbureau.gc.ca**).

SPOTLIGHT ON REAL PEOPLE   Buddy Belt

Like most pet owners, Roxanne Pettipas loved Buddy, her miniature dachshund, and was frustrated every time she took him for a walk and he started to choke on his harness. After searching through many Toronto pet stores, this former art teacher found that none of the pet harnesses on the market were suitable for Buddy. Pettipas decided to invent her own—and Buddy Belt was born. Buddy Belt is a leather harness designed to reduce stress on a pet's neck—its unique design has only one buckle and reduces pressure on a pet's throat or trachea.

Buddy Belt was an idea that came just at the right time. The pet industry in Canada is booming. The current market is estimated to be about $4 billion to $5 billion a year, with more strong growth expected. Canadians are spending a record number of dollars to keep their pets healthy and happy.

Pettipas's company, Class Act Productions Inc., took a slow and deliberate approach to growth. At first, she ran minimal advertising in high-end pet magazines and relied heavily on her website to land business. Although pet owners are buying everything from jewellery to specialty food products for their pets, Class Act has chosen to focus on its core product, Buddy Belt, and a few related leather accessories such as leashes and key chains.

With prices ranging from $50 to $130, Buddy Belt is definitely at the top end of the market. Similar products at big box retailers sell for less than $20. For now, Class Act Productions is relying on its patented design, which uses a special "O-ring" to ensure a custom fit, and its strong brand name in the market to command such premium prices. Buddy Belt is only available online or at high-end boutique retailers.

Now five years old, Class Act expects to sell 20 000 harnesses to about 200 high-end retailers. The company has just begun shipping to Japan and Paris and has its sights set on the lucrative U.S. market. The company has recently doubled its office and factory space to accommodate this anticipated growth.[31]

1. Class Act Productions chose a premium pricing strategy for the Buddy Belt. What are the pros and cons of choosing this pricing strategy?
2. As Class Act Productions continues to expand internationally, what pricing strategy would you recommend for the future?

Exhibit 9.17

Suzy Shier Inc. was recently fined $1 million for misleading price advertising.

Deceptive Pricing Practices

Unscrupulous businesses may attempt to advertise or promote prices in a deceptive way. The Competition Act specifies that sellers cannot make a representation to the public that is false or misleading in a material respect. Thus, a retailer or other supplier must not claim that its prices are lower than a competitor's, unless it is true. Firms cannot promote a going-out-of-business sale unless they are going out of business. Similarly, sellers cannot make false or misleading representation as to the ordinary selling price of a product. For example, a retailer cannot promote a 50 percent–off sale unless it has sold a substantial volume of the product at the "regular" or higher price within a reasonable period of time. An "introductory low price" cannot be promoted unless the price goes up to its "regular" level within a reasonable period of time. What is "reasonable" and "substantial" is a matter for the civil courts to decide. The Canadian Competition Bureau recently fined women's fashion retailer Suzy Shier Inc. $1 million for misleading consumers about how much they were saving on items marked "on sale" (Exhibit 9.17).[32] In another instance, Canada's Competition Bureau ruled that Sears Canada Inc. violated Canada's Competition Act through exaggerated claims of possible savings to consumers in 1999 tire-sale advertising. The Bureau said that Sears Canada "could not have truly believed that its regular tire prices were genuine," as it had sold less than 2 percent of the tires at the regular price before advertising them as on sale.[33]

bait and switch An illegal marketing practice in which an advertised price special is used as bait to get customers into the store with the intention of switching them to a higher-priced item.

Another deceptive pricing practice is the **bait and switch**, a tactic in which a retailer advertises an item at a very low price—the *bait*—to lure customers into the store, does not have reasonable quantities available, and then tries to get customers to buy a different, more expensive, item—the *switch*. They might tell the customer, "The advertised item is really poor quality. It doesn't have important features. There have been a lot of problems with that one. I can tell you're a really smart shopper—you know poor quality when you see it." Simply encouraging consumers to purchase a higher-priced item is an acceptable sales technique—called "trading up"—but it is a civil offence to advertise a lower-priced item when there are not reasonable quantities available. It is not considered "bait-and-switch" when a product is not available because of circumstances beyond the retailer's control or when customers are offered a "rain cheque," a promise to fulfill at a later date, when supplies are replenished.

Other deceptive practices are selling a product at a price above the advertised price and double ticketing, or the selling of a product at a price that exceeds the lowest of two or more prices tagged on, or applied to, a product. Selling at a price above the advertised price is a civil court issue, while double ticketing is a criminal offence.

Predatory Pricing

predatory pricing The strategy of selling products at unreasonably low prices to drive competitors out of business.

Predatory pricing is a strategy of selling products at unreasonably low prices to drive a rival out of the market or substantially reduce competition, then raising prices to recoup the sacrificed returns and earn higher profits. Although predatory pricing is a criminal offence under section 50(1)(c) of the Competition Act, setting prices for the purpose of taking business away from competitors is normal competition. It is very difficult to prove that low prices are "unreasonable" or that an intentional "strategy" is being followed, and few organizations have been charged under this section of the Act.

A low price is not necessarily a predatory price. **Loss-leader pricing**, for example, is a retailer's strategy of offering products below cost to draw consumers into its store. Once in the store, the consumers are expected to buy other items with higher margins. The city of Vancouver, for example, has a reputation for having the lowest CD prices in the world. Stores like A&B Sound and Future Shop compete aggressively with international chains like HMV and Virgin Records. A $12.79 CD brings customers into the stores, where they tend to buy $30 to $40 worth of CDs, and may buy stereo equipment or other electronic products while they are there.[34] In another example, the recent launch of the seventh and final Harry Potter book, *Harry Potter and the Deathly Hallows*, was much anticipated. The sticker price on the book was $45; however, it was discounted deeply by retailers across Canada. The book sold at Costco for $25.99 and through Chapters/Indigo at $24.30. At those prices, retailers were making little if any profit. They used the discounted book to draw consumers into their store, where hopefully they would purchase other higher priced books as well.[35]

loss-leader pricing The pricing strategy of setting prices below cost to attract customers into a store.

Price Discrimination

The Competition Act also prohibits **price discrimination**. Price discrimination is a supplier practice of granting price concessions or other advantages to one purchaser, but not making them available to competing purchasers that are buying articles of like quality and quantity.[36] It applies only to the sale of goods, not leases, licences, or the consignment of goods or the sale of services. Dry cleaners charge more to clean a woman's shirt than a man's shirt. Movie theatres charge students and seniors less than other adults. These practices are not illegal. Price discrimination only applies to competing business purchasers, not end users or consumers, and it does not apply to concessions (such as discounts, rebates, guarantees, or shipping costs) negotiated on a particular transaction. As with the predatory pricing statute, price discrimination, a criminal offence, is difficult to prove. The Consumers Group for Fair Gas Prices, for example, took the case of Porter's Automotive Parts and Service in Foxtrap, Newfoundland, to the Competition Bureau, alleging that the major Canadian gasoline suppliers were selling gas to their own corporate-owned gas stations at a lower price than to the independents. The Competition Bureau found no evidence to support the allegation that gas suppliers had charged Porter's a higher price than another dealer in the area buying a similar volume.[37]

price discrimination The illegal practice of offering the same product of like quality and quantity to different business customers at different prices, thus lessening competition.

Price Maintenance

Price maintenance, or price fixing, occurs when two or more companies conspire to keep prices at a certain level. The Federal Court of Canada imposed a fine of $2.25 million on Chinook Group Limited of Toronto for its participation in an international conspiracy to fix prices and share markets for chlorine chloride, an important additive widely used in the animal feed industry.[38] A criminal offence under section 61 of the Competition Act, price maintenance can take two forms: horizontal and vertical.

price maintenance The collaboration of two or more firms in setting prices, usually to keep prices high.

HORIZONTAL PRICE FIXING *Horizontal price fixing* occurs when competitors making the same product jointly determine what price they will charge. This kind of price fixing keeps prices high by eliminating competition. Canadian courts convicted and fined the head of a Swiss vitamin and fine chemicals company, who conducted conversations with other multinational vitamin-producing companies to fix prices and allocate sales volumes for numerous bulk vitamins and related products.[39] In industries such as the Canadian gasoline industry, in which there are few sellers, there may be no specific price-fixing agreement, but sellers will still charge the same price to "meet the competition." Such parallel pricing is not of itself considered price fixing. There must be an exchange of pricing information between sellers to indicate price-fixing actions. Korean Airlines, South Korea's largest airline, and British Airways were recently fined US$300 million each for fixing prices for passenger and cargo flights.[40]

Ethical Decisions in Marketing

The Competition Act prohibits a company from predatory pricing—selling below cost to drive a competitor out of business. The Competition Bureau (**www.competitionbureau.gc.ca**) expressed concerns when Air Canada purchased Canadian Airlines and ended up with an 80 percent share of the air travel market. There was concern that, as WestJet moved to introduce flights in central and eastern Canada, Air Canada would reduce fares to a point that would drive the competition out.[41] In 2002, the Competition Bureau investigated Air Canada, alleging that Air Canada engaged in predatory pricing in 2000 and 2001 on some eastern Canadian routes in an attempt to drive away discount competition. In general, predatory pricing charges are hard to prove because reducing prices to stimulate business is the very essence of competition. After an investigation, even though the Competition Bureau ruled that Air Canada's fares on the routes in question were less than its operating costs in a bid to prevent WestJet from expanding into eastern Canada, there were no penalties attached to the finding.[42] Should a company have the right to charge whatever it would like for its products—even if it loses money in the short run—if this pricing decision is part of its overall business strategy?

VERTICAL PRICE FIXING Sometimes manufacturers or wholesalers attempt to force retailers to charge a certain price for their product. This is called *vertical price fixing*, a criminal offence under the Competition Act. Retail stores are free to set whatever price they choose without interference or coercion by the manufacturer or wholesaler. Manufacturers and wholesalers can provide a "suggested retail price," but they cannot retaliate against retailers who choose not to follow the suggestion. Manufacturers or wholesalers are free to set prices when they own the retail outlet. The same is true for consignment selling, in which retailers do not actually ever own the product but simply agree to offer it for sale and to accept a percentage of the selling price for their efforts.

BID RIGGING **Bid rigging** is collusion between suppliers responding to a request for bids or tenders, where the suppliers reduce or eliminate competition in the bidding process and trade off opportunities to "win" the business with margins that are higher than would otherwise be attained. This might include: suppliers agreeing to submit token bids that are priced too high; suppliers abstaining from bidding or withdrawing bids; pre-selected suppliers submitting the lowest bid on a systematic or rotating basis; or suppliers not competing in designated geographic regions or for specific customers. These activities are all criminal offences.

bid rigging Collusion between suppliers responding to bid requests to lessen competition and secure higher margins.

MAKING PRICING DECISIONS

Pricing decisions, like product decisions, are interrelated with all other marketing mix decisions and are made with an understanding of the internal and external decision environment. Let's take a look at these relationships.

Marketing Mix Considerations

PRICE AND PRODUCT The price of the product must cover the costs of doing business, but price also sends a *signal* about product quality. For example, the prices of Rolex and Gucci watches, such as the one in Exhibit 9.18, tell consumers much about the products—that they're made from durable, precision parts—and that those who can afford them are probably in an upper-income class. And although experts and the media often try to tell women that most makeup and skin care products have identical ingredients and are pretty much the same, the premium prices charged for certain brands continue to convince consumers that higher price means a better product. Sometimes it does, and sometimes it doesn't.

The stage of the product's life cycle also affects pricing. Early in the life cycle, a single firm may be the only producer of a highly desirable product. This firm is a *monopoly supplier*, so it's able to charge a premium price. Later, as competitors enter the market, prices often go down. For example, Novell Inc. sold Netware 4.0 to business customers. This product, which links up to 1000 PCs into a common network, sold for as much as $48 000 in the early growth phase, but, as the market grew, Microsoft decided to enter with a product similar to Novell's but priced at $35 000 less.[43]

PRICE AND DISTRIBUTION We must study pricing decisions from the viewpoint of each member of the channel of distribution—the manufacturers, wholesalers, and retailers—that help get the product to consumers. Will the pricing plan allow each channel member to be successful in reselling the product to end customers? Is the **margin** a wholesaler or

margin The difference between the cost of the product and the selling price of the product.

retailer earns—the difference between their cost and their selling price—too low to cover their costs?

Manufacturers usually want channel partners to perform marketing, selling, and physical distribution tasks. By taking their costs into account, channel members can figure out the margin they need to operate at a profit; a margin that covers the channel member's shipping costs, inventory costs, customer credit, overhead, and marketing and selling costs. Marketers must take these margins into consideration in deciding on a final selling price for a product. In any case, manufacturers are legally restricted from forcing channel partners to resell a product at a given price, for such control would hamper competition and hurt consumers. So, a pricing plan must appeal to channel partners on its own merits.

Consider the plight of such Canadian magazine wholesalers as Metro News or The News Group, which are intermediaries between publishers and magazine retailers. Traditionally, publishers received 50 percent of the retail price, distributors (which take the magazines from the publishers and deliver them to the wholesalers) 10 percent, and wholesalers 40 percent, which was split evenly with retailers. Retailers, in an attempt to increase their own profitability and combat price discounters, have recently sought relationships with wholesalers outside their sales region and have demanded an additional 4 to 8 percent of the split.[44] To win contracts in this more competitive marketplace, wholesalers have increased their marketing costs, cut prices, and engaged in mergers and acquisitions. They are now seeking better terms from the publishers, who are already facing financial pressures from new media and international competitors. The publishers now need to rethink their channel and pricing strategy.

The relationship between place and price also means that marketers select retail channels that match their product's price and image. For example, a shopper would not expect to find a Rolex watch in Sears or Wal-Mart, nor expect to see Timex watches on display at Birks.

PRICE AND COMMUNICATION Pricing is strongly related to communication activities, if for no other reason than the firm needs to be sure it has enough revenue to pay for its advertising and promotion. It is just as important that the advertising strategies justify the cost of the product. For example, an ad for an expensive fragrance should project luxury, quality, and status imagery to convince shoppers that they are getting "quality" for their money. Even ads for high-end building materials, such as the Corian countertops in Exhibit 9.19, create a luxury appeal through advertising.

PRICE AND RELATIONSHIP MANAGEMENT Pricing is also strongly tied to relationship management. High-priced products often have sufficient margins to support a closer and more responsive relationship with customers. SMED, a Calgary-based builder of office interiors, for example, entertains key clients and prospective clients at a $14-million alpine retreat and takes them salmon fishing in the Queen Charlotte Islands to build relationships and gain client trust.[45] Individualized attention on such a grand scale is not possible when lower margins or purchase volumes result in less profit per customer.

Exhibit 9.18

Gucci knows that its high price means a quality timepiece for many consumers.

Environmental Considerations

THE ECONOMY Economic trends have an important role in directing pricing strategies. The business cycle, inflation, economic growth, and consumer confidence all help to determine whether one pricing strategy or another will succeed. But the upswings and downturns in a national economy do not affect all product categories or all regions equally. In 2007 the strengthening of the Canadian dollar relative to the U.S. dollar made American imports relatively inexpensive but made Canadian exports expensive for American consumers.

The last time you loved something
this much, you married it.

Shown in Glacier White.
Corian® is a DuPont registered trademark.
Only DuPont makes Corian®.

Warm. Expressive. Good-looking. Willing to make a long-term commitment. Highly desirable qualities. Especially in a countertop. Which is why Corian® is compatible with every room in the house. From kitchen to bathroom to bedroom. Of course, it doesn't hurt that it's also stain-resistant, hygienic and easy to clean. After all, you may have kids.

Visit us at www.corian.com or call
1-800-4-CORIAN® (1-800-426-7426)

CORIAN®
DUPONT

Exhibit 9.19

Even for building materials such as Corian countertops, advertising must justify the cost of high-end products.

Marketers need to understand how economic trends will affect their particular business.

During recessions, consumers grow more price sensitive. They switch to generic brands to get a better price and patronize discount stores and warehouse outlets. Even wealthy households, relatively unaffected by recession, tend to cut back on conspicuous consumption, if for no other reason than to avoid attention. As a result, to keep factories in operation during periods of recession, many firms find it necessary to cut prices to levels at which costs are covered but the company doesn't make a profit. Unfortunately, price sensitivity tends to persist for a time even when a recession ends.[46] During such periods, marketers need to consider what pricing strategies will be helpful in regaining pre-recession sales and profit levels.

Recession had an even greater impact on Japanese consumers in the early 1990s. Unlike Canadian consumers, the Japanese were used to paying high prices all the time to satisfy an inefficient, multilayered distribution system. However, the recession opened the door to discount retailing. Specialty retailers bought directly from manufacturers and were able to sell goods at least a third below department stores' prices. The trend has gained momentum, and bargain hunting is becoming a consumer sport in Japan.[47]

Economic trends also influence a firm's ability to increase prices, because they affect what consumers see as an acceptable or unacceptable price range for a product. For example, inflation accustoms consumers to price increases; but they can grow fearful for the future and whether they will have enough money to meet basic needs. In such a case, they may cut back on purchases. Then, as in periods of recession, inflation may cause marketers to lower prices and temporarily sacrifice profits to maintain sales levels. On the other hand, hyperinflation of 30 to 40 percent a month, such as Brazil experienced in the 1990s, causes consumers to spend all their money as fast as they receive it. Pricing is particularly challenging in a hyperinflation environment.

CONSUMERS Another important environmental influence on price is consumer behaviour. Much of what we've said about pricing depends on economists' notions of a customer who evaluates price in a logical, rational manner. For example, the concept of demand is expressed by a smooth demand curve, which assumes that if a firm lowers a product's price from $10 to $9.50 and then from $9.50 to $9 and so on, customers will simply buy more and more. In the real world, though, it doesn't always work that way. Let's look at consumer considerations in setting prices.

Buyers' Pricing Expectations Often consumers base their perceptions of price on what they perceive to be the customary or fair price. For example, for many years a candy bar or a pack of gum was five cents. Consumers would have perceived any other price as too high or low. It was a nickel candy bar—period. When costs went up or inflation kicked in, the candy makers shrank the size of the bar instead of changing the price. Eventually, inflation prevailed and consumers' salaries rose, and the candy bar goes for 15 to 20 times one nickel today—a price that consumers would have found unacceptable even a decade ago.

When the price of a product is above or even sometimes when it's below what consumers expect, they are less willing to purchase the product. If the price is above their expectations, they will perceive it as a rip-off. If it is below expectations, consumers may think the product quality is unsatisfactory. By understanding the pricing expectations of their customers, marketers are better able to develop pricing strategies that meet those expectations.

Exhibit 9.20

Most consumers have an internal reference price when it comes to buying food staples like bread.

Sometimes consumers' perceptions of the customary price of a product depend on their **internal reference price**—based on past experience, consumers have a set price or a price range in their mind that they refer to in evaluating a product's cost. The reference price may be the last price paid, or it may be the average of all the prices they know of similar products (Exhibit 9.20). No matter what the brand, the normal price for a standard loaf of sandwich bread is about $1.49. In some stores it may be $1.39 and in others $1.59, but the average is $1.49. If consumers find a loaf of bread priced much higher than this—perhaps $2.99—they will feel it is overpriced and grab a competing brand. If they find bread priced significantly lower—perhaps $0.59 or $0.69—they may shy away from the purchase, wondering "what is wrong" with the bread.

internal reference price A set price or a price range in consumers' minds that they refer to in evaluating a product's price.

Marketers may try to influence consumers' expectations of what a product should cost by using reference-pricing strategies. For example, manufacturers may show their price compared to competitors' prices in advertising. Similarly, a retailer will display a product next to a higher-priced version of the same or a different brand. The consumer must choose between the two products with different prices. Two quite different results are likely.

On the one hand, if the prices (and other characteristics) of the two products are fairly close, it is likely that the consumer will feel the product quality is similar. This is called an *assimilation effect*. The customer might think, "The price is about the same; they must be alike. I'll be a smart shopper and select the one that saves me a few dollars." And so the customer chooses the item that is priced lower, because the low price made it look attractive next to the high-priced alternative. This is why store brands of deodorant, vitamins, pain relievers, and shampoo sit beside national brands (see Exhibit 9.21), often accompanied by a shelf sign pointing out how much shoppers can save by purchasing the store brands.

On the other hand, if the prices of the two products are far apart, a *contrast effect* may result. In this case the consumer feels that the large difference in price means that there is a large difference in quality. "Gee, this lower-priced one is probably not as good as the higher-priced one. I'll splurge on the more

Exhibit 9.21

Reference pricing strategies: Pharmacists sometimes need to explain why a brand-name drug costs more than a generic drug.

expensive one." Using this strategy, an appliance store may place an advertised $800 refrigerator next to an $1199 model to make the customer believe that the "bottom of the line" model just won't do.

Price-Quality Inferences Imagine that you are in a shoe store looking for a new pair of running shoes. You notice one pair priced at $89.99. On another table you see a second pair displayed. It looks almost identical to the first pair, but the price is only $24.95. Which pair do you want? Which pair do you think is the better quality? Many of us will pay the higher price, because we believe the bargain-basement shoes won't be worth the price—at any price.

Consumers make *price-quality inferences* about a product when they use price as a cue or an indicator for quality. If consumers are unable to judge the quality of a product through examination or prior experience—direct evidence—they will usually assume that the higher-priced product is the higher-quality product.

Does it make sense to believe that a product is better quality just because it has a higher price tag? The answer is: sometimes. In many cases, it is true that a higher-priced product is better. Many of us have bought a bargain-priced pair of sneakers, a private-label brand of cereal, or a less expensive brand of cellophane tape only to be disappointed. These experiences lead rational decision makers to associate price with quality, when quality cannot be otherwise perceived, especially when they have little prior experience in evaluating the item.

THE PRICE ELASTICITY OF DEMAND Marketers also need to know how sensitive customers are to *changes* in price. In particular, it is critical to understand whether a change in price will have a large or a small impact on demand. How much can a firm increase or decrease its price before seeing a marked change in sales? If the price of a pizza goes up $1, will people switch to subs or burgers? What would happen if the price goes up $2? $3? $5? **Price elasticity of demand** is a measure of the sensitivity of customers to changes in price: If the price changes by 10 percent, what will be the percentage change in demand for the product? The word *elasticity* reminds us that changes in price usually cause demand to stretch or retract like a rubber band.

> **price elasticity of demand** The percentage change in unit sales that results from a percentage change in price.

Price elasticity of demand is calculated as follows:

$$\text{Price elasticity of demand} = \frac{\text{percentage change in quantity demanded}}{\text{percentage change in price}} = \frac{(Q_1 - Q_2)/Q_1}{(P_1 - P_2)/P_1}$$

Elastic and Inelastic Demand Sometimes customers are very sensitive to changes in prices, and a change in price results in a substantial change in the quantity demanded. In such cases, demand is said to be **elastic**. In other situations, a change in price has little or no effect on the quantity that consumers are willing to buy, and demand is said to be **inelastic**.

> **price elastic** When a percentage change in price results in a larger percentage change in the quantity demanded.

For example, using the formula above, suppose the pizza maker finds (from experience or from marketing research) that lowering the price of her pizza by 10 percent (from $10 per pie to $9) will cause a 15 percent increase in demand. She would calculate the elasticity of demand as 0.15 divided by 0.10 (or 15 divided by 10). The price elasticity of demand would be 1.5. If the price elasticity of demand is greater than 1, demand is elastic; that is, consumers respond to the price decrease by demanding more. Or, if the price increases, consumers will demand less.

> **price inelastic** When a percentage change in price results in a smaller percentage change in the quantity demanded.

When demand is elastic, changes in price and in total revenues (total sales) work in opposite directions. If the price is increased, revenues decrease. If the price is decreased, there will be an increase in total revenues. With elastic demand, the demand curve shown in Figure 9.6 is more horizontal. For the pizza maker, with an elasticity of demand of 1.5, a decrease in price will increase her total sales.

In some instances, demand is inelastic so that a change in price results in little or no change in demand. For example, if the 10 percent decrease in the price of pizza resulted in only a 5 percent increase in pizza sales, then the price elasticity of demand calculated would be 5 divided by 10, which is 0.5 (less than 1), and our pizza maker faces *inelastic demand*. When demand is inelastic, price and revenue changes are in the same direction; that is, increases in price result in increases in total revenue, whereas decreases in price result in

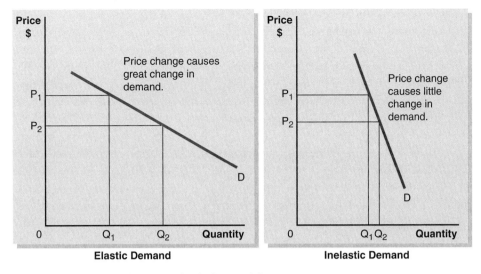

Figure 9.6 Price Elastic and Inelastic Demand Curves

Price elasticity of demand represents how demand responds to changes in prices. If there is little change in demand, then demand is said to be price inelastic. If there is a large change in demand, demand is price elastic.

decreases in total revenue. With inelastic demand, the demand curve shown in Figure 9.6 becomes more vertical. Generally, the demand for necessities is inelastic. Even large price increases do not cause us to buy less food or to give up our telephone.

If demand is price inelastic, can marketers keep raising prices so that revenues and profits will grow larger and larger? And what if demand is elastic? Does it mean that marketers can never raise prices? The answer to these questions is "no." Elasticity of demand for a product often differs for different price levels and with different percentages of change. In the 1950s and 1960s, the price of gasoline was less than 12 cents a litre. There were the rare "gas wars" (see Exhibit 9.22), when the price of gas was less than 9 cents a

Exhibit 9.22

Because demand for gasoline was price elastic, competing service stations fought for valuable customers with low, low prices in the 1960s. Now, gasoline is thought to be inelastic—at least within the range of 70 to 90 cents a litre.

litre. In those years, if the price of gasoline had increased 20 percent or more, demand would have decreased as consumers refused to pay the higher prices and simply stayed home—demand was elastic at the low price. If the price of gasoline dropped 10 cents, many consumers would decide to take more trips, drive across the country and see Victoria, Prince Edward Island, or Niagara Falls. Today, gasoline prices are seldom less than 95 cents a litre, and consumers have become used to changes in gasoline prices of 5 to 10 cents a litre or more. Now a 20 percent price change is a common occurrence, making gasoline demand *price inelastic*.

Influences on Demand Elasticity Other factors can affect price elasticity and sales. Consider the availability of *substitute* goods or services. If a product has a close substitute, its demand will be elastic; that is, a change in price will result in a change in demand, as consumers move to buy the substitute product. For example, Coke and Pepsi may be considered close substitutes by all but the most die-hard cola fans. If the price of Pepsi goes up, many people will buy Coke instead. Marketers of products with close substitutes are less likely to compete on price, recognizing that doing so could result in less profit for everyone as consumers switch from one brand to another.

Price elasticity also depends on the time period marketers are considering. Demand that is inelastic in the short term may become elastic in the long term. In general, the longer the time period, the greater the likelihood that demand will be more elastic. Here again, the role of substitutes matters because longer time periods make it possible for substitutes to enter the market. If the price of oil increases, there may not be much immediate change in the quantity demanded. However, in the long term, demand will build for alternatives for home heating, such as gas, electric, and solar power. Utilities may build more electric power plants, and auto manufacturers will develop viable electric cars and buses, and hybrid cars such as the one shown in Exhibit 9.23.

There is also an *income effect* on demand. This means changes in income affect demand for a product, even if its price remains the same. For *normal goods*, such as clothing and housing, and for luxury goods, demand is income elastic. This means that as income increases, the amount purchased increases. For necessities such as salt, toilet tissue, and toothpaste, demand is income inelastic, because changes in income do not have much impact on demand. Consumers can't do without these products. For some *inferior goods,* as income increases, demand decreases; if, in a period of economic recession, household income decreases, there is likely to be an increase in sales of dried beans, an inexpensive source of protein, whereas the number of steaks consumed goes down. But if the economy improves and incomes rise, consumers will be able to afford and demand steaks instead of beans.

Finally, the changes in prices of *other* products affect the demand for an item, a phenomenon called *cross-elasticity of demand*. When products are substitutes for each other, an increase in the price of one will increase the demand for the other. For example, if the price of bananas goes up, consumers may instead buy more strawberries, blueberries, or apples. However, when products are complements—that is, when one product is essential to the use of a second—then an increase in the price of one decreases the demand for the second. For example, if the price of gasoline goes up, consumers may drive less and, thus, demand for tires will also decrease.

CONSUMER TRENDS Culture and demographics determine how consumers think and behave and so have a large impact on all marketing decisions. Marketers who

Exhibit 9.23

The adoption of hybrid cars or electric cars is an example of how technologies and environmental change may make gasoline prices elastic again.

continuously monitor the consumer environment are in a position to make better pricing decisions. These are some current trends:

- Consumers have grown disinterested in fancy stores with big markups. Grey Advertising agency calls these consumers "precision shoppers." They are more choosy, less inclined to shy away from lesser-known brands, and drawn to warehouse stores that offer inexpensive self-serve products.[48] Marketers of everything from autos to suits are scrambling to find ways to offer value and build bonds with customers who are weary of glitzy promotions and overpriced merchandise.

- Consumers want to be able to afford tokens of success. In the last decade, sales of products such as Lee Valley tools, Calvin Klein fragrances, and BMW cars soared because they offered consumers a unique prestige product image—driving a BMW tells other drivers that "you've made it." Much of the success Starbucks has enjoyed is a result of its gourmet coffee being an "affordable luxury."

- Many of the women who opted for a career in their twenties are hearing the ticking of their biological clocks as they enter their late thirties and early forties. But couples having babies later in their lives are often better off financially than younger parents, and they are far more willing to spend whatever it costs to give their babies the best. For producers of products for babies and children, this means that price resistance is rather low within the group. Such parents have no problem spending $50 or more for a Beatrix Potter musical crib mobile and don't even flinch at the $75 price tag on a Wedgwood china Peter Rabbit cereal bowl and mug.

THE COMPETITION Decision makers must always consider how the competition will respond to their pricing actions. They know that consumers' expectations of what constitutes a fair price depend on what the competition is charging. The Marriott hotel chain, for example, monitors the room rates of Hilton, Hyatt, and other chains.

In the cut-throat fast-food industry, when Burger King trotted out its 99-cent Whopper, McDonald's retaliated with a 55-cent Big Mac (see Exhibit 9.24), and third-place Wendy's increased promotion of its 99-cent chicken nuggets and Double-Stack cheeseburgers.[49] It's not always a good idea to fight the competition with lower and lower prices. Pricing wars, like those in the fast-food industry, can change consumers' perceptions of what is a "fair" price, leaving them unwilling to buy at previous price levels. This will be a challenge in Coke's new premium pricing strategy as years of discounting have conditioned consumers to expect to pay less than $2.99 for a two-litre bottle. In addition, when firms focus on price competition, they often ignore the need to satisfy other customer wants. For instance, many consumers have become dissatisfied with traditional burgers at any price and are looking for restaurants that offer better-tasting meals.

The type of competitive environment in which an industry operates—whether it's an oligopoly, monopolistic competition, or pure competition—also influences price decisions. Generally, firms that do business in an oligopoly, in which the market has few sellers and many buyers, are more likely to adopt *status quo* pricing objectives, in which the pricing of all competitors is similar. Such objectives are attractive to oligopolistic firms because avoiding price competition allows all players in the industry to remain profitable. The Canadian gasoline industry is an oligopoly, in which a few large petroleum refiners, such as Irving Oil, Shell, and Petro-Canada, control most of the market.

Exhibit 9.24

In a price war strategy, McDonald's reduced the Big Mac's price to 55 cents when part of a Meal Deal.

In a state of monopolistic competition, in which there are many sellers each offering a slightly different product, it is possible for firms to differentiate products and to focus on non-price competition. Thrifty Foods, a Vancouver Island grocery chain, for example, faces competition from Canada Safeway, the Real Canadian Superstore (Loblaws), Save-On-Foods, Costco, other warehouse clubs, and other independent food retailers. This level of competition makes it difficult for Thrifty Foods to compete on price. Instead it focuses on being competitively priced with superior quality, choice, service, and retail innovation. To combat consumer perceptions that its prices were higher than others, the company introduced a new tag line, "We never lower our standards—just our prices," and has experienced increased market share despite increased competition from big-box discounters.

Firms in a purely competitive market have little opportunity to raise or lower prices. Rather, the price of soybeans, corn, or fresh peaches is directly influenced by supply and demand. When bad weather hurts crops, prices go up. And prices for almost any kind of fish have increased dramatically since health-conscious consumers began turning away from beef and other red meat.

INTERNATIONAL ENVIRONMENTAL INFLUENCES Different situations influence pricing decisions by firms conducting international trade, including the *currency exchange rate*. Japanese auto sales in Canada soared by 36 percent in 1997, and total Japanese imports doubled.[50] This increase in market share was fuelled by a lower yen and higher U.S. dollar that made North American models more expensive for Canadian consumers.

price subsidies Government payments made to protect domestic businesses or to reimburse them when they must price at or below cost to make a sale. The subsidy can be a cash payment or tax relief.

In international markets, national or local government strategies can lead to differences in the prices competitors charge for products in global markets. Governmental **price subsidies** to domestic industries, in the form of either an outright payment or a tax relief, allow some firms to sell their products at prices often below production costs. Prairie farmers face this situation as low grain prices and U.S. and European subsidies have combined to put Canadian farmers at a severe competitive disadvantage; they are seeking as much as $1 billion in federal and provincial aid to make up for lost revenue.[51] American forest companies claim that Canada's software lumber is unfairly subsidized and have successfully lobbied for import restrictions.[52]

Want to take a luxury cruise? There'll be plenty of room thanks to European taxpayers. Between 1997 and 2000, European shipbuilders built over 30 new cruise ships. Cruise ship prices are low because of European Union government subsidies (up to 9 percent of the price of the vessels) designed to keep ship-building labour on the job.[53]

PRICING WITH ELECTRONIC COMMERCE

As we have seen, pricing for "bricks-and-mortar" firms is a complex decision process. But with the advent of the Internet, a whole new set of options appeared. Many experts suggest that technology is creating a pricing revolution that might change pricing forever—and create the most efficient market ever, some say. Because sellers are connected to buyers around the globe as never before through the Internet, corporate networks, and wireless setups, marketers can offer consumers deals tailored to a single person at a single moment.[54]

For firms that want to sell to other businesses (B2B firms), the Internet means that they can change prices rapidly to adapt to changing costs. For consumers who have lots of stuff in the attic they need to put in someone else's attic (C2C e-commerce), the Internet means an opportunity for consumers to find ready buyers. And for B2C firms, firms that sell to consumers, the Internet offers other opportunities. In this section we will discuss some of the more popular Internet pricing strategies.

Dynamic Pricing Strategies

dynamic pricing Pricing strategy in which the price can easily be adjusted to meet changes in the marketplace.

One of the most important opportunities offered by the Internet is **dynamic pricing**, where the price can easily be adjusted to meet changes in the marketplace (Exhibit 9.25).

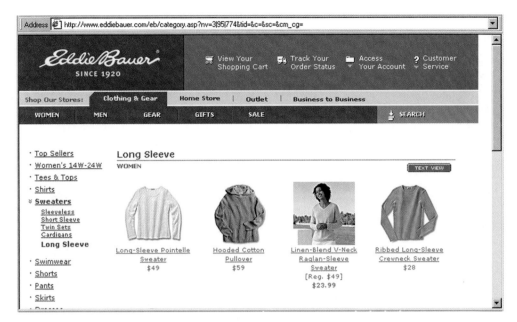

Exhibit 9.25

Online retailers have an advantage over bricks-and-mortar retailers in that they can use dynamic pricing. They can easily and quickly change prices to adjust to supply, demand, and costs.

Posting merchandise for sale on the web means the costs of price changes are negligible. If a retail store wants to change prices, new price tags must be placed on items, new store display signage and media advertising must be created and displayed, and new prices input into the store's computer system. For business-to-business marketers, catalogues and price lists must be printed and distributed to salespeople and to customers. These activities can be very costly to a firm, so firms simply don't change their prices very often. Because the cost of changing prices on the Internet is practically zero, firms are able to respond quickly and, if necessary, frequently, to changes in costs, changes in supply, and/or changes in demand. For example, Tickets.com adjusts concert ticket prices based on supply and demand.

Because it's so easy to change prices on the Internet, firms can test different pricing strategies. For example, if a firm wants to see if a 5 percent increase in price will affect sales, it might try the new pricing strategy on every twentieth customer and then see if the rate of sales decreases among that group of customers. As a result, the company reports it has been able to increase revenue by as much as 45 percent.[55]

AUCTIONS

Hundreds of Internet **online auctions** allow shoppers to bid on everything from Beanie Babies to health and fitness equipment to a Wayne Gretzky hockey stick. Auctions provide a second Internet pricing strategy. Perhaps the most popular auctions are the C2C auctions such as those on eBay. The eBay auction is an open auction, meaning that the buyers all know the highest price bid at any point in time. In many Internet auction sites the seller can set a reserve price, a price below which the item will not be sold.

Many B2B sites offer reverse-price auctions in which buyers ask sellers to submit quotations for a desired product. The supplier with the lowest bid wins the sales. Priceline.com offers customers goods and services in first-price, sealed-bid auctions (Exhibit 9.26). This means that potential buyers may offer a single price to a potential seller of a product (such as an airline ticket). In the case of Priceline.com, bidders guarantee their bids with a credit card. Priceline then checks to see if any airline is willing to sell a ticket for or below the bid price.

online auctions E-commerce that allows shoppers to purchase products through online bidding.

Exhibit 9.26

Priceline.com uses a "first price" auction strategy for airline tickets, hotel rooms, and even cruises. Customers make a bid and Priceline checks to see if any suppliers are willing to sell at that price.

PRICE DISCRIMINATION

For years, some catalogue marketers have sent out more than one catalogue version with different prices based on what they know different customer segments are willing to pay. Customers in one area code may receive a catalogue with prices that are 10 or 15 percent higher on many items than customers who live in a different area code. This practice, called

Real People, Real Decisions

How It Worked Out at TELUS

Leonard Hendricks and his team chose Option 2, the market-based pricing model. TELUS wanted to enter the market with pricing in line with its competitors. This pricing model was chosen to ensure that TELUS would not be seen as too "cheap" (which would compromise the TELUS brand if the product was priced too low) or alternatively that the product would not be priced too high (and customers would not take TELUS's desire to enter this market seriously).

The end result? TELUS ended up winning several large contracts to provide service to ISPs. These contracts provide millions of dollars of profitable revenue a year to TELUS's new non-traditional operating area. Customers experienced few problems because of TELUS's experience. The Dial VPOP product enabled the company to sell additional services to the target market of ISPs.

What lessons has Leonard learned the most in his career? "Underestimating the critical need to communicate your strategy, ideas, plans, and decision rationale. It sounds trite, but you can't over-communicate. In any organization, it is the people that enable your best ideas or plans to succeed.

And, it is people that generally cause them to fail," says Leonard.

What advice does he have for students in preparing for a productive career? Leonard says, "Find things that interest you and pursue them. They may not be directly related to what you are studying, but don't let that stop you. If you are bored or aren't challenged you won't be successful. The thing I enjoy most about the telecommunications industry is the constant change and learning opportunities. Continual learning keeps me challenged, which is the key to enjoying your job." He also says, "Make the time before/during/after school to go to another country and travel (and work). The life experience will help tremendously, and once you start working it is very difficult to get a long period of time to do it."

Finally, do not forget that marketing is everyone's job. It is not the sole domain of the marketing department. A good marketing plan unites the entire business organization. As a marketing strategist, it is your job to champion the customer within your organization and to educate others on the salient points contained within the marketing plan.

price discrimination, is even more easily implemented on the web in situations in which Internet marketers know more about customers who shop on the web and can segment them easily and quickly.

Price discrimination means that marketers classify customers based on some characteristic that indicates what they are willing or able to pay. Movie theatres offer lower prices to children and *Maclean's* magazine offers college students lower subscription rates. The downside is that customers who pay the higher price usually aren't thrilled about this if they find out. When customers found out that Amazon.com was testing prices using a price discrimination strategy, they were outraged. The random price test charged some customers 3 to 5 percent more than other customers for DVD movies. Amazon.com refunded $3.10 each to more than 6000 customers.

Pricing Advantages for Online Shoppers

The Internet also creates unique challenges for marketers in terms of prices. As we've already discussed, consumers and business customers are gaining more control over the buying process. With the availability of search engines and "shopbots" they are less at the mercy of firms handing out prices that they must accept. The result is that customers have become more price sensitive. For example, online drugstores have been stealing customers from traditional pharmacies by offering drastically lower prices: As one illustration, a comparison study found Rogaine priced at $53.99 at Rite Aid while at the same time the same anti-baldness product could be purchased online for $47.39 at More.com.[56] (That's a hair-raising difference!)

Detailed information about what products actually cost manufacturers, available from sites such as **consumerreports.org**, can give consumers more negotiating power when shopping for new cars and other big-ticket items. Finally, e-commerce can potentially lower consumers' costs due to the gasoline, time, and aggravation saved by avoiding a trip to the mall.

CHAPTER SUMMARY

1. **Explain the importance of pricing and how prices can take both monetary and non-monetary forms.**

Price, the amount of outlay of money, goods, services, or deeds given in exchange for a product, can be monetary or non-monetary. Bartering occurs when consumers or businesses exchange one product for another. Pricing is important to firms, because it creates profits and influences customers to purchase. Pricing decisions are tied to decisions about the rest of the marketing mix. Prices must allow channel members to cover their costs and make a profit. Prices vary during stages in the product life cycle. Prices must cover the cost of promotions, and promotions must justify the product price.

2. **Understand the pricing objectives that marketers typically have in planning pricing strategies.**

Effective pricing objectives are designed to support corporate and marketing objectives and often focus on sales (to maximize sales or to increase market share), or they may specify a desired level of profit growth or profit margin. At other times, firms may develop pricing objectives for competitive effect, to increase customer satisfaction, or to communicate a certain image to prospective customers. Pricing objectives need to be flexible to adapt to different geographic areas and time periods.

3. **Understand the pricing policies used to achieve different pricing objectives.**

The most commonly used pricing policies are based on cost. Though easy to calculate and "safe," cost-based strategies do not consider demand, the competition, the stage in the product life cycle, plant capacity, or product image. Cost-based strategies include cost-plus pricing—markup on cost or markup on selling price—and price-floor pricing, and these help organizations achieve profit or target return objectives.

Key Terms

- bait and switch, p. 316
- bartering, p. 295
- bid rigging, p. 318
- break-even analysis, p. 337
- captive pricing, p. 311
- competitive effect objective, p. 298
- contribution margin, p. 337
- cost of ownership, p. 308
- cost-plus pricing, p. 300
- cumulative quantity discounts, p. 314
- customer satisfaction objective, p. 298
- demand-based pricing, p. 302
- demand curve, p. 302
- dynamic pricing, p. 326
- experimental pricing, p. 305
- fixed costs, p. 301
- f.o.b. delivered pricing, p. 311
- f.o.b. origin pricing, p. 311
- freight absorption pricing, p. 311

Pricing strategies based on demand require that marketers estimate demand at different prices to be certain they can sell what they produce. Such strategies include target cost pricing, which starts with the desired price and then the product (and its costs) is designed to meet that price. Yield management sets different prices for different market segments, based on their willingness and ability to pay. Variable (custom) pricing is when prices are negotiated on a customer-by-customer basis. Skimming strategy attempts to maximize profits by charging a high price for new products.

Strategies to achieve market share objectives include value pricing (everyday low pricing), frequent discounting, penetration pricing (for new products), and trial pricing (for new products). All these strategies involve low prices to stimulate demand. Firms that focus on customer needs in developing pricing strategies may consider everyday low price (EDLP) or value pricing strategies. If a new product has unique customer benefits and demand is inelastic, a firm can charge a high skimming price to recover research, development, and promotional costs. If the firm needs to encourage more customers and discourage competitors from entering the market, it may use a very low penetration price. Trial pricing means setting a low price for a limited time.

Strategies to achieve competitive objectives include a price leader strategy, often used in an oligopoly where it is best for all to avoid competition. In parity pricing, a firm sets the same price as competitors. Finally, strategies to achieve image enhancement or positioning objectives include premium pricing and prestige pricing.

4. Apply pricing tactics to set price points.

There are numerous tactics marketers use in setting prices. These include two-part pricing, where individual products like cellphones have an initial cost and a usage cost (time). Pricing for multiple products includes price bundling (selling two or more products together for one price) and captive pricing, where there is a base price plus ongoing supply or operating costs—such as with a printer and toner or ink. Geographic pricing takes into account different tactics for charging for delivery costs. Price discounts are the trade, quantity, cash, and seasonal discounting tactics used to stimulate demand from customers and distributors. Psychological pricing tactics include odd (even) number pricing and price lining—the tactic of having a standard range of prices for a product line, such as found for televisions and computers.

5. Understand key implementation and legal issues with respect to pricing.

Most marketers seek to avoid unethical or illegal pricing practices. Deceptive pricing practices include illegal bait-and-switch pricing and superficial discounting. The federal Competition Act prohibits predatory pricing, price discrimination, horizontal or vertical price maintenance, and bid rigging.

6. Understand some of the environmental factors that affect pricing strategies, including the Internet.

Like other elements of the marketing mix, pricing is influenced by a variety of internal and external environmental factors. External factors include economic trends, such as inflation and recession, and the firm's competitive environment, such as the number and size of competing firms. Pricing can also be influenced by consumer behaviour and changing consumer trends, and by differences in international market environments. Internal environment considerations include product costs and other elements of the marketing mix. The Internet provides opportunities for dynamic pricing, auctions, and price discrimination, but creates challenges for marketers in that customers have easy access to competitor prices.

CHAPTER REVIEW

Marketing Concepts: Testing Your Knowledge

1. Explain how pricing decisions are important to firms.
2. Explain variable costs, fixed costs, average variable costs, average fixed costs, and average total costs.
3. What is break-even analysis? How do marketers use break-even analysis?

4. What are some common pricing objectives and strategies to achieve them?

5. What are the advantages and disadvantages of pricing strategies based on demand? Explain yield management.

6. For new products, when is skimming pricing more appropriate and when is penetration pricing the best strategy? When would trial pricing be an effective pricing strategy?

7. Explain key pricing tactics used by marketers and when they would be appropriate.

8. Explain these unethical or illegal pricing practices: bait and switch; predatory pricing; price discrimination; price maintenance; bid rigging.

9. How are pricing decisions interrelated with other elements of the marketing mix?

10. What are some ways in which external environmental factors affect price planning?

11. Why do marketers use trade or functional discounts, quantity discounts, cash discounts, and seasonal discounts in pricing to members of the channel? What is dynamic pricing? Why does the Internet encourage the use of dynamic pricing?

12. Explain these psychological aspects of pricing: price–quality inferences, odd–even pricing, internal reference price, and price lining.

13. What is price elasticity and what external influences affect demand elasticity?

14. What are the pricing implications of the Internet?

Marketing Concepts: Discussing Choices and Issues

1. Governments sometimes provide price subsidies to specific industries; that is, they reduce a domestic firm's costs so that they can sell products on the international market at a lower price. What reasons do governments (and politicians) use for these government subsidies? What are the benefits and disadvantages to domestic industries in the long run? How about to international customers? Who would benefit or lose if all price subsidies were eliminated?

2. Critics of business often accuse marketers of taking advantage of consumers by setting prices that are far above the cost of producing the good or service—sometimes 10 or 20 or more times the cost. How do you feel about this? What reasons might a manufacturer of luxury products have for setting very high prices? Why might a pharmaceutical firm set the prices of its life-saving medicines higher than the cost of production requires?

3. With a price leadership strategy, firms can avoid price competition and yet not be guilty of illegal collusion—getting together to set prices. Although it is legal, is a price leadership strategy ethical? How does a price leadership strategy hurt and how does it help the industry? What benefits does it provide and what problems does it pose for customers?

4. Everyday low pricing strategies have met with limited success. What do you think are the advantages and disadvantages of EDLP? Are some products more suited to it than others? Why have customers not been more responsive to EDLP? What do you think its future will be?

5. Two-part pricing and payment pricing are pricing tactics that are designed to make price more palatable to customers and to better meet their needs. But do these policies always benefit consumers? What are the advantages and disadvantages of these pricing approaches for the average consumer? For business customers?

6. Technology is said to be creating a pricing revolution. How is electronic commerce changing pricing strategies? In what ways are such changes good for customers? In what ways are the changes good for sellers?

7. In pricing new products, marketers may choose a skimming or a penetration pricing strategy. While it's easy to see the benefits of these practices for the firm, what is the advantage or disadvantage of the practice for consumers? For the industry as a whole?

Marketing Practice: Applying What You've Learned

1. Assume that you are the director of marketing for a large Rocky Mountain ski resort. It is essential that the resort maintain a high occupancy rate during the skiing season. Pricing is an important part of your marketing strategy, because the demand for rooms at your resort is very price elastic. For this reason, you feel that you should develop contingency pricing plans for use during changes in the economic environment (inflation and recessions, for example).

List the economic conditions that might warrant changes in the pricing strategy, and give your recommendations for each possibility.

2. Assume that you are the assistant director of marketing for a firm that manufactures a line of hair-care products (e.g., shampoos, conditioners). This morning, your boss came into your office and announced that she is going to recommend a dramatic price increase. You respond by saying, "Well, I guess that means we need to totally revamp our marketing plan." To this, she replies, "No, all we're going to do is raise the price. We're not going to mess with anything else." After she leaves you think, "I've got to convince her that we can't make pricing decisions without considering the other elements of the marketing mix. It's all interrelated."

   In a role-playing situation with one of your classmates, explain to your boss why you think the marketing department should consider the implications of the price increase on the other marketing mix elements, what you feel these implications are, and what recommendations for change might be suggested.

3. As the vice-president for marketing in a firm that markets computer software, you must regularly develop pricing strategies for new software products. Your latest product is a software package that automatically translates any foreign-language e-mail messages into the user's preferred language. You are trying to decide on the pricing for this new product. Should you use a skimming price, a penetration price, or something in between? With a classmate taking the role of another marketing professional with your firm, argue in front of your class the pros and cons of each alternative.

4. Assume that you are working in the marketing department of a firm that manufactures furnaces and air conditioners. Previously, your firm has limited its operations to manufacturing units for other OEM companies. Now your firm is expanding. You will be manufacturing your product for sale with your own brand name and will be selling to heating and air-conditioning distributors across the country. What pricing objectives, strategies, and tactics will you adopt?

5. Assume that you and your friend have decided to go into business together manufacturing wrought-iron birdcages. You know that your fixed costs (rent on a building, equipment, for example) will be $60 000 a year. You expect your variable costs to be $12 per birdcage.

   a. If you plan on selling the birdcages to retail stores for $18, how many must you sell to break even; that is, what is your break-even quantity?

   b. Assume that you and your partner feel that you must set a goal of achieving $10 000 profit with your business this year. How many units would you have to sell to make that amount of profit?

   c. What if you feel that you will be able to sell no more than 5000 birdcages? What price will you have to charge to break even? To make $10 000 in profit?

Marketing Mini-Project: Learning by Doing

Organizations develop pricing strategies to meet pricing objectives. These objectives may be related to sales, profit, the competition, customer satisfaction, or the image of the product. The purpose of this mini-project is to help you understand how different pricing objectives are important in marketing planning.

Many universities are having trouble filling up their existing dormitory space, as more and more students choose to live off campus in houses or in apartments. Identify your university's existing pricing objectives and develop recommendations for changes.

1. First, with two or three of your classmates, interview someone who participates in your university's pricing of dormitory space. It may be the vice-president for student affairs, the dean of students, the director of student life, or the vice-president for business and finance. Try to find out:

   a. The current prices charged for dormitory space.

   b. What the pricing objectives for dormitory space are.

   c. How the prices are calculated.

   d. The part that costs, demand, customer satisfaction, and competitive housing prices play in setting the dorm prices.

2. Next talk with students in your school to find out:

   a. Students' attitudes toward the prices charged for dormitory space.

   b. What a customer-pleasing price would be for dormitory space.

   c. The type and price of alternative housing used by students.

   d. Any other relevant student attitudes toward dormitory housing.

3. Develop a report that includes your findings and the recommendations you would make to your university. Be sure to focus on the pricing objectives currently in use and the alternative objectives that might be considered. What pricing strategies do your findings suggest? Present your results to your class.

Real People, Real Surfers: Exploring the Web

Barter exchanges are organizations that facilitate barter transactions between buyers and sellers. Many of the Canadian exchanges are members of the International Reciprocal Trade Association (IRTA) or the American National Association of Trade Exchanges (NATE).

First, visit the IRTA (**www.irta.com**) or NATE (**www.nate.org**) webpages. Using links from those homepages to member exchanges or using an Internet search engine, locate and explore several barter exchange webpages. Based on your Internet experience, answer the following questions.

1. What are the benefits to a business of joining a barter exchange?

2. What types of products are bartered?

3. How does a trade actually work with a barter exchange?

4. How does the exchange make its money? Who pays the exchange, and how much is charged?

5. Assuming the goal of barter exchange websites is to attract new members, evaluate the different websites you visited. Which website do you think was best? What features of the site would make you want to join if you were the owner of a small business? What features of the other sites made them less appealing than this one?

Visit the MyMarketingLab website at **www.pearsoned.ca/mymarketinglab**. This online homework and tutorial system puts you in control of your own learning with study and practice tools directly correlated to this chapter's content.

Would you pay $265–$300 for a pair of jeans? You'd be surprised how many people will. "People are willing to pay a lot of money if the jeans look good because it's like a bathing suit," explains Erica Yeu, a buyer for Contemporary Casual at Holt Renfrew. She goes on to say, "Once you find the right one, you're willing to pay a bit more just to get that perfect jean." True Religion truly exemplifies the power of premium high-fashion clothing and, specifically, the demand for stylish jeans at any price.

True Religion is a company that began operations in 2001 selling high-fashion jeans priced from $265 per pair to a whopping $650 or more per pair. Since then, the company has racked up some very impressive growth, with sales now topping $100 million annually. In addition, True Religion's earnings have grown by an average of over 900 percent in the most recent three quarters. Clearly, selling jeans at $265 and up is a very lucrative business.

To understand the meteoric success of True Religion Jeans, start by considering its marketing strategy. First, True Religion Jeans targets the market of people willing to pay a premium price for the *prestige factor* inherent in its brand. The prestige comes largely from celebrities who wear the jeans—something like "prestige by association." As with the Kingsley brand of baby clothes, which got a big boost in buzz when Brad Pitt and Angelina Jolie's daughter was photographed wearing them, True Religion has benefited from stars Jessica Simpson, Eva Longoria, Jessica Alba, and Katie Holmes wearing its jeans. While the demand for blue jeans in general is price elastic, the primo publicity True Religion Jeans gets from top movie or television stars acts to reduce price elasticity and inspire people to go to extreme lengths to buy a pair.

Despite all the early success of True Religion Jeans, you have to wonder just how long it can last. The market for high-fashion jeans at a premium price is fairly limited. How many people out there are willing to do something as drastic as get a part-time job just to afford a pair? Some consumers admit that they have trouble affording other items they need to purchase (like food, for example) after buying the jeans. It's likely that in the long run, True Religion can't count on consumers like this to keep building the business. Instead, the company will probably have to rely on high-income consumers as its primary market. This strategy is risky because these consumers tend to be far more fashion and trend conscious than they are brand loyal. Eventually the stars wearing these jeans will move on to some other fashion statement, taking with them much of True Religion's fickle consumer base. Perhaps a different item of clothing or designer will usurp True Religion's popularity in the near future. Currently, other stars like Angelina Jolie and Lindsay Lohan are making J Brand pants the "in" pair to wear, too. If this continues, what will be True Religion's next move?

A real problem for companies selling prestige-priced fashion clothing is that when the clothing goes out of style, it's often sold on websites like eBay or other discount clothiers like **overstock.com**. It's hard to charge premium prices in those venues! To date, True Religion has spent an enormous amount of time, effort, and money cultivating relationships with the owners of high-end fashion stores and boutiques as retail partners for its product. The value of those relationships will instantly evaporate once the jeans become available on discount websites.

For now, True Religion seems to be banking on a group of consumers who want their clothes to scream "I have money" or "I am somebody." How can the company build on that consumer sentiment with a future approach to pricing that ensures long-term success for the brand?

Sources: Lisa Schmeiser, "How true religion got to blue jeans heaven: Upscale jeans maker focuses on quality and savvy salesmanship," *Investors Business Daily*, 12 December 2005: A10; Megan Molitor, "Label hunting," *Kansas State Collegian*, 20 January 2006; Stephanie McGrath, "True blue: The jean craze has infected everybody, from celeb 'It Girls' to your average janes," *The Toronto Sun*, 26 February 2006: S10.

Things to Think About

1. What is the decision facing True Religion?

2. What factors are important in understanding this decision situation?

3. What are the alternatives?

4. What decision(s) do you recommend?

5. What are some ways to implement your recommendation?

To develop marketing strategies to meet the goals of an organization effectively and efficiently, it is essential that marketers understand and use a variety of financial analyses and costs. This Appendix provides an overview of how marketers view costs as well as an overview of basic financial analysis.

A MARKETER'S VIEW OF COSTS

It is very important for marketers to understand the profit model and how marketers view costs. If you have taken an accounting course, you are likely familiar with the calculation for net income shown in Figure 9A.1. Marketers look at the financial world a bit differently to make marketing decisions (Figure 9A.1). Marketers split the cost of goods sold (i.e., the total cost to make and sell the products that have been sold by an organization in a particular time period) into two components: fixed costs and variable costs.

Fixed costs are the costs incurred to make and sell the first unit of a product. They do *not* vary with the number of units produced and they have to be paid up front, even if the organization does not sell any of the units produced. Fixed costs include rent, plant and equipment, utilities and overhead, advertising and other marketing communication expenses, the salaries of a firm's executives, managers, and employees, and any other costs that have to be paid up front and do not change with the level of production.

Variable costs are the costs that change depending on the number of units produced. That is, they are the costs involved in making and selling one more unit of a product (other than the first). Variable costs for a manufacturer of bookcases like Palliser Furniture, for example, would include construction materials such as wood, nails, and glue; finishing materials like paint or varnish; packaging (boxes, shrinkwrap, etc); piecework labour (wages paid by the number of pieces finished or hourly wages allocated to the number of units produced); shipping; and sales commission (wages paid to sales staff based on the number of units sold).

In reality, calculating variable costs is often quite complex. For example, as the number of bookcases a factory produces increases or decreases, the variable costs may change. If the company buys just enough lumber for one bookcase, the lumberyard will charge top dollar. If it buys enough for 100 bookcases, it will get a better deal. And if it buys enough for thousands of bookcases, it may cut variable costs even more. Even the cost of labour goes down with increased production, as manufacturers are likely to invest in labour-saving equipment that allows workers to produce bookcases faster. At some point diseconomies of scale will be reached, and using the bookcase example, the demand for the labour, lumber, or nails required to produce the bookcases may exceed the supply, causing the average cost per bookcase to rise. Because variable costs are related to the number of units produced, marketers often use the average variable cost across a production range, or they use sensitivity analysis to calculate financial impacts of different production level scenarios.

Marketers split these costs up to make pricing decisions. At a minimum, the price charged must cover the variable costs—otherwise the company loses money on each transaction. The difference between the price charged by a manufacturer and its variable costs is its **contribution margin (CM)**. It is called a contribution margin because these funds, in excess of the variable costs, contribute to paying off the fixed costs incurred up front. The contribution margin for each unit sold times the number of units sold is the **total contribution** received by the organization. The total contribution less fixed costs is net profit before tax. Marketers know that they have to cover all their fixed costs to stay in business. As we will see below, marketers sometimes use the concept of **total unit cost** (variable costs plus average fixed costs per unit) to ensure that prices cover all the costs incurred.

Accounting View	Marketing View
Sales Revenue – Costs of Goods = Gross Margin	Sales Revenue – Variable Costs = Contribution Margin per Unit
Gross Margin – Operating Expenses = Net Income Before Taxes (Operating Income)	Contribution Margin × Units Sold = Total Contribution Margin
	Total Contribution Margin – Fixed Costs = Net Income Before Taxes (Operating Income)

Figure 9A.1 Marketing Versus Accounting Views of Costs

BREAK-EVEN ANALYSIS

Break-even analysis is a technique marketers use to examine the relationship between cost and price and to determine what sales volume must be reached at a given price before the company breaks even. The break-even point is the point at which the company doesn't lose any money and doesn't make any profit; all costs are covered, but there isn't a penny extra. A break-even analysis allows marketers to identify how many units of a product they will have to sell at a given price to begin to be profitable.

Figure 9A.2 demonstrates break-even analysis for a bookcase manufacturer like Palliser. The vertical axis represents the amount of costs and revenue in dollars, and the horizontal axis shows the quantity of goods produced and sold. In this break-even model, we assume that there is a given total fixed cost and that variable costs do not change with the quantity produced.

In this example, the total fixed costs (for the factory, the equipment, and electricity) are $200 000, and the average variable costs (for materials and labour) are constant. The figure shows the total costs (variable costs plus fixed costs) and total revenues if varying quantities are produced and sold. The point at which the total revenue and total costs lines intersect is the *break-even point*. If sales are above the break-even point, the company makes a profit. Below that point, the firm suffers a loss.

To determine the break-even point, the firm first needs to calculate the *contribution per unit,* or the difference between the price the firm charges for a product

contribution margin (CM)   The price an organization receives less its variable costs.

total contribution   Contribution margin multiplied by the number of units sold.

total unit cost   Variable costs plus average fixed costs per unit.

break-even analysis   A method for determining the number of units that a firm must produce and sell at a given price to cover all its costs.

(the revenue per unit) and the variable costs. This *contribution margin* is the amount the firm has after paying for the wood, nails, paint, and labour to contribute to meeting the fixed costs of production. For our example, assuming that the firm sells its bookcases for $100 each and that variable costs are $50 per unit, contribution per unit is $100 − $50 = $50. Using the fixed cost for the bookcase manufacturing of $200 000, we can now calculate the firm's break-even point in units of the product.

$$\text{Break-even point (in units)} = \frac{\text{total fixed cost}}{\text{contribution per unit to fixed costs}}$$

$$\text{Break-even point (in units)} = \frac{\$200\,000}{\$50} = 4000 \text{ units}$$

Thus, the firm must sell 4000 bookcases at $100 each to meet its fixed costs and to break even. In a similar way, we can calculate the break-even point in dollars. This shows us that to break even, the company must sell $400 000 worth of bookcases.

$$\text{Break-even point (in dollars)} = \frac{\text{total fixed cost}}{1 - \dfrac{\text{variable cost per unit}}{\text{price}}}$$

$$\text{Break-even point (in dollars)} = \frac{\$200\,000}{1 - \dfrac{\$50}{\$100}} = \frac{\$20\,000}{1 - 0.5}$$

$$= \frac{\$20\,0000}{0.5} = \$400\,000$$

Now that we understand the profit model and how marketers view costs, we can discuss how marketers determine or set pricing objectives, strategies, price points, and terms and conditions.

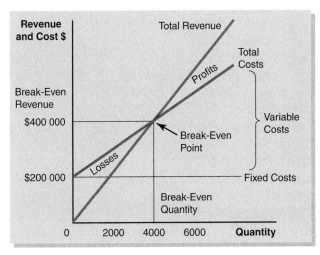

Figure 9A.2 Break-Even Analysis

Using break-even analysis, marketers can determine what sales volume to reach before the company makes a profit. This company needs to sell 4000 bookcases at $100 each to break even.

Using Break-Even Analysis to Set Price Objectives

Marketers who seek to achieve a target level of profit or target return on investment use the concept of break-even analysis in setting specific price objectives. Often a firm will set a *profit goal*, which is the dollar profit figure it desires to earn. The "break-even" point may be calculated with that dollar goal added to the fixed costs. This is not really a break-even point because it includes profits; but by adding the desired profit to fixed costs in the break-even equation, marketers can determine how many units would need to be sold at a particular contribution margin (price − variable costs) to achieve that level of profit. For example, if the bookcase manufacturer feels it is necessary to realize a profit of $50 000, the firm's calculations would be as follows:

$$\text{Break-even point (in units with target amount included)} = \frac{\text{total fixed cost} + \text{target profit}}{\text{contribution per unit to fixed costs}}$$

$$\text{Break-even point (in units)} = \frac{\$200\,000 + \$50\,000}{\$50}$$

$$= 5000 \text{ units}$$

Sometimes the target return or profit goal is expressed as a *percentage of sales*. For example, a firm may say that it wants to make a profit of at least 10 percent on sales. In such cases, this profit is added to the variable cost in calculating the break-even point. In our example, the company wants to earn 10 percent of the selling price of the bookcase, or 10% × $100 = $10 per unit. We add this $10 to the variable costs of $50 and calculate the new target amount as we calculated the break-even point before. The contribution per unit becomes:

$$\text{Contribution per unit} = \text{selling price} - (\text{variable costs} + \text{target profit})$$

$$= \$100 - (\$50 + \$10) = \$40$$

$$\text{Break-even point (in units)} = \frac{\text{total fixed cost}}{\text{contribution per unit to fixed costs}}$$

$$\text{Break-even point (in units)} = \frac{\$200\,000}{\$40} = 5000 \text{ units}$$

Marketers who want to maximize profits sometimes use a technique called **marginal analysis**, where demand is forecast at different price levels and the profit expected in each price–demand scenario is calculated. Although the procedure is straightforward, it is often diffi-cult to develop sufficiently accurate forecasts, and variable costs can fluctuate with shortages, inclement weather, and other uncontrollable events.

COST-PLUS PRICING

As discussed earlier in this chapter, the most common cost-based approach to pricing a product is cost-plus pricing, in which a marketer totals the unit cost for the product and then adds an amount to cover desired profit. The first step requires that the unit cost be estimated reasonably well and that the level of output does not change much. For this and the other examples, we will consider how a small manufacturer and a retailer price a line of jeans. As Table 9A.1 shows, we will assume that the jeans manufacturer has a fixed cost of $2 000 000 to make 400 000 pairs of jeans, or $5 per pair. Variable costs for the jeans are $20 per pair, making the total cost $25 per pair.

The second step is to calculate the markup. There are two methods for calculating the markup percentage: markup on cost and the more popular markup on selling price. In *markup on cost pricing*, just as the name implies, a percentage of the cost is added to the cost to determine the selling price.

Markup on cost: For markup on cost, the calculation is:

$$\text{Price} = \text{total cost} + (\text{total cost} \times \text{markup percentage})$$

In our jeans example, if the manufacturer wants a profit of $2 000 000, what markup percentage would it use? The $2 000 000 is 20 percent of the $10 million total cost. To find the price, the calculation would be:

$$\text{Price} = \$25 + (\$25 \times 0.20) = \$25 + \$5 = \$30$$

(Note that in the calculations, the markup percentage is expressed as a decimal; that is, 20% = 0.20.)

Markup on selling price: As we noted, sometimes firms use a different calculation method—markup on selling price. Wholesalers and retailers more frequently use markup on selling price in pricing their products because the markup percentage becomes the seller's gross margin. For example, if a retailer knows it needs a 40 percent margin to cover overhead and profits, the retailer will calculate its price as a 40 percent markup on selling price.

Let's say a retailer buys the jeans from the manufacturer for $30 per pair. If the retailer requires a 40 percent markup on selling price, we would calculate the retailer's price as follows.

$$\text{Price} = \frac{\text{cost}}{1 - \text{markup percentage}}$$

As we see in Table 9A.1, the price of jeans with the markup on selling price is $50.00.

Table 9A.1 Markup on Cost: An Example for a Jeans Manufacturer

marginal analysis A method that uses costs and demand to identify the price that will maximize profits.

Fixed Costs

Management and other non-production-related salaries	$750 000
Rent	600 000
Insurance	50 000
Depreciation on equipment	70 000
Supplies	30 000
Advertising	500 000
Total fixed costs	$2 000 000
Number of units (pairs of jeans) produced	400 000
Fixed costs per unit	$5.00

Variable Costs

Cost of materials (fabric, zipper, thread, etc.)	$7.00
Cost of production labour	10.00
Cost of utilities and supplies used in production process	3.00
Variable cost per unit (pair of jeans)	$20.00
Total cost (fixed cost per unit plus variable cost per unit)	$25.00

Markup on Cost

Formula: Price = total cost + (total cost × markup percentage)

Price = $25.00 + ($25.00 × 0.20) = $25.00 + $5.00 = $30.00

Just to compare the difference in the final prices of the two markup methods, Table 9A.2 also shows what would happen if the retailer uses a markup on cost method. Using the same product cost and price with a 40 percent markup on cost would yield $42, a much lower price. The markup on selling price gives you the percentage of the selling price represented by the markup ($20 is 40 percent of the selling price of $50). The markup on cost gives you the percentage of the cost represented by the markup ($12 is 40 percent of the cost of $42). But what happens when costs go up? Do marketers increase their prices? If they do, consumers are likely to rebel. One solution is to keep the price constant but provide a bit less of the product. Frito-Lay, maker of salty snack foods, offset increasing production costs by cutting the contents by 6.7 to 7.5 percent per bag of Fritos, Cheetos, and potato chips.[57] To keep consumers from complaining that packages aren't full, a company may make the package ever-so-slightly smaller. In a similar move, Procter & Gamble once reduced the number of disposable diapers in its Luvs and Pampers packages by an average of 13 percent. Let the buyer beware!

BASIC FINANCIAL ANALYSIS

To develop marketing strategies to meet the goals of an organization effectively and efficiently, it is essential that marketers understand and use a variety of financial analyses. This section of the Appendix provides some of these basic financial analyses, including a review of the income statement and balance sheet as well as some basic performance ratios. In addition, this section includes an explanation of some of the specific calculations that marketers use routinely in determining price.

Table 9A.2 Markup on Cost and Markup on Selling Price: An Example of a Retailer's Pricing

Markup on Selling Price		Markup on Cost	
Retailer's cost for a pair of jeans	$30.00	Retailer's cost for a pair of jeans	$30.00
Markup percentage	40%	Markup percentage	40%
		Formula: Price = total cost + (total cost × markup percentage)	
Formula: Price = $\frac{cost}{(1.00 - markup\ percentage)}$		Price = $30.00 + ($30.00 × 0.40) = $30.00 + $12.00 = $42.00	
Price = $\frac{\$30.00}{(1.00 - .40)} = \frac{\$30.00}{0.60} = \$50.00$			

Income Statement and Balance Sheet

The two most important documents used to explain the financial situation of a company are the income statement and the balance sheet. The *income statement* (which is sometimes referred to as the *profit and loss statement*) provides a summary of the revenues and expenses of a firm—that is, the amount of income a company received from sales or other sources, the amount of money it spent, and the resulting income or loss that the company experienced.

The major elements of the income statement are:

Gross sales: the total of all income the firm receives from the sales of goods and services.

Net sales revenue: the gross sales minus the amount for returns and promotional or other allowances given to customers.

Cost of goods sold (sometimes called the *cost of sales*): the cost of inventory or goods that the firm has sold.

Gross margin (also called *gross profit*): the amount of sales revenue that is in excess of the cost of goods sold.

Operating expenses: expenses other than the cost of goods sold that are necessary for conducting business. These may include salaries, rent, depreciation on buildings and equipment, insurance, utilities, supplies, and property taxes.

Operating income (sometimes called *income from operations*): the gross margin minus the operating expenses. Sometimes accountants prepare an *operating statement*, which is similar to the income statement except that the final calculation is the operating income—that is, other revenues or expenses and taxes are not included.

Other revenue and expenses: income and/or expenses other than those required for conducting the business. These may include such items as interest income/expenses and any gain or loss experienced on the sale of property or plant assets.

Taxes: the amount of income tax the firm owes calculated as a percentage of income.

Net income (sometimes called *net earnings* or *net profit*): the excess of total revenue over total expenses.

Table 9A.3 shows the income statement for an imaginary company, DLL Incorporated. DLL is a typical merchandising firm. Note that the income statement is for a specific year and includes income and expenses from January 1 through December 31 inclusive. The following comments explain the meaning of some of the important entries included in this statement.

- DLL Inc. has total or gross sales during the year of $253 950. This figure was adjusted, however, by deducting the $3000 worth of goods returned and special allowances given to customers and by $2100 in special discounts. Thus the actual or net sales generated by sales is $248 850.

- The cost of goods sold is calculated by adding the inventory of goods on January 1 to the amount purchased during the year and then subtracting the inventory of goods on December 31. In this case, DLL had $60 750 worth of inventory on hand on January 1. During the year the firm made purchases in the amount of $135 550. This amount, however, was reduced by purchase returns and allowances of $1500 and by purchase discounts of $750, so the net purchase is only $133 300.

There is also an amount on the statement labelled "Freight-In." This is the amount spent by the firm in shipping charges to get goods to its facility from suppliers. Any expenses for freight from DLL to its customers (Freight-Out) would be an operating expense. In this case, the Freight-In expense of $2450 is added to net purchase costs. Then these costs of current purchases are added to the beginning inventory to show that during the year the firm had a total of $196 500 in goods available for sale. Finally, the inventory of goods held on December 31 is subtracted from the goods available, for a total cost of goods sold of $136 200. For a manufacturer, calculation of the cost of goods sold would be a bit more complicated and would probably include separate figures for such items as inventory of finished goods, the "work-in-process" inventory, the raw materials inventory, and the cost of goods delivered to customers during the year.

- The cost of goods sold is subtracted from the net sales revenue to get a gross margin of $112 650.

- Operating expenses for DLL include the salaries and commissions paid to its employees, rent on facilities and/or equipment, insurance, depreciation of capital items, and the cost of operating supplies. DLL has a total of $31 125 in operating expenses, which is deducted from the gross margin. Thus DLL has an operating income of $81 525.

- DLL had both other income and expenses in the form of interest revenues of $1500 and interest expenses of $2250, making a total other expense of $750, which was subtracted from the operating income, leaving an income before tax of $80 775.

- Finally, the income before tax is reduced by 40 percent ($32 310) for taxes, leaving a net income of $48 465. The

Table 9A.3 DLL Inc. Income Statement for the Year Ended December 31, 20XX

Gross Sales			$253 950
Less: Sales Returns and Allowances		$ 3 000	
Sales Discounts		2 100	5 100
Net Sales Revenue			$248 850
Cost of Goods Sold			
Inventory, January 1, 20XX			$ 60 750
Purchases	$135 550		
Less: Purchase Returns and Allowances	1 500		
Purchase Discounts	750		
Net Purchases	$133 300		
Plus: Freight-In	2 450	135 750	
Goods Available for Sale		196 500	
Less: Inventory, December 31, 20XX		60 300	
Cost of Goods Sold			$136 200
Gross Margin			112 650
Operating Expenses			
Salaries and Commissions		15 300	
Rent		12 600	
Insurance		1 500	
Depreciation		900	
Supplies		825	
Total Operating Expenses			31 125
Operating Income			81 525
Other Revenue and (Expenses)			
Interest Revenue		1 500	
Interest Expense		(2 250)	(750)
Income before Tax			80 775
Taxes (40%)			32 310
Net Income			$ 48 465

40 percent is an average amount for federal and provincial corporate income taxes incurred by most firms.

The *balance sheet* lists the assets, liabilities, and stockholders' equity of the firm. Whereas the income statement represents what happened during an entire year, the balance sheet is like a snapshot; it shows the firm's financial situation at one point in time. For this reason, the balance sheet is sometimes called the *statement of financial position*.

Table 9A.4 shows DLL Inc.'s balance sheet for December 31. Assets are any economic resource that is expected to benefit the firm in the short or long term. Current assets are items that are normally expected to be turned into cash or used up during the next twelve months or during the firm's normal operating cycle. Current assets for DLL include cash, securities, accounts receivable (money owed to the firm and not yet paid) inventory on hand, prepaid insurance, and

supplies: a total of $84 525. *Long-term assets* include all assets that are not current assets. For DLL, these are property, plant, equipment, furniture, and fixtures less an amount for depreciation, or $45 300. The total assets for DLL are $129 825.

A firm's *liabilities* are its *economic obligations*, or debts that are payable to individuals or organizations outside the firm. *Current liabilities* are debts due in the coming year or in the firm's normal operating cycle. For DLL, the current liabilities—the accounts payable, unearned sales revenue, wages payable, and interest payable—total $72 450. *Long-term liabilities* (in the case of DLL, a note in the amount of $18 900) are all liabilities that are not due during the coming cycle. *Stockholders' equity* is the value of the stock and the corporation's capital or retained earnings. DLL has $15 000 in common stock and $23 475 in retained earnings for a total stockholders' equity of $38 475. Total liabilities always equal total assets—in this case, $129 825.

Table 9A.4 DLL Inc. Balance Sheet: December 31, 20XX

Assets

Current Assets

Cash		$ 4275	
Marketable Securities		12 000	
Accounts Receivable		6 900	
Inventory		60 300	
Prepaid Insurance		300	
Supplies		150	
Total Current Assets			84 525

Long-Term Assets—Property, Plant and Equipment

Furniture and Fixtures	$42 300		
Less: Accumulated Depreciation	4 500	37 800	
Land		7 500	
Total Long-Term Assets			45 300
Total Assets			$129 825

Liabilities

Current Liabilities

Accounts Payable	$70 500		
Unearned Sales Revenue	1 050		
Wages Payable	600		
Interest Payable	300		
Total Current Liabilities		72 450	

Long-Term Liabilities

Note Payable		18 900	
Total Liabilities			91 350

Stockholders' Equity

Common Stock		15 000	
Retained Earnings		23 475	
Total Stockholders' Equity			38 475
Total Liabilities and Stockholders' Equity			$129 825

IMPORTANT FINANCIAL PERFORMANCE RATIOS

How do managers and financial analysts compare the performance of a firm from one year to the next? How do investors compare the performance of one firm with that of another? Often, a number of different financial ratios provide important information for such comparisons. Such ratios are percentage figures comparing various income statement items to net sales. Ratios provide a better way to compare performance than simple dollar sales or cost figures for two reasons. They enable analysts to compare the performance of large and small firms, and they provide a fair way to compare performance over time, without having to take inflation and other changes into account. In this section we will explain the basic operating ratios. Other measures of performance that marketers frequently use and that are also explained here are the inventory turnover rate and return on investment (ROI).

Operating Ratios

Measures of performance calculated directly from the information in a firm's income statement (sometimes called an operating statement) are called the *operating ratios*. Each ratio compares some income statement item to net sales. The most useful of these are the *gross margin ratio, the net income ratio, the operating expense ratio, and the returns and allowances ratio*. These ratios vary widely by industry but tend to be important indicators of how a firm is doing within its industry. The ratios for DLL Inc. are shown in Table 9.A5.

- The *gross margin ratio* shows what percentage of sales revenues are available for operating and other expenses and for profit. With DLL, this means that 45 percent, or nearly half, of every sales dollar is available for operating costs and for profits. The *net income ratio* (sometimes called the *net profit ratio*) shows what percentage of sales revenues are income or profit. For DLL, the net income ratio is 19.5 percent. This means that the firm's profit before taxes is about 20 cents of every dollar.

Table 9A.5 (Hypothetical) Operating Ratios for DLL Inc.

Gross margin ratio	=	gross margin / net sales	=	$112 650 / 248 850	=	45.3%
Net income ratio	=	net income / net sales	=	$ 48 465 / 248 850	=	19.5%
Operating expense ratio	=	total operating expenses / net sales	=	$ 31 125 / 248 850	=	12.5%
Returns and allowances ratio	=	returns and allowances / net sales	=	$ 3000 / 248 850	=	1.2%

- The *operating expense ratio* is the percentage of sales needed for operating expenses. DLL has an operating expense ratio of 12.5 percent. Tracking operating expense ratios from one year to the next or comparing them with an industry average gives a firm important information about how efficient its operations are.

- The *returns and allowances ratio* shows what percentage of all sales are being returned, probably by unhappy customers. DLL's returns and allowances ratio shows that only a little over 1 percent of sales are being returned.

Inventory Turnover Rate

The *inventory turnover rate*, also referred to as the stock-turn rate, is the number of times inventory or stock is turned over (sold and replaced) during a specified time period, usually a year. Inventory turnover rates are usually calculated on the basis of inventory costs, sometimes on the basis of inventory selling prices, and sometimes by number of units.

For our example, DLL Inc., we know that for the year, the cost of goods sold was $136 200. Information on the balance sheet enables us to find the average inventory. By adding the value of the beginning inventory to the ending inventory and dividing by 2, we can compute an average inventory. In the case of DLL, this would be

$$\frac{\$60\,750 + \$60\,300}{2} = \$60\,525$$

Thus

$$\text{Inventory turnover rate (in cost of goods sold)} = \frac{\text{costs of goods sold}}{\text{average inventory at cost}}$$

$$= \frac{\$136\,200}{\$60\,525} = 2.25 \text{ times}$$

Return on Investment (ROI)

Firms often develop business objectives in terms of return on investment, and ROI is often used to determine how effective (and efficient) the firm's management has been. First, however, we need to define exactly what a firm means by investment. In most cases, firms define investment as the total assets of the firm. To calculate the ROI we need the net income found in the income statement and the total assets (or investment), which is found on the firm's balance sheet.

Return on investment is calculated as follows:

$$\text{ROI} = \frac{\text{net income}}{\text{total investment}}$$

For DLL Inc., if the total assets are $129 825, then the ROI is

$$\frac{\$48\,465}{\$129\,825} = 37.3\%$$

Sometimes return on investment is calculated by using an expanded formula.

$$\text{ROI} = \frac{\text{net profit}}{\text{sales}} \times \frac{\text{sales}}{\text{investment}}$$

$$= \frac{\$48\,465}{\$248\,850} \times \frac{\$248\,850}{\$129\,825} = 37.3\%$$

This formula makes it easy to show how ROI can be increased and what might reduce ROI. For example, there are different ways to increase ROI. First, if the management focuses on cutting costs and increasing efficiency, profits may be increased while sales remain the same.

$$\text{ROI} = \frac{\text{net profit}}{\text{sales}} \times \frac{\text{sales}}{\text{investment}}$$

$$= \frac{\$53\,277}{\$248\,850} \times \frac{\$248\,850}{\$129\,825} = 41.0\%$$

But ROI can be increased just as much without improving performance simply by reducing the investment—by maintaining less inventory, for instance.

$$\text{ROI} = \frac{\text{net profit}}{\text{sales}} \times \frac{\text{sales}}{\text{investment}}$$

$$= \frac{\$48\,465}{\$248\,850} \times \frac{\$248\,850}{\$114\,825} = 42.2\%$$

Sometimes, however, differences among the total assets of firms may be related to the age of the firm or the type of industry, which makes ROI a poor indicator of performance. For this reason, some firms have replaced the traditional ROI measures with *return on assets managed* (ROAM), *return on net assets* (RONA), or *return on stockholders' equity* (ROE).

PRICE ELASTICITY

Price elasticity, discussed in Chapter 9, is a measure of the sensitivity of customers to changes in price. Price elasticity is calculated by comparing the percentage change in quantity to the percentage change in price.

$$\text{Price elasticity of demand} = \frac{\text{percentage change in quantity}}{\text{percentage change in price}}$$

$$E = \frac{(Q_2 - Q_1)/Q_1}{(P_2 - P_1)/P_1}$$

where Q = quantity and P = price.

For example, suppose the manufacturer of jeans increased its price from $30 a pair to $35. But instead of 40 000 pairs being sold, sales declined to only 38 000 pairs. The price elasticity would be calculated as follows:

$$E = \frac{(38\,000 - 40\,000)/40\,000}{(\$35 - 30)/\$30} = \frac{-0.05}{0.167} = 0.30$$

Note that elasticity is usually expressed as a positive number even though the calculations create a negative value.

In this case, a relative small change in demand (5 percent) resulted from a fairly large change in price (16.7 percent), indicating that demand is inelastic. At 0.30, the elasticity is less than 1.

On the other hand, what if the same change in price resulted in a reduction in demand to 30 000 pairs of jeans? Then the elasticity would be

$$E = \frac{(30\,000 - 40\,000)/40\,000}{(\$35 - 30)/\$30} = \frac{-0.25}{0.167} = 1.50$$

In this case, because the 16.7 percent change in price resulted in an even larger change in demand (25 percent), demand is elastic. The elasticity of 1.50 is greater than 1. Note: Elasticity may also be calculated by dividing the change in quantity by the average of Q1 and Q2 and dividing the change in price by the average of the two prices. We, however, have chosen to include the formula that uses the initial quantity and price rather than the average.

Economic Order Quantity

The amount a firm should order at one time is called the *economic order quantity* (EOQ). Every time a firm places an order, there are additional costs. By ordering larger quantities less frequently, the firm saves on these costs. But it also costs money to maintain large inventories of needed materials. The EOQ is the order volume that provides both the lowest processing costs and the lowest inventory costs. The EOQ can be calculated as follows:

1. Determine the *order processing cost*. This is the total amount it costs a firm to place an order from beginning to end. Typically, this might include the operating expenses for the purchasing department, costs for follow-up, costs of record keeping of orders (data processing), costs for the receiving department, and costs for the processing and paying of invoices from suppliers. The simplest way to calculate this is to add up all these yearly costs and then divide by the number of orders placed during the year.

2. Next, calculate the *inventory carrying cost*. This is the total of all costs involved in carrying inventory. These costs include the costs of capital tied up in inventory, the cost of waste (merchandise that becomes obsolete or unusable), depreciation costs, storage costs, insurance premiums, property taxes, and opportunity costs.

The formula for calculating EOQ is

$$EOQ = \sqrt{\frac{2 \times \text{units sold (or annual usage)} \times \text{ordering cost}}{\text{unit cost} \times \text{inventory carrying cost (\%)}}}$$

For example, suppose an office supply store sells 6000 cases of pens a year at a cost of $12 a case. The cost to the store for each order placed is $60. The cost of carrying the pens in the warehouse is 24 percent per year (this is a typical inventory carrying cost in many businesses). Thus, the calculation is

$$EOQ = \sqrt{\frac{2 \times 6000 \times \$60}{\$12 \times 0.24}} = \sqrt{\frac{\$720\,000}{\$2.88}} = 500$$

The firm should order pens about once a month (it sells 6000 cases a year or 500 cases a month).

The Bait in Rebates

You open the morning paper, flip through the flyers, and see rebates everywhere for many different products. You can save $50 on the purchase of a camera or $100 when you buy a TV. Mail-in rebates are a tool marketers use to entice customers to buy their products.

Companies are well aware that mail-in rebates generate higher volumes of sales because of the lower price the consumer will end up paying for their products. With so many choices for similar products, retailers are always trying to get an edge on the competition. One edge that is quite effective is the mail-in rebate. John Shalino, Marketing Manager for Sony, admits mail-in rebates help increase the sales in the store by offering a reduced price for a product as long as the consumer is willing to go through the steps in redeeming their rebate. The truth, however, is that customers make purchase decisions based on the discounted price, then don't follow through on redeeming the rebate. Redemption rates are often in the range of one to five percent, but can go as high as 40 percent. This low redemption rate is what makes the mail-in rebate so appealing for manufacturers. It allows the product to be sold at two different prices, a price that is lower for customers who are more price sensitive and willing to mail in the rebate, and the regular price for those less price sensitive consumers who cannot be bothered.

When a rebate is actually mailed to receive the redemption, it never goes to the manufacturer; instead, it makes its way to a kind of middleman called a fulfillment house. Marco Sales and Incentives, a fulfillment house, receives mail-in rebates for many companies, sorts through them, ensures every requirement has been met, and if so, finally issues a cheque to the consumer for the amount of the rebate.

When Garrett Luelling was buying a printer from Staples he was convinced by the sales associate that he could get a higher quality printer for the same price as the lower quality printer as long as he sent in his mail-in rebate. After getting home Garrett did just that: he filled out all the necessary paperwork and mailed in his $50 rebate. After several months he got a reply saying he had mailed the wrong bar code. Garrett completed the paperwork and mailed it again, a year after the purchase and he still had not gotten a cheque. Two weeks after an interview with Mr. Matyas, Staples' president, Garrett received his $50 rebate.

While Carol de Ville of Marco Sales and Incentives says all the paperwork is necessary to reduce fraud, many companies are trying to move to an online rebate system to make it easier for consumers to claim their rebates. Manufacturers say this system will give them an edge on the competition. Of course, if more people redeem rebates, they become less attractive as a pricing tactic.

Questions

1. If companies know that rebate redemption rates are very low, is it ethical for them to use this pricing tactic? Why or why not?
2. In what purchase contexts do you think consumers are more or less likely to redeem rebates? Why do you think behaviour differs in these contexts?
3. Have you ever bought something based on the rebate, and then didn't complete the redemption requirements? If so, how did this affect your attitude toward the brand? If not, how might this behaviour affect consumer attitudes toward brands?
4. Should the use and redemption requirements of rebates be subject to any industry or government regulation? Why or why not?

Source: This case was prepared by Brock Smith and Michael Rawluk and is based on "The Bait in Rebates," *Marketplace* #8, 2005.

Inkjet Cartridges

One of the most expensive liquids on earth is in most of our homes, yet many people do not know what it is. A fancy bottle of champagne, at $165, and a nice perfume, at $75, come nowhere near the cost of the ink in printer cartridges. A cartridge contains about one tablespoon of ink and sells for about 12 times more per millilitre than the champagne. An attractive Epson printer, at $75, consumes almost $78 of ink per month in typical home business use.

The pricing model used for printers and their inkjet cartridges is called the razors-and-blades model. Gillette has been very good at using this model. By selling the razor and first set of blades at a low price, it locks in consumers so that they have to buy Gillette's replacement blades, which are priced very high. The blades, similar to replacement printer cartridges, are called consumables. Consumables ensure that a manufacturer has a steady source of income after the initial sale and are the money-maker in the industry.

The average computer owner will buy four cartridges per year for their printer, which works out to one billion per year totalling $20 billion in sales. At Epson, Don Cameron says the cost is reasonable and should be thought of as a price per page. This price per page is said to be only 3.7 cents per page, comparable to the cost of a photocopy, but that is for a standard 5 percent coverage of ink, which is not the typical usage of most printer owners. Cameron explains that the price of inkjet cartridges considers the cost of research and development, shipping, marketing to Canadians, and the average number of cartridges the average consumer buys.

Jim Bradbury is one consumer who goes through a lot of ink while restoring old family photos and completing other photographic work. Bradbury does not agree that the pricing model is reasonable. He believes the ink costs are too high, so he has decided to purchase his refills on the Internet from cheaper generic suppliers, thus reducing his cost from about $55 to $15 per cartridge. Others consumers are doing the same. NOMI Computer Sense collects, refills, and resells used inkjet cartridges. A test compared a refilled cartridge to a brand new HP cartridge and found that the HP printed 25 pages more, but cost $10 more as well. When both the printouts were taken to an expert it was discovered that the HP had better colours and images. However, there was no difference in the text between the two cartridges.

Epson has also frustrated consumers over its "Smart Chip," a chip placed in the cartridge monitoring the level of ink remaining. The chip will say that the cartridge is empty when there is still about 20 percent of the ink left. The cartridge will not work at this point unless a "chip resetter" is used to fool the cartridge into thinking it is full, allowing the consumer to use *all* the ink in the cartridge. Other manufacturers suggest that using generic ink will either damage the printer or result in poor quality results.

Although running the cartridge to empty can be damaging to the printer heads, and while there may be a difference in print quality, Bradbury says all the money he saves buying the generic cartridges and running them to empty is far more than the money he would spend on buying a new printer a little sooner than he might have to if he used branded ink.

Questions

1. How would you describe the computer printer industry's pricing strategy using concepts from the text?
2. Do you think this strategy is appropriate? Why or why not?
3. What are some alternative pricing strategies? What would be the relative advantages and disadvantages of these alternative strategies?
4. What segments might exist in this market, and how might they differ in ink purchase and consumption behaviour?

Source: This case was prepared by Brock Smith with the assistance of Michael Rawluk and is based on "Inkjet Cartridges," *Marketplace* #9, 2004.

PART IV

Delivering, Communicating, and Implementing the Value Proposition

You learned in Part III how marketers make product and pricing decisions—which are at the heart of the value proposition. In this part, you will learn how marketers deliver and communicate that value proposition to their target customers. You may be tempted to think that once a business develops a marketing strategy, its job is done. Think again. Implementing the strategy and evaluating whether you are performing to plan is a significant challenge. Consequently, this book concludes with a summary chapter that puts all the marketing decisions together, shows you how to write an effective marketing plan, and discusses implementation and evaluation issues.

Dimension Lumber

Weldwood
the measure of quality

Species:	SPF	Spruce-Pine-Fir
	DFir	Douglas Fir

MC: All lumber is kiln-dried(KD) to a maximum moisture content of 19%

Grade stamp: All lumber products graded #3 or Utility and higher have a grade stamp showing the grading agency, mill number, species, grade, and "KD – HT" (Kiln-Dried and Heat-Treated). This means lumber is dried to a maximum moisture content of 19% and achieves a minimum core temperature of 56 °C for a minimum of 30 minutes.

Economy grades are not grade stamped, but are stamped "HT" (Heat-Treated).

Products:

KD SPF –CLS/ALS dimension lumber graded to NLGA rules or better

NOMINAL SIZE	ACTUAL SIZE	PKG SIZE	LENGTHS	#2 & BTR	STD & BTR	#3	UTILITY	ECONOMY
2 x 3	1 ½" x 2½"	399	8' to 16'	✔		✔		✔
2 x 4	1 ½" x 3½"	294	8' to 20'	✔	✔	✔	✔	✔
2 x 6	1 ½" x 5½"	189	8' to 20'	✔		✔		✔
2 x 8	1 ½" x 7¼"	147	8' to 20'	✔		✔		✔
2 x 10	1 ½" x 9¼"	105	8' to 20'	✔		✔		✔
2 x 12	1 ½" x 11¼"	84	8' to 20'	✔		✔		✔

KD DFir –CLS/ALS dimension lumber graded to NLGA rules or better

NOMINAL SIZE	ACTUAL SIZE	PKG SIZE	LENGTHS	#2 & BTR	STD & BTR	#3	UTILITY	ECONOMY
2 x 4	1 ½" x 3½"	294	8' to 20'	✔	✔	✔	✔	✔
2 x 6	1 ½" x 5½"	189	8' to 20'	✔		✔		✔
2 x 8	1 ½" x 7¼"	147	8' to 20'	✔		✔		✔
2 x 10	1 ½" x 9¼"	105	8' to 20'	✔		✔		✔

Specialty products:
MSR (Machine Stress Rated) Lumber
DFir Lamstock – L3 & Btr
"Hiline" appearance grade lumber
Odd length lumber – 7' to 15'
Rough Grn SPF timber – 4 x 4 to 10 x 10 – 9' to 16'

Packages
Poly-wrapped packages (except economy grades)
Steel-strapped

Grading agencies: AFPA, CLMA, NFPA

Weldwood of Canada Limited
604. 662. 2790
www.weldwood.com

CHAPTER 10
Channels and Supply Chain Strategy

CHAPTER OBJECTIVES

WHEN YOU HAVE COMPLETED YOUR STUDY OF THIS CHAPTER, YOU SHOULD BE ABLE TO

1. Explain what a distribution channel is and what functions distribution channels perform.

2. Describe some of the types of wholesaling intermediaries found in distribution channels.

3. Discuss the steps in planning distribution channel strategies and channel management.

4. Describe what a supply chain is, how it is related to a value chain, and how logistics is used to implement the supply chain management.

Real People, Real Decisions

Meet **Mike Nomura**, a Decision Maker at Weldwood of Canada

Mike Nomura is the manager of Marketing & Customer Development, Offshore Export, for Weldwood of Canada, a large forest products company based in Vancouver, British Columbia. Mike went to school in both the Japanese and Canadian school systems, attended the British Columbia Institute of Technologies (Wood Science), and took post-graduate marketing courses before getting his first job as a technician at an R&D company specializing in super-conductor–based medical and geological exploration machines.

Mike identified the forest industry as an industry with major earnings potential in British Columbia, and he went after the export market where he could use his bicultural background. While his technical degree gave him a good foundation in the forest products industry, allowing him to get his foot in the door to his first lumber job, he feels nothing can beat on-the-job experience.

Over a five-year period beginning in 1994, he increased sales by over 250 percent. Although 1997 and 1998 saw dramatic downturns in lumber exports to Japan, Mike and his team were alone in achieving an increase in market share during this period. This can be attributed to Mike's relentless focus on the needs of the customer.

This single-minded customer focus was put to the test when one of Weldwood's key customers in Japan decided to dramatically shift its channel of distribution strategy. Weldwood of Canada's offshore department was enjoying a good, solid business relationship with one of the largest homebuilders and developers of wood-frame apartments in Japan—Daito Trust Construction. Daito builds more than 10 000 units annually, and the majority of building materials had been sourced and supplied by its material procurement group, Trans-Pac Housing, in Vancouver. Weldwood had worked extremely hard to capture a large portion of Trans-Pac Housing's business (and, ultimately, Daito's trust).

In 2002, Daito caught many of its suppliers off guard when it announced that it was permanently closing its Vancouver office, and that it would now be conducting all material procurement activities directly from Japan. The company created a brand-new department, with all new personnel, and it seemed as though the relationships built with its Vancouver office over the years simply would evaporate.

It was indeed starting over for Weldwood—Daito chose to deal with *all* available suppliers, not only in Canada, but worldwide. Weldwood found itself in a tough situation, because Daito's position was that "Whoever can provide the most attractive deals will get our business." Mike knew that if he was going to continue serving this company, he had to get creative, and fast!

After conducting a careful assessment of the customer's needs, Mike decided to present Daito with four options.

Option 1: Weldwood would effectively replace the old Trans-Pac, and fulfill all of its functions.

Weldwood would purchase on Daito's behalf, provide quality control, and take responsibility for loading and shipping to various ports in Japan. This option carried a lot of risk. Weldwood would be stepping away from its traditional role of supplying wood products to take on purchasing and warehousing, as well as quality control, for other suppliers' products. The advantage was that Weldwood would become the exclusive supplier and would control 100 percent of Daito's requirements.

Option 2: Find ways to enjoy the same relationship with Daito that Weldwood had with Trans-Pac.

Weldwood would continue to supply its portion, close to 50 percent of Daito's needs, and deal directly with Daito. The difference would be that while Trans-Pac had previously handled shipping, Weldwood would offer to manage shipping its portion to Daito directly. This option carried the least risk, but little gain. Protecting the status quo, Weldwood would continue to enjoy the relationship with Daito that it had with Trans-Pac, with the addition of shipping revenues.

Option 3: Do nothing, with the confidence that Weldwood would prove to be a supplier of choice once Daito reviewed the options, and the relationship would be maintained as with Trans-Pac before them.

This option required the least effort, waiting for Daito to come to Weldwood. The likelihood of continuing to supply 50 percent of the customer's needs was a definite possibility, without the cost or effort of starting from scratch with a new business proposal, which may or may not be accepted. However, this option could turn into a "pricing game" with other suppliers.

Option 4: Partner with another supplier to cover Weldwood's inability to supply certain products that Daito required.

Along with another firm, Weldwood would attempt to provide almost all of Daito's requirements. This option would require a high degree of coordination between two competing suppliers, and would be logistically demanding. Products from both would have to be coordinated and bundled together, and shipped on a "just-in-time" basis, to avoid costly warehousing. The advantage was that Weldwood would control a much larger portion of Daito's requirements than in the past, and would be able to charge a premium for the extra service provided. The amount of coordination and effort required to make things work could be daunting. Weldwood would be responsible for the quality of everything that was shipped to Daito, whether it produced the product or not.

Now, join Mike and his team at Weldwood. Which option would you choose, and why?

CHANNELS OF DISTRIBUTION: THE FINAL FRONTIER

Channels of distribution may be the final "frontier" for competitive success. After years of hype, many consumers no longer believe that "new and improved" products really are new and improved. Competitors usually easily match aggressive pricing strategies. Advertising and other forms of marketing communications are so commonplace that they have lost much of their impact. Marketers know that channels of distribution may be the only one of the four Ps for which there is an opportunity for sustainable competitive advantage. With companies like Wal-Mart that masterfully use the power of channel distribution, marketing is now going back to its roots. In fact, when the study of marketing was first initiated at the turn of the twentieth century, it was first and foremost the study of the channels area. Moreover, marketing was then known as distribution.[1]

Book retailers are well aware of the major criteria people use to choose a bookstore: selection, availability, pricing, and knowledgeable staff. Because the convenience of buying a book is important to customers, book retailers such as Chapters and Indigo try to make channels of distribution a competitive advantage. By channels, we mean making goods and services available where and when customers need and want them. Banks and trust companies, for example, make it easy for people to access their services by locating instant tellers where people are likely to need money: at malls, grocery stores, and airport lounges. Canadian Imperial Bank of Commerce, for example, teamed up with Loblaw Companies Limited to offer "President's Choice Financial," an in-store no-fee banking service with low mortgage rates and no-minimum-balance savings accounts paying interest above CIBC's own products.[2] The other major banks also have kiosks in supermarkets—this makes good sense since as many as 10 000 to 30 000 shoppers pass by each week.[3]

For those who don't even have time to run out to the grocery store, the Internet is fast becoming an important place for consumers to shop for everything from tulip bulbs, Montreal smoked meat, and mortgages to exotic vacations. Chapters.indigo.ca and Amazon.com, among others, make books available to consumers any time and any place. Expedia.ca offers vacation packages directly to consumers (Exhibit 10.1). It does so by being a wholesaler between vacation package suppliers (such as Sunquest, Transat Holidays, and

Exhibit 10.1

Expedia.ca offers vacation packages directly to consumers at a discount. Expedia.ca is the "intermediary" between vacation providers and consumers.

Air Canada Vacations) and consumers. The Internet enables even small firms with limited resources to enjoy the same competitive advantages as their largest competitors in terms of making their products available to customers around the globe.

This chapter is about the science and art of distributing goods and services to customers. First, we'll discuss distribution channels and how marketers make smart decisions in developing distribution strategies. We'll also talk about supply chains and the importance of supply chain strategy for business success.

THE IMPORTANCE OF DISTRIBUTION: YOU CAN'T SELL WHAT ISN'T THERE!

You have identified and profiled your target market(s). You have created your product and priced it. You're not done. You need to get it to your customer. In today's marketplace, marketers must work hard to get their products to consumers, who no longer have the leisure time available to "shop till they drop" for goods and services. You also want to structure your channel(s) so that it can adapt rapidly to competitive changes. For example, the Internet forced many companies to change their distribution model.[4]

What Is a Distribution Channel?

channel of distribution The series of firms or individuals that facilitates the movement of a product from the producer to the final customer.

A **channel of distribution** is a series of firms or individuals that facilitates the movement of a product from the producer to the final customer. In many cases, channels include an organized network of manufacturers, wholesalers, and retailers that develop relationships and work together to make products conveniently available to buyers.

Distribution channels come in different shapes and sizes. The bakery around the corner where you buy your cinnamon rolls is a member of a channel, as is the baked goods section at the local supermarket, the espresso bar at the mall that sells biscotti to go with your double mocha cappuccino, and the bakery outlet store that sells day-old rolls at a discount.

A channel of distribution consists of, at a minimum, a producer—the individual or firm that manufactures or produces a good or service—and a customer. This is a *direct channel*. For example, when you buy a kilogram of strawberries at a farm where they're grown, that's a direct channel. Firms that sell their own products through catalogues, 800 numbers, the Internet, or factory outlet stores use direct channels.

channel intermediaries Firms or individuals such as wholesalers, agents, brokers, and retailers that help move a product from the producer to the consumer or business user.

But channels often are *indirect*, because they include one or more **channel intermediaries**, firms or individuals such as wholesalers, agents, brokers, and retailers that in some way help move the product to the consumer or business user. For example, strawberry farmers may choose to sell their berries to a produce wholesaler that, in turn, sells cases of the berries to supermarkets and restaurants that, in turn, sell to consumers.

Channel Objectives

The first step in deciding on a distribution plan is to develop appropriate objectives that support the organization's overall marketing goals. How can distribution work with the other elements of the marketing mix to increase profits? To increase market share? To increase volume of sales?

In general, the overall objective of any distribution planning is to make a firm's product available when, where, and in the quantities customers want and need at a minimum cost. More specific distribution objectives, however, depend on characteristics of the product and the market. For example, if the product is bulky, a primary distribution objective may be to minimize shipping costs. If the product is fragile, a goal may be to develop a channel that minimizes handling. In introducing a new product to a mass market, a channel objective may be to provide maximum product exposure or to make the product available close to where customers live and work. Sometimes marketers make their product available where similar products are sold so that consumers can compare prices.

Evaluating the Environment

After setting the distribution objectives, marketers must consider their internal and external environments. The organization must examine such issues as its own ability to create distribution channels, what channel intermediaries are available, the ability of customers to access these intermediaries, and how the competition distributes its products. Should a firm use the same retailers as its competitors? Sometimes, to ensure customers' undivided attention, a firm sells its products in outlets that don't carry the competitors' products. In other cases, a firm uses the same intermediaries as its competitors because customers expect to find the product there. Finally, by studying competitors' distribution strategies, marketers can learn from their successes and failures. For example, if the biggest complaint of competitors' customers is delivery speed, developing a system that allows same-day delivery can make the competition pale in comparison.

Choosing a Distribution System

Planning distribution strategies means making at least three decisions. Distribution planning includes decisions about the number of levels in the distribution channel, but distribution strategies also involve decisions about channel relationships—whether a conventional system or a highly integrated system will work best. A final decision relates to the distribution intensity or the number of intermediaries at each level of the channel.

CONVENTIONAL, VERTICAL, AND HORIZONTAL MARKETING SYSTEMS Participants in any distribution channel form an interrelated system. To develop a successful distribution strategy, marketers must consider the different types of systems and select the one that best meets their needs. In general, these systems take one of three forms: conventional, vertical, and horizontal marketing systems.

A **conventional marketing system** is a multiple-level distribution channel in which members work independently of one another. Their relationships are limited to simply buying and selling from one another. Each firm seeks to benefit with little concern for other channel members. Even though channel members work independently, most conventional channels are highly successful. For one thing, all members of the channel are working for the same goals—to build demand, reduce costs, and improve customer satisfaction. And the channel members know that it's in everyone's best interest to treat other channel members fairly.

A **vertical marketing system (VMS)** is a channel in which there is cooperation among channel members at two or more levels of the channel—the manufacturing, wholesaling, and retailing levels. Firms in a VMS work together and depend on each other, like links in a chain. Members share information and provide services to other members, recognizing that such coordination makes everyone more successful in reaching a desired target market.

There are three types of vertical marketing systems: administered, corporate, and contractual. In an administered VMS, channel members remain independent but voluntarily agree to work together. In a corporate VMS, firms have ownership control of some or all of a distribution channel, such as when a manufacturer buys agent companies.

In a contractual VMS, cooperation is enforced by contracts, legal agreements that spell out each member's rights and responsibilities and how they will cooperate. In a wholesaler-sponsored VMS, wholesalers get retailers to work together under their leadership in a voluntary chain. Retail members of the chain use a common name, cooperate in advertising and other promotion, and even develop their own private-label products. Examples of wholesaler-sponsored chains are IGA (Independent Grocers' Alliance) food stores, Ace Hardware stores, and Island Farms Dairy (BC).

In other cases, retailers themselves organize a cooperative marketing channel system. A *retailer cooperative* is a group of retailers that has established a wholesaling operation to help them compete more effectively with the large chains. Each retailer owns shares in the

conventional marketing system A multiple-level distribution channel in which channel members work independently of one another.

vertical marketing system (VMS) A channel of distribution in which there is cooperation among members at the manufacturing, wholesaling, and retailing levels.

wholesaler operation and is obligated to purchase a certain percentage of inventory from the cooperative operation. The Calgary Co-op and True Value Hardware Stores are examples of retailer cooperatives.

Franchise organizations are a third type of contractual VMS. In these organizations, channel cooperation is explicitly defined and strictly enforced through contractual arrangements in which a franchiser (a manufacturer or a service provider) allows an entrepreneur to use the franchise name and marketing plan for a fee. In most franchise agreements, the franchiser provides a variety of services for the franchisee, such as helping train employees, giving access to lower prices for needed materials, and helping pick a location with visibility. In return, the franchiser receives a percentage of revenue from the franchise owner. Usually the franchisees are also allowed to use the franchiser business format, but they are required to follow that format to the letter.[5] For example, a McDonald's franchisee is not allowed to change the menu or the physical decor of the restaurant. It's important that customers know that they can get the same Big Mac in Toronto that they will find in Corner Brook, Newfoundland.

Canada is the franchise capital of the world—with more than 1300 franchise operations and 64 000 outlets generating more than a million jobs and $100 billion a year in revenues.[6] Although relatively high-cost food-service franchises ($60 000 to $1 million) represent about 40 percent of all outlets, some of Canada's hottest franchises are in consumer and business services—website design, window cleaning, tutoring, maid services, dog walking, and house painting—with franchise fees under $30 000.

From the manufacturer's perspective, franchising a business is a way to develop widespread product distribution with minimal financial risk while, at the same time, maintaining control over product quality. From the entrepreneur's perspective, franchises, such as The Great Canadian Bagel, shown in Exhibit 10.2, are a popular way to get a start in business.

horizontal marketing system An arrangement within a channel of distribution in which two or more firms at the same channel level work together for a common purpose.

In a **horizontal marketing system**, two or more firms at the same channel level agree to work together to get their product to the customer. Air Canada and Lufthansa, for example, cooperate in providing passenger air service. To increase passenger volume for both airlines, they share a common flight code. This means that travel agents who book passengers on one of the airline's flights will be more likely to book a connecting flight on the other airline. To increase customer benefits, they also share frequent-flyer programs and airport clubs.[7]

Exhibit 10.2

The Great Canadian Bagel is a franchise bagel shop that is a Canadian icon.

Functions of Distribution Channels

Distribution channels perform a number of different functions that make the flow of goods from the producer to the customer possible. These functions must be handled by someone, be it the producer, a channel intermediary, or even the customer. They can be shifted from one member of the channel to another, such as when customers pick up new chairs from the warehouse instead of having them delivered to their home, but they cannot be eliminated. Channels that include one or more intermediaries can often accomplish certain distribution functions more effectively and efficiently than can a single organization.

Channels provide form, time, place, information, and possession utility for customers. They make desired products available when, where, and in the sizes and quantities that customers want them. Utilities in marketing and distribution measure the ability of a good or service to satisfy a customer's needs or wants.[8] Economic utility can be divided into five types: form, time, place, information, and possession. First, the creation of **form utility** encompasses all activities used to change the appearance or composition of a good or service with the intent of making it more attractive to potential and actual users. Secondly, **time utility** consists of the increased satisfaction created by marketing through making products available at the time consumers want them. Thirdly, **place utility** plays a significant role as well. It is the increased usefulness created by making a product available at a location preferred by consumers. Fourthly, **information utility** is defined as the value given to a product that provides the user with useful information. And finally, the increased usefulness created by making it possible for a consumer to own, use, and consume a product is called **possession utility**, or sometimes ownership utility.[9]

Take, for example, flowers such as those shown in Exhibit 10.3. The flowers are harvested and electronically sorted by growers, auctioned to buyers in Amsterdam, shipped by air to importers in Mississauga, where they are inspected for insects and disease, transported to wholesalers around the country, and finally distributed to local florists who make them available to their customers. The channel members—the growers, the auction house, the importers, the wholesalers, and the local florists—all work together to create just the right bouquet for flower lovers.

A second function of distribution channels is increasing the efficiency of the flow of goods from producer to customer. How would we buy groceries without our modern system of

form utility All activities used to change the appearance or composition of a good or service with the intent of making it more attractive to potential and actual users.

time utility All activities that increase satisfaction by making products available at the time consumers want them.

place utility Increased usefulness created by making a product available at a location preferred by consumers.

information utility The value given to a product that provides the user with useful information.

possession (ownership) utility Increased usefulness created by making it possible for a consumer to own, use, and consume a product.

Exhibit 10.3

An efficient distribution system facilitates getting flowers from greenhouses to flower lovers—all in the same day.

Exhibit 10.4

Canadian Tire stores provide an assortment of products and services to customers.

supermarkets? We'd have to get our milk from a dairy, our bread from a bakery, our tomatoes and corn from a local farmer, and our flour from a flourmill. And forget about specialty items, like Granola bars or Coca-Cola. The companies that make these items would have to handle literally millions of transactions to sell to every individual who craved a junk-food fix.

Distribution channels create efficiencies by reducing the number of transactions necessary for goods to flow from many different manufacturers to large numbers of customers. This occurs in two ways. With **bulk breaking**, wholesalers and retailers purchase large quantities (usually cases) of goods from manufacturers but sell only one or a few at a time to many different customers. Channel intermediaries also reduce the number of transactions by **creating assortments**—providing a variety of products in one location—so that customers can conveniently buy many different items from one seller at one time (Exhibit 10.4).

Figure 10.1 provides a simple example of how distribution channels reduce hassles in our lives. This illustration includes five manufacturers and five customers. If each producer sold

bulk breaking Dividing larger quantities of goods into smaller lots to meet the needs of buyers.

creating assortments Providing a variety of products in one location to meet the needs of buyers.

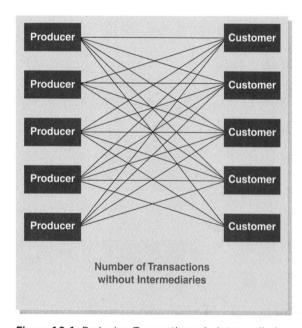

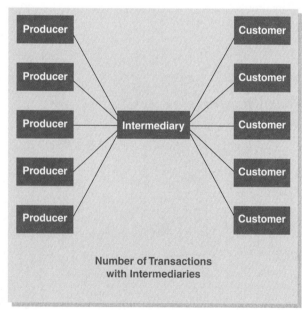

Figure 10.1 Reducing Transactions via Intermediaries

One of the functions of distribution channels is to provide an assortment of products. Because the customers can buy a number of different products at the same location, this reduces the total costs of obtaining a product.

its product to each individual customer, 25 different transactions would have to occur, which is a very inefficient way to distribute products. But with a single intermediary who buys from all five manufacturers and sells to all five customers, the number of transactions is cut to 10. If there were 10 manufacturers and 10 customers, an intermediary would reduce the number of transactions from 100 to just 20. Do the math: Channels are efficient.

Channel intermediaries also perform a number of **facilitating functions**, which make the purchase process easier for customers and manufacturers. For example, intermediaries often provide important customer services, such as offering credit to buyers. Most of us like to shop at department stores because, if we are not happy with the product, we can take it back to the store, where customer service personnel are happy to give us a refund (at least in theory). These same customer services are even more important in business-to-business markets in which customers purchase larger quantities of higher-priced products than in consumer markets. Some wholesalers and retailers assist the manufacturer by providing repair and maintenance service for products they handle. An appliance, television, stereo, or computer dealer may serve as an authorized repair centre, provide maintenance contracts, and sell essential supplies to customers (Exhibit 10.5).

Finally, international distribution channels can make global marketing easier. Even small companies can be successful in global markets by relying on distributors that know local customs and laws.

We've discussed what a distribution channel is and some of the functions it performs. What are the different types of channel intermediaries and channel structures?

Exhibit 10.5

Many distribution channel members provide customer services. Appliance and electronics retailers such as Best Buy provide repair and warranty services for the products they sell.

THE COMPOSITION AND STRUCTURE OF CHANNELS

How can you get your hands on a new U2 T-shirt? There are several ways. You could pick one up at your local music store or directly over the Internet (eBay.ca for example). You might buy an "official U2 concert T-shirt" from vendors during a show. Alternatively, you might get a "deal" on a bootlegged, unauthorized version of the same shirt being sold from a suitcase by a shady person standing *outside* the stadium before and after the event. Each of these distribution alternatives traces a different path from producer to consumer. Let's look at the different types of wholesaling intermediaries and at different channel structures. We'll focus on retailers, which are usually the last link in the chain, in the next chapter.

Types of Wholesaling Intermediaries

Wholesaling intermediaries are firms that handle the flow of products from the manufacturer to the retailer or business user. There are many different types of consumer and business-to-business wholesaling intermediaries. Some of these are independent, but manufacturers and retailers can own them, too. Table 10.1 summarizes the important characteristics of each.

INDEPENDENT INTERMEDIARIES **Independent intermediaries** do business with many different manufacturers and many different customers. Because they are not owned or controlled by any manufacturer, they make it possible for many manufacturers to serve customers throughout the world while keeping prices low.

Merchant wholesalers are independent intermediaries that buy goods from manufacturers and sell to retailers and other business-to-business customers. Because merchant wholesalers **take title** to the goods—they actually have legal ownership of the goods—they assume certain ownership risks and can suffer losses if products get damaged, become out of date or obsolete, are stolen, or just don't sell. At the same time, because they own the

---

facilitating functions Functions of channel intermediaries that make the purchase process easier for customers and manufacturers.

wholesaling intermediaries Firms that handle the flow of products from the manufacturer to the retailer or business user.

independent intermediaries Channel intermediaries that are not controlled by any manufacturer but rather do business with many different manufacturers and many different customers.

merchant wholesalers Intermediaries that buy goods from manufacturers (take title to them) and sell to retailers and other business-to-business customers.

take title To accept legal ownership of a product and the accompanying rights and responsibilities of ownership.

Table 10.1 Types of Intermediaries

Intermediary Type	Description	Advantages
Independent intermediaries	Do business with many different manufacturers and many different customers	Used by most small- to medium-sized firms
Merchant wholesalers	Buy (take title of) goods from producers and sell to organizational customers; either full or limited function	Allow small manufacturers to serve customers throughout the world while keeping costs low
Rack jobbers	Provide retailers with display units, check inventories, and replace merchandise for the retailers	Useful when retailers require merchandising services from manufacturers
Cash-and-carry wholesalers	Provide products for small business customers who purchase at wholesaler's location	To distribute low-cost merchandise for small retailers and other business customers
Truck jobbers	Deliver perishable food and tobacco items to retailers	For perishable items when delivery and some sales functions are required
Drop shippers	Take orders from and bill retailers for products drop-shipped from manufacturer	Facilitate transactions for bulky products
Mail-order wholesalers	Sell through catalogues, telephone, or mail order	For products sold to small organizational customers at a reasonable price
Merchandise agents and brokers	Provide services in exchange for commissions	Sellers do not give up legal ownership of product
Manufacturers' agents	Independent salespeople; carry several lines of non-competing products	Supply sales function for small and new firms
Selling agents Export/import agents	Handle entire output of one or more products	Handle all marketing functions for small manufacturers
Commission merchants	Receive commission on sales price of product	Primarily in agricultural products markets
Merchandise brokers Export/import brokers	Identify likely buyers and bring buyers and sellers together	In markets where there are lots of small buyers and sellers
Manufacturer owned	Operations limited to one manufacturer	Control
Sales branches	Like wholesalers, maintain some inventory in different geographic areas	When firms must provide service to customers in different geographic areas
Sales offices	Carry no inventory; in different geographic areas	Reduce selling costs and provide better customer service
Manufacturers' showrooms	Products attractively displayed for customers to visit	When desirable for customers to examine merchandise at a central location

Source: Adapted from J. Thomas Russell and W. Ronald Lane, *Kleppner's Advertising Procedure*, 11th ed. (Upper Saddle River, NJ: Prentice Hall, 1990); William Wells, John Burnett, and Sandra Moriarty, *Advertising: Principles and Practice*, 3d ed. (Upper Saddle River, NJ: Prentice Hall, 1995).

products, they are free to develop their own marketing strategies, including setting the prices they charge their customers.

Full-service merchant wholesalers, as the name suggests, provide a wide range of services for their customers. These services may include delivery, credit, product-use assistance, repairs, advertising and other promotion support, and market research. Full-service wholesalers often have their own sales force to call on businesses and organizational customers.

One type of full-service merchant wholesaler is a *rack jobber* (Exhibit 10.6). Rack jobbers supply retailers with such specialty items as health and beauty products, magazines, and books. Rack jobbers get their name because they own and maintain the product display racks in grocery, drug, and variety stores. These wholesalers visit their retail customers on a regular basis to maintain levels of stock and refill their racks with merchandise.

In contrast, *limited-service merchant wholesalers* provide fewer services for their customers. Like full-service wholesalers, they take title to merchandise, but they are less likely to provide such services as delivery, credit, or marketing assistance to retailers.

- *Cash-and-carry wholesalers* provide low-cost merchandise for retailers and industrial customers that are too small for other wholesalers' sales representatives to call on. Customers pay cash for products and provide their own delivery. Some popular cash-and-carry product categories include groceries, office supplies, building materials, and electrical supplies.

Exhibit 10.6

Rack jobbers are full-service merchant wholesalers. These intermediaries own and maintain product display racks in retail stores.

- *Truck jobbers* carry their products to small business customer locations for their inspection and selection. Truck jobbers often supply such perishable items as fruit, vegetables, and meats to small grocery stores. The bakery truck jobber calls on supermarkets, checks the stock of bread on the shelf, removes any outdated items, and suggests how much bread the store needs to order.

- *Drop shippers* are limited-function wholesalers that take title to the merchandise but never actually take possession of it. Drop shippers take orders from and bill retailers and industrial buyers, but the merchandise is shipped directly from the manufacturer. Because they take title to the merchandise, they assume the same risks as other merchant wholesalers. Drop shippers are important to both the producers and customers of bulky products such as coal, oil, or lumber.

- *Mail-order wholesalers* sell products to small retailers and other industrial customers, often located in remote areas, through catalogues rather than a sales force. They usually carry products in inventory and require payment in cash or by credit card before shipment. Mail-order wholesalers supply such products as cosmetics, hardware, sporting goods, and general merchandise.

- **Merchandise agents or brokers** are another major type of independent intermediary. Agents and brokers provide services in exchange for commissions. They may or may not take possession of the product, but they never take title— they do not accept legal ownership of the product. Agents normally represent buyers or sellers on an ongoing basis, whereas clients employ brokers for a short period of time. PayPal, shown in Exhibit 10.7, performs payment processing for online vendors, auction sites, and other corporate users, for which it charges a fee.

merchandise agents or brokers Channel intermediaries that provide services in exchange for commissions but never take title to the product.

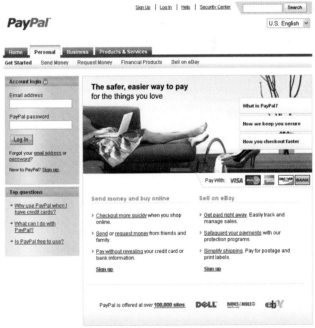

Exhibit 10.7

PayPal is an e-commerce broker allowing payments and money transfers to be made through the web. It serves as an electronic alternative to traditional paper methods such as cheques and money orders.

- *Manufacturers' agents*, also referred to as *manufacturers' reps*, are independent salespeople who carry several lines of non-competing products. They have contractual arrangements with manufacturers, which outline territories, selling prices, and other specific aspects of the relationship. These agents have little, if any, supervision and are compensated with commissions based on a percentage of what they sell. Manufacturers' agents often develop strong customer relationships and provide an important sales function for small and new companies.

- *Selling agents*, including export-import agents, market a whole product line or one manufacturer's total output. They are often seen as independent marketing departments because they perform the same functions as full-service wholesalers but do not take title to products. Unlike manufacturers' agents, selling agents have unlimited territories and control the pricing, promotion, and distribution of their products. Selling agents are found in the furniture, clothing, and textiles industries.

- *Commission merchants* are sales agents who receive goods, primarily agricultural products, such as grain or livestock, on consignment—they take possession of products without taking title. Although sellers may state a minimum price they are willing to take for their products, commission merchants are free to sell the product for the highest price they can get. Commission merchants receive a commission on the sales price of the product.

- *Merchandise brokers* (including export-import brokers) are intermediaries that facilitate transactions in markets such as real estate, food, and used equipment in which there are many small buyers and sellers. Brokers identify likely buyers and sellers and bring the two together in return for a fee received when the transaction is completed.

MANUFACTURER-OWNED INTERMEDIARIES Sometimes manufacturers set up their own channel intermediaries. In this way, they can have separate business units that perform all the functions of independent intermediaries *and* maintain complete control over the channel.

- *Sales branches* are manufacturer-owned facilities that, like independent wholesalers, carry inventory and provide sales and service to customers in a specific geographic area. Sales branches are found in such industries as petroleum products, industrial machinery and equipment, and motor vehicles.

- *Sales offices* are manufacturer-owned facilities that, like agents, do not carry inventory but provide selling functions for the manufacturer in a specific geographic area. Because they allow members of the sales force to be located close to customers, they reduce selling costs and provide better customer service.

- *Manufacturers' showrooms* are manufacturer-owned or leased facilities in which products are permanently displayed for customers to visit. Manufacturers' showrooms are often located in or near large merchandise marts, such as the furniture market in High Point, North Carolina, where Palliser Furniture goes to showcase its products.

Types of Distribution Channels

Firms face many choices when structuring distribution channels. Should they sell directly to consumers and business users? Would they benefit by including wholesalers, retailers, or both in the channel? Would it make sense to sell directly to some customers but use retailers to sell to other customers? There is no single best channel for all products. The marketing manager must select a channel structure that creates a competitive advantage for the firm and its products based on the size and needs of the target market. Here are some factors marketers need to consider.

In developing place or distribution strategies, marketers first consider different **channel levels**, or the number of distinct categories of intermediaries that make up a channel of distribution. Many different factors have an impact on this decision. What channel members are

channel levels The number of distinct categories of intermediaries that populate a channel of distribution.

Major Types of Channels of Distribution

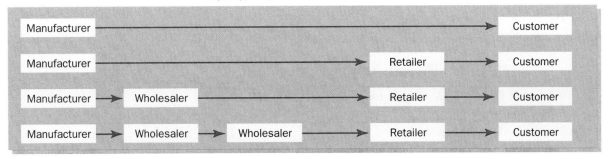

Typical Consumer Channels

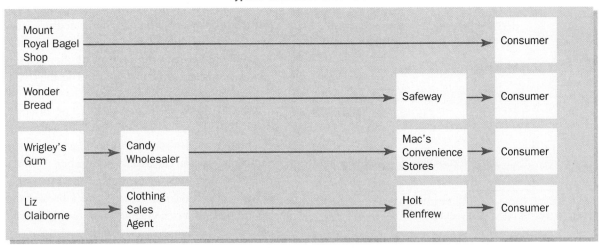

Business-to-Business Channels

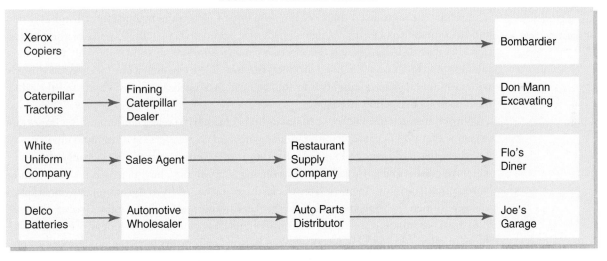

Figure 10.2 Different Types of Channels of Distribution

Channels differ in the number of channel members that participate.

available? How large is the market, how frequently do consumers purchase the product, and what services do they require?

Figure 10.2 summarizes the different structures a distribution channel can take. The producer and the customer are always members, so the shortest channel possible has two levels. Using a retailer adds a third level; a wholesaler adds a fourth level; and so on. Different channel structures exist for both consumer and business-to-business markets.

CONSUMER CHANNELS The simplest channel is a direct channel. Why do some manufacturers sell directly to customers? One reason is that a direct channel may allow the

Exhibit 10.8

The Internet allows ING Direct Canada to reach customers around the globe, making it a legitimate competitor against bigger chartered banks.[10]

perishability management A strategy that considers the characteristics of any given product or service that is perishable, that cannot be stored, and that must be sold at particular moments in time.

manufacturer to serve its customers better and at a lower price than is possible using a retailer. By using direct channels, strawberry farmers make sure their customers have fresher strawberries than if they sell the berries through a local supermarket. Customers, on the other hand, can directly interact with farmers and get more information about the product being sold to them. Furthermore, if the farmers sell the berries through a supermarket, their price will be higher because of the supermarket's costs of doing business and required profit on the berries. In fact, sometimes the direct channel is the *only* way to sell the product, because using intermediaries may increase the price above what consumers are willing to pay. **Perishability management** of products is also an important contributing factor in the development of direct channels.

One of the newest means of selling direct is through the Internet. In 2007, ING Direct Canada celebrated its 10th anniversary. Customers can bank online or can call a toll-free number, 24 hours a day, 7 days a week. The company provides Canadians with a choice in banking and a break from banking fees, service charges, and low interest. It offers a very conventional product and service through a unique distribution channel (Exhibit 10.8). ING Direct is now Canada's largest direct bank, with over 1.6 million customers and more than $24 billion in total assets.

Another reason to use a direct channel is control. When the manufacturer handles distribution, it maintains control of pricing, service, and delivery—all elements of the transaction. Because distributors and dealers carry many products, it can be difficult to get their sales force to focus on selling one product. But in a direct channel, a producer works directly with customers, gaining insights into trends, customer needs and complaints, and the effectiveness of its marketing strategies.

Why do manufacturers choose to use indirect channels to reach consumers? An important reason is that often customers are familiar with certain retailers or other intermediaries—it's where they always go to look for what they need. Getting customers to change their normal buying behaviour—for example, convincing consumers to buy their laundry detergent or frozen pizza from a catalogue or over the Internet instead of from the corner supermarket—might be difficult, although e-commerce grocery businesses (such as OnlineGrocer.ca, based in Ottawa) are finding that many consumers will change their behaviour if presented with the right offer.[11] In addition, intermediaries help manufacturers in all the ways described earlier. By creating utility and transaction efficiencies, channel members make manufacturers' lives easier and enhance their ability to reach customers.

The *manufacturer–retailer–consumer channel* in Figure 10.2 is the shortest indirect channel. GE uses this channel when it sells small appliances through such large retailers as Zellers and Sears. Because the retailers buy in large volume, they can buy at a low price, which they pass on to shoppers. The size of these retail giants also means that they can provide the physical distribution functions, such as transportation and storage, which wholesalers handle for smaller retail outlets.

The *manufacturer–wholesaler–retailer–consumer channel* is a common distribution channel in consumer marketing. For example, a single ice-cream factory can supply four or five regional wholesalers. These wholesalers then sell to 400 or more retailers, such as grocery stores. The retailers in turn each sell the ice cream to thousands of customers. In this channel, the regional wholesalers combine many manufacturers' products to supply to grocery stores. Because the grocery stores do business with many wholesalers, this arrangement results in a broad selection of products.

BUSINESS-TO-BUSINESS CHANNELS Business-to-business distribution channels, as the name suggests, facilitate the flow of goods from a producer to an organizational or business customer such as a factory or a hospital. Generally, business-to-business channels parallel consumer channels—they may be direct or indirect. The simplest indirect channel in industrial markets is the single intermediary—a merchant wholesaler referred to as an *industrial distributor* rather than a retailer—buying products from a manufacturer and selling them to business customers.

Direct channels are more common in business-to-business markets than in consumer markets, because business-to-business marketing often means selling high-dollar, high-profit items—a single piece of industrial equipment may cost hundreds of thousands of dollars— to a market made up of only a few customers. In such markets, it pays for a company to develop its own sales force and sell directly to customers at a lower cost than if it used intermediaries. The Internet is used as a direct channel in business-to-business markets as well. For example, for standardized goods such as car parts, automobile manufacturers use the Internet to ask competing suppliers to bid on a piece of business. The supplier who can meet manufacturer specifications at the lowest price wins the bid.

DISTRIBUTION CHANNELS FOR SERVICES Because services are intangible, there is no need to worry about storage, transportation, and the other functions of physical distribution. In most cases, the service travels directly from the producer to the customer. However, some services do need an intermediary, an *agent* who helps the parties complete the transaction. Examples include insurance agents, stockbrokers, and travel agents.

DUAL DISTRIBUTION SYSTEMS Figure 10.2 shows simple distribution channels; but life is rarely that simple. Manufacturers, dealers, wholesalers, retailers, and customers alike may actually interact with more than one type of channel. These are *dual* or *multiple distribution systems.*

The pharmaceutical industry provides a good example of multiple channel usage (Exhibit 10.9). Pharmaceutical companies distribute their products in at least three channel types. First, they sell to hospitals, clinics, and other organizational customers directly. These customers buy in quantity, purchase a wide variety of products, and, because pills are dispensed one at a time rather than in bottles of 50, require different product packaging than when the products are sold to other customers. Pharmaceuticals' second channel is an

Exhibit 10.9

Pharmacies represent one of many channels used by the pharmaceutical industry.

indirect consumer channel in which the manufacturer sells to large drug retailer chains that distribute the medicines to their stores across the country. Some of us would rather purchase our prescriptions in a more personal manner from a local independent drugstore. In this channel, the manufacturer sells to drug wholesalers that in turn supply these independents.

We have discussed what distribution channels and channel intermediaries are and the role of channel members in the distribution of goods and services. We know that not all channels are alike: Some are direct and simple, but indirect channels can be quite complex. The next section is about how marketers plan channel strategies to meet customer needs better than the competition—the all-important competitive advantage.

PLANNING A CHANNEL STRATEGY

Do customers want products in large or small quantities? Do they insist on buying them locally, or will they purchase from a distant supplier? How long are they willing to wait to get the product? Intelligent marketers want to know. Distribution planning is best accomplished when marketers follow the steps in Figure 10.3. In this section, we'll look at what influences distribution decisions, and discuss how firms select distribution strategies and tactics.

Firms that operate within a channel of distribution—manufacturers, wholesalers, and retailers—may do some distribution planning. In this section, our perspective focuses on distribution planning of producers or manufacturers rather than intermediaries, because they, more often than intermediaries, take a leadership role in creating a successful distribution channel.

Intensive, Exclusive, and Selective Distribution

Distribution strategy decisions also mean determining how many wholesalers and retailers will carry the product within a given market. This may seem like an easy decision: Distribute the product through as many intermediaries as possible. However, if the product goes to too many outlets, there may be inefficiency and duplication of efforts. For example, if there are too many Honda dealerships in town, there will be many unsold Hondas sitting on dealer lots, and no single dealer will be successful. But, if there are not enough wholesalers or retailers carrying a product, total sales of the manufacturer's products (and profits) will not be maximized. If customers have to drive hundreds of kilometres to find a Honda dealer, they may settle for a Ford or a Chevy. Thus, a distribution objective may be to either increase or decrease the level of market penetration.

The three basic choices are intensive, exclusive, and selective distribution. The **channel width** and market coverage that a channel member provides is crucial.[12] Figures 10.4 and 10.5 summarize the key decision factors—company, customers, channels, constraints, and competition—and how they help marketers determine the best fit between distribution system and marketing goals. **Channel length** is also considered in a distribution strategy.

Intensive distribution aims at maximizing market coverage by selling a product through all wholesalers or retailers that will stock and sell the product. An intensive distribution channel's coverage is considered as being wide. Marketers use intensive distribution for such products as chewing gum, soft drinks, milk, and bread that are quickly consumed and must be frequently replaced. Intensive distribution is necessary for these products, because availability is more important than any other consideration in customers' purchase decisions.

In contrast to intensive distribution, **exclusive distribution** means limiting distribution to a single outlet in a particular region. An exclusive distribution channel's coverage is considered as being narrow. Marketers sell pianos, cars, executive training programs, television programs, and many other products with high price tags through exclusive distribution arrangements. These strategies are typically used with products that are high priced and have considerable service requirements and when there is a limited number of buyers in any single geographic area. Exclusive

channel width The extent to which a channel covers a market either by distributing the product through the largest number of intermediaries or to only one in the market.

channel length The number of levels or different types of intermediaries used in a distribution strategy.

intensive distribution Selling a product through all suitable wholesalers or retailers that are willing to stock and sell the product.

exclusive distribution Selling a product through only a single outlet in a particular region.

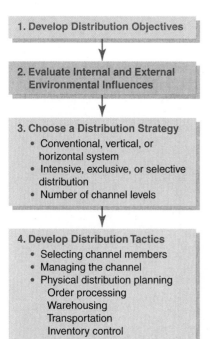

Figure 10.3 Steps in Distribution Planning

Distribution planning begins with setting channel objectives and includes developing channel strategies and tactics.

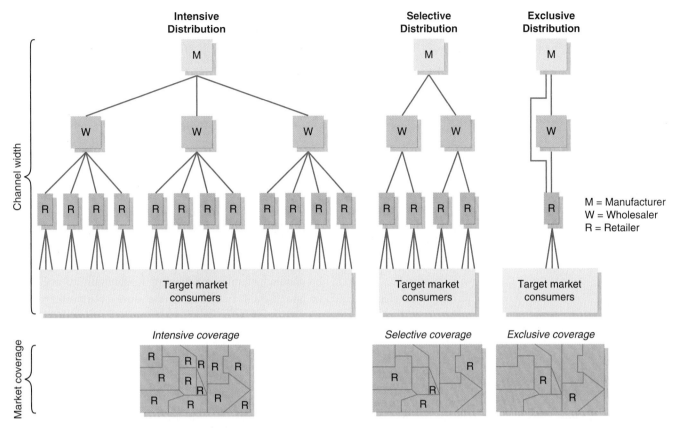

Figure 10.4 Three Specific Strategies for Market Coverage

distribution enables wholesalers and retailers to recoup the costs associated with long selling processes for each customer and, in some cases, extensive after-sale service.

Not every situation neatly fits a category in Figure 10.5. For example, consider professional sports. Customers might not shop for games in the same way they shop for pianos. They might go to a game on impulse, and they don't require much individualized service. Nevertheless, professional sports employ exclusive distribution. The team's cost of serving customers is high, due to those million-dollar player salaries and multimillion-dollar stadiums.

Market coverage that is less than intensive distribution, but more than exclusive distribution, is **selective distribution**. Selective distribution fits when demand is so large that exclusive distribution is inadequate, but selling costs, service requirements, or other factors make intensive distribution a poor fit. Selective distribution strategies are suitable for shopping products, such as household appliances, computers, and electronic equipment, for which consumers are willing to spend time visiting different retail outlets to compare product alternatives. For producers, selective distribution means freedom to choose

selective distribution Distribution using fewer outlets than in intensive distribution but more than in exclusive distribution.

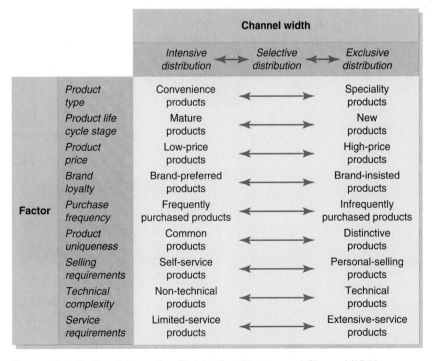

Figure 10.5 Factors Influencing Distribution Strategy and Channel Width

only those wholesalers and retailers that have a good credit rating, provide good market coverage, serve customers well, and cooperate effectively. Wholesalers and retailers like selective distribution because it results in higher sales and profits than are possible with intensive distribution in which sellers often have to compete on price.

Developing Distribution Tactics

As with planning for the other marketing Ps, the final step in distribution planning is developing the distribution tactics necessary to implement the distribution strategy. These decisions are usually about the type of distribution system to use—a direct or indirect channel, a conventional or an integrated channel. Distribution tactics relate to the implementation of these strategies, such as selecting individual channel members and managing the channel.

SELECTING CHANNEL PARTNERS When firms agree to work together in a channel relationship, they become partners in what is normally a long-term commitment. Like a marriage, it is important to both manufacturers and intermediaries to select channel partners wisely or they'll regret the match later. In evaluating intermediaries, manufacturers try to answer such questions as: Will the channel member contribute substantially to our profitability? Does the channel member have the ability to provide the services customers want? What impact will a potential intermediary have on channel control? For example, what small- to mid-sized firm wouldn't jump at the chance to have its products distributed by retail giant Canadian Tire? With Canadian Tire as a channel partner, a small firm could double, triple, or quadruple its business. Actually, more than one firm, recognizing that size means power in the channel, has decided against Canadian Tire, because it is not willing to relinquish control of its marketing decision making.

Another important consideration in selecting channel members is competitors' channel partners. For example, because people spend time comparing different brands when purchasing certain products (consumer durable goods, for example), firms need to make sure their products are displayed near similar competitors' products. If most competitors distribute their electric drills through mass merchandisers, a manufacturer has to make sure its brand is there as well.

fair trade A strategy that creates opportunities for producers of goods and commodities who have been economically disadvantaged or marginalized by conventional distribution systems.

A firm's dedication to social responsibility and **fair trade** may also be an important determining factor in the selection of channel partners (Exhibit 10.10). Many firms have developed extensive programs to recruit minority-owned channel members.

Exhibit 10.10

Fair trade involves transparent management and commercial relations to deal fairly and respectfully with partners in a distribution channel.

Generally speaking, channel partner recruitment is not rocket science, but it does require a professional and robust selection process that is managed with discipline and shared ownership. In essence, any firm needs to motivate its channel partners. Remember, the objective here is to obtain an unfair share of the overall talent pool, thereby forcing competitors to settle for second-best channel partners. You need to keep your channel partners wanting to push your products by way of incentives and power symmetries. It gets more complicated when a multi-channel system is set up.

CHANNEL MANAGEMENT Once a manufacturer develops a channel strategy and aligns channel members, the day-to-day job of managing the channel begins. The **channel captain** is the dominant firm that controls the channel. A firm becomes the channel leader because it has power relative to other channel members. This power comes from different sources:

- A firm has *economic power* when it has the ability to control resources.
- A firm such as a franchiser has *legitimate power* if it has legal authority to call the shots.
- A firm has *reward* or *coercive power* if it engages in exclusive distribution and has the ability to give profitable products and to take them away from the channel intermediaries.

channel captain A firm at one level of distribution that takes a leadership role, establishing operating norms and processes that reduce channel conflicts, reduce costs, and enhance delivered customer value.

Although producers have traditionally held the role of channel captain, a firm at any level of distribution can emerge as a channel leader. When retailers were much smaller than they are now, manufacturers tended to assume leadership in consumer goods markets. Procter & Gamble, for instance, developed customer-oriented marketing programs, tracked market trends, and advised retailers on the mix of products most likely to build sales. As large retail chains evolved and began harnessing customer data via technology, such giant retailers as Wal-Mart Canada, Canadian Tire, and Rona began to assume a leadership role.

Because manufacturers, wholesalers, and retailers depend on one another for success, channel cooperation helps everyone. High intermediary profit margins, training programs, cooperative advertising, and expert marketing advice are invisible to end customers but are important motivating factors in the eyes of wholesalers and retailers.[13] Victoria's Rogers' Chocolates, for example, has found ways to help its retail channel partners become more successful. By improving the speed and accuracy of reorders, retailers are able to maintain inventory levels necessary to satisfy customers while avoiding ordering errors.

Relations among members in a channel are not always wonderful. Because each firm has its own unique set of objectives, channel conflict may threaten a manufacturer's distribution strategy. Such conflict most often occurs between firms at different levels of the same distribution channel. Incompatible goals, poor communication, and disagreement over roles,

SPOTLIGHT ON REAL PEOPLE Grand & Toy

Garry Wood is the CEO of one of the largest commercial office products companies in Canada. Grand & Toy has been in operation for over 120 years; it operates over 70 retail stores and 7 distribution centres, and deals with over 4000 suppliers. Grand & Toy was seeking to better its point-of-sale (POS) system to support the ever-growing demands of the market and an increasingly knowledgeable customer base. Wood wanted a fully integrated POS system for Grand & Toy that included accounting, inventory management, open-to-buy forecasting, customer relationship management (CRM), service management, rental, and payroll modules. The new system was successfully implemented and allowed Grand & Toy to start groundbreaking marketing initiatives. The new POS solution has led to increased sales associate satisfaction and customer service and better relationships with its suppliers. For Grand & Toy suppliers, demand is now easier to predict. Sales are now processed faster and orders to suppliers are customized to address fluctuating demands. Wood is pleased with the results, and feels that Grand & Toy is now truly the channel captain.[14]

1. What distribution channel does Grand & Toy use?
2. What other channels are available to the firm?
3. How does Grand & Toy's distribution strategy differ from that of other office supply retailers?

responsibilities, and functions cause conflict. For example, a manufacturer is likely to feel that the firm would enjoy greater success and profitability if intermediaries carry only its brands, but the intermediaries likely believe they will do better if they carry a number of brands.

Distribution Channels and the Marketing Mix

How are decisions about channel of distribution interrelated with the other three Ps? For one thing, channel decisions affect pricing. Marketers that distribute products through mass merchandisers such as Zellers and Canadian Tire will have different pricing objectives and strategies than those that sell to specialty stores. This is why customer relationship management (CRM) solutions within the channel are important. Sound CRM strategies help firms communicate and adapt to changes in demand.

Distribution decisions can sometimes give a product a distinct position in its market. For example, Peter van Stolk, the creator of Jones Cola, realized that he couldn't compete with the US$200 million Coke and Pepsi spent on advertising, so he chose to try to increase sales through unusual distribution channels. Rather than remain unnoticed on supermarket shelves and convenience stores, van Stolk chose to distribute his product in tattoo and body-piercing parlours, hair salons, sex shops, and fashion stores—anywhere that Coke and Pepsi won't go or won't be taken.

SUPPLY CHAIN MANAGEMENT

Marketing textbooks tend to depict the practice of marketing as 90 percent planning and 10 percent implementation. In the real world, many managers would argue that this ratio should be reversed. Marketing success is very much the art of getting the timing right and delivering on promises. That's why marketers place so much emphasis on efficient **logistics**, the process of designing, managing, and improving the movement of products through the supply chain. Logistics includes purchasing, manufacturing, storage, and transport. To understand logistics, we must first examine the concept of supply chain management.

The Supply Chain

The **supply chain** includes all the firms that engage in activities that are necessary to convert raw materials into a good or service and put it in the hands of a consumer or business customer. Thus, **supply chain management** is the management of flows among the firms in a supply chain to maximize total profitability.

The difference between a supply chain and a channel of distribution is the number of members and their function. A supply chain consists of those firms that supply the raw materials, component parts, and supplies necessary for a firm to produce a good or service *plus* the firms that facilitate the movement of that product to the ultimate users of the product, that is, the channel members. As shown in Exhibit 10.11, a supply chain can be complicated, and sophisticated software is often needed to ensure that a link in the chain does not break. Figure 10.6 provides a simple example of a supply chain for a computer maker such as Hewlett-Packard. Of course, Hewlett-Packard uses hundreds of suppliers in manufacturing its computers, and sells those items through hundreds of online and off-line retailers worldwide. And it is noteworthy

logistics The process of designing, managing, and improving the movement of products through the supply chain.

supply chain All the firms that engage in activities necessary to turn raw materials into a good or service and put it in the hands of the consumer or business customer.

supply chain management The management of flows among firms in the supply chain to maximize profitability.

value chain The concept of a supply chain that looks at how each firm receives inputs, adds value to these inputs, and then passes them along to the next firm in the value chain.

procurement management Procuring goods and services from external suppliers in a strategic fashion.

Ethical Decisions in Marketing

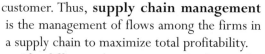

When a firm engages in illegal distribution practices, the marketer loses in a number of ways. The effort spent in building a distribution system is lost, competition gains ground, and courts may impose high fines on a guilty firm. To avoid costly setbacks, marketers must understand the basic legal constraints of channel arrangements. Here are some of the most common offenders:

- Exclusive-dealing contracts: a written agreement allowing the retailer to carry a firm's products only if it does not carry other brands.
- Exclusive territories: an agreement stating that only one wholesaler or retailer will be allowed to sell the manufacturer's products in that geographic area.
- Tying contracts: an agreement in which a producer requires that a wholesaler or retailer purchase one or more of its other products along with the desired product.

Why do you think these practices spell bad business, and for whom?

that the role individual firms play within the supply chain depends on your perspective. If we are looking at Hewlett-Packard's supply chain, Intel is a supplier and Best Buy is a member of its channel of distribution. From Intel's perspective, Hewlett-Packard is a customer. From the perspective of Best Buy, Hewlett-Packard is a supplier.

Another way to look at the supply chain is as a value chain. The **value chain** concept looks at the supply chain from the perspective of adding value.[15] As a product "flows" from a producer to the consumer, other firms add value by providing supporting materials (such as packaging), **procurement management**, financing, a physical space to store or display the item, and so on. So, every firm in the channel of distribution occupies a position on a value chain whether that firm is "upstream" (involved fairly early on in the process) or "downstream" (involved relatively closer to the point where the product reaches the consumer).

With globalization, firms are compelled to outsource. **Outsourcing** is contracting with another firm or person to do a specific task at a cheaper price. Almost every firm outsources nowadays (Exhibit 10.12). As such, value chains are now more globalized than ever. Typically, the task outsourced is considered non-core to the business. Some advantages to be expected from outsourcing are lower costs, better focus on core competencies, and an increased access to intellectual capital.[16] Of course, outsourcing has attracted criticism in recent years due to loss of manufacturing jobs in developed countries and insecure working environments in developing countries.[17]

Let us see how a value chain works in our computer example. Intel takes raw materials such as silicon and adds value by turning them into chips. Intel ships these chips to Hewlett-Packard, which combines them with the other components of a computer, again adding value. Best Buy takes the finished product and adds value by providing display, sales support, repair service, financing, and so forth for the customer. Ideally, then, the product that a consumer "catches" in the value stream has been transformed as it journeys from the source of the stream to its end. Wal-Mart understands the importance of an efficient distribution and logistics management system that in turn creates value for customers and offers them low prices (Exhibit 10.13).

Exhibit 10.11

A supply chain can be complicated, and sophisticated software is often needed to ensure that a link in the chain doesn't break.

outsourcing Transferring a firm's task to an external supplier at a cheaper price.

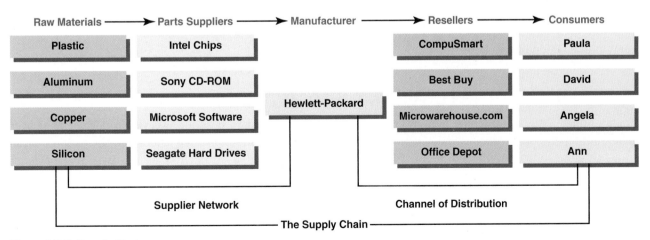

Figure 10.6 Supply Chain

Exhibit 10.12

More firms are now outsourcing tasks unrelated to their core competencies to reduce production costs.

Exhibit 10.13

Sound logistics helped Wal-Mart become the biggest company in the world.

THE LOWDOWN ON LOGISTICS

Logistics was originally a military term used to describe everything needed to deliver troops and equipment to the right place, at the right time, and in the right condition. In business, logistics is similar in that its objective is to deliver exactly what the consumer wants—at the right time, in the right place, at the right price. The application of logistics is essential to the efficient management of the supply chain. Just as it's said that "An army travels on its stomach" (meaning it cannot function without adequate supplies), so a business relies on efficient planning to be sure it has what it needs to contribute its part to the value chain.

Logistics Functions

In developing logistics strategies, marketers must make decisions related to the five functions of logistics: order processing, warehousing, materials handling, transportation, and inventory control. For each decision, managers must consider how to minimize costs while maintaining the service customers want.

ORDER PROCESSING Order processing includes the series of activities that occurs between the time an order comes into the organization and the time a product goes out the door. After an order is received, it is typically sent electronically to an office for record keeping and then to the warehouse to be filled. When the order reaches the warehouse, personnel there check to see if the item is in stock. If it is not, the order is placed on back-order status. That information is sent to the office and then to the customer. If the item is available, it is located in the warehouse, packaged for shipment, and scheduled for pickup by either in-house or external shippers.

Many firms have automated this process. Once an order is in the system, all the other steps occur automatically. Inventories are continuously updated in computer databases so that a sales representative who calls on customers, or telemarketers who take orders by phone, know immediately whether the product is in stock.

WAREHOUSING Whether we speak of fresh-cut flowers, canned goods, or computer chips, at some point goods (unlike services) must be stored. Storing goods allows marketers to match supply with demand. For example, toys and other gift items are big sellers at Christmas, but toy factories operate 12 months of the year. **Warehousing**—storing goods in anticipation of sale or transfer to another member of the channel of distribution—enables marketers to provide time utility to consumers by holding onto products until consumers need them (Exhibit 10.14).

Part of developing effective logistics is deciding how many warehouses a firm needs, where, and what type they should be. A firm determines the location of its warehouse(s) by the location of customers and access to major highways, airports, or rail transportation. The number of warehouses often depends on the level of service customers require. If customers generally require fast delivery (today or tomorrow at the latest), then it may be necessary to store products in a number of different locations where they can be delivered to the customer within a few days.

Firms use private and public warehouses to store goods. With private warehouses, firms have a high initial investment but they also lose less inventory due to damage. Public

> **warehousing** Storing goods in anticipation of sale or transfer to another member of the channel of distribution.

Exhibit 10.14

By warehousing goods, marketers can match supply with demand.

materials handling The moving of products into, within, and out of warehouses.

warehouses are an alternative, allowing firms to pay for a portion of warehouse space. Most countries offer public warehouses in all large cities and many smaller cities to support domestic and international trade. A *distribution centre* is a warehouse that stores goods for short periods of time and that provides other functions, such as breaking bulk.

MATERIALS HANDLING **Materials handling** is the moving of products into, within, and out of warehouses. When goods come into the warehouse, they must be physically identified, checked for damage, sorted, and labelled. Next they are taken to a location for storage. Finally, they are recovered from the storage area for packaging and shipment. The goods may be handled over a dozen separate times. Procedures that limit the number of times a product must be handled decrease the likelihood of damage and reduce the cost of materials handling.

TRANSPORTATION Logistics decisions take into consideration the modes of transportation and the individual freight carriers a firm needs to use to move products among channel members. Making transportation decisions entails a compromise between minimizing cost and providing the service customers want. As shown in Table 10.2, modes of transportation, including railroads, pipelines, water transportation, motor carriers, and airways, differ in the following ways:

- *Dependability:* the ability of the carrier to deliver goods safely and on time.
- *Cost:* the total transportation costs for moving a product from one location to another, including any charges for loading, unloading, and in-transit storage.
- *Speed of delivery:* the total time for moving a product from one location to another, including loading and unloading.
- *Accessibility:* the number of different locations the carrier serves.
- *Capability:* the ability of the carrier to handle a variety of different products (e.g., large and small, fragile and bulky).
- *Traceability:* the ability of the carrier to locate goods in shipment.

Each mode of transportation has strengths and weaknesses that make it a good choice for different transportation needs.

Table 10.2 A Comparison of Transportation Modes

Transportation Mode	Dependability	Cost	Speed of Delivery	Accessibility	Capability	Traceability	Most Suitable Products
Railways	average	average	moderate	high	high	low	heavy or bulky goods such as automobiles, grain, steel
Water	low	low	slow	low	moderate	low	bulky, non-perishable goods such as automobiles
Trucking	high	high for long distances; low for short distances	fast	high	high	high	a wide variety of products, including those that need refrigeration
Air	high	high	very fast	low	moderate	high	high-value items such as electronic goods and fresh flowers
Pipeline	high	low	slow	low	low	moderate	petroleum products and other chemicals
Internet	high	low	very fast	potentially very high	low	high	services such as banking, information, and entertainment

Railways. Railways are best for carrying heavy or bulky items, such as coal and other mining products, agricultural products, forest products, steel, automobiles, and large machines over long distances. Railways are about average in their cost and provide moderate speed of delivery. Although rail transportation provides dependable, low-cost service to many locations, trains simply cannot carry goods to every community in the country, and they can't go over the oceans. These problems with rail transportation have been solved in recent years. *Piggyback services* allow low-cost rail transportation for shipping to a larger number of destinations. Truck trailers are loaded onto trains and carried as close to their destination as possible. Truck, train, and ship transportation have been similarly combined to provide *fishyback services*. Combining truck and air transportation is called *birdyback service*. Problems of excessive handling and damage have been reduced by *containerization*, in which large quantities of goods are sealed in large protective containers for transit.

Water. Ships and barges, like railways, carry large, bulky, nonperishable goods and are very important in international trade. Water transportation is quite low in cost but is very slow.

Trucking. Arnold Bros. Transport Ltd. promises "On the road and on time!" Trucks or motor carriers, such as those operated by Arnold Bros. in Exhibit 10.15, are the most important carrier for consumer goods, especially for shorter hauls. Motor carrier transportation allows flexibility because trucks can travel to those locations missed by boats, trains, and planes. Trucks are also able to carry a wide variety of products, including perishable items.

Exhibit 10.15

Arnold Bros. Transport Ltd. is one of Canada's largest independent transportation companies and a leading player in the North American transportation scene.

Although costs are fairly high for longer-distance shipping, trucks are economical for shorter deliveries. Because trucks provide door-to-door service, product handling is minimal, reducing the chance of product damage.

Air. Air transportation is the fastest and most expensive transportation mode. It is ideal for moving high-value items, such as some mail, electronic goods, fresh-cut flowers, and live lobsters. Passenger airlines, air-freight carriers, and express delivery firms such as Federal Express and Parcel Post provide air transportation. Air transportation, especially the overnight services provided by express delivery firms, is becoming more and more important in the development of international markets—particularly for e-commerce where customers expect fast delivery. Ships, however, remain the major mover of international cargo, with Vancouver, Halifax, and Montreal being Canada's busiest ports.

Pipeline. Pipelines are used to carry such petroleum products as oil and natural gas and a few other chemicals. Pipelines primarily flow from oil or gas fields to refineries. They are very low in cost, require little energy, and are not subject to disruption by weather.

Internet. The Internet is revolutionizing many distribution channels. Although scientists haven't yet figured out how to transport goods electronically, marketers of services such as banking, news, and entertainment are taking advantage of distribution opportunities provided by the Internet. Small entrepreneurs as well as larger firms such as Roots, Molson Canada, and the Bank of Montreal have set up websites to make their products readily available to a worldwide market.

INVENTORY CONTROL A final activity of physical distribution is **inventory control**, developing and implementing a process to ensure that the firm always has goods available to meet customers' demands—no more and no less. Firms store goods, or create an inventory, for many reasons. For manufacturers, the pace of production may not match seasonal demand, and it may be more economical to produce snow skis year round than to produce them only during the winter season. For channel members that purchase goods from

inventory control Activities to ensure that goods are always available to meet customers' demands.

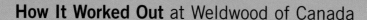

Real People, Real Decisions

How It Worked Out at Weldwood of Canada

Weldwood presented all options to Daito, with emphasis on Option 4 as the favourite. Weldwood's weakness was an inability to supply sufficient "studs" (a wood product used in home construction) for Daito's needs, so it partnered with a competitor that could guarantee sufficient product supplies. The result was a new relationship where Weldwood arranged for a wide variety of building materials and products—including some the company didn't even produce—to be packaged and delivered to Daito's various job sites in Japan.

Thus, Mike was able to offer the customer a more comprehensive product mix and provide "one stop" shopping. Further, Mike promised the customer various other services such as quality control and shipping coordination at a cost. His overall strategy was to expand Weldwood's business with the customer and maximize the returns on goods and services provided.

Weldwood was able to offer Daito considerable goods and services at a profit, while Daito still realized considerable savings. The arrangement has worked out very well for Weldwood. Its sales volumes have more than doubled, with very attractive net margins.

Mike succeeded in this case because he has learned over time that assessing the customer's needs correctly can be very difficult; sometimes customers themselves do not know what their needs are or where the solutions may lie.

Mike's advice for career success is to know what gives you the most fulfillment and pursue your dreams. In his own case he derives the most satisfaction by concluding large deals and knowing that his actions have a significant impact on the growth of a certain housing segment. He loves being accountable for the entire marketing strategy—market development, pricing, channels, and marketing communications.

manufacturers or other channel intermediaries, it may be economical to order a product in quantities that don't exactly parallel demand. For example, delivery costs make it prohibitive for a retail gas station to place daily orders for just the amount of gas people will use that day. Instead, stations usually order truckloads of gasoline, holding their inventory in underground tanks. Finally, the consequences of stock-outs may be very negative. Hospitals must keep adequate supplies of blood, IV fluids, drugs, and other supplies on hand to meet emergencies, even if some items go to waste.

Inventory control has a major impact on the costs of physical distribution. If supplies of products are too low to meet fluctuations in customer demand, a firm may have to make expensive emergency deliveries or lose customers to competitors. If inventories are above demand, unnecessary storage expenses and the possibility of damage or deterioration occur.

Increasingly, manufacturers are turning to quick-response, continuous replenishment, and just-in-time inventory management systems to ensure that their products are available for customers when and where they are needed and to improve the bottom lines of all channel partners. VF Corporation, maker of Lee and Wrangler jeans, uses a computerized market-response system that keeps records on what consumers buy each day from the register scanners of each of its key retail partners, automatically enters an order based on what items have been sold, and ships new jeans to arrive within three days.[18]

Key Terms

- **bulk breaking**, p. 356
- **channel captain**, p. 367
- **channel intermediaries**, p. 352
- **channel length**, p. 364
- **channel levels**, p. 360
- **channel of distribution**, p. 352

CHAPTER SUMMARY

1. **Explain what a distribution channel is and what functions distribution channels perform.**

A distribution channel is a series of firms or individuals that facilitates the movement of a product from the producer to the final customer. Channels provide time, place, and ownership utility for customers and reduce the number of transactions necessary for goods to flow from many manufacturers to large numbers of customers by breaking bulk and creating assortments. Channel members make the purchasing process easier by providing important customer services.

2. **Describe some of the types of wholesaling intermediaries found in distribution channels.**

   Wholesaling intermediaries are firms that handle the flow of products from the manufacturer to the retailer or business user. Merchant wholesalers are independent intermediaries that take title to a product and include both full-function wholesalers and limited-function wholesalers. Merchandise agents and brokers are independent intermediaries that do not take title to products. Manufacturer-owned channel members include sales branches, sales offices, and manufacturers' showrooms.

   Distribution channels vary in length from the simplest two-level channel to longer channels with three or more channel levels. Consumer distribution channels include direct distribution, in which the producer sells directly to consumers, and indirect channels, which may include a wholesaler and/or a retailer. Business-to-business channels may also be either direct or indirect and often include industrial distributors. Distribution channels for services are usually direct but may include an agent intermediary. Many firms are part of more than one type of channel, participating in dual or multiple distribution systems.

3. **Discuss the steps in planning distribution channel strategies.**

   Marketers begin channel planning by developing channel objectives and considering important environmental factors. Conventional marketing systems include multiple levels of intermediaries that work independently. Vertical marketing systems (VMS) are channels in which there is cooperation at the different levels and may be administered, corporate, or contractual. Horizontal marketing systems are composed of firms at one channel level that work together.

   Distribution planning also includes decisions about the number of channel members at each level. Intensive distribution includes all possible intermediaries, exclusive distribution has only one intermediary per region, and selective distribution includes a few but not all outlets in a region. Distribution tactics include the selection of individual channel members and management of the channel.

4. **Describe what a supply chain is, how it is related to a value chain, and how logistics is used to implement the value chain.**

   The supply chain includes all the firms that engage in activities that are necessary to turn raw materials into a good or service for a consumer or business customer, including those in the marketing channel of distribution. Every firm occupies a position on a value chain. Companies add value to inputs received from firms upstream. Logistics is the process of designing, managing, and improving supply chains, including all those activities that are required to move products through the supply chain. Logistics activities include order processing, warehousing, materials handling, transportation, and inventory control.

CHAPTER REVIEW

Marketing Concepts: Testing Your Knowledge

1. What is a channel of distribution? What are channel intermediaries?
2. Explain the functions of distribution channels.
3. List and explain the types of independent and manufacturer-owned wholesaling intermediaries.
4. What is a direct channel? An indirect channel?
5. Explain the steps in distribution planning.
6. What are conventional, vertical, and horizontal marketing systems?
7. Explain intensive, exclusive, and selective forms of distribution.
8. What is a channel captain?
9. What is a supply chain? How is it related to a value chain?
10. What activities are involved in logistics?
11. What are the advantages and disadvantages of shipping by rail? By air? By ship? By truck?

Marketing Concepts: Discussing Choices and Issues

1. You have probably heard someone say, "The reason products cost so much is because of all the intermediaries." Do intermediaries increase the cost of products? Would consumers be better or worse off without intermediaries?

2. Many entrepreneurs choose to start a franchise business rather than "go it alone." Do you think franchises offer the typical business person good opportunities? What are some positive and negative aspects of purchasing a franchise?

3. As colleges and universities are looking for better ways to satisfy their customers, an area of increasing interest is the distribution of their product—education. Describe the characteristics of your school's channel(s) of distribution. What types of innovative distribution might make sense for your school to try?

Marketing Practice: Applying What You've Learned

1. Assume that you have recently been hired as the director of marketing for a medium-sized furniture manufacturer. Your firm specializes in producing small tables and chests, each of which is made unique with a hand-painted design. As your firm is beginning to expand into new regions of the country, you must consider whether an intensive, selective, or exclusive distribution system is best for your product.

   a. Develop an outline listing the pros and cons of each type of system for your product.

   b. Decide which you will recommend, and say why.

2. As the one-person marketing department for a candy manufacturer (your firm makes high-quality, hand-dipped chocolates from only natural ingredients), you are considering making changes in your distribution strategy. Your products have previously been sold through a network of food brokers who call on specialty food and gift stores. But you think that it would be good for your firm to develop a corporate VMS (vertical integration). In such a plan, a number of company-owned retail outlets would be opened across the country. The president of your company has asked that you present your ideas to the company executives. In a role-playing situation with one of your classmates, present your ideas to your boss, including the advantages and disadvantages of the new plan compared to the current distribution method.

3. Assume that you have recently been given a new marketing assignment by your firm. You are to head up development of a distribution plan for a new product line—a series of do-it-yourself instruction CDs for home gardeners. These CDs would show consumers how to plant trees and shrubbery and bulbs, how to care for their plants, how to prune, and so on. You know that in developing a distribution plan, it is essential that you understand and consider a number of internal and external environmental factors. Make a list of the information you will need before you can begin developing the distribution plan. How will you adapt your plan based on each of these factors?

Marketing Mini-Project: Learning by Doing

In Canada, the distribution of most products is fairly easy. There are many independent intermediaries (wholesalers, dealers, distributors, and retailers) that are willing to cooperate to get the product to the final customer. Our highway system combines with rail, air, and water transportation to provide excellent means for moving goods from one part of the country to another. In many other countries, the means for distribution of products are far less efficient and effective.

For this mini-project, you and one or more of your classmates should first select a consumer product, probably one that you normally purchase. Then use either or both library sources and other people (e.g., retailers, manufacturers, dealers, classmates) to gather information to do the following:

1. Describe the path the product takes to get from the producer to you. Draw a model to show each of the steps the product takes. Include as much as you can about transportation, warehousing, materials handling, order processing, and inventory control.

2. Select another country in which the same or a similar product is sold. Describe the path the product takes to get from the producer to the customer in that country.

3. Determine if the differences between the two countries cause differences in price, availability, or quality of the product.

4. Make a presentation to your class on your findings.

Real People, Real Surfers: Exploring the Web

Chapters.indigo.ca (**www.chapters.indigo.ca**) is one of many book retailers that are seeking to develop a competitive advantage through distribution, by offering customers online shopping services. Some other leaders in Internet shopping are Amazon.com (**www.amazon.com**) and Barnes & Noble (**www.bn.com**).

Explore these or other book and music selling sites. Based on your experience, answer these questions.

1. Describe the online shopping services offered by Chapters.

2. Describe the online shopping services offered by the other retailers you have researched.

3. What differences do you see in the online shopping services offered to consumers by the different booksellers?

4. Distribution planning seeks to make products available to customers when and where they want them. Do all customers want book-shopping services available on the Internet? What book-related services do you think consumers and business customers want on the Internet? What services do you think they would prefer through a different distribution channel? Which segments of customers do you think prefer online book shopping to the in-store experience?

5. Of the booksellers you have studied, which do you think provides a competitive advantage for customers like yourself, and why?

6. What is your overall opinion of the bookseller websites you visited? What is it about the sites that makes them appealing to potential customers? Is adequate information about the service provided? Is one site easier to navigate than the other? Based on the design of the website, which customers do you think each bookseller is most interested in attracting?

Visit the MyMarketingLab website at **www.pearsoned.ca/mymarketinglab**. This online homework and tutorial system puts you in control of your own learning with study and practice tools directly correlated to this chapter's content.

Steven Poirier, vice-president of sales and marketing for Moosehead Brewery, considered his options for increasing sales of the popular Moosehead brands of beer. Having operated as a craft brewery for 127 years in Saint John, New Brunswick, Moosehead Brewery now distributes its beer to every province in Canada, except Saskatchewan and Quebec, and sells it internationally in over 60 countries. Although Moosehead is a profitable company, Poirier and the other executives realized that there was still unused capacity in their production facilities. To increase efficiency, Moosehead investigated the viability of additional distribution markets. Quebec seemed like the next logical step for distribution. The province is densely populated, with 7.3 million residents, and is the second largest beer consumption market in Canada, consuming 5.3 million hectolitres a year. As Quebec and New Brunswick are neighbouring provinces, distribution costs would be significantly lower than shipping to other markets.

Poirier considered the company's usual marketing strategy. Moosehead's basic strategy focuses on selling its product as a premium Canadian lager. Its approach in each market differs, based on volume, market conditions, as well as distributor and government regulations. Within Canada, Moosehead starts out with a strong licensee push to generate trial and awareness, as this is the most cost-effective way to promote the product. It then begins to overlay advertising through print, radio, and billboards and signs. It could use a similar strategy in Quebec, taking into account language and cultural differences.

Poirier, very familiar with the Canadian food and beverage industry—having worked for Bacardi Rum and McCain Foods—realized that there would be challenges to distributing Moosehead products in Quebec. New Brunswick and Quebec have historically struggled with high inter-provincial trade barriers, and there were strong labour and corporate lobby groups that wanted to keep Moosehead out of the province.

The push against Moosehead is being led by a smaller Quebec brewery, whose product is not selling well in the New Brunswick market. The Quebec company believes that the New Brunswick regulations are causing the poor sales. Their product, however, is sold at a very high premium price and is a Belgian-style beer, quite different in taste from English-style ales and lagers. It is also difficult to compare the regulations of out-of-province product, as the New Brunswick and Quebec practices are structured differently.

New Brunswick marks up out-of-province beer by an additional $59 per hectolitre, but also guarantees 100 percent retail distribution. Quebec, however, is not involved in the liquor industry, so it does not offer any distribution services. Subcontracting the distribution costs a company a minimum of $48 per hectolitre, but this does not provide any guarantee of listings. To list the product, most breweries need to account for another $24 per hectolitre. Moosehead believes that these factors will contribute to higher costs when selling in Quebec. However, the provincial regulators do not recognize this.

Other challenges involve physical distribution and channel management. In British Columbia and Ontario, all alcoholic beverages are sold through government-owned liquor distribution branches (LDB). Trucks carrying Moosehead beer have relatively few stops to deliver product to the LDBs. In-store promotions are typically coordinated centrally and are similar for each of the government retail outlets, making promotion management fairly straightforward. In Alberta and Quebec, however, alcohol is sold to independent retailers or retail chains. Each retailer is responsible for negotiating contracts as well as for obtaining and promoting product. The breweries also have to assume the cost of warehousing the inventory. Selling beer in these provinces is similar to selling other retail products, such as cola or toothpaste, and requires a stronger channel management program. Moosehead would also have to ensure that the labels follow Quebec language regulations.

To balance these challenges, Moosehead already has very high brand awareness in Quebec. Its initial studies indicate that retailers are very interested in stocking Moosehead beer, and the company is confident that it will attain high-volume sales. Sales are excellent in areas surrounding Quebec. Although the two major Canadian breweries enjoy a 90 percent market share, Moosehead has the largest market share of the "smaller breweries." Poirier feels he could maintain Moosehead's premium image and pricing in the Quebec market because of this brand awareness.

After much thought and analysis, Poirier thought that entering the Quebec market made sense for Moosehead. It was not clear, however, how best to do this. Poirier knew that he needed to devise a market entry strategy for Quebec, make marketing mix decisions consistent with this strategy and the Quebec market, and focus particularly on distribution and relationship management issues. There would be implementation issues, but he didn't know if any of these would be insurmountable.

Things to Think About

1. What marketing mix and market entry strategy would you recommend for Moosehead?

2. How would you manage Moosehead's relationships with Quebec retailers and other key stakeholders?

3. What issues, barriers, or limitations would need to be overcome to implement your strategy? Do any of these seem insurmountable?

4. What additional research or analysis would you want to conduct before implementing your launch strategy?

CHAPTER 11
Retailing and Etailing

CHAPTER OBJECTIVES

WHEN YOU HAVE COMPLETED YOUR STUDY OF THIS CHAPTER, YOU SHOULD BE ABLE TO

1. Define retailing and describe how retailers evolve over time.

2. Describe how retailers are classified.

3. Understand the importance of store image to a retail positioning strategy, and explain some of the actions a retailer can take to create a desired image in the marketplace.

4. Describe the major forms of non-store retailing.

5. Describe the opportunities and barriers to etailing.

Real People, Real Decisions

Meet **Dawn Robertson**, a Decision Maker at Federated Direct

Dawn Robertson is president and chief merchandising officer at Federated Direct. After obtaining a Bachelor of Science degree in Fashion Merchandising from Auburn University in 1977, Dawn secured a job as a buyer and executive trainee with Davidson's, then a division of R.H. Macy & Co. Before joining Federated, Dawn was president and chief executive officer of McCrae's, a division of Saks, Inc.

Discount stores, catalogue companies, and online upstarts have been grabbing business right and left from department stores. Being the president and chief merchandising officer at Federated Direct, the Federated department stores' consumer catalogue and e-commerce division, Dawn Robertson looked for ways to outperform these rivals. She saw one opportunity for growth in the bridal business, especially since increasing numbers of baby boomers' kids would be at the age to get married over the next decade. Since Federated added an Internet component to its bridal registry operation, the total bridal business (both in-store and online) now reported to her.

Dawn was convinced that, under the right conditions, Federated could acquire new customers and win the lifetime loyalty of millions of brides and grooms. In fact, her research showed that over half of women who get engaged shop at new stores as they prepare for the Big Day—and three years later 96 percent of them are still shopping at those stores. That's a relationship worth cultivating.

Even though Federated Stores, which included Macy's East and West, Bloomingdale's, Rich's, Lazarus, Goldsmiths, Burdines, and The Bon Marché, were recognized as the leaders in bridal registry, younger consumers in greater numbers were going to newer, cooler specialty stores. To make matters worse, Dawn knew that a poor bridal registry experience could poison the relationship brides, grooms, and their wedding guests have with a store. She also recognized that Federated was not alone in seeing the potential of this business: Competition is fierce as retailers such as Bed, Bath and Beyond; Target; and Crate and Barrel lure droves of engaged couples to their registries.

Two other trends factored into Dawn's thinking: (1) Offering engaged couples personalized bridal consulting, once the advantage of the department store, was eroding as web-savvy women were doing research online, (2) With the exception of certain brands of china, specialty and discount stores were carrying the same merchandise as traditional department stores at cheaper prices.

So, Dawn reviewed customer feedback gathered from 15 000 customer surveys, 10 focus groups, and evaluations of competitors conducted by Federated staff. The research found that consumers liked Federated's bridal merchandise overall, but in-store service and visual displays were in need of work. And, unlike some of its competitors' private label offerings, Federated store brands did not evoke an emotional connection with its customers. Dawn also learned that brides- (and grooms-) to-be love using the scanning gun that lets them scan in the items they want to register without the need for a salesperson. However, this cool tool was no longer novel or rare. Many stores, even discounters, offered a self-scan option.

Dawn had three options to enhance Federated's bridal services business.

Option 1: Offer a total bridal solution.

Maintain the existing bridal registry business (the product offerings and service), but invest in buying bridal dress and tuxedo businesses, while developing alliances with a national florist and a bridal magazine to make Federated the "Total Bridal Location." This strategy would differentiate Federated from its competitors by offering a broad selection of services that the bride and groom need. But this option would require a significant investment. And these extra businesses would not be a core competency—it's difficult for big retailers to compete with smaller stores on customer service.

Option 2: Slowly enhance registry offerings.

Improve Federated's bridal offerings slowly without adding significant investment. Focus on providing better in-store training to sales representatives and better merchandise selection, particularly in the china and crystal categories that make up 50 percent of bridal sales. This conservative financial strategy would slightly increase sales and bridal registrations without draining the company of time and money. However, this strategy would not deter competitors from taking away bridal registry market share, and it would not establish Federated as a leader in this category.

Option 3: Completely redo the bridal registry.

Totally revamp Federated's core bridal business and give it a new marketing push. This strategy would require significant change in merchandise selection, pricing policies, and customer service. Such a radical move could either succeed beautifully or fail miserably. It would take management's time away from other initiatives, cost a lot of money, and be difficult to execute across both Federated's bricks-and-mortar and online operations.

Now, put yourself in Dawn Robertson's shoes: Which option would you choose, and why?

RETAILING: SPECIAL DELIVERY

Shop till you drop! For many people, obtaining the product is half the fun. Others would rather walk over hot coals than spend time in a store. Marketers need to find ways to deliver products and services that please both types of consumers. **Retailing** is the final stop on the distribution path—the process by which goods and services are sold to consumers for their personal use.

A retail outlet is often more than simply a place where you buy something. The retailer adds or subtracts value from the offering with its image, inventory, service quality, location, and pricing policy. In many cases, the shopping experience is what is being bought as well as the products we take home. That's what visitors to the Discovery Channel store in Washington, DC, get when they meet up with a life-size model of a *Tyrannosaurus rex* on the main floor of the four-level store. The place feels like a museum, with such attractions as a cockpit from a vintage World War II plane.[1] Similarly, part of Ikea's strategy is to make its stores a shopping destination with experiences that encourage shoppers to spend more time there.

Retailers are a special breed of marketers. They assemble and present products, often from many different manufacturers, in ways that make them appealing and accessible. And they often develop unique and exciting store images that are similar to the product branding strategies we've already discussed. In this chapter, we explore the different types of retailers, comparing and contrasting them along some key dimensions, keeping in mind that today's shoppers have many retail choices—boutiques, department stores, ordering by phone, and clicking on a website. How does a retailer—whether a traditional one operating a store or a non-store retailer selling via television, phone, or computer—lure the consumer? These important marketing questions get more difficult to answer as the competition for customers intensifies. We start with an overview of where retailing has been and where it's going.

retailing The final stop in the distribution channel by which goods and services are sold to consumers for their personal use.

Retailing: A Mixed (Shopping) Bag

Retailing is big business. About one in eight Canadian workers is employed in retailing, and the sales from more than 217 000 retail stores represent about 9.54 percent of Canada's gross domestic product—and that percentage is growing.[2] Although we tend to associate huge chains like Ikea, Canadian Tire, and the Bay with retailing activity, most retailers (about 75 percent) are independent small businesses.[3] Some retailers, such as Home Depot and Costco, are also wholesalers, and provide goods and services to businesses as well as end consumers. We saw how the wholesaling process works in the previous chapter. Now, we'll focus on the process that delivers goods and services to individuals for their personal use (Exhibit 11.1).

The Evolution of Retailing

Retailers have taken many forms over time, including the simple peddler who hawked his wares from a horse-drawn cart, a majestic urban department store, an intimate boutique, and a huge hypermarket that sells everything from potato chips to snow tires. Old types of retailers routinely give way to new variations, as economic, social, and cultural developments change the face of society. That horse-drawn cart has been replaced by the cart that sits in the middle of your local mall, selling new-age jewellery or monogrammed golf balls to passersby en route to grab a plate of sushi in the food court or catch a movie at a state-of-the-art theatre. As times change, different types of retailers emerge, often replacing older, outmoded types. How can we understand and predict what the dominant types of retailing will be tomorrow or 10 years from now to be sure that we keep in step?

THE WHEEL OF RETAILING One of the oldest and simplest explanations for these changes is the **wheel-of-retailing hypothesis**. This states that new types of retailers find

wheel-of-retailing hypothesis A theory that explains how retail firms change, becoming more upscale as they go through their life cycle.

Exhibit 11.1

Retailing is big business indeed. Retailers in Canada are now selling $400 billion worth of goods across the country. Retailers like lululemon athletica provide many benefits to consumers. Some save people time or money by providing an assortment of merchandise under one roof. Others search the world for the most exotic delicacies, allowing shoppers access to goods they would otherwise never see. Still others, such as Chapters and Indigo bookstores, provide us with interesting environments in which to spend our leisure time and, they hope, our money.

it easiest to enter the market by offering goods at lower prices than competitors.[4] After they gain a foothold, they gradually trade up, improving their facilities, increasing the quality of merchandise, and offering amenities like parking and gift wrapping. This upscaling results in greater investment and operating costs, so the store must raise its prices to remain profitable, which then makes it vulnerable to still newer entrants that can afford to charge lower prices. And so the wheel turns. The wheel of retailing helps explain the development of some, but not all, forms of retailing. For example, some retailers never trade up; they simply continue to occupy a niche as discounters. Others, such as upscale specialty stores, start out at the high end. Let's take a look at a more satisfying explanation.

THE RETAIL LIFE CYCLE Retailers sell products; but in a way, retailers also *are* products, because they provide benefits such as convenience or status to consumers and must offer a competitive advantage over other retailers to survive. A better way to understand how retailers evolve is the **retail life cycle**. Like the product life cycle, this perspective recognizes that retailers are born, they live, and eventually they die. The life cycle approach allows us to categorize retail stores in terms of the conditions they face at different points in the cycle.[5]

In the *introduction* stage, the new retailer is often an aggressive entrepreneur who takes a unique approach to doing business. This may mean competing on the basis of low cost, as the wheel of retailing suggests. However, the new guy on the block may enter the market by offering a distinctive assortment or a different way to distribute items, such as through the Internet. In this initial stage, profits are low due to high development costs.

As the business enters the *growth* stage, the retailer catches on with shoppers, and sales and profits rise. But a new idea doesn't stay new for long. Others start to copy it, and competition increases, so the retailer needs to expand what it offers. Often the retailer responds by opening more outlets and developing systems to distribute goods to these new stores, which may cut profits, as the firm invests in new buildings and fixtures.

retail life cycle A process that focuses on the various retail life cycle stages from introduction to decline.

Exhibit 11.2

Full-service gas stations fight off decline by adding products to their retail mix.

In the *maturity* stage, the industry has overexpanded, and intense competition makes it difficult to maintain customer loyalty. Profits decline, as retailers resort to price cutting to keep their customers. This pattern applies to department stores like the Bay and fast-food chains like McDonald's. Office supply superstores are entering the mature phase of the retail life cycle, which means they need to find ways of differentiating themselves other than price. For example, Office Depot enlisted the help of cartoon character Dilbert, the stereotypical cubicle dweller, to forge a distinctive identity, claiming: "Business is crazy. Office Depot makes sense."[6]

In the *decline* stage, retail businesses, like the general store or the peddler, become obsolete, as newer ways of doing business emerge. The outmoded retailer does not have to fold its tent at this stage: Marketers that anticipate these shifts can avert decline by changing to meet the times. For example, full-service gas stations had difficulty competing with self-service discount outlets. Many responded by adding variety stores to their retail mix for drivers wanting to buy a tank of gas and groceries at the same location, as seen in Exhibit 11.2. Canada Safeway is doing the opposite—adding gasoline to its retail mix.[7]

The Evolution Continues: What's "in Store" for the Future?

As our world continues to rapidly change, retailers are scrambling to keep up. Three important factors motivate innovative merchants to reinvent the way they do business.

DEMOGRAPHICS As noted in Chapter 2, keeping up with changes in population characteristics is at the heart of many marketing developments. Retailers can no longer afford to stand by and assume that their customer base is the same as it has always been. They are coming up with new ways to sell their products to diverse groups. Major demographic factors altering the face of retailing include:

- *Convenience for working women:* Some retailers are expanding their hours of operation, because many harried women have time to shop only at night. Others, including dry cleaners and pharmacies, are adding drive-up windows to meet demands for convenience and security. In some areas, from financial services to interior decorating and clothing,

Exhibit 11.3

Retailers are increasingly using technology. Self-checkout counters distract customers into thinking they spend less time in line waiting.

enterprising individuals have turned time shortage into a business opportunity by offering their services as shopping consultants for those unwilling or unable to shop on their own. Many major department stores also fill this need by offering the services of their own in-house consultants at no charge.

- *Catering to specific age segments:* Retailers are recognizing that there are many opportunities to specialize in providing for the needs of different age groups. For example, boomers tend to shop and make purchases based on trusted brands, and retailers recognize that.[8] Ikea offers an example of how retailers cater to a specific age segment. Ikea is responding to its me-too rivals by developing Children's Ikea, which sells furniture and related products for kids. The company recruited psychologists to assist in creating 600 new products for this market, from egg-shaped cribs to fabric dolls.[9]

- *Recognizing ethnic diversity:* Although members of every ethnic group can usually find local retailers that understand and cater to their specific needs, larger companies must tailor their strategies to the cultural makeup of specific areas. George Michel, president of the Toronto-based Burger King Restaurants of Canada, for example, recognized that catering to multiculturalism would benefit the company. With 25 percent of the Toronto population being of Chinese descent, Michel began the "Now we're speaking the same language" ad campaign in Cantonese, focusing on strategic locations. Burger King also rolled out its veggie burger to ethnic markets to appeal to non-beef-eating East Indian and East Asian markets.[10] Canada's Aboriginal peoples represent an under-served market niche. In the three Prairie provinces they make up at least 10 percent of the population, half of them are under 30, their education levels are soaring, and land-claim settlements (across Canada) are forecast to be $15 billion by 2010.[11]

TECHNOLOGY Technology is revolutionizing retailing. In-store video channels entertain customers by giving messages about local events or showing ads.[12] Some stores feature talking posters that contain a sensor that speaks up when a shopper approaches.[13] Other stores (Exhibit 11.3) are experimenting with wireless networks that allow shoppers to scan in their own items as they shop, eliminating the need for checkout lines.[14] When shoppers enter a store, whatever chip-enabled device they are carrying—a cellphone, Palm computer, or smart card—interacts with a store's computer system to update the shopper's buying profile and provide the shopper with individualized communications, coupons, and other incentives.[15] And widespread use of the personal computer has turned many homes into virtual malls, as consumers surf the web from the comfort of their own chairs.

Some of the most profound changes are not even visible to shoppers, such as advanced electronic **point-of-sale (POS) systems**, which collect sales data, are hooked directly into the store's inventory control system, and place timely orders to ensure that the store does not stock out of an item. Birks jewellers, for example, uses its new POS system for this purpose; but in the future, the chain expects to use it for such marketing applications as analyzing trends and planning local sales.[16]

Other technological innovations will radically change the way we shop in the future. Leading retailers predict that in the year 2010, each consumer will have a personal preference card so that a store will know your tastes, clothing sizes, and even your current household decor. When shopping for furniture, a design consultant will call up a 3-D image of your living room and show you how your new purchases will actually look in the room. Or, forget about endlessly trying on clothes—holographic imaging will let you "see" yourself

point-of-sale (POS) systems Retail computer systems that collect sales data and are hooked directly into the store's inventory control system.

in a new suit or dress.[17] As Exhibit 11.4 shows, sophisticated body scanners already exist that can read a person's exact dimensions and send this information to machines that produce clothing precisely tailored to individual proportions.

GLOBALIZATION As we know, the world is becoming a smaller place. Retailers are busy expanding to other countries and bringing with them innovations and management philosophies that change the way local firms do business. Many international retailers, such as Ikea, Blockbuster Entertainment, Home Depot, and Toys "R" Us (Exhibit 11.5), are prominent in Canadian retailing, while some Canadian retailers such as Roots, La Senza, and Mark's Work Wearhouse have made significant inroads in the United States and other parts of the world.[18] Cinnaroll Bakeries Ltd., a western Canadian cinnamon bun retailer, has 10 Cinnzeos franchises in the Philippines and has signed an agreement for 50 more Cinnzeos throughout Southeast Asia.[19]

Of course, an understanding of global retailing means recognizing that retailing differs from country to country. In many developing countries, the retailing industry is made up of small individual retailers (Exhibit 11.6). In many parts of the developing world, kiosks or small street-corner stands sell cigarettes, soft drinks, snacks, and batteries—the products of convenience stores.

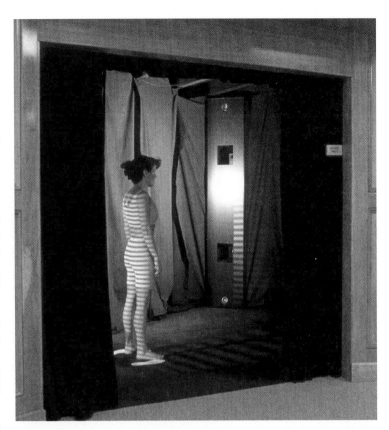

Exhibit 11.4

Body scanners can read a person's exact dimensions and send this information to machines that produce precisely tailored clothing.

Exhibit 11.5

International retailers, such as Toys "R" Us, are prominent in Canadian retailing.

Exhibit 11.6

In planning expansion to other countries, companies must consider the way retailing is done in each country. In China, many independent retailers take their merchandise to open markets in pedicarts.

TYPES OF RETAILERS

We've seen that exciting things are happening in the world of retailing. But the field of retailing covers a lot of ground—from mammoth department stores to sidewalk vendors to websites. This section provides an overview of the different types of retailers. Retail managers need to understand the competitive environment in which they operate to make decisions about the ways to offer their merchandise to the public and to compare the productivity of their business to similar retailers.

Classifying Retailers by What They Sell

One of the most important strategic decisions a retailer makes is *what* to sell—its **merchandise mix**. This choice is similar to settling on a market segment: If a store's merchandise mix is too limited, it may not have enough potential customers; if it is too broad, the retailer runs the risk of being a "jack of all trades, master at none." A retailer's **merchandise assortment**, or merchandise mix, is the variety and selection of products it sells. It has both breadth and depth.

Merchandise breadth, or variety, is the number of different product lines available. A *narrow assortment*, such as that found in convenience stores, means that its customers can buy only a limited selection of product lines, such as candy, cigarettes, and soft drinks. A *broad assortment*, such as that in a warehouse store, means there is a wide range of items, from eyeglasses to barbecue grills.

Merchandise depth is the variety of choices available for each specific product. A *shallow assortment* means that the selection within a product category is limited, so a factory outlet store may sell only white and blue men's dress shirts all made by the same manufacturer and only in standard sizes. In contrast, a men's specialty store may feature a *deep assortment* of dress shirts, but not much else, in exotic shades and in hard-to-find sizes. Figure 11.1 illustrates these assortment differences for one product, science fiction books.

The strategy of carrying a mixture of merchandise items that are not directly related to each other is called **scrambled merchandising**. This strategy is exemplified by Blockbuster

merchandise mix The total set of all products offered for sale by a firm, including all product lines sold to all consumer groups.

merchandise assortment The range of products sold.

merchandise breadth The number of different product lines available.

merchandise depth The variety of choices available for each specific product.

scrambled merchandising A merchandising strategy that offers consumers a mixture of merchandise items that are not directly related to each other.

Entertainment Group, which defines its merchandise mix in terms of products a customer might want when spending an evening at home, including food items and other goods. In addition to stocking your favourite James Bond video, the stores sell candy, soda, and even private-label popcorn to complete the couch potato experience.

In deciding what merchandise assortment to offer, retailers need to strike a balance between the profitability of the mix and ensuring that they have the depth and breadth required to satisfy their customers. On the profitability side, they consider the markup on particular items, projected sales volume, and gross margin (revenues minus cost of goods sold, calculated as a percentage of sales). Gross margin, however, does not consider the costs of operating the store. Knowing a store's gross margin is useful, because it is a performance measure that allows the retailer to compare how it is doing relative to similar stores. The retailer also can compare how much different product lines within the store are contributing to profits. Usually, stores that mark up items substantially will have higher gross margins than those that sell products closer to what they actually cost the store to buy.

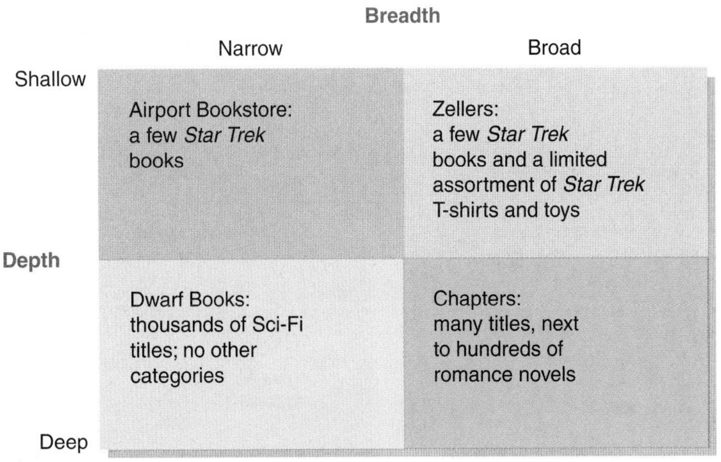

Inventory turnover, or *stock turn*, is the average number of times a year a retailer expects to sell its inventory. For example, a candy store owner can expect to sell the "same" pack of gum hundreds or thousands of times a year. A jewellery store owner may need to sell only one diamond ring per year to make the same profit as the gum retailer selling a thousand packs a year. So the candy store owner hopes to sell a greater volume of merchandise to compensate for razor-thin margins. All retailers, regardless of gross margin, try to

Figure 11.1 Merchandise Selection for Science Fiction Books

Retail stores are often classified based on the breadth and depth of their merchandise assortment. In this figure, the two dimensions are used to classify types of bookstores that carry science fiction books.

inventory turnover The average number of times a year a retailer expects to sell its inventory.

Marketing Metrics

Measuring Value

Retail stores like Jos. Bank typically measure store performance by looking at sales per square foot and by looking at comparable store sales on a year-to-year basis. While the comp-store sales have proven useful in measuring the progress of new stores and the value of locations, sales metrics are not enough.

Unlike catalogue retailers that can measure catalogue fill rates to determine whether they are meeting customer demand, bricks-and-mortar retailers have a difficult time tracking the number of customers who enter a store with the intent to purchase but who walk out with nothing. Now, companies are developing customer intelligence programs that use video camera systems as a way to count traffic in

retail stores. These programs count the number of shoppers that enter the store and compare these data with the number of transactions the POS system processes during the same time frame. This new measure allows retailers to understand the conversion rate of customers walking through the door. To further track why conversion rates are less than 100 percent, retailers can use the POS system to monitor each stock-keeping unit (SKU) and record the exact time stock runs out. By judging the demand for an SKU on a weekly basis, retailers can use a metric they call weighted in-stock percentage to help them assess just how "hot" a given item is compared to other merchandise the store is selling at the same time.

Exhibit 11.7

Convenience stores such as 7-Eleven offer consumers just that, convenience, by carrying a limited number of frequently purchased items.

encourage more rapid turnover, because this helps guarantee that their merchandise will be "fresh" and that expenses associated with storing the products will be minimized.

Overly rapid turnover, however, results in greater costs, because products must be bought in smaller quantities. The retailer, then, can't take advantage of volume discounts offered by the manufacturer or wholesaler, and delivery charges are higher for small shipments. Successful retailers try to balance gross margin and inventory turnover. The Gap, for example, started by selling items with thin profit margins, such as inexpensive jeans and T-shirts. When competitors began imitating this strategy, the company boosted profits by modifying its merchandise mix to include more higher-margin items, such as hats and handbags.[20]

STORE TYPES We have seen that retailers differ in the breadth and depth of their assortments. Let's review some of the major forms these retailers take.

Convenience stores, such as Mac's or 7-Eleven, are neighbourhood retailers that carry a limited number of frequently purchased items, including basic food products, newspapers, and sundries (Exhibit 11.7). They cater to consumers willing to pay a premium for the ease of buying staple items close to home. In other words, they meet the needs of those who are pressed for time, who buy items in smaller quantities, or who shop at irregular hours.

Supermarkets, such as Loblaws, Sobeys, and Safeway, are food stores that carry a wide selection of edible and non-edible products. Although the large supermarket is a fixture in North America, it has not caught on to the same extent in other parts of the world. Europeans, for example, are used to walking or bicycling to small stores near their homes. They tend to have smaller food orders per trip and to shop more frequently. Wide variety is less important than quality and local ambience, though those habits are changing as huge hypermarkets have grown in popularity.

Specialty stores, such as La Senza, Mark's Work Wearhouse, and the Running Room (Exhibit 11.8), have narrow and deep inventories. They do not sell a lot of product lines, but they offer good selection of brands within the lines they do sell. Some retailers are even establishing specialty store-within-stores, such as the Bay's in-store vitamin boutique.

An example of a specialty store that has adapted to changes in technology is Blockbuster Video. Blockbuster has adopted a *clicks and mortar* marketing strategy to keep up with competitors that are entering Blockbuster's traditional marketplace. Utilization of a website along with a physical presence allows Blockbuster to rent to a larger clientele and allows its customers flexibility in rental products. Its adoption of technology was required to compete with Netflix.com, an online rental firm that is a direct competitor in the rental industry. There are also non-traditional competitors in the form of cable and digital television providers. Communications providers such as Shaw Cable, Rogers, SaskTel, Telus, and Bell ExpressVu all offer video-on-demand products with their current selection of television channel packages. The technology that provides Blockbuster Video with a competitive advantage could also be the technology that hurts it. Software piracy is an outside threat to its rental business that increases as access to technology becomes readily available. Blockbuster had to change from an older model of doing business to a newer method to compete with competitors and software piracy.

Exhibit 11.8

The Running Room is a specialty store targeting jogging, cycling, walking, and other fitness enthusiasts.

General merchandise discount stores, such as Zellers and Wal-Mart, offer a broad assortment of items at low prices and with minimal service. Some discount stores, such as Winners, Army & Navy, and Toronto's Honest Ed's, are **off-price retailers**. These stores obtain surplus merchandise from manufacturers and offer these brand-name, fashion-oriented goods at low prices.

Warehouse clubs, such as Costco and the Loblaws warehouse stores, are a new version of the discount store. These establishments do not even pretend to offer any of the amenities of a store; a bargain mentality is reinforced by merchandise that is displayed, often in its original box, in a cavernous, bare-bones facility. These clubs often charge a modest membership fee to consumers and small businesses, which buy a broad assortment of food and non-food items in bulk sizes. The typical warehouse shopper is likely to have a large family and a relatively high income and can afford to pay several hundred dollars to "stock up" on staples during one shopping trip.[21]

Factory outlet stores, such as Danier Leather Factory Outlet, are another type of discount retailer. These stores are owned by a manufacturer and sell off its defective merchandise or excess inventory.[22] Although the assortment is not wide, because a store carries only products made by one manufacturer, a recent trend is for different factory outlet stores to cluster together in the same location to form an *outlet mall*.

Department stores, such as the Bay and Sears, sell a broad range of items and offer a deep selection organized into different sections of the store. Department stores have encountered serious problems in recent years, exemplified by the bankruptcy of Eaton's and its subsequent sale to Sears. Specialty stores have lured department store shoppers away with deeper, more cutting-edge fashion selections and better service. They have also been squeezed by mass merchandisers, catalogues, and e-commerce retailers, which can offer many of the same items at lower prices, because they don't have to shoulder expenses involved in elaborate fixtures or high salaries for knowledgeable salespeople.

Hypermarkets combine the characteristics of warehouse stores and supermarkets. Popular in Europe and Latin America, these huge establishments are several times larger than other stores. A supermarket might be 3700 to 4600 square metres, whereas a hypermarket takes up 18 500 to 28 000 square metres, the equivalent of four football fields. They offer one-stop shopping, often for over 50 000 items, and feature restaurants, beauty

off-price retailers Retailers that buy excess merchandise from well-known manufacturers and pass the savings on to customers.

hypermarkets Retailers with the characteristics of both warehouse stores and supermarkets; hypermarkets are several times larger than other stores and offer virtually everything from grocery items to electronics.

Exhibit 11.9

Continente, a Spanish hypermarket, offers one-stop shopping and includes a variety of smaller stores within the store.

salons, and children's play areas (Exhibit 11.9). They haven't caught on as well in North America, where so many discount stores, malls, and supermarkets are available, and consumers find the hypermarkets to be so large that finding items and checking out is too time-consuming.[23]

DEVELOPING A STORE POSITIONING STRATEGY: RETAILING AS THEATRE

Although stores can be distinguished by the breadth and depth of their assortments, we are less likely to say "I'll go to that store because its assortment is broad" than to say "That place is neat, I like going there." Stores can entertain us, they can bore us, they can make us angry or make us sad. In today's competitive marketplace, retailers have to do more than offer good inventory at reasonable prices. They need to position their stores so that they offer a competitive advantage over other stores also vying for the shopper's attention. Let's see how they do that.

Walk into REI, a Seattle-based store that sells gear for climbing, cycling, skiing, and camping. REI is more than that, though. The store features a 20-metre-high, artificial climbing rock, a vented area for testing camp stoves, and an outdoor trail to check out mountain bikes. Buying a water pump? Test it in an indoor river. Eyeing that new Gore-Tex jacket? See how it holds up in a simulated rainstorm.[24]

Many retailers recognize that much of what they do is really theatre. At a time when it is possible to pick up a phone or log onto a website to buy many items, a customer must have a reason to make a trip to a store instead. True, you can probably buy that jacket over the Internet, but try getting your computer to rain on it.

Shoppers are an audience to entertain. The "play" can cleverly employ stage sets (store design) and actors (salespeople) that together create a "scene." For example, think about buying a pair of sneakers. Athletic shoe stores are a far cry from the old days, when a tired shoe salesman waded through box after box of shoes as kids ran amok across dingy floors. Now salespeople may be dressed in black-striped referee outfits, and stores like Foot Locker are ablaze with neon, with the shoes displayed in clear acrylic walls appearing to float.[25] All these special effects make the buying experience less about buying and more about having an experience. As one marketing strategist commented, "The line between retail and entertainment is blurring."[26]

Ontario's Liquor Control Board (LCBO) recognized the importance of entertainment to attract customers and motivate purchases (Exhibit 11.10). It created a 1850-square-metre mega liquor store in Toronto's Bayview Village shopping centre, which has 1600 different wines, 250 foreign and domestic beers, music-listening stations, a gift-wrapping centre, and a demonstration kitchen for cooking presentations and wine-tasting seminars—turning what was once a mundane trip to the liquor store into a great shopping experience.[27] Such retailers are focusing on **experiential marketing**. What tools are available to the retailing playwright?

Exhibit 11.10

Retailers like Ontario's Liquor Control Board (LCBO) invest more in experiential marketing.

Store Image

When people think of a store, they often have no trouble describing it in the same terms they might a person. They use words like *exciting*, *depressed*, *old-fashioned*, *tacky*, or *elegant*. **Store image** is how the target market perceives the store—its market position relative to the competition. For example, Holt Renfrew's department store is seen by many as chic and fashionable, especially compared to a more traditional competitor such as the Bay (Exhibit 11.11). These images don't just happen. Just as brand managers do for products, store managers work hard to create a "personality."

experiential marketing A holistic approach to marketing predicated on the fact that consumers make both rational and emotional buying decisions.

store image The way a retailer is perceived in the marketplace relative to the competition.

Exhibit 11.11

Holt Renfrew's department store is seen by many Canadian consumers as chic and fashionable.

In developing a desirable store image, the resourceful retailer has a number of choices. Ideally, all these elements should work together to create a clear, coherent picture that meets consumers' expectations of what that particular shopping experience should be.

atmospherics The use of colour, lighting, scents, furnishings, and other design elements to create a desired store image.

Atmospherics is the use of colour, lighting, scents, furnishings, sounds, and other design elements to create a desired setting. Marketers manipulate these to create a certain "feeling" about the retail environment. U.S. retailer Kinney, whose Colorado stores sell high-end outdoor clothing, has taken this to an extreme. Its stores are designed to make the shoppers feel they're out in nature: The stores pipe in new-age background music, interrupted occasionally by the sound of a thunderstorm or a babbling brook. Motion sensors in the ceiling activate displays as a shopper approaches—a person who walks near an arrangement of beach shoes, for example, may hear the sound of waves crashing.[28] The owners of these stores believe that getting people "into the mood" makes them more likely to buy what they see.

STORE DESIGN: SETTING THE STAGE The elements of store design should correspond to management's desired image. A bank lobby needs to convey respectability and security, because people need to be reassured about the safety of their money. In contrast, a used bookstore might create a disorderly look, so shoppers will think treasures lie buried beneath piles of tattered novels. One of the most innovative restaurant store designs in Canada is the Richtree Market restaurant in Toronto's BCE Place. This 400-seat restaurant has several rooms, each decorated in different styles, such as French bistro. The cafeteria-style restaurant offers stations throughout the store where customers can watch their dinner of sushi, spit-roasted Cornish hen, or fresh pasta being prepared. An in-store bakery, ice-cream parlour, and fruit and vegetable stand allow customers to complete their grocery shopping after dinner, a feature especially attractive to busy business people.

Some specific design decisions management must make are:

traffic flow The direction in which shoppers move through the store and what areas they pass or avoid.

- *Store layout.* This is the arrangement of merchandise in the store. The placement of fixtures such as shelves, racks, and cash registers is important, because store layout determines **traffic flow**—how shoppers move through the store and what areas they pass or avoid. A *grid layout*, usually found in supermarkets and discount stores, consists of rows of neatly spaced shelves that are at right angles or parallel to one another. This configuration is useful when management wants to systematically move shoppers down each aisle, ensuring that they pass through such high-margin sections as deli and meat. Figure 11.2 illustrates how a grid layout in a supermarket helps to regulate traffic flow. A typical strategy is to place staple goods in more remote areas. The designers know that traffic will move to these areas, because staples are purchased frequently. They try to place impulse goods in spots shoppers will pass on their way elsewhere; then they place eye-catching displays to catch people's attention. In contrast, a *free-flow layout* is more often used in department and specialty stores, because it is conducive to browsing. A retailer might arrange merchandise in circles or arches or perhaps in separate areas, each with its own distinct image and merchandise mix.

- *Fixture type and merchandise density.* Just as we form impressions of people from the way they decorate their homes, our feelings about stores are affected by furnishings, fixtures (shelves and racks that display merchandise), and even how much "stuff" is packed into the sales area. Generally, clutter conveys a lower-class store. Upscale stores allocate space for sitting areas, dressing rooms, and elaborate displays of merchandise. A southern California shopping centre called the Lab attracts its target audience of mall rats aged 18 to 30 by using unusual furnishings—concrete walls, a fountain made of oil drums, and an open-air living room filled with thrift-shop furniture—to craft a laid-back image its patrons call "the anti-mall."

- *The sound of music.* An elegant restaurant softly playing Mozart in the background is worlds apart from a raucous place such as the Hard Rock Café, where loud rock 'n' roll is essential to the atmosphere. One owner of a 7-Eleven convenience store discovered the power of music when he figured out how to deter groups of teenagers who were loitering in his store. He piped in "classics" from the 1940s and 1950s, and soon they were gone.[29]

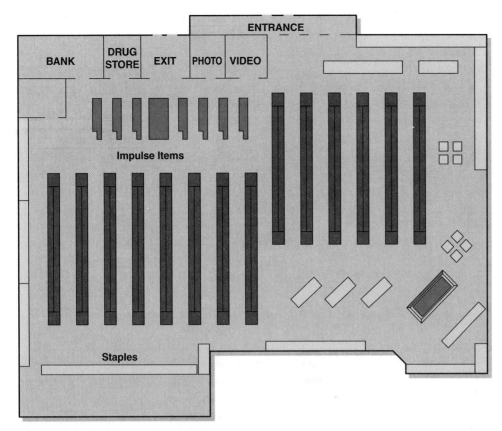

Figure 11.2 A Typical Grid Layout for a Supermarket

A grid layout encourages customers to move up and down the aisles, passing many different products, and is often used by supermarkets and discount stores.

- *Colour and lighting.* Marketers use colour and lighting to set a mood. Red, yellow, and orange are warm colours (fast-food chains use a lot of orange to stimulate hunger), whereas blue, green, and violet signify elegance and cleanliness. Light colours make one feel more serene, whereas bright colours convey excitement. Nova Scotia's Bolands food stores, for example, moved all their fruits and vegetables onto one 3.5-metre wall of produce, painted the wall black, and highlighted the whole section with spotlights. This treatment, as well as the addition of a few new and exotic varieties of produce, drew customers to the produce and increased sales.[30]

THE ACTORS: STORE PERSONNEL Store personnel should complement a store's image. Each employee has a part to play, complete with props and costumes. Movie theatres sometimes dress ushers in tuxedos, and many store employees are provided with scripts to use when they present products to customers. At the Loblaws store at Toronto's Queen's Quay (Exhibit 11.12), for example, counter staff help to create a fun and entertaining atmosphere by engaging customers with banter and hucksterisms—with the seafood counter clerk, for example, yelling "Fresh fish, get your fresh fish here."[31]

Although the presence of knowledgeable sales personnel is important to shoppers, they generally rate the quality of service they receive from retail personnel as low, often because stores don't hire enough people to wait on their customers.[32] In one survey, 62 percent of shoppers said they had decided to not buy a product in a store in the past six months because sales clerks were unavailable to help them.[33] Retailers are working hard to upgrade service quality, though they often find that the rapid turnover of salespeople makes this a difficult goal to achieve. Perhaps they can learn from Japanese retailers: A visitor to a Japanese store is greeted by an enthusiastic, polite employee who bows profusely.[34]

Exhibit 11.12

Counter staff at this Loblaws complement the store's image by helping to create an engaging atmosphere.

PRICING POLICY: HOW MUCH FOR A TICKET TO THE SHOW? When consumers form an image of a store in their minds, the *price points*, or price ranges, of its merchandise often play a role. Ed Mirvish used humour and poetry to communicate his concept of Honest Ed's, for example: "Honest Ed's for the birds—his prices are cheap, cheap, cheap." Similarly, Daffy's, a U.S. off-price retailer, advertises: "Friends Don't Let Friends Pay Retail." In recent years, department stores have been hurt by consumers' desires for bargains. The response of many department stores was to run frequent sales, a strategy that often backfired because many consumers would buy *only* when the store held a sale. Many stores, such as Zellers and Home Depot, have reduced the number of sales they run in favour of an everyday low-pricing (EDLP) strategy. Loblaws supports its premium shopping experience with prices that are often slightly higher than the competitors'. It has recognized, however, that premium merchandise and pricing need to be supported by premium store designs, and that the building itself contributes a lot to the customer experience.[35]

Building the Theatre: Store Location

Realtors list the three most important factors in buying a home as "location, location, and location." The same is true in retailing. Wal-Mart's success is not due to what it is but *where* it is. Wal-Mart was the first mass merchandiser to locate in small and rural market areas. When choosing a site, its planners consider such factors as proximity to highways and major traffic routes. By carefully selecting "undiscovered" areas, the company has been able to negotiate inexpensive leases in towns with expanding populations, an important strategy for Wal-Mart because it means access to markets hungry for a store that offers such a wide assortment of household goods.[36] The same goes for fast-food giant McDonald's. This section reviews some important aspects of retail locations.

TYPES OF STORE LOCATIONS As Figure 11.3 shows, there are four basic types of retail locations—a business district, a shopping centre, a free-standing entity, and a non-traditional location.

- *Business districts.* A *central business district (CBD)* is the traditional downtown business area in a town or city. Many people are drawn to the area to shop or work, and public transportation is usually available. CBDs have suffered in recent years due to concerns about

A central business district is often found in downtown areas. Although North American retailers have been deserting city centres for the past 20 years, these downtown areas are now staging a comeback. Such sophisticated developments as Toronto's St. Lawrence Market (shown here) and Queen's Quay, Winnipeg's The Forks, and Vancouver's Granville Market are bringing shoppers back to the city cores.

A shopping centre features one or more anchor stores, usually major department stores that initially attract shoppers, who then discover the other small, specialty stores in the centre. Shopping centres have the advantages of (1) providing heavy traffic flow (especially for small stores that would not attract so many people if they were on their own), (2) the sharing of costs (such as advertising and promotion) among tenants, and (3) a clean (and usually safe) environment. It seems likely that large malls will continue to evolve as entertainment centres and for recreational shopping, featuring a greater mix of movie theatres, restaurants, and hobby and bookstores. The West Edmonton Mall is the world's largest retail centre, featuring a wide variety of shopping and entertainment experiences.

A freestanding store is not located near other stores. This locational strategy, used by some big chains like Kids "R" Us, has the advantage of offering a lack of direct competition, lower rents, and adaptability. The store has the freedom to alter its selling space to accomodate its own needs. On the other hand, the store had better be popular because it cannot rely on the drawing power of neighbour stores to provide it with customer traffic.

A non-traditional location offers products to shoppers in convenient places. Canadian banks and financial institutions are opening branches and kiosks in large grocery stores. McDonald's has located inside Wal-Mart stores to entice customers to take a McBreak from shopping.

Source: Chip Walker, "Strip malls: Plain but powerful," *American Demographics*, October 1991, 48(4).

Figure 11.3 Types of Store Locations

Different types of store locations are best for different types of retailers. Retailers choose from among central business districts, shopping centres, freestanding stores, and non-traditional locations.

security, lack of parking, and the lack of customer traffic on evenings and weekends. To combat these problems, many cities provide such incentives as tax breaks to encourage the opening of stores and entertainment areas like Toronto's St. Lawrence Market, as shown in Figure 11.3. These vibrant developments are called *festival marketplaces*, and they have done much to reverse the fortunes of aging downtown areas.

• *Shopping centres.* A shopping centre is a group of commercial establishments owned and managed as a single property. They range in size and scope from *strip centres* to massive *super-regional centres*, such as the West Edmonton Mall, shown in Figure 11.3, North America's largest retail centre—a 492 370-square-metre complex complete with a theme-room hotel, amusement park, water park, full-sized indoor skating rink, deep sea adventure area that houses dolphins and submarines, casino, and shooting gallery.[37] Strip malls offer quick and easy access to basic conveniences such as dry cleaners and video rentals, though shoppers seeking more exotic goods need to look elsewhere. Shopping

Exhibit 11.13

Sunglass Hut uses kiosks to provide shades to the masses.

malls offer variety and the ability to combine shopping with entertainment. On the other hand, rents tend to be higher, so it's difficult for stores such as home-improvement centres to be profitable. In addition, small specialty stores may find it hard to compete with a mall's *anchor stores*, the major department stores that typically draw many shoppers.

- *Free-standing retailers.* Some stores, usually larger ones such as Kids "R" Us (Figure 11.3), are free-standing, located by themselves in a separate building. These retailers benefit from lower rents and fewer parking problems. However, the store must be attractive enough on its own to be a destination point for shoppers, because it can't rely on spillover from consumers visiting other stores at the same place.

- *Non-traditional store locations.* Innovative retailers find new ways to reach consumers. Many entrepreneurs use *carts*, small, movable stores that can be set up in many locations including inside malls, airports, and other public facilities, or *kiosks* that are slightly larger and offer store-like facilities, including telephone hookups and electricity. As Exhibit 11.13 shows, Sunglass Hut sells nothing but sunglasses in its kiosk. Its assortment is narrow and deep. Carts and kiosks are relatively inexpensive and a good way for new businesses to get started. Mall operators need to be careful about regulating carts, because they may block a store or sell merchandise that is incompatible with a desired image.

SITE SELECTION: CHOOSING WHERE TO BUILD Retailers used to simply choose to build a store on a site where an adequate number of people saw it. Sam Walton, the founder of Wal-Mart, used to fly over an area in a small plane until he found a spot that appealed to him. No more. Now such factors as long-term population patterns, the location of competitors, and the demographic makeup of an area factor into retailers' decisions. The choice of where to open a new store should reflect the company's overall growth strategy. It should be consistent with long-term goals and be in a place that allows the company to best support the outlet. For example, a chain with stores and an extensive warehouse system in Ontario may not be wise to open a new store on Vancouver Island, because the store would be an "orphan" cut off from the company's supply lines.

Location planners look at many factors when selecting a site. A store's targeted consumer segment is a key determinant of where it locates. For example, a new, growing community would be appealing for hardware stores that can supply hammers and drywall to home owners, whereas upscale dress stores and travel agencies might find better locations in more established areas where people have the income to spend on fashion items and vacations. Planners also want to find a place that is convenient to customers in the store's **trade area**, the geographic zone that accounts for the majority of its sales and customers.[38] A *site evaluation* considers such specific factors as traffic flow, number of parking spaces available, ease of delivery access, visibility from the street, local zoning laws that determine the types of buildings, parking, and signage allowed, as well as such cost factors as the length of the lease and the amount of local taxes.

Planners also consider such population characteristics as age profile (Is the area witnessing an influx of new families?), community life cycle (Is the community relatively new, stable, or in decline?), and mobility (How often are people moving in and out of the area?). Planners also have to consider the degree of competition they will encounter by locating in one place rather than another.

trade area A geographic zone that accounts for the majority of a store's sales and customers.

ETAILING AND OTHER NON-STORE RETAILING

Many products are readily available in places other than traditional "bricks and mortar" stores. For example, the familiar Avon ladies, who sell cosmetics and other beauty products to millions of women around the world, show that a retailer need not be a store. Avon is continuing to explore new ways to give customers access to its products. Customers can place orders by phone, fax, catalogue, via the Internet, or through a sales representative. Avon has even tested a 30-minute infomercial to sell its products on television.[39]

Avon's success at giving customers alternatives to traditional store outlets illustrates the increasing importance of **non-store retailing**, which is any method a firm uses to complete an exchange that does not require a customer visit to a store. North Americans spend almost $70 billion through catalogues, TV shopping channels, the Internet, and other non-store formats.[40] Many retail stores even offer non-store alternatives to buying their merchandise, such as using catalogues and websites. As the founder of the Neiman-Marcus department store acknowledged: "If customers don't want to get off their butts and go to your stores, you've got to go to them."[41]

non-store retailing Any method used to complete an exchange with a product end user that does not require a customer visit to a store.

Two major types of non-store retailing are **etailing** and **direct marketing**. Customers are exposed to merchandise through print, broadcast, or electronic media and then purchase the products over the Internet, by phone, or by mail. In this section, we'll review the major forms of non-store retailing, starting with the newest—buying on the Internet.

etailing Offering products for sale directly to consumers via the Internet.

direct marketing Exposing a consumer to information about a good or service through a non-personal medium and convincing the customer to respond with an order.

ETAILING

Throughout this book, we have talked about electronic commerce—conducting business transactions and communication over networks and through computers. In the chapter on customer (organizational) buying behaviour we discussed electronic commerce's place in business-to-business (B2B) markets. In this chapter, our focus is on etailing, electronic commerce in business-to-consumer (B2C) markets.

Industry Canada and market research firms forecast annual growth of 50 to 70 percent through 2010 and expect worldwide e-commerce sales of US$1.9 to $3 trillion.[42] So even in the aftermath of some "dot.bombs," there is a lot of excitement about etail opportunities.

WHO SHOPS ONLINE? Almost 65 percent of Canadians have tried to buy something online.[43] Traditionally (a couple of years ago), Internet shoppers tended to be better educated, younger men who were better off financially. Increased access to the Internet at work, school, libraries, and home, however, has reduced demographic differences in online shopping. The profile of online consumers now mirrors those of other shoppers: Online shoppers

Marketing Metrics

E-commerce marketers often want to measure a metric they call the conversion rate, which is the percentage of visitors to an online store who purchase from it. This is a useful metric, but if this rate is low, it doesn't help the retailer understand the possible factors affecting the website's performance. So, in addition to knowing the conversion rate, researchers compute other metrics called microconversion rates that enable them to pinpoint more precisely what may need to be improved in the online shopping process. This technique first breaks down the shopping experience into the stages that are involved between visiting a site and actually making a transaction.

Product impression: Viewing a hyperlink to a webpage presenting a product

Click-through: Clicking on the hyperlink and viewing the product's webpage

Purchase: Actually buying the item

The researchers then calculate microconversion rates for each transition between stages to come up with additional metrics that can pinpoint specific problems in the shopping process:

Look-to-click rate: How many product impressions are converted to clickthroughs? This can help the etailer determine if the products featured on the website are the ones that customers want to see.

Click-to-basket rate: How many clickthroughs result in a product being placed in the shopping basket? This metric helps to determine if the detailed information provided about the product is appropriate.

Basket-to-buy rate: How many basket placements are converted to purchases? This metric can tell the etailer which kinds of products are more likely to be abandoned in the shopping cart instead of being bought. It can also pinpoint possible problems with the checkout process, such as forcing the shopper to answer too many questions or making her wait too long for her credit card to be approved.

bots Electronic robots or shopping agents that help consumers find products and prices on the Internet.

are now, on average, older, increasingly female, less affluent, and less highly educated than they once were.[44]

WHY DO THEY SHOP ONLINE? Consumers shop online to achieve a variety of benefits, known as the six Cs: cost, choice, convenience, customization, communication, and control (see Figure 11.4). Many consumers shop online to get lower prices and to reduce the psychological cost of comparison shopping: Product information is just a click away, and there are **bots**, electronic shopping agents that help consumers find the lowest prices.

Other consumers shop online because of choice and convenience—accessibility to products from around the corner to around the world, the ability to buy them from the comfort of their home or office, and the ability to have their purchases delivered right to their homes or, in the case of gifts, directly to others, gift-wrapped with a personalized card. Lingerie sellers, like La Senza (Exhibit 11.14), and La Vie en Rose, provide a convenient, more private online shopping experience that is particularly attractive to men buying lingerie for women.[45] They make it convenient by using standard sizing, offering easy-to-follow sizing charts, making products out of Lycra which accommodates different sizes and shapes, and having flexible return policies.

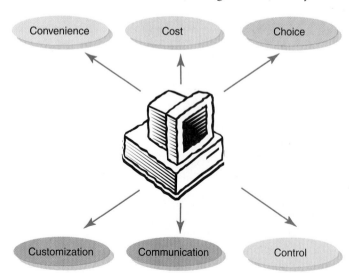

Figure 11.4 The Six Cs of Etailing

Still others are attracted to buying online because of their ability to have interactive communication with etailers. **Push technology** allows marketers to automatically send customers relevant information, specified by consumer preferences; while e-mail, chat rooms, and call centres allow consumers to talk back.

Pizza 73 is a pizza company in western Canada that is utilizing technology to gain a competitive advantage. Customers are able to register their name, address, and preferences through the Pizza 73 website. All contact information is stored in Pizza 73's contact centre database and the webpage is linked with its point-of-sale system. All sales go through the company POS, regardless of whether the sale is taken by telephone, website, or walk-in clientele at its physical storefront locations. Dedicated contact centre staff process orders to allow the cooking staff to concentrate on quality food production. During the information gathering process, the customer's e-mail address and telephone number are taken so that future specials or offers that match up to the customer's past purchase preferences will be sent out to drum up new sales. Pizza 73 can now target its push marketing campaigns to make them more effective.

Exhibit 11.14

Lingerie retailer La Senza stresses convenience as a main benefit of shopping online.

Online shopping gives customers greater control over the shopping experience, and allows them to engage etailers on their own terms and make more informed purchase decisions. Internet **portals**, such as **Canoe.ca** and **Sympatico.ca**, assist consumers in navigating the Internet, finding products, and making informed choices. Finally, **search engines** such as **yahoo.com**, **ask.com**, and **Google.ca** are Internet tools often used by consumers to find etailers. When a consumer "Googles" shoes, for example, he or she expects to see a list of shoe retail and/or etail stores. Marketers of retailing companies make sure that the store they represent is shown at the top of the list on the first page of search results to increase sales.

WHAT DO THEY BUY? Although still in its infancy, electronic commerce has transformed the way we shop. Buyers now have access to millions of stores around the world without leaving their computers, and often they can easily get crucial information before making a purchase. For example, Intel is working on a site for Ticketmaster that allows the customer to move around a virtual replica of a concert hall or a sports arena to test the view from different seats before buying tickets: Try doing that over the phone.[46] Clearwater Fine Foods of Nova Scotia sells fresh lobster, shipped to your door anywhere in North America within 24 hours. Ordering might be done by fax, but it's easier to track your dinner over the Internet using software supplied by courier companies like UPS and Federal Express.

Travel services, banking services, computer hardware and software, financial services, collectibles, autos, health and beauty products, toys, books, and videos are fast-moving online items. Products that can actually be delivered electronically over the Internet, such as computer software, news, music, videos, electronic games, financial services, airline and other tickets, and maybe even books are naturals for etailing—the convenience of buying these products online may soon make other forms of distribution obsolete.

Table 11.1 illustrates other consumer products that have the potential to do well online. This is not an exhaustive list. Every day innovative entrepreneurs are demonstrating business models for selling new product categories online.

Critical Success Factors

We are just beginning to see the enormous potential of electronic commerce in retailing. The success of this non-store format will depend on the ability of retailers to offer sites that are entertaining and informative, and that are worth revisiting again and again even after the novelty wears off. Blast Radius, a Vancouver-based web design company with production offices in Toronto, New York, San Francisco, Los Angeles, and Amsterdam, won gold and silver

push technology Internet tools that allow marketers to send information they think is relevant to consumers directly to their computers.

portals Gateways to the Internet that assist consumers in navigating the Internet and customizing their experience.

search engines Internet tools that maintain databases of websites and use programs to collect information in order to help users find webpages on a given subject.

Table 11.1 Consumer Products That Have Had Success or Have the Potential to Do Well Online

Characteristic	Description	Example
Straight rebuys	Consumers have product and brand experience and just want another one as conveniently and cost effectively as possible	packaged goods, household items, health, flowers, personal care products
Commodities	No or few perceived differences between brands and price is a key buying criteria	produce, electricity, recycling services, telephone services
"Low-touch" items	Items that don't need to be tried on or fitted, felt, or smelled (although once body shapes and sizes are determined, even custom clothes can be bought online)	
Have high retail margins	Direct to consumer distribution may provide significant cost savings	toys, cosmetics, clothes
Can be customized	Can be targeted to very narrow audiences around the world	computers, cars, clothing, music
Expensive to inventory	Difficult and expensive to offer wide selections in traditional retail settings	cars, computers, household appliances
Invite comparison shopping	Products that are highly differentiated or where there are many options and where consumers can save time and effort by comparing product features and prices	consumer electronics, household furniture and fixtures
Difficult to find	Where supply is limited or geographically inaccessible	collectibles, specialty goods, antiques, art

Clio awards for the interactive sites it designed for Casio.[47] These sites keep consumers involved, bring them back, and help build brand loyalty. A segment of a critical success factor is a firm's website domain name. In the early days of the Internet, individuals were purchasing domain names on speculation that the Internet was the market of the future. Microcell Communications, the company behind the Canadian mobile telephone provider Fido, offered a firm that owned the domain name fido.com $20 000 for that web address. Web addresses that are catchy or representative of a firm's name or business are the Internet version of a store location. A colourful, user-friendly website with a good layout will also ensure the success of a website. Just as in retailing, colours and background graphics are as important as colour and lighting in a store. Bright, friendly websites will draw more customers to them than a dark website.

More than ever, consumers can communicate among themselves through sites like **YouTube.com** (Exhibit 11.15) and social networking sites like **Facebook.com** and **MySpace.com**. At these sites, video clips and blogs, often produced and written by consumers, are rapidly disseminated throughout the world. While etailers can cheaply test products and advertisements online at these sites, consumers now have access to more information than ever before. The online world is a very dynamic marketplace and it is very difficult for any etailers to keep up.

Guerrilla marketing strategies will use websites such as those mentioned above to get their message out. They provide "free" webspace for content providers. Guerrilla marketers are using the Internet for a tried and true method of marketing: word-of-mouth advertising.

Exhibit 11.15

Sites like YouTube allow consumers to share information, but also allow etailers to test-market certain products and advertisements at little or no cost.

Branding (discussed in Chapter 8) is particularly important in etailing, as customers need to know what to look for online and need some way to assess the trustworthiness of online suppliers. That's why many etailers are spending, on average, 32 percent of revenues on marketing communications, where traditional retailers typically spend about 5 percent.[48]

A second critical success factor is building loyalty. This is where Canadian etailers excel, with 47 percent of their revenues coming from repeat customers compared to 31 percent for U.S. etailers.[49] As Figure 11.5 shows, speed of delivery, cost of delivery, responsiveness of customer service, and return policy are key factors driving customer satisfaction, a key determinant of customer loyalty. We will have more to say about the relationship between customer satisfaction and customer loyalty in Chapters 4 and 6.

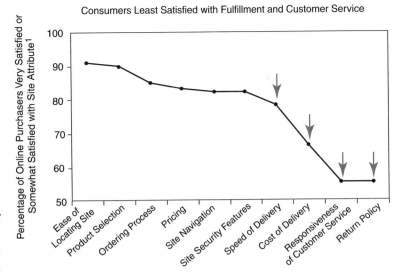

Consumers Least Satisfied with Fulfillment and Customer Service

Figure 11.5 Determinants of E-Customer Satisfaction

An example of branding where an etailer has built up customer loyalty is Chapters/ Indigo books. The large selection and quick and reliable delivery of books directly to the door have built up customer loyalty to a base of customers who either don't like going to the storefront location or live in remote locations.

Branding and customer loyalty are also key issues for traditional retailers. Where etail organizations really stand out is in their **scalability**, their ability to get bigger without a big rise in expenses. Once a website is set up, it is accessible anywhere in the world. It also allows marketers such as **Bluenile.com** to almost infinitely expand the depth and breadth of their product assortment, as long as they can deliver the product to the customer (see the Spotlight on Real People, on page 404).

One thing to watch when utilizing etailing is network congestion. The web hosting company must be able to handle and process incoming traffic. Logarithmic growth rates are not unheard of in emerging Internet services. If the web hosting firm does not have the bandwidth or processing power on the web server to process the information, the effect that this can have on a website is similar to closing the doors on a business.

Another problem is that people need "touch-and-feel" information before buying many products. For this reason, companies such as Tupperware, Amway, and Mary Kay discourage Internet sales. Executives at Tupperware want shoppers to be able to "burp" their plastic containers to appreciate their airtight qualities.[50] This is one reason why Just White Shirts and Black Socks of Mississauga decided to open a bricks-and-mortar warehouse outlet in Toronto to support its Internet and mail-order sales (Exhibit 11.16)—some buyers just have to touch the fabric and feel the weight of the cotton.[51]

Many consumers are still reluctant to buy over the Internet due to their concerns about security. They are understandably reluctant to provide such sensitive information as credit card numbers. Technological advances such as digital signatures, 128-bit encryption, and secure hypertext transfer protocol (https) may help to ensure that valuable personal information is secure, and pre-paid e-cards may reduce the risk of others using your credit card number.[52] The governments of Ontario and Saskatchewan have passed e-commerce bills to ensure that electronic contracts, documents, and signatures have the same legal effect as non-electronic versions to protect both consumers and businesses.[53]

As major marketers beef up their presence on the web, some are concerned that inventory sold online will cannibalize store sales. That is not a concern of Future Shop: This electronics retailer has one of Canada's busiest websites, with over 100 000 visits each month.

scalability The ability of organizations to get bigger without a big rise in expenses.

SPOTLIGHT ON REAL PEOPLE   Bluenile.com

Amy Smith is what happens when true love meets the Internet. The 31-year-old fell in love with an engagement ring she saw at Tiffany & Co., the high-end jewellery store. When she got home she went to Blue Nile, a jewellery etailer, and after using the site's guides to master the four Cs of diamonds (colour, cut, clarity, and carats), she picked one costing US$10 000. But what surprised this consumer was that **bluenile.com** beat Tiffany & Co.'s price by almost $6000. Amy thought to herself, "Why are the offline retailers so expensive?"

Welcome to the web's second act, being led by jewellery etailers such as Blue Nile Inc., founded by Mark Vadon, a discouraged engagement ring shopper, and Ben Elowitz.

Founded in 1999, bluenile.com went public in May 2004. Selling diamonds, double-strand pearl necklaces, sterling silver bangle bracelets, and more, online jewellers made up about $2 billion of the industry's $45 billion in revenues in 2006. These etailers are textbook examples of how the web fundamentally undercuts traditional ways of doing business.

They run their business by knocking out the intermediaries and expensive stores to lower costs, then offering the consumer lower prices. Amazon.com, for example, is betting it can make money on 15 percent markups instead of the industry's usual 60 percent to 100 percent. "We believe over time customers figure these things out," says Thomas J. Szkutak, Amazon's chief financial officer.[54]

1. Do you think upscale retailers such as Tiffany & Co. face troubles from online retailers, or do you think their image and cachet afford them protection?

2. Some authors argue that neighbourhood jewellery stores face the biggest threat from jewellery etailers. Do you agree? What can neighbourhood stores do to insulate themselves from the online attack?

3. What other goods and services do you think are prime candidates for following Blue Nile's business model? Provide a rationale for your choice.

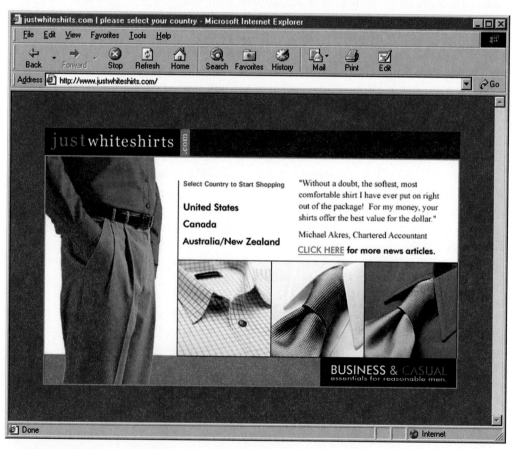

Exhibit 11.16

Some non-store retailers are opening traditional storefronts to support their brands.

The site is fully integrated with its stores in a "clicks and mortar" concept, so that consumers can decide to buy online or just browse online and go to a traditional Future Shop store to purchase. The retail stores provide their customers with a tangible point of reference, places where they can go and see the products.[55]

Manufacturers also face a problem. If they sell their products directly on the web, they will anger stores that carry their merchandise. Companies such as Mattel are experimenting with online marketing and are finding that consumers appreciate access to hard-to-find items, such as Share a Smile Becky, a wheelchair-bound friend of Barbie that many small toy stores don't stock. Still, these companies must be sure they don't antagonize the many stores on which they still rely to sell their products.[56]

In addition, electronic retailing has the potential to increase price competition, because the web surfer can look for the same branded item offered on numerous websites and just buy it wherever it's cheapest, regardless of whether the business is located next door or on another continent. Indeed, shopping bots already scan cyberspace for bargains; these electronic agents (such as the ones found at **www.compare.net** and **www.webmarket.com**) automatically access many sites and compare prices.

Direct Marketing

Although etailing has gained significant attention in the marketplace, there are more established forms of non-store retailing, by which customers are exposed to merchandise through print or electronic media and then purchase the products by phone or mail. Let's look at the most popular types of direct marketing, starting with the oldest—buying through the mail. The communications functions of direct marketing will be discussed in Chapter 13.

MAIL ORDER In 1872, Aaron Montgomery Ward and two partners put up $1600 to mail a one-page flyer that listed their merchandise with prices, hoping to spur a few more sales for their retail store.[57] The mail-order industry was born. Today, consumers can buy just about anything through the mail. Mail order comes in two forms: catalogues and direct mail.

Catalogues A **catalogue** is a collection of products offered for sale in book form, usually consisting of product descriptions accompanied by photos or illustrations of the items. Catalogues came on the scene within a few decades of the invention of movable type in the fifteenth century, but they've come a long way since then.[58] The early Canadian catalogues pioneered by innovators such as Sears and Eaton's were designed for people in remote areas who lacked access to stores.

> **catalogue** A collection of products offered for sale in book form, usually consisting of product descriptions accompanied by photos or illustrations of the items.

Today, the catalogue customer is likely to be an affluent career woman with access to more than enough stores but who does not have the time or desire to go to them. Canadians spend about $3 billion through domestic and foreign catalogues.[59] Catalogue mania extends well beyond clothing and cosmetics purchases. Dell and Gateway, direct-selling computer companies, each have annual sales of over $1 billion. Bridgehead, an Ottawa-based Oxfam affiliate, has a catalogue that features housewares, gifts, foods, and other items imported through "fair trade" deals from the Third World. Large retailers such as Canadian Tire and Ikea continue to make extensive use of catalogues to make shopping more convenient for consumers. The trend, however, is to replace catalogues with Internet sales.[60] Zellers, though, uses catalogues and the Internet to reach key target audiences. It created a new Zellers Special Delivery Baby Catalogue and online baby-gift registry. Baby-related tips are offered throughout the catalogue courtesy of *Today's Parent* magazine, and there is as an integrated loyalty program for Club Z members and their babies.[61]

Direct Mail Unlike a catalogue retailer that offers a variety of merchandise through the mail, **direct mail** is a brochure or pamphlet offering a specific product or service at one point in time. Although e-mail is increasingly used for the same purpose, Canada Post expects to continue to deliver about 4.7 billion pieces of direct mail each year.[62] A direct mail offer has an advantage over a catalogue because it can be personalized. Direct mail is widely used by charities, political groups, and other not-for-profit organizations.

> **direct mail** A brochure or pamphlet offering a specific product or service at one point in time.

Direct Selling

direct selling An interactive sales process in which a salesperson presents a product to one individual or a small group, takes orders, and delivers the merchandise.

Direct selling occurs when a salesperson presents a product to one individual or a small group, takes orders, and delivers the merchandise. This form of non-store retailing works well for such products as vacuum cleaners, nutritional products, and educational materials—products that require a great deal of information to sell. Most people involved in direct selling are independent agents who buy the merchandise from the company and then resell it to consumers.

DOOR-TO-DOOR SALES Although door-to-door selling is popular in some countries such as China, it is declining in North America, because few women are home during the day and those who are home are reluctant to open their doors to strangers. Companies that used to rely on door-to-door sales have had to adapt their retailing strategies. Finding that many of its female customers work during the day, Avon now sells to them at the office during lunch and coffee breaks (Exhibit 11.17). Similarly, Tupperware features rush-hour parties at the end of the workday and finds that about 20 percent of its sales come from outside the home. An employee of Mary Kay cosmetics, which has also adopted this strategy, offered another explanation for its success: "Working women buy more in the office because they are not looking at the wallpaper that needs replacing. They feel richer away from home."[63]

PARTIES AND NETWORKS About three-quarters of direct sales are made in the consumer's home, sometimes at a home shopping party, at which a company representative makes a sales presentation to a group of people who have gathered at a friend's.[64] People who attend may get caught up in the "group spirit," buying things they would not normally buy if alone.[65] This technique is called a **party plan system**.

party plan system A sales technique that relies heavily on people getting caught up in the "group spirit," buying things they would not normally buy if alone.

The nature of social networking lends itself to better communications among a group of likeminded people. For example, an Avon representative could use Facebook to set up a group to advise clients of upcoming meetings and to establish a forum where people would be able to exchange ideas and tips among themselves. To join a group, the administrators need to invite you or you have to ask to join the group.

Exhibit 11.17

Avon was able to develop a retailing network with consumers.

Another form of non-store retailing, epitomized by the Amway Company, is **multilevel marketing**, or network marketing. In this system, a master distributor recruits other people to become distributors as well. Master distributors sell the company's products to the people they entice to join and receive commissions on all the merchandise sold by the people they recruit. Despite the growing popularity of this technique, some network systems are illegal. They are really **pyramid schemes** in which the initial distributors profit by selling merchandise to other distributors, and very little product ever gets bought by consumers.[66]

TELEMARKETING Telemarketing is direct selling conducted over the telephone. It is definitely easier and less expensive than door-to-door selling. Recent surveys indicate that one out of six North Americans felt it difficult to resist a telemarketing pitch; on the other hand, about one in three complained of feeling cheated at one time by a telemarketer.[67]

ELECTRONIC MAIL Electronic mail, or e-mail as it is more commonly known, is used to market products today. Unsolicited e-mail is known as **spam**. As the Internet has grown, the use of e-mail to market goods has also grown. E-mail is a very cheap form of communications; all that is required is an Internet connection and an e-mail account. Direct e-mailing does have credibility issues though, as Internet pharmacies and organized crime rings have been known to sell pharmaceuticals or stock "pump and dump" scams through e-mail.

Automatic Vending

Coin-operated vending machines are a tried-and-true way to sell convenience goods, especially cigarettes and drinks. These machines are appealing because they require minimal space and personnel to maintain and operate.

Some of the most interesting innovations are state-of-the-art vending machines, which dispense everything from Ore-Ida french fries to software. French consumers can even purchase Levi's jeans from a machine called Libre Service, which offers the pants in 10 different sizes. Due to their frenetic lifestyles, the Japanese are avid users of vending machines. These machines, a cluster of which can be found on many street corners, dispense virtually all of life's necessities, plus many luxuries people in other countries would not consider obtaining from a machine. The list includes jewellery, fresh flowers, frozen beef, pornography, business cards, underwear, and even the names of possible dates.[68]

In general, vending machines are best suited to the sales of inexpensive merchandise and food and beverages. Most consumers are reluctant to buy pricey items from a machine. New vending machines may spur more interest, however, as technological developments such as video kiosk machines that let people see the product in use, the ability to accept credit cards as payment, and inventory systems that signal the operator when malfunctions or stock-outs occur loom on the horizon.

Direct-Response Television

Almost as long as there has been television there has been **direct-response TV (DRTV)**—television programming that is intended to elicit direct orders, typically by phone, from viewers. Where the original DRTV pioneers were entrepreneurs who couldn't get their products into traditional channels, their approach of selling products on TV was so successful that it soon became mainstream for more established companies and brands.[69] DRTV is still an important marketing tool for two reasons: It works and it is measurable, so you can tell how well it is working. The latest use of technology in direct response television is utilized by *Canadian Idol* and MuchMusic. *Canadian Idol* and MuchMusic are using simple message service (SMS) or text messaging to vote for a favourite entertainer or music videos. SMS is growing at an incredible rate worldwide and is the one type of communications that is fairly cheap to use and operate. Viewers can respond to what is displayed on the television screen in real time with their mobile telephone. Marketers even use the *Canadian Idol* website to promote services. For example, there is

multilevel marketing A system in which a master distributor recruits other people to become distributors, sells the company's product to the recruits, and receives a commission on all the merchandise they sell.

pyramid schemes An illegal sales technique in which the initial distributors profit by selling merchandise to other distributors, with the result that consumers buy very little product.

telemarketing A sales technique in which direct selling is conducted over the telephone.

spam Unsolicited electronic massages sent in bulk.

direct-response TV Television programming, such as infomercials or shopping channels, which elicits direct orders for products from the viewing public.

Ethical Decisions in Marketing

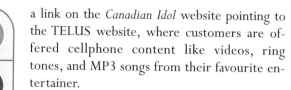

When consumers shop online, they leave an electronic trail that provides lots of personal information. From that data, programmers can trace your name, phone number, address, e-mail, and the types of goods that interested you when you searched their website. A company interested in that specific information would like to buy the data from the company that owns the website. Companies are always looking to get in touch with customers and find out about purchasing patterns.

Should the company make the sale? Do you believe the company has the right to use that information in-house? What rules would you impose on companies that want to share such information?

a link on the *Canadian Idol* website pointing to the TELUS website, where customers are offered cellphone content like videos, ring tones, and MP3 songs from their favourite entertainer.

HOME SHOPPING NETWORKS Television channels that exist solely to sell products let shopping junkies indulge themselves without leaving their living rooms.[70] In Canada, shoppers can frequent the Home Shopping Channel; the U.S. equivalent is QVC, which sells products at the rate of $39 per second around the clock. To date, the typical North American home shopping customer is in a low-income bracket, and the most frequently purchased product is inexpensive jewellery.

Personal Information

The Canadian government introduced the Personal Information Protection and Electronic Documents Act (PIPEDA), which lays out a framework for firms to work within regarding personal information. The Act came into effect in 2004. This Act impacts marketers any time they are gathering customer information such as names, phone numbers, and credit card information. The firm that is taking the information must advise the customer as to how that information is being used and in what capacity.

Real People, Real Decisions

▶ How It Worked Out at Federated Direct

Dawn chose Option 3. Federated developed a strategy to revamp its bridal registry business. To attract younger couples and change shoppers' perceptions of its bridal registry, the retailer developed a list of the "Top 10 Reasons to Register with Federated." These reasons were the core of the marketing strategy:

1. Creating your registry is FUN, FAST, and EASY—With the latest technology, including touch-screen kiosks, in-store scanner guns, and online registrations.
2. Personalized service—Meet with professional bridal consultants at our Premier Stores to customize a registry that fits your lifestyle.
3. Best selection—Of china, crystal, flatware, housewares, and home textiles under one roof!
4. Locking in Low Registry Prices Is a Piece of Cake!—On the day that you register, you will lock in the lowest price of the last 60 days for the next year to be used by you and your guests.
5. Guests Buy Gifts With Ease . . . And Confidence—By visiting 400 stores of the most highly recognized nameplates across the USA, shopping online, or by calling our toll-free number.

6. Great Brands You Know . . . And Trust—Choose from the most respected national brand names plus our own exclusive brands that you won't find anywhere else.
7. New, Exciting Shower Gifts—A selection of great gift ideas is available through our special shower gift in-store displays.
8. Reliable Delivery—The most popular items are always in stock and shipped to you within five days.
9. Special Savings—With our additional 10% off completion program for brides in all Home areas.
10. Hassle-Free Returns—With our one-stop return desk.

Early returns showed a dramatic increase in the number of bridal registrations across the stores. Dawn is hopeful that Federated's revamped courtship of brides and grooms will be a match made in heaven!

The gutsy move made by Dawn is no surprise, given her motto in life: "Dream big and dare to fail," a quote from the explorer Norman Vaughan. Dawn's advice is to make a commitment to a course of action, regardless of what you do in life, and give it your best.

Exhibit 11.18
Macy's revamped bridal registry offers younger couples what they want.

CHAPTER SUMMARY

1. **Define retailing and describe how retailers evolve over time.**

   Retailing is the process by which goods and services are sold to consumers for their personal use. The wheel-of-retailing hypothesis suggests that new retailers compete on price and, over time, become more upscale, leaving room for other new, low-price entrants. The retail life cycle theory suggests that retailing institutions are introduced, grow, reach maturity, and then decline. Three factors that motivate retailers to change are changing demographics, technology, and globalization.

2. **Describe how retailers are classified.**

   Retailers can be classified according to the type of products sold, whether they carry items having high or low gross margins and high or low turnover rates. Merchandise assortment is described in terms of breadth and depth, which refer to the number of product lines sold and the amount of variety available for each.

3. **Understand the importance of store image to a retail positioning strategy, and explain some of the actions a retailer can take to create a desired image in the marketplace.**

   Store image is the result of many elements working together to create a desirable shopping experience and to ensure that shoppers view a store favourably compared to the competition. Colour, lighting, scents, furnishings, and other design elements, or atmospherics, are used to create a "feel" for a store environment. Atmospheric decisions include store layout, which determines traffic flow and influences the desired customer behaviour in the store; the use of store fixtures and open space; the use of sound to attract (or repel) certain types of customers; and the use of colour and lighting that can influence customers' moods. The number and type of store personnel are selected to complement the store image. Pricing of products sold in the store contributes to shoppers' perceptions. A store's location also contributes to its image: Major types of retail locations include central business districts, shopping centres, free-standing retailers, and non-traditional locations such as kiosks.

Key Terms

- atmospherics, p. 394
- bots, p. 400
- catalogue, p. 405
- direct mail, p. 405
- direct marketing, p. 399
- direct-response TV, p. 407
- direct selling, p. 406
- etailing, p. 399
- experiential marketing, p. 393
- hypermarkets, p. 391
- inventory turnover, p. 389
- merchandise assortment, p. 388
- merchandise breadth, p. 388
- merchandise depth, p. 388
- merchandise mix, p. 388
- multilevel marketing, p. 407
- non-store retailing, p. 399
- off-price retailers, p. 391
- party plan system, p. 406
- point-of-sale (POS) systems, p. 386

4. Describe the major forms of non-store retailing.

Non-store retailing includes etailing and direct marketing, such as traditional mail-order shopping, direct-selling, vending machines, direct-response television shopping, and online shopping. Mail-order retailing includes catalogues and direct-mail advertisements sent to consumers. Popular direct selling techniques include the home shopping party, door-to-door sales, and telemarketing. The growing electronic marketplace uses both the power of more traditional television infomercials and home shopping networks and the growing popularity of computer online services and the World Wide Web.

5. Describe the opportunities and barriers to etailing.

Etailing, online exchanges between companies and consumers, is growing rapidly. Etailing benefits include greater convenience and greater product variety for consumers and opportunities for specialized businesses, lower business costs, and instantaneous delivery of some products for marketers. For consumers, the downside of etailing is that they have to wait to receive products, security issues, and the inability to touch and feel products. For Internet-only marketers, success on the Internet may be difficult to achieve, whereas cannibalization may be a problem with traditional retailers' online operations.

CHAPTER REVIEW

Marketing Concepts: Testing Your Knowledge

1. How does the wheel-of-retailing hypothesis explain changes in retail outlets? How does the retail life cycle concept explain these changes?
2. What are some environmental trends that will have a major impact on the future of retailing?
3. How are gross margins and turnover rates used to classify retailers? Describe the differences in merchandise assortments for convenience stores, supermarkets, specialty stores, discount stores, department stores, and hypermarkets.
4. What is meant by store atmospherics? How can the elements of atmospherics be used to increase the store's success? How are store personnel a part of store image?
5. What are the different types of store locations? What are the advantages and disadvantages of each?
6. How do retail store location planners evaluate potential store sites?
7. Describe the major types of non-store retailing.
8. Describe some of the changes that are expected in the growing electronic marketplace.
9. Explain the different types of direct marketing.

Marketing Concepts: Discussing Choices and Issues

1. The wheel-of-retailing theory suggests that the normal path for a retailer is to enter the marketplace with lower-priced goods and then to increase quality, services, and prices. Why do you think this happens? Is it the right path for all retailers? Why or why not?
2. Discount retail stores such as Wal-Mart seem to be getting larger and larger. Is there an optimal size for retailers? Can retail stores get too big? Why or why not?
3. Owners of stores that make effective use of atmospherics believe that getting people "in the mood" makes them more likely to buy. Do you feel that store atmospherics influence your purchase behaviour? Is this sort of planned store setting ethical?

Marketing Practice: Applying What You've Learned

1. All your life you've wanted to be an entrepreneur and own your own business. Now you're ready to graduate and you've decided to open a combination coffee shop and bookstore in a location near your college or university. You know that to attract both the student market and

other customers from the local community, you will have to carefully design the store image. Develop a detailed plan that specifies how you will use atmospherics to create the image you desire.

2. In your job with a marketing consulting firm, you are often asked to make recommendations for store location. Your current client is a local caterer that is planning to open a new retail outlet for selling take-out gourmet dinners. You are examining the possible types of locations: the central business district, a shopping centre, a free-standing entity, or some non-traditional location. Outline the advantages and disadvantages of each type of location. Present your recommendations to your client.

3. Assume you are the vice-president of marketing for Elegant Evenings, a chain of women's lingerie stores. Your firm sells exclusive designer lingerie in boutiques located in shopping malls across the country. With a changing marketplace, your firm is considering whether there is a need to develop some type of non-store retailing operation. You consider the opportunities for marketing your products via

   a. catalogues

   b. direct mail

   c. television infomercials

   d. television home shopping network

   e. World Wide Web

   Outline the pros and cons of each for your firm.

4. Assume you are the director of marketing for a national chain of convenience stores. Your firm has about 80 stores located in central and eastern Canada. The stores are fairly traditional both in design and in the merchandise they carry. Because you want to be proactive in your marketing planning, you are concerned that your firm may need to consider significant changes due to the current demographic, technological, and global changes in the marketplace. You think it is important to discuss these things with the other executives at your firm. Develop a presentation that includes:

   a. a discussion of the demographic changes that will affect your stores.

   b. a discussion of the technological changes that will affect your stores.

   c. a discussion of how global changes may pose problems and opportunities for your organization.

   d. your recommendations for how your firm might meet the challenges faced in each of these areas.

Marketing Mini-Project: Learning by Doing

This project is designed to help you understand how store atmospherics play an important role in consumers' perceptions of a retail store.

1. Select two retail outlets where students in your college or university are likely to shop. Try to select two stores that have different images but that sell the same types of products.

2. Visit each store and write down a detailed description of its atmosphere—colours, materials used, types of displays, lighting fixtures, product displays, store personnel, and so on.

3. Survey some of the students in your college or university. Develop a brief questionnaire asking about the perceptions of the two stores you are studying. Include questions about the quality of merchandise, prices, competence and friendliness of the store personnel, attitude of management toward customer service, and so on. What is the "personality" of each store?

4. Develop a report of your findings. Compare the description of the stores with the results of the survey. Explain how the different elements of the store atmosphere create each store's image.

Real People, Real Surfers: Exploring the Web

Many retailers have Internet sites. The Hudson's Bay Company (**www.hbc.com/bay**), Sears (**www.sears.ca**), and Future Shop (**www.futureshop.com**) are three examples. Explore these or other retailer sites and answer the following questions.

1. Describe each retailer's website. What information is available on each site? How easy was each to navigate? What information did you find interesting and useful on each site? What did you find that you didn't expect to find at a retailer site? What was lacking at each site?

2. How do the retailers' websites communicate the image or personality of their stores? How are they alike? How are they different? If you had no information except that available on the web, would you know what types of products are sold, whether the products sold are expensive, prestige products or low-priced products, and what types of consumers each retailer is attempting to attract to its stores? How does each site use graphics or other design elements to represent the "setting," as retailers do in their stores? How do they communicate the type of consumer they consider to be their primary market?

3. Why do you think customers visit a retailer's website? To find a local store? To learn about career opportunities? To find out whether a certain product is available in the store? To shop online? Or for some other reason? How well does each site you explored satisfy these customer needs?

4. What recommendations would you make to each retailer to improve its website?

Visit the MyMarketingLab website at **www.pearsoned.ca/mymarketinglab**. This online homework and tutorial system puts you in control of your own learning with study and practice tools directly correlated to this chapter's content.

Restaurants are always on the lookout to boost sales and satisfy demand quickly. To do that, some fast-food operators are using sophisticated online ordering systems that promise to make take-out seamless for both restaurant and customer. Toronto-based Pizza Pizza is trying to perfect its approach to e-business. In one year, Pizza Pizza fulfills more than 28 million orders and participates in events attended by more than 15 million people. To sell pizza online, one specific model is a website that can actually accept orders from customers and fax them to a local store for fulfillment. That would be Pizza Pizza's old method. With such a model, staff still had to manually enter orders and collect payments at pickup. A more sophisticated method is a web-based network that integrates with the point-of-sale system. It processes credit payments and sends the order directly to the kitchen. This method is much faster and more reliable.

The new system seems to work well. The new technology used by Pizza Pizza has the ability to take out the human element of order taking, since most mistakes were made when orders were taken over the phone. To order, an ordinary consumer clicks one of the store locations on a drop-down menu on the online ordering interface. The next step is to log in, then either set up an account with credit information or go to the online menu page. The order can actually be made days in advance, provided the store is open.

Pizza Pizza considers that online customers are virtual cashiers. They take care of payment themselves, freeing the staff to handle in-store business. In addition, consumers who are attracted to the online ordering method are highly educated, and online tickets are often substantially larger than phone orders. Pizza Pizza regularly has online orders as large as $1000. It has also noticed that the simplicity of online ordering has led to continual repeat business. Once an account is set up, a customer's loyalty is more likely.

Source: Based on James Scarpa, "Web ordering gets more functionality, use among operators," *Nation's Restaurant News*, 41(10), 5 March 2007: 11.

Things to Think About

1. Do you think Pizza Pizza's initiative of selling pizzas online is a good idea? Do you think it will help or hinder the company in the long run? How?

2. Do you think any type of food could be sold online? Why?

3. Do you think Pizza Pizza might alienate its core customers by selling the same products online? Is there a niche market for pizza online ordering? Why?

4. How do you think Pizza Pizza's competition will react to this initiative? Why?

CHAPTER 12
Integrated Marketing Communications

CHAPTER OBJECTIVES

WHEN YOU HAVE COMPLETED YOUR STUDY OF THIS CHAPTER, YOU SHOULD BE ABLE TO

1. Explain the concept of integrated marketing communications and its implementation.

2. Understand the characteristics of integrated marketing communications.

3. Explain the important role of database marketing in integrated marketing communication.

4. Explain the steps involved in developing a communication plan.

5. List, describe, and contrast the elements of the communication mix.

6. Explain how marketing communication strategies can be evaluated.

7. Explain the content and purpose of a communication brief.

Real People, Real Decisions

Meet **David Edward**, a Decision Maker at Cormark Communications

David Edward is president of Cormark Communications, a full-service agency that practises integrated marketing communications, with offices in London, Toronto, and Calgary. It is a member of Maxxcom, a communications holding company, which has created the fourth largest advertising network in Canada. Cormark provides communications counsel, strategic planning, advertising, promotion, and direct marketing to a diverse client base in the financial services, life sciences, agriculture, business-to-business, packaged goods, and retail sectors.

After earning a BBA from Wilfrid Laurier University, Edward gained 16 years of agency management experience with Ogilvy & Mather, Saatchi & Saatchi, and Grey Canada, managing such clients as Toyota, British Airways, SmithKline Beecham, American Express, and Effem Foods. In addition to his presidential duties, Edward takes an active role in the strategic management of key accounts like Pfizer Animal Health.

The Cormark Pfizer Animal Health Team was given the task of launching a new pharmaceutical product for the treatment of arthritis in dogs. Rimadyl had been successfully launched in the U.S. market the previous year, and Pfizer was looking for similar success in Canada.

The U.S. campaign was a high-budget, multilayered communication campaign that targeted both consumers and veterinarians. Media included television, magazines, direct mail, video production, in-clinic collateral, and veterinary detail pieces. The benchmark had been established, and a successful strategy and campaign had been developed. Cormark's task was to ensure similar success for Pfizer's first major direct-to-consumer launch of a product in Canada. A typical new product launch could take six months to plan and execute—Cormark and Pfizer Canada had 90 days. The agency had three options.

Option 1: Cormark could use existing U.S. materials.

The U.S. agency responsible for the launch of Rimadyl was also a member of the Maxxcom network. Cormark had access to all materials, the strategy, and the teams responsible for the U.S. launch. There were no issues in sourcing material. In fact, Cormark's professional relationship with the U.S. agency meant materials could be sourced and used at a savings for the Pfizer Canada client. Cormark used this relationship to understand the strategy and how the materials were used in the marketplace. Given the success in the United States and the market similarities, using the U.S. materials would offer several benefits. It would be cost efficient—costs sunk into production of material could be allocated to media spending or other marketing activities to promote the launch—and time efficient—time otherwise spent on the production of communications materials could be spent on other marketing activities, particularly important given the

launch timetable. In addition, using the materials would seem to provide some guarantee of success in the Canadian market.

Option 2: Cormark could build on a good thing by taking the best of the available U.S. launch materials and adapting them for use in Canada.

Given the variety of materials and the multitude of messages, it could tailor a campaign for Canada that would be based on the "best of the best." This option would ensure a role for the agency in the launch. Materials could be adapted to address perceived market differences or any differences in consumer behaviour that might exist between Canadians and Americans. Costs would be minimized, as adaptation would be limited to copy platforms and claims. Strategic direction and major sunk production costs would be preserved. In the interests of synergy, North–South relationships, and cost, this option would be a pragmatic way to preserve Canadian identity in the communications.

Option 3: Cormark could create new communications materials for the Canadian launch, thus taking advantage of the learning in the United States and building on its success.

With the U.S. results in hand and access to the strategy, Cormark could create materials designed to beat the U.S. benchmark and provide Pfizer Canada the opportunity to better the U.S. results with a Canadian success story. A case could be made that market conditions and consumer behaviour were not identical to those in the U.S. launch. In the United States, Rimadyl was a first-in-class product belonging to a new generation of non-steroid anti-inflammatory drugs (NSAIDs), while in Canada Rimadyl was second to market. In addition, there was the important French market to consider in Canada, which often requires a separate strategy and communications materials. A "made in Canada" solution would ensure that Cormark and Pfizer Canada controlled the launch and managed the launch process to Canadian standards and Canadian expectations. An investment in new Canadian materials takes a longer-term view of the market in terms of payback and assumes that original work meets the financial hurdles and budget requirements for the launch.

Cormark and Pfizer Canada concluded that all the options could be achieved in the 90-day launch timetable. They conducted qualitative research with consumers and veterinarians to probe usage and attitudes: The Cormark team concluded that the U.S. strategy and its key messages were effective with Canadian consumers, who were generally similar to their U.S. counterparts, but the Canadian veterinarians held different perspectives.

Now, join David Edward and the Cormark–Pfizer decision team. Which option would you choose, and why?

TAILORING MARKETING COMMUNICATIONS TO CUSTOMERS

See how many of the following you can answer:

1. Name the tiger that says, "They're grrrrrreat!"

2. Name one or more products for which Tiger Woods is a spokesperson.

3. What character is featured in Eveready battery ads?

4. At Burger King, you can have it "_____," whereas at Harvey's the burgers are a "_____."

5. Which paper towel brand is "The Quicker Picker-Upper"?

Did you get them all right? You owe your knowledge about these and a thousand other trivia questions to the efforts of people who specialize in marketing communication.

To reach customers, it is essential to get to know them and to talk their language—to communicate well. Sometimes, it's as simple as creating an image for your product or company that matches customer preferences. For example, when research showed that the image of courier service UPS Canada was that of a boring, traditional, and old-fashioned company, they knew that change was needed. A new communications campaign was developed to liven up UPS's image. It focused on their trusted and approachable drivers overcoming all obstacles to deliver their packages, with a tag line "Moving at the speed of your business." It worked. Customers now use words like "dynamic" and "contemporary" to describe the company.[1]

The coordination of a marketer's efforts to influence attitudes or behaviour used to be commonly called **promotion**. While this term fits well as one of the four Ps of the marketing mix, it implies a one-way (asymmetrical) conversation from marketer to customer. Promotion-oriented companies focus on disseminating favourable information about products and services to mass audiences, or on using research to develop messages to persuade specific, targeted audiences to engage in desired behaviour.[2] Today, technologies ranging from the Internet to digital wireless communication to "smart" products allow marketers to become much more interactive with customers. Many consumers expect to enter into a dialogue with an organization—to be informed, not manipulated, and to be assisted in making decisions, not sold.

promotion The coordination of a marketer's communication efforts to influence attitudes or behaviour toward a product or service.

Marketing communications is the term now used most frequently to describe the vital roles of informing consumers and customers about the relative value of products, and developing trust and other relational bonds that facilitate ongoing exchange relationships. Marketing communications plays these roles for every type of business, whether its goal is to sell suits to executives or to encourage government to decrease taxes on gasoline. New two-way (symmetrical) approaches to communication strategies help build better relationships—there is greater mutual understanding with two-way ongoing dialogue, more balance in relationships, and consequently greater commitment to brands and companies on the part of consumers and customers that usually results in greater long-term profitability.[3]

marketing communications Informing consumers and customers about the relative value of products, and developing trust and other relational bonds that facilitate ongoing exchange relationships.

Marketing communications can take many forms—quirky television commercials, sophisticated magazine ads, Internet banner ads using the latest interactive technology, glaring billboards, funky T-shirts, or blimps drifting lazily over football stadiums. Some of these communication activities are intended to communicate key messages to a target audience. Others provide incentives to buy specific products. In each case, the communication is intended to accomplish specific goals:

- Communications *inform* consumers about new goods and services, and where they can be obtained.[4]

- Communications *remind* consumers to continue using products.

- Communications *persuade* consumers to choose one product over others.

- Communications *create* complex brand images and identities in the minds of consumers.

- Communications *build* relationships with customers.

INTEGRATED MARKETING COMMUNICATIONS

In the past, companies made little effort to coordinate the messages consumers received. An advertising campaign would run independently of a sweepstakes, which in turn had no relation to a series of company-sponsored community events. The consumer, however, does not see these items in isolation but instead as one stream of communication. It was often confusing and ineffective. But let's see how the rules have changed in the marketing communication business.

Coordinating Communication Messages

integrated marketing communications (IMC) IMC is the practice of unifying all marketing communication tools and corporate and brand messages to communicate in a consistent way to and with stakeholder audiences.

Many marketing experts now believe that integrating all forms of marketing communications is essential for successful marketing, as shown in Figure 12.1. **Integrated marketing communications (IMC)** is the practice of unifying all marketing communication tools and corporate and brand messages to communicate in a consistent way to and with stakeholder audiences.[5] In a survey of marketing executives, IMC was rated the most important factor in marketing strategy—more important than consumer lifestyle changes, economic trends, new retail formats, or globalization.[6]

The IMC philosophy recognizes that customers absorb information about a product or an organization from many sources, not all of which are formal communication messages or even under the marketer's control. It takes the recipients' perspective—anticipating every opportunity in which they see information about the good, service, or organization—and then ensures that each of these exposures communicates the desired message and elicits the intended response.[7] As Figure 12.1 illustrates, this approach still relies on a variety of communication tools and approaches, but it emphasizes that some are planned, some are unplanned, that all marketing mix decisions and contact points (such as the cleanliness of washrooms, convenience of parking, or even employee appearances) send messages to consumers or business customers, and that all are used in harmony to reach targeted consumers. Figure 12.1 also suggests that different elements in an IMC strategy may have greater or lesser relevance to consumers or customers during different stages of their decision process from pre-purchase, to purchase, to post-purchase evaluation.

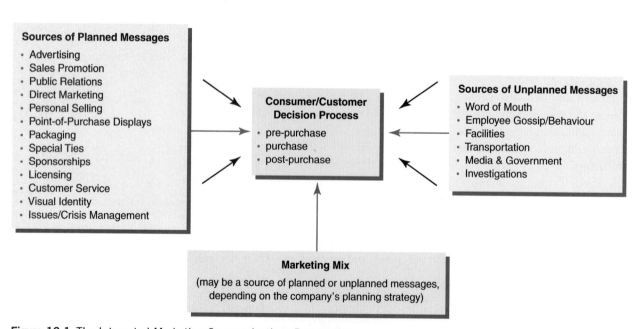

Figure 12.1 The Integrated Marketing Communications Perspective

Adapted from Figure 1.2, *Introduction to Marketing Communications*, First Canadian Edition, John Burnett, Sandra Moriarty, and E. Stephen Grant, Prentice Hall, 2001.

Exhibit 12.1

Lucky Brand Jeans used an innovative IMC approach to garner attention for the opening of its new Montreal store.

When Lucky Brand Jeans (an American brand) opened its new store in Montreal, it used some innovative communication strategies to garner attention. According to a company spokesperson, "Lucky Brand Jeans is very rooted in rock 'n' roll and the '70s era" (Exhibit 12.1). The target for this premium brand is 30- to 55-year-olds. To capture the attention of its target audience, Lucky Brand hired a "street team" to camp out in front of the store from 9 a.m. to 9 p.m. the Wednesday before the opening, and then again at 7:30 a.m. the next day. The company believed that having people wait in line outside a store is reminiscent of fans lining up for tickets to a concert. This ploy was an attempt to garner the attention of its target audience on the way to work. The store opening was also supported by print ads and transit advertising. The plan worked—close to 2000 people went through the store on opening day (compared to average traffic of 450 people a day in other stores).[8]

The IMC approach can assign relatively more importance to aspects of communication other than advertising. Some executives are reluctant to divert part of their communication budget from glamorous ads to coupons or contests, and some advertising agencies don't want to relinquish this piece of their business to other companies specializing in running sweepstakes or hosting town hall meetings. Utilizing an IMC approach, marketers plan and then execute marketing communication programs that create and maintain long-term relationships with customers by satisfying customer needs. This means that they use promotion tools to build ongoing loyal relationships with customers or other stakeholders, rather than simply causing a one-time product purchase or short-term change in behaviour.[9]

Brand managers and associate brand managers develop communication strategies at lower levels after senior planners have already developed the larger marketing strategy. But the IMC approach requires that upper-level management view other aspects of the marketing mix, such as packaging or pricing decisions, as part of the communication strategy. A successful IMC approach requires a company-wide commitment, from the CEO down, to putting the customer first and communicating interactively with customers in many different channels. Some firms find it hard to change their habits.

Some advertising agencies have not bought into the concept of IMC. Since they often do not have the full services required to deliver comprehensive programs, the solutions they offer their clients focus on their area of specialization, such as advertising or public relations.

So why is IMC so important today? A few years ago, marketers could effectively communicate with consumers by placing a few ads on major television networks and perhaps in a few popular magazines. Today, with increased global competition, customers are bombarded with more and more marketing messages—over 1400 advertising messages *every day*. And the sheer number of media outlets is also mushrooming. Marketers can choose from literally hundreds of cable and satellite stations, each of which can deliver its messages to a selected portion of the television viewing audience. All this means that consumers are less likely to be influenced by any single marketer-generated message. At the same time, technology now enables even small firms to develop and effectively use customer databases, giving firms greater opportunities for understanding customers and for developing one-to-one communication programs. And technology gives customers the ability to communicate among themselves about products and companies and even to view ads on the Internet and TV at their leisure.[10]

Characteristics of IMC

To fully understand what IMC is all about and before a firm can begin to implement an IMC program, it is essential that managers understand some important characteristics of IMC.

IMC CREATES A SINGLE UNIFIED VOICE Perhaps the most important characteristic of IMC is that it creates a single unified voice for a firm. If we examine the traditional communication program of a typical consumer goods firm—say, a manufacturer of frozen foods—we see that it often develops communication tactics in isolation. If its marketers decide they need advertising, what do they do? They hire an ad agency to produce great advertising. Or they may even hire several different ad agencies to develop advertising aimed at different target markets. They may also realize they need public relations activities, so they hire a public relations firm. Then some other genius decides to sponsor a sweepstakes and hires a sales promotion firm to do this. The sales department hires a different firm to develop trade show materials, and someone in the corporate communication department hires a sports-marketing firm to work on sponsoring an auto race.

Each of these firms may well do a good job, but each may also be sending out a different message. The customer can't help but be confused. What is the product? What is the brand image? Whose needs will this product satisfy? IMC strategies present a *unified selling proposition* in the marketplace by eliminating duplication and conflicting communication. Because a company develops an IMC program as a whole, there is a focus on *all* communication elements—advertising, public relations, sales promotion, and so forth—speaking with one voice, creating a single and powerful brand personality.

Having a single brand message, however, doesn't mean that marketers don't communicate to different segments of the market or to different stakeholder groups with different tactics. They can communicate the same brand message to employees with a story in the company newsletter about how local workers have helped flood victims, to loyal customers via direct mail that explains how to make their home safe for toddlers, and to prospective customers through mass media and Internet advertising.

The one-voice/one-message focus of IMC also considers other less obvious forms of communication. For example, a firm's communication includes the letters it sends to vendors and customers (even the stationery the company uses), the way company personnel talk on the phone with clients or customers, the uniforms that delivery people or other employees wear, signage, and other policies and procedures that may have an unintended effect on consumers' perceptions of the firm.

IMC BEGINS WITH THE CUSTOMER The customer is the primary focus of the communication, *not* the goals of the company or the creative genius of the communication specialists.

First and foremost, the goal of IMC is to provide the information customers want when they want it, where they want it, and in the amount needed. Sometimes that's as simple as letting consumers "vote" on the shows or products they want to see, as when fans of the hit TV comedy *Friends* were allowed to choose their six favourite episodes at a website when the producers decided to end the series.[11]

IMC SEEKS TO DEVELOP RELATIONSHIPS WITH CUSTOMERS As mass-marketing activities have become less effective, many marketers are finding that the road to success is through one-to-one marketing, in which the focus is on building and maintaining a long-term relationship with each individual customer. To achieve this, marketers must continuously communicate with each customer or else risk losing him or her to the competition.

What we said earlier bears repeating—*it is easier and less expensive to keep an existing customer than to attract a new one.* Thus, IMC firms also measure their success by share of customer, not share of market, and by the lifetime value of a customer. This means prioritizing customers so that greater resources go to communicating with high-value buyers or clients.

Because IMC is also about building and maintaining relationships with customers, IMC strategies often rely on CRM programs. With these tools, marketers have the information they need to better understand customers and to deliver unique messages to each consumer—messages that meet the needs of each consumer and that build relationships.

IMC INVOLVES TWO-WAY COMMUNICATION Traditional communication programs were built on one-way communication activities. Television, magazine, newspaper, and outdoor advertising spouted clever messages at the consumer, but there was little if any way for the consumer to talk back. Today, we know that one-way, impersonal communication is highly ineffective at building long-term relationships with customers. Instead, marketers seek first to learn what information customers have and what additional information they want and then develop communication tactics that let them share information with their customers.

IMC FOCUSES ON STAKEHOLDERS, NOT JUST CUSTOMERS As we discussed in Chapter 1, stakeholders are any individuals or organizations that are important to the long-term health of an organization. Some of these stakeholders include employees, suppliers, stockholders, the media, trade associations, regulators, and even neighbours. One reason these other stakeholders are so important is that customers and prospective customers don't learn about a company and its products just from the firm. Their attitudes, positive or negative, are also heavily influenced by the mass media, government regulatory bodies, or even their neighbour who happens to work for the company. Thus, while the primary stakeholder is usually the customer, myriad other groups or individuals can significantly influence customers' attitudes and behaviours.

IMC GENERATES A CONTINUOUS STREAM OF COMMUNICATION A major characteristic of an IMC strategy is that tactics using many different elements of the communication program—advertising, publicity, personal selling, sales promotion, customer testimonials, and so on—are included in a single IMC plan. As a result, IMC strategies provide a continuous stream of communication. Instead of consumers being bombarded with messages from various sources for a week or two and then hearing nothing from the brand for months, IMC planning ensures that consumers receive information on a regular basis and in the right amount.

IMC MEASURES RESULTS BASED ON ACTUAL FEEDBACK Many IMC boosters suggest that the only adequate measure of a promotional campaign's effectiveness is to evaluate the return on investment on communication dollars (earlier we referred to this as "marketing ROI"). This means that if a firm spends $1 million on advertising, it should be able to determine what dollar amount of revenue the firm receives as a result of that expenditure. While this type of relationship between promotion dollars and revenues may be difficult to measure exactly because of things such as the long-term effects of advertising and other marketing communications, most firms are seeking measures of accountability for their communication budgets and demand results.

IMC and Database Marketing

The effective use of databases is crucial for building relationships with consumers, a key characteristic of IMC. The development of a customer database allows an organization to learn about the preferences of its customers, fine-tune its offerings, and build an ongoing relationship with its market.

Some companies have maintained a customer database for years, but until recently most have not linked the database with their marketing communication activities. **Database marketing** is the creation of an ongoing relationship with a set of customers with an identifiable interest in a good or service and whose responses to promotion efforts become part of the ongoing communication process.

Let's look at an example of how an IMC firm might make effective use of database marketing. What if you ordered a dozen roses to be delivered to a friend for his or her birthday last year? You (and your friend) have become a part of the florist's database. What are the possibilities for the florist? First, the database is a gold mine of information. By examining (the *data mining* we discussed in Chapter 4) the records of thousands of customers, including you, the florist can find out which customers order flowers frequently (heavy users) and which order only occasionally (light users). They can identify customers who order flowers for themselves, usually when they entertain. They know which customers order flowers only for funerals, and which send flowers to their sweethearts (or ex-sweethearts if you forget!). And they can determine what type of customer accounts for their greatest sales and their greatest profits. This helps them to develop a better understanding of their target markets.

Of course, using the information in the database for understanding a firm's market is only the beginning. Even more important is how firms such as our florist use the database to create that one-to-one communication with their target markets. So you, our florist's customer, may get a call or an e-mail next year reminding you of your friend's birthday and asking if you want the same dozen roses (well, actually, fresh ones of the same type) sent again this year. The customer who entertains frequently may receive a brochure before the New Year's holiday season that shows various table arrangements. Heavy users might receive a special thank-you for their business and an offer to receive a free arrangement after purchasing 12 arrangements. And by the way, what about your friend who received flowers but who has never purchased from our florist? Since we may assume that a consumer who likes to receive flowers will sooner or later want to purchase them as well, she becomes part of the florist's prospective customer database. As such, she may receive a catalogue of the most popular arrangements or perhaps a coupon for a discount on her first order.

The following list explains what database marketing can do.[12]

- **Database marketing is interactive: Interactive marketing** elicits a response from consumers, be it filling out an order form or calling an 800 number for product information. For example, H. J. Heinz sent a mail piece to female cat owners that asked the provocative question, "Does he sleep with you?" If the woman completes a brief survey that tells the company more about her pet food preferences, she receives a personalized thank-you note that mentions her pet by name.[13] She is also entered into the company's database so that she will receive future communications about her feline friend. This type of interactivity gives marketers more than one opportunity to develop a dialogue with the customer and possibly to create add-on sales by engaging the customer in a discussion about the product and related items or services in which she might be interested.

- **Database marketing builds relationships:** It's easier for the marketer to build promotion programs that continue over time with database marketing because the marketer can best adapt them in light of consumers' responses. *The best predictor of who will buy a product is knowing who bought it in the past.* That's why *Reader's Digest*'s 12 full-time statisticians sort its customers by likelihood of purchase and predict the probability that each will respond to a given offer.[14] Once sophisticated database marketers know who has already purchased, they can keep in touch with these consumers on an ongoing basis. They can reward

database marketing The creation of an ongoing relationship with a set of customers who have an identifiable interest in a good or service and whose responses to promotional efforts become part of future communication attempts.

interactive marketing A promotion practice in which customized marketing communications elicit a measurable response from individual receivers.

loyal customers with money-saving coupons and keep them informed of upcoming prizes and promotions. As one executive whose company tracks big-ticket customers explained, "They are members of a club, but they don't know they are members."[15]

- **Database marketing locates new customers:** In some cases, a marketer can create new customers by focusing communications on likely prospects with characteristics similar to current users. For example, Dial sent coupon mailings about rust stains to neighbours of people in Des Moines, Iowa, and Omaha, Nebraska, who use its Sno-Bol toilet bowl cleaner. The brand's sales volume jumped 81 percent in a 12-week period.[16]

- **Database marketing stimulates cross-selling:** Database marketers can find it easy to offer related products to their customers. Interest in one product category boosts the odds that the customer is a good candidate for similar items. This explains why companies bombard consumers with mail offers for computer software, magazines, or clothing after they purchase a similar product over the phone or through a catalogue. Hershey Direct, a division of Hershey Foods Corp. that sells limited-edition collectible elf figurines (not the chocolate kind), tested its database by sending some mailings to only its most serious collectors, while its other mailings measure the potential of other database segments.[17] Some mailings have included questionnaires regarding specific collectible interests such as plates and music boxes to help the company decide on future product offerings.

- **Database marketing is measurable:** A common complaint of many marketers is the difficulty of pinpointing the impact a promotion had on the target market—what is a specific promotion's ROI? Who can say for sure that a single TV commercial motivated people to switch colas? But the database marketers know exactly who received a specific message, so they are able to measure the effectiveness of each communication.

- **Responses are trackable:** The marketer can assess the proportion of message recipients who responded, compare the effectiveness of different messages, and compile a history of which consumers are most likely to respond over time. Farm equipment manufacturer John Deere targeted 20 000 farmers who were loyal to other brands. Using a list of farmers who owned competing equipment, Deere sent prospects a series of four mailings spaced over eight weeks, each with an inexpensive gift such as a stopwatch that was related to the theme of saving time and money by replacing existing equipment. The campaign brought 5800 farmers into the showroom, yielding a 29 percent response rate. Nearly 700 of these consumers bought new equipment, resulting in more than $40 million in new business.[18]

COMMUNICATION

Like other marketing mix decisions, marketing communication strategy is based on a solid understanding of the target market, the decision environment, and marketing concepts, principles, and theory. In this next section we will explore the central communication theory and models on which communication decisions are based.

The Communication Model

With either one-way or two-way communication, the consumer is the focal point: A message is transmitted on some medium from a sender to a receiver who (it is hoped) is paying attention and understands the sender. Regardless of how messages are sent, whether as a hat with a Roots logo on it or a sales pitch from an Aveda representative, messages are designed to capture receivers' attention and relate to their needs. With two-way communication, the receiver sends a message back to the original sender, opening a dialogue between the parties.

Any ways that marketers reach out to consumers, from simple highway billboards to customized messages sent via e-mail to busy executives, are part of the basic communication process. The **communication model** specifies that a number of elements are necessary for communication to occur—a source, a message, a medium, and a receiver. Figure 12.2 shows the communication model.

communication model The elements necessary for meaning to be transferred from a sender to a receiver.

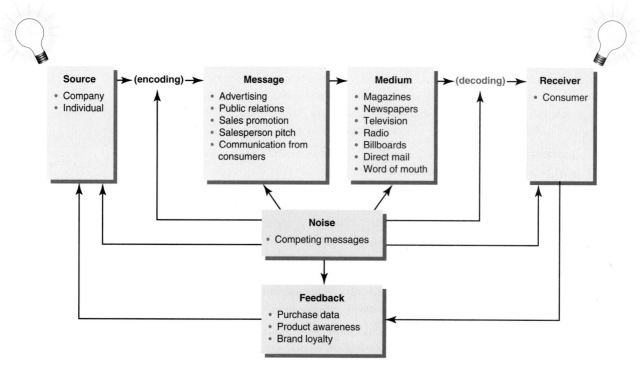

Figure 12.2 The Communication Model

The communication model explains how ideas are translated into messages and transmitted from the marketer (the source) to the consumer (the receiver) who (we hope) understands what the marketer intended to say.

encoding The process of translating an idea into a form of communication that will convey meaning.

ENCODING BY THE MARKETER It is one thing for marketers to create an idea about a product in their minds and quite another to express that idea so that other people get the same picture. **Encoding** is the process of translating an idea into a form of communication that will convey the desired meaning. Consider how different companies have used a dog to symbolize their brands. Microcell's Fido, a personal communication (PCS) product, has successfully used dogs in its communications to help us draw linkages to its services being as faithful and companionable as "man's best friend." RCA has introduced a second dog (a puppy) into its logo to communicate that it's always innovating—the best of old and new. And Greyhound Bus Lines has successfully used a greyhound dog to convey fast and sleek service. Many other animals have been used by many other companies to convey brand meaning: Can you think of some?

source An organization or individual that sends a message.

THE SOURCE The **source** is the organization or individual sending the message. Marketers must choose a real person (e.g., company president Galen Weston for Loblaws), hire an actor or model (e.g., Canadian country singer Shania Twain for Revlon), or create a character (e.g., Mr. Peanut for Planters Peanuts) who will represent the source.

message The communication in physical form that goes from a sender to a receiver.

AIDA model The communication goals of attention, interest, desire, and action.

THE MESSAGE The **message** is the actual communication sent from a sender to a receiver. The message should ideally accomplish four objectives (though a single message can rarely do all of these): It should get *attention*, hold *interest*, create *desire*, and produce *action*. These communication goals are known as the **AIDA model**, which will be discussed further later in this chapter. Messages may include both verbal and nonverbal elements, such as beautiful background scenery or funky music. These elements must be carefully constructed so that they can connect with a wide variety of consumers or business customers. In contrast, the message a salesperson delivers can be carefully tailored for each individual customer, and the salesperson can respond to questions or objections.

medium A communication vehicle through which a message is transmitted to a target audience.

THE MEDIUM No matter how the message is encoded, it must then be transmitted via a **medium**, a communication vehicle used to reach members of a target audience. This vehicle can be television, radio, a magazine, personal contact, a billboard, or even a product logo printed on a coffee mug (Exhibit 12.2). Ideally the attributes of the product should match those of the medium. For example, magazines with high prestige are more effective at communicating messages about overall product image and quality, whereas specialized magazines do a better job of conveying factual information.[19]

DECODING BY THE RECEIVER Communication cannot occur unless there is a **receiver** to intercept the message. Assuming that the customer is even paying attention—a big assumption in our overloaded, media-saturated society—the meaning of the message is interpreted in light of that individual's unique experiences. **Decoding** is the process whereby a receiver assigns meaning to a message. We hope that the target consumer will decode the message the way we had intended. Effective communication occurs only when the source and the receiver have a mutual *frame of reference*. They must share the same understanding about the world. Grabbing the receiver's attention is more likely if the message source is someone the receiver likes, the message is creatively executed, and the medium is one the receiver typically notices. Furthermore, it helps if the subject of the message is something that is personally relevant. The most enticing shampoo ad in the world probably won't be noticed by a bald man.

To improve the abilities of organizations to focus their communication efforts on receptive receivers, companies are slicing the mass market into smaller and smaller target audiences. In a truly interactive environment, communication efforts will look more like door-to-door selling than like television advertising. Even the Coca-Cola Company, which has long been known for extravagant network productions, is looking for alternatives to big-budget, mass-market commercials. One recent campaign, produced by Creative Artists Agency, has 24 ads in many moods and styles developed for 20 different television networks. These range from one done in a "quick-cut" style for MTV to a *Star Trek*–style spot called "Spaceship," intended to appeal to teenage boys.[20] These changes make sense, because the more recipients can identify with the message, the greater the probability they will reach for a Coke.

NOISE The communication model also acknowledges that messages often are blocked by **noise**, which is anything that interferes with effective communication. Competing marketing communications cause noise, as do other things happening in the environment that divert the receiver's attention. Marketers try to minimize noise by placing their messages where there is less likely to be distractions or competition for consumers' attention. For example, companies such as Calvin Klein often buy a block of advertising pages in a magazine to be sure the reader sees only pictures of their clothing. Some advertisers are now using black and white ads in colour magazines or on television to break through the noise. Corporate Communications Limited, Aliant Telecom, and Halifax Regional Police, for example, teamed up to create an anti-bullying public service announcement (Exhibit 12.3). The television spot shows white words on a plain black background with voiceovers of bullying taunts from both boys and girls and the tag line: "Just because you don't see it, doesn't mean it's not going on."

FEEDBACK To complete the communication loop, the source receives **feedback**, or reactions, from receivers. These reactions to the message help the marketer gauge the appeal's

The only way you're ever gonna take me

The exclusive WWE™ phone – just $74*
Get inside the ring with WWE™ ringtones, screensavers, updates and the WWE™ Mobile Madness™ Hardcore game. Only from Solo. Ask us for details.

Solo

mysolo.ca

Exhibit 12.2

Electronic devices like PDAs and cellphones are now being used as communication medium by marketers. Bell Mobility recently partnered with World Wrestling Entertainment Canada to offer a phone for WWE fans, enabling the WWE to target electronic communication.

receiver The organization or individual that intercepts and interprets the message.

decoding The process by which a receiver assigns meaning to the message.

noise Anything that interferes with effective communication.

feedback Receivers' reactions to the message.

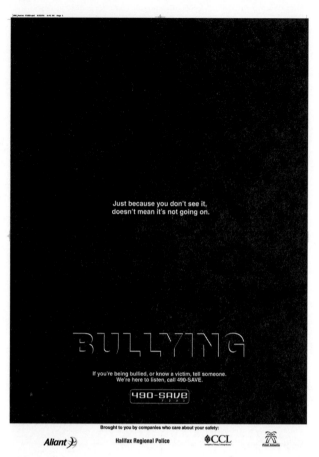

Just because you don't see it,
doesn't mean it's not going on.

BULLYING

If you're being bullied, or know a victim, tell someone.
We're here to listen, call 490-SAVE.

490-SAVE

Brought to you by companies who care about your safety:

Aliant   Halifax Regional Police   CCL   Print Atlantic

Exhibit 12.3

Distinctive black and white ads can help break through the noise of colour images.

effectiveness and fine-tune it. Obtaining feedback reminds us of the importance of conducting marketing research to verify that a firm's strategies are working. The area of feedback is where newer symmetrical communication techniques based on IMC outperform the traditional asymmetrical approaches. By listening to the feedback provided by consumers and customers, organizations can be more responsive to the information needs of consumers and develop closer and stronger relationships with them. As we discussed in Chapter 5, developing these relationships has become increasingly important for marketers.

The FCB Grid

There are many other communication frameworks and models. In Chapter 5 we introduced the FCB grid that categorized consumer decisions as being primarily thinking (cognitive) or feeling (affective) and high involvement or low involvement. This model has useful communication implications as different communication strategies and tactics are appropriate in each of the four quadrants (Figure 12.3).

High involvement–thinking decisions, for example, call for informative communication strategies and tactics such as comparative advertising or demonstrations, and detail-accommodating media such as print, infomercials, and the Internet. Low involvement–feeling decisions, on the other hand, call for image-oriented strategies and tactics such as lifestyle advertising or sex appeals and immediate response media such as point-of-purchase displays. We will further discuss communication strategies and tactics later in this chapter.

		Thinking (Rational / Cognitive)	Feeling (Emotional / Affective)
High Involvement	Creative Strategy	**Informative Communication** Specific information Demonstrations Comparative advertising	**Affective Communication** Strong creative execution Visual appeals Impactful communication
	Media Strategy	Long copy formats Magazine & newspaper Infomercials Internet	Large spreads (Space) Inserts & other special images Television & other rich media Interactive media
Low Involvement	Creative Strategy	**Habitual Communication** Reminder communication Repetition Memorable music and slogans	**Reactive Communication** Attention-getting Impulse-trigger Image-oriented
	Media Strategy	Small-space ads TV shorts or radio Point of sale	Billboards / outdoor Point of sale Newspaper

Figure 12.3 FCB Grid Communication Implications

There are a number of limitations associated with the FCB grid, including its simplicity, its inability to differentiate product attitudes and motivations from brand attitudes and motivations, and its lack of recognition of the need to create brand awareness before brand attitudes.[21] There are more sophisticated models such as the Rossiter and Percy RPG grid,[22] but these models are best left to advanced marketing communication classes. Because of its simplicity, the FCB grid is widely used and provides a useful way to think about marketing communication strategy. It also relates nicely to value creation strategies. "Thinking" decisions are concerned with functional value and cost-sacrifice value while "feeling" decisions are concerned with experiential and symbolic value.

DEVELOPING COMMUNICATION PLANS AND BRIEFS

A marketing manager has to identify the specific combination of communication tools that will meet the company's objectives in the most effective and cost-efficient way. To ensure that companies develop an IMC strategy, the smart manager first develops a **communication plan**, a framework for developing, implementing, and controlling the firm's communication activities.[23]

Communication agencies typically have three main functional areas: communication strategy, creative, and media placement. Large agencies may also have in-house market research and Internet/mobile communication capability. Communication planning and strategy is the domain of the "suits"—the account management people with business diplomas and degrees who understand target audiences, marketing strategy, communication theory, and how to develop the strategic elements of a communication plan. An effective communication plan addresses the elements illustrated in Figure 12.4. A communication brief is a summary (typically three or four pages) of the elements in Figure 12.4 that is used by the creative team to ensure that the creative execution is on-strategy.

> **communication plan** A framework that outlines the strategies for developing, implementing, and controlling the firm's communication activities.

Step 1: Identify the Target Audience

Marketing communication strategy is designed to achieve marketing objectives such as those discussed in Chapter 2 and, as previously discussed, is based on an understanding of the decision environment and specific target markets. We will discuss the influences of the decision environment after reviewing communication mix alternatives. The target market is identified from research and segmentation decisions, which we discussed in Chapter 4. A **target audience** is the group or set of individuals or organizations with whom you want to communicate. This may be the same as the target market, but often target audiences are more specific. For example, the target market for Burton Snowboards may be status-conscious boarders, 15 to 25 years old, but the target audience for a specific communication campaign may be female status-conscious boarders, 15 to 25 years old, living in greater Vancouver.

> **target audience** A highly segmented group of people who receive and respond similarly to marketing messages.

There may be more than one target audience within a target market. For example, the audiences may have different media watching and reading habits, may live in different geographic areas reached by different TV or radio stations, or may be persuaded by different types of information or appeals. Target audience profiles are also typically more detailed than target market profiles— particularly in the areas of media use and communication strategy and tactic preferences or responsiveness. For example, an account executive working on a campaign for Pioneer Stereo was assigned to hang out with guys who were likely prospects to buy car stereos. His observations resulted in an advertising campaign that incorporated the phrases they used to describe their cars: "My car is my

1. Identify the Target Audience
2. Establish Communication Objectives
3. Determine Communication Strategy Approach
4. Develop Key Messages and Positioning Statement
5. Design the Communication Mix
6. Determine and Allocate Budget
7. Implement Creative Strategy
8. Evaluate

Figure 12.4 Stages in Developing the Communication Plan

holy temple, my love shack, my drag racer of doom. . . ."[24] To make our communications more effective we need to know the target audience's values, attitudes, interests, opinions, and anything else that might affect how they receive, process, store, and use information. This additional information helps marketers to hone their integrated communication strategies to successfully reach consumers with the right message, in the right place, at the right time, and with the right offer.

Step 2: Establish Communication Objectives

The point of developing a communication strategy is to connect the marketing plan to consumers, to let them know that the organization has a product to meet their needs in a timely and affordable way. It's bad enough when a product comes along that people don't want or need; perhaps a bigger marketing sin is to have a product that they do want, but fail to let them know about it. As creative as some advertisers or salespeople are, it is rare that any one communication element could cause a consumer who has never heard of a product to become aware of it, prefer it over competing products, and buy it on the spot. An exception is novelty or impulse items, which are bought on a whim. Think of this communication road as an uphill climb (see Figure 12.5)—as the hill gets steeper, the later steps, which are forming a preference for the product and actually buying it, get tougher. During this climb, many people drop out, so only a small proportion of the target market actually reaches the top of the hill to become loyal customers. Each part of this path can entail different communication objectives to "push" people to the next level in their decision processes (see Chapters 5 and 6 for a review of decision models).

To understand how this process works, consider how a company would have to adjust its communication objectives as it tries to establish a presence in the market for a new men's cologne called Hunk. Let's say that the primary target market for the cologne is single men, aged 18 to 24, who care about their appearance and who are into health, fitness, and working

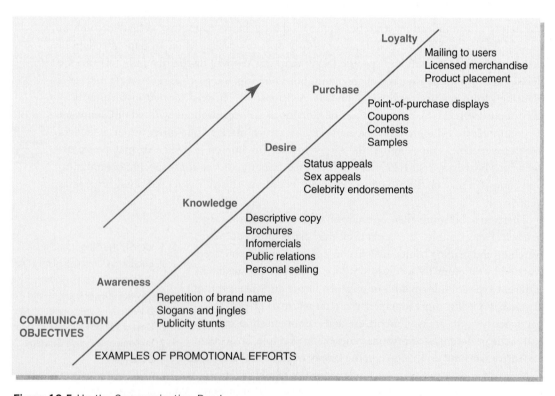

Figure 12.5 Up the Communication Road
Communication objectives seek to move consumers up the communication road.

out. The company would want to focus more on some communication methods (such as advertising) and less on others (such as personal selling). These are some steps the company might take to promote Hunk:

- *Create awareness.* The first step is to make members of the target market aware that there's a new brand of cologne on the market. This would be accomplished by simple, repetitive advertisements in magazines, on television, and on the radio that feature the brand name (Exhibit 12.4). The selection of the specific magazines, television shows, and radio stations would be based on knowing what men 18 to 24 years old are reading, watching, and listening to. The company might even undertake a *teaser campaign*, in which interest is heightened by not revealing the exact nature of the product (e.g., newspaper ads that simply proclaim, "Hunk is coming!"). The communication objective might be to create an 80 percent awareness of Hunk cologne among 18- to 24-year-old men in the first two months in the three Prairie provinces.

- *Inform the market.* The next step would be to provide prospective users with knowledge about the benefits the new product has to offer; that is, how it is positioned relative to other fragrances (see Chapter 8). Perhaps the cologne has a light, slightly mentholated scent that smells vaguely like liniments men use after a workout. Communication efforts would focus on messages and images that emphasize this position. The objective at this point might be to communicate the connection between Hunk and muscle building, so that 75 percent of the target market becomes interested in the product.

Exhibit 12.4

This ad for Fibre Source bars by Nature Valley was part of an integrated campaign designed to make consumers aware of a new product on the market.

- *Create desire.* The next task is to create favourable feelings toward the product and to convince at least some portion of this group that it is preferable to other colognes they now wear. Communications at this stage might emphasize splashy advertising spreads in magazines, perhaps including an endorsement by a well-known celebrity "hunk," such as Arnold Schwarzenegger. The specific objective might be to create positive attitudes toward Hunk cologne among 50 percent of the target market and brand preference among 30 percent of the target market.

- *Encourage trial.* The company now needs to get some of the men who have formed a preference for the product to splash it on. A communication plan might encourage trial by mailing samples of Hunk to members of the target market, inserting scratch-and-sniff samples in bodybuilding magazines, placing elaborate displays in stores that dispense money-saving coupons, or even sponsoring a contest in which the winner gets to have Arnold Schwarzenegger as his personal trainer for a day. The specific objective now might be to encourage trial of Hunk among 25 percent of 18- to 24-year-old men in the first two months in the three Prairie provinces.

- *Build loyalty.* Now, the company must focus on building loyalty: convincing customers to keep buying the cologne after they've gone through the first bottle. Communication efforts must maintain ongoing communications with current users to reinforce the bond they feel with the product. This will be accomplished with some mix of strategies, including periodic advertising, special events for users, and maybe even the development of a workout clothing line bearing the fragrance's logo. The objective might be to develop and maintain regular usage of Hunk cologne over 18 months among 10 percent of 18- to 24-year-old men in the three Prairie provinces.

In Chapter 8 we discussed the concept of the product life cycle. Marketers recognize that different communication objectives are particularly relevant in each life cycle stage. In the introduction stage, marketers need to make consumers or customers aware of their offering and help them become knowledgeable about it. In the growth stage, when competition increases, marketers pay most attention to creating desire and differentiating their brands. In the maturity stage, the focus is mostly on increasing market share, encouraging trial from new users or encouraging non-users to switch brands, and building loyalty. In the decline stage the focus is predominantly on encouraging loyal customers to repeat their purchases and increase consumption. It should be noted, however, that all communication objectives are evident in marketing campaigns at each stage of the product life cycle, as marketers need to help consumers complete their decision process at each stage.

Step 3: Determine Communication Strategy/Approach

The communication strategy describes the overall approach to the communication. For example, when LG Canada launched its new line of high-definition televisions, it built a golf hole in downtown Montreal and invited people to take a swing. Participants whose shot landed within 52 inches of the hole were entered into a draw to win a 52-inch HD television. This launch campaign also included television ads, print ads, and Internet ads.[25]

push strategy Moving products through the channel by convincing channel members to offer them.

IMC is one way to describe an overall strategy. Another is whether the strategy is a push strategy or a pull strategy. A **push strategy** means that the company wants to move its products by convincing channel members to offer them and entice their customers to select these items. In this case, promotion efforts will "push" the products from producer to consumers by focusing on personal selling, trade advertising, and sales promotion activities such as exhibits at trade shows.

pull strategy Moving products through the channel by building desire for the products among consumers, who convince retailers to stock the items.

In contrast, a company relying on a **pull strategy** is counting on consumers to desire its products and thus convince retailers to respond to this demand by stocking them. In this case, efforts will focus on media advertising and consumer sales promotion to stimulate interest among end consumers who will "pull" the product onto store shelves and then into their shopping carts.

Whether we use a push or a pull strategy and how the promotion mix for a product is designed must vary over time because some elements work better at different points in the product life cycle than others.

Step 4: Develop Key Messages and Positioning Statement

Once the overall approach to the communication strategy is established, marketers need to decide what they want to communicate to their audience(s). In Chapter 3 we discussed the concept of positioning. A positioning statement is a one- to three-sentence summary of the product positioning—how you want a product to be known in the minds of customers as being different from, and better than, competitive offers.

Benjamin Moore, for example, recently changed its corporate positioning statement to "Benjamin Moore is in the business of helping discerning customers create an atmosphere, express their style and personality, and add value to their homes, through the use of colour."[26]

It then conducted extensive research to understand its target audience of home decorators, and learned that home decorators constantly scour magazines, rip out pages, and put them into a file for later use, seeking inspirational decorating ideas for their home. It captured its positioning for this audience in the expression "Colour as Inspiration," and developed a personalized "My Scrapbook" feature on the Benjamin Moore website.

Communication purists would suggest that the positioning statement should focus on the one, maybe two, ways in which a marketing organization wants its product to be differentiated for a particular audience. Under this perspective, the positioning statement is similar to the concept of a unique selling proposition (USP)—the number one message a marketer wants to convey to an audience. A good example of a USP is "M&M's melt in your mouth, not in your hands." Recently, Subaru launched its new Impreza model. It positioned the car as "the Japanese car the Germans wish they had made." The positioning aims to reinforce the automaker's Japanese heritage, while associating it with the excellent engineering of German cars.[27]

Other key messages are what you want to communicate to your target market, and these are typically listed in a communication plan in order of priority. That way, the marketer can evaluate the communication media and assess how many messages can be reasonably communicated by that media. Billboards, for example, can typically accommodate only one message. A 30-second radio spot might accommodate three or four messages. Magazine and newspaper ads can accommodate more messages.

Step 5: Design the Communication Mix

The communication mix section discusses the themes and approach(es) that will break through the perceptual screens, get the attention of the target audience, and be consistent with the overall strategy and positioning.

An **advertising appeal** is the central idea of the ad and a **creative concept** is how that idea will be expressed through visuals, text, music, and other design elements. While advertising appeals and creative concepts are typically the domain of the creative department within an agency (see below), a communication plan needs to set some boundaries on the creative process to ensure that the creative is on strategy and is consistent with the communication objectives, target audience, and positioning.

The message should ideally accomplish four objectives (although a single message can rarely do all of these). It should hold attention, hold interest, create desire, and produce action. These communication goals are known as the AIDA model (Figure 12.6). Here we'll review some different forms the message can take, as well as how the information in the message can best be structured.

advertising appeal The central idea or theme of a communication message.

creative concept How the advertising appeal will be expressed through visuals, text, music, and other design elements.

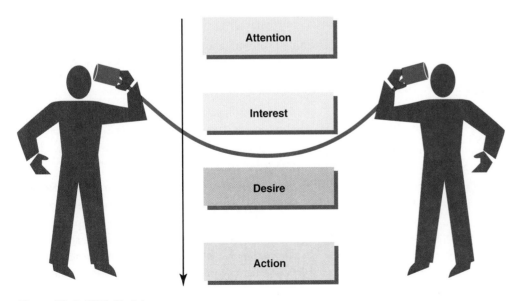

Figure 12.6 AIDA Model

TYPE OF APPEAL Because there are many ways to say the same thing, marketers must choose what type of appeal, or message strategy, they will use when encoding the message. To illustrate how the choice of an appeal can result in a different communication, compare two strategies selected by rival car companies to promote similar automobiles. A few years ago, Toyota and Nissan both introduced a large luxury car that sold for over $50 000. Toyota's advertising for its Lexus model used a *rational appeal*, which focused on the technical advancements in the car's design. This approach is often effective for promoting products that are technically complex and that are a substantial investment.

In contrast, Nissan's campaign for its Infiniti model used an *emotional appeal*, an attempt to arouse good feelings in the consumer. The new car was introduced with a series of print and television ads, which focused on the Zen-like experience of driving and featured long shots of serene landscapes. As one executive with the campaign explained, "We're not selling the skin of the car; we're selling the spirit."[28]

STRUCTURE OF THE APPEAL Many marketing messages are similar to debates or trials, in which someone presents arguments and tries to convince the receivers to shift their opinions accordingly. The way the argument is presented can be important. Most messages merely present one or more positive attributes about the product or reasons to buy it: These are *supportive arguments* or *one-sided messages*. An alternative is to use a *two-sided message*, with both positive and negative information. Two-sided ads can be quite effective, but marketers do not use them very often.[29] A related issue is whether the argument should draw conclusions: Should the ad say only "our brand is superior," or should it add the message that the consumer should buy the brand? The answer depends on the consumer's motivation to think about the ad and the complexity of the arguments. If the message is personally relevant, people will pay attention to it and spontaneously draw their own conclusions. However, if the arguments are hard to follow or the person's motivation to follow them is lacking, it is safer for the ad to make these conclusions explicit.[30]

Communication experts come up with many ingenious ways to express a concept (Exhibit 12.5). Consistent with the FCB grid, some marketers use an emotional appeal complete with dramatic colour or powerful images, whereas others bombard the audience with facts. Some feature sexy people or stern-looking experts (even professors from time to time). Different appeals can work for the same product, from a bland "talking head" to a montage of animated special effects. An attention-getting way to say something profound about cat food or laundry detergent is more art than science, but we can describe some common appeals.

- *Informative Appeal:* Gives consumers one or more clear reasons why one product is a good choice for solving a problem. The format focuses on a need and points out how the product can satisfy it.

- *Comparative Advertising*: A *comparative advertisement* explicitly names two or more competitors. The Pepsi challenge is an example of a comparative advertising campaign that has been used successfully over a long period of time. Comparative ads like the Pepsi challenge can be very effective, but there is a risk of turning off consumers who don't like the

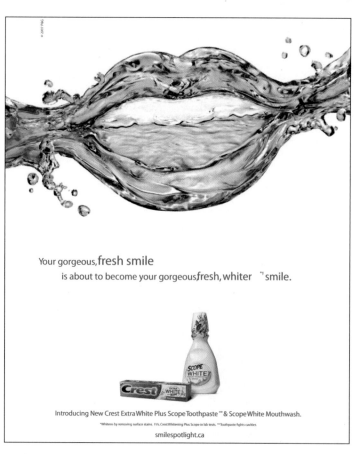

Your gorgeous, **fresh smile**
is about to become your gorgeous, fresh, whiter ⁗ smile.

Introducing New Crest Extra White Plus Scope Toothpaste ™ & Scope White Mouthwash.

ᵃWhitens by removing surface stains. ᵀᵛ% Crest Whitening Plus Scope in lab tests. ⁗ Toothpaste fights cavities.

smilespotlight.ca

Exhibit 12.5

Advertising creatives find unique ways to express a concept.

negative tone. This is especially a problem in cultures that don't take kindly to impolite messages. For instance, Tokyo's five major television networks pulled a Pepsi comparative ad because Japanese viewers found it offensive to be too blunt.[31]

- *Demonstration:* The ad shows a product "in action" to prove that it performs as claimed: "It slices, it dices!" This appeal helps sell products that people "use." The ad in Exhibit 12.6 demonstrates the poor performance of unnamed Goodyear tire competitors in a very creative and attention-getting way.

- *Testimonial:* A celebrity, an expert, or a "typical person" states the product's effectiveness. The use of *celebrity endorsers* is a common but expensive strategy. It is particularly effective for mature products, which need to differentiate themselves from competitors. 3M Canada, for example, used comedian Steve Smith (otherwise known as Red Green) as the spokesperson for one of its mature products—the Scotch brand duct tape.[32] Chrysler dropped Celine Dion (and walked away from a US$14-million contract!) as a celebrity endorser of its Pacifica crossover car (part SUV, station wagon, and minivan) after finding she was too young to appeal to the Pacifica's target market.[33]

- *Slice-of-Life:* A slice-of-life format presents a (dramatized) scene from everyday life. Today, advertisers are trying to expand their definition of "everyday life." An ad for Spray 'n' Wash Stain Stick from Dow Chemical, for example, shows a mother and her Down syndrome child. The mother comments, "The last place we need another challenge is the laundry room." One advertising critic described the spot as "the most crassly contrived slice-of-life in advertising history." But the American National Down Syndrome Congress applauded the ad and awarded Dow its annual media award.[34]

Exhibit 12.6

This Goodyear tire ad demonstrates the benefit of having Goodyear tires.

- *Lifestyle:* A lifestyle format shows a person or persons attractive to the target market in an appealing setting (Exhibit 12.7). The advertised product is "part of the scene," implying that the person who buys it will attain the lifestyle. For example, a commercial shown on MuchMusic might depict a group of snowboarders having fun and then taking time to drink a McCain fruit drink. A fantasy format is a variation of the lifestyle approach in which the viewer is encouraged to imagine being transported to a novel or exotic situation. Ads for some Canadian lotteries show fantasy lifestyles that ticket purchasers can achieve if they win the lottery. R K Swamy/BBDO used a lifestyle appeal to sell Apple's Performa by focusing on how the computer empowers children to pursue their potential. It created print ads and television commercials that plugged the Performa by showing parents and children using it to expand their horizons. The goal was to create ad messages that are warm and friendly, "feel-good" ads that would humanize the technology behind Apple's products and show potential buyers how the home computer could improve their lives.

Exhibit 12.7

Lifestyle advertising shows consumers who are attractive to the target market in an appealing setting. Here, Cheer focuses on family living in an appeal for clean laundry.

communication mix The major elements of marketer-controlled communications, including advertising, sales promotions, marketing public relations, direct marketing, and personal selling.

- *Fear Appeals:* This format highlights the negative consequences of using or not using a product. Fear appeals are often used to get the attention of audiences for social messages like not drinking and driving, not smoking, and safe sex. The Quebec government and its agency Marketel, for example, recently developed a campaign to help increase awareness of AIDS and expose the source of the danger. While the images are provocative and disturbing, the intent was to get their audience's attention. Fear appeals are also used by private-sector marketers, but typically with less disturbing images aimed at illustrating the problem of not buying a particular good or service. The British Columbia Automobile Association, for example, developed a campaign that humorously showed the problems of not having a BCAA membership, and being stranded in potentially scary situations.

- *Sex Appeals:* Some ads appear to be selling sex rather than products. This was the case in a recent ad for Carlsberg beer, run by Labatt Breweries of Canada, in which three women are shown discussing a boyfriend's willingness to perform a particular sexual act. These ads and many others rely on sexuality to get consumers' attention.

- *Humorous Appeals:* Humorous ads can be an effective way to break through advertising clutter. But humour can be tricky: What is funny to one person may be offensive to another. Different cultures also have different senses of humour.

COMMUNICATION MIX We've discussed integration as key to effective communication strategy. Now let's look at the elements that marketers must coordinate in their IMC efforts. Within the marketing mix, the communication elements that the marketer controls or influences are the **communication mix**. These include advertising, sales promotions, public relations, direct marketing, personal selling, and word of mouth. The term *mix* implies that a company's communication strategy is focused on more than one element, so part of the challenge is to combine these different communication tools effectively. Another challenge is to ensure that the communication mix works in harmony with the overall marketing mix, which combines elements of communication with distribution, price, and product decisions to position the firm's offering in people's minds. These other marketing mix elements, after all, also communicate. A product design, for example, can send a powerful message: Honda Motor Company introduced to the Japanese market a model called the City, which it deliberately designed to attract young drivers. The car featured a very high roof that made the City look like a toy. This playful quality appealed to Japan's young consumers, and the design theme was reinforced by fun and carefree communication messages.[35]

COMMUNICATION MIX ELEMENTS Marketing communications can be categorized along two basic dimensions: the type of communication and the source (see Table 12.1). From the

Table 12.1 Types of Marketing Communications

		Identified as Marketer	Not Identified as Marketer
METHOD OF TRANSMISSION	**Mass Media**	Advertising, Sales promotion	Public relations
	Personal	Personal selling	Word of mouth

SPOTLIGHT ON REAL PEOPLE   From Diesel to Sid Lee

The traditional advertising agency is on the decline, with new innovative agencies springing up to keep pace with the changing environment. On the scene since 1993, Diesel Marketing was one of the premier marketing agencies in Montreal. That's why it came as a surprise to many when the agency decided to change its name to Sid Lee in 2006. The agency felt that "Diesel" was a brand associated with jeans or oil barrels—not communications. Sid Lee is far from an ordinary communications firm. Rather, it calls itself a "commercial creativity firm" that helps clients with everything from store design to stunts to ad work. In addition, staying ahead of consumer trends is important to Sid Lee. "Over the past 10 years, consumers have evolved more rapidly than agencies have," explains Jean-François Bouchard, the president/founding partner.

Sid Lee changed more than just its name—it changed the way people look at advertising. The Sid Lee philosophy is that advertising should be seen as a tool, as opposed to a tool box. Sid Lee sees "commercial creativity" as the toolbox—and it can include a lot more than just advertising. Consistent with this attitude, Sid Lee is involved in more than just advertising—it's also involved in retail architecture, experiential marketing, and industrial design. The agency started as a design firm that evolved into an advertising agency. It later added interactive marketing to the mix. In a recent project, Sid Lee orchestrated the redesign of a new SAQ (Quebec liquor board) store. This innovative new store groups wines according to types rather than regions and includes an "entertainment-educational experience" that explains wine to consumers. Clearly, Sid Lee is involved in much more than traditional advertising. The approach is working—Sid Lee has recently won many acclamations, including Best of Show at the Digital Marketing Awards and the Boomerang Award, which celebrates the best in Quebec digital work.[36]

1. Why is Sid Lee's approach consistent with the IMC philosophy?
2. What allows a small agency like Sid Lee to compete with large national and international agencies?

customer's perspective, there are two types of communication: Marketers are trying to deliver a message about their product or organization, or they are providing an incentive to purchase or otherwise change consumer behaviour.[37] The customer identifies the source of these messages or incentives as either the organization or a presumed independent source, such as friends, magazine editorials, or expert opinion. There are also two main methods of transmitting messages and incentives—those that communicate to a mass audience and those that communicate person to person. This latter distinction is becoming blurred, however, as the Internet, smart checkout scanners, and interactive television enable what have traditionally been considered tools of mass media—advertising, sales promotion, and public relations—to be used to reach individual consumers with personal appeals. In this section, we'll briefly describe the elements of the communication mix, which are covered in more detail in Chapter 13. Some of the pros and cons of each element are also presented in Table 12.2.

Advertising For many, **advertising** is the most familiar and visible element of the communication mix. Advertising is non-personal communication from an identified sponsor using paid space, primarily in mass media. Because it can convey rich and dynamic images, such as the ones in the Olay Body Wash ad in Exhibit 12.8, advertising creates and reinforces a distinctive brand identity. This helps marketers to both persuade customers to select their product and build bonds with buyers by presenting them with familiar brand images and logos time after time. Advertising is also useful in communicating factual information about the product or reminding consumers to buy their favourite brand. However, advertising sometimes suffers from a credibility problem, because cynical consumers tune out messages they think are biased or are intended to sell them something they don't need. It can also be very expensive for firms, so they must take great care to ensure their messages are effective.

advertising Non-personal, paid communication from an identified sponsor, primarily using mass media.

Personal Selling The most personal way to communicate with consumers is by direct interaction, which can occur in person, by phone, or even over an interactive computer link. Personal selling occurs when a company representative comes in direct contact with a

Table 12.2 A Comparison of Elements of the Communication Mix

Communication Element	Pros	Cons
Advertising	The marketer has control over what the message will say, when it will appear, and who is likely to see it.	Often expensive to produce and distribute. May have low credibility and/or be ignored by audience.
Sales promotion	Provides incentives to retailers to support one's products. Builds excitement for retailers and consumers. Encourages immediate purchase and trial of new products. Price-oriented promotions cater to price-sensitive consumers.	Short-term emphasis on immediate sales rather than a focus on building brand loyalty. The number of competing promotions may make it hard to break through the promotional clutter.
Public relations	Relatively low cost. High credibility.	Lack of control over the message that is eventually transmitted, and no guarantee that the message will ever reach the target. Hard to track the results of publicity efforts.
Personal selling	Direct contact with the customer gives the salesperson the opportunity to be flexible and modify the sales message to coincide with the customer's needs. The salesperson can get immediate feedback from the customer.	High cost per contact with customer. Difficult to ensure consistency of message when it is delivered by many different company representatives. The credibility of salespeople often depends on the quality of their company's image, which has been created by other promotion strategies.

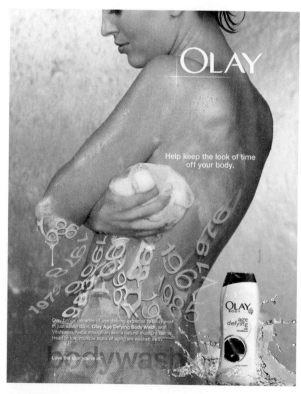

Exhibit 12.8

Olay Body Wash uses vivid imagery to attract customers to its advertising.

customer or group of customers to inform them about a product or service and to encourage them to make a purchase. This type of communication activity is most often seen in the business-to-business market, but everyone has experienced a door-to-door representative selling Girl Guide cookies or sales clerks in clothing stores asking if they can be of assistance. Salespeople are a valuable communication medium, because customers can ask questions and the salesperson can immediately address objections and relay product benefits.

Personal selling can be tremendously effective, especially for big-ticket consumer items and for industrial products for which the "human touch" and developing tailored solutions is essential. It can be so effective that some marketers, if given a choice, might well abandon other forms of communication and simply dispatch a salesperson to every customer's house or office. Unfortunately, this form of communication is also the most expensive, and it can be difficult to ensure that all salespeople are delivering the same message with the same impact.

Direct Marketing Direct marketing was introduced in Chapter 11 as a form of non-store retailing. The tools of direct marketing—catalogues, direct mail, the Internet, and direct response television—also play a significant communication role and are part of the communication mix. Some of these tools, such as the Internet and direct mail, are interactive: They can be customized to elicit measurable direct responses from individual customers and allow marketers to provide further customized information based on that response. Use of these interactive tools is called **interactive marketing**. The desired response is typically an order—a first-order response. But other intermediate responses might be desired, such as a request for more information, agreeing to a sales demonstration, or providing feedback on a provided sample—second-order responses. Coupon Radio, a car radio system that is now being tested, lets drivers request more information (e.g., about a band they hear on the radio, or to get names and addresses of retailers that sell an advertised product), all while cruising along in their cars.[38] It may sound strange, but another kind of second-order response is a request to *not* receive any more information from the company. We assume that a priority of any communication campaign is to get more customers. Interactive marketers sometimes operate with the opposite goal in mind: to *reduce* their customer base. They know that their efforts will be most effective when they are communicating only with customers who are interested in what they have to offer.

Direct marketing typically focuses on short-term, single transaction responses or a set of responses leading to a purchase decision. Database marketing, as discussed earlier in the chapter, focuses on building ongoing relationships and brand loyalty over time. The secret to effective direct marketing is developing an effective customer database, which contains enough detail in its target market profiles about customer needs, wants, interests, preferences, purchase behaviour, consumption behaviour, and media habits to enable the marketer to tailor messages to very specific categories of consumers. In the case of direct mail, messages are often personalized, not only by using the consumers' name and address, but also by using personal information from the database in the content of the message.

Public Relations **Public relations** is a set of communication tools that organizations use to establish and maintain contact with the various publics (stakeholders) on whom their success depends. Public relations components of the communication mix seek to nurture a long-term positive relationship between the organization and its customers, suppliers, distributors, employees, shareholders, legislators, and other parties who affect or are affected by the achievement of the organization's objectives, and a positive image for the organization and its products in the long term. Public relations efforts are often associated with **publicity**—writing press releases and developing relationships with journalists who write stories or articles about an organization and its products. The communication results of publicity efforts are typically identified by consumers as being from an independent source. As pictured in Exhibit 12.9, for the recent launch of *The Simpsons Movie*, marketers used

interactive marketing Two-way communications, in which customized marketing communications elicit a measurable response from individual customers.

public relations Communications strategies to build good relationships with an organization's publics.

publicity Unpaid communication about an organization appearing in the mass media.

Exhibit 12.9

Promoters of *The Simpsons Movie* used an innovative publicity campaign to garner attention for their new movie.

biodegradable paint to depict Homer Simpson next to the Cerne Abbas Giant in Dorset, Southern England. Homer was painted next to the ancient giant creature carved in the chalk bedrock. The publicity stunt garnered significant media attention and coverage.

Public relations activities also include staging events, commissioning surveys of people's feelings about issues related to a product, signing and working with a celebrity spokesperson, and responding to product recalls or other crises. These are all activities that consumers identify with the organization. Tourism PEI, for example, recently used roving PEI ambassadors to tour New Brunswick tourist attractions in specially detailed cars (suggesting fun adventure) to entice Quebecers visiting New Brunswick to come over to PEI during their holiday. This PR campaign was highly successful, but drew the wrath of New Brunswick tourism officials and government ministers.

Event marketing is a growing area of integrated marketing communication, as more and more firms use events as part of their communication mix. Events can often break through the clutter associated with some communication mix elements to deliver a clear and impactful brand message to consumers. For example, every year, Guinness Beer holds an event on Parliament Hill lobbying the government to make St. Patrick's Day a national holiday. The event garners significant media coverage for Guinness each year. Marketers at Guinness say that events such as this have contributed to a 20 percent sales increase for the brand.[39] Events are an effective way to garner media attention and to allow consumers to interact directly with the brand.

Sales Promotion Sales promotions are programs, such as contests or store demonstrations, that marketers design to build interest in or encourage purchase of a product or service during a specified time period. Unlike other forms of communication that are message oriented, sales promotions are incentives, which are primarily intended to stimulate immediate action, such as coupons, rebates, or bonuses that might stimulate a purchase. Increasingly, however, organizations such as airlines (e.g., Air Canada), grocery stores (e.g., Canada Safeway), and gas stations (e.g., Petro-Canada) are using continuity or loyalty programs, which give discounts, bonuses, or redeemable "points" to members or frequent customers with the intention of building long-term loyalty to the organization. Sales promotions are a form of mass appeal, because they target groups of consumers or retailers to receive special offers or merchandise, invite these people to participate in some activity, or call attention to some event or product feature.

The Internet and Other Elements The IMC concept, illustrated in Figure 12.1 on page 418, suggests that marketers can use many other communication elements to communicate messages and incentives to customers—word-of-mouth communication, brand placement (such as in movies or on TV shows), third-party endorsements (such as Greenpeace recommending an environmentally friendly product), and third-party incentives (such as government subsidies for buying emergency preparedness kits). Marketers don't control third-party endorsements or incentives, but they can influence the third parties through public relations and political lobbying. Chapter 13 discusses the growing area of Internet advertising in detail.

Buzz Appeals In addition to the tried-and-true methods described above, many marketers are starting to figure out that they must find alternatives to traditional advertising—especially when talking to young consumers who are very cynical about the efforts of big corporations to buy their allegiance. For these and other "hard-to-get" consumers, marketers must find new "out-of-the-box" tactics. In addition, traditional advertising media are so saturated that marketers are scrambling to find new, unexpected places to place their messages. Some recent attempts include:

- Nickelodeon is stamping images of SpongeBob Squarepants and Dora the Explorer onto packs of fruit.

- US Airways is selling ad space on motion-sickness bags.

- A woman rented out her forehead on eBay; a casino paid $10 000 to tattoo an ad there.

- CBS is advertising new shows on eggs, using a laser technology that etches images onto the shells.[40]

These cutting-edge techniques come under a variety of names, including word-of-mouth marketing, viral marketing, and buzz and guerrilla marketing.

Buzz, Word-of-Mouth, and Viral Marketing Everywhere you turn in marketing today, it seems someone is talking about "buzz." In fact, we hear so much about buzz and its counterparts viral marketing and word-of-mouth marketing that it's hard to know exactly what all the terms mean. The Word of Mouth Marketing Association (WOMMA), founded in 2004, provides the following definitions:[41]

- **Word of mouth (WOM):** The act of consumers providing information to other consumers.

- **Word-of-mouth marketing:** Giving people a reason to talk about your products and making it easier for that conversation to take place.

- **Buzz marketing:** Using high-profile entertainment or news to get people to talk about your brand.

- **Viral marketing:** Creating entertaining or informative messages that are designed to be passed along in an exponential fashion, often electronically or by e-mail.

In more general terms, marketers think of **buzz** as everyday people helping their marketing efforts by talking about a product or a company to their friends and neighbours.[42] As the examples in Table 12.3 illustrate, companies today are spending millions to create consumer buzz. Companies such as Dell have named word of mouth (WOM) marketing managers, and WOMMA membership boasts most of the top consumer brand companies.[43] According to advertising agency JWT Worldwide, over 85 percent of the top 1000 marketing firms now use some form of word-of-mouth tactics.[44]

Of course, buzz isn't *really* new. Many refer to the *Mona Lisa* as one of the first examples of buzz marketing. In 1911 the famous painting was stolen from the Louvre and became the

word of mouth (WOM) The act of consumers providing information to other consumers.

word-of-mouth marketing Giving people a reason to talk about your products and making it easier for that conversation to take place.

buzz marketing Using high-profile entertainment or news to get people to talk about your brand.

viral marketing Creating entertaining or informative messages that are designed to be passed along in an exponential fashion, often electronically or by e-mail.

buzz Word of mouth communication that is viewed as authentic and generated by customers.

Table 12.3 How Some Marketers Have Created Buzz

Company Buzz	Marketing Tactic
General Mills	In the 1930s General Mills created the Betty Crocker character. When the Betty Crocker weekly radio show was aired, consumers spread the word. Betty Crocker still gets letters every day.[45]
Burger King	At BK's website **www.subservientchicken.com**, consumers could have fun typing in orders for a man in a chicken suit to follow. The site attracted 418 million visitors who stayed on an average of 6 minutes.[46] Result: Young people saw Burger King as a more empathetic and relevant company.
Nike	Nike was supposedly the "brains" behind a cool, illegal warehouse club in Berlin.[47]
Hasbro	Consumers were encouraged to play Monopoly on the streets of London.[48] The fines and clean-up fees Hasbro paid to the city were far less than the advertising costs the company would have incurred in a traditional campaign.
Puma	The company encouraged consumers to stencil its cat logo all over Paris.
Audi	For the introduction of its A3 model, Audi staged a fake car heist at the New York Auto Show. Posters placed near the heist appealed to consumers for help and sent them to a website where they could participate in an alternate reality game (ARG) and find hidden clues to solve the mystery.[49]
Kellogg's	The company gave a video of never-before-seen ads for Pop-Tarts to 12 000 "tween" girl influencers.[50]
America's Next Top Model (television series)	To promote the launch of its fourth season, the series used **alloy.com**, a website aimed at teen girls, to find 500 "insider" girls who could generate buzz about the show. Alloy monitors the chat on its site and identified 7000 girls who had shown an interest in the show in their "chats." From the initial 7000, Alloy.com identified 500 who were the most popular on instant messaging buddy lists. These 500 were given party kits and asked to invite four friends to their homes for gatherings themed around *America's Next Top Model*.[51]
Procter & Gamble	P&G sent product and information to 250 000 teens who were not paid but were free to form their own opinions and talk about the products.[52]
Microsoft	When introducing its new Halo 3 video game, Microsoft gave gamers identified as influencers bits of information about the game before its release so that they could talk about the product with other avid gamers who, conveniently, are also heavy users of chat rooms and video game message boards.[53]

topic of consumer talk around the globe, giving the previously little-recognized painting fame that exists until today. When you think of the effect of consumers talking one-on-one nearly a century ago, imagine the exponential increase in influence of the individual consumer "connectors" or "e-fluentials" who use blogs and other computer-generated media to increase their reach.[54] Compared to traditional advertising and public relations activities, these endorsements are far more credible and thus more valuable to the brand.

Buzz works best when companies put unpaid consumers in charge of creating their own messages. As Table 12.4 shows, WOMMA considers the hiring of actors to create buzz deceptive and unethical. This is just what Sony Ericsson Mobile Communications did when the company hired 60 actors to go to tourist attractions. Their role was to act like tourists

Table 12.4 Positive and Unethical Word-of-Mouth Marketing Strategies

Positive Word of Mouth Marketing Strategies	Unethical Word of Mouth Marketing Strategies
1. Encouraging communication Developing tools to make telling a friend easier Creating forums and feedback tools Working with social networks	**1. Stealth Marketing** Any practice designed to deceive people about the involvement of marketers in a communication.
2. Giving people something to talk about Information that can be shared or forwarded Advertising, stunts, and other publicity that encourages conversation Working with product development to build WOM elements into products	**2. Shilling** Paying people to talk about (or promote) a product without disclosing that they are working for the company; impersonating a customer.
3. Creating communities and connecting people Creating user groups and fan clubs Supporting independent groups that form around your product Hosting discussions and message boards about your products Enabling grassroots organizations such as local meetings and other real-world participation	**3. Infiltration** Using fake identities in an online discussion to promote a product; taking over a website, conversation, or live event against the wishes or rules set by the proprietor.
4. Working with influential communities Finding people who are likely to respond to your message Identifying people who are able to influence your target customers Informing these individuals about what you do and encouraging them to spread the word Good-faith efforts to support issues and causes that are important to these individuals	**4. Comment Spam** Using automated software ("bots") to post unrelated or inappropriate comments to blogs or other online communities.
5. Creating evangelist or advocate programs Providing recognition and tools to active advocates Recruiting new advocates, teaching them about the benefits of your products, and encouraging them to talk about them	**5. Defacement** Vandalizing or damaging property to promote a product.
6. Researching and listening to customer feedback Tracking online and offline conversations by supporters, detractors, and neutrals Listening and responding to both positive and negative conversations	**6. Spam** Sending bulk or unsolicited e-mail or other messages without clear, voluntary permission.
7. Engaging in transparent conversation Encouraging two-way conversations with interested parties Creating blogs and other tools to share information Participating openly on online blogs and discussions	**7. Falsification** Knowingly disseminating false or misleading information.
8. Co-creation and information sharing Involving consumers in marketing and creative (feedback on creative campaigns, allowing them to create commercials, etc.) Letting customers "behind the curtain" have first access to information and content	

Source: "Word of Mouth 101: An Introduction to Word of Mouth Marketing" (accessed July 17, 2006, at **www.womma.org/wom101.htm**).

and get unsuspecting passersby to take their photos using the new Sony Ericsson camera phone, and then hype the phone. WOMMA now has rules that state that anyone talking up products should identify the client for whom they work.[55] Some critics say buzz marketing should never be directed at children and teens, as these consumers are more impressionable and easier to deceive than adults.[56]

Companies also must be careful using buzz marketing because campaigns can backfire. This is what happened with McDonald's "Lincoln Fry" buzz campaign. The company used its blog to spread the word about a couple who found a McDonald's fry that looked like Abraham Lincoln. When consumers learned that the blog and the couple were bogus, the buzz turned negative.[57] Of course, marketers don't have a hand in creating all the buzz around a product. WOMMA refers to buzz resulting from buzz marketing campaigns as "amplified WOM," while it calls buzz that occurs naturally "organic WOM." Organic buzz allowed Procter & Gamble to discover that its Home Café coffee maker had a tendency to start fires after 3000 buzz agents complained.[58] Naturally occurring buzz also can create negative publicity, as when ex-journalist Jeff Jarvis detailed on a blog his problem getting a $1600 PC fixed due to poor service from Dell.[59] To create positive buzz, companies need to have a total customer focus, and to empathize and care about their customers.

Guerrilla Marketing A few years back, some companies with smaller advertising budgets developed innovative ways of getting consumers' attention. These activities—from putting advertising stickers on apples and heads of lettuce to placing product-related messages on the backs of theatre tickets and flags on a golf course—became known as **guerrilla marketing**. No, this term doesn't refer to marketers making monkeys out of themselves (that's "gorilla marketing"). A guerrilla marketing strategy involves "ambushing" consumers with promotional content in places where they are not expecting to encounter this kind of activity.[60]

Today, big companies are buying into guerrilla marketing strategies big time. Burger King recently began a guerrilla marketing campaign to increase sales in its Asia-Pacific stores by 25 percent.[61] The company sent CDs with quirky marketing suggestions to local restaurant

> **guerrilla marketing** Marketing activity in which a firm "ambushes" consumers with promotional content in places they are not expecting to encounter this kind of activity.

Marketing Metrics

For many marketers, building a word-of-mouth campaign is the easy part. Measuring its effectiveness is much more difficult.

In 2003, Frederick Reichheld's article in the *Harvard Business Review*, entitled "One Number You Need to Grow," caught the attention of marketers all over the world. In this article, Reichheld defined two influential consumer groups that he termed "promoters" and "detractors." He then went on to develop a new metric called the Net Promoter Score (NPS), which is based on just one survey question—the likelihood of recommending a business or brand. The Net Promoter Score can be used to measure the loyalty of a company's customers. This simple approach looks at the responses to a firm's willingness-to-recommend question, typically measured on a zero-to-10 scale. Consumers who score nines and 10s are "promoters" and are very willing to recommend the brand to others, those who score sevens and eights are "neutrals," and the rest are "detractors." By subtracting the number of detractors from the number of promoters, the firm can calculate its net promoter score.

The idea is simple: Find out how likely a brand is to be recommended, and you will have a good indicator of how well the brand will grow. NPS clearly correlates with financial performance, and a number of companies now use this as an important performance metric. As word-of-mouth continues to become a more important part of the communication mix, marketers are trying to find new metrics to measure the impact of word-of-mouth on financial performance.[62]

managers. These included putting "I♥BK" on T-shirts and placing the shirts on Ronald McDonald, placing large footprints from McDonald's stores to Burger King outlets, placing signs on empty benches saying "Gone to BK –Ronald," and placing large signs at BK locations that are near KFC locations that read, "It's why the chicken crossed the road."

INFLUENCES ON THE COMMUNICATION STRATEGY, TACTICS, AND MIX Some products need personal selling, whereas others are best sold in other ways. Industrial goods and services, as well as big-ticket consumer items, are more likely to have a greater emphasis on personal selling in their communication mix, whereas it would be too costly for Colgate to hire door-to-door salespeople to promote its toothpaste. Many consumer products, such as cologne, tend to rely more on advertising, especially when the buyer selects the brand because of an image the manufacturer has carefully created for it. Using consumer sales promotion techniques such as coupons and premiums is very important to Procter & Gamble's sales of Tide detergent, but those same tactics would cheapen the image of Rolex or Mercedes. To compete for shoppers' attention, many companies allocate part of their communication efforts to in-store displays and even live product demonstrations to add the personal touch.

The communication mix must vary over time, because some elements are better for accomplishing the marketer's objectives at different points in time than are others. As we saw in the Hunk cologne example, the stage of the product life cycle (see Chapter 8) influences the communication mix.

In the introduction phase, the objective is to build awareness of the product among consumers and to rely on a push strategy. Advertising is the primary communication tool for creating awareness, and a publicity campaign to generate news reports about the new product may help. At this stage, sales promotion can be used to encourage consumers to try a new product or service. Distributors are also often given incentives to stock the new item.

In the growth phase, communication efforts must start to focus on communicating specific product benefits. Advertising increases, whereas sales promotions that encourage trial often decline, because people are more willing to try the product without being offered an incentive.

The opposite pattern often occurs during the maturity phase in which many people have tried or used the product. As sales stabilize, the goal is to persuade people to switch from a competitor's product, often when they see few important differences between competitors in a category. Sales promotions, particularly coupons and special price deals, increase—but sales promotion is not the only way to gain market share in a mature market. Familiprix, a Quebec pharmacy chain, managed to increase sales by 23 percent and awareness from 19 percent to 52 percent in a mature market through a series of 15-second ads demonstrating, with humour, the positioning that Familiprix pharmacies are close by and understand health issues. The ads depicted common family health issues and a Familiprix pharmacist jumping to the rescue exclaiming "Ah! Ha! Familiprix!" The campaign became such a pop-culture sensation that consumers, schoolchildren, and media personalities began adopting the tag line in their conversations.[66]

Ethical Decisions in Marketing

Consumers are spending increasingly more time in front of the TV and computer screen gaming, and marketers who don't want to be shut out are pushing their way right into the media. "The gaming industry's financial influence is irrefutable. Larger than the motion picture box office in terms of revenue, and growing at three times the pace, gaming is a path to more than 145 million customers of all ages," states Jack Clues, CEO of ad agency SMG.[63] The allure of video games for marketers is twofold, as they provide an interactive avenue to target a coveted demographic, in an immersive content that keeps consumers engaged. Dole bananas has had huge success and recognition for stamping its logo on all the hundreds of bananas collected in the popular kids' Nintendo game Super Monkey Ball. Both Burton and McDonald's are a few of the advertisements scattered on the sidelines of the most popular game in the world, the FIFA soccer series.[64] Canadians spent $152 million on video games in the first two months of 2007, a 61 percent increase over the same period last year.[65] This trend is expected to continue—and advertisers will continue to take advantage of it. What do you think—is this is a communication vehicle marketers should not ignore or should games be ad free?

All bets are off during the decline phase. As sales plummet, the company dramatically reduces spending on all elements of the communication mix. Sales will be driven by the continued loyalty of a small group of users who keep the brand alive until it is sold to another company or discontinued as part of a harvesting strategy (see Chapter 2). The decline in sales further discourages the company from investing any more money in promoting the product, which may be left to wither on the vine. Alternatively, the company may decide to try to revive the brand and dedicate a modest budget to restoring sales.

This was the case with Clorox Canada. Market research found that by the late 1990s, the Glad garbage bags brand was timeworn. Clorox needed to revive its whole line of garbage bags and food protection products: It decided to go "retro" and revived a famous Canadian ad icon, the Man from Glad. Clorox took him out of the old suburban setting and placed him in the technical surroundings of a high-performance testing lab, where he watched technicians demonstrate the strength and dependability of Glad products to the slogan "Glad. Depend on it." Canadians watched new Man from Glad television ads, read magazine ads, saw promotions in their local grocery store, and responded very positively. The re-emphasis on the Man from Glad has put Glad close to surpassing its main competitor to take over the top position in the disposable container category.[67]

Step 6: Determine and Allocate Budget

While setting a budget for marketing communication might seem easy, in reality it's not that simple. Determining and allocating communication budgets involves determining the total communication budget and allocating how much to spend on specific promotion activities. Communication budgets do not determine communication strategy but communication budgets do inform strategy, in that marketers need to be aware of what can be achieved with a particular budget. The strategies and tactics used to communicate with a $50 000 budget may be the same as the strategies and tactics used to communicate with a $500 000 budget, but the impact will be different as the $500 000 can buy more, and perhaps different, exposure to an audience. Table 12.5 shows examples of what different media cost for single placement (one ad, one time). Costs fall significantly when multiple placements are booked and most media sell packages of space, bundling attractive time slots with less attractive time slots at a discounted rate. However, as you can see from the "list" prices, communication is not inexpensive. Knowing the approximate budget for a communication campaign helps marketers decide what communication mix elements can realistically be used.

Table 12.5 Media Cost Examples

30-Second Television: National Exposure		Magazine Full-Page, 4-Colour	
CTV—*Survivor*	$209 000	*Maclean's*	$32 600
CBC—*The National*	$8000	*BC Business*	$4630
TSN—PGA Golf	$1200	*EnRoute*	$7500
Teletoon (National)	$500–$3000	*Chatelaine*	$43 840
MuchMusic (12 p.m.–6 p.m.)	$525	*Toronto Life*	$12 960
		Famous Magazine	$25 000

Newspaper ¹/₂-Page, Black + 1-Colour		30-Second Radio	
The Globe and Mail (National)	$8204	Montreal CINW—AM	$75–$105
The Gazette (Montreal)	$2446	Vancouver CKNW	$135 (afternoon)
Times Columnist (Victoria)	$929	Edmonton CFCW—AM	$117–$147
		Toronto CJCL—AM	$130–$235
		Fredericton CFXY—FM	$56–$62

Note: Rates are approximate and change frequently. Significant volume- and package-based discounts are available.

In an ideal world, setting the budget for communications would be simple: Spend whatever it takes to accomplish the stated objectives. In reality, firms often view communication costs as an expense rather than as an investment that will lead to greater profits. When sales are declining or the company is operating in a difficult economic environment, it is often tempting to cut costs by reducing spending on advertising, sales promotions, and other "soft" activities whose contributions to the bottom line are hard to quantify. When this is the case, marketers must try to justify these expenses to others in the firm.

Economic approaches to budgeting rely on marginal analysis (discussed in Chapter 9), in which the organization spends money on communications as long as the revenues realized by these efforts continue to exceed the costs of the communications themselves. This perspective assumes that promotions are always intended solely to increase sales when, in fact, these activities may have other objectives, such as enhancing a firm's image. Also, the effects of communications often lag. For example, a firm may have to spend a lot on communications when it first launches a product without seeing any return on this investment for quite a while. Because of these limitations, most firms rely on two budgeting techniques: top down and bottom up.

Top-down budgeting techniques require top management to establish the overall amount that the organization wishes to devote to communication activities, and this amount is then divided among advertising, public relations, and other communication departments.

The most common top-down technique is the **percentage-of-sales method**, in which the communication budget is based on last year's sales or on estimates for this year's sales. The percentage is an industry average provided by trade associations that collect objective information on behalf of member companies. The advantage of this method is that it reminds the organization that spending on communication does result in profits.

Unfortunately, this method implies that sales cause communication outlays, rather than viewing sales as the outcome of communication efforts. As sales drop, firms might be reluctant to spend more on communication, when the drop might be due to environmental changes, such as a change in economic conditions or a rival's recent introduction of a new product. If so, cutting communication spending might not help the firm in the long run.

The *competitive-parity method* is simply matching whatever competitors are spending. Some marketers think this approach is justified, saying that the decision simply mirrors the best thinking of others in the business. However, this method often results in each player maintaining the same market share year after year. This method also assumes that the same dollars spent on communication by two different firms will yield the same results, but spending a lot of money doesn't guarantee a successful communication. Firms certainly need to monitor their competitors' communication activities, but they must combine this information with their own objectives and abilities.

The problem with top-down techniques is that budget decisions are based more on established practices than on communication objectives. Another approach is to begin at the beginning: Identify communication goals and allocate enough money to accomplish them. That is what **bottom-up budgeting techniques** attempt. For example, some marketers construct a *payout plan* that attempts to predict the revenues and costs associated with a product over several years and matches communication expenditures to this pattern—spending more on communication in the first year to build market share, for example, and then less after the product catches on.

This bottom-up logic is at the heart of the **objective-task method**, which is gaining in popularity. Using this approach, the firm first defines the specific communication goals it hopes to achieve, such as increasing by 20 percent the number of consumers who are aware of the brand. It then tries to determine what kind of communication efforts it will take to meet that goal. Although this is the most rational approach, it is hard to implement, because it obliges managers to specify their objectives and attach dollar amounts to them. This method requires careful analysis and a bit of "guesstimating."

top-down budgeting techniques Allocation of the promotion budget that is based on the total amount to be devoted to marketing communications.

percentage-of-sales method A method for promotion budgeting, in which the promotion budget is based on a percentage of either last year's sales or on estimates for this year's sales.

bottom-up budgeting techniques Allocation of the promotion budget that is based on identifying promotional goals and allocating enough money to accomplish them.

objective-task method A promotion budgeting method in which an organization first defines the specific communication goals it hopes to achieve and then tries to calculate what kind of promotional efforts it must take to meet these goals.

Exhibit 12.10

Many companies have shifted their promotional dollars to sponsor sporting events, such as NASCAR racing.

ALLOCATE THE BUDGET TO A SPECIFIC COMMUNICATION MIX Once the organization has decided how much to spend on communications, it must divide its budget among the elements in the communication mix. Although advertising used to get the lion's share of the communication budget, sales promotions are now playing a bigger role in marketing strategies. As MasterCard's vice-president of promotions observed, marketers who once relied on sales promotions solely to create a short-term response now see them as "a permanent, integral part of the brand."[68] For example, although the typical NASCAR racing car, such as the one in Exhibit 12.10, is covered with the logos of tobacco and motor oil companies, other marketers such as Hewlett-Packard, Universal Studios, and even banking giant HSBC (Hong Kong and Shanghai Banking Corp.) are changing their communication mix by sponsoring racing teams. They are joining the race to capture the attention of the 460 million people who watch these events as they are broadcast to 201 countries.[69] Several factors influence how companies divide up the communication pie:

- *Organizational factors:* Characteristics of the specific firm influence how it allocates its money. These characteristics are the complexity and formality of the company's decision-making process, preferences within the company for advertising versus sales promotions or other elements in the communication mix, past experiences with specific communication vehicles, as well as the "comfort level" of the firm's advertising and communication agencies with developing different kinds of marketing communications. Nestlé, the giant Swiss company, for example, shifted about 20 percent of its advertising budget into sales promotion and direct-response efforts over a two-year period after the company determined that its communication dollars would be more effective there.[70]

- *Market potential:* Consumers in some markets will be more likely to buy the product. For example, the marketers of Hunk might find that men in blue-collar occupations would be more interested in the product than men in professional occupations. It makes sense for marketers to allocate more resources to television shows, radio stations, magazines, and other media or communication vehicles that also target people in blue-collar occupations.

- *Market size:* As a rule, larger markets are more expensive places in which to communicate. The costs of buying media (such as spots on local television) are higher in major metropolitan areas. But the sheer density of highly populated areas makes it easier to reach large numbers of consumers at the same time. Advertising is good for mass-market products, whereas personal selling is good for specialized or highly technical products.

Step 7: Implement Creative Strategy

Creative strategy is the process that turns a concept into a communication piece or element. It's one thing to know what a company wants to say about itself and its product, and quite another to figure out exactly how to say it. The creative process has been described as the "spark between objective and execution." The Novell ad in Exhibit 12.11 demonstrates how even business-to-business products, such as computer software and services, can come to life with the right creative strategy.

It is unlikely that one communication element can achieve all the communication objectives discussed previously, so marketers work in campaigns—a set of related elements that collectively deliver the objectives desired. Each element in a campaign (a television ad, a newspaper ad, a brochure, etc.) typically has a different objective. The goal of a campaign is to present a series of messages and repeat it to a sufficient degree that the audience will progress through the AIDA stages described earlier in this chapter. To do this, the creative team (art directors, mechanical artists, copywriters, photographers, and others) must develop a "big idea," a concept that expresses aspects of the product, service, or organization in a tangible, attention-getting, memorable manner. Then the concept must be executed in different media—such as print advertising, point-of-purchase materials, packaging, etc. Recognizing the concept of

Exhibit 12.11

Business products like software can be given a distinctive identity through advertising.

diffusion of innovation (Chapter 7), campaign elements need to be repeated—where the innovators may have acted already and tried a product, there will be many in the early and late majority who are not yet aware of a product.

MEDIA SCHEDULING AND PLACEMENT **Media planning** is a problem-solving process for getting a message to a target audience in the most effective fashion. The decisions include audience selection and where, when, and how frequent the exposure should be. There is no such thing as one perfect medium for marketing communications. The choice depends on the specific target audience, the objective of the message, and the budget. For the communication to be effective, the media planner must match up the profile of the target market with that of specific media vehicles. For example, 80 percent of Chinese Canadian consumers in Vancouver read Chinese Canadian newspapers.[71] Thus, a marketer trying to reach this segment might allocate a significant share of the communication budget to buying space in these newspapers.

The media planner's first task in deciding where to place the communication is to find out when and where people in the target market are most likely to be exposed to the communication. This is the **aperture**, the best "window" to reach that type of person. For example, many people who drive to work in the morning listen to the radio, so their aperture would include this medium at this time. Sun-Rype, for example, wanted to reach Moms with a message that its product "Fruit to Go" was nutritious (100 percent fruit) and reach kids with a message that these snacks were cool and tasty. Magazine ads, such as the one in Exhibit 12.12, were chosen as the way to reach both audiences, separately, with specific messages. Mom-targeted media included lifestyle and parenting magazines, while magazines distributed through schools, movie theatres, and direct to home were used to reach kids.[72]

Media Choices There are numerous paid and unpaid media outlets for communicating to audiences. Paid media such as television, radio, print, and outdoor media will be discussed in Chapter 13—when we further discuss communication tactics.

A company's website is becoming an increasingly important way to communicate interactively with consumers and support other forms of advertising. Kellogg Canada has set up several websites to support its advertising and communication goals for individual products. For example, the site for Kellogg's Special K cereal uses the slogan from its television and magazine ads, "Look good on your own terms," and is designed for women, the cereal's primary target market. As users enter the site, they are shown an ad for Special K before the webpage loads. Once on the site, visitors can see recipes using the product, participate in chat rooms, or ask questions of fitness and nutrition experts. Through its website, Kellogg Canada is able to reinforce advertising activities in more traditional media and potentially reach new consumers with its ads and other promotional messages.

Media Scheduling: When to Say It After choosing the advertising media, the planner then creates a **media schedule** that specifies the exact media to use, when, and how often the message should appear. Figure 12.7 shows a hypothetical media schedule for the communication of a new video game. Note that much of the advertising reaches its target audience in the months just before Christmas, and that much of the expensive television budget is focused on

media planning The process of developing media objectives, strategies, and tactics for use in an advertising campaign.

aperture The best place and time to reach a person in the target market group.

media schedule The plan that specifies the exact media to use and when.

Exhibit 12.12

Sun-Rype used targeted magazines to reach Moms and kids with different messages.

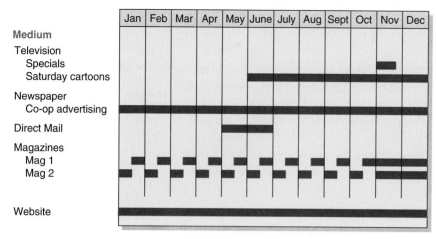

Figure 12.7 A Media Schedule for a Video Game

advertising during specials just before the holiday season. The company's website is used in the media schedule as a constant reinforcement of the paid advertising placed in other media.

The media schedule outlines the planner's best estimate of which media will be most effective in attaining the advertising objective(s), and which specific media vehicles will do the most effective job. The media planner considers such factors as the match between the demographic and psychographic profile of a target audience and the people reached by a media vehicle, the communication activities of competitors, and the capability of a medium to convey the desired information adequately. The planner must also consider the compatibility of the product with editorial content: After all, viewers might not respond well to a lighthearted ad for a new snack food during a sombre documentary on world hunger.

advertising exposure The degree to which the target market will see an advertising message placed in a specific vehicle.

When analyzing media, the planner is interested in assessing **advertising exposure**, the degree to which the target market will see an advertising message in a specific medium. Media planners talk in terms of **impressions**, which measure the number of people who will be exposed to a message placed in one or more media vehicles. For example, if one million people watch a miniseries on CTV, each time an advertiser runs an ad during that program, it receives one million impressions. If the advertiser's spot runs four times during the program, the impression count would be four million, even though some of these impressions would represent repeated exposure to the same viewers.

impressions The number of people who will be exposed to a message placed in one or more media vehicles.

reach The percentage of the target market that will be exposed to the media vehicle.

To calculate the exposure a message will have if placed in a certain medium, planners consider two factors: reach and frequency. **Reach** is the percentage of the target market that will be exposed to the media vehicle. This measure is particularly important for widely used products when it's important to get the message to as many consumers as possible. **Frequency** is the number of times a person in the target group would be exposed to the message. This is important with products that are complex or are targeted to relatively small markets for which multiple exposures to the message are necessary to make an impact.

frequency The number of times a person in the target group will be exposed to the message.

For example, say a media planner wants to get Club Med advertising to university and college students. The advertiser learns that 25 percent of that target market reads at least a few issues of *Rolling Stone* each year (reach). The advertiser may also determine that these students are likely to see three of the twelve monthly ads that Club Med will run in *Rolling Stone* during the year (frequency). Now, the planner calculates the magazine's **gross rating points (GRPs)** by multiplying reach times frequency, which in this case compares the effectiveness of *Rolling Stone* to alternative media. By using this same formula, the planner can then compare the GRP number of another magazine or the GRP of placing an ad on television or on a bus or any other advertising medium.

gross rating points (GRPs) A measure used for comparing the effectiveness of different media vehicles: average reach times frequency.

Although some media vehicles deliver superior exposure, they may not be cost efficient. More people will see a commercial aired during the Stanley Cup playoffs than during a 3:00 a.m. rerun of a horror movie. But the advertiser could run late-night commercials every night for a year for the cost of one 30-second Stanley Cup spot. For example, a 30-second ad on CBC that would be shown across the country could cost as little as $100 or as much as $46 000, depending on when it was run. Similarly, a 30-second ad on TSN could be as little as $100 or as much as $20 000.[73]

To compare the relative cost-effectiveness of different media and of spots run on different vehicles in the same medium, media planners use a measure called **cost per thousand (CPM)**. This figure compares the relative cost-effectiveness of different media vehicles that have different exposure rates and reflects the cost to deliver a message to 1000 people. For example, the cost for a Canadian company to do banner advertising on DoubleClick averages $30 to $40 CPM.[74] A medium's popularity with consumers determines how much advertisers must pay to put their message on it. Television networks are concerned with getting good ratings, because their advertising rates are determined by how many viewers their programming attracts. Similarly, magazines and newspapers try to boost circulation and websites to justify raising ad rates.

Media Scheduling: How Often to Say It After deciding where to advertise, the planner must decide when and how often. What time of day? Frequently for a few weeks, or occasionally for a long time? After selecting the media schedule, the planner turns to the overall pattern the advertising will follow.

A *continuous schedule* maintains a steady stream of advertising throughout the year. This is most appropriate for products that sell on a regular basis, such as shampoo or bread. Some advertising professionals maintain that continuous advertising sustains market leadership even if total industry sales fall.[75] On the downside, some messages can suffer from *advertising wearout*, because people tune out the same old ad messages.

A *pulsing schedule* varies the amount of advertising throughout the year, based on when the product is likely to be in demand. S.C. Johnson & Son, for example, uses a pulsing schedule to communicate its Off! brands of bug repellents more heavily in the summer months. *Flighting* is an extreme form of pulsing in which advertising appears in short, intense bursts alternating with periods of little to no activity. It can produce as much brand awareness as a steady dose of advertising at a much lower cost, if the messages from the previous flight were noticed and made an impact.

Step 8: Evaluate

The final stage in developing a communication plan is to set criteria and methods to determine whether the plan is working. The marketer needs to determine whether the communication objectives are adequately translated into marketing communications that are reaching the right target market.

It would be nice if a marketing manager could simply report, "Our new $3 million communication campaign for our revolutionary glow-in-the-dark surfboards resulted in $15 million in new sales!" Unfortunately, it is not so easy. Because there are many factors at work in the marketing environment, other events such as a manufacturing problem encountered by a rival board manufacturer, a coincidental photograph of a movie star riding one of the boards, or even renewed interest in surfing may have caused those new sales instead.

A retail advertiser once complained: "I am certain that half the money I spend on advertising is completely wasted. The trouble is, I don't know which half."[76] Despite this admonition, there are ways to monitor and evaluate the company's communication efforts. The catch is that the effectiveness of some forms of communication is easier to determine than others. As a rule, sales promotions are the easiest to evaluate because they occur during a fixed period of time and can be directly tied to sales.

Direct measures of advertising effectiveness are difficult to design. It is hard to determine just how many sales were the result of a specific ad campaign. Advertising researchers measure brand awareness, recall of product benefits communicated through advertising, and even the image of the brand before and after an advertising campaign. **Post-testing** is conducting research on consumers' responses to advertising messages they have seen or heard (as opposed to pretesting, which collects reactions to messages before they're actually placed in

cost per thousand (CPM) A measure used to compare the relative cost-effectiveness of different media vehicles that have different exposure rates: the cost to deliver a message to 1000 people or homes.

post-testing Research conducted on consumers' responses to actual advertising messages they have seen or heard.

"the real world"). Ironically, many creative ads that are quirky or even bizarre make an advertising agency look good within the industry but are ultimately unsuccessful, because they don't communicate what needs to be said about the product itself. As one consultant observed, "There is so much emphasis on the creative aspect of the ads, sort of 'Aren't we clever?' that the message is lost."[77]

In some cases, the ads are popular but they send the wrong message to consumers. For example, a lot of people remember Joe Isuzu, the lying car salesman whose television commercials were popular for two years but were no help to Isuzu's car sales during that time.[78] As one advertising executive explained, "The humor got in the way. All you remembered was that car salesmen are dishonest, and the car salesman you remembered most was from Isuzu."[79] Three measures of the impact of an advertisement are *unaided recall*, *aided recall*, and *attitudinal measures*. **Unaided recall** tests, by telephone survey or personal interview, how much of an ad a person remembers during a specified period of time, sometimes by asking the person to write down what the ad said. An **aided recall** test uses clues to prompt answers. For example, a researcher might show a group of consumers a list of brands and ask them to choose which items they have seen advertised within the past week. **Attitudinal measures** probe a bit more deeply by testing consumer beliefs or feelings about a product before and after being exposed to messages about it. If, for example, Dove antiperspirant's ads about the product being good for the skin make enough consumers believe that this is an important attribute for antiperspirants, marketers can consider the advertising campaign successful.

Measuring the effectiveness of marketing communications is easier if the audience is requested to respond in some way—such as calling a 1-800 number or going to a website. For example, in the Adobe ad in Exhibit 12.13, the company wants people to visit the "defytherules" site; if Adobe wanted to measure the effectiveness of the ad, it might use number of visits to the website advertised as one measure of this. Most often, however, advertisers research consumer response to advertising through post-testing. The effectiveness of banner advertising is even easier to measure, since the number of visitors coming to a website through a banner ad is directly measurable.

A firm can analyze and compare the performance of salespeople in different territories, though again it is often difficult to rule out other factors that make some sales forces more effective than others. Public relations activities are perhaps the hardest to assess, because they often are intended to result in building favourable relationships over a longer period of time.

EVALUATING INTEGRATED MARKETING COMMUNICATIONS The IMC perspective takes a broad view of the world: Learning about a good or service comes from many sources, and beliefs develop over time. For these reasons, traditional measurement techniques that focus on the impact of one message at one point in time are not adequate to assess the impact of an entire communication program. Instead, marketers track consumer responses to communication efforts and interactions with the brand and/or company over time.[80] They also conduct research to assess consumer attitudes toward the brand and/or organization. Although they don't always accurately predict purchases, customers' attitudes toward an item still are important pieces of information, especially when changes in attitudes are tracked over time. Ideally these pieces of information are collected on an ongoing basis and fed back into a database, where they will be used to update and refine the integrated strategy.[81]

unaided recall A research technique conducted by telephone survey or personal interview that asks how much of an ad a person remembers during a specified period of time.

aided recall A research technique that uses clues to prompt answers from people about advertisements they might have seen.

attitudinal measures A research technique that probes a consumer's beliefs or feelings about a product before and after being exposed to messages about it.

Exhibit 12.13

The number of people visiting the "defytherules" website would be one way of measuring the effectiveness of this ad.

COMMUNICATION BRIEFS

Communication plans are internal documents created by organizations that provide rationale for, and guide, their communication strategy for a specified period of time. People in an in-house creative department or communication/advertising agency do not have time to read a lengthy communication plan. They rely on a communication brief, which is typically a one- to three-page summary of the elements of a communication plan that precedes creative execution—and for small projects it may replace the communication plan if the other elements of the plan are considered in the brief. The advantage of writing a formal communication brief, rather than just explaining the strategy for a campaign to the creative team, is that verbal explanations can be misinterpreted or modified in sequential telling within the creative team. If a lot of time is wasted in wrestling projects back on track (and at rates of $100 to $150 dollars an hour for each person in the room), it can be very expensive not having a clear understanding of the creative task. It is not easy capturing the essence of a 15- to 25-page communication plan in a one- to three-page brief, but as one marketing executive suggested, "The creative has to be brief so the brief has to be creative."[82] The idea is to set the strategic parameters in which the creative team operates and to gain agreement from the client that the brief represents the intended strategy. One retired president of a large New York agency described the brief as needing to be "as hard and brilliant as a diamond, and as tight and confining as a pair of handcuffs."[83] For example, the heart of the creative brief for the now acclaimed Absolut Vodka campaign (Exhibit 12.14) was "You can do anything you want creatively, but you must always show the product and no headline can be longer than two words and one of those words must be Absolut."[84]

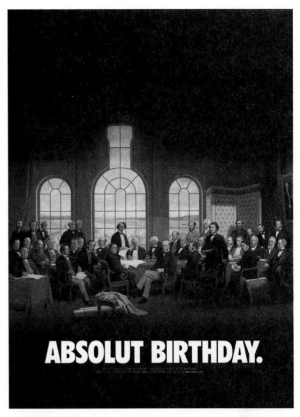

Exhibit 12.14

A very tight creative brief helped focus the creative team to create the famous Absolut Vodka campaign.

Real People, Real Decisions

▶ **How It Worked Out** at Cormark Communications

The Cormark team chose Option 2, maintaining the U.S. strategic platform but rebuilding key sections of the strategy to meet the needs of the Canadian marketplace. They concluded that the communications materials were directionally right but needed some modification to fit the Canadian marketplace and regulatory context, particularly for the veterinary market. They based this decision primarily on their market research. The hybrid option of customizing the U.S. strategy allowed Cormark and Pfizer Canada to control the Canadian product launch and move directionally correct and successful U.S. material to strategically accurate and insightful material that was right for the Canadian market.

There were two significant differences in the Canadian launch program. One was the significantly smaller budget requiring tighter targeting of messaging for efficiency. The second was a higher degree of emotion in the message. Cormark learned through research that consumers were moved by the restoration of the dog–owner relationship that could be achieved by the use of the product.

In implementing the strategy, Cormark developed a launch blueprint for Canada. The agency determined the key audiences within the broader consumer and veterinarian target markets and determined how best to reach them. Within three months of launch, Rimadyl exceeded the annual volume objective. Post-campaign research indicated that awareness by the target markets was higher than expected. Rimadyl is well on its way to becoming a major product in the category. Since the launch, other international markets have requested the Canadian launch materials for their own local use.

CHAPTER SUMMARY

1. Explain the concept of integrated marketing communications and its implementation.

Integrated marketing communications (IMC) programs allow marketers to communicate with consumers on a continual basis by coordinating the communication messages and media. IMC often uses customer databases to stay in touch with the market. In an IMC strategy, contact management means that communications occur when customers will be receptive to them. The type of message is influenced by the communication objectives, the characteristics of the customer group, and the exposure situation. The effectiveness of the IMC strategy may be assessed through transactional data, by customers' second-order responses, or by customer attitudes. Some marketers resist IMC because it requires changing accepted ways of doing things, decreases emphasis on advertising, puts an increased focus on communications, and requires major changes in advertising agencies.

2. Understand the characteristics of integrated marketing communications.

Integrated marketing communications (IMC) includes the planning, development, execution, and evaluation of coordinated, measurable, persuasive brand communications. IMC programs mean that a firm's marketing communication programs include a single unified voice, begin with the customer, seek to develop relationships with customers, use targeted communication, use two-way communication, focus on all stakeholders rather than customers only, rely on the effective use of databases, generate a continuous stream of communication, and measure results based on actual feedback.

3. Explain the important role of database marketing in integrated marketing communication (IMC).

The effective use of databases, key to an IMC strategy, allows organizations to learn about its customers, fine-tune its offerings, and build an ongoing relationship with its market. Database marketing is interactive—that is, it requires a response from consumers and it builds relationships, allowing the marketer to adapt to consumers' needs. Database marketing provides a means to locate new customers and to stimulate cross-selling of related products. With database marketing, a company can measure the impact of its communication efforts and track which consumers responded.

4. Explain the steps involved in developing a communication plan.

A communication plan is an internal document that develops the communication strategy for an organization, product line, or brand. It starts with a summary of the marketing objectives and situational context, then specifies the target markets and profiles the target audiences. Communication objectives are then identified, followed by a description of communication strategy, positioning and key messages, and tactics (themes or approaches) that will be used to break through perceptual screens of receivers. A communication mix is then chosen, informed by a budget reality check. This part of the plan is often summarized in a communication brief for the creative team in order to keep the creative on strategy. The plan concludes with specification of the creative execution, media scheduling and placement, budget allocation, and evaluation criteria and methods.

5. List, describe, and contrast the elements of the communication mix.

The five major elements of marketing communications are known as the communication mix. Personal selling provides direct contact between a company representative and a customer. Direct marketing is direct impersonal communication focused on short-term, single-transaction responses or a set of responses leading to a purchase decision. Advertising is non-personal, paid-for communication from an identified sponsor using mass media. Sales promotions stimulate immediate sales by providing incentives to the trade or to consumers. Publicity and public relations activities seek to influence the attitudes of various publics.

6. **Explain how marketing communication strategies can be evaluated.**

   Marketers need to conduct research to determine if specific advertisements are effective. Post-testing research may include recall tests or attitudinal measures, which examine whether the message had an influence on the target market. If the communication has a direct response element to it (1-800 number, website sign-in, etc.), it is easier to measure its effectiveness.

7. **Explain the content and purpose of a communication brief.**

   A communication brief is a summary of a communication plan that is used by the creative team to develop the creative concept and execution for a campaign. The brief typically summarizes the elements of the communication plan up to creative execution, but it might also include summaries of the other elements if the brief is used instead of a formal communication plan.

CHAPTER REVIEW

Marketing Concepts: Testing Your Knowledge

1. What is integrated marketing communications (IMC)?
2. What is marketing communication? What are the goals of communication?
3. How does communication theory help marketers develop more effective communication strategies?
4. List and describe the elements of the communication mix.
5. What are word-of-mouth marketing, buzz marketing, and viral marketing? Why are such activities gaining in popularity?
6. Explain what guerrilla marketing means.
7. What is database marketing? How do marketers use databases to better meet the needs of their customers?
8. List and explain the steps in the development of a communication plan.
9. Why should communication objectives be phrased in terms of communication tasks? What are some examples of communication task objectives?
10. How does the communication mix vary with push versus pull strategies? How does it vary in different stages of the product life cycle (PLC)?
11. Explain each of the following budgeting methods:
    a. percentage-of-sales method
    b. competitive-parity method
    c. objective-task method
12. What are some methods for evaluating the effectiveness of marketing communication?

Marketing Concepts: Discussing Choices and Issues

1. Increasingly, marketers are seeking new ways to communicate with consumers. Advertising is being placed on washroom walls, in high-school cafeterias, and even in the halls of university and college classroom buildings. Develop debate arguments for and against this proliferation of commercial messages.

2. One reason to build a database is to advance a political or social agenda by identifying and mobilizing a core of supporters. For example, Philip Morris has built a database with 26 million names, which the tobacco company uses to rally customers to the cause of smokers' rights. What are the ethical issues related to this use of databases?

3. Advertisers who spend millions of dollars for ads during special events such as the Olympics may be more interested in achieving aesthetic goals—having the most highly rated ad—than in selling products. Does it make sense for advertisers to focus on aesthetic goals rather than on marketing goals? Explain.

- promotion, p. 417
- publicity, p. 437
- public relations, p. 437
- pull strategy, p. 430
- push strategy, p. 430
- reach, p. 448
- receiver, p. 425
- source, p. 424
- target audience, p. 427
- top-down budgeting techniques, p. 444
- unaided recall, p. 450
- viral marketing, p. 439
- word of mouth (WOM), p. 439
- word-of-mouth marketing, p. 439

4. With an IMC program, firms need to coordinate all their marketing communication activities. What do you see as the problems inherent in implementing this?

5. Consumers are becoming concerned that the proliferation of databases is an invasion of an individual's privacy. Do you feel this is a valid concern? How can marketers use databases effectively and, at the same time, protect the rights of individuals?

6. Some argue that IMC is just a passing fad in marketing communications. What do you think?

Marketing Practice: Applying What You've Learned

1. As a marketing consultant, you are frequently asked by clients to develop recommendations for communication strategies. Outline your recommendations for the use of different communication mix elements for one of the following products:

   a. a new brand of laundry detergent

   b. a familiar brand of cereal

   c. a political candidate

   d. equipment for a new manufacturing facility

2. As the director of marketing for a small firm that markets specialty salad dressings, you are in the process of developing a communication plan. With one or more of your classmates, develop suggestions for each of the following. Then, in a role-playing situation, present your recommendations to the client.

   a. communication objectives

   b. a method for determining the communication budget

   c. the use of a push strategy or a pull strategy

3. As an account executive for a communication services firm, you have been assigned to a new client, a manufacturer of a popular brand of toothpaste. As you begin development of the creative strategy, you are considering different types of appeals:

   a. informative appeal

   b. comparative advertising

   c. a fear appeal

   d. a celebrity endorsement

   e. a slice-of-life ad

   f. sex appeal

   g. humour

   Outline the strengths and weaknesses of using each of these appeals for advertising the toothpaste.

4. As the marketing manager for a chain of bookstores, you are interested in developing a database marketing plan. Give your recommendations for the following:

   a. How to generate a customer database

   b. How to use the database to better understand your customers

   c. How to increase sales from your existing customers using your database

   d. How to get new customers using your database

5. As a member of the marketing department for a manufacturer of sports equipment, you have been directed to select a new agency to do the communications for your firm. You have asked two agencies to submit proposals. One agency recommends an integrated marketing communications plan, and the second agency has developed recommendations for a traditional advertising plan. Write a memo to explain each of the following to your boss.

   a. What is different about an integrated marketing communication plan?

   b. Why is the IMC plan superior to merely advertising?

   c. Why do some agencies resist changing from traditional communication planning?

Marketing Mini-Project: Learning by Doing

The purpose of this mini-project is to give you an opportunity to experience the advertising creative process.

1. With one or more classmates, create (imagine) a new brand of an existing product, such as a laundry detergent, toothpaste, perfume, or soft drink.

2. Develop a communication brief for this new product.

3. Develop at least three creative concepts for implementing the strategy summarized in your brief and mock-up magazine ads as one element of a campaign. Your magazine ads should have a headline, a visual, and copy to explain your product and to persuade customers to purchase your brand.

4. Present your brief and ads to your class. Discuss the advertising appeal you selected, and explain your ad executions.

Real People, Real Surfers: Exploring the Web

Much of the advertising you see every day on television and in magazines is created by communication services companies and advertising agencies. Some of these companies are large, some very small. Some offer clients specialized services, such as "new media" advertising, while others offer a wide variety of services. To make their company stand out from the others, the different agencies develop unique personalities or corporate philosophies. Visit the websites of several large and small Canadian communication companies.

Cossette Communications Group (www.cossette.com)
BBDO Canada (www.bbdo.ca)
Amoeba Corporation (www.amoebacorp.com)
Palmer Jarvis DDB (www.palmerjarvisddb.com)
Sonic Boom (www.sonicboom.com)
Critical Mass (www.criticalmass.com)

Explore the websites to see how they differ. Then answer these questions.

1. What is the mission of each company? How does each company attempt to position itself?

2. Who are some of the major clients of the firm?

3. How does the site demonstrate the creative ability of the company? Does the site do a good job of communicating the mission of the company? Explain.

4. If it is available, tell a little about the history of the company.

5. Of the companies you visited, which would you most like to work for and why?

6. As a client, based on your exploration of the websites, which company would you choose for your business and why?

What do Robert DeNiro, Tiger Woods, Kate Winslet, Laird Hamilton, and Mike Krzyzewski all have in common? Let's see, Robert DeNiro is one of the greatest living actors; Tiger Woods is arguably the best golfer ever; Kate Winslet is a multiple Academy Award nominee; Laird Hamilton is perhaps the greatest surfer to have ever lived; and Mike Krzyzewski is a Hall of Fame basketball coach. However, being famous and best in their field are not the only things these folks have in common. They also all carry the American Express credit card and have been in television or print commercials promoting the card in the company's "My Life, My Card" campaign.

By using famous and recognizable people in its ads, American Express is trying to capture the attention of current and potential consumers. The fast pace of today's busy lifestyles and the rapid changes in information technology mean that, more than ever, companies like American Express have to rely on the familiar faces of celebrities to get their messages across. Each of the AMEX ads includes brief biographical information on the celebrity such as where they live, profession, greatest triumphs or greatest disappointments, and basic philosophy of life. The final point of each ad is how the American Express card helps enable the individual to pursue what is important to him or her. American Express is communicating to its current and potential customers that they are just like these celebrities—simply trying to live life at its best. So, the slogan "My Life, My Card" is perfect for the ad campaign.

However, advertising is not the only element of the promotion mix that American Express is using to get its message across. In Mexico, for example, AMEX uses sales promotion to offer one free airline ticket for each ticket purchased with the American Express card. In Europe the company has set up "AMEX Travelcast" hubs in tourist areas such as train stations. These hubs take advantage of the growing podcast phenomenon by allowing travellers to download maps and videos to their MP3 players. The downloaded maps feature foreign exchange bureaus and retailers that accept the American Express card. The company also has used the Internet to broadcast "webisodes," which are five-minute video stories featuring comedian Jerry Seinfeld, resulting in over three million visitors to its website. Finally, AMEX uses personal selling to attract restaurant owners to its Restaurant Partnership Program, which provides savings and benefits to owners that accept the American Express card.

Unfortunately for American Express, its "My Life, My Card" advertising campaign isn't without competition. Visa has been running ads for some time now with the slogan "Life takes Visa," which is a clever variation on the same theme communicated by the American Express ads. American Express's other main competitor, MasterCard, uses its "Priceless" line of commercials that are aimed at encouraging customers to use the card to create priceless moments. Promotional ads expressing the same theme by these competitors diminish the impact of American Express's ads somewhat and have the potential to confuse consumers about which card provides the best means to pursue life's rewards.

The company's previous campaign, "The American Express card. Don't leave home without it," had a long run of popularity and is still a well-known advertising saying. But will the current campaign enjoy the same success? How long will people stay connected to the "My Life, My Card" message, along with its accompanying celebrities?

Perhaps American Express needs to look for creative ways to utilize other elements of the promotion mix to develop a truly integrated marketing communication strategy that augments its advertisements. Otherwise, over the long haul American Express may end up investing a lot of money in advertising but still fail to achieve its long-term marketing communication goals.

Sources: Brian Steinberg, "Now showing: Clustered ad spots on television," *The Wall Street Journal*, 15 February 2006, B3; Business Wire Inc., "American Express launches the restaurant partnership program with savings, access and information," *Business Wire*, 8 June 2006; Centaur Communications Ltd., "Amex expands tourist podcast after Turin Olympics success," *New Media Age*, 2 March 2006, 2; Dan Sewell, "Companies use online magazines to woo customers," *Associated Press Financial Wire*, 2 January 2006; Sentido Comun, "American Express launches new promotion campaign in Mexico," *Latin American News Digest*, 14 February 2006.

Things to Think About

1. What is the decision facing American Express?

2. What factors are important in understanding this decision situation?

3. What are the alternatives?

4. What decision(s) do you recommend?

5. What are some ways to implement your recommendation?

CUCINAetc.

CUCINA*etc*.™

ENGLISH EDITION   COOKING THE ITALIAN WAY

ALLA GRIGLIA
Grill to Perfection

TOSCANA
A Culinary Tour

MENU CLASSICO
From *Campania* to You

www.cucinaetc.com

5,95 $ - No 5

0 55113 57038 4   01

CHAPTER 13
Communications Mix and Tactics

Real People, Real Decisions

Meet **Mario Demers**, a Decision Maker at Saputo Dairy Products Canada

Mario Demers is the national marketing director of Saputo Dairy Products Division (Canada). Founded in 1954, Saputo is a Montreal-based cheese and food products company that has rapidly grown through acquisition since going public in 1997. After acquiring Dairy World (the B.C.-based company that owned Dairy Land and Armstrong Cheese), Saputo is now the leading dairy processor in Canada and one of the most important cheese producers in North America and Argentina. Mario graduated in 1985 with a BBA in Marketing from the Université du Québec à Montréal. Prior to joining Saputo in 2001, he spent 11 years at Quebecor Inc. as a marketing and sales director, and one year as marketing director at the TVA Network.

The challenge Mario faced was that Saputo had developed or acquired a number of regional cheese brands, but none had national recognition, and there was no marketing vision or synergy. Saputo was well known in Quebec and some parts of Ontario for its Italian cheeses such as Mozzarella, Parmesan, and Ricotta. Armstrong was well known for its Cheddar in western Canada. Bari is a fighter brand known in western Canada, primarily in British Columbia.

Mario recognized that maintaining a large portfolio of small cheese brands was an expensive proposition from a marketing communications point of view, as each brand had its own positioning and would need to be supported with a separate communication strategy. He thought it would make more strategic and financial sense to rationalize the brands into three groups: the Italian cheeses under the Saputo brand name, Canadian and English cheeses (e.g., Cheddar, Colby, Monterey Jack) under the Armstrong brand, and French and other European cheeses (e.g., Brie, Camembert, Swiss) under the Cayer brand. This brand rationalization would require some time, however, as the other brand names were liked and sought by both regional customers and regional distributors as a "local" alternative to large international brands like Kraft and Black Diamond. But Mario recognized the advantages of having three family brands: the ability to position each family differently, to leverage the current strong reputations of individual cheeses to build brand equity for a family of related cheeses, and to share brand reputation with any new products added to the three lines. The question became how to manage the transition. Mario considered two options.

Option 1: A series of national mass media advertising campaigns.

Mario thought that the rationalization of the brands could be achieved through a series of large-scale television, print, and radio campaigns introducing consumers to the Saputo Corporation and the three brand families. The main advantage of a mass media approach was the relative speed at which the branding strategy could be introduced to consumers.

Most consumers across Canada were already familiar with one of the three family brands, and positive associations with that brand would likely be transferred to the unfamiliar brands. This approach, however, would be very expensive—in the range of $500 000 for each six-week campaign, and $4 million to $5 million in total to get sufficient reach and frequency. This is Kraft's approach, and it can be quite effective in generating brand recognition so that when consumers see the brand in the store, they have a positive predisposition to purchase it. However, frequent campaigns are necessary to keep a brand in consumers' minds. Also, large-scale television, print, and radio campaigns do not guarantee that the product will be listed by grocery chains and independent retail stores. Consequently, this alternative might need to be implemented on a region-by-region basis where the Saputo sales force was successful in getting listings for all three of the product lines. This might prove difficult as some retailers had established relationships with other regional or specialty brands and might be unwilling or unable to break contracts to free up shelf space for Saputo products they had not previously carried.

Option 2: A product-placement IMC approach.

Mario thought that another effective approach would be to promote the three families of Saputo cheeses more slowly by reaching current and new users through product placement in a cooking show. There has been a significant increase in interest in cooking as the baby boomer generation reaches the prime ages for home entertaining and people of the echo-boom generation are setting up apartments and learning to cook for themselves. Rather than compete with other cheese brands for product placement opportunities on established cooking shows, Saputo could create its own cooking show to increase general cheese consumption, and specifically to increase Saputo cheese consumption. This would be done first in Italian on a specialty channel (TLN—Telelatino) to reach the large Italian communities in Quebec and Ontario (almost 1 million people) who were the main customers of Saputo's Italian cheeses. Then, after listing agreements were developed for the three cheese families, the show would be produced in English on TLN and other base cable carriers to reach both the bilingual Italian communities and other English-speaking consumers in the rest of Canada.

Although Mario estimated that it would cost $16 000 to $20 000 to produce each 30-minute cooking show segment, he would have control over the product placement and there would be opportunities for sponsorship and advertising revenue from complementary manufacturers such as cooking appliance companies, kitchen supply stores, and producers of food complements like pasta or wine. Mario's concept was to feature one cheese and one recipe in each

30-minute show, and allocate six minutes to advertising Saputo brands and directing consumers to Saputo retailers. The retailer featured each week would feature the Saputo cheese in its store flyer and consumers would be reminded of the cheese and recipe with in-store signage and demonstrations. This alternative had the advantages of being scaleable (starting small and then expanding the number of shows produced and where they were shown), being memo-

rable to consumers (tied to valued content), and having a direct benefit to the grocery retailers (which would aid in securing listing agreements). The question in Mario's mind was whether they could generate sufficient viewership to warrant the production costs and get the attention of the retailers and sponsors.

Now join the Saputo team: Which option would you choose and why?

COMMUNICATIONS MIX REVISITED

In the previous chapter we discussed the range of decisions involved in developing a marketing communication strategy. In this chapter we revisit the communications mix to get a deeper understanding of the tactical tools available to marketers to get their messages in front of audiences. While advertising is often the most visible of communication mix elements, organizations that follow an IMC strategy recognize that other elements can be highly effective—and that is the choice facing Mario Demers at Saputo Dairy Products Canada. Microcell Solutions, for example, supports its Fido (cellular phone system) brand's communications strategy with a strong public relations program, sales promotion, and personal selling (Exhibit 13.1). In the greater Toronto area, Microcell's objective was to increase awareness and trial of Fido and leverage the emotional relevancy of the brand to reach customers one-to-one.[1] The company linked a variety of experiences—key messages, images, sounds, and activities—to the brand under the theme "Fun & Freedom." It launched the campaign with a "Fido mobile," a vintage 1942 bus pulled by a dozen dogs, which attracted significant media attention. Fun & Freedom events were held throughout greater Toronto—augmented by free photographing of prospective customers and their pets, having dogs perform tricks to demonstrate Fido's features and benefits, and allowing prospective customers to make free calls anywhere in Fido's coverage area. Fido also chose to involve Canine Vision Canada in the campaign, because both Fido and guide dogs represent freedom to their masters. Advertising supported the public relations efforts by visually linking Fido to fun and freedom imagery, such as sunglasses, beach balls, and fireworks. Sales promotions, including a grand prize sweepstakes and at-event contests for T-shirts, baseball caps, Fido phones, and airtime packages, further enhanced the overall strategy. The campaign was successful in making the Fido brand personally relevant to thousands of pet owners. Having a better understanding of these communication mix elements will allow you to make more informed communication mix decisions.

Exhibit 13.1

Microcell Solutions uses public relations to support its integrated marketing communications strategy.

ADVERTISING

Wherever we turn, we are bombarded by ads in the form of television commercials, radio spots, banner ads on the Internet urging us to "click here," or huge billboards screaming "Buy Me!" As indicated in the previous chapter, advertising is non-personal communication paid for by an identified sponsor using mass media to persuade or inform an audience.[2] Advertising is the most common element of a communication mix because it can be fun to create, glamorous to be involved with, and often involves large budgets, travel, and celebrities. It gives a marketing manager or executive something tangible that says "I helped create that" inspiring, magical, humorous, provocative, or otherwise creative piece of art. Be honest, wouldn't you rather spend $200 000 of someone else's money creating a television ad with Shania Twain or Justin Timberlake than developing a coupon or hiring another sales rep? Of course, actually creating the television ad can be time consuming, heavily detail-oriented, and boring (such as waiting for the paint on the set to dry or taking five or six hours of retakes to shoot a three-second scene), but overall, advertising attracts a lot of a communication budget because it is fun to do.

Of course, advertising is also very effective. Advertising is often unparalleled in its ability to demonstrate products (particularly services), use sights and sounds to create desire, and repeat the message as often as deemed necessary for it to have an impact on receivers. Advertising is such a big part of our culture that it both reflects and shapes our culture, and it is so effective that there are laws limiting its use for vulnerable audiences like children and the promotion of socially undesirable products like cigarettes. And that's also why Canadian businesses spend close to $12.6 billion a year on advertising.[3]

We talked about the planning that goes behind the creation of advertising in Chapter 12. Here we will discuss how to create effective advertising and how to evaluate or critique its effectiveness.

Creating Advertising

A poor strategy or poor execution can result in annoying, boring, or otherwise ineffective advertising. You know, the ones you flip the TV channel to avoid watching or the ones you don't even look at when reading your favourite magazine.

When people give examples of effective advertising, they are likely to recall the provocative poses in Calvin Klein ads, the charming dialogue between Frank and Gordon, or vomiting Playland customers—advertising that was memorable because it stood out and uniquely appealed to its intended audience. These are all examples of **product advertising**, in which the message focuses on a specific good or service. Product advertising usually has one of three purposes: to educate people about the new product and what it does; to convince the target audience to try it or choose it over other options; or to ensure that people won't forget about the product and the things they already know about it. **Institutional advertising** promotes the activities, personality, or point of view of an organization or company, as in the ad for Pfizer shown in Exhibit 13.2. Another use of institutional advertising is to build demand for a product category, such as the Canadian egg producers' ads that encourage consumers to "Get Cracking."

Some institutional messages state a firm's position on an issue in order to sway public opinion, a strategy called **advocacy advertising**.[4] For example, the R.J. Reynolds company ran an ad titled "Of Cigarettes and Science," which attempted to refute arguments about the relationship between smoking and health. **Public service advertisements** (PSAs) are advertisements the media runs free of charge for not-for-profit organizations that serve society in some way, or to champion an issue such as increasing literacy or discouraging drunk driving. The ad in Exhibit 13.3 created by Toronto ad agency Downtown Partners was first produced for the Red Cross and World First Aid Day. The ad tries to convince Canadians to learn first aid and CPR—the tag line is "Know what to do. Learn First Aid." Often advertising agencies will take on one or more public service campaigns on a pro bono basis (for free).

product advertising An advertising message that focuses on a specific good or service.

institutional advertising An advertising message that promotes the activities, personality, or point of view of an organization or company.

advocacy advertising A type of public service advertising provided by an organization that is seeking to influence public opinion on an issue because it has some stake in the outcome.

public service advertisements Advertising run by the media without charge for not-for-profit organizations or to champion a particular cause.

Exhibit 13.2

Institutional advertising can be used to build a corporate reputation.

WHO CREATES ADVERTISING? An **advertising campaign** is a coordinated, comprehensive plan that carries out promotion objectives and results in a series of advertisements placed in media over a period of time. For example, the long-running advertising campaign for Buckley's Mixture—"It tastes awful. And it works"—has included both print advertising and a series of humorous television commercials that all work together to build brand loyalty for the cough medicine. In fact, the Buckley's campaign is considered one of the most effective in Canadian advertising history. The brand is the number-one selling cough syrup in Canada, even though it spends far less on advertising every year ($458 600) than its closest competitor, Robitussin DM ($1.7 million).[5]

Exhibit 13.3

This shocking ad by the Red Cross asks Canadians to "Know what to do. Learn First Aid."

Creating and executing an advertising campaign often requires many companies working together and a broad range of skilled people to do the job right. Some firms may do their own advertising by creating an *in-house agency*. In many cases, though, the firm retains one or more outside advertising agencies to develop advertising messages on its behalf. A *limited-service agency* provides one or more specialized services, such as media buying or creative development (we'll see what these tasks are later). A *full-service agency* provides most or all of the services needed to mount a campaign, including research, creation of ad copy and art, media selection, and production of the final messages. In keeping with the move to integrated communications strategies discussed in Chapter 12, most Canadian advertising agencies have transformed themselves into full-service *communications services companies*, which provide clients with advice and service in all areas of communications decision making, including advertising. Many different tasks are required to produce an advertising campaign. The ad in Exhibit 13.4 humorously illustrates the "birth" of an advertising concept, highlighting some of the major players who participate in the delivery. Big or small, an advertising agency or communications services company joins the talents of specialists who together craft a message and make the communications concept a reality.

> **advertising campaign** A coordinated, comprehensive plan that carries out promotion objectives and results in a series of advertisements placed in media over a period of time.

- *Account Management:* The *account executive*, or *account manager* or *suit*, is the "soul" of the operation. This person develops the campaign's strategy for the client. The account executive supervises the day-to-day activities on the account, and is the primary liaison between the agency and the client. The account executive has to ensure that the client is happy while verifying that people within the agency are executing the desired strategy.

- *Creative Services:* *Creatives* are the "heart" of the communications effort. These are the people who actually dream up and produce the ads. They include the agency's creative director, copywriter, and art director. Creatives are the artists who breathe life into marketing objectives and craft messages that (hopefully) will excite, arouse, or interest consumers.

- *Research and Marketing Services:* Researchers are the "brains" of the campaign. They collect and analyze information that will help account executives develop a sensible strategy. They assist creatives in getting consumer reactions to different versions of ads, or by providing copywriters with details on the target group.

- *Media Planning:* The media planner is the "legs" of the campaign. The media planner helps to determine which communications vehicles are the most effective and recommends the most efficient means for delivering the ad by deciding where, when, and how often it will appear.

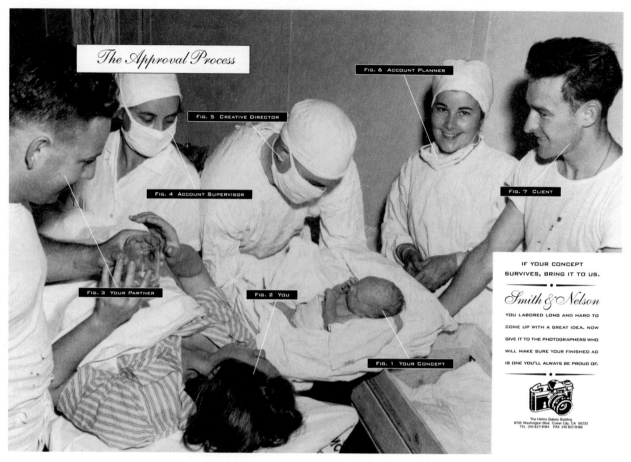

Exhibit 13.4

This trade ad illustrates the "birth" of an advertising concept.

Media Choices

What does a 130-centimetre television with Dolby Surround Sound have in common with a matchbook? Each is a media vehicle that permits an advertiser to communicate with a potential customer. Depending on the intended message, each medium has its advantages and disadvantages. Let's look at the major categories of media. The pros and cons of each type are summarized in Table 13.1.

TRADITIONAL MEDIA

Television Because of television's ability to reach so many people at once, this medium is a favourite choice for regional or national companies. Ninety-nine percent of Canadians live in households that have a TV, and 65 percent of Canadians live in households with more than one TV. On an average day, 86 percent of Canadians watch TV at least once.[6] There are two English (CBC and CTV) and two French (Radio-Canada and TVA) national television networks in Canada, which can offer both regional and national advertising exposure. There are 18 regional networks, three of which are in French. Yet another option for TV advertising is specialty channels, which provide a specific programming format (The Comedy Network) or audience (Women's Television Network) and can, therefore, provide easy access to a particular market segment. In 2007, 36 percent of homes in Canada reported that they subscribed to pay TV.[7]

One disadvantage of advertising on television is cost. In addition to the cost of placing ads in media, production costs range from $80 000 to $250 000 for a 30-second television ad.[8] This high cost of production has led some companies to consider advertising on TV without using commercials. *Product placement* is a method of advertising on television (and in movies),

Table 13.1 Pros and Cons of Selected Media Vehicles

Vehicle	Pros	Cons
Television	• Extremely creative and flexible. • Network TV is the most cost-effective way to reach a mass audience. • Cable and satellite TV allow the advertiser to reach a selected group at relatively low cost. • A prestigious way to advertise. • Can demonstrate product in use. • Can provide entertainment and generate excitement. • Messages have high impact because of the use of sight and sound.	• The message is quickly forgotten unless it is repeated often. • The audience is increasingly fragmented. • Although the relative cost of reaching the audience is low, prices are still high on an absolute basis—often too high for smaller companies. A 30-second spot on a prime-time TV sitcom costs well over $250 000. • Fewer people are viewing network television. • People switch from station to station zapping commercials. • Rising costs have led to more and shorter ads, causing more clutter.
Radio	• Good for selectively targeting an audience. • Is heard out of the home. • Can reach customers on a personal and intimate level. • Can use local personalities. • Relatively low cost, both for producing a spot and for running it repeatedly. • Because of short lead time, radio ads can be modified quickly to reflect changes in the marketplace. • Use of sound effects and music allows listeners to use their imagination to create a vivid scene.	• Listeners often don't pay full attention to what they hear. • Difficulty in buying radio time, especially for national advertisers. • Not appropriate for products that must be seen or demonstrated to be appreciated. • The small audience of individual stations means ads must be placed with many different stations and must be repeated frequently.
Newspapers	• Wide exposure provides extensive market coverage. • Flexible format permits the use of colour, different size ads, and targeted editions. • Ability to use detailed copy. • Allows local retailers to tie in with national advertisers. • People are in the right mental frame to process advertisements about new products, sales, etc. • Timeliness, i.e., short lead time between placing ad and having it run.	• Most people don't spend much time reading the newspaper. • Readership is especially low among teens and young adults. • Short life span—people rarely look at a newspaper more than once. • Very cluttered ad environment. • The reproduction quality of images is relatively poor. • Not effective in reaching specific audiences.
Magazines	• Audiences can be narrowly targeted by specialized magazines. • High credibility and interest level provide a good environment for ads. • Magazines have a long life and are often passed along to other readers. • Visual quality is excellent. • Can provide detailed product information with a sense of authority.	• Expensive: with the exception of direct mail, the highest cost per exposure. The cost of a full-page, four-colour ad in a general-audience magazine typically exceeds $100 000. • Long deadlines reduce flexibility. • The advertiser must generally use several magazines to reach the majority of a target market. • Clutter.
Outdoor	• Most of the population can be reached at low cost. • Good for supplementing other media. • High frequency when signs are located in heavy traffic areas. • Effective for reaching virtually all segments of the population. • Geographic flexibility.	• Hard to communicate complex messages because of short exposure time. • Difficult to measure advertisement's audience. • Controversial and disliked in many communities. • Cannot pinpoint specific market segments.
Direct response	• Ads can target extremely narrow audiences. • Messages can be timed by the advertiser at his or her convenience. • Easy to measure the effectiveness of ads.	• High cost per exposure. • Target lists must be constantly updated. • Ads lack credibility among many consumers.

Sources: Adapted from Thomas J. Russell and Ron Lane, *Kleppner's Advertising Procedure*, 15th ed. Upper Saddle River, NJ: Prentice Hall, 2002; Terence A. Shimp, *Advertising, Promotion and Supplemental Aspects of Integrated Marketing Communications*, 6th ed., Australia: Thomson Southwestern, 2003; and William Wells, John Burnett, and Sandra Moriarty, *Advertising: Principles and Practice*, 6th ed. Upper Saddle River, NJ: Prentice Hall, 2003.

Exhibit 13.5

Commercial free and supported by subscriber fees, satellite radio's presence in Canada has not had a measurable impact on traditional radio.

where the product is seen as part of the TV show (or movie) rather than in a separate ad. Recent product placements in Canadian TV shows include Nortel phones used on *The Newsroom*, Ruffles Chips on *Degrassi: The Next Generation*, Rona building products used in the Quebec home renovation show *Ma Maison Rona*, and Sony Ericsson phones being used on *Train 48*. MMI Product Placement, the largest product placement company in Canada, claims that the advantages of product placement include image reinforcement when a "star" uses the product, brand awareness, extensive reach (during reruns as well as during first runs), and the protection of the product from zapping (since consumers often use zapping to avoid ads, not TV shows).[9]

Radio One advantage of radio advertising is flexibility. Marketers can change commercials quickly, often on the spot by an announcer and a recording engineer.[10] Radio is attractive to advertisers seeking low cost and the ability to reach specific consumer segments. There are hundreds of radio stations in Canada, with formats ranging from contemporary hits to classical.[11] The growth of online radio also presents future opportunities for reaching large numbers of consumers in a cost-effective manner. Radio reaches 92 percent of Canadians 12 years old and older in an average week. While we have seen a slight decline in radio listenership among teens and young adults, weekly reach has remained relatively constant for most demographic groups.[12] As part of a multi-media campaign, TD Canada Trust used radio to help launch a promotion to give away five appliances to 61 winners across the country (Exhibit 13.5). A ballot to enter the contest was given out with each eligible application for a home equity line of credit or a mortgage. TD Canada Trust used radio to cost-effectively reach customers across the country.[13]

Satellite radio arrived in Canada in late 2005. There are currently two major players selling satellite radio in Canada—Sirius Canada and XM Radio. Satellite radio is commercial free and is supported through subscriber fees. Although some industry experts expected satellite radio to take market share from traditional radio, since its launch, satellite radio has had little measurable impact on traditional radio.[14]

Newspapers The newspaper is one of the oldest media vehicles. Retailers in particular have relied on newspaper ads since before the turn of the century to inform readers about sales and deliveries of new merchandise. Newspapers are an excellent medium for local advertising and for events (such as sales) that require a quick response. Many newspapers, such as *The Globe and Mail* and the *National Post*, offer online versions of their papers to expand their exposure.

Magazines Magazine ads provide high-quality images and can reach specific segments of consumers. New technologies such as *selective binding* allow publishers to personalize their editions so that advertisements for local businesses can be included in issues mailed to specific locations. *Desktop publishing* software allows magazines to close their pages just before going to press—no more long lead times that used to plague advertisers that wanted to hit their market with timely information.

Directories Directory advertising is the most "down-to-earth," information-focused advertising medium. Today, the *Yellow Pages* has revenues of over $9.5 billion, and more than

6000 directories are published in North America alone. These listings are usually references used just before the consumer makes the decision to buy, so the advertiser has the opportunity to influence the buyer immediately before the decision.

INTERNET ADVERTISING The web gives marketers the ability to reach customers in new and exciting ways. Online advertising has grown to over $801 million a year in Canada,[15] with major firms like General Mills, Inc. and Kraft Foods increasing their spending and the number of brands they promote online. The reason? The Internet had the third highest media consumption time among Canadian adults—just behind television and radio. Sixteen percent of the time Canadian consumers spend with all media is now online.[16] Online advertising offers several advantages. First, the Internet provides new ways to finely target customers. Web user registrations and *cookies* allow sites to track user preferences and deliver ads based on previous Internet behaviour. In addition, because the website can track how many times an ad is "clicked," advertisers can measure how people are responding to online messages. Finally, online advertising can be interactive—it lets consumers participate in the advertising campaign, and in some cases they can even become part of the action. Viewers who logged on to a special website were able to "direct" TV commercials for the Ford Probe by picking the cast and plotlines that would be used to create actual spots. Similarly, during its "whatever.com" campaign, Nike sent consumers to the web to pick the endings of three cliffhanger TV spots.[17]

Specific forms of Internet advertising include banners, buttons, pop-up ads, search engines and directories, and e-mail (Table 13.2).

- **Banners: Banners** are rectangular graphics at the top or bottom of webpages.
- **Buttons: Buttons** are small banner-type advertisements that a company can place anywhere on a page.

banners Internet advertising in the form of rectangular graphics at the top or bottom of webpages.

buttons Small banner-type advertisements that can be placed anywhere on a webpage.

Table 13.2 Internet Advertising

Banners	Banners, those rectangular graphics at the top or bottom of webpages, were the first form of web advertising. Although the effectiveness of banners remains in question (banners now receive less than a 1 percent click-through rate), they are still the most popular form of web advertising. One study that tested the impact of banner ads at top websites reported a dramatic increase in brand awareness after just one exposure and significant positive impact on intent to purchase.[18] Experts suggest banners that contain animation, effectively use colour, call for action (i.e., "click here"), and create a sense of urgency are more effective.
Buttons	Buttons are small banner-type advertisements that can be placed anywhere on a page. Early in the life of the Internet, buttons encouraging surfers to "Download Netscape Now" became a standard on many websites and were responsible for much of Netscape's early success.
Sponsorships	Sponsorships, much like the sponsorships of traditional radio and television programming, provide visibility for the company but, unlike banners and buttons, are not aimed at getting web users to visit their sites. Ford sponsors a site that provides answers to women's major concerns about buying cars, safety, maintenance, and leasing rather than buying. Johnson & Johnson and its Huggies brand sponsor a parenting area on iVillage.
Search Engines and Directory Listings	Just as the *Yellow Pages* and other directories are advertising media, so too are search engines and online directory listings. Increasingly, firms are paying search engines for more visible or higher placement on results lists.
Pop-up Ads	A pop-up ad is an advertisement that pops up on the screen while a webpage is being loaded or after it is loaded. Because pop-up ads take the centre of the screen while surfers are waiting for the desired page to load, they are difficult to ignore. A pop-up ad opens a separate Internet window. Web advertisers are typically charged only if people click through the windows.
E-mail	For advertising, e-mail is becoming as pervasive as radio and television, and is one of the easiest ways of communicating with consumers.

pop-up ad An advertisement that appears on the screen while a webpage is being loaded or after it has loaded.

e-mail A process of sending messages in electronic form.

spamming Sending unsolicited e-mail to five or more people not personally known to the sender.

permission-based marketing E-mail advertising in which online consumers have the opportunity to accept or refuse the unsolicited e-mail.

- **Search engine and directory listings:** Just as the *Yellow Pages* and other directories are advertising media, so too are search engines and online directory listings. Who have you Googled today? In Canada 35 percent of online advertising revenue comes from search engine advertising.[19]

- **Pop-up ads:** A **pop-up ad** is an advertisement that appears on the screen while a webpage is being loaded or after it has loaded.

- **E-mail:** For advertising, **e-mail** is becoming as pervasive as radio and television. It is one of the easiest ways of communicating with consumers because marketers can send unsolicited e-mail advertising messages to thousands of users by **spamming**—sending unsolicited e-mail to five or more people not personally known to the sender. Many websites that offer e-mail give surfers the opportunity to refuse unsolicited e-mail via junk e-mail blockers. This **permission-based marketing** gives the consumer the power to opt in or out. Marketers in the United States send about 200 billion e-mails to consumers every year, so they hope that a good portion of these will be opened and read rather than being sent straight to the recycle bin.[20]

Search Engine Marketing Search engines like Google are the primary destination for people wanting to find things on the Internet. Getting your website to show up in search engines is one of the most important things you can do in online marketing. The process of increasing a website's performance in search engines is known as search engine marketing, or SEM. The top three search engines, Google, Yahoo, and MSN, account for most of the Internet search traffic, with Google alone accounting for over half of the world's Internet searches. Therefore, when we talk about SEM, it is usually easiest just to talk about increasing a website's performance in Google. Google provides a full range of good SEM tools, and most of the concepts transfer to any search engine.

Search engines use complex algorithms to sort through billions of webpages on the Internet. They send out robots known as "spiders" that crawl through the web reading information and storing their findings in the search engine's database. Users then go to the search engine and enter a search term, called a query. The search engine then delivers a long list of websites it thinks are somehow related to the query. The pages these results are shown on are called search engine results pages or SERPs, and the position of a result in the SERPs is called a rank. Website owners can pay to have their website show up in the "paid" or "sponsored" results section, which can be found along the right-hand side or top of Google's SERPs. The main list of results, known as "organic" or "natural" results, appears down the left of the SERPs. It is most desirable to have your site appear in the organic results section because these links are free and generally attract more clicks than paid results.

Search Engine Optimization (SEO) A typical search in Google will return hundreds of millions of results, but all that really matter are the first 10 to 50. Once your site has been indexed, the real challenge becomes battling your way to the top of the organic results. Search Engine Optimization (SEO) is the process of improving a website's rank in organic search engine results.

Using techniques that legitimately improve a site's search engine visibility through website design or content improvements is known as White Hat SEO. Using tricks solely for the purpose of boosting organic search rankings is known as Black Hat SEO, and can result in a website being banned from search engines like Google. Black Hat techniques include things like making text the same colour as the background so that it is invisible to users but still appears in the website's code. Some Black Hat techniques can get your site to the top of the results quickly, but once you get labelled as a search engine spammer it can be tough to ever get back into the top 50.

When you're optimizing your site for search engines, it may help to consider the four Rs of SEO:

- **Readability:** Can search engines find and read your website?

- **Relevance:** Based on a given query, what are the chances the searcher is looking for information on a page in your website?

- **Reliability:** How credible is your website?
- **Reputability:** How popular is the page on your website?[21]

MOBILE MEDIA In this age of the Internet, it seems as if we just get used to a dozen or so new terms when they are replaced by an equal number of new ones. M-commerce is a new buzzword that many marketers are talking about. The "m" stands for mobile. **M-commerce** is the promotional and other e-commerce activities transmitted over mobile phones and other mobile devices such as personal digital assistants (PDAs).[22]

M-commerce is prevalent in Europe and Asia. Text messaging in the Philippines is replacing traditional phone calls because of convenience and cost savings. According to the Philippine Long Distance Telephone Co., an estimated one million text messages are sent every day.[23]

M-commerce has made its way to Canada and the United States. Even the *MTV Music Video Awards* now include a wireless advertising campaign to promote the event. Millions of consumers who use such networks as Telus, Bell Mobility, Palm, and OmniSky will get messages urging them to tune in.[24]

What's the big attraction? Canadians have embraced wireless phones; these devices have become one of the fastest growing consumer products in Canada. In 2007, 74 percent of 18–34-year-olds in Canada had access to a wireless device. This is up dramatically from 45 percent in 2000. While young people in particular are big users of wireless devices, the number of Canadians with access to a wireless device has grown in all age categories, with 72 percent of 35–54-year-olds and 48 percent of adults aged 55 and older having access to a wireless device.[25]

More and more companies are using cellphones as another way to reach consumers with advertising. This technique, known as *short-messaging system marketing (SMS)*, is becoming increasingly popular in Canada. Lancôme recently ran a national text message marketing campaign for its new line of eye makeup, Color Design. The campaign targets consumers 18 to 35 years old. Ads were placed in women's washrooms in restaurants and bars, inviting consumers to text message "Color" to a six-digit code. They then received an instant message with a toll-free number to call to book a free Lancôme Eye Design makeup session at the Bay. Consumers then received a second message reminding them of their makeup session. At the appointment they received a Color Design eye shadow, worth $19.[26]

McDonald's used SMS marketing to encourage consumers to try its new deli sandwich. The promotion was centred on the World Ski and Snowboard Festival in Whistler, British Columbia. Signage around the event invited users to "Text in to get toasted." After consumers sent the text as directed, the message they got back was "Congratulations, you've won a coupon for a free deli sandwich," with instructions to visit the on-site McDonald's kiosk for a coupon that could be redeemed there, or later at another restaurant. More than 7000 samples of Toasted Deli Sandwiches were distributed during the weekend event. McDonald's sales in Whistler rose by 38 percent overall, with an average increase in Toasted Deli Sandwich sales of 12 percent. The campaign was a success![27]

M-commerce messages can reach specific types of consumers. A campaign for readers of *Men's Health* magazine sent a customized daily menu via cellphone to help interested readers curb calories.[28] So what are the advantages of m-commerce to consumers? First, m-commerce provides incredible consumer convenience. You can use your mobile phone to buy tickets for a concert without standing in line. You can even buy soft drinks from a vending machine through the phone—a service already available in Europe.[29]

But the potential for m-commerce is even greater. Perhaps you're in the market for a new computer. You visit a local retailer and decide what you want. While you're there, you use your mobile phone or PDA to check prices of the same computer on the Internet. If you decide you have the best price, you'll be able to handle the transaction on your phone as well, paying for the computer through a secure Internet connection.

For marketers the opportunities for m-commerce are even more exciting. Using sophisticated *location-based technologies* including satellites, a retailer will be able to know when you

m-commerce Promotional and other e-commerce activities transmitted over mobile phones and other mobile devices such as personal digital assistants (PDAs).

are only a few blocks away from her store and she can send you messages about a special sale.[30] And as you pass McDonald's, your phone will beep to remind you how great a Big Mac combo would taste right about now. Of course, such opportunities bring a whole host of privacy issues that must be settled before these scenarios can become a reality.

In the past, SMS campaigns were typically one way—once the mobile campaign was over, advertisers ended the mobile relationship. Advertisers are now starting to see the benefits of an ongoing relationship with customers who have, in effect, initiated a relationship when they texted a code to the advertiser. Molson, for instance, deploys SMS campaigns at most major events where it is a sponsor. The "Canadian Rocks" campaign, for example, enticed audiences at the Molson Amphitheatre in Toronto with the opportunity to upgrade their seats to the "best seats in the house." All that consumers had to do was type the Molson short code and a specific keyword promoted at the event into their cell to be notified just before the headliner hit the stage. Molson continued the relationship by sending a text to all users who responded to the promotion asking them if they'd like to receive ongoing information about music and join the Molson "Insider" program, which provides them with special insider benefits. Molson has enjoyed an opt-in rate of 15–30 percent with this SMS program—very impressive.

One study predicts that despite the slow start, about 90 million North Americans will be participating in m-commerce by 2007, generating more than $50 billion in revenues.[31] That's opportunity calling!

out-of-home media Communications media that reach people in public places.

OUT-OF-HOME MEDIA **Out-of-home media** such as blimps, transit ads, and billboards reach people in public places. This medium works best when it tells a simple, straightforward story.[32]

Marketers are constantly searching for new ways to get their messages out to busy people. Ads in movie theatres are popular with certain advertisers. For example, since TV viewers are also frequent movie goers, several TV networks, such as Global and the Discovery Channel (Canada), use ads in movie theatres to promote new shows.[33] In addition, *place-based media*, which transmits messages in public places, can be an effective way to reach a captive audience. Exhibit 13.6 shows part of an ad for the Bank of Montreal Financial Group. Kitchener, Ontario–based Timeline Technologies operates video screens that transmit ads while consumers are pumping gas at gas stations. Igrabber is a Canadian company that sells ad space on more than 1000 mini-billboards in laundromats across the country.[34]

pre-testing A research method that seeks to minimize mistakes by getting consumer reactions to ad messages before they appear in the media.

Exhibit 13.6

Place-based media such as rink-boards can be an effective way to communicate to a captive audience.

Developing Effective Advertising

Once the creative team has developed a campaign concept, how does the agency know if the ideas will work? Advertisers try to minimize mistakes by getting reactions to ad messages before they are actually placed. Much of this **pre-testing**, the research that goes on in the early stages of a campaign, centres on gathering basic information that will help planners make sure they've accurately defined the product's market, consumers, and competitors. This information comes from quantitative sources, such as syndicated surveys, and qualitative sources, such as focus groups, which we discussed in Chapter 4.

As the campaign takes shape, the players need to determine how well the specific advertising concepts under development will perform.

Copy testing measures the effectiveness of ads. It seeks to determine whether consumers are receiving, comprehending, and responding to the ad according to plan. There are several copy-testing techniques.

- *Concept testing* helps determine if initial ideas will work. Respondents, who are often drawn from the target market for which the ad is intended, evaluate different creative ideas or rough copies of ad layouts.

- *Test commercials* let consumers respond to a rough version of what a television message will look like. This preliminary treatment may take the form of an *animatic* or *storyboard*, such as the one shown in Exhibit 13.7, which is a series of sketches showing frame by frame what will happen in the finished commercial.

- *Finished testing* is testing audience reactions to a fully produced commercial to see if it has motivated them to buy the product. This occurs before the commercial actually airs on television. Because production of a "real" commercial is expensive, most testing is conducted before this point.

CRITIQUES OF ADVERTISING You might like advertising that your friends do not and one of your friends might like an ad that you do not. Liking or disliking an ad does not determine its effectiveness. While formal measures of communication and advertising effectiveness involve an assessment of the outputs and outcomes of the communication effort (Chapter 12), advertising critique involves an assessment of the quality of the communication strategy and its execution, to the extent that these are reflected by the ad. Following the communication plan outline (see Figure 12.4, page 427), an advertising critique has eight main elements (Table 13.3).

Advertising is highly effective when all the elements in Table 13.3 are done well, are coordinated and consistent with each other, and come together with impact and creativity that supports the intended strategy. When one or more elements are not done well, the results can be a disaster. Next time you are reading a newspaper or magazine, look for ads that you think are not effective—what didn't the creator(s) do well?

copy testing A marketing research method that seeks to measure the effectiveness of ads by determining whether consumers are receiving, comprehending, and responding to the ad according to plan.

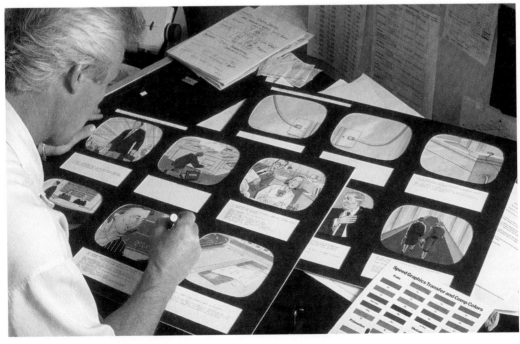

Exhibit 13.7

A storyboard presents preliminary ideas for an advertisement.

Table 13.3 Elements of an Advertising Critique

Target Audience	Is the target audience clear? When we dislike an ad it is often because we are not in the target audience—the ad was not meant for us, it does not strike a chord, and we just don't "get it."
Communication Objectives	Are the objectives clear? Advertising needs to be assessed against its objectives. Does the ad do what is intended for its audience? If the objectives of an ad are not clear, it is unlikely to be very effective.
Overall Communications Strategy	How appropriate is the overall communications strategy, given the intended audience and objectives? Is an IMC, push or pull, or one-way or two-way symmetrical or asymmetrical strategy appropriate?
Positioning Statement and Key Messages	Does the ad clearly position the product and are the key messages clear and appropriate for the desired positioning of the brand, media used, and creative concept? If not, then the ad is not very effective. Every element in a communication strategy should reinforce the overall brand positioning.
Communication Tactics	Is the theme, approach, or tactics used to break through perceptual screens and get the attention of the audience appropriate given the audience, communication objectives, brand positioning, messages, and media? Ineffective ads do not break through the noise or do so in a way that is annoying or otherwise creates negative attitudes toward the brand. The German ad in Exhibit 13.8, for example, gets the reader's attention but could result in negative attitudes toward Cinemaxx.
Communications Mix/Media	Is advertising the most effective way to achieve the communication objectives with the intended audience and is the media selected, the ad placement, and scheduling appropriate given the other strategic elements?
Creative Execution	Is the creative concept appropriate for the audience, communication objectives, positioning, media, and messages? Cost-effective communication also has lasting power—it doesn't get old or stale too quickly. Humour, for example, wears out quickly.
Evaluation	Does the ad include a call to action that would help the marketing organization track responses to the ad (e.g., a 1-800 number or web address)? An ad is more effective if its creators can demonstrate its impact.

Exhibit 13.8

This German ad for a movie theatre reminds us that "Not everywhere that's dark shows great movies." As some readers might be turned off by the imagery, a concept like this one would need to be pre-tested.

public relations (PR) Communications strategies to build good relationships and corporate image with an organization's stakeholders, including consumers, stockholders, and legislators.

PUBLIC RELATIONS

Chapter 12 noted that **public relations (PR)** helps build mutually beneficial long-term relationships and improve the image of an organization with key stakeholders—consumers, the media, shareholders, legislators, and interest groups. Public relations is crucial to an organization's ability to create and sustain favourable relationships, corporate goodwill, and overall image. There are many types of public relations that focus on different activities and stakeholders:

- *Publicity and media relations:* unpaid communications about an organization and/or its products appearing in the mass media.

- *Corporate public relations:* managing the overall reputation and image of the organization.

- *Crisis management:* plans for the management of corporate crises, including boycotts, recalls, natural disasters, and strikes.

- *Employee relations:* internal programs designed to foster positive relationships among and between organization employees.

- *Financial relations:* effective communications directed toward investors, regulators, and other financial stakeholders.

- *Public affairs:* lobbying efforts aimed at influencing policy decisions at the federal, provincial, and municipal levels of government.

- *Community relations:* grassroots management of relationships with local community stakeholders, including business owners, major employers, schools, kids' groups, and community organizations.

Although public relations is a powerful element of the communications mix, marketers often overlook it, primarily because it doesn't have the creative and visual appeal of creating an "ad." Public relations is powerful because it is interactive, helping to foster relationships. It allows corporations to build social goodwill, which can often protect them against future public issues and concerns. It also provides a higher level of credibility and believability when the communication is presented through third parties like reporters, experts, celebrities, or independent organizations such as the Consumers' Association of Canada. Finally, public relations provides an inexpensive way to reach not only consumers but also other stakeholders important to the interests of an organization.

Objectives of Public Relations

Public relations specialists need to operate at many levels to ensure that various stakeholders receive coordinated and accurate messages about the firm. As we saw with the Fido example, public relations strategies are often used in concert with advertising, sales promotions, and personal selling to accomplish various communication objectives.

INTRODUCING NEW PRODUCTS When Al Galbraith earned the chance to sell 246 homes in the village at Cornwallis Park, a former military base in Nova Scotia, he enlisted a PR agency to help him develop an innovative public relations and advertising campaign. It was expected to take two years to sell the well-maintained, three- and four-bedroom homes, some of which had ocean views; Galbraith sold them all in seven weeks. One key was price—the homes were $29 900 to $49 900. A second key was getting media attention. Galbraith and his PR agency created news releases to capture the public-interest angles— the developer was targeting former servicemen and other retirees who didn't have a lot of money, and was revitalizing a down-trodden region of Nova Scotia; these were picked up across the country.[35] Wendy's Restaurants used the reality show *The Apprentice* to launch its Western BK Steak Burger. The product was featured in a challenge in an episode of *The Apprentice* and was launched the next day.[36]

SUPPORTING CURRENT PRODUCTS Ocean Spray Cranberries Ltd. sponsored research at Harvard Medical School that confirmed the "folk wisdom" that cranberry juice is an effective way to treat urinary tract infections. With the help of PR agency Cohn & Wolfe in Toronto, Ocean Spray sent press kits to food editors and other writers with a focus on health and seniors' lifestyles to promote the study published in the *New England Journal of Medicine* and to offer interviews with the leader of the research team, Dr. Jerry Avorn.[37] The strategy was to promote the product category, not the brand, but sales of Ocean Spray cranberry juice increased significantly after the PR program.

INFLUENCING GOVERNMENT LEGISLATION Concerned about public outcry over the price of gasoline, Petro-Canada and other distributors developed a PR campaign to explain that more than half the price consumers pay for gasoline is tax.[38] This was intended, in part, to deflect public influence onto the federal and provincial governments.

ENHANCING THE IMAGE OF AN ORGANIZATION OR ENTITY Faced with international criticism about possible human rights abuses and restriction of trade, the Chinese government established an office in charge of "overseas propaganda" to present a more favourable image of China to the rest of the world.[39]

CALLING ATTENTION TO A FIRM'S INVOLVEMENT WITH THE COMMUNITY To help improve their corporate image, Canadian insurance companies, such as Royal Insurance, are providing financial aid and employees' time to support community initiatives, such as injury awareness campaigns, sailing regattas, block parent associations, and neighbourhood

Exhibit 13.9

A sponsored event is a form of public relations. Changes in the Canadian law now ban tobacco companies like du Maurier from sponsoring cultural or sporting events.

watches. These companies have realized what other organizations that support little league teams, youth associations, and community events have known all along—being involved in community interests helps win friends and influence people.[40] Many companies find value in sponsorship of large-scale events, such as the Olympic Games, the HSBC Celebration of Light (formerly the Benson & Hedges Symphony of Fire), the Montreal International Jazz Festival (Exhibit 13.9), or the Molson Indy. Public relations specialists work behind the scenes to ensure that a sponsored event receives ample press coverage and exposure for the organization. Changes to Canadian sponsorship law banned the tobacco company sponsorship of cultural or sporting events and left many events searching for new sponsors. Attracting new sponsors has proven difficult for some events as sponsor organizations are increasingly questioning the value of such sponsorship, setting specific measurable communication objectives for their sponsorship and basing sponsorship decisions on return on investment.

DEMONSTRATING SOCIAL RESPONSIBILITY With help from Toronto-based social marketing firm Manifest Communications, Swedish telecom giant Ericsson launched a program called Ericsson Response, a worldwide initiative to aid the cause of disaster relief by providing mobile and satellite telephone systems to humanitarian relief workers.[41] Crabtree & Evelyn of London, Ontario, donates $2 for every bath gel sold in the month of October to the Canadian Breast Cancer Foundation, which helps raise the company's visibility.[42]

DEVELOPING POSITIVE EMPLOYEE OR INVESTOR RELATIONS Petro-Canada uses PR to influence, albeit indirectly, government legislation. It has also undertaken an internal communications program in an effort to enlist its 4500 employees in the cause to redirect public concern about gas prices—recognizing that its employees are the best ambassadors.[43] Husky Injection Moulding Systems introduced a program that allows its 3000 workers to earn company shares for acting green and helping others. While this has social responsibility and community involvement messages, it also makes employees more committed to the organization and helps shape organization culture.[44] Electronic bulletin boards, newsletters, golf tournaments, and staff picnics are among many vehicles used to develop positive employee relations. Company tours, open houses, annual reports, quarterly reports, annual general meetings, technical briefings, and one-on-one interviews are some of the methods used to develop relationships with investors and potential investors.

HANDLING COMMUNICATION ISSUES AND CRISES A few years ago, PepsiCo was rocked by claims that hypodermic needles had been found in Diet Pepsi cans. The company assembled a crisis team to map out a response and supplied video footage of its bottling process to reassure people that foreign objects could not be inserted at the factory. The claims turned out to be false, and PepsiCo ran ads designed to let people know there was nothing to worry about. Pepsi's calm, coordinated response averted a public relations disaster. Similarly, Bridgestone/Firestone Canada Inc. decided to act proactively and voluntarily recalled a million sport utility vehicle (SUV) tires when it was learned that some Firestone tires had failed in the United States under conditions of high temperatures, high speed, and low tire pressure. This PR initiative cost Bridgestone/Firestone over $212 million in Canada but is expected to foster stronger long-term relationships with SUV owners.[45] McDonald's, on the other hand, decided to sue a London, England–based environmental group in the 1980s to prevent it from publishing a pamphlet that accused McDonald's of numerous wrongdoings. McDonald's won the suit, but it took 10 years and cost $23 million in legal fees, and the proceedings were covered by the global media for a decade. Supporters of the defendants established a website that is still frequently updated to bring public scrutiny to McDonald's business practices.[46]

Planning a Public Relations Campaign

A public relations campaign is a coordinated effort to communicate with one or more of the firm's stakeholders. It requires a three-step process of developing objectives, executing, and evaluating.

The organization must first develop clear objectives for the PR program that define the message it wants people to hear. Raincoast Books, for example, wanted to ensure that it got the "most bang for the time" in terms of favourable publicity surrounding J.K. Rowling's visit to Canada. After determining the objective, the PR specialists create a campaign strategy, which includes these elements:

- A statement of the problem
- A situation analysis
- Specification of target audiences (publics)
- Messages to be communicated
- Specific program elements to be used
- A timetable and budget
- Discussion of how the program will be evaluated

The International Apple Institute, a trade group devoted to increasing the consumption of apples, had to decide if a campaign should get consumers to cook more with apples, drink more apple juice, or buy more fresh fruit. Because fresh apples brought a substantially higher price per kilogram to growers than apples used for applesauce or apple juice, the group decided to push the fresh fruit angle. It used the familiar theme "An apple a day . . ." and mounted a focused campaign to encourage people to eat more apples by placing articles extolling the fruit's health benefits in consumer media.

Execution of the campaign means deciding precisely how the message should be communicated to the stakeholder(s) of interest. An organization can get out its positive messages in many ways (Table 13.4), ranging from news conferences and sponsorship of charity or

Table 13.4 Tools of Public Relations

Interactive	Proactive	Responsive	Indirect & Associative
E-mail	Newsletters	Letters to Customers	Social/Cause Advertising
Websites	News Releases	Annual Reports	Public Service Announcements
Open Houses	Video News Releases	Bulletin Boards	Celebrity Endorsements
Ceremonies	Disaster Planning	Suggestion Boxes	Product Placements
Meetings	Issues Management	Surveys	Fundraising
Events	Lobbying	Environmental Scanning	Sponsorships
Speeches/Addresses	Brochures		Advertorials
Trade Shows & Exhibits	Pamphlets		
News Conferences			
Annual General Meeting			
Corporate Social Events			
Employee Volunteering			

Note: Categories are illustrative; public relations tools can be used in different ways to reach different objectives.

CLIMBING THE 1776 STAIRS OF THE CN TOWER TAKES STRENGTH, STAMINA AND DETERMINATION. IT ALSO USUALLY TAKES LEGS.

ON SEPT 26, JEFF ADAMS WILL CLIMB THE 1776 STAIRS OF THE CN TOWER IN HIS WHEELCHAIR TO HEIGHTEN AWARENESS OF THE NEED FOR A BARRIER-FREE SOCIETY. SUPPORT THE CLIMB, BUY A STEP. VISIT WWW.STEPUPTOCHANGE.COM

CANADIAN FOUNDATION FOR PHYSICALLY DISABLED PERSONS

Exhibit 13.10

PR messages can be communicated in many ways, such as using strong visuals like the CN Tower in this ad by the Canadian Foundation for Physically Disabled Persons.

publicity Unpaid communication about an organization appearing in the mass media.

press release Information that an organization distributes to the media about its activities, intended to appear as publicity.

sporting events to creating attention-getting promotional events. Palmer Jarvis DDB Toronto created the public service announcement in Exhibit 13.10 for the Canadian Foundation for Physically Disabled Persons. It uses a strong visual to communicate the social issue of wheelchair access.

Public Relations Program Elements

Sometimes, these efforts involve lobbying government officials to persuade them to vote a certain way on pending legislation, or writing speeches for company executives to deliver. PR specialists may provide input on corporate identity materials, such as logos, brochures, building design, and even stationery, which communicate a positive image for the firm. Or the organization can simply try to get media exposure for the achievements of an employee who has done some notable charity work or for a product it developed that saved someone's life. For example, the Canadian pharmaceutical firm Boehringer Ingelheim (Canada) Ltd. sent large My Buddy dolls wearing respirator masks to Canadian pediatricians. The dolls helped doctors ease their young patients' fears about putting a mask over their mouths and noses. In return, Boehringer Ingelheim received a lot of favourable publicity when newspapers across the country featured the campaign.

As the My Buddy doll example illustrates, **publicity** is a powerful PR tool. The most common way for public relations specialists to communicate to the media is through a **press release**, a description of some event that an organization produces itself and sends to the media in the hope that a reporter will write an article about it. A newer version of this idea is a video news release (VNR), aimed at the broadcast media, that tells the story in a film format. Some of the most common types of press releases are:

- *Timely topics* deal with hot topics in the news. Levi Strauss promoted casual Fridays (and presumably sales of its casual dress pants such as Dockers and Slates) by highlighting how different corporations around the country are adopting a relaxed dress code.

- *Research stories* summarize research projects, such as articles that universities send out that highlight recent breakthroughs by faculty members or public opinion polls that are released by political parties. Ralston Purina released the results of a survey that asked people how they show love to their pets: It was picked up by media across the country, earning 22 million impressions based on readership, viewership, and circulation of the media.[47]

- *Consumer information releases* provide information to help consumers make better product decisions. The British Columbia Ministry of Health's Food Safe Program distributes helpful tips about properly preparing foods for Thanksgiving, barbecuing, and other seasonal activities.

Internal public relations activities aimed at employees often include company newsletters and closed-circuit television. These sources of information help keep employees informed about company plans, successes, changes, and so on. Often company newsletters are distributed outside the firm to suppliers or others outside the company.

sponsorship A PR activity through which companies provide financial support to help fund an event in return for publicized recognition of the company's contribution.

Sponsorships are PR activities through which companies provide financial support to help fund an event in return for publicized recognition of the company's contribution

Marketing Metrics

The traditional measurement of the effectiveness of public relations has been a metric called "ad value equivalency" or AVE. AVE is a long-held PR measurement process that equates the amount of editorial coverage a product, service, or issue receives with what a marketer would have to spend in advertising dollars to reach the same audience. Although this measurement has been the industry standard for many years and is used by many companies today, others say that it is antiquated, inaccurate, misleading, and impossible to standardize. Recently, the Canadian Public Relations Society developed a completely new system for measuring the value of public relations—*Media Relations Ratings Points*—that omits ad value equivalency. The MRP system has already been taken up by Canadian marketers, including the Bank of Montreal, Coca-Cola, Johnson & Johnson, and Visa Canada.[48]

(Exhibit 13.11). Many companies today find that their promotion dollars are far better spent on sponsoring a golf tournament, a building, an athlete or team, a symphony concert, or global events such as the Olympics or World Cup soccer competition. These sponsorships are particularly effective because consumers often connect their enjoyment of the event with the sponsor, thus creating brand loyalty. Sony Canada recently signed a $10 million 20-year title sponsorship agreement with Toronto's Hummingbird Centre— now called the Sony Centre for the Performing Arts. The centre will be renovated and equipped with state-of-the-art Sony products.

Because different events cater to different consumers, sponsorships are a good way to target specific market segments. Philishave, for example, is the official electric shaver of the Toronto Maple Leafs and Raptors—using the team websites and events to promote its association with the teams and endear itself with Toronto sports fans.

The Olympic Games offer interesting sponsorship opportunities as every two years there is worldwide media coverage of a summer or winter Olympic Games. Visa Canada has jumped on the Olympic bandwagon with a sponsorship program called "Team Visa." The program entails long-term support of 19 athletes as well as financial, media, and sports mentoring from financial advisers and retired Olympic athletes. Visa ran ads featuring each sponsored athlete prior to the 2008 Beijing Olympics to foster public interest and support. The program will continue for the 2010 Vancouver Winter Games.[49]

guerrilla marketing Promotional strategies that "ambush" consumers with promotional content in places they are not expecting it.

Guerrilla marketing, which was introduced in Chapter 12, involves "ambushing" consumers with promotional content in places they are not expecting to encounter this kind of activity. The Canadian Tourism Commission (CTC) recently undertook guerrilla marketing to encourage Canadians to "explore Canada." Building on its new theme, "Keep Exploring," the CTC targeted Canadians who usually vacation outside of the country to let them know about all the places they can explore in Canada. The program launched on Canada Day, with performances

Exhibit 13.11

Corporate sponsorship of events or facilities, like Air Canada's sponsoring of the Air Canada Centre in Toronto, can help marketing organizations build brand loyalty.

Exhibit 13.12

RCA Records used guerilla marketing to create buzz around Christina Aguilera.

of original poetry by two spoken-word artists on stage at the celebrations in Ottawa. Street teams "ambushed" Canadians at select events and festivals across the country throughout the summer to encourage them to explore Canada. The teams are armed with viewfinders showcasing images of some of Canada's "hidden" destination gems, and giveaways include magnets touting an interactive contest, as well as CDs and a screensaver.[50]

Today, big companies are buying into guerrilla marketing strategies big time. When RCA Records wanted to create a buzz around pop singer Christina Aguilera, the label hired a team of young people to swarm the web and chat about her on popular teen sites like **alloy.com** and **gurl.com**. They posted information casually, sometimes sounding like fans. Just before one of her albums debuted, RCA also hired a direct marketing company to e-mail electronic postcards filled with song snippets and biographical information to 50 000 web addresses. The album quickly went to number one on the charts.

One barrier to greater reliance on public relations campaigns by many organizations is the PR focus on long-term relationships across a wide variety of stakeholders, making it difficult to assess the effectiveness of specific program elements. For example, no one knows precisely what impact a series of appearances by company executives on talk shows or sponsorship of a charity event has on sales: Any one effect cannot be isolated. Marketers do, however, use such research tools as focus groups, interviews, and quantitative surveys (described in Chapter 4) to measure PR effectiveness by tracking changes in attitudes, opinions, and behaviours over time. Measuring media exposure from publicity efforts is relatively more straightforward, although it is more difficult to gauge what impact that coverage has had. Table 13.5 describes some of the most common publicity measurement techniques.

Table 13.5 Measuring Effectiveness of Publicity Efforts

Method	Description	Pros	Cons
In-house assessments conducted by a PR manager	Analyze media coverage in publications, looking for number and prominence of mentions	Relatively inexpensive because the major cost is the manager's time	Cannot guarantee objectivity in the analysis; crucial to specify up front what the relevant indicators are
Awareness and preference studies	Assess company's standing in the minds of customers relative to competition	Good for broad-based strategy setting or to demonstrate the progress of a large program	Difficult to connect results to specific PR events and to identify which actions had what level of impact on awareness; very expensive
Measurement of print and broadcast coverage generated by PR activities	The basic measurement tool in PR	Provides a quantifiable measure of press coverage; relatively inexpensive	Quantitative only; does not consider the *content* of the press coverage
Impression counts	Measure the size of the potential audience for a given article	Because a similar measure is used to assess advertising effectiveness, this method provides a common measure for comparison	Usually limited to the circulation of selected publications, so this method does not include pass-along readership; can be expensive

Source: Adapted from Deborah Holloway, "How to select a measurement system that's right for you," *Public Relations Quarterly*, Fall 1992: 15–17.

SALES PROMOTION

Walking into your student union, you have to be prepared to be ambushed by people eager for you to enter a contest, taste a new candy bar, or take home a free T-shirt with a local bank's name on it. These are examples of **sales promotions**, programs marketers design to build interest in or encourage you to purchase a product or service during a specified time period.[51] Sales promotions can sometimes be elaborate and far-reaching. Pepsi-QTG Canada launched the "Get Your Game On with Sidney Crosby" promotion. Consumers of Pepsi brands such as Lay's, Pepsi, Doritos, and Gatorade had a chance to win the grand prize—a meeting with Sidney Crosby, the rising Canadian hockey star—during a game in Atlanta. The contest gave away one prize every hour for 56 days—this prize level is very high relative to most contests. Consumers who bought specially branded packages had the chance to win one of 1344 prizes after finding an entry or UPC code and registering online. In addition to the grand prize, prizes included NHL video games, Xbox 360 systems, televisions, replica jerseys signed by Crosby, and four NHL All-Star Game VIP experiences in Atlanta. To publicize the contest, ads ran on TSN and NHL networks.[52]

How does a sales promotion differ from advertising? They are similar in that they are both paid messages from identifiable sponsors intended to bring about a change in behaviour or attitudes. In some cases, the sales promotion itself is publicized using a traditional advertising medium, such as the Diet Coke commercials that ran after *Friends*. But although many advertising campaigns are carefully crafted to create long-term positive feelings about a brand, company, or store, sales promotions tend to focus on more short-term objectives, such as an immediate boost in sales of Diet Coke. There are exceptions, however. Perpetual promotions like McDonald's Monopoly game, Canadian Tire's "Canadian Tire money," and Tim Hortons' "Roll up the rim to win" contest are all examples of sales promotions targeted to support or reward an existing customer base, rather than boost short-term sales.[53] Marketers also recognize that a series of short-term sales promotions can help to create long-term brand associations, image, and equity.

> **sales promotion** A program designed to build interest in or encourage purchase of a product during a specified time period.

Sales promotions are very useful if the firm has an immediate objective, such as quickly bolstering sales for a brand or encouraging consumers to try a new product. The objective may be to create enthusiasm among dealers who carry the product by convincing them to take a chance on a new product or provide more shelf space for an item they already carry. Thus, like advertising, sales promotions can be targeted to channel partners and to the firm's own employees in the form of trade promotions as well as to end consumers.

Trade Promotions

Trade promotions take one of two forms. Some sales promotions give the retailer a discount on the product's cost or on the expense of advertising it to encourage the store to stock the item and to make sure it's given a lot of attention. Other sales promotions generate awareness and increase sales by creating enthusiasm among salespeople.

DISCOUNTS AND DEALS One form of trade promotion is a price break. A manufacturer can reduce a channel partner's costs through sales promotions that give a discount on its own products. For example, a manufacturer can offer a

Ethical Decisions in Marketing

Mattel, the world's largest toy maker, faced its share of bad press in 2007. About nine million Mattel toys were recalled worldwide over concerns that the toys contain magnets that could be swallowed by children or could have "impermissible" levels of lead in paint. The recall in Canada affects approximately 890 000 magnetic toys and action figures. Mattel attributes the problem to a Chinese painting subcontractor that violated Mattel's standards and used paint from a non-authorized third-party supplier. The Mattel recall comes in the wake of other high-profile recalls of brands manufactured in China—Menu Foods had to recall pet food that was contaminated with poisonous melamine and caused serious injury and illness to pets, and counterfeit brand-name toothpaste shipped from China was shown to contain a toxic chemical used in antifreeze. This has shaken consumer confidence in brands with the "Made in China" label. In response, Mattel is implementing a "three-point check system" that involves testing every batch of paint at every vendor and increasing unannounced random inspections. Only time will tell if Canadian consumers are convinced that Mattel's actions are good enough. A Decima poll taken shortly after the Mattel recalls showed that only 32 percent of Canadians consider products from China safe. What would you do if you were on the public relations team at Mattel?[54]

Table 13.6 Sales Promotion Techniques: A Sampler

Technique	Primary Target	Description	Example
Trade shows	Trade	Many manufacturers showcase their products to convention attendees.	The National Kitchen and Bath Association organizes several shows a year. Manufacturers display their latest wares to owners of kitchen and bath remodelling stores.
Incentive programs	Trade	A prize is offered to employees who meet a prespecified sales goal or who are top performers during a given period.	Mary Kay cosmetics awards distinctive pink cars to its top-selling representatives.
Point-of-purchase displays	Trade and consumers	In-store exhibits make retail environments more interesting and attract consumers' attention.	As sombre music plays in the background, a huge plastic rat draped in a black shroud lies next to a tombstone to promote the Farnam Company's Just One Bite rat poison.
Push money	Trade	Salespeople are given a bonus for selling a specific manufacturer's product.	A retail salesperson at a cosmetics counter at a Nordstrom store in Seattle gets $5 every time she sells a bottle of Glow by J-Lo.
Promotional products	Trade and consumers	A company builds awareness and reinforces its image by giving out items with its name on them.	Coors distributors provide bar owners with highly sought-after "Coors Light" neon signs.
Cross promotion/ cooperative promotions	Trade and consumers	Companies team up to promote their products jointly.	Burger King promotes its Spidey Sense game in conjunction with Columbia Pictures' *Spider Man 2*.
Coupons	Consumers	Certificates for money off on selected products, often with an expiration date, are used to encourage product trial.	Crest offers $5 off its WhiteStrips.
Samples	Consumers	Retailers might get a demonstration product to help in sales presentations; consumers get a free trial size of the product.	A free small bottle of Clairol Herbal Essences shampoo arrives in the mail.
Contests/ sweepstakes	Trade and consumers	A sales contest rewards wholesalers or retailers for performance; consumers participate in games or drawings to win prizes; builds awareness and reinforces image.	Publisher's Clearing House announces its zillionth sweepstakes.
Special/bonus packs	Consumers	Additional product is given away with purchase; rewards users. Note that bonus packs usually mean the package must be altered in some way to accommodate the extra merchandise.	Maxell provides 10 free blank CDs with purchase of a pack of 50.
Gifts with purchase	Consumers	A consumer gets a free gift when a product is bought; reinforces product image and rewards users.	A free makeup kit comes with the purchase of $20 worth of Clinique products.

merchandise allowance A promotion that reimburses the retailer for in-store support of the product.

case allowance A discount to the retailer or wholesaler based on the volume of product ordered.

trade shows Events at which many companies set up exhibits to show their products, give away samples, distribute product literature, and troll for new business contacts.

merchandise allowance, which reimburses the retailer for in-store support such as shelving. A **case allowance** provides a discount to the retailer or wholesaler based on the volume of product ordered.

INDUSTRY BOOSTING AND BOASTING Other types of trade sales promotions increase the visibility of a manufacturer's products to channel partners (Table 13.6). Whether an elaborate exhibit at a convention or a coffee mug with the firm's logo mailed to clients, these efforts seek to keep the company's name topmost when distributors and retailers make decisions about which products to stock and push. These forms of sales promotions include:

- *Trade shows.* Hundreds of industry **trade shows** are held in Canada each year, and over 9000 shows are held in the United States. These are major vehicles for manufacturers to show off their product lines to wholesalers and retailers.[55] Large trade shows are often held in big hotels or convention centres where many companies set up elaborate exhibits to show their products, give away samples, distribute product literature, and troll for new business contacts. Some large Canadian companies, such as Home Hardware Stores Ltd. and Shoppers Drug Mart, focus their marketing strategies on private trade shows where key suppliers can interact more closely with buyers and store managers and do more deal making than is possible in a standard show where suppliers interact with many competing customers.[56]

- *Promotional products.* We have all seen them—coffee mugs, visors, T-shirts, key chains, and countless other doodads emblazoned with a company logo. These are *promotional products.* Unlike licensed merchandise sold in stores, these goodies are given away free to build awareness of the sponsor. Although some of these freebies are distributed directly to consumers, many, like the 3M Post-it notes in Exhibit 13.13, are intended for channel partners, such as retailers and vendors, to build name recognition and loyalty.

- *Incentive programs.* In addition to motivating distributors and customers, some promotions are designed to light a fire under the firm's own sales force. These incentives, known as **push money**, may come in the form of cash bonuses, trips, or prizes. Mary Kay cosmetics is famous for giving its more productive distributors pink cars as a reward for their efforts. Involving employees in a promotion is a great way to get them excited about what they sell. When Frito-Lay sponsored a promotion giving away six million bags of its new Nacho Cheese Doritos around the United States in one day, one objective was to psych up its own employees. Frito-Lay had its salespeople distribute the free goodies to people on the street, and a full-page ad in *USA Today* featured employees who worked on the brand.[57]

Exhibit 13.13

Many businesses put their logos on Post-it notes, used as a promotional item to keep their name in front of customers.

Consumer Promotions

Since 1970, Gillette has run the Gillette Cavalcade of Sports promotion, using large prizes, huge displays, and major sports stars to draw consumers across Canada into retail outlets to buy popular and less well-known Gillette products. Each year, it fine-tunes the $2 million promotion to keep it fresh, but the basic strategy is impact—go big or go home. Year after year it works, and the company experiences a 30 percent dollar sales increase during the event.[58]

Gillette's efforts and the Fido example, discussed earlier in the chapter, illustrate how major companies are creating unusual and attention-getting forms of promotion. As with trade promotions, sales-boosting efforts try to stimulate purchases by attracting consumers with price breaks or attracting their attention with novel incentives.

PRICE-BASED CONSUMER PROMOTIONS Many sales promotions aim for consumers' wallets. They emphasize short-term price reductions or refunds, thus encouraging people to choose a brand—at least while the deal is on.

- *Coupons.* Try to pick up any Wednesday newspaper without spilling a pile of coupons. Coupons are certificates redeemable for money off a purchase and are the most common price promotion. Indeed, they are the most popular form of sales promotion overall. Over 3.6 billion coupons are distributed annually in Canada, with redemptions valued at $134 million.[59] Consumers can also now find coupons online at sites like **www.savingyoumoney.com**.

- *Price deals, refunds, and rebates.* Manufacturers often offer temporary price reductions to stimulate sales. This price deal may be printed on the package itself, or it may be a price-off flag or banner on the store shelf. Sometimes companies offer **rebates**, which allow the customer to recover part of the product's cost directly from the manufacturer.

push money A bonus paid by a manufacturer to a salesperson for selling its product.

rebates Sales promotions that allow the customer to recover part of the product's cost from the manufacturer.

Chapters Inc. offered a new twist on the common "scratch & save" promotion by offering web surfers a chance to scratch a real-sounding card on its website.

- *Special packs.* Another form of price promotion is giving the shopper more of the product instead of lowering its price or bundling another product for the same price.[60] Kraft Canada, for example, recently included Famous Players movie coupons in a Post cereal promotion.

ATTENTION-GETTING CONSUMER PROMOTIONS Attention-getting consumer promotions stimulate interest in and publicity for a company's products. Labatt Breweries, for example, recently made a 14-stop tour of Ontario parks and beaches to promote its Kokanee brand of beer. The tour included a 7.5-metre-high inflatable glacier, bikini and muscleman contests, ultimate Frisbee games, and kayak races.[61] Some typical types of attention-getting promotions are:

- *Contests and sweepstakes.* A contest is a test of skill, while a sweepstakes is based on chance. Guinness Import Company's "Win Your Own Pub in Ireland" contest gave away an actual pub to winners of the essay contest "Why Guinness Is My Perfect Pint."[62] Tim Hortons' "Roll up the rim to win" contest has become so ingrained in Canadian culture that Tim Hortons ran an advertising campaign in which a traveller "proved" Canadian citizenship by spouting the "Roll up the rim to win" slogan.[63] A Kool-Aid promotion helped launch Kool-Aid Magic, a Kool-Aid product aimed at 6- to 12-year-olds that changes colour when water is added.

premium An item included without charge with a purchased product.

- *Premiums.* **Premiums** are items offered for free to people who have bought a product. A premium is often a novelty item, such as the free, removable tattoos called Barqtoos that Barq's root beer gives away to its customers. A Pokemon card in a box of cereal, a replica Stanley Cup in cases of Labatt's Blue, or a movie pass in Humpty-Dumpty potato chips are all examples of premiums. The latest craze in premiums is prepaid phone cards that enhance brand identification. Phone cards make ideal premiums, because they are compact in size, brand logos or graphics provide opportunities for repeat exposure, and the issuer can track card usage and build databases by determining where calls originate.[64] Labatt struck retail (and promotion award) gold for its Coldies—bottles of Labatt Blue dressed in a sleeve designed like one of 30 NHL teams (Exhibit 13.14).

sampling Distributing trial-size versions of a product for free to encourage people to try it.

point-of-purchase (POP) promotion The use of signs or displays to influence purchases at the store.

- *Sampling.* How many people at one time or another have managed to scrape together an entire meal by scooping up free food samples at their local grocery store? **Sampling** gets people to try a product by distributing trial-size versions in stores, on street corners, or through the mail. Effem, the Canadian subsidiary of Mars Corp. that owns the Whiskas brand of cat food, used sampling to encourage cat owners to try Whiskas' wet pack product. It sent 250 000 samples to cat owners and increased sales by 20 percent.[65]

  - *Point-of-purchase promotion.* A **point-of-purchase (POP) promotion** attempts to influence consumers in the store by catching their attention with displays or signs.[66] Marketers are challenged to come up with new and innovative POP displays that will grab people's attention. For example, Bausch & Lomb conducted a promotion in Spain to encourage consumers with good vision to buy contact lenses to change their eye colour. The in-store display allowed shoppers to see what they would look like with five different colours of eyes before they actually inserted the contacts.[67] POP activities also include the use of *in-store media*, including placards on shopping carts or even closed-circuit television, which promote specific products. As the CEO of one company that produces these in-store messages put it, "Does it make any sense to spend millions of dollars talking to people in their living rooms and cars and then let them wander around a supermarket with 30 000 product choices without something to remind them to buy your product?"[68]

Exhibit 13.14

Labatt "Coldies" are an example of a premium promotion.

LOYALTY GENERATING PROMOTIONS *Continuity programs, membership programs,* and *loyalty programs* are all terms used to describe the practice of awarding discounts, bonuses, or such other incentives as redeemable "points" to frequent and other high-value customers. These programs are increasingly recognized as the best retention-marketing tactic. They are used to recognize the importance of customers, reward their on-going patronage, establish long-term ties or bonds to the organization, and encourage loyalty. An added benefit is the organization's ability to observe and track their purchase behaviour. More than 71 percent of Canadian consumers participate in at least one loyalty program, and over 67 percent take part in four or five different programs.[69] While some companies such as Air Canada (Aeroplan) and Petro-Canada (Petro-Points) have independent loyalty programs, smaller companies are able to participate in joint programs such as Air Miles, where points earned from purchases from a variety of participating organizations can be redeemed for travel on a number of sponsor airlines or for merchandise (such as theatre tickets) from member organizations.

Promotion Strategy

Ideally, the objective of every sales promotion should be to cement the product's position in the marketplace. This may mean building awareness for a new product, enticing retailers to stock it, or kick-starting sales for an item during Christmas season. Once marketers have determined the objectives of a sales promotion, they must decide what the program will look like. If the objective is to encourage users of a competing product to try the item, a sampling program might work best. If the objective is to encourage loyal users to increase their interest in the brand, the firm might sponsor a contest or sweepstakes. If the company wants to increase its shelf space allocation, it might try a price break to retailers. Many marketers also are discovering the virtues of **cross-promotion**, in which two or more companies combine forces to create interest in their different products or services using a single promotional tool. Duracell, for example, recently teamed up with the Canadian Association of Fire Chiefs (Exhibit 13.15) to promote fire safety and support Duracell's Trusted Everywhere positioning.

cross-promotion Two or more companies combining forces and using a single promotional tool to create interest in their products or services.

A key issue for marketers is over-redemption: having too many customers redeem coupons, satisfy contest requirements, or buy cross-promoted product.[70] The classic example of this was Maytag Corporation's 1993 offer of free round-trip airline tickets to British customers who bought Hoover-brand appliances. The company placed severe restrictions on the dates of travel to limit redemption but hadn't counted on unemployed people buying the appliances just to go on the trip. It cost Maytag US$36 million to honour the promotion, and it then faced a flood of "nearly new" second-hand Hoover appliances being sold by customers who never really wanted the appliance. Marketers can now buy over-redemption insurance.

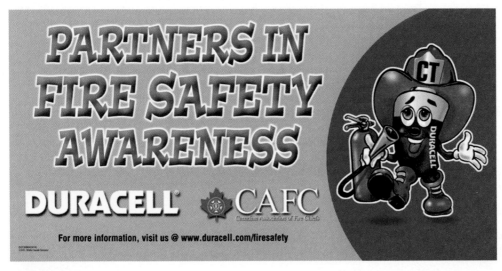

Exhibit 13.15

A cross-promotion lets companies join forces to communicate about their products.

Exhibit 13.16

Cox Target Media is a firm that specializes in direct mail coupon promotions under the ValPak brand.

DIRECT MARKETING

We discussed direct marketing in Chapter 11 as a non-store form of retailing. Direct marketing also serves a communications function, as direct mail and catalogues are print-based media that can be specifically targeted to customers and consumers (Exhibit 13.16). The Whiskas sampling program described earlier was successful because the company was able to mail samples to 250 000 cat owners by buying access to a database of potential customers, by having its own database from previous promotions, and by soliciting sample requests on its website. As discussed in Chapter 12, the key to successful direct marketing is having a solid database that allows organizations to select potential recipients who match the desired target profile.

Direct mail is becoming increasingly popular as a communications vehicle that supports other elements in a campaign. Rocky Mountaineer Railtours, for example, sent a direct mail piece to 20 000 empty nest couples who had previously requested a brochure. It drew a conversion of 3 percent (203 bookings and 511 guests) and incremental revenue of $1 million—a 25:1 return on investment.[71]

Direct mail is also used extensively in business-to-business contexts. Hewlett-Packard, for example, used direct mail to both channel partners and end users as part of an integrated campaign to promote its SureStore AutoBackup Storage System for computer networks. For channel partners, it sent a box whose front copy read "Opening This Box Is Guaranteed to Make You Richer." Inside the box were a $5 bill, product feature brochures, and a demo CD.

SPOTLIGHT ON REAL PEOPLE   Cara's Winning Combo

Gabriel Tsampalieros, CEO of Cara Operations, the parent company of some of the best-known Canadian restaurant chains, uses extensive consumer research and targeted marketing techniques to ensure that the company meets and understands customer demands. Cara Operations has evolved from a Railway News Company in 1883 to a successful restaurant company that now boasts an impressive list of chains, including Swiss Chalet, Harvey's, Second Cup, Kelsey's, Montana's, Outback Steakhouse, and Milestone's. Tsampalieros says that Cara has its bases covered. "When you play in a geography like Canada with its limited population, you recognize that to grow to a certain size, you have to have flexibility to play in different price points." Cara Operations envisions itself being the leading restaurant company in Canada; with this in mind, it created a central branding and research team in 1999. This team fully evaluated each brand, researched consumers' needs, and developed marketing campaigns and tactics to support their findings. These included a "brand intelligence gathering capability" that cost $3 million annually and meant developing a back-of-house support system for the front-line brands. They gather information from 21 different sources, including focus groups, individual surveys, 7000 consumer interviews per year, and syndicated sources. The results of this branding initiative are becoming apparent today, and Cara's leading brand, Swiss Chalet, is spearheading the restaurant pack. Through restaurant upgrades, new menu offerings, takeout and delivery channels, increased advertising, special offers such as Häagen-Dazs Ice Cream, and enhanced website interactivity, Cara hopes to attract younger customers, revitalize its image, and boost sales. Tsampalieros explains that each individual chain is going through some major marketing efforts, with tailor-made campaigns and initiatives aimed at restaurant-specific goals. Through marketing efforts, re-branding, and brand clarification strategies, Cara hopes to attain its vision of becoming the leading restaurant company in Canada.[72]

1. How does Cara's market information support its marketing and communication decisions?
2. How else might Cara incorporate communications mix activities to enhance brand positioning?

Business executives and IT managers were also sent personalized direct mail pieces that directed them to a promotional website for the product. The campaign achieved a 6 percent response rate (1 percent to 3 percent is typical) from the business executives and resulted in a 32 percent increase in sales.[73]

A key benefit of direct marketing initiatives is the opportunity to elicit a measurable response from prospects or customers by directing them to a 1-800 number, a website, or another way for customers or consumers to respond such as by mail or by fax. When a specific call to action is included in direct mail it becomes **direct-response marketing**—marketing activity aimed at generating a measurable response via marketing communications.

direct-response marketing Marketing activity aimed at generating a measurable response via marketing communications.

PERSONAL SELLING

The final piece of the promotion pie is personal selling, which is a far more intimate way to talk to the market. **Personal selling** is a company representative coming in direct contact with customers to inform them about a good or service to get a sale. Many organizations rely heavily on this immediate form of communication. The "personal touch" can be a lot more influential than information we get from mass media. And, for business-to-business marketers such as Xerox, personal selling accounts for a big chunk of sales. Many industrial products and services are too complex or expensive to be adequately explained or demonstrated in an impersonal trade advertisement.

personal selling The part of the promotion mix that involves direct contact between a company representative and a customer.

Another advantage of relying on a good sales force is that salespeople are the firm's eyes and ears in the field. They pay attention to which competitors' salespeople are calling on customers, what new competing products have been delivered to their customers, and what new literature is on the customers' desks. Personal selling has special importance for students, because many graduates with a marketing background will enter sales jobs. Let's take a close look at how personal selling works and how sophisticated salespeople work hard to develop long-term relationships with customers.

The Role of Personal Selling

When a man calls a 1-800 number to order a new desktop PC configured with a snappy DVD drive so his kids can play the latest Hollywood blockbuster, he is dealing with a company salesperson. When he sits in on a presentation at work by a computer technician who demonstrates a new spreadsheet software package, he is dealing with a company salesperson. And when that same man agrees over dinner at a swanky restaurant to buy a new computer network for his company, he also is dealing with a company salesperson.

For many firms, some form of personal selling is essential for a transaction (the sale) to occur, so this type of communication is an important part of an organization's overall marketing plan. Generally, a personal sales effort is more important when a firm engages in a *push strategy*, in which the goal is to push the product through the channel of distribution. As a vice-president at Hallmark Cards observed, "We're not selling *to* the retailer, we're selling through the retailer. We look at the retailer as a pipeline to the hands of consumers."[74] Personal selling also is likely to be crucial in business-to-business contexts when direct interaction with upper-level management is required to clinch a big deal—and often when intense price negotiations will occur before the deal is signed. In addition, inexperienced buyers may need the hands-on assistance that a salesperson can provide. Organizations selling products that consumers buy infrequently, such as computers, lawn mowers, and college educations, often place greater emphasis on personal selling, as do firms selling complex or very expensive products that need a salesperson to explain, justify, and sell them.

If personal selling is so effective, why don't firms just scrap their advertising and sales promotion budgets and hire more salespeople? There are some drawbacks that limit the role played by personal selling in the communications mix.

First, when the dollar amount of individual purchases is low, it doesn't make sense to use personal selling. The cost per contact with a customer is much higher than with other forms of communication. After all, the median cost for a typical sales call is over $3200, due to salary, travel, a company car, and other expenses.[75] In comparison, the cost per contact of a national television commercial is low, even though the total cost to run the ad is high. A 30-second, prime-time commercial may be $30 000 to $40 000 (plus production costs), but with millions of viewers, the cost may be only $10 or $15 per 1000 viewers—little more than a penny per viewer.

Because salespeople—even if they are *really* energetic—can call on only a limited number of customers in a day, reliance on personal selling is effective only when a reasonable number of the customers the salespeople do see make a purchase. Because the cost of field salespeople is so great, **telemarketing**, in which person-to-person communication takes place via the telephone, fax machine, or e-mail, is growing in popularity. Pharmaceutical companies Novartis, Janssen-Ortho, and Becton Dickinson, for example, make extensive use of telemarketing to launch new products. Armed with a good database and software that can handle 8000 to 10 000 outbound faxes per hour, they can communicate product information to all the 6500 pharmacies and dispensaries in Canada within one hour. They then follow up the same or next day with phone calls from a team of professional, knowledgeable telemarketers who can each place about 80 calls per day. This enables the pharmaceutical companies to effectively reach their target audience with timely information far more quickly than a regiment of in-store reps.[76]

telemarketing The use of the telephone or fax to sell directly to consumers and business customers.

Technology and Personal Selling

Personal selling is supposed to be, well, "personal." By definition, a company uses personal selling for marketing communications in situations when one person (the salesperson) interacts directly with another person (the customer or prospective customer) to communicate about a good or service. All sorts of technologies are available to enhance the personal selling process. However, as anyone making sales calls knows, technology cannot and should not *replace* personal selling. As we'll discuss later in this chapter, nowadays a key role of personal selling is to manage customer *relationships*—and remember that relationships occur between people, not between computers (as much as you love your MySpace).

However, without doubt a bevy of technological advancements has made it easier for salespeople to do their jobs more effectively. One such technological advance is *customer relationship management (CRM) software*. For years now, *account management software* such as ACT and GoldMine has helped salespeople. These programs are inexpensive, easy to navigate, and allow salespeople to track all aspects of customer interaction. Currently, many firms are turning to "on demand" online CRM applications, which are more customizable and integrative than ACT or GoldMine yet are less expensive than major company-wide CRM installations. These widely used online CRM products include SalesForce and SalesNet, both of which are user-friendly for salespeople. A key benefit of online CRM systems is that the firm "rents" them for a flat fee per month (at SalesForce.com, $65 per user), avoiding major capital outlays.[77] Recently, sales organizations began using a new-generation system called *partner relationship management (PRM)* that links information between selling and buying firms. PRM differs from CRM in that both supplier and buyer firms share at least some of their databases and systems to maximize the utility of the data for decision-making purposes. Firms that share information are more likely to work together toward win-win solutions.

Beyond CRM and PRM, numerous other technology applications are enhancing personal selling, including teleconferencing, videoconferencing, and improved corporate websites that include FAQ (frequently asked questions) pages that answer many customer queries. Many firms also use intranets and blogs to facilitate the interface of internal and external communication.

Voice-over Internet protocol (VoIP)—using a data network to carry voice calls—is beginning to get a lot of use in day-to-day correspondence between salespeople and customers. With VoIP, the salesperson on the road can plug into a fast Internet connection and then start making and receiving calls just as if he or she were in the office. Unlike using cellphones, there are no bad reception areas, and unlike using hotel phones, there are no hidden charges. One popular VoIP product is Skype, whose tag line is "The whole world can talk for free." According to its website, Skype "is a little piece of software that allows you to make free calls to other Skype users and really cheap calls to ordinary phones." Skype even offers bargain rates to fixed lines and cellphones outside North America.[78]

The type of salespeople and the roles they perform vary in different firms. The person who processes a computer purchase over the phone is an **order taker**, a salesperson whose primary function is to facilitate transactions that the customer initiates. Most retail salespeople are order takers; but often wholesalers, dealers, and distributors also employ salespeople to wait on customers. The computer technician is a **technical specialist**, who contributes expertise in the form of product demonstrations, recommendations for complex equipment, and set-up of machinery. The technical specialist's job is to provide *sales support* rather than actually closing the sale, meaning that the technical specialist promotes the firm and tries to stimulate demand for a product to make it easier for others to actually make the deal.

Sometimes a person whose job is to lay this groundwork is known as a **missionary salesperson**.[79] Missionary salespeople promote the firm and try to stimulate demand for a product but don't actually complete a sale. And this support person may even be part of a sales team. Xerox, for example, competes for big accounts by sending out teams of specialists: Each Team Xerox includes customer service personnel, financial experts, and even top management in the case of important customers.[80] Finally, the person who actually convinces the customer to shell out for the computer network, probably after several weeks or months of discussions, is an **order getter**. Order getters work creatively to develop relationships with customers or to generate new sales. These salespeople find new customers, persuade customers to buy, and close the sale. Some marketers, such as Tupperware and Mary Kay Cosmetics, recruit people to become order getters within their personal network of friends, family, and acquaintances (Exhibit 13.17). This network or multilevel marketing approach can be highly effective since the "sales rep" is someone who customers in the network know and trust.

order taker A salesperson whose primary function is to facilitate transactions that the customer initiates.

technical specialist Sales support personnel with a high level of technical expertise who assist in product demonstrations.

missionary salesperson A salesperson who promotes the firm and tries to stimulate demand for a product but does not actually complete a sale.

order getter A salesperson who works creatively to develop relationships with customers or to generate new sales.

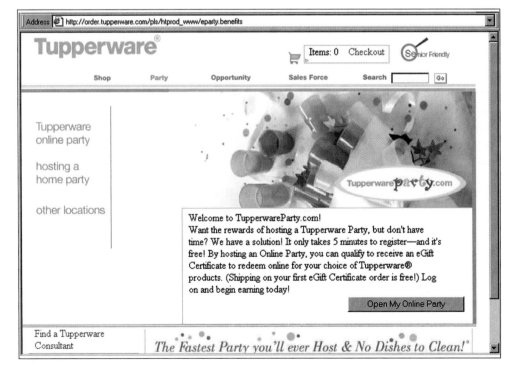

Exhibit 13.17

Tupperware parties used to be housebound. Now they can be held online!

Exhibit 13.18

Jacques Gatien uses in-store product demonstrations to show customers how useful his products are.

Approaches to Personal Selling

Personal selling is one of the oldest forms of communication, but the image of this profession has been tarnished by smooth-talking hucksters who would say anything to make a sale. In the latter part of the twentieth century, personal selling has largely redeemed itself as a profession. In most industries, it has moved from a transactional, hard-sell marketing approach to a relationship marketing approach.

TRANSACTIONAL MARKETING: PUTTING ON THE HARD SELL The *hard sell* is a high-pressure process. We've all been exposed to the pushy electronics salesperson who puts down the competition by telling shoppers that if they buy elsewhere they will be stuck with an inferior sound system that will fall apart in six months. These hard-sell tactics are a form of **transactional selling**, a sales technique that focuses on making an immediate sale with little or no attempt to develop a relationship with the customer. As customers, we feel manipulated by the hard sell and resent it. This technique and its depiction in movies like *GlenGarry Glen Ross* and plays like *Death of a Salesman* also contribute to the negative image many of us have of obnoxious salespeople. But not all transactional marketers are obnoxious. Jacques Gatien, president of Atlantic Promotions of Longueuil, Quebec (see Exhibit 13.18), has earned a reputation as the "jovial huckster." He is the brains behind a $115 million company that sells products like the Oskar snowbrush, Pant Saver car mat, Starfrit Rotato, T-Rex rake, and other useful products, using a combination of advertising and in-store demonstrations. His motto is: "The more you can use a demonstration to sell a product, the easier it is to sell."[81]

RELATIONSHIP SELLING: COUNTERING THE TARNISHED IMAGE Rather than transactional selling, today's professional salesperson is more likely to practise **relationship selling**—seeking to develop a mutually satisfying relationship with the customer.[82] Relationship selling involves winning, keeping, and developing customers. *Winning* customers means converting interested prospects into people who are convinced that the product or service holds value for them. *Keeping* customers means ensuring that the product or service delivers what was promised. *Developing* customers means satisfying them so that they can be counted on to provide future business.[83]

transactional selling A form of personal selling that focuses on making an immediate sale with little or no attempt to develop a relationship with the customer.

relationship selling A form of personal selling in which the salesperson seeks to develop a mutually satisfying relationship with the consumer so that they can work together to satisfy each other's needs.

The Role of Personal Selling in the Communications Mix

The salesperson's job can be made easier with support from public relations and advertising. The business customer, having already seen the supplier's advertisements or product releases, is likely to welcome that vendor's representative. Responses to toll-free numbers included in advertising and sales promotions can provide hot sales leads to follow up with prospective customers who have already expressed interest in learning more about the product. And many salespeople obtain valuable leads at industry trade shows attended by thousands of prospective customers.

THE SELLING PROCESS Selling is seldom boring. Every customer, every sales call, and every salesperson is unique. Some salespeople are successful primarily because they know so much about what they sell. Others are successful because they've built strong relationships with their customers over time, and these people look forward to their visits to "chew the fat." And most salespersons understand and engage in a series of activities necessary to bring about a transaction.

Sales of complex or expensive products require careful planning. To be successful in these, the salesperson must follow the **creative selling process**—seeking out customers, analyzing their needs, determining how product attributes provide benefits, and then deciding how best to communicate that information to the targeted customers. As Figure 13.1 shows, there are seven steps in the process.

PROSPECT CUSTOMERS **Prospecting** is the process of identifying and developing a list of potential customers, called *prospects* or *sales leads*. Leads can come from existing customer lists, telephone directories, and commercially available databases. The local library usually contains directories of businesses (including those published by provincial and federal agencies) and directories of association memberships. Some companies generate sales leads through their advertising or sales promotions by letting customers request more information. One way to generate leads is through *cold calling*, when the salesperson contacts prospects "cold," without prior introduction or permission. Because it always helps to know someone rather than starting off cold, salespeople might instead seek *referrals* from other customers. Current clients who are satisfied with their purchase often give referrals, which is yet another reason to maintain good customer relationships.

QUALIFY PROSPECTS Just because people are willing to talk to a salesperson doesn't mean they will turn out to be good sales leads. Along with identifying potential customers, salespersons need to **qualify prospects** to determine how likely they are to become customers. Salespeople qualify prospects by asking themselves such questions as: Are the prospects likely to be interested in what I'm selling? Are they likely to switch their allegiance from what they are currently using? Is the potential sales volume large enough to make a relationship with them profitable? Can they afford the purchase? If they must borrow money to buy my product, is their credit history acceptable?

DO A PRE-APPROACH The **pre-approach** consists of compiling background information about prospective customers and planning the sales interview. Important purchases are not made lightly, so it is foolish for a salesperson to blindly call on a qualified prospect and risk losing the sale due to a lack of preparation. Salespeople try to learn as much as possible about qualified prospects before initiating a sale, such as their past history of purchases, their current needs, and, in some cases, personal information about their likes and dislikes.

Salespeople can find information about a prospect from a variety of sources. In the case of larger companies, financial data, names of top executives, and other information about a business can be found in such publications as *Standard & Poor's 500 Directory* or the *Million Dollar Directory*. The inside scoop on a prospect, however, frequently comes from informal sources, such as non-competing salespeople who have dealt with the person before. This background information helps salespeople to plan their strategy and the goals they will try to achieve when the prospect is contacted.

MAKE THE APPROACH After the groundwork has been laid with the pre-approach, it is time to **approach**, or contact, the prospect. During the important first minutes when the salesperson initiates contact with the prospective customer, several key events occur. The salesperson tries to learn even more about the prospect's needs, create a good impression, and build rapport. If the salesperson made contact with the prospect through a referral, the salesperson will probably acknowledge this connection: "Barbara Price with Amida Industries suggested I call on you."

During the approach, the customer is deciding whether the salesperson has something beneficial to offer. The old saying, "You never get a second chance to make a good first impression," certainly rings true in this situation. A professional appearance is a signal to the prospect that the salesperson means business and is competent to handle the sale. Successful salespeople are always well groomed and wear appropriate business dress; they don't chew gum, use poor grammar or inappropriate language, mispronounce the customer's name, or seem uninterested in the job.

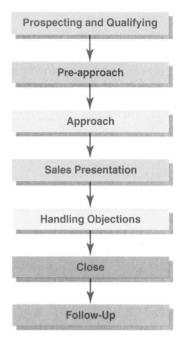

Figure 13.1 Steps in the Creative Selling Process

In the creative selling process, salespeople follow a series of steps to ensure successful long-term relationships with customers.

creative selling process The process of seeking out customers, analyzing their needs, determining how product attributes might provide benefits for them, and then communicating that information.

prospecting A part of the selling process that includes identifying and developing a list of potential or prospective customers.

qualify prospects A part of the selling process that determines how likely prospects are to become customers.

pre-approach A part of the selling process that includes developing information about prospective customers and planning the sales interview.

approach The first step of the actual sales presentation in which the salesperson tries to learn more about the customer's needs, create a good impression, and build rapport.

sales presentation The part of the selling process in which the salesperson seeks to persuasively communicate the product's features and the benefits it will provide after the sale.

MAKE THE SALES PRESENTATION Many sales calls involve a formal **sales presentation**, in which the salesperson lays out the benefits of the product and why it is better than what competitors are offering. *Proof statements*, such as data on past sales, testimonials, guarantees, or research results, help to make the salesperson's pitch credible. And in the most effective sales presentations, the salesperson gets the would-be customer to participate by asking questions or, as we saw with Jacques Gatien, allowing the customer to try the product.

Some sales presentations are canned, which means a script has been written in advance and the same message is delivered to every prospect. This technique often provides a series of verbal prompts to which the customer is expected to respond in the desired manner. For example, office supplies salespeople might start all their pitches with, "Would you like to see a new line of products that will revolutionize the way you run your office?" That standardized approach works fine in some cases, but the most effective sales presentations are those that are tailored to the specific needs of the customer. For example, a salesperson instead might say, "Would you be interested in getting better-quality report binders at a lower price?" after discovering during the pre-approach that the office manager was under pressure from the boss to cut costs on office supplies.

Such technologies as laptop and palm computers, presentation software, digital projectors, and the Internet are enhancing the ability of salespeople to make effective presentations. "Web-push" technology, for example, transmits information via any combination of telephone and Internet-enabled communication formats to a desktop computer, allowing presenters to simultaneously talk to, visually interact with, and otherwise communicate with remote audiences using in-sync multiple media formats.[84] Many marketing organizations, such as Fujitsu Siemens Computers and Tourism Queensland, are putting multimedia product presentations on the Internet, allowing customers and consumers to view them with more convenience (Exhibit 13.19).

OVERCOME CUSTOMER OBJECTIONS It is rare that a prospect accepts whatever the salesperson has to say and immediately makes an order. The effective salesperson anticipates *objections*, or reasons why the prospect is unwilling to commit to a purchase, and is prepared to overcome them by providing additional information or persuasive arguments. In fact, the salesperson should *welcome* objections, because they show that the prospect is at least interested enough to have considered the offer and seriously weigh its pros and cons. Handling the objection successfully may move a prospect to the decision stage. For example, the salesperson might say, "Ms. Robbins, you've said before that you don't have room to carry our new line of sleeping bags, although you admit that you may be losing some sales by carrying only one brand with very few different models. If we could determine how much business you're losing, I'd be willing to bet you'd make room for our line, wouldn't you?"

Exhibit 13.19

Tourism Queensland offers multimedia sales presentations to travel agents and consumers wanting more information on Queensland tourism products.

CLOSE THE SALE A common mistake made by salespeople is that they work very hard to open the door for the prospect but don't get the prospect to walk through that door. **Sales closing** occurs when the salesperson asks the customer straight out to buy the product and complete the transaction.

There are a variety of techniques good salespeople use to close the sale. A *last objection close* asks customers if they are ready to purchase, providing any concerns they have about the product can be addressed: "Are you ready to order if we can show you a 20 percent cost savings associated with using this software?" In a *trial close*, on the other hand, the salesperson acts as if the purchase is inevitable; all that's left is to wrap up the details: "What quantity would you like to order?" In some cases, the salesperson applies a bit more pressure by using a *standing-room-only close*, in which the salesperson indicates that if the customer does not buy now, there may not be the opportunity in the future. No matter what technique is used, it's important to close the sale rather than just assume the transaction will happen "magically" on its own.

FOLLOW-UP AFTER THE SALE **Sales follow-up** includes arranging for delivery, payment, and purchase terms. It also means the salesperson is making sure the customer received the order and is satisfied. Follow-up also allows the salesperson to *bridge* to the next purchase. Once a relationship develops with a customer, the selling process is only beginning. Even as one cycle of purchasing draws to a close, a good salesperson is already laying the foundation for the next one.

Sales Management

No firm can succeed with just one star salesperson. Personal selling is a team effort, and this form of communication usually requires careful planning to ensure that a firm's salespeople are in the field when and where customers need them. **Sales management** is the process of planning, implementing, and controlling the personal selling function of an organization. These are some major decisions sales professionals who oversee this function must make.

SETTING SALES FORCE OBJECTIVES Sales force objectives state what the sales force is expected to accomplish and when. Sales managers develop specific sales force performance objectives, such as "acquire 100 new customers," "generate $100 million in sales," or even "reduce travel expenses by 2 percent." Some firms also state goals for customer satisfaction, new customer development, new product suggestions, training, or community involvement.

Sales managers also work with their salespeople to develop individual goals. *Performance goals* are measurable outcomes, such as total sales and total profits per salesperson. *Behavioural goals* specify the actions salespeople must accomplish, such as the number of prospects to identify, the number of sales calls they need to make, and the number of sales presentations they must deliver.

CREATING A SALES FORCE STRATEGY A sales force strategy specifies how the firm will structure, size, and compensate its sales force. Each salesperson has the responsibility for a **sales territory**, a set group of customers. The territory structure allows salespeople to have an in-depth understanding of customers and their needs because they call on the same people repeatedly and get to know them on a personal level. The most common way to structure territories is by geographic boundaries to minimize travel and other field expenses. Thus, a sales territory might be Regina, Saskatchewan, the Prairie provinces, western Canada, or even all of Canada.

If the product line is technically complex or quite diverse, however, it may be better to structure sales territories based on different classes of products rather than location. This enables the salesperson to provide greater expertise to a set of customers with similar needs. Still another structure is industry specialization, in which salespeople focus on a single industry or a small number of industries. For example, IBM went from a geographic sales force structure to one in which its salespeople were assigned to one of 14 different industries. In making the change, IBM executives cited a need to have salespeople who "speak the language of its customers and understand their industries."[85]

sales closing The stage of the selling process in which the salesperson asks the customer to buy the product.

sales follow-up After-sales activities that provide important services to customers.

sales management The process of planning, implementing, and controlling the personal selling function of an organization.

sales territory A set of customers often defined by geographic boundaries, for whom a particular salesperson is responsible.

Putting a salesperson out in the field is an expensive proposition; so the number of people pounding the pavement for the company affects its profitability. For this reason, determining the optimal number of salespeople is an important decision. A larger sales force may increase sales, but it will also increase costs. A smaller sales force will keep costs down, but this strategy can backfire—competitors with larger sales forces may be able to develop stronger customer relationships, because each of their salespeople doesn't have to call on as many customers.

RECRUITING, TRAINING, AND REWARDING SALESPEOPLE Because the quality of a sales force can make or break a firm, recruiting and hiring the right set of people to do the job is a top priority for sales managers. Many firms recruit people who are strategic thinkers, who have technical knowledge pertaining to the industry, and who have excellent interpersonal skills.[86] Companies use various methods to screen potential salespeople. Interviews reveal communication skills, interpersonal skills, and information about interests and capabilities. Paper-and-pencil tests can determine quantitative skills and competence in areas not easily assessed through interviews.

Although some people feel that a successful salesperson is born, not made, even the most skilled communicator has much to learn. *Sales training* allows salespeople to learn about the organization and its products and to develop the skills, knowledge, and attitudes necessary for high levels of performance. For example, training programs at Xerox focus on ways to identify customer problems. The Xerox Document University, a training facility with 250 classrooms and a curriculum of 180 courses, provides an 11-week training program for new salespeople and continuing training throughout the salesperson's career.[87] The publisher Southwestern Company runs a different sort of sales training program: Every summer, almost 4000 college students attend the company's sales school where they attend pep rallies (Exhibit 13.20), meet with sales managers, and learn how to sell books door-to-door.

An important way to motivate salespeople is by paying them well, and often this means tying compensation to performance. There are several payment systems commonly used to motivate salespeople. A *straight commission plan* is payment based solely on a percentage of sales the person closes. Under a *commission-with-draw plan*, earnings are still based on commission

Exhibit 13.20

Sales schools train college students to sell by finding novel ways to motivate them.

but the salesperson also receives a regular payment, or "draw," which may be charged against future commissions if current sales are inadequate to cover the draw. With a *straight salary compensation plan*, the salesperson is paid a set amount regardless of sales performance. Sometimes straight salary plans are augmented by use of a *quota-bonus plan*, in which salespeople are paid a salary plus a bonus for sales they make above their assigned quota.

In addition to basic compensation, many managers find that a variety of other incentives can also enhance the sales force effort tremendously. Such incentives can range from a free trip to the Caribbean for the top salesperson and his or her family to products like barbecues or steaks (Exhibit 13.21), or the always-appreciated extra cash. IBM invites all of its sales representatives who achieve their sales quotas and their spouses, or significant other, to "Club"—a three-day vacation/sales meeting at an expensive resort.

Although most salespeople like to work independently, supervision is essential for an effective sales force. Sales managers often require salespeople to develop monthly, weekly, and daily *call reports*, plans of action detailing which customers were called upon and what happened during the call. These reports allow the sales manager to track what the salespeople are doing in the field, and they provide marketing managers with timely information about customers' responses, competitive activity, and changes in the firm's customer base.

Exhibit 13.21

Omaha Steaks markets to organizations looking for innovative incentive items.

Real People, Real Decisions

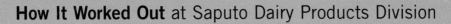

How It Worked Out at Saputo Dairy Products Division

Mario and the Saputo executives chose Option 2—to develop their own weekly cooking show, called *Cucina,* focused on Italian cuisine and how consumers could use Saputo cheeses to make fabulous dishes. They hired a well-known food personality in the greater Toronto area named Rita DeMontis, who has been food editor at the *Toronto Sun* for over 25 years; guest chef personalities from famous restaurants; and a producer who was a food lover to help select recipes and ensure Saputo products were showcased in the best possible way.

This approach required less of an investment, could be tried for limited commitment and then reassessed, was focused on building demand through increased product use, and helped support the sales force in getting listings for the Saputo brand of Italian cheeses across the country. A similar strategy could then be used to develop demand for the Armstrong and Cayer family brands across the country—either by changing the theme of the show to more general cuisine, or developing a second show featuring Canadian cuisine with Armstrong products or multicultural cuisine with Armstrong and Cayer products.

Mario started with a series of six-minute cooking spots, in Italian, in a one-hour news/sports show on TLN (part of basic cable in Toronto). Research on viewer attitudes demonstrated sufficient demand to produce 13 30-minute shows, in English, also on TLN. These shows in turn had sufficient following to justify the production of 39 episodes the next year, which attracted more than 100 000 viewers per show, key sponsors, and new distributors. With the ability to measure week-to-week changes in sales compared to the previous year using ACNielsen data, Mario was able to demonstrate the financial impact of the strategy—sales at least tripled and sometimes increased tenfold.

Interest in the show was so high that Saputo began producing and selling a cooking magazine (now with distribution of 50 000 copies) and is selling DVD copies of its shows through major book retailers like Chapters. Mario recently negotiated to bring the *Cucina* show to Global, providing national exposure to his brands, an expected 400 000 viewers, and the ability to customize the Saputo advertising by region—which was not possible previously.

Implementation of the strategy was not without its challenges. What proved most difficult was coordinating a schedule that aligned featured stores and cheeses, and then creating or finding appropriate recipes.

Key Terms

CHAPTER SUMMARY

1. Explain the advantages and disadvantages of alternative advertising media.

Television is an excellent medium for demonstrating goods, and particularly services, for mass audiences. It is highly flexible from a creative concept perspective, but very expensive. Radio is a cost-effective way to reach selective audiences and spots can be created and changed quickly, but products cannot be demonstrated and listeners do not often pay full attention to radio ads. Newspapers provide extensive market coverage and allow for informative appeals. People do not spend much time reading newspapers, however, and they are typically thrown away once read. Magazines have a longer shelf life than newspapers, may be passed on to other readers, and may be more targeted, but magazine ads can be expensive. Internet banner advertising, buttons, and pop-ups can be cost-effective with measured results, but they are easily ignored. Outdoor advertising (primarily billboards) can be effective in reaching broad audiences with simple messages but are not effective for complex messages.

2. Critique advertising.

The elements that go into a communication plan can be used as criteria to critique advertising. These include an evaluation of the target audience, communication objectives, overall communications strategy, positioning and key messages, communication tactics, choice of communications mix/media, creative execution, and ease of evaluation.

3. Explain the role of public relations and describe the steps in developing a public relations campaign.

The purpose of public relations is to build mutually beneficial long-term relationships and improve the image of an organization with key stakeholders, including consumers, the media, shareholders, legislators, and interest groups. An important part of this is managing publicity. Public relations is important in introducing new products; influencing legislation; enhancing the image of a city, region, or country; and calling attention to a firm's community involvement.

A public relations campaign begins with setting objectives, creating and executing a campaign strategy, and planning how the PR program will be evaluated. PR specialists often use print or video news releases to communicate timely topics, research stories, and consumer information.

4. Explain what sales promotion is and describe some of the different types of trade and consumer sales promotion activities.

Sales promotions are short-term programs designed to build interest in or encourage purchase of a product. Trade promotions include merchandise allowances, trade shows, promotional products, and incentive programs, including push money. Consumer sales promotions include coupons, price deals, rebates, special packs, contests and sweepstakes, premiums, sampling programs, point-of-purchase promotions, and continuity (loyalty) programs.

5. Explain the important role of personal selling in the marketing effort and list the steps in the personal selling process.

Personal selling occurs when a company representative directly informs a client about a good or service to get a sale. Personal selling is more important for push strategies. Because of the high cost per customer contact for field sales, telemarketing is growing in popularity. Different types of salespeople include order takers, technical specialists, missionary salespeople, and order getters. Today's salesperson is less likely to practise transactional selling, that is, hard-sell tactics. Instead, salespeople today often engage in relationship selling, seeking to develop mutually satisfying relationships with customers.

The steps in the personal selling process include prospecting, qualifying the prospects, the pre-approach, the approach, making the sales presentation, overcoming customer objections, closing the sale, and follow-up after the sale.

6. Explain the job of the sales manager.

Sales management means planning, implementing, and controlling the selling function. The responsibilities of a sales manager are setting sales force objectives and creating a sales force strategy, including specifying sales territories, recruiting, training, and rewarding salespeople.

CHAPTER REVIEW

Marketing Concepts: Testing Your Knowledge

1. What is advertising and what is its role in marketing?
2. What are the strengths and weaknesses of television, radio, newspapers, magazines, out-of-home media, and the Internet for advertising?
3. How can advertisers make sure their advertising is effective before it is placed in the media, and what criteria can be used to critique advertising?
4. What is public relations, what is publicity, and when are they likely to be an important part of the communication mix?
5. What is sales promotion? When is sales promotion more likely to be an important part of the communication mix?
6. Explain some of the different types of trade sales and consumer promotions marketers frequently use.
7. What is the role played by personal selling within the total marketing function?
8. What is the difference between transactional selling and relationship selling?
9. List the steps in the creative selling process.
10. Describe the major decisions made by sales managers.

Marketing Concepts: Discussing Choices and Issues

1. Some people are turned off by advertising because they say it is obnoxious, that it insults their intelligence, and that advertising claims are untrue. Others argue that advertising is beneficial and actually provides value for consumers. What are some arguments on each side? How do you feel?
2. Technology through the Internet, television remotes, DVDs, and digital television is giving today's consumers more and more control over the advertising images they see. What are the implications of this for advertising as an industry?
3. Some critics denounce public relations specialists, calling them "flacks" or "spin doctors," whose job is to cover up the truth about a company's problems. What is the proper role of public relations within an organization? Should PR specialists try to put a good face on bad news?
4. Companies sometimes teach consumers a "bad lesson" with the overuse of sales promotion. As a result, consumers expect the product always to be "on deal." What are some examples of products for which this has occurred? How do you think companies can prevent this?
5. In general, professional selling has evolved from hard sell to relationship selling. Does the hard-sell style of selling still exist? If so, in what types of organizations? What do you think the future holds for these organizations? Will the hard sell continue to succeed?
6. M-commerce allows marketers to engage in *location commerce*, in which they can identify where consumers are and send them messages about a local store. Do you think consumers will respond positively to this? What do you think are the benefits for consumers of m-commerce?

Marketing Practice: Applying What You've Learned

1. Assume that you are working in the media department of an advertising agency. You have been asked your opinion on which media to use for advertising for a local retail-clothing store.
   a. Write a memo that compares newspapers, magazines, television, radio, and outdoor advertising as vehicles for this media plan.
   b. Write a memo assessing the appropriateness of each of these media for advertising a national brand of dog food.
2. As a public relations professional employed by your college or university, you have been asked to develop recommendations for improving your school's public relations program. Write a memo to your college or university president with your recommendations.

3. Assume that you are a member of the marketing department for a firm that produces several brands of household cleaning products. Your assignment is to develop recommendations for trade and consumer sales promotion activities for a new brand of laundry detergent. Develop an outline of your recommendations for sales promotions for the new detergent.

4. Timing is an important part of a sales promotion plan. When is the best time to mail out samples, to offer trade discounts, to sponsor a sweepstakes? Assume the introduction of the new laundry detergent in question 3 is planned for April 1. Place the activities you recommended in question 3 on a 12-month calendar. In a role-playing situation, present your plan to your supervisor. Be sure to explain why you have included certain types of promotions and the reasons for your timing of each promotion activity.

5. You have been newly hired as a field salesperson by a firm that markets college and university textbooks. As part of your training, your sales manager has asked that you develop an outline of what you will say in a typical sales presentation. Write that outline.

6. As a sales manager for a firm that sells heavy construction equipment, you are evaluating the current sales force compensation plan. Currently, salespeople are paid straight commission, but you are thinking that moving to straight salary or a combination salary and commission plan might be better.

   a. With one of your classmates taking the other side, present your arguments for each option in a role-playing situation.

   b. In a similar role-playing situation, present arguments for different compensation plans that might be used in a retail-clothing store.

   c. In a similar role-playing situation, present arguments for different compensation plans that might be used by a new car sales force.

Marketing Mini-Project: Learning by Doing

Many college and university students say that they are "absolutely, completely lost" when it comes to knowing what type of job they want, much less how to look for the ideal job. This project gives you experience in the beginning steps in the creative selling process; but in this case, your potential customers are potential employers and the "product" you will be selling is yourself. You might find the information included on the Pearson Education Canada Companion website (**www.pearsoned.ca/solomon**) helpful for this project.

1. Your first task is to identify a list of characteristics of jobs you might find attractive—your target market. You may consider such characteristics as:

   a. Geographic location

   b. Size of company (local, regional, national, international)

   c. Type of business

   d. Job responsibilities

   e. Skills required

2. One method used by salespeople for identifying potential job prospects is through networking. Therefore, with one or more members of your class, seek to talk with other people for their suggestions and to find out if they know of any jobs that have the characteristics you have outlined for your target market.

3. Using the resources of your school or your college or university library, generate a list of potential employers that seem to match your target market.

4. Using library resources or personal contacts if available, find out as much as you can about each potential employer.

5. Based on the information you have gathered, classify these employers as A, B, or C leads. "A" leads warrant more of your time and effort. "C" leads warrant the least level of time and effort, because you have determined that their fit with your target market is not very good.

6. With your group, present your findings to your class.

Real People, Real Surfers: Exploring the Web

A problem that has confronted marketers for several years is how to efficiently distribute coupons. Some companies find the Internet to be a useful medium for this. In fact, a number of websites have been developed solely for the purpose of distributing coupons, including:

www.valpak.com
www.coupons.com
www.happycoupons.com
www.simplybestcoupons.ca

Visit several of these websites, or use an Internet search engine to identify other coupon sites. Then evaluate the different sites you've visited by answering the following questions.

1. Generally describe each coupon website you visited. What kinds of coupons were there? How do consumers take advantage of the offers?

2. What about the design of each website is most useful to you as a consumer?

3. Do you think the coupons offered by the websites are useful to many consumers? Do you think consumers visit the website on a regular basis? What do you think would be some of the characteristics of the type of consumer most likely to be a regular visitor to these sites?

4. As a marketer, would you be likely to try to distribute coupons for your products over the websites? Why or why not?

5. How would you improve each of the websites you visited?

Founded in 1998 by a group of athletes and headed by Chip Wilson, founder of surf and skateboard brand Westbeach, Vancouver-based lululemon athletica has become a retailing phenomenon in Canada. With 57 stores in four countries and 1700 employees, it has become one of the fastest-growing apparel companies in the world. The company sells yoga-inspired apparel and accessories designed for both women and men. The company owes much of its success to the dramatic increase in the popularity of yoga. In Canada, between 2001 and 2006 participation in yoga increased 136 percent, making it the number one trend in sport.

lululemon athletica has achieved this success without huge marketing budgets and with minimal traditional advertising. The company chooses local (preferably free) community papers to announce its store openings. Relying heavily on word-of-mouth, the company identifies role models, including yoga instructors and other female athletes and community role models, to act as ambassadors for its brand. These community leaders are chosen because they embody the active and healthy lifestyle that is at the heart of the lululemon athletica brand. They are given a lululemon athletica clothing allowance for a year. They are asked to wear and provide feedback on the clothing. They also spread the word within the community—educating the community on the benefits of lululemon athletica clothing. These ambassadors are also used to hire and train staff for the new location. This community engagement is a pillar of the lululemon brand.

In addition to strong WOM, Wilson has a knack for pulling together stunts that get people talking about the brand. For a Vancouver store opening, the first 30 people who showed up in the buff were awarded a free top and bottom. More than 40 Vancouverites arrived in robes and were told to get naked and stand outside the store for 30 seconds. The store made headlines—even getting coverage on CNN.

For a recent store opening in Toronto, lululemon athletica launched a yoga-themed scavenger hunt, inviting consumers to apply, along with a friend, for their chance to win a $1500 shopping spree. lululemon athletica selected 20 teams from all the entrants, who were asked to explain, in 100 words or less, why they should be chosen to participate. The event was kicked off with *Canadian Idol* judges Zach Werner, Jake Gold, and Farley Flex at the starting line. The scavenger hunt featured yoga challenges in predetermined checkpoints, and contestants were allowed to travel only by foot or public transportation. All contestants wore lululemon athletica "Get Off Your Asana" T-shirts.

The lululemon athletica brand lends itself well to word-of-mouth advertising because the product is clearly of superior quality. Their active wear is constructed of anti-microbial wicking fabrics, using sewing machines that cost around $25 000 that make flat seams, ensuring it is non-abrasive to the wearer. While the clothing is primarily made for athletes, it can be used by anyone for any activity or as street wear.

The company is looking to grow aggressively in the United States in the near future, with as many as 60 new stores over the next two years. More than a few Canadian companies have tried to make the move south of the border with less than positive results. lululemon athletica is looking to duplicate the grassroots marketing strategy that served it so well in Canada and is confident that its winning formula will translate well in the U.S. market.

At the same time, the company cannot lose focus on the Canadian market. Industry experts warn that it is difficult to maintain momentum at the retail level over the long term. Competition is on the rise, with companies such as Lotuswear springing up to capitalize on the "street wear" trend. How long can lululemon athletica stick with its grassroots marketing campaigns before they wear thin?

Sources: Grant Surridge, "Lululemon leaps in market debut," *National Post*, 28 July 2007: FP1; Aideen McCormick, "Yoga numbers," *Calgary Herald*, 19 August 2007: D2; Joanne Blain, "Street yoga," *The Vancouver Sun*, 31 July 2007: C1.

Things to Think About

1. What is the decision facing lululemon athletica?

2. What factors are important to understanding this decision situation?

3. What are the alternatives?

4. What decision(s) do you recommend?

5. Using the model provided in Chapter 12, devise an integrated marketing communications plan for lululemon athletica.

CHAPTER 14
Developing and Implementing a Marketing Plan

CHAPTER OBJECTIVES

WHEN YOU HAVE COMPLETED YOUR STUDY OF THIS CHAPTER, YOU SHOULD BE ABLE TO

1. Explain why firms develop and implement marketing plans.

2. Describe the steps involved in developing and implementing a marketing plan.

3. Highlight dos and don'ts in developing a strong marketing plan.

4. Understand the importance of monitoring customer satisfaction and customer retention.

5. Describe what causes customer satisfaction and dissatisfaction.

6. Describe methods to measure customer satisfaction.

7. Explain why business organizations go beyond measuring customer satisfaction to monitoring customer retention.

Real People, Real Decisions

Meet **Jaimie Love,** a Decision Maker at j.love handbags

Jaimie Love loves sewing. She grew up in Calgary and was taught to sew by her grandmother when she was only four years old. She immediately fell in love with it and spent many hours making clothes for her dolls. In her teenage years she took as many home economics courses as Central Memorial High School offered, and it was always her strongest and favourite subject. Jaimie knew that she wanted to pursue a career in fashion design, but rather than taking Fine Arts in university, she decided to go to the University of Victoria (UVic) to take a B.Com. in entrepreneurship and learn what it takes to start and run a successful business. Jaimie chose UVic because of the cultural diversity, real-life work experience, international opportunities, and integrative cohort structure—and it was a pretty nice place to live.

After arriving at UVic, school became a priority, so sewing was put on hold until the summer after her second year. It was the first summer that Jaimie stayed in Victoria, and she decided it was time to become serious about sewing. Handbags were always her favourite thing to sew, so she researched all the outdoor markets in Victoria and applied with her handbags to attend the Government Street Market. Sales were quite slow, but that did not discourage Jaimie, as the women who attended the Government Street Market tended to be older than the women Jaimie thought would be most interested in the handbags. The following fall she set up a booth at an on-campus market and sold more than 50 handbags in two days. She continued to sell handbags to friends, classmates, and co-workers, but due to hectic school and work schedules she stopped participating in markets.

After completing her "core" courses, Jaimie took UVic's integrative, five-course Entrepreneurship specialization—the program she had been particularly interested in when choosing to come to UVic. The program began in May with a 10-day Innovation Project, where Jaimie and her classmates were challenged with starting a new venture and making as much economic, social, and/or environmental value as possible within 10 days (while going to school full time). She offered her sewing talents to her team and they made a respectable profit in the 10 days. The concept that she was most passionate about was custom handbags—unique pieces of art inspired by the customer in consultation with the designer. The feedback she had gotten from her friends, peers, and current customers was that having a unique item was important—particularly if it communicated something about the style and taste of the buyer.

The rest of the summer was a mix of entrepreneurship theory, practical experiences, and opportunities to build specific entrepreneurial skills, all designed to help Jaimie become an expert entrepreneur within five years of graduation. One of the required assignments was to create a marketing plan (and then a business plan) for a new venture. This was Jaimie's opportunity to create the foundations for the business she had always wanted to start: j.love handbags.

After a month of research—both secondary (industry and competitor) research and primary (qualitative consumer) research—Jamie had focused on four business models for j.love handbags:

Option 1: Supplier to established fashion retail stores.

One option was to focus on product design and manufacturing and sell her handbags through current fashion retailers that focused on the same target market as Jaimie. This would allow Jaimie to focus on the creative side of the business: both product design and branding—and that was the part she liked most. She could make prototypes and solicit listings with fashion boutiques and then either outsource the manufacturing to sewers in China, or as sales grew, establish her own mass manufacturing capability. This option would allow her to start small—having a few outlets carrying her brand—but would also allow her to expand quickly by hiring salespeople to manage relationships with distributors, and someone to manage the manufacturing relationships. Jaimie thought that this option would probably make her the most money, but one key disadvantage of this option was that it was basically the same concept as all the other handbag producers. It would be difficult to offer custom handbags in volume without losing control over the customer relationship. She thought that most retailers would just want to sell handbags, not spend time with customers to help them design their own. On the other hand, the potential for having a large scale national or even international brand was appealing.

Option 2: Create a boutique.

Another option was to create a small boutique where Jaimie could interact with customers and make custom handbags. She would have a line of pre-made handbags for those customers who did not want to wait and pay more for a custom bag, but this way she would get to interact with customers directly. While this approach would be more personally satisfying, it would also be a much smaller scale business. In the beginning Jaimie would be the designer, manufacturer, sales rep, and store manager. If the concept proved profitable others could be hired over time to handle some of these tasks, but the concept would still be limited by the number of hours in her day. On the other hand, it would be a lot less risky and would give her direct feedback from customers as she refined her concept and designs.

Option 3: Create a boutique, then franchise.

Once the boutique concept was proven to be successful, she could expand via a franchise model. Jaimie would provide the business concept, design expertise, branding expertise, manufacturing, and relationships with suppliers to help others establish similar boutique operations across the country and perhaps internationally. The key challenge with this option was to have a sufficiently strong brand name that others would want to create and sell j.love handbags rather than their own. Jaimie thought that her marketing training and experience would enable her to do this. The ideal franchisees would be those who were interested in fashion accessories and good with customers, but who could not create the handbags themselves or develop the same level of brand recognition. This option would mean a lot more focus on recruiting franchisees and managing franchisee relationships, and less time interacting with customers. But it could be very rewarding financially.

Option 4: Etail sales.

Rather than investing in physical space, Jaimie wondered if this concept could be implemented online. Jaimie didn't know if customers would buy a handbag online. Her experience had been that customers like to feel the material, try on the strap, and walk around with the bag before buying it. However, with a liberal return policy, these issues might be overcome. Certainly it would be relatively easy to create a website where customers could build their own handbag by selecting styles, fabrics, colours, and options. This would allow Jaimie to solicit customers anywhere in the world. There would not be the same interpersonal relationships with customers, but there would also not be the problems of running a retail business and a manufacturing business at the same time. She could hire someone with etail expertise and concentrate on the design and manufacturing aspects of the business.

Faced with needing to write a marketing plan and a business plan, Jaimie needed to decide which business model she was going to pursue. Which option would you choose and why?

"IF YOU FAIL TO PLAN, YOU PLAN TO FAIL"

Whether a firm is a not-for-profit organization like the United Way, a family-based retailer like Army & Navy, or a major manufacturer like Bombardier, planning for the future is the key to prosperity. Success in the competitive world of business is not accidental; businesses that succeed do so because they are capable of developing and implementing *superior* strategies in the marketplace. A recent study tracking the fate of 160 businesses over a 10-year time period found exactly that—organizations that outperformed their industry peers did so because they developed superior strategies and executed those strategies flawlessly.[1]

As we saw in Chapter 2, business organizations develop plans at three levels: strategic, marketing, and functional. We also saw that the marketing plan is a crucial document that links the high-level strategic plan with the functional (or operational) plans developed by various functions such as sales, HR, production, and finance.

This chapter is devoted entirely to the topic of developing and implementing marketing plans. Read this chapter carefully and practise the exercises at the end of the chapter, and you will be in a position to develop winning marketing plans on your own!

WHY DEVELOP A MARKETING PLAN?

The development of a marketing plan enables a business to set priorities regarding markets it wants to compete in (market segments), customers it wants to serve (target customers), and how it plans to serve those customers (marketing mix decisions).

Without such priorities, the firm will not have a viable product at a price customers are willing to pay, the means to get that product to the place customers want it, and a way to promote the product to the right customers. In other words, without the development of a sound **marketing plan**, the business tends to drift.

WHAT HAPPENS WHEN A BUSINESS DOES NOT DEVELOP A MARKETING PLAN?

The underlying goal of all marketing strategies and plans is to create a **competitive advantage** for the business—to take what the company does really well and outperform the competition, thus providing customers with a benefit the competition cannot. A competitive advantage gives customers a reason to choose one product over another again and again.

marketing plan A document that describes the marketing environment, outlines the marketing objectives and strategy, identifies who will be responsible for carrying out each part of the marketing strategy, and describes how the strategy will be adjusted to respond to a changing marketplace.

competitive advantage The ability of a firm to outperform the competition, providing customers with a benefit the competition cannot.

Table 14.1 Negative Consequences of Not Developing Marketing Plans

1. **The business tends to drift.**
   Lacking superior strategies, the business continually underperforms.

2. **There is a lot of "pie-in-the-sky" thinking, but no formal strategy.**
   Without formal strategies to compete in a tough marketplace, the business thinks about success, but it never comes to fruition.

3. **The business tends to waste resources trying one tactic after another.**
   Without a plan of action, the business attempts many things without knowing in advance the likehood of their success.

4. **The business lacks a "playbook."**
   A marketing plan is like a playbook for a sports team. Without a playbook, there is no accountability within different functions.

5. **There is no unity within the organization.**
   Lacking a "glue" that binds the business together, different functions work to optimize specific interests instead of focusing on the customer.

Without a formal marketing plan outlining superior marketing strategies, most businesses underperform for years. Eventually, many of these firms go out of business. As we have repeated before, success in the competitive world of business is *earned*; it is not a right. When a business organization conducts itself without developing formal marketing plans, it faces many negative consequences, such as outlined in Table 14.1.[2] Without a formal marketing plan, businesses tend to engage in a lot of "pie-in-the-sky" thinking: "The market is worth $1 billion. All we have to do is capture 1 percent of it." This may be true, but without a formal strategy, how is the business going to capture any of it?

As a result, businesses without formal marketing plans tend to try one tactic, and if that does not work, they try another. They end up wasting resources. A sound marketing plan enables a business to utilize its limited resources in an optimum fashion.

As also shown in Table 14.1, a marketing plan is like a "playbook" for a sports team. Imagine the fate of a football team without a playbook! There would be complete chaos on the field. Similarly, as you will see when we turn to the topic of actually developing a marketing plan, a marketing plan clearly outlines a detailed set of tactics to implement each marketing strategy. So, everyone within the business knows exactly what they have to do and how long they have to do it.

Finally, as we saw in Chapter 2, the marketing plan provides a common foundation for the development of other functional plans (e.g., sales, HR, production, finance). Therefore, without a formal marketing plan there is no unity among the different functions in a business. Each function is motivated to act in its best interests, and not in the collective interests of the customer.

Table 14.1 explored the negative consequences of not developing superior marketing strategies encoded in the form of marketing plans. On the other hand, as shown in Exhibit 14.1, successful firms such as Sony succeed by understanding customer needs and developing superior offerings to satisfy those needs.

Exhibit 14.1

Sony succeeds by understanding customer needs and developing superior offerings to satisfy those needs.

When Sony initially came out with a digital camera, it quickly captured over a 40 percent share of the market, even though its camera's picture quality was inferior to the competition's. This is because Sony developed a superior marketing plan based on its understanding of customer needs. It correctly recognized that customers would be willing to sacrifice picture quality for ease of use. So, it developed a camera that would enable users to insert floppy disks into the camera, take pictures, and instantly upload the pictures on their computers without the fuss of memory cards or cables.

HOW TO DEVELOP STRONG MARKETING PLANS: THE MARKETING PLAN TEMPLATE

Table 14.2 outlines a practical template you can use to develop sound marketing plans. As can be seen from the marketing plan template, a typical marketing plan has nine different sections. A good marketing plan can be written in about 8 to 10 pages, single spaced (plus exhibits), if focused on one target market. It is important to familiarize yourself with the general layout of the marketing plan. Although it may look complicated, the marketing plan actually is a very simple document that has *four* major sections, as outlined in Figure 14.1.

The four sections are:

1. Identify value creation opportunities in the marketplace by understanding customers, competitors, your own organization, and other factors in the internal and external environment.
2. Specify the value proposition by identifying your objectives, target market, and positioning strategy.
3. Create, communicate, and deliver the value by designing marketing mix strategies.
4. Realize the value by developing tactical plans, systems to monitor performance, and contingency plans for corrective action; then evaluate the value created for both the customer and the organization using market research and financial and other analysis.

The four major sections of the marketing plan play an important role in that the output from one section forms the input for the next section. Let us turn to this topic next.

Using the Marketing Plan Template

Now that we have examined the marketing plan's overall structure, let us examine each of the nine sections to see why they are there and what role they play in the overall marketing plan development.

Ethical Decisions in Marketing

Marketers invest considerable time, effort, and money attracting customers, but large and small organizations alike have found that some customers are simply not worth having. Some customers can actually cost you money—taking more resources to service and satisfy them than the profit generated on their purchases. Consultant Ian Gordon suggests that organizations should "fire" the customers they lose money on.[3]

It is not hard to find out who these 25 to 30 percent of customers are. Many companies have a mountain of customer information gathered from scanners and smart cash registers, credit card summaries, call centres, and customer feedback programs that can be mined with simple software tools to identify the most profitable and least profitable customers. Clearnet, for example, tries to assess the value of every customer. It steeply discounts the sales of cellphones to attract a long-term stream of monthly phone usage. If a customer is not generating sufficient revenue to warrant Clearnet's investment in the phone, Clearnet first tries to get them to use it more and then tries to reduce the cost of servicing the customer by reducing service levels. As a last resort, it will cut off the phone service, buy back the phone for what the customer paid for it, and politely suggest that another service provider would better meet that customer's needs.[4] In the airline industry, WestJet has cut unprofitable routes while Air Canada is mandated to keep basic service levels, even if it loses money on them. The Bank of Montreal, like most financial institutions, uses research and Customer Relationship Management (CRM) software to help it develop highly detailed segment profiles—helping it to group customers by their profitability, and focus attention on retaining the most profitable customers.

Identifying market segments and choosing target markets is central to marketing strategy. However, there are some controversial and potentially discriminatory practices when it comes to serving the needs and wants of some customers and not others. What do you think? Is it acceptable for organizations to "fire" customers or not do business with those in less desirable segments? Is it acceptable for companies to identify their most profitable customers and focus their efforts on retaining those customers, or should customers be treated equally?

Table 14.2 Marketing Plan Template

i.   Executive Summary
ii. Table of Contents
iii. Situation/Environment Analysis
    SWOT Summary
    Segmentation
    Positioning Maps
    Other Analysis
iv. Opportunity Identification/Assessment
    & Assumptions
v.   Objectives
vi. Marketing Strategy
    Target Market Selection
    Target Market Profiles
    Positioning
        Strategic Orientation
        Differentiation
        Defendability
        Brand Personality
vii. Marketing Mix Decisions (by Target Market)
    Product Decisions
        Concept
        Product Line
        Service Strategy
        Branding
        Package & Label
    Pricing Decisions
        Objectives
        Policy
        Price Points & Tactics
        Terms & Conditions
    Distribution Decisions   (Retail Distribution)
        Objectives   Objectives
        System   Store Image
        Channel Mgmt   Store Design
        Supply Chain Mgmt   Merchandising
        CRM   Staffing/Personnel
                Store Location/Hours

    Communication Decisions
        Audience & Objectives
        Approach
        Key Messages & Tactics
        Communication Mix
        Budget & Allocation
        Implementation
viii. Implementation & Evaluation
    Plan the Implementation
        Action Plans (Tactical Considerations)
        Task Schedule (timeline, responsibilities)
        Evaluation & Control Plan
           Goals/Benchmarks by period
           Tracking Systems & Measures
        Contingency Plan/Corrective Actions
        Research Plan (to test key assumptions)
        Budget & Financial Projections
    Evaluation
        Value to the Organization
           Financial Analysis
           Cost-Benefit Analysis
           Go–No Go Decision
        Value to the Customer
           Perceived Value
           Purchase Intentions
           Value in Use
           Customer Satisfaction
           Customer Retention
ix. Appendices
    SWOT Details
    Detailed Segment Profiles
    Annotated Pro-Forma Income Statement
    Other Supporting Material

SECTION I. EXECUTIVE SUMMARY The Executive Summary section is a one-page summary of the marketing plan. It outlines to the reader:

- The key strategic issues or challenges facing the business (from your SWOT analysis)
- Your objectives and key strategies to achieve these objectives
- Key expected outcomes (financial and non-financial)

Therefore, reading the Executive Summary tells us what objectives will be pursued and how, and what rewards await us at the end of the plan period if we implement our strategies well. The Executive Summary should be able to be read as a stand-alone document. It is not an introduction, it is a snapshot of your plan. An executive summary is typically one page or less in length. It typically does not include the rationale for your decisions (this is in the body of your plan).

SECTION II. TABLE OF CONTENTS After the Executive Summary section, a Table of Contents section appears so that one can see what areas the plan covers. This helps the reader navigate more easily through the marketing plan.

Figure 14.1 Major Sections of a Marketing Plan

	Text Chapter
Identify Value Opportunities	**Sections iii, iv**
–opportunity identification/assessment	CH 1, 3
–situation/environment analysis	CH 2, 5, 6
–assumptions	
Specify the Value	**Sections v, vi**
–objectives to be achieved	CH 2
–marketing strategy	CH 3
–segmentation	
–positioning	
Create, Communicate, & Deliver the Value	**Section vii**
–marketing mix decisions	CH 8–13
Implement & Evaluate the Value	**Sections viii, ix**
–implementation	CH 14
–evaluation	CH 14

SECTION III. ENVIRONMENTAL ANALYSIS In this section of the plan we provide the foundation of analysis on which our plan is built. This section typically has four key elements.

1. *SWOT Analysis Summary.* Your full SWOT analysis should go in an exhibit. What you want to report here are the key factors in the internal and external environment that influence your marketing strategy decisions. Recall from Chapter 2 that SWOT analysis involves identifying the strategic implications of key environmental factors. It is the relevance of those strategic implications that determine how important they are to your marketing decisions. Note that the environmental analysis on which the SWOT analysis is based is also often included in an appendix so that the readers and users of the plan can be confident that the plan is based on a solid understanding of the decision environment.

2. *Segmentation.* Your SWOT analysis would have included a consumer analysis, but here you should identify the major segments in the market (which you need to define or specify here); justify your segmentation approach; and estimate the relative size of these segments (providing evidence to support your estimates if possible). A short (three- or four-sentence) description of each segment (key attributes and differentiating factors) will help the reader understand what the segments are all about. These profile summaries should briefly identify the key needs, wants, and preferences of the segments and how these may be changing over time.

3. *Positioning Maps.* Your SWOT analysis would have included competitor analysis, but a series of positioning maps that illustrate the relative positioning of key brands in the market will help communicate the competitive landscape. Annotating your positioning maps with assessments of the competing organizations and brands can be helpful.

4. *Other Analysis.* As you progress through your marketing and business education you will learn more tools and concepts that can help you and readers of the plan better understand the decision environment. Some key concepts in this text such as diffusion of innovation, the product life cycle, services considerations, the BCG Growth-Share Matrix, and the FCB grid could also be used effectively to understand the decision environment.

As you can see, up to this point we have assessed the marketplace and come to certain conclusions about what major issues we will have to address during the next year. At this point it should be fairly clear what actions we will need to take to serve the market well and be an effective competitor. In other words, the marketing plan should *almost* write itself (with your help!).

SECTION IV. OPPORTUNITY IDENTIFICATION, ASSESSMENT, AND ASSUMPTIONS In this section, we draw conclusions from our analysis and specify what opportunity (or problems/issues) we plan to take advantage of, or address, in our marketing plan. We justify our focus on this/these opportunities (or problems) and not others, and clearly state what market(s) we plan to serve with what product(s), using what technologies (know-how). If possible, we quantify this opportunity by using market research to assess how attractive it is, what piece of the market we can expect to attain, what slice of the market our competitors already have, and other factors that may impact our ability to create value for customers. However, it is not always possible to have conducted extensive market research before writing a plan, so we also identify here any key assumptions about the market, the opportunity, and the decision environment on which our plan is based.

SECTION V. OBJECTIVES TO BE ACHIEVED BY THE MARKETING PLAN In the previous section we identified the major issues to be addressed by the marketing plan. However, if we left it at that, we would not have any way of monitoring the success or failure of the marketing plan. Therefore, we need to establish certain objectives to be achieved by the plan.

In this section we begin by establishing financial objectives to be achieved by the marketing plan. These objectives are stated in the form of revenues and profits (which might be a break-even target for a not-for-profit organization). Next, we convert these financial objectives into actionable marketing objectives and highlight other functional objectives, if appropriate (e.g., sales, HR). Objectives should be SMART: Specific, Measurable, Actionable, Realistic, and Time bounded. Writing down financial objectives by themselves will not ensure that we actually achieve them. We have to perform some marketing actions to make an impact in the marketplace and thereby achieve our financial objectives. These marketing objectives enable us to develop specific marketing actions. We turn to this in the next section.

SECTION VI. MARKETING STRATEGIES This section is the engine that drives the marketing plan. It outlines our efforts to specify the value proposition for customers by selecting our target market(s), developing detailed profiles of our target market(s), then specifying the positioning that we want to establish in the minds of those customers. You should provide rationale for why you have selected the target markets you have chosen and why you rejected other viable alternatives. Recall from Chapter 3 that positioning involves specifying the basis of differentiation for your brand, your strategic orientation (how you will compete, create value, and develop competitive advantage), how you will be able to defend your desired positioning, and your brand personality. The strategies tell us generally how we will compete and achieve our objectives. They are executed by our specific marketing mix decisions.

SECTION VII. MARKETING MIX DECISIONS This section is the heart of the marketing plan. It outlines our specific decisions for creating value for our customers (and consequently ourselves). As discussed in Chapters 7 through 13 of the text, each marketing mix element (product, pricing, distribution, and communication) involves a set of decisions, which are summarized in Table 14.2. You should provide a brief rationale for each decision that you make, drawing on your analysis, understanding of your target market, and marketing concepts, tools, and principles. Although a marketing plan is an internal document (used within an organization), the rationale is important to include, both to justify the conclusions to other stakeholders within the organization and to provide a basis from which others can critique the plan. A recommendation without the rationale for why it makes sense in a particular context is not worth the paper it is written on. If you are writing a plan that targets more than one market segment, organize your marketing mix discussion by target market (i.e., write a complete marketing mix section for each market segment).

SECTION VIII. IMPLEMENTATION AND EVALUATION In this section we examine our strategies from the previous section and, for *each* strategy, we delineate our tactical action plans for how the strategy will be executed. We have to be very specific about what needs to be done (action steps), when it will be done, who will do it, what resources will be needed, and what we will do in case of "roadblocks" to our plan. This often includes a task schedule that specifies who will do what, by when. An evaluation and control plan specifies how the results will be assessed. Performance benchmarks (targets) need to be specified (with a timeline) to determine whether or not the strategy has been successful. Systems are specified for tracking the monitoring information and measures are identified for the key variables of interest—such as customer satisfaction or loyalty. You will learn more about this later in this chapter.

A marketing plan is a living, breathing document. As such, it needs to be monitored constantly to ensure goals are being met and progress is being made. If the targets are not met then corrective action needs to be taken, and this is the focus of a contingency plan—what you will do if the original strategy and tactics do not work as expected. Because you have had to make some key assumptions to write your plan, you need a section that outlines: (a) which of these assumptions need to be tested (an assessment which is based on **sensitivity analysis**), and (b) your research plan to get the needed information. Finally, we need to specify what it will cost to implement the plan. A budget is created that specifies what resources are needed, where those resources will come from, and how they will be spent (sources and uses of funds statement). Also typically included is a pro-forma (forecast) income statement that specifies the expected revenues, expenses, and profit (or loss) from implementing the plan. This pro-forma income statement needs to be annotated (footnoted) to explain the key assumptions in the financial analysis—such as the sales forecast and costs, and how you came up with the numbers you have used.

> **sensitivity analysis** An analytic technique of testing how important an assumption is. Financial analysis is conducted under different assumptions for a key value. If the same marketing decision would be made under any assumption of the value, then the results are not sensitive to that value. If your decision would change depending on the number used, then research is needed to determine the correct value.

Many marketing plans go astray because they lack a detailed implementation section. This is the way we assign responsibility for implementing the plan and ensuring that the plan does not get placed on a shelf somewhere to be forgotten.

Before we implement a marketing plan we need to assess whether it makes sense to do so at all. We really can't make that assessment until the plan is written because the likely success of the plan depends on the strategies and tactics that we have devised. We make this assessment from two perspectives: value to the organization and value to the customer. As a marketing organization, our "prime directive" is to achieve the long-term goals of the organization. Thus we need to assess whether our plan helps us do that. Specifically, we conduct financial analysis by examining the pro-forma income statement created in the previous section and comparing the expected results to either organization standards (Microsoft, for example, only enters markets where it can expect dominant market share), internal cost of capital (comparing the returns to a standard expected return), or the returns of other projects (comparing the expected outcomes to the expected outcomes of other projects). This financial analysis might also include scenario analysis where best case, worst case, and perhaps other scenarios (differences in assumptions for key figures in the analysis) are compared.

Also typically included is a cost-benefit analysis. Cost-benefit analysis compares all the advantages of implementing the plan to all the disadvantages. Some of these advantages and disadvantages are quantitative (number based) and some are qualitative (judgment based). The data for the cost-benefit analysis comes from your SWOT analysis, consumer analysis, competitive analysis, and all the other analyses conducted in creating your plan. More sophisticated approaches try to quantify the qualitative factors so that the cost-benefit of one project can be compared objectively to the cost-benefit of another project.

In the end, the decision makers have to make a recommendation. That is, they have to decide whether or not to implement the plan. The rationale for this decision comes from the previously conducted financial analysis and cost-benefit analysis, drawing on marketing concepts, tools, and principles.

Value is also assessed from the customer's perspective. In the end, no one will buy what you have to offer unless they think it is more valuable than the money they have in their pocket (or bank account). Market research is conducted to test perceived value and purchase

value-in-use analysis Analysis that quantifies the cost-benefit analysis from the customer's perspective, specifying what the customer will gain or save by using the product relative to the cost of buying, using, and disposing of the product. After the plan has been implemented, markets track customer satisfaction and retention as indicators of customer value creation.

intentions. **Value-in-use analysis** attempts to quantify the cost-benefit analysis from the customer's perspective, specifying what the customer will gain or save by using the product relative to the cost of buying, using, and disposing of the product.

SECTION IX. APPENDICES By now you will have realized that a lot of analysis goes into writing a marketing plan. Readers of the plan do not want to sort through pages and pages of analysis. They want to know that the analysis has been done well, can be relied upon, and what conclusions should be drawn from it. Consequently, a lot of the analytic details can go in an appendix—available for review but not burdensome for the reader. Typical appendices include environmental analysis, SWOT details, detailed segment profiles, an annotated pro-forma income statement, other analyses or supporting material such as positioning maps, and other details such as illustrative communication elements. Be sure to reference appendix material in the main body of the plan. It is also important to summarize the content of each appendix in the marketing plan when you refer to it, so that the reader does not have to look at the appendix to understand the main conclusion(s) from that analysis.

DOS AND DON'TS IN DEVELOPING A STRONG MARKETING PLAN

Table 14.3 lists dos and don'ts that need to be followed to develop strong marketing plans.

As we discussed in Chapter 2, the marketing plan is the foundation upon which all other plans are built. Therefore, keep the focus of the marketing plan on *major* strategies and tactics to be implemented during the time period (i.e., one year) to create value for your customers. *Do not try to do it all next year.* As has been wisely suggested, you are better off being short on strategy and long on implementation, rather than the other way around.[5]

A good marketing plan should be a highly *actionable* document. So, keep the plan short (approximately 10–15 pages, single spaced) and simple. As necessary, individual "brand" plans may be developed for each product (e.g., goods, services offered, programs) or separate plans can be created for each target market. Do not provide information that is interesting but does not directly impact your strategies to serve customers.

To ensure you have a short and actionable plan, focus on the implications, the "so what" of data, and not on the data itself. Spend time gathering relevant information (section III) and then spend a *lot* of time thinking about what the information means (section IV). This time, invested up front, is well spent and will enable you to develop meaningful strategies and tactics as you write the plan. Unfortunately, many marketing plans end up being very voluminous and not actionable because the marketing strategist focused on the data rather than their implications. Try not fall into this trap.

Table 14.3 Dos and Don'ts in Developing Strong Marketing Plans

Do:

Focus on key strategies and tactics

Provide rationale for every decision

Keep the marketing plan short and actionable

Focus on the implications, the "so what" of data, and not on the data itself

Develop the marketing plan for a period of one year, but meet periodically to assess progress and examine marketing plan assumptions.

Do not:

Try to write about multiple target markets at the same time

Forget that the marketing plan template is directional

Forget that marketing is everyone's job

Forget that the implementation details are as important as the strategy

SPOTLIGHT ON REAL PEOPLE   Sangam Dairy

Anil Rao, the managing director of a small dairy in India, has to develop a marketing plan. His dairy buys milk directly from farmers, packages the milk in plastic pouches, and sells the product through India's weak channels of distribution. The problem with plastic pouches is that because the "cold chain" (refrigeration in the channel of distribution) is not well developed in India, milk has a tendency to spoil, and therefore homemakers boil (and often re-boil) the milk before using it.

Rao is thinking of introducing milk in an innovative packaging format from Europe. Although still needing refrigeration, the new packaging can stand non-refrigerated formats better than the plastic pouch. Rao's biggest challenge is how to communicate the superior benefits of his package (i.e., no need to boil milk before use), change entrenched household behaviour, and charge a price premium for his product.

1. What recommendations do you have for Rao in terms of marketing plan development?
2. What factors should Rao keep in mind as he develops his marketing strategy?
3. Which elements of the marketing mix do you think should be emphasized in this problem? Are all elements equally important? In either case, provide a rationale for your answer.

The marketing plan should be developed for a period of one year. However, it is necessary to meet periodically (e.g., every quarter) to assess progress and make any corrections to the plan.

Do not forget that the marketing plan template in this chapter is *directional*. This means that you should not view the template as a checklist. Examine each section carefully and assess what it is asking of you. For example, in the section on situational/environmental analysis, only one thing is paramount: Where is there an opportunity to create value? The rest (e.g., consumer analysis, competitor analysis, industry analysis) is merely background material to help you in your analysis of how best to create this value.

"BUSINESS SUCCESS IS NOT DETERMINED BY THE PRODUCER BUT BY THE CUSTOMER"

Years ago, Thomas Bonoma, a Harvard professor, coined the term "marketing inertia" to describe a business organization's inability to adapt to market changes.[6] He argued that a firm's success makes it complacent such that managers are reluctant to tamper with marketing strategies that have been successful in the past. The thinking is, "If it ain't broke, why fix it?"

In this book we have provided you with frameworks, concepts, and marketing tools to be successful. So, it is only fitting that in this last chapter, we show you how to avoid getting trapped by your own success.

Ultimately, it is the customer who determines whether a business succeeds or not. It is for this reason that business organizations pay so much attention to the topic of this chapter— customer satisfaction and customer retention.

IMPORTANCE OF MONITORING CUSTOMER SATISFACTION AND CUSTOMER RETENTION

Research has shown that customer retention (customer loyalty) is the single most important driver of long-term financial performance.[7] But what is the key to customer retention? As shown in Figure 14.2, it is customer satisfaction, which explains why business organizations are so concerned about monitoring customer satisfaction and customer retention. To be successful, a business needs loyal (retained) customers. This is because retained customers are less costly to serve and tend to be more price insensitive.

Figure 14.2 Importance of Monitoring Customer Satisfaction and Customer Retention

Exhibit 14.2

Lexus cares about its customers.

Think about your own behaviour for a minute. Do you have favourite brands? The firms that supply those brands do not need to spend precious marketing communication dollars to attract you because you are already familiar with the brands. Further, it is possible that, in spite of a price increase, you will continue to be loyal to this brand.

As demonstrated in Figure 14.2, customer satisfaction is the key to customer retention. According to Philip Kotler,[8] a highly satisfied customer:

- Stays loyal longer
- Buys more as the company introduces new products and upgrades existing products
- Talks favourably about the company and its products
- Pays less attention to competing brands and advertising, and is less sensitive to price
- Offers product/service ideas to the company
- Costs less to serve than new customers because transactions are routinized

Given the crucial role played by customer satisfaction and customer retention, it is no wonder companies take these topics seriously, as demonstrated by the Lexus ad in Exhibit 14.2.

Lexus is well known in the industry for its high standards of customer care. When the brand was initially introduced in the mid-1980s it took on luxury car brands from Germany by going above and beyond to satisfy the customer. For example, shortly after its launch, a minor defect was discovered in the car. Lexus immediately issued a recall notice, went to each Lexus owner's home, picked up the car, performed the minor repair, and delivered the car (after a thorough wash) back to its home. Such customer service has helped propel Lexus into the ranks of established luxury automobiles.

CAUSES OF CUSTOMER SATISFACTION AND DISSATISFACTION

customer satisfaction The difference between a customer's needs and expectations and the customer's perception that the good or service has met those needs and expectations.

Customer satisfaction can be defined as the consumer's fulfillment response. It is a judgment that a product or service feature, or the product or service itself, provides a pleasurable level of consumption-related fulfillment.[9] Satisfaction is the difference between a customer's needs and expectations and the customer's perception that the good or service has met those needs and expectations. Figure 14.3, adapted from a well-known concept in services marketing called service quality, shows this.[10]

Failure to meet the customer's needs and expectations results in dissatisfaction. According to Figure 14.3, a customer can be dissatisfied because the good or service does not meet expectations. But the customer can also be dissatisfied *even though* the good or service performs as it should if the customer's *perception* is that it does not perform as it should. For this reason, we show in Figure 14.3 that communicating with the customer is key. *Customer communications can influence both customer expectations and customer perceptions.* HSBC knows this very well. As can be seen from Exhibit 14.3, its advertising is clearly aimed at shaping customer expectations about what they can expect from the bank: local expertise.

Let us examine Figure 14.3 in more detail to see how a business can shape customer satisfaction and dissatisfaction.

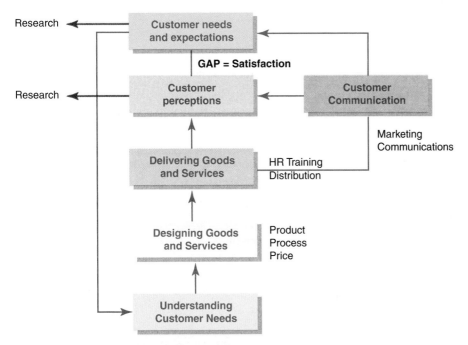

Figure 14.3 Customer Satisfaction and Dissatisfaction

Source: Adapted from the Service Quality Model proposed by Parasuraman, Zeithaml, and Berry (1985).

Understanding Customer Needs

At the heart of any successful strategy to monitor customer satisfaction is the firm's ability to understand the needs and expectations of its customers. Most successful business organizations use a combination of the methods listed in Table 14.4. Many average or underperforming firms either do a poor job of understanding customer needs, or do a poor job of incorporating customer needs into their strategies.[11]

Designing Goods and Services to Satisfy Customer Needs

Unless a business organization has done a first-rate job of understanding customer needs, it cannot develop goods and services to satisfy its customers. Clorox, for example, uses its understanding of customer needs to make life a little easier for its customers.

Delivering Goods and Services

The way in which a good or service is delivered affects customer perceptions and, in this way, impacts satisfaction. Business organizations go to great lengths to ensure that the delivery of goods and services to customers is seamless. Harry Rosen, a high-end clothier across Canada, demonstrates this point in its ad seen in Exhibit 14.4. Harry Rosen not only makes it easy to find the perfect gift through its stores or online, but reassures customers through its no-hassle return policy that shopping at its stores is a breeze.

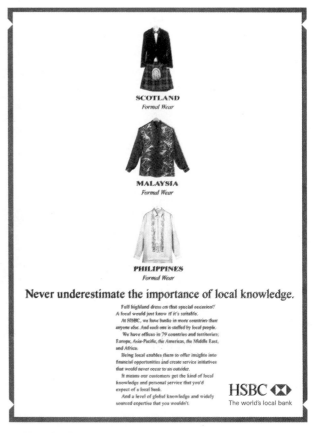

Exhibit 14.3

HSBC is shaping customer expectations.

Table 14.4 Tools to Understand Customer Needs

Marketing Research

As discussed in Chapter 4, many qualitative as well as quantitative marketing research tools are available at a firm's disposal. Common methods to understand customer needs are focus groups and surveys.

Frontline Personnel

Employees who come in direct contact with the customer (e.g., sales force, customer service, technical service) are excellent sources of customer information. Unfortunately, these sources are not very well utilized in many organizations. To fully utilize these sources, it is important to develop formal mechanisms to capture, store, and disseminate frontline personnel information.

Customer Complaints

Strong marketing organizations make it easy for their customers to complain or offer suggestions. Procter & Gamble, for example, provides toll-free phone numbers and websites so that customers can register a complaint or a suggestion. Such corporations correctly recognize that a customer complaint is actually a form of free marketing research.

Exhibit 14.4

Harry Rosen: Excellence in delivering goods and services.

Table 14.5 Tools to Measure Customer Satisfaction

Customer Satisfaction Surveys
Most customer satisfaction surveys have three sections:
(1) a global satisfaction index with the good, service, or firm (typically measured on a 5-point scale, with "Very Dissatisfied" and "Very Satisfied" being the two end points)
(2) a detailed evaluation of the goods and services offered by the firm
(3) intentions to repurchase the firm's offerings

Mystery Shopping
A form of marketing research, mystery shopping involves a researcher buying the firm's goods and services and assessing the purchase experience vis-à-vis the firm's competitors.

Customer Complaint Analysis
Analyzing customer complaints is another way to understand customer satisfaction.

Lost Customer Analysis
Some business organizations contact customers who have stopped being repeat purchasers to assess what went wrong. This provides a good assessment of customer satisfaction levels and what needs to be done to retain customers.

TOOLS TO MEASURE CUSTOMER SATISFACTION

As described in Chapter 4, there are different ways to measure customer satisfaction. Some are shown in Table 14.5. Validity is a key challenge, however. General questions can be interpreted differently by different respondents, and they might not really be answering the same question. For example, imprecise words like "quality" mean different things to different people. In a hotel, quality could mean high-end furniture and fixtures to one respondent and customer service responsiveness to another. Customer service is another term that means different things to different people. When designing a customer satisfaction survey we try to be as precise as possible in what attributes we want customers to rate, and then choose among prioritized attributes to keep the number of questions reasonable.

There is also the issue of variability. Some respondents hold stronger convictions than others, so the same rating, such as 4 out of 5, might be given by one respondent whose response would not vary over time, and by another respondent whose response might change depending on how they feel on a particular day.

MOVING FROM CUSTOMER SATISFACTION TO CUSTOMER RETENTION
Why Is Monitoring Customer Satisfaction Not Enough?

We discussed in Chapter 4 that complete customer satisfaction is required to retain customers, and research shows that respondents who give a score of 5 (out of 5) are six times more likely to be repeat buyers than ones who give a score of 4. This is why marketers focus on customer satisfaction as a key determinant of customer loyalty, but the focus is on customer loyalty and retention.

Figure 14.4 demonstrates how the competitive environment affects the satisfaction–loyalty relationship. As can be seen from the figure, any drop from total satisfaction (e.g., in the automotive industry) results in a precipitous drop in customer loyalty.

How Should You Use Customer Satisfaction Research?

Table 14.6 outlines three stages of actions a firm can take, depending on the bulk of responses to a customer satisfaction survey.

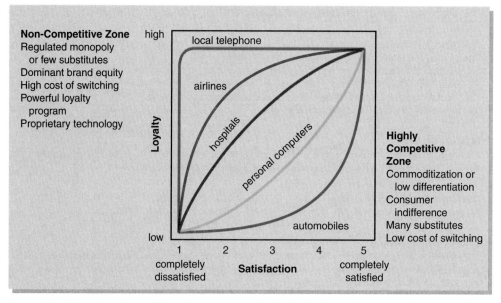

Figure 14.4 How the Competitive Environment Affects the Satisfaction–Loyalty Relationship

Table 14.6 How to Use Customer Satisfaction Information

	Bulk of Responses	Strategic Response
Stage 1	2–3 (dissatisfied)	Deliver the basic product or service elements as expected of anyone in the industry.
Stage 2	3–4 (neutral)	Provide an appropriate range of supporting services. Develop proactive service recovery to make amends when something goes wrong.
Stage 3	4–5 (satisfied)	Understand and achieve results in customers' terms.

Source: Based on Thomas O. Jones and W. Earl Sasser, Jr., "Why satisfied customers defect," *Harvard Business Review*, November–December 1995: 88.

Real People, Real Decisions

▶ How It Worked Out at j.love handbags

When writing her business plan, Jaimie Love chose Option 3: Create a boutique, then eventually franchise. Her passion is the design of handbags, and for now, she really wants the close personal customer relationships that a boutique store would offer—not just because she loves people, but because customer involvement in the design process often results in a superior, more valued product. After proving the concept, she would consider franchising—but only if she could keep a hand in the first store and continue to hone her design sense with the immediate feedback of customers. Developing a strong brand name would be a challenge, but that is a challenge she wants to take on.

She could make prototypes and solicit listings with fashion boutiques (Option 1), but she would not really have any competitive advantage over other handbag designers, other than the uniqueness of her designs, which would be relatively easy for others to copy. Her unique differentiation was in interacting with customers to create a unique design. She did not think this could be done effectively with commission sales representatives in someone else's store, or online.

Jaimie has one more academic term and a cooperative education work term to complete before graduating with her B.Com. degree. She plans to continue sewing handbags in between trips to other parts of the world, where she will source fabrics, beads, and other materials and establish supplier relationships.

According to Table 14.6, a dissatisfied customer (scores of 2 or 3) is not even receiving the basic good or service expected by customers in the industry. This is the equivalent of ordering a meal in a restaurant and not receiving one. Such customers are best served by reviewing the delivery of basic goods and services and making changes to keep pace with industry and technological trends.

A score of 3 or 4 indicates a neutral customer, one who is satisfied with the basic good or service but desires a set of supporting services (e.g., procedures in place when service delivery fails). This is similar to going to a restaurant where you are happy with the food and service, except that when the restaurant gets busy, the level of service tends to fall short. A neutral customer is best served by putting in place proactive service standards to handle situations when service delivery fails.

Finally, a score of 4 or 5 indicates a completely satisfied customer. Companies that excel at this define the good or service experience from the customer's perspective.

Lexus is a good example. It recognized that most dealerships define the experience of getting a car fixed from their own (i.e., internal) perspective. But customers define the experience as the hassle of going to the dealership and dropping off the car, the inconvenience of going without a car, and the hassle involved in picking the car up. So, Lexus, in its quest to completely satisfy the customer, picks up the car at the customer's home or office, repairs and cleans the car, and drops it back at the customer's location.

CHAPTER SUMMARY

Key Terms

1. **Explain why firms develop and implement marketing plans.**

   Smart businesses know that "If you fail to plan, you plan to fail." Firms, both in the for-profit and not-for-profit sector, develop and implement marketing plans because it is through sound marketing planning that they are able to utilize their resources most effectively and achieve their marketing objectives. Organizations that do not develop and implement marketing plans tend to drift because they lack superior strategies and, therefore, the business continually underperforms. A sound marketing plan is like a "playbook" for a sports team. It provides a common direction for all functions and, in this way, unites the entire organization.

   - competitive advantage, p. 503
   - customer satisfaction, p. 512
   - marketing plan, p. 503
   - sensitivity analysis, p. 509
   - value in use analysis, p. 510

2. **Describe the steps involved in developing and implementing a marketing plan.**

   The marketing planning process, as demonstrated by the marketing plan template, begins with a thorough analysis of the external environment facing the firm. This includes the current market situation to ascertain marketplace attractiveness, competitor analysis, analysis of the macro environment (such as cultural or technological trends), and analysis of customer needs and trends. Taken together, the external analysis provides the firm with a set of opportunities and threats.

   Next, the business evaluates the external opportunities and threats by completing a SWOT analysis. Based on the SWOT analysis, the business organization highlights key issues it must address the following year and develops some key financial and non-financial objectives it wants to achieve. The next steps in the development and implementation of a marketing plan are to formulate marketing strategies using the marketing mix elements, outline detailed tactical plans, provide budgets and profit/loss statements, and put in place mechanisms to control the implementation of the plan.

3. **Highlight dos and don'ts in developing a strong marketing plan.**

   A strong marketing plan is an actionable marketing plan. To achieve this, the marketer should focus on the key strategies and tactics, keep the plan short and simple, focus on data analysis (and not the data themselves), understand that the marketing plan template is *not* a checklist, and educate the rest of the organization on the needs of the customer and major sections of the marketing plan.

4. **Understand the importance of monitoring customer satisfaction and customer retention.**

   Research has shown that customer retention (customer loyalty) is the single most important driver of long-term financial performance. Loyal customers tend to be less price sensitive and firms do not have to spend marketing communication dollars in attracting these customers. Customer satisfaction is the single most important factor that impacts customer retention. It is for this reason that firms spend time monitoring customer satisfaction and customer retention.

5. **Describe what causes customer satisfaction and dissatisfaction.**

   Customer satisfaction may be defined as the difference between what a customer expects from a good or service and the customer's perception that the good or service met prior expectations. So, when perceptions equal expectations, we say the customer is satisfied. When there is a mismatch between customer perceptions and expectations, the customer is dissatisfied.
   To satisfy a customer, a business organization needs to do four things well. They are:

   1. Understand customer needs and expectations in an accurate fashion.
   2. Develop goods and services to match customer needs.
   3. Deliver goods and services in a manner that the customer expects.
   4. Influence customer needs (and expectations) and customer perceptions via marketing communications.

6. **Describe methods to measure customer satisfaction.**

   There are four main methods used to measure customer satisfaction.

   1. *Customer Satisfaction Surveys.* Most customer satisfaction surveys have three sections: a global satisfaction index with the good, service, or firm (typically measured on a five-point scale—"Very Dissatisfied" and "Very Satisfied" being the two end points); a detailed evaluation of the goods and services offered by the firm; and intentions to repurchase the firm's offerings.
   2. *Mystery Shopping.* A form of marketing research, mystery shopping involves a researcher buying the firm's goods or services and assessing the purchase experience against the firm's competitors.
   3. *Customer Complaint Analysis.* Analyzing customer complaints is another way to understand customer satisfaction.
   4. *Lost Customer Analysis.* Some business organizations contact customers who have stopped being repeat purchasers to assess what went wrong. This provides a good assessment of customer satisfaction levels and what needs to be done to retain customers.

7. **Explain why business organizations go beyond measuring customer satisfaction to monitoring customer retention.**

   Research has shown that merely satisfying customers is not enough; the ultimate goal should be customer retention. This is because even satisfied customers can migrate to the competition. Only totally satisfied customers become repeat purchasers.

CHAPTER REVIEW

Marketing Concepts: Testing Your Knowledge

1. Draw a figure explaining the relationship between a strategic plan, marketing plan, and functional plan.
2. List five reasons why firms should develop marketing plans.

3. List the steps needed to develop and implement a sound marketing plan.

4. Why is it important to have a control section in a marketing plan?

5. Provide a definition of customer satisfaction in your own words.

6. What is the difference between customer satisfaction and customer retention? Why are these terms so important to a business organization?

7. What are some ways in which we can measure customer satisfaction? Describe the pros and cons of each.

8. Why do we focus on customer retention? What are some factors that affect customer retention?

Marketing Concepts: Discussing Choices and Issues

1. In this chapter, we asserted that the marketing plan provides a common foundation for the development of other functional plans. Do you see any problems with this approach?

2. Can you think of any situations where a business may not want to develop a marketing plan?

3. Critique the marketing plan template provided in this chapter. Are there any sections missing? If so, what are they? If not, provide a rationale for your answer.

4. In this chapter we argue that customer satisfaction and retention are key to business success. Do you agree? Describe situations where these variables may not be the best options for a firm.

5. Can you design a method to measure customer satisfaction that we have not discussed in this chapter?

Marketing Practice: Applying What You've Learned

1. Search on the Internet for a marketing plan. Read and critique the plan.

2. Working with four to six classmates, select a product that you all use. Identify the different brands used by each person in the group and find out what product attributes contribute to satisfaction or dissatisfaction. Summarize your findings.

3. You have been asked by your college or university's admission director for help in conducting a student satisfaction study. Advise her on the main study methods you can use in this situation.

Marketing Mini-Project: Learning by Doing

The purpose of this project is to gain an understanding of developing marketing plans through actual experience.

1. Select one of the following:

   a. An existing product (e.g., Crest toothpaste, John Deere tractors)

   b. An existing business (e.g., Apple computers, your local dry-cleaning establishment)

   c. A product or business you want to launch

2. Next, develop a marketing plan for your product or business. For an existing product you may have to draw certain conclusions based on your research. For example, comparing toothpaste brands in a supermarket will enable you to understand pricing, packaging, and positioning. Depending on your product or business choice, you may not have the capability to develop detailed tactical plans (e.g., for Crest toothpaste, it will be hard to develop tactical plans; for your local dry-cleaning establishment this should present no problem).

3. Present your results as a set of recommendations the product or business should follow to be a better competitor.

Real People, Real Surfers: Exploring the Web

For the four products listed below, visit the company's website and answer these questions.

- Harley Davidson motorcycles
- Levi's jeans
- Boeing aircraft
- McDonald's

1. What objectives does the organization hope to achieve in the next five years?
2. What customers does the organization want to serve?
3. What is the external environment facing the firm (e.g., competitors, macro environmental factors)?
4. Do you think the organization's strategies are consistent with its external environment?
5. Develop a report based on your findings and present your recommendations to the class.

Visit the MyMarketingLab website at **www.pearsoned.ca/mymarketinglab**. This online homework and tutorial system puts you in control of your own learning with study and practice tools directly correlated to this chapter's content.

Robin Pierce, David Jawl, Erin Hay, and Leah Maxwell have an idea for a new value proposition in the costume jewellery market. Binski & Bia's mission is "to change the way in which jewellery is purchased by allowing women to customize their jewellery to match their fashion forward personal style and express their individuality on an everyday basis." Binski & Bia plans to differentiate itself from the competition by offering customers a customized jewellery service that fuses current fashion trends and personal style to satisfy a variety of fashion appetites.

Binski & Bia have three key marketing objectives.

1. Create strong brand awareness to distinguish its customization niche in the fashion accessory market.

2. Establish customer loyalty to promote repeat purchases of the Binski & Bia product line.

3. Generate a reputation as being the leading jewellery company that offers customized products that are trendy and constructed from high-quality materials at reasonable prices.

Binski & Bia plans to target young female professionals. This segment consists of young female professionals aged 25 to 35 who make above the Canadian average in annual income, as well as young socialites (teenage and university-student girls who have access to money). These women have a disposable income that they typically spend on shopping for current trends, socializing, and self-betterment. They live an "urban lifestyle," consider themselves to be fashion savvy, stay up on current fashion trends, and take note of popular celebrity lifestyles. They are independent, self-confident, and value their health, beauty, and individualism. The young female professional will shop at popular retail stores and boutiques approximately four times a month and usually shops with one or more people. These women are familiar with using online applications and are comfortable shopping online, making such purchases, on average, three times per year.

Young female professionals love fashion accessories and take great pride in putting together different outfits that involve noticeable and unique jewellery. They enjoy developing their own personal style and making exclusive purchases because they want to own things that others do not. They also care strongly about the quality of goods they purchase. Name brands are not a requirement, but they are motivated to make purchases if they trust the reputation of a brand because they do not like spending money on goods that will not last long.

Binski & Bia's position in the jewellery marketplace will focus on offering its customers a combination of two values: experiential/hedonic value and cost/sacrifice value. Experiential/hedonic value will be part of the Binksi & Bia positioning mix for a number of reasons. Jewellery is a luxury item that makes consumers feel good about their appearance. However, although this absolutely applies to the product, it does not position the company differently in the marketplace. The customization aspect is the key experiential value aspect of the product concept. The experiences around customized jewellery before, during, and after the purchase are where Binski & Bia truly stands out from the other jewellery distributors at this price range. Prior to the jewellery purchase, customers may analyze their unique style and how they would want to express themselves. During the purchase, the customer is actually going through the simple steps of mixing and matching different pieces. For those few minutes the customer becomes a fashion designer, and is given the freedom of expression through a new medium—jewellery. After the purchase is made, the experience can further be enhanced as the consumer will feel increased satisfaction by having a piece of jewellery whose every aspect satisfies (i.e., the chain is just right, the pendant is just right, and the colours are just right according to the customer). The experience of the piece can be enhanced further if the consumer wishes to mix and match the pieces with her own jewellery, or if it is used as an interesting conversation piece at a social event. Binski & Bia is really positioning itself as delivering extensive experiential value in the jewellery marketplace—a marketplace where the experience of self-expression is minimal.

Binski & Bia want to differentiate itself as a fun, trendy, unique, innovative, and affordable provider of high-quality products. This is supported through the products themselves in their identifiably high-quality materials and their assembly by skilled professionals. The distribution channels will also support this image. They are unique to the industry, and include home parties, step-by-step in-store displays, and online jewellery services. Each of these distribution channels will be designed and delivered in a highly professional yet fun manner. The brand will also be supported through the highly visible silver logo, displayed on bright coloured boxes, uniforms, and in-store displays.

Binski & Bia will offer a variety of jewellery styles in the form of necklaces, bracelets, earrings, and rings. As Binski & Bia's primary value proposition is the offering of customized jewellery, the selection of materials for the customer to use to design the jewellery will consist of an assortment of chains, pendants, stones, gems, pearls, semi-precious stones, and clasps. Due to the fact that Binski & Bia is a trend-oriented and fashion-forward company, the product line will be constantly changing and have a short life span. This will mean that items will need to be quickly added and dropped from the line. The company will need to stay on top of trends and changes in the fashion industry. This will also allow the company to add product extensions once it has built a stable clientele.

Binski & Bia's pricing strategy is to price at a level that indicates value and premium high-quality products, while simultaneously offering a competitive and affordable price within its market. In terms of competition, Binski & Bia's pricing is in the range of its primary competitor, Blue Ruby. However, Binski & Bia offers added value through its customization feature, which gives it a competitive advantage. Binski & Bia is also priced higher than Aldo, one of its mainstream competitors; the strategy behind this is to insinuate that Binski & Bia's products are of higher quality and more unique.

Jewellery will be marked up 50 to 100 percent of total product cost (materials, labour, and supplies). Various factors will contribute to a higher retail markup. Items that take longer to produce, items that are more intricate, pieces with more expensive materials, and pieces that include special pendants designed by Binski & Bia will have higher markups than other standard jewellery items. Of the total price of the product, 5 percent will be the cost of the materials and 25 percent will be the cost of the labour used to produce it. The remaining 70 percent will be allocated to fixed costs, to other associated variable costs, and to profit for the company.

As Binski & Bia has limited startup capital, its goal is to start creating brand awareness and making sales without having a retail store of its own for the first three years. To do this, Binski & Bia will initially distribute its products through home parties and through its online store. Payment for Binski & Bia products will be accepted in the form of cash, debit card, and credit card (Visa and MasterCard). Online purchases, however, can be made only by credit card.

In the first year Binski & Bia products will be sold using two avenues: home parties and through an online store. The home parties will fit into the fun and social aspect of the young female professional profile. The overall experience will be unique, enjoyable, and creative. The online store will provide a means for the Internet-savvy young female professionals to order additional material, make new purchases, and choose models to customize their jewellery so that they stay current with the fashion trends.

The second year will bring an opportunity for the company to grow. Binski & Bia will set up display stands where the jewellery can be purchased within stores. These stands will follow the step-by-step customization process characteristic of Binski & Bia. They will include a selection of base pieces, a selection of additions, and a selection of clasps. Lengths, sizes, and colours will also be customizable. Some examples will be shown to assist the customer with ideas and some pre-made jewellery will be available. Prices for each separate material will be displayed prominently so that customers are fully aware of how much their final design will cost. Because of the interactive and complete nature of the display stands, they will be managed by existing store employees.

Binski & Bia's communication objective is to create brand awareness and establish its leadership in the industry. The key message that Binski & Bia wants to send to its customers is that it's a fashion-forward, high-quality jewellery company that offers a new way of purchasing and wearing jewellery through its simple step-by-step process. Binski & Bia wants to create a brand image of a fun, innovative, and unique company that offers must-have products. Because it's able to allocate only 8 percent of its budget to marketing and advertising it will have a very limited budget for these tasks. The marketing and advertising will need to be innovative, focused, and creative.

Binski & Bia will evaluate its progress in three key ways related to the organization's objectives. Most of the evaluation will relate to the online activity, as the company hopes to have most of its activity online within the first three years.

- To monitor customer satisfaction and loyalty, the company will track repeat purchases; for example, for all online purchases, a minimum level of person information must be entered on the website, including e-mail address. Therefore, an appropriate database that tracks the number of purchases per e-mail address will be created.

- To monitor brand awareness, Binski & Bia will survey the target market and consumers as to how familiar they are with the product. Surveys will be conducted in a number of ways such as online, in high-traffic shopping areas, and cold calling to both individuals in the target market and local retailers that sell similar fashion trends.

- Customer satisfaction will be a continual concern. Focus groups will be used for prototyping and feedback prior to launching any new collection. After each online purchase, a questionnaire will be sent with the final confirmation to follow up on the customer's experience of the purchasing process. Images may be sent to the company for further ideas and suggestions. This will also give Binski & Bia information on what the target consumers want. Customer satisfaction will also be sought after home parties are hosted. A short customer satisfaction card will be distributed to the guests and a more in-depth survey offered to the host as a means to garner feedback.

The team has $50 000 to commit to starting this venture, but it still needs to work out a marketing budget and launch strategy.

Things to Think About

1. Critique the marketing strategy laid out by the Binsky & Bia team.

2. What needs to be done to develop a formal marketing plan?

3. Would you invest in this business? Why or why not?

4. What are the strategic issues facing this organization?

Ginch Gonch

A few years ago Jason Sutherland purchased some designer underwear and, after wearing them a few times, they shrank, became very uncomfortable to wear, and fell apart after three washes. Jason's entrepreneurial mind came up with the idea of a brand that was all about being cheeky, having fun, and being okay with sexuality. After selling his house, taking out loans, and finding investors, Jason had raised $2 million to start Ginch Gonch. Knowing that the success of the product depended on brand reputation, Jason took out full-page advertisements in designer magazines before he even had a product to sell. Armed with orders, he began production, and since then sales have been skyrocketing, first in the gay market segment, then spreading into heterosexual markets.

With distribution in 17 countries, demand for Ginch Gonch is now high and Jason is having trouble filling all the orders. In fact, 40 percent of orders are not being filled at all. Jason has run into some cash flow problems and his manufacturer is not producing enough products for him to sell. Jason has been forced to lay off staff and cut the salaries of other employees to help reduce costs. To remedy this problem Jason has done what many young companies do, turn to their manufacturer looking for a partnership. Jason is hoping to sell the concept of Ginch Gonch to Venicio Rezalas, a production manager from El Salvador who was invited out to Jason's head office in Vancouver. But Jason is concerned about giving up too much of the ownership of his company. Rezalas is in a strong bargaining position as Ginch Gonch owes his company money, and Jason is unable to pay, unless they can get more production from him to make more sales.

After meeting Vancouver retailers that carry Ginch Gonch, and the Ginch Gonch staff, Rezalas expresses interested in investing in Ginch Gonch. While the details still need to be worked out, Rezalas returns to El Salvador leaving Jason with high hopes that his company has the investing and production capacities needed by Ginch Gonch to enable future growth.

Jason travels to El Salvador to meet with Rezalas to further discuss the investment. However, when he arrives he discovers Rezalas has not held up his end of the production agreement, forcing the investment discussions to take a back seat. The current production levels are not high enough for Ginch Gonch to fulfill the orders already placed. Unfortunately, production levels are only able to satisfy key stores, leaving 17 stores in Australia, 42 in Spain, and 50 in Germany with orders unfilled. However, Rezalas is building a new factory and believes in the potential for Ginch Gonch. He decides to invest $1 million in the company. Jason is very happy with this outcome because now production and cash flow problems are no longer an issue. Furthermore, he only had to give up 10 percent of his company, much less than the 30 percent initially asked for by Rezalas.

Questions

1. How does Ginch Gonch compete in its market? How is it positioned and how is that positioning defended?
2. What might the supply chain look like for Ginch Gonch?
3. How might the marketing mix for Ginch Gonch differ if targeting different segments?

Source: This case was prepared by Brock Smith and Michael Rawluk and is based on "Ginch Gonch," *Venture* #2, 2005.

Montreal Sandwich

Lina's Sandwiches is a franchise operation from Paris, where there are 29 locations. The concept is simple: luxury sandwiches sold in an appealing ambience. The Lina's Sandwiches franchise "book" is complete, with details on how to set up the store, prepare sandwiches, and serve the customer. However, the book is silent on the subject of how to actually raise the cash to start up the business. Frederick, the entrepreneur, has borrowed from his mother, a friend, and a local bank. Frederick is thinking big, with plans to expand across Canada.

But starting a retail store is no easy task, as Frederick soon finds out. First, you have to get the required licences from the government. Then, you have to line up contractors to do the actual construction of the retail establishment. Frederick does his own research, visiting other restaurants to see how they create a certain atmosphere, and what is on their menus. Finally, reliable suppliers have to be lined up.

Frederick goes shopping for restaurant equipment and realizes, with shock, just how expensive things are. He quickly goes $80 000 over budget, so he has to make adjustments to his dream store: the washroom is chopped, and he has to settle for less expensive heating and air conditioning systems, and cheaper furniture. But this is not enough. He still has to finance another $40 000 to $50 000. Fortunately, his friend steps in to make up the difference.

The opening of the store is constantly delayed. Frederick does not open in the fall, as originally anticipated, but in early January.

Questions

1. Do you think Frederick made the right choice of retail location for his store (Place Ville Marie in Montreal)? Why or why not?

2. What problems does Frederick run into before he even opens his retail store? What do you think he could have done to minimize some of his problems?

3. If you were a banker lending money to Frederick, what would you expect to see in his retail "business plan"?

4. Your best friend wants to start a retail store. Make a list of critical success factors necessary for a retail operation to succeed.

Source: This case was prepared by Ajay Sirsi and is based on "Montreal Sandwich," *Venture* #893.

EXECUTIVE SUMMARY

j.love handbags is a unique, upscale boutique that enables fashion-savvy women to participate in the process of creating a one-of-a-kind handbag that reflects their own style, personality, and needs. This custom handbag boutique offers 10 style prototypes and over 50 different fabrics to choose from. Customers see, feel, and experience different styles while working through the design process.

The marketing strategy will be based on an experiential image branding approach intended to generate lasting customer relationships and brand loyalty comparable to that of competitors. The three-step approach to marketing will utilize many resources to increase brand awareness, introduce the custom handbag concept, and encourage customers to benefit from the unique nature of the products. Marketing for j.love handbags will focus on its unique product concept and its affordability.

Two different market segments have been identified in the target market: the Mall Rats and the Urbanites. These segments exhibit different purchasing patterns and consumer behaviours. However, marketing efforts to reach these distinct groups will be uniform.

An in-depth competitor analysis revealed that j.love handbags' two main competitors are 1154 Lill Studio, because of its similar business concept, and Matt & Nat for its ability to recognize current trends. The two largest risks facing the business are a possible failure to penetrate existing brand loyalties and difficulty in creating brand awareness. The innovative concept behind j.love handbags will likely minimize the effects of these two risks.

A marketing budget has been established based on projected annual sales, and it was determined that start-up costs would total approximately $18 500, including pre-launch marketing and advertising.

SITUATIONAL ANALYSIS
Mission and Vision

j.love handbags is committed to delivering unique, hand-made, and affordable products based on a superior industry knowledge, a real understanding of customers' needs and wants, and a genuine enthusiasm for sewing a quality handbag. We offer fashion-savvy women the opportunity to design their own handbag. Knowledgeable seamstresses help each client navigate the different style and fabric choices to create a unique accessory that expresses her individuality. Our aim at j.love handbags is to create an atmosphere of creativity and self-expression that enables women in today's society to be a part of their product's creation. Our vision is to foster creativity, self-expression, and individuality in an affordable and non-restricting way.

SWOT Summary

Strengths	Weaknesses
• Specialized service	• Limited production capabilities
○ Unique value	○ Scalability challenges
• Affordable products	• Made in Canada production philosophy
○ Impulse-purchase appeal	○ Restricts profitability
• Innovative product concept	• Easily imitated by competition
○ Differentiated niche focus	○ Need entry barriers and differentiation
Opportunities	**Threats**
• Concept new to Canadian fashion industry	• Intense competition and existing brand loyalties
○ First-mover advantage	○ Hard to get consumer attention
• Vancouver emerging as Canada's fashion capital	• Inadequate marketing and pre-launch advertising
○ Could leverage this success to other markets	○ Need creative use of resources
• Capitalize on providing women with an outlet for self-expression	• Retail industry very price sensitive
○ Long-term need	○ Selling direct makes more sense
	○ Margins may not support customized service
	• Customers unwilling to wait two to three weeks for a handbag
	○ Need in-house production

The SWOT analysis indicates that there is potential to create a niche custom brand in Victoria and Vancouver, and perhaps to leverage this to other markets. The challenges include getting consumer attention, selling the customized value to support higher than standard margins, and erecting barriers against others copying the concept. Although scalability could be an issue for investors, I envision this as a lifestyle business, not as a huge profit generator. Although customers will have to wait for delivery of their handbags, I believe the appeal of a custom handbag will outweigh the pain of the wait. By making the bags in-house, I give up margin but hope to gain satisfaction and sales volume because I can get the bags to my customers within a week. This is a new concept to the Canadian fashion scene, so I am hoping to gain a first mover advantage. In the event that existing or new companies imitate the customization concept, I will have already established myself as its originator in Canada.

Macro/General Environment

In a recent article written by a local media publication, Vancouver was declared the emerging fashion capital of Canada. The fast-growing trend among designers to "go green" by using recycled fabrics and renewable, earth-friendly alternatives is generating a great deal of media attention.

The Canadian consumer is influenced not only by American fashion but by European fashion, too. European fashion is often coveted by the Canadian consumer who is also willing to pay a premium for European brands, believing them to be more design driven and up to date.

Handbags are a staple in most women's wardrobes, but not all women are fashion conscious and not all women care about the self-expression and personal differentiation that a custom-made bag provides. The fashion trend among younger women in Victoria and Vancouver, however, is self-expression and uniqueness without spending a lot of money: smart hip.

Consumer Analysis

The average woman owns at least six handbags, and in the past year 44 percent of American women aged 13 and over bought a handbag either for herself or someone else. In 2004, it was reported that, on average, women bought three handbags during the year and typically spent between $40 and $65 on each one.

Based on the fact that discount stores accounted for only 20 percent of retail sales in Canada, Canadian consumers are typically not discount shoppers. Well over 50 percent of all apparel purchases by Canadians are made at specialty retailers, including multi-label chain stores and independent boutiques.

There are many segments in the fashion accessory market. Benefit segmentation identifies four key segments:

1. **Mall Rats/style seekers.** Mall Rats are women between the ages of 16 and 22 years who have limited disposable income and are in either high school or university, or working in a non-career-related job. These consumers typically care about how they are viewed by society and, more importantly, their peers. A status hierarchy exists among them and is measured, to some extent, by the products they purchase and wear. Most women in this segment have a desire, stronger in some than in others, to stand out and show their individuality in an effort to avoid getting lost among cookie-cutter styles and copycat fashions. The segment often shops as a social activity with no intention of purchasing anything. These consumers frequent the downtown core, mainly on weekends, and have a moderate to strong interest in fashion and clothing. This segment is estimated to include about 50 percent of young women.

2. **Urbanites/professional image seekers.** Urbanites are busy, career-oriented women aged 23 to 40 with disposable income and some interest in fashion, but little time to shop. They do not place great emphasis either on what others think of them or on their personal style, but they do care enough to want to look professional and well put together. Since Urbanites work full time, they do not often shop for the sake of the activity, but rather for practical reasons and the need for new items. They have some fashion sense, which they rely on. They won't pay for a high-end handbag that isn't functional. This segment is estimated to include about 50 percent of working women.

3. **Paris Wanna B's/status seekers.** Paris Wanna B's are status-seeking women of all ages whose self-image and self-concept are tied to getting on, or staying on, the fashion "A-list." They spend a lot of money on looking good and must have the latest fashions. They buy many high-end handbags for the labels. They are not price conscious and only really care about fitting into their social circle. This segment is estimated to include 10 to 15 percent of women.

4. **Grab & Go/utility seekers.** Grab & Go women don't care much about fashion or about what others think of them. They have one, maybe two, handbags that are used all the time until they wear out. These women are of all ages, but tend to be mothers with small children or students who don't see a need to

make a statement with a handbag. This segment is estimated to make up 20 to 25 percent of all women.

Competitor Analysis

I have identified three different categories of competition: custom-made handbags, handbag boutiques, and handbag designers. Each of these categories presents a threat to j.love handbags, and some competitors have a presence in more than one category. I have identified the competitors that I feel pose the largest challenge to my company in each category.

In the category of custom made handbags, there are two handbag companies, both based in the United States and with an online presence, that offer customers the opportunity to customize their handbags: 1154 Lill Studio and Freddy and Ma. Studying these two companies, I find that 1154 Lill Studio closely mimics what I am striving to do, making it a direct threat to my business.

There is a handful of handbag boutiques in Victoria, none of which features only one designer, but two boutiques that I feel are important to analyze are She She Bags, a store that exclusively sells handbags from a wide variety of designers, and Violet Veldor, a small downtown boutique offering handmade one-of-a-kind fashion accessories. Violet Veldor features Canadian designers whose handbags are unique, fashionable, and reasonably priced, making them similar to j.love handbags.

Lastly, the category of handbag designers includes many names. However, there is one Canadian designer, Matt & Nat, who is capitalizing on the immensely popular global trend of "going green" in fashion by creating a line of vegan-friendly handbags. Another handbag designer that I feel needs to be reckoned with is Coach, known for eloquent simplicity and classic shapes and styles in their designs. Customers of this brand trust its quality and commitment to excellence. Since Coach is an international brand with over 40 years of success, I decided that Matt & Nat was a brand that was small enough to focus on while being large enough to worry about. All of these brands appear on a positioning map in Appendix 2.

1154 LILL STUDIO 1154 Lill Studio started the custom-made handbag concept at a street market in Chicago in 1999. They operate boutiques in Chicago, Boston, and Kansas City, and have an interactive, easy-to-navigate website. They strive to provide an unequalled creative, personal, and interactive experience centred on the design of custom handbags and accessories, and on the production of a fresh, high-quality product that represents their customers' unique styles. They consider themselves to be the originator and front runner in the custom handbag industry. They boast an impressive array of styles and fabrics to choose from and offer prices in the range of $60 to $185 for the average handbag. A summary of their strategy can be found in Appendix 1.

MATT & NAT Matt & Nat, the design inspiration of Canadian designer Inder Bedi, was formed in Montreal in 1997. Matt & Nat is a fashion-forward line of vegan handbags that embodies balance, European and North American cultural influences, and the old and the new, while being functional, yet alternative. It have a strong presence in the Canadian market and recently entered into the European market with a branch in London, England. Matt & Nat uses the highest quality synthetic materials to mimic the look and feel of leather and suede without sacrificing the lives of animals. Priced reasonably, Matt & Nat handbags offer an affordable substitute to leather without compromising design. A summary of its strategy can be found in Appendix 1.

Industry Analysis

The Canadian economy is incredibly strong at the moment and is expected to lead most developed nations in economic growth. The fashion sector, in particular, has seen strong growth and the number of new companies entering the Canadian market is increasing quickly. One reason for this is the increased strength of the Canadian dollar compared to the U.S. dollar.

The Canadian apparel market totalled nearly $20 billion dollars in 2005. This represented an increase of 2.6 percent over 2004. The Canadian market is centred in three metropolitan areas: Toronto, Montreal, and Vancouver. Approximately one third of Canada's 33 million citizens lives in these three metropolitan areas. The areas also account for approximately 40 percent of all apparel sales. This means that a brand can penetrate a significant portion of the Canadian market by focusing on just three places.

The fashion industry is an important part of the Canadian economy because it encompasses fashion innovation, design, manufacture, and the retailing of apparel and accessories. The United States' accessories industry was estimated to be worth approximately US$58.2 billion in 2006, with the world apparel trade totalling an astounding US$276 billion.

A key threat to Canadian and American fashion manufacturing is an expected reduction in duties on clothing and other textile items made in China and other parts of Asia. Downward pressure on prices is expected to impact the United States before it does Canada.

OPPORTUNITY IDENTIFICATION/ ASSESSMENT AND ASSUMPTIONS

Given this situation, I see four main approaches to entering this industry.

My preferred option is to create a small boutique where I could interact with customers and make custom handbags. There would be a line of pre-made handbags for those customers who did not want to wait or to pay more for a custom bag. While this approach would be personally satisfying, it would also result in a much smaller-scale business. In the early stages, I would be designer, manufacturer, sales representative, and store manager. If the business proved profitable, others could be hired to handle some of these tasks, but the concept would still be limited by the number of hours in my day. On the other hand, this approach would be a lot less risky and would provide me with direct feedback from customers, which is critical for refining concepts and designs. If the boutique proved successful, there would be opportunities for expansion via a franchise model. I would provide the business concept, design and branding expertise, manufacturing, and relationships with suppliers to help others establish similar boutique operations across the country and perhaps internationally. I would maintain control of the first store and continue to develop my design sense based on the immediate feedback of customers. The key challenge with this option is in having a sufficiently strong brand name so that others would want to create and sell j.love handbags rather than their own.

I rejected the option of being a supplier to established fashion retail stores that focus on the same target market. While this would allow me to focus on the creative side of the business, both product design and branding, manufacturing would have to be outsourced, perhaps to China or other parts of Asia, in order to keep costs down and as a result quality control might be hard to maintain. It would allow me to start small, but it would also allow me to expand quickly by hiring people to manage relationships with both the distributors and with the manufacturers. The potential for a large-scale national or international brand is appealing, but this model is followed by all the other handbag producers and I, therefore, wouldn't have any competitive advantage. It would be difficult to offer custom handbags in large volumes without control over the customer relationship. It would also be difficult to find retailers willing to spend time designing custom handbags with customers.

I also considered an etail format, but rejected that idea because handbags are very personal and customers are not likely to make purchases online. Customers like to feel the material, try the strap, and walk around with the bag before buying it. Also, there would not be any interpersonal relationships with customers.

MARKETING OBJECTIVES

I have four main marketing objectives:

1. To become the front runner in the Canadian custom handbag industry, in both sales and brand awareness.

   - There is only an advantage in being first into this market if I am able to create barriers to entry through a strong brand name. My specific objective is to have 30 percent unaided awareness among Mall Rats in the first year and 50 percent in the second year, as measured by office and school intercept surveys.

   - My competitive advantage is in customization. To consider my concept successful, I would expect more than 65 percent of my handbag sales to be custom orders by the end of the first year.

2. To break even by the end of the first year and make a profit of at least $50 000 in the second.

   - This is a lifestyle business, but it needs to generate a reasonable income if the concept is to be franchised. I envision my franchisees to be younger moms who want to run a business as a second income for the family.

   - To achieve these figures, I need to sell an average of seven handbags a day (2100 in total) in the first year, and nine handbags a day (2800 in total) in the second year.

3. To create a satisfied, loyal customer base with a 20 percent return rate.

   - Educating new customers on the merits of custom handbags will be a relatively expensive task compared to selling to repeat customers. My specific objective is to achieve a 90 percent satisfaction rate as measured by a follow-up email question, "Would you recommend this product to others?" Of the sales in the first year, 20 percent should come from repeat customers and in the second year this should increase to 30 percent.

MARKETING STRATEGY
Target Markets

I will focus on two major customer segments within my original target market of 16- to 40-year-old, fashion conscious women who own at least one handbag each: the Mall Rats and the Urbanites. Of these two, my primary target market is the Urbanites. Urbanites have more disposable income than do the Mall Rats, make decisions faster, and have a better idea of what they want. Mall Rats, my secondary target market, are more individualistic, more fashion conscious, and spend more time shopping than do other segments. They don't have as much disposable income as the Urbanites do, but they spend a higher proportion of it on fashion and fashion accessory items. However, they tend to browse more, making them more expensive to serve. Paris Wanna B's require more resources and designer reputation than I could provide, and Grab & Go utility seekers won't see the value in a custom handbag. The Mall Rats and the Urbanites are both relatively large segments of the market and they can be reached through a variety of low-cost media options, including in-mall signage. Mall Rats, in particular, are reachable through cellphone-based viral marketing techniques and social networking websites.

Segment Profile: Urbanites

WHO THEY ARE Urbanites are busy, career-oriented women in the 23 to 40 age range. They are fashion minded and have disposable income, but may not have time to shop. They do not place a great emphasis on what others think of them or their style, but they do care enough to want to look professional and well put together. Since Urbanites work full time, they do not often shop for the sake of the activity but rather for practical reasons.

WHAT THEY WANT AND WHY Urbanites seek a professional style of handbag that is durable and of a superior quality. They are drawn to handbags in a fabric that holds its shape, such as leather, suede, or high-quality synthetic variations so that they can fit files and folders into them. Lacking the time to shop often, Urbanites look for handbags that will withstand a lot of wear and tear and that are multi-purpose, match a variety of outfits, and functional in various situations. They seek handbags with closures and multiple inside pockets, possibly including a laptop compartment, and of a size allowing the bag to function both as a work tote and as an errand runner. Urbanites are typically drawn to neutral handbags in classic prints and with features that will match many outfits while remaining professional in style. They do not alternate their handbags as often as the Mall Rats do. Rather, they change handbags if the current one starts to wear out or when there is a change in the season.

WHEN AND WHERE Urbanites are busy, so time is important to them. They shop for handbags after work or on the weekend and value a quick, in-and-out visit that keeps them away from crowded malls. They typically enter a given store with the intent to purchase a handbag every four to six months, or as needed. They are often quite loyal to specific brands and stores, mainly as a result of positive past experience. Besides visiting downtown boutiques while out of the office, the Urbanites are quite fond of on-line shopping. Online handbag companies give this segment the flexibility to shop whenever they want, help them avoid overcrowded stores, and provide access to numerous different brands in one location. Members of this segment use their handbags daily but may have smaller, less professional-looking bags for weekend and evening events.

HOW THEY BUY THE PRODUCT When the need arises for customers in this segment to purchase a new handbag, they often browse stores alone, or with a female friend. Initially, the purchase is a moderately high-involvement decision for them, but in the end the purchase decision is made on an emotional basis. There is some social risk in making a poor choice, so they will put a considerable amount of thought into the decision, and they will assess the handbag's quality and durability because of the infrequency of these purchases. The consumers in this segment are willing to spend more money on their handbags, in the range of $75 to $120, because they do not purchase them often and value the quality of the product. Although they do not tend to spend as much time shopping as other segments do, they will take the time to comparison shop other stores and brands to ensure they are buying the best quality bag with all the desired features for their money. The Urbanites do not necessarily place much emphasis on media attention or celebrity endorsement; however, high quality is generally associated with celebrities so they may seek brands in the media spotlight while searching for a bag that will last.

HOW THEY USE THE PRODUCT These successful women will be seen toting their handbag everywhere they go: to the office, to meetings, work events, and while running errands. They may have a smaller, more unique handbag that gets some attention on the weekends when they're going out for dinner or catching up with friends. Although this segment includes somewhat fashion-conscious professionals, they use their handbags primarily for functionality rather than fashion appeal.

Segment Profile: Mall Rats

WHO THEY ARE This segment is composed of women between the ages of 16 and 22 who have limited disposable income and are in either high school or university, or working in non-career-related jobs. These consumers typically care about how they are viewed by society and, more importantly, their peers. A status hierarchy exists among them and is measured to some extent by the products they purchase and choose to wear. Most women in this segment have a desire, stronger in some than in others, to stand out and show their individuality in an effort to avoid getting lost among cookie-cutter styles and copycat fashions. The segment often shops as a social activity, without intending to purchase anything. These consumers frequent the downtown core, mainly on weekends, and have a moderate to strong interest in fashion and clothing.

WHAT THEY WANT AND WHY The Mall Rats are enthusiastic about making fashion statements and enjoy being the new fashion trendsetters. Since a large portion of this segment attends school on a regular basis, they seek handbags that fit into this environment. This means the handbag must have the capacity to carry multiple books and binders for extended periods of time. Inside pockets for cellphones, pens, and other personal effects and a secure closure are the two most important functional features of their handbags. The Mall Rats have little disposable income, so affordability is held in high regard. This group is more likely to change their style on a regular basis, making them excellent candidates for repeat purchases. This segment evaluates a handbag based on its uniqueness, ability to represent personal style, and the chances of fellow Mall Rats owning the same one.

WHEN AND WHERE The Mall Rats frequent shopping hot spots primarily on the weekend and in the evenings as a way of interacting with friends, other Mall Rats. They usually lack a developed intention to purchase a handbag and are often victim to the internal dilemma of the impulse buy. On the rare occasions that they are shopping with a purpose, it is almost always for one of two reasons: to find a handbag to match a newly purchased outfit or to combat the feeling of boredom with their wardrobes. These customers use handbags on a daily basis, taking them to school, work, and social events such as shopping, movies, parties, or after-school events. The Mall Rats use handbags around their friends, peers, and co-workers, and the opinions of all of these people are important to them. Members of this segment often own many handbags, generally those of a lower price and quality, and constantly alternate between different styles. These young consumers purchase their handbags from stores in the mall where they receive more generic, less unique products or from downtown boutiques that offer a unique alternative in exchange for a steeper price. Online companies would not be attractive to this particular segment because a large portion of the segment may not have a credit card for purchasing products electronically and because handbags are more of an impulse buy for this segment they are not likely to look up handbag retailers on the internet.

HOW THEY BUY THE PRODUCT The Mall Rats tend to travel in groups of more than two but fewer than five. They will enter a store and, with a quick scan, decide within the first few seconds whether it is worth their time. They make impulse purchases based on an emotional reaction to an item. If a product grabs their attention, either for its colour or pattern, they will pick it up and listen to the opinions of the others. If the group likes it, the purchaser will continue to investigate all of the features, try it on a couple times, look in the mirror, and then check the price tag. If it is moderately priced, approximately $40 for this segment, she will consider a few additional things, such as whether or not anybody else has it, the likelihood of anybody else buying it, and, lastly, whether it suits her. The group offers feedback throughout the process. It is an emotionally based decision, not based on need, and there is no inclination to comparison shop. If the brand or store has received media attention in the past or been known for celebrity association, the sale is more likely to take place as the item's value as a status symbol will be higher. If a Mall Rat is currently bored with her wardrobe or style, has had a bad day, or has a reason to celebrate, handbags (like other fashion accessories) are an easy and inexpensive way to remedy the situation. Handbags are purchased regularly, and past purchases are rarely considered when the purchaser is faced with a new, "must-have" bag.

HOW THEY USE THE PRODUCT The Mall Rats carry their handbags with them throughout the day, especially when they are required to carry a number of items. A new handbag is a source of pride and these consumers are not afraid to talk about and draw attention to their new fashion accessory. Those within the segment who bought a handbag for its value as a fashion statement will surely attend school and social events carrying their new possession.

Positioning: Basis of Differentiation

j.love handbags will position itself as the first Canadian handbag company to enter the custom handbag industry as a new and innovative concept. This concept is also relatively new in the United States, where only two companies that offered it could be found. The main basis of differentiation for this product over those of other manufacturers is customization. The main source of differentiation from other downtown street-front boutiques will be the relative affordability of j.love handbags: a customized handbag that will sell for about the same price as a mass-produced item. This can be done by someone, such as myself, who has both the design talent and the ability to make the handbags, thereby eliminating middlemen. This positioning is also consistent with the target customers who are unable to spend hundreds of dollars on a handbag. The product will also be high quality and durable, and include a strong customer service element, such as allowing for minor repairs. The fact that they are made in Canada will also differentiate the brand. In summary, this brand is about "Affordable Self-Expression with Personal Meaning."

Strategic Orientation

j.love handbags intends to enter the market as a leader in the absence of the custom-made concept in Canada's fashion industry. Being an industry leader with good resources and having the skills and know-how will hopefully lead to rapid growth for j.love handbags. I will confront the competition with this new product concept, one that will ensure differentiation in what is known as a copycat industry. j.love will compete primarily through a customer intimacy and brand image strategy focused on creating symbolic value (self-expression and personal meaning) with some functional value (custom features and benefits). j.love handbags will create a competitive advantage by understanding the unique handbag needs and wants of customers, by facilitating meaningful interactions with customers, and by offering custom handbags tailored to the individual. Drawing on features such as a cozy, intimate, and fashionable physical space; a personable, caring staff and proprietor; and relationship-facilitating accompaniments like a cup a tea for the Urbanites or trendy bottled drinks for the Mall Rats, we aim to engage and befriend customers. By becoming involved in the design process, customers will be able to express their personalities in their handbags and create personal meaning with lifestyle-focused features.

Defendability

This positioning can be defended by my core competencies: advanced sewing ability, high level of creativity, and customer orientation. These competencies will enable me to relate to my target markets and make unique products that are valued. Being a skilled comparison and discount shopper will enable me to purchase cost-effective materials in order to price products in an affordable manner. I am a highly relational person and can make all sorts of people comfortable quickly. As business picks up, sewers will be hired to help make the handbags. This may prove challenging, but I expect to be able to find skilled workers among recent immigrants. The challenge in franchising this business is to find partners with similar competencies as the expected volumes and margins will not support a large-scale operation. To support this positioning on a limited budget, much creativity, the resources of others, and the support of connectors and super saleswomen in the target markets are all essential.

Brand Personality

j.love handbags will be known for creativity, self-expression, and innovation. j.love is independent, stylish, and smart. At the same time it is bold, spirited, and feminine.

MARKETING MIX

Since the basis of j.love handbags is the concept of custom-made fashion accessories, the marketing efforts will be the same for both target markets. Since the customer will ultimately decide what their product will look like, marketing efforts will focus on the concept rather than on the products.

Product

OBJECTIVES/POLICIES j.love handbags is a boutique that offers fashion savvy females the opportunity to design their own handbags. This focus provides competitive advantage. Consequently, j.love's main product focus will be handbags. Other fashion accessories, such as hair scrunchies, will be sold in the store and a customized version will be considered and added to the product line if there is value in it and if the manufacturing process involves sewing. The main product objective is to start with 10 base styles and then add at least 3 new base styles per year. It is expected that 65 percent of handbag sales will be custom orders by the end of the first year.

CONCEPT j.love handbags is an upscale boutique that offers clients both the option of customizing their own handbag or of buying one that has been designed and created by a member of the highly skilled design team. Consistent with the needs of the target markets, the core product is fashionable, functional self-expressive. The value of j.love handbags for fashion-minded women is in the opportunity for customizing a handbag that is then perfectly suited to their own personality and style. It eliminates the chances of purchasing a new item that any other woman might already have or ever will have. It allows consumers to update their wardrobes in an affordable manner and own high-quality handmade items.

The actual product is the custom handbag itself. The customization process is made possible by providing a display of approximately 10 different style prototypes in muslin, an inexpensive and neutral fabric used for constructing test garments. By showing customers a prototype of each style, they can view and model the styles before deciding on which one to purchase. The fabric selection process will be similar to that for choosing a paint colour or carpeting. A small flip book of over 50 different fabrics in various colours, patterns, and textures will be available, allowing customers to envision the final product. In addition to choosing their own style and fabric, customers will have choice among the various hardware options for inside pocket styles, types of closures, buttons, snaps, rings, and rivets. Each handbag will be available for pick up at the store in two to three weeks. All handbags, regardless of style, will be lined and have two inside pockets (one for a cell phone and one with a zipper), a snap or zipper closure, and one additional detail or feature that differentiates it from other handbags. Thus, no two bags will be identical. Of the ten featured styles, one or two of them will be limited-edition styles, meaning they will be changed every few months to maintain the creativity and innovation of the custom concept. Fabric that is cost effective will be sought while at the same time a high level of quality will be maintained to support the affordable appeal of j.love handbags. With direct material costs being low, extra time can be spent on each handbag, thus ensuring that only premium care will go into the process.

Consistent with the customer intimacy brand image strategy, the augmented product will include a personal relationship with the designer; relationship-enhancing activities, like offering trendy beverages; the creative experience of being involved in the design process; a location with an inviting and inspiring physical environment that supports the independent, stylish, bold, spirited, and feminine brand image through the lighting, fixtures, fabrics, textures, colours, and music; upscale feminine packaging; and a five-year warranty. These attributes are valued by customers, but they are not the main reason they would want a j.love handbag.

PRODUCT LINES The first product line will be the pre-made and custom handbags based on 10 basic design prototypes that have been created and are endlessly customizable by means of fabric and notion choices. Ten basic styles provide a reasonable range of selection and individuality without being confusing to customers. Each of the basic design prototypes represents a product line and will have a brand name that conveys meaning about the style and the owner. For example, one style might be called "earth goddess" to reflect the use of natural materials and dyes. Three new design prototypes will be added each year, while the lowest-selling styles will be dropped, but kept in reserve. Other impulse-purchase fashion accessory product lines such as hair bows, scrunchies, and jewellery made by others will be available.

SERVICE STRATEGY The service customers receive will be an important aspect of j.love handbags, and especially of the customization concept. All employees hired will have backgrounds both in retail selling and in sewing and design, and they will be comfortable in both fields. The people hired to represent the business will be outgoing and willing to assist customers in the process of creating their handbags. The goal is to create an atmosphere that is both interactive and inviting, and one that will encourage customers to come in with friends, sit down, and spend some time designing handbags together. The objective is for the store experience to be a social event as opposed to just another purchase in a day of shopping. Customer satisfaction will be an integral part of building customer relationships and I would like to be as flexible as possible when it comes to custom orders. If a customer does not see what she wants, every effort will be made to accommodate her needs. A more-than-reasonable yet professional return policy will maximize customer

satisfaction. All pre-made handbags may be returned up to 30 days after the purchase date with the original receipt and the tags attached. The bag must be in the same condition it was in when sold. Custom-made handbags will be exchangeable for up to 60 days after the purchase. In the rare event that a handbag breaks at any time within five years, it can be brought back to the store for free repair.

BRANDING STRATEGY j.love was not chosen as the brand name for vanity reasons but to reflect the personal relationship that I will have with each customer and with each handbag made. The name is short, easy to remember, and feminine sounding. It also works well as a family brand (j.love handbags, j.love scrunchies, j.love jewelry, etc.), and my family name (Love) has a lot of potential in creative campaigns (i love j.love; love it; love at first glance, etc.).

PACKAGING AND LABEL Creating an image and brand will be an important part of the success of j.love handbags. Fabric tags with the company name and logo printed onto them will be made and sewn into each handbag. The packaging is also important and will not be overlooked. Price tags, shopping bags, and business cards will all be custom-printed with the name **j.love handbags** and a small logo, which is still to be designed but will convey a stylish, spirited, and feminine image. Another way to create a strong and lasting brand image is to offer a fabric with the name j.love silkscreened or embroidered into it for use in what would be known as the signature handbag. Purchases will be wrapped in tissue paper and sealed with a small sticker, and then placed in a paper bag with handles; tissue paper and paper bags, rather than plastic bags, are associated with higher-end stores.

Price

OBJECTIVES The main pricing objective is to support my positioning of affordable self-expression with personal meaning. However, as this is a lifestyle business, there is also a returns objective of at least $50 000 a year by the second year. Profit maximization is not an appropriate objective because it is not consistent with my desire to be personally involved with customers and the creation of their handbags, and also because affordability is important to the target segments. High volume is also an inappropriate objective because the production capacity does not exist.

POLICY Consistent with an affordable positioning pricing objective, a value-pricing policy will be implemented where I maintain reasonable margins with handbags that provide excellent value. A pricing competition with low-end imports is not desirable, but I also won't have the brand loyalty or the demand to support premium pricing.

Customers should perceive the handbags as a good deal (high value for reasonable money) so that they will recommend them to their friends. A cost-plus approach is not appropriate here as materials and notions have widely different costs, and customers will perceive greater value and be willing to pay disproportionately more for higher-end materials.

PRICE POINTS AND TACTICS The prices for the pre-made designs will range from $40 to $100, depending on the style and materials. The custom handbags will be priced slightly higher due to the specialized nature of the product, within the range of $50 to $120, again depending on style, materials, and features added. To avoid wasted production, customers will be required to pay for their custom handbag when they place the order rather than when they pick it up. Shipping will also be available to out-of-town customers for an additional charge based on a full cost recovery. Styles will be grouped into four categories (price lining) and will have a base price ending in ".00" ($30.00, $50.00, $70.00, $90.00). Materials and notions will also be offered using a pricie lining strategy, with four categories that reflect the average differences in costs (e.g., materials: $10, $15, $20, $25; notions: $2, $5, $10, $15). Round numbers make it easier for customers to add up the cost of the different options they are considering. Simplified pricing is important because the target customers must have a clear idea of what price range they are shopping in and odd-number pricing adds stress to the buying decision.

The average selling price is expected to be $69 and the average variable costs (materials and sewing labour) to be $29. With first-year fixed costs expected to be $102 100, break-even sales will be achieved on 2100 units sold, or 7 handbags a day. With sales of nine handbags a day, profits of $63,000 should be achieved in year two.

Periodic sales and promotions will be used to attract customers to the store and increase the turnover of less popular fabrics or out-of-season pre-made bags. Storewide sales will be held semi-annually to reduce the inventory of seasonal fabrics and make room for new trends. This is easily accomplished by temporarily putting higher-value materials into a lower price category or by providing a percentage discount on the total cost of a handbag that uses a sale fabric. Target customers are motivated by sale items, but they are more likely to buy a better bag at the price point they were willing to pay. To encourage customers to come back and make a repeat purchase, there will be a frequent shopper card for j.love handbag purchasers. Customer will receive a free bag with a value of up to $40 if they have previously purchased five handbags.

TERMS AND CONDITIONS Customers will expect to be able to pay by Visa or MasterCard, but a small bonus item will be offered for cash payments as it will cost 2 to 3 percent of the transaction when credit cards are used. Customers will pay for all items when ordering them. If the exchange rate continues to be close to parity, American cash will be accepted at par.

Distribution and Supply Chain Management

OBJECTIVES The main distribution objective is to secure a retail location with high visibility to Mall Rat and Urbanite foot traffic. Handbags are an impulse purchase and on-street or in-mall signage will bring significant traffic to the store. Once the concept is proven with the first store, the objective will be to expand by opening stores in major urban centres across Canada.

LOCATION j.love handbags' first location will be either in a street-front boutique located in the downtown core of Victoria or in a mid-scale mall. The preferred location is a small downtown storefront because Urbanites walk around downtown during their lunch breaks as they shop or do errands, and they also go back downtown at night for dinner or to attend cultural events. There is also a significant tourist base that fits the Urbanite profile.

STORE IMAGE AND DESIGN The goal for the store is to provide an atmosphere of warmth and comfort that makes customers want to come in and stay awhile. It will be a small space to avoid the look of scarcity so often associated with expensive products. It will be bright, clean, and decorated in a simple, classic, and elegant way so that the product stands out. I would favour a space that is large enough to include a small studio, perhaps on a slightly raised level, where all the fabric and notions would be stored and production would take place. Having the sewing studio in the boutique would support the idea of handmade, customized products as customers could see the construction process taking place right in front of them.

HOURS AND STAFFING Open hours would be from 11:00 a.m. to 6:00 p.m. on Tuesday, Wednesday and, Saturday, and 11:00 a.m. to 9:00 p.m. on Thursday and Friday. These hours are when Urbanites and Mall Rats are most likely to shop. One staff member will be hired for 200 hours per month to help greet customers and interact with them, and ring in orders. Mondays and morning hours before 11:00 a.m. will be used for making, or supervising the making of, the bags.

SUPPLY CHAIN MANAGEMENT Standard materials and notions will be sourced through a local wholesaler until the business is large enough to warrant buying trips. Through relationship building, the wholesaler will be made aware of the types of materials and notions that are needed and will look out for novel items on my behalf.

The hours before 11:00 a.m. will also be used for purchasing non-standard materials and notions.

Communication

OBJECTIVES The main communication objectives are to

1. Create awareness of the brand among Urbanites and Mall Rats
   a. A specific objective is to have 30 percent unaided awareness among Urbanites and Mall Rats in the first year and 50 percent in the second year, as measured by office and school intercept surveys.
2. Generate 50 store visits per day.
   a. Sales of seven to ten handbags a day are needed to meet financial objectives. Fifty store visits per day are needed with a 15- to 20-percent conversion rate.

APPROACH j.love handbags will primarily exercise a pull strategy to inform customers and increase awareness of the custom handbag concept. As I will not be working with distributors, appealing directly to customers to come into the store makes sense. Without the resources for two-way communication except through in-store consultations, communication of the benefits of customization and participation in the design process will be mainly one way (except for customer satisfaction research) and symmetrical.

POSITIONING STATEMENT, KEY MESSAGES, AND TACTICS j.love handbags offers affordable fashion self-expression with personal meaning. Our key messages are

1. affordable customization that allows you to express yourself—create a statement of your personal style
2. stylish handbag designs for every occasion and season—a whole new meaning to the expression "bag lady"
3. design fun—be part of the design process and unleash the creative you
4. quality Canadian craftsmanship—quality you can trust and rely on, five year guarantee

These messages were chosen to reflect and communicate our "Affordable Self-Expression with Personal Meaning" positioning. They have yet to be refined and tested through focus groups. Emotional appeals and feminine wit will be the main tactics to get the attention of target customers. While handbag purchases start as moderate involvement decisions for Urbanites, the ultimate purchase decision is made on an emotional basis (e.g., I'll feel better if I buy it; I want it). Mall Rats generally make the decision emotionally. Feminine wit is appropriate because, consistent with the brand personality, the target customers are smart, spirited, independent, and feminine. They like to feel hip, even if it is just while out shopping.

j.love is also bold, so bold colours will be used in the communication strategy. The first campaign will focus on creating brand awareness and will use the tag line "i love j.love."

COMMUNICATIONS MIX Several months prior to the opening of the boutique, a website will be created that describes the concept and informs viewers of the anticipated store opening. On or shortly after the launch of the physical store location, the website will also offer online handbag customization and a selection of pre-made designs. The intent is not for customers to order online, but for them to be able to see the different handbag styles and begin to make custom choices on their own before coming into the store for expert advice. A website is a cost-effective way to keep communication current because the targeted customers are web savvy.

Publicity will be a primary focus as the story of a young female entrepreneur should be newsworthy to local reporters. Media coverage will be facilitated by a media kit for reporters and by sending a gift of a handbag to female local on-air personalities. I also plan to have a launch event where I make a custom handbag for a high-profile celebrity, such as Pamela Anderson or Nelly Furtado, who would use the bag for a month and then donate it to raise money for a local charity. I will also donate certificates for custom handbags to charity fundraisers of interest to my customers, such as the local office of the Canadian Breast Cancer Society or high school and university women's organizations. By doing this, my brand will be seen by many potential customers. I can also leverage the resources of others by partnering with other, complementary, fashion retailers and putting their signage in my store if I can put my signage in theirs.

Most of the communications budget will go into street and store signage. j.love needs to look stylish and welcoming in order to catch the attention of women passing buy. They may not make a purchase the first time they come in, but my tags and bags will direct them to the website, where they can explore options without feeling pressured.

With a limited communication budget, radio is the best option for paid space. I plan to develop 15-second radio ads for morning and after school drive-time placement on local light rock stations. I also plan to develop a cellphone text message viral marketing element for Mall Rats as part of the "i.love j.love" campaign. Details of this plan are still being worked out.

For Valentine's Day, I plan to deliver boxes of individually wrapped chocolates with "i.love j.love" and the store's web address on them to offices within a three block radius of the store for distribution to their staff members and customers.

BUDGET AND ALLOCATION The marketing communications budget is as follows:

Start Up

Signage & Visual Identity		$4000
Launch Event	2000	
Viral Marketing	2500	

Monthy

Radio Advertising		1000 to 1250
Publicity & Donations	250	

Yearly

Valentine's Promotion	1500

IMPLEMENTATION AND EVALUATION

ACTION PLAN AND TASK SCHEDULE I won't be starting my store until I finish a one-year fashion design program. I plan to implement my concept in February of 2010, after finishing that program.

The most important implementation issue is location. The next year and a half will be spent scouting appropriate locations and determining which of them might be available near the desired start-up time. A six-month lease with options to extend for a year or beyond is preferred. Six months should be sufficient time to determine if the concept is going to be successful.

Some of this time will also be spent making a pre-made inventory of 200 units so that there is a two month's supply on hand at launch. Having more than two months' worth of pre-made inventory is not a good idea because it's not known which styles will be most popular.

Approximately four months before the intended launch date, a creative agency will be hired to work with me on the store's visual identity, signage, packaging, media kit, and radio advertisements. A creative boutique with experience in fashion retailing and a reputation for bold, stylish, eye-catching creativity will be approached for this. A creative boutique agency is a better choice than a full-function agency because I can provide a lot of the strategic thinking, and it is undesirable to be the smallest account of a big agency. A computer science student with an interest in marketing will be hired to help with the technical aspects of the viral marketing campaign. At the same time, I will be buying fabric and notions and hiring an assistant to help run the store when it opens.

Approximately a month before the intended launch date of j.love handbags, I will write a short press release and create a media kit that will be sent to all the local reporters and possibly some newspapers in Vancouver. To find a celebrity to participate in my launch event, I will use my personal network and tap into the network of faculty and mentors at the University of Victoria.

EVALUATION AND CONTROL There are four possible ways to evaluate whether marketing efforts, as described in this plan, are generating enough interest and sales to be worth their expense.

1. The objectives of 30 percent unaided awareness among Urbanites and Mall Rats in the first year and 50 percent in the second year will be measured using office and school intercept surveys. A university student who has taken a market research course will be hired to do this work so that the interviewer will be unbiased. An office building and a school will be randomly selected and permission for the survey will be sought from the building owner or major tenant, and from the school principal. At each location, approximately 100 people would be intercepted and asked to identify places to shop for handbags. Our ranking in this unaided list will be recorded, as will the first five stores named, in order to determine what the considerations set of the customers is.

2. Store visits and conversion rates will be tracked. The objective is 50 store visits per day and this is expected to be achieved by the end of the second month. If this volume is not achieved, then the communication strategy and concept must be reviewed.

3. Sales of seven to ten handbags a day are necessary to meet the financial objectives. Sales will be tracked by product type and an evaluation of average daily sales will be done at the month's end.

4. To track the effectiveness of the communication mix, an attempt will be made to measure what communication vehicle brought customers to the store: street signage, website, publicity, radio ads, or sales promotion. Customers in the store will be asked those questions.

Following are several aspects that must be monitored closely, especially in the first year of business:

- Expenses, monthly and annual: to ensure that spending remains within the marketing budget and is allocated evenly throughout the year

- Repeat business: computerized records of all customers will help determine if any are repeats

- Customer satisfaction: sending a questionnaire to customers via email or mail, with an incentive for their honest answers, can help determine which areas are generating satisfaction and which need improvement.

CONTINGENCY PLAN There are many difficulties and risks that j.love handbags may experience if the proper precautions are not taken. The following are the major risk areas in which this business might encounter difficulties:

- finding suitable employees
- covering monthly expenses in the event of lower than expected sales
- securing cost-effective relationships with fabric suppliers
- generating brand awareness

- meeting demand, given the nature of handmade products
- managing all aspects of the business equally and simultaneously
- generating visibility, in the event of a non-street-front location
- unexpected and excessive cost increases
- overly aggressive and debilitating actions by competitors
- a parallel entry by a new or existing competitor

If target sales figures are not reached by the end of the first four months, market research will be conducted to determine if it is a communications issue or a product issue. (It is unlikely to be a pricing issue.) If it is a product concept issue, then the business will be closed. If it is a communications issue, $4000 will be invested in a new campaign over two subsequent months in an effort to increase sales. If this attempt to reach break-even sales is unsuccessful within six months, the business will be closed and other venture concepts explored.

Pro Forma Income Statement

	Avg Price	Sales/day	Year 1	Year 2	Sales/day
Sales Revenue					
Pre-Made Handbags	$55	2 units	$33 000	$49 500	3 units
Custom Handbags	75	5 units	112 500	157 500	7 units
Other Merchandise	10	5 units	15 000	21 000	7 units
Average Hand Bag Price	69				
Total Sales Revenue			$160 500	$222 000	
Variable Costs					
Pre-Made Handbags	$25		$11 250	$15 000	
Custom Handbags	30		31 500	45 000	
Other Merchandise	5		7 500	20 000	
Average Handbag Variable Cost	29				
Total Variable Cost			$50 250	$80 000	
Total Contribution			$110 250	$142 000	
Start-Up Fixed Costs					
Leasehold Improvements	$3 000				
Permits & Incorporation	1 500				
POS & Computer	2 000				
Samples & Style Book	500				
Fabric & Notions Samples	1 500				
Launch Event	2 000				
Market Research	1 500				
Signage & Visual Identity	4 000				
Viral Marketing	2 500				
Total Start-Up			$18 500		
Monthly Fixed Costs					
Marketing Communications	$1 200			$1 500	
Rent & Utilities	2 500			2 500	
Wages (200 hours @ $15)	3 000			3 000	
Office Supplies & Overhead	500			500	
Contingency	300			300	
Total Monthly Costs			$7 500	$7 800	
Total Fixed Costs			$90 000	$90 000	
Yearly					
Valentine's Promotion			$1 500	$1 500	
Market Research			500	500	
Total Fixed Costs			$108 500	$90 000	
Net Profit Before Tax			−$250	$50 000	

RESEARCH PLAN Informal focus groups have been conducted with the Mall Rat segment, and these have generated positive feedback on both the concept and the designs. More than 80 pre-made bags have already been sold through a sales booth on campus and at an off-campus craft fair. However, before the concept is launched it will be tested again by first conducting two focus groups, one of Urbanites and one of Mall Rats in Greater Victoria, and then by conducting a mall intercept survey. A professional moderator will conduct the focus groups. The main purpose of these is determining a) what the segment thinks of the concept, b) whether these individuals would buy a custom j.love handbag (why or why not), and c) what price point they would expect to pay for a custom handbag. A professional does not need to be hired for the mall intercept survey. This survey could be used to determine purchase intentions and an estimated demand for the product from women in these two target markets.

BUDGET AND FINANCIALS A marketing budget is provided in a two-year pro forma income statement. In summary, sales of two pre-made handbags and five custom handbags per day in the first year, at an average selling price of $69, are expected. I also expect to sell $50 worth of other merchandise per day. Assuming 300 sales days in the year, total expected revenue is $160 500 in the first year. In the second year, sales of ten handbag units and seven other merchandise units a day are expected for total revenues of $222 000. The average variable cost per handbag is $29, which includes $15 for manufacturing. It takes a skilled sewer about 30 minutes to make a handbag. An amount of $18 500 in one-time start-up costs has been budgeted, along with $7500 in monthly fixed costs ($7800 in the second year) and $2000 in yearly fixed costs for a total of $108 500 in fixed costs in the first year and $90 000 in the second year. This is expected to generate a $250 loss in the first year and a $50 000 profit in the second year. With a six-month first lease, store operating expenses are expected to be $63 500. These funds can be raised through family.

Financial Analysis

A two-year pro forma income statement is shown. First year break-even point is seven handbag sales per day and just over $50 of other merchandise sales per day. Second-year break-even point is five handbag sales per day, but higher sales are anticipated. These are attainable figures as seven handbags a day is an average of only one per hour.

Cost-Benefit Analysis and Overall Recommendation

There are a number of advantages to this venture. I would be able to do something for a living that I love to do; my creative talents would be developed and used to help people express their own creativity; there would be valuable opportunities for interesting social interactions; and it would be an opportunity to use the entrepreneurial expertise I developed at university. One store is expected to generate a reasonable profit for a lifestyle business, and there is potential to exceed financial projections and potential in the franchising concept. There is, of course, some risk in doing this. All or part of the entire $63 500 investment could be lost. There is some social and family relationship risk in the potential for failure, but my family is very supportive and $63 500 is a manageable investment.

The potential upsides significantly outweigh the potential downsides, and I plan to implement the concept as soon as I am finished design school.

Competitive Analysis

1154 LILL STUDIO STRATEGY

Objectives

- Allow customers to use their creativity.
- Foster self-expression and individuality.
- Create a comfortable community among customers and employees.
- Build trust with customers to encourage them to come back.
- Continually innovate and grow as a company.
- Remain the front runner in the custom-handbag industry.

Strategy

- Use only the highest quality materials.
- Use a local design team, chosen by the owner.
- Offer over 25 styles and over 100 samples of fabric to choose from.
- Guarantee orders to be completed within three to four weeks.
- Offer only a limited return policy: 14 days for Lill designs, final sale on custom bags.
- Price products from $26 to $185, based on style not fabric chosen.
- Change fabric selection every few weeks.
- Frequently review company mission and values by entire company to ensure they are being met.
- Diversify by offering handbag home parties and bridal packages.

Strengths and Weaknesses

- It is the originator and front runner in the custom-handbag industry.
- Maintains strong company values.
- Uses only high-quality materials for bags.
- Ensures a high standard of quality by using a local design team.
- Obtains celebrity endorsements and media attention.
- Owns trademarks on innovative handbag party concept.
- Maintains an aesthetically pleasing, easy-to-navigate website.
- The price range is expensive for most consumers.

Potential Reactions

- Ill feelings may be generated by perception of a copy-cat concept.
- There is potential to enter the Canadian market.
- The company may feel confident because of perceived customer loyalty.

MATT & NAT

Objectives

- Make a difference in the world and in the fashion industry.
- Differentiate itself from competitors.
- Offer quality, leather-like bags without sacrificing the lives of animals.
- Foster self-expression and individuality.

- Grow and expand internationally.
- Successfully expand its product line to include vegan friendly items.

Strategy

- Use only the finest synthetic leather.
- Be vegan friendly while remaining fashion forward.
- Publicly support earth-friendly associations, such as PETA.
- Maintain a price range of $25 to $150.
- Obtain a large amount of media attention.

Strengths and Weaknesses

- Combines fashion with a worthy cause.
- Maintains a high standard of quality.
- Attracts frequent media attention and celebrity endorsement.
- Products are reasonably priced.
- Synthetic materials are not as durable as leather.
- Website does not emphasize the vegan nature of the company.
- Website lacks vital information and is not easy to navigate.
- Production in China may contradict company's stated philosophies.

Potential Reactions

- Consumers may fail to notice the company right away.
- It's not threatened by competitors because concepts are quite different.

Positioning Map

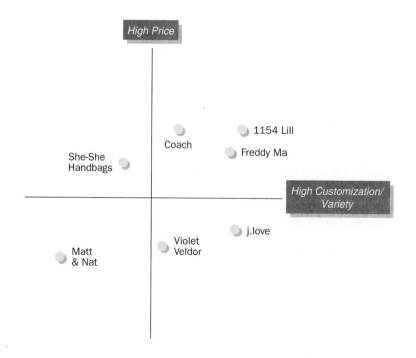

REFERENCES

www.corporate.canada.travel
The Official Business Site of the Canadian Tourism Commission

www.csca.ryerson.ca
The Center for the Study of Commercial Activities

www.plunkettresearch.com
Industry Statistics, Trends and In-depth Analysis of Top Companies

www.freddyandma.com

www.1154lillstudio.com

www.mattandnat.com

www.bcstats.gov.bc.ca
The central statistical agency of the Province of British Columbia

www.reuters.com
The world's largest international multimedia news agency

www.ambottawa.um.dk

ENDNOTES

Chapter 1

1. www.marketingpower.com, 2004.
2. Rebecca Camber, *Daily Mail*, 2 May 2006: 29.
3. Peter F. Drucker, *Management*, New York: Harper & Row, 1973.
4. Peter F. Drucker, *Management: Tasks, Responsibilities, Practices*, New York: Harper & Row, 1972: 64–5.
5. Evan Shannon, "3BR w/VU of asteroid belt," *Wired*, April 2006: 130.
6. Ani Hadjian, "Communicate, innovate," *Fortune*, Autumn/Winter 1993: 25.
7. Linda Grant, "Mattel gets all dolled up," *U.S. News & World Report*, 13 December 1993: 72(4).
8. Adapted from Carly Fiorina's talk given at the Schulich School of Business, York University, October 28, 2003.
9. www.finewaters.com/Newsletter/November_2007/Claridge's_to_offer_Comprehensive_Water_Menu.asp.
10. Bill Saporito, "Behind the tumult at P&G," *Fortune*, 7 March 1994: 74(6).
11. Bob Tedeschi, "Brand Building on the Internet," 25 August 2003, www.nyt.com.
12. "McCain drops genetically altered spuds," *Calgary Herald*, 29 November 1999: D5.
13. Cf. M.K. Khoo, S.G. Lee, and S.W. Lye, "A design methodology for the strategic assessment of a product's eco-efficiency," *International Journal of Production Research*, 39, 2001: 2453–74; C. Chen, "Design for the environment: A quality-based model for green product development," *Management Science*, 47(2), 2001: 250–64; McDonough Braungart Design Chemistry LLC, "Cradle to Cradle Design Paradigm," http://www.mbdc.com/c2c_home.htm; Elizabeth Corcoran, "Thinking green," *Scientific American*, 267: 6, 1992: 44–46; Amitai Etzioni, "The good society: Goals beyond money," *The Futurist*, 2001: 68–69; M.H. Olson, "Charting a course for sustainability," *Environment*, 38: 4, 1996: 10–23.
14. Jeff Lowe, *The Marketing Dashboard: Measuring Marketing Effectiveness*, Venture Communications, February 2003, www.brandchannel.com/images/papers/dashboard.pdf; G.A. Wyner, "Scorecards and more: The value is in how you use them," *Marketing Research*, Summer: 6–7; C.F. Lundby and C. Rasinowich, "The missing link: Cause and effect linkages make marketing scorecards more valuable," *Marketing Research*, Winter 2003: 14–19.
15. Adapted from C.F. Lundby and C. Rasinowich, "The missing link," *Marketing Research*, Winter 2003: 18.
16. Theodore Levitt, "Marketing myopia," *Harvard Business Review*, July–August 1960: 45–56.
17. *Canadian Business*, 26 December 1997: 66–7.
18. Jean Halliday, "Mustang fans help Ford give new model free ride," *Advertising Age*, 24 May 2004: 4.
19. Michael E. Porter, *Competitive Advantage: Creating and Sustaining Superior Performance*, New York: Free Press, 1985.
20. Suzanne Vranica, "Marketers' new idea: Get the consumer to design the ads," *The Wall Street Journal*, 14 December 2005: B1.
21. *Times Colonist*, 5 June 2007: D1.
22. Wikipedia.com, 16 April 2006.
23. Parts of this section are adapted from Michael R. Solomon, *Consumer Behavior: Buying, Having, and Being*, 7th ed., Upper Saddle River, NJ: Prentice Hall, 2007.
24. "Columbine video game upsets victim's father," CNN.com, 17 May 2006.
25. William Leiss, Stephen Kline, and Sut Jhally, *Social Communication in Advertising: Persons, Products, and Images of Well-Being*, Toronto: Methuen, 1986; Jerry Mander, *Four Arguments for the Elimination of Television*, New York: Morrow, 1977.
26. George Stigler, "The economics of information," *Journal of Political Economy*, 1961: 69.
27. William Leiss, Stephen Kline, and Sut Jhally, *Social Communication in Advertising: Persons, Products, and Images of Well-Being*, Toronto: Methuen, 1986.
28. Thomas C. O'Guinn and Ronald J. Faber, "Compulsive buying: A phenomenological explanation," *Journal of Consumer Research* 16, September 1989: 154.
29. Laurie J. Flynn, "Web site for Chap Stick addicts," *New York Times on the Web*, 1 November 1999.
30. Jane Macartney, "Slave labour scandal shocks Chinese: Workers locked in brickworks, many just children," *The Ottawa Citizen*, 16 June 2007: A10.
31. Andrew Wahl, "Tickets to rise," *Canadian Business*, 30 April 1999: 26–32.

Chapter 2

1. www.madd.org, accessed 30 May 2006.
2. http://www.campbellsoupcompany.com/pdf/campbell_2007_annual_report.pdf.

3. Kerry A. Dolan, "The Soda with buzz," *Forbes*, 28 March 2005: 126.

4. Christina Binkley, "Hotels? 'Go to the Mattresses': Marriott is latest to make huge bet on better bedding," *Wall Street Journal*, January 25, 2005: D1.

5. Patrick Barwise and John U. Farley, "Which marketing metrics are used and where?" Working Paper Series, Report No. 03-111, Cambridge, MA: Marketing Science Institute, 2003.

6. Pallovi Gogoi, "Chipotle's IPO: One hot tamale," *Business Week Online*, 23 September 2005.

7. B. Mainprize, K. Hindle, B. Smith, and R. Mitchell, "Caprice versus standardization in venture capital decision making," *The Journal of Private Equity* 7(1), Winter 2003: 15–25.

8. This quote is based on Lisa Schmidt, "How WestJet lost its shine," *Calgary Herald*, 30 May 2006.

9. Tom Seery, "RV makers targeting new niche," *Post and Courier* (Charleston, SC), 25 May 1997: 1–2D.

10. Jeremy Kahn, "The world's most admired companies," *Fortune*, 26 October 1998, 206–16.

11. An influential argument for this perspective can be found in Theodore Levitt, "The globalization of markets," *Harvard Business Review*, May–June 1983: 92–102.

12. Juliana Koranteng, "Reebok finds its second wind as it pursues global presence," *Advertising Age International*, January 1998: 18.

13. Terry Mills, "Planning in pictures," *Marketing Magazine Online*, 10 May 2004.

14. Terry Clark, "International marketing and national character: A review and proposal for an integrative theory," *Journal of Marketing* 54, October 1990: 66–79.

15. Norihiko Shirouzu, "Snapple in Japan: How a splash dried up," *Wall Street Journal*, 15 April 1996: B1(2).

16. Sara Hope Franks, "Overseas, it's what inside that sells," *Washington Post National Weekly Edition*, 5–11 December 1994: 21.

17. William Echikson, "The trick to selling in Europe," *Fortune*, 20 September 1993: 82.

18. Nikhil Deogun and Jonathan Karp, "For Coke in India, Thums Up is the real thing," *Wall Street Journal*, 29 April 1998: B1(2).

19. Sinclair Stewart, "Tim Hortons brews new U.S. campaign," *Strategy Magazine*, 27 September 1999: 3.

20. Sak Onkvisit and John J. Shaw, *International Marketing: Analysis and Strategy*, 2nd ed., New York: Macmillan, 1993.

21. "Kodak alleges Fuji photo is dumping color photographic paper in the U.S.," *Wall Street Journal*, 22 February 1993: B6.

22. Choe Sang-Hun, "Wal-Mart selling stores and leaving South Korea," *The New York Times Online*, 23 May 2006.

23. www.thebodyshop.ca.

24. www.mec.ca.

25. Quote by John Shad, former chairman of the U.S. Securities and Exchange Commission, in N. Craig Smith and John A. Quelch, *Ethics in Marketing*, Homewood, IL: Richard D. Irwin, 1993.

26. "Shareholders and general public say corporations should balance profits with social responsibilities, poll reveals," press release, Canadian Democracy and Corporate Accountability Commission, http://www.corporate-accountability.ca, 9 January 2002.

27. www.dow.com.

28. www.mbnet.mb.ca/crm/lawcac01.html.

29. www.geocities.com/WallStreet/Floor/3105/RIGHTS.html.

30. Mark Abley, *The Ice Storm*, Toronto: McClelland & Stewart, 1998.

31. Advertising Standards Canada, "1998 Ad Complaints Report," www.canad.com.

32. www.environmentalchoice.com.

33. Catherine Arnst, Stanley Reed, Gay McWilliams, and De'Ann Weimer, "When green begets green," *BusinessWeek*, 10 November 1997: 98–106.

34. Nancy Arnott, "Marketing with a passion," *Sales and Marketing Management*, January 1994: 64–71.

35. www.avon.com/about/women/global/current_programs.html.

36. www.equalopportunity.on.ca/enggraf/business/labert.html.

37. Patricia Digh, "America's largest untapped market: Who they are, the potential they represent," *Fortune*, 2 March 1998: S1–S12.

Chapter 3

1. Industry Canada, *Small Business Quarterly*, Spring 2000, www.strategis.ic.gc.ca.

2. Eve Lazarus, "Sizing up the sizzle," *Marketing Magazine*, 5 June 2000: 17.

3. "Seizing the occasion," *Marketing Magazine Online*, 13 August 2001.

4. Craig Saunders, "Peachtree invests in brand-building," *Strategy Magazine*, 27 March 2000: 1.

5. Judann Pollack, "Kraft's Miracle Whip targets core consumers with '97 ads," *Advertising Age*, 3 February 1997: 12.

6. Bill Guns, president, SRI Consulting, personal communication, 1998.

7. Environics Research Group website, www.erg.environics.net/tribe/default.asp.

8. Caitlin Kelly, "A jones for a soda: Peter van Stolk is bottling success in Fufu Berry and

Vanilla Coke flavours," *The Ottawa Citizen*, 15 January 2000: B2.

9. Jennifer Lawrence, "Gender-specific works for diapers—almost too well," *Advertising Age*, 8 February 1993: S-10.

10. Keith Morgan, "Designed by women, Volvo concept car will please both sexes," *The Montreal Gazette*, 30 March 2004: E1.

11. Astrid Van Den Broek, "Not so tough a sell," *Marketing Magazine*, 19/26 July 1999.

12. Kathleen Martin, "Boys Read," *Marketing Magazine*, 20 January 2003.

13. David K. Foot and Daniel Stoffman, *Boom, Bust and Echo 2000: Profiting from the Demographic Shift in the New Millennium*, Toronto: Macfarlane Walter & Ross, 1998.

14. David K. Foot and Daniel Stoffman, *Boom, Bust and Echo 2000: Profiting from the Demographic Shift in the New Millennium*, Toronto: Macfarlane Walter & Ross, 1998.

15. David K. Foot and Daniel Stoffman, *Boom, Bust and Echo 2000: Profiting from the Demographic Shift in the New Millennium*, Toronto: Macfarlane Walter & Ross, 1998: 124.

16. "Kids with cash," *Marketing Magazine*, 29 November 1999: 76.

17. Liza Finlay, "A lot more than just a piggy bank," *Marketing Magazine*, 4/11 January 1999: 14.

18. Alan Cohen, "Swimming against the tide," *Fast Company*, January 2005: 80–84.

19. Robert Scally, "The customer connection: Gen X grows up, they're in their 30's now," *Discount Store News*, 25 October 1999: 38.

20. Mary Beth Grover, "Teenage wasteland," *Forbes*, 28 July 1997, 44–45.

21. Mary Beth Grover, "Teenage wasteland," *Forbes*, 28 July 1997, 44–45.

22. Tracy A. Rickman and Michael R. Solomon, "Anomie goes online: The emo microculture," presented at the Association for Consumer Research, October 2006.

23. Charles M. Schaninger and William D. Danko, "A conceptual and empirical comparison of alternate household life cycle markets," *Journal of Consumer Research* 19, March 1993: 580–94.

24. James Careless, "Condos find their niche," *Marketing Magazine*, 25 January 1999: 12.

25. Statistics Canada, *The Population Census of Canada, 2000*, www.statcan.ca.

26. Michael R. Solomon, Judith L. Zaichkowsky, and Rosemary Polegato, *Consumer Behaviour: Buying, Having and Being*, Canadian Edition, Toronto: Prentice Hall Canada Inc., 1999: 476.

27. Danny Kucharsky, "Quebec's distinct specialty TV," *Marketing Magazine*, 20 March 2000: 22.

28. Statistics Canada, "1996 Census: Ethnic origin, visible minorities," *The Daily*, 17 February 1998.

29. Deanie Kolybabi, "Time for a closer look at the aboriginal market," *Marketing Magazine*, 22 September 2003.

30. Julie McCann, "Native niches," *Marketing Magazine*, 14 September 1998: 15–7.

31. Ken Waldie, "Out of the gate, financing aboriginal enterprises," *Summit*, November 1998: 56.

32. Statistics Canada, "1996 Census: Ethnic origin, visible minorities," *The Daily*, 17 February 1998.

33. Eun-Mi (Liz) Adams, "The big piece of the mosaic," *Marketing Magazine*, 21 June 1999: 16–7.

34. Statistics Canada, *2001 Census: Household Income Groups (24) in Constant 2000 Dollars*.

35. Eun-Mi (Liz) Adams, "The big piece of the mosaic," *Marketing Magazine*, 21 June 1999: 16–7.

36. Astrid Van Den Broek, "Cozying up to kosher," *Marketing Magazine*, 5 June 2000: 18–9.

37. "Terra Boots to take down billboards," CBC News Online, 8 October 2003, www.cbc.ca/stories/2003/10/08.

38. David Menzies, "It's only advertising," *Marketing Magazine*, 12 January 2004.

39. "The rich list: How the rich spend their money," *National Post*, 22 April 2000, www.nationalpost.com/content/features/richlist/spend.html.

40. Jo Marney, "When the urge hits," *Marketing Magazine*, 29 March 1999.

41. Canada Post website, www.canadapost.ca/cpc2/dirmlfiles/geopost.pdf.

42. Thomas V. Bonoma and Benson P. Shapiro, *Segmenting the Organizational Market*, Lexington, MA: Lexington Books, 1983.

43. Sinclair Stewart, "Grand & Toy launches The Stockroom," *Strategy Magazine*, 7 June 1999: D10.

44. Bruce Gillespie, "Get Ready for the new wave," *National Post*, 24 November 2003: FE.01.F.

45. Debbie Shork, "A matter of taste," *Marketing Magazine*, 22 May 2000: 14.

46. Heather Paris and Henry Wong, "Toyota sells functional fun," *Marketing Magazine*, 20 March 2000: 27.

47. Jeannette Hanna, "How to expand your brand," *Marketing Magazine*, 1 April 2002.

48. William Echikson, "Aiming at high and low markets," *Fortune*, 22 March 1993: 89.

49. Worldine, *Marketing Magazine Online*, May 21, 2001.

50. Becky Ebenkamp, "No dollars for bowling," *Brandweek*, 27 March 2000: 56–8.

51. Kathleen Martin-James, "Peak pita performance," *Marketing Magazine*, 10 April 2000: 18.

52. Michael Treacy and Fred Wiersama, "Customer intimacy and other value disciplines," *Harvard Business Review*, January–February 1993: 84–93.

53. Ian P. Murphy, "Beverages don't mean a thing if they ain't got that zing," *Marketing News*, 14 April 1997: 1.

54. "The university crunch," *Maclean's Magazine*, 18 November 2002: 21–62.

55. Eve Lazarus, "Lemon-aid," *Marketing Magazine*, 11 October 1999: 15.

56. Martin R. Lautman, "End-benefit segmentation and prototypical bonding," *Journal of Advertising Research*, June/July 1991: 9–18.

57. "Cassies Awards: Listerine Mouthwash and PocketPaks," *Marketing Magazine Online*, 18 November 2002.

58. Chris Powell. "Selling together: A new study by Group M and CTV suggests TV ads achieve better recall when matched with product placement," *Marketing Magazine Online*, 6 June 2005.

59. Shawna Cohen, "Energizing elixirs," *Marketing Magazine*, 3 April 2000: 12–3.

60. Chris Daniels, "Little porn shop going mainstream," *Marketing Magazine*, 29 May 2000.

Chapter 4

1. Natalia Williams, "Canadian Tire: Canadian idol," *Strategy Magazine*, November 2006: 42.

2. Chris Flanagan, "Proof positive," *Marketing Magazine*, 17 May 1999: 15.

3. "Happy Mother's Day: Here's a ticket to Antarctica," Canada NewsWire, 8 May 2007.

4. Daniel Erasmus, "A common language for strategy series: Mastering information management," *National Post (National Edition)*, 18 September 2001: M10.

5. S.J. Diamond, "Trend tracking," *Los Angeles Times*, 29 March 1993: E1.

6. BrainReserve, www.faithpopcorn.com, accessed 5 June 2007.

7. Statistics Canada website, www.statcan.ca/english/IPS/Data/63—224-XPB.html.

8. SurveySite website, www.surveysite.com.

9. Yumiko One, "An ad for smudge-proof makeup rubs a big marketer the wrong way," *Wall Street Journal*, 12 April 1996: B1.

10. www.businessobjects.com/company/customers/spotlight/bigelow.asp, accessed 22 May 2006.

11. Anthony Boright, "Banking on the web," *Marketing Magazine*, 7 February 2005.

12. Peter R. Peacock, "Data mining in marketing: Part I," *Marketing Management*, Winter 1998: 9–18.

13. Peter R. Peacock, "Data mining in marketing: Part I," *Marketing Management*, Winter 1998: 9–18.

14. Paul C. Judge, "Do you know who your most profitable customers are?" *Business Week Online*, 14 September 1998, accessed at www.Businessweek.com/1998/37/B3595144.html.

15. Philip Kotler and Ronald E. Turner, *Marketing Management: Analysis, Planning, Implementation and Control*, Canadian 9th ed., Toronto: Prentice-Hall Canada.

16. Paul Ferriss, "'Ice cream' powers Mercedes-Benz," *Marketing Magazine*, 9 June 2003: 2.

17. Cyndee Miller, "Sometimes a researcher has no choice but to hang out in a bar," *Marketing News*, 3 January 1994: 16(2).

18. Lauren Sherman, "Dancing into the hearts of teens," *Marketing Magazine*, 20 January 2003: 10.

19. Rebecca Harris, "Do focus groups have a future?" *Marketing Magazine*, 6 June 2005.

20. Annetta Miller, "You are what you buy," *Newsweek*, 4 June 1990: 59(2).

21. "Special report: Research: What role should research play?" *Strategy Magazine*, 1 September 1997: 23.

22. Terry Taciuk, "Guiding consumer apathy," *Marketing Magazine Online*, 5 May 2003.

23. Rebecca Harris, "Better latte than never," *Marketing Magazine*, 14 May 2007.

24. Jack Weber, "Absorbing some changes," *Quirk's Article #101*, November 1994, accessed via www.quirks.com, 26 January 1998.

25. "Special report: Research: What role should research play?" *Strategy Magazine*, 1 September 1997: 23.

26. "Special report: Research: What role should research play?" *Strategy Magazine*, 1 September 1997: 23.

27. Nancy Vonk, "Fun with dull numbers," *Marketing Magazine*, 10 April 2000: 26.

28. Mark MacDonald, "Workshops improving service," *Nanaimo Daily News*, 29 April 2003: A4.

29. "Wal-Mart chooses ACNielsen's consumer panel services," *Frozen Foods Age*, August 2006: 8.

30. Srikumar Rao, "Diaper-beer syndrome," *Forbes*, 6 April 1998: 128(3).

31. Erica Zlomislic, "Special report: Legitimate researchers combat 'sugging,'" *Strategy Magazine*, 14 April 1997: 40.

32. Terry Poulton, "Virgin Mobile flaunts number portability victory," mediaincanada.com, accessed 6 June 2007.

33. Fawzia Sheikh, "Kiosks ASK shoppers for their views," *Marketing Magazine*, 15 February 1999: 3.

34. Annette Bourdeau, "No more pencils. No more (note)books," *Strategy Magazine*, February 2006: 34.

35. Rebecca Piirto Heath, "The digital interviewer," *Marketing Tools*, August 1997: 28(3).

36. Peter Krasilovsky, "Surveys in cyberspace," *Marketing Tools*, November/December 1996: 18(4).

37. Lisa D'Innocenzo, "Cosying up to shoppers," *Strategy Magazine*, November 2006: 32.

38. Chris Daniels, "Real life research," *Marketing Magazine*, 17 May 1999: 15–6.

39. Chris Daniels, "Real life research," *Marketing Magazine*, 17 May 1999: 15–6.

40. "Bait Car: Media Innovation Awards," *Marketing Magazine*, 5 November 2003.

41. Mike Galetto, "Turning trash to research treasure," *Advertising Age*, 17 April 1995: I-16.

42. Lisa D'Innocenzo, "Cosying up to shoppers," *Strategy Magazine*, November 2006: 32.

43. Bruce L. Stern and Ray Ashmun, "Methodological disclosure: The foundation for effective use of survey research," *Journal of Applied Business Research* 7, 1991: 77–82.

44. Alan E. Wolf, "Most colas branded alike by testy magazine," *Beverage World*, 31 August 1991: 8.

45. Janet Simons, "Youth marketing: Children's clothes follow the latest fashion," *Advertising Age*, 14 February 1985: 16.

46. Gary Levin, "New adventures in children's research," *Advertising Age*, 9 August 1993: 17.

47. Alan Radding, "Consumer worry halts databases," *Advertising Age*, 11 February 1991: 28.

48. Alan Radding, "Consumer worry halts databases," *Advertising Age*, 11 February 1991: 28.

49. Amanda Maltby, "Adapting to Canada's new privacy rules," *Marketing Magazine*, 3 November 2003: 16–8.

50. Nikki Swartz, *Information Management Journal*, Mar/April 2007: 8.

51. Jan Larson, "It's a small world, after all," *Marketing Tools*, September 1997: 47–51.

52. Tara Parker-Pope, "Nonalcoholic beer hits the spot in Mideast," *Wall Street Journal*, 6 December 1995: B1(2).

53. Michael R. Solomon, Greg Marshall, and Elnora W. Stuart, *Marketing: Real People, Real Choices*, Upper Saddle River, NJ: Prentice Hall, 2008.

54. SurveySite website, www.surveysite.com.

55. Michael R. Solomon, Greg Marshall, and Elnora W. Stuart, *Marketing: Real People, Real Choices*, Upper Saddle River, NJ: Prentice Hall, 2008.

56. Jean Halliday, "Automakers involve consumers," *Advertising Age*, 31 January 2000: 82.

57. Sue Cummings, "Online music surveys look for future hits," *New York Times Online*, 2 February 2001.

58. Jack Neff, "P&G weds data, sales," *Advertising Age*, 23 October 2000: 76.

59. James Heckman, "Turning the focus online," *Marketing News*, 28 February 2000: 15; Judith Langer, "'On' and 'offline' focus groups: Claims, questions," *Marketing News*, 5 June 2000: H38.

60. Dana James, "Precision decision," *Marketing News*, 27 September 1999: 24–25.

61. Erik Bruenwedel, "Poll position," *Brandweek*, 20 March 2000: 82.

Chapter 5

1. James R. Bettman, "The decision maker who came in from the cold," in Leigh McAllister and Michael Rothschild (eds.), *Advances in Consumer Research* 20, Provo, UT: Association for Consumer Research, 1990; John W. Payne, James R. Bettman, and Eric J. Johnson, "Behavioral decision research: A constructive processing perspective," *Annual Review of Psychology* 4, 1992: 87–131; Robert J. Meyer and Barbara E. Kahn, "Probabilistic models of consumer choice behavior," in Thomas S. Robertson and Harold H. Kassarjian (eds.), *Handbook of Consumer Behavior*, Englewood Cliffs, NJ: Prentice Hall, 1991: 85–123.

2. "Condoms cause concern among student consumers," *Chronicle, The University of B.C. Alumni Magazine* 53(2), Summer 1999.

3. Mary Dickie, "Yahoo! Canada bows new lifestyle site," *Media in Canada*, 8 July 2007.

4. Susannah Patton, "Web metrics that matter," *CIO Magazine*, November 2002, www.cio.com.

5. Merlin Stone et al., "The effect of retail customer loyalty schemes—Detailed measurement or transforming marketing?" *Journal of Targeting, Measurement and Analysis for Marketing*, March 2004: 307; "Customer experience is the marketing tool that counts," *Marketing Week*, 5 April 2007: 19.

6. Richard Vaughn, "How advertising works: A planning model revisited," *Journal of Advertising Research*, 26(1): 57–66.

7. "Touch looms large as a sense that drives sales," *Brand Packaging*, May/June 1999: 39–40.

8. Abraham H. Maslow, *Motivation and Personality*, 2nd ed., New York: Harper & Row, 1970.

9. Clayton Alderfer, *Existence, Relatedness, & Growth*, New York: Free Press, 1972.

10. Robert A. Baron and Donn Byrne, *Social Psychology: Understanding Human Interaction*, 5th ed., Boston: Allyn & Bacon, 1987.

11. Rebecca Piirto Heath, "You can buy a thrill: Chasing the ultimate rush," *American Demographics* I, June 1997: 47–51.

12. Linda L. Price and Nancy Ridgway, "Development of a scale to measure innovativeness," in Richard P. Bagozzi and Alice M. Tybout (eds.), *Advances in Consumer Research* 10, Ann Arbor, MI: Association for Consumer Research, 1983: 679–84; Russell W. Belk, "Three scales to measure constructs related to materialism: Reliability, validity, and relationships to measures of happiness," in Thomas C. Kinnear (ed.), *Advances in Consumer Research* 11, Ann Arbor, MI: Association for Consumer Research, 1984: 291; Gordon R. Foxall and Ronald E. Goldsmith, "Personality and consumer research: Another look," *Journal of the Market Research Society* 30(2)

1988: 111–25; Ronald E. Goldsmith and Charles F. Hofacker, "Measuring consumer innovativeness," *Journal of the Academy of Marketing Science* 19(3) 1991: 209–21; Terence A. Shimp and Subhash Sharma, "Consumer ethnocentrism: Construction and validation of the CETSCALE," *Journal of Marketing Research* 24, August 1987: 282.

13. Emily Yoffe, "You are what you buy," *Newsweek,* 4 June 1990: 59.

14. Jeffrey F. Durgee, "Self-esteem advertising," *Journal of Advertising,* 14(4) 1986: 21.

15. Mark Etting, "How to make perfect patties," *Marketing Magazine,* 26 October 1998: 47.

16. Gavin O'Malley, "Teens online doing homework, text messaging and watching TV," *Advertising Age,* 12 June 2006.

17. Crissandra Ayroso, "TV still rules kids' media habits," *Media in Canada,* 9 February 2007.

18. Benjamin D. Zablocki and Rosabeth Moss Kanter, "The differentiation of life-styles," *Annual Review of Sociology I,* 1976: 269–97.

19. Alan R. Hirsch, "Effects of ambient odors on slot-machine usage in a Las Vegas casino," *Psychology & Marketing* 12(7), October 1995: 585–94.

20. Marianne Meyer, "Attention shoppers!" *Marketing and Media Decisions* 23, May 1988: 67.

21. Eben Shapiro, "Need a little fantasy? A bevy of new companies can help," *The New York Times,* 10 March 1991: F4.

22. Brad Edmondson, "Pass the meat loaf," *American Demographics,* January 1989: 19.

23. Robert La Franco, "Wallpaper sonatas," *Forbes,* 25 March 1996: 114; Louise Lee, "Background music becomes hoity-toity," *The Wall Street Journal,* 22 December 1995: B1(2).

24. Joanne Bales, "More than a makeover," *Marketing Magazine,* 13 June 2005.

25. Bernice Kanner, "Trolling in the aisles," *New York,* 16 January 1989: 12; Michael Janofsky, "Using crowing roosters and ringing business cards to tap a boom in point-of-purchase displays," *The New York Times,* 21 March 1994: D9.

26. Stephanie Whittaker, "Stopping them cold," *Marketing Magazine,* 5 April 1999.

27. Wendy Cuthbert, "Gadgets and gizmos," *Strategy Magazine,* 27 September 1999: 21.

28. John P. Robinson, "Time squeeze," *Advertising Age,* February 1990: 30–3.

29. Leonard L. Berry, "Market to the perception," *American Demographics,* February 1990: 32.

30. Richard W. Pollay, "Measuring the cultural values manifest in advertising," *Current Issues and Research in Advertising,* 1983: 71–92.

31. Michael Adams, "Clouds over Canada: The new social climate," www.erg.environics.net/news/default.asp?aID=400.

32. "Cashing in on the new nationalism," *Marketing Magazine,* 22 May 2000: 26.

33. Shawna Steinberg, "Oh, Canada in the spotlight," *Marketing Magazine,* 2 November 1998: 10–1.

34. Mary Dickie, "Change is brewing," *Strategy Magazine,* July 2007: 13.

35. Annette Bourdeau, "Mr. Retail: Lou Pium, director of marketing, Wal-Mart," *Marketing Magazine,* October 2005: 16.

36. Chris Daniels, "Canucks vs. Yanks," *Marketing Magazine,* 22 May 2000: 26–7.

37. Elliot Ettenberg, "Red, white, and red, eh," *Marketing Magazine,* 10 November 2003: 8.

38. Tony Spencer, "Going Canadian," *Marketing Magazine,* 7 September 1998: 23.

39. Helena Katz, "Distinctly Quebecois," *Marketing Magazine,* 26 April 1999: 13.

40. Jack Kohane, "Wampole Canada taps into sappy idea," *Marketing Magazine,* 5 October 1998: 2.

41. Danny Kucharsky, "Migrating to Montreal," *Marketing Magazine,* 14/21 July 2003: 8.

42. Trevor Hofmann, "What's in a name? GM embarrassed over LaCrosse," *Canadian Auto Press,* 25 October 2003, www.auto123.com/en/info/news/news,view.spy?artid=18027.

43. Brandon Watson, "The new frontiers," *Marketing Magazine,* 21 June 1999: 14.

44. Malcolm Dunlop and Christine Comi, "Multicultural explosion," *Strategy Magazine,* 11 February 2002.

45. Astrid Van Den Broek, "Speaking the same language," *Marketing Magazine,* 21 June 1999: 13.

46. Michelle Warren, "Telus, Fat Free tailor Indian ad effort," *Marketing Magazine,* 17 November, 2003: 3.

47. "Female Consumerism: What women want," *Brand Strategy,* 18 December 2006: 40.

48. Joanne Thomas Yaccato, "Through the gender lens," *Marketing Magazine,* 30 June/7 July 2003: 14.

49. Robert Beaudoin and Daniel Charron, "Answering the needs of female drivers," *Marketing Magazine,* 30 June/7 July 2003: 16.

50. Chris Daniels, "The rise of men's mags," *Marketing Magazine,* 22 September 2003: 18.

51. Stefanie Balogh, "Sexualised role models are unhealthy—Pop culture portrayals of women are leading to depression and eating disorders," *The Courier Mail* (Australia), 22 February 2006: 16.

52. Shari Graydon, "Good for the gander," *Marketing Magazine,* 2 October 2006.

53. "Canada's hole-y grail," *Marketing Magazine,* 6 September 1999: 30.

54. "Green thinking," *Marketing Magazine,* 11 June 2007: 20.

55. Rebecca Harris, "Turning green," *Marketing Magazine,* 11 June 2007.

56. Annette Bourdeau, "A green future: Three eco-friendly trends you should keep your eye on," *Strategy Magazine*, May 2007: 38.

57. Richard P. Coleman, "The continuing significance of social class to marketing," *Journal of Consumer Research* 10, December 1983: 265–80.

58. J. Michael Munson and W. Austin Spivey, "Product and brand-user stereotypes among social classes: Implications for advertising strategy," *Journal of Advertising Research* 21, August 1981: 37–45.

59. Stuart U. Rich and Subhash C. Jain, "Social class and life cycle as predictors of shopping behavior," *Journal of Marketing Research* 5, February 1968: 41–9.

60. Michael Shnayerson, "The champagne city," *Vanity Fair*, December 1997: 182–202.

61. Nathan Kogan and Michael A. Wallach, "Risky shift phenomenon in small decision-making groups: A test of the information exchange hypothesis," *Journal of Experimental Social Psychology* 3, January 1967: 75–84; Nathan Kogan and Michael A. Wallach, *Risk Taking*, New York: Holt, Rinehart and Winston, 1964; Arch G. Woodside and M. Wayne DeLozier, "Effects of word-of-mouth advertising on consumer risk taking," *Journal of Advertising*, Fall 1976: 12–9.

62. Donald H. Granbois, "Improving the study of customer in-store behavior," *Journal of Marketing* 32, October 1968: 28–32.

63. Robert D. Hof, "Special report: Internet communities," *Business Week*, 5 May 1997: 63(8).

64. Len Strazewski, "Tupperware locks in new strategy," *Advertising Age*, 8 February 1988: 30.

65. Kathleen Debevec and Easwar Iyer, "Sex roles and consumer perceptions of promotions, products, and self: What do we know and where should we be headed," in Richard J. Lutz (ed.), *Advances in Consumer Research* 13, Provo, UT: Association for Consumer Research, 1986: 210–4; Lynn J. Jaffe and Paul D. Berger, "Impact on purchase intent of sex-role identity and product positioning," *Psychology & Marketing*, Fall 1988: 259–71.

66. Kathleen Debevec and Easwar Iyer, "Sex roles and consumer perceptions of promotions, products and self"; Deborah E.S. Frable, "Sex typing and gender ideology: Two facets of the individual's gender psychology that go together," *Journal of Personality and Social Psychology* 56(1), 1989: 95–108; Lynn J. Jaffe and Paul D. Berger, "Impact on purchase intent of sex-role identity and product positioning," Keren A. Johnson, Mary R. Zimmer, and Linda L. Golden, "Object relations theory: Male and female differences in visual information processing," in Melanie Wallendorf and Paul Anderson (eds.), *Advances in Consumer Research* 14, Provo, UT: Association for Consumer Research, 1986: 83–7; Leila T. Worth, Jeanne Smith, and Diane M. Mackie, "Gender schematicity and preference for gender-typed products," *Psychology & Marketing* 9, January 1992: 17–30.

67. James Pollock, "Home Hardware drops handyman slogan," *Marketing Magazine*, 24 February 1997: 2.

68. Everett M. Rogers, *Diffusion of Innovations,* 3rd ed., New York: Free Press, 1983.

69. Patti Summerfield, "WOM Study: 15% of consumers generate more than 1/3 of buzz," *Media in Canada*, mediaincanada.com, accessed 4 June 2007.

70. Steven A. Baumgarten, "The innovative communicator in the diffusion process," *Journal of Marketing Research* 12, February 1975: 12–8.

71. Lynn Fletcher, "The buzz on buzz," *Marketing Magazine*, 23 August 2004.

72. Eric Blais, "Birth of buzz," *Marketing Magazine*, 13 September 2004.

73. Robert V. Kozinets, "E-tribalized marketing?: The strategic implications of virtual communities of consumption," *European Management Journal* 17(3), June 1999: 252–64.

74. Tom Weber, "Net's hottest game brings people closer," *The Wall Street Journal Interactive Edition*, 20 March 2000.

75. Quoted in Marc Gunther, "The newest addiction," *Fortune*, 2 August 1999: 123.

76. Greg Jaffe, "No MTV for Widespread Panic just loads of worshipful fans," *The Wall Street Journal Interactive Edition*, 17 February 1999.

77. Amy Harmon, "Illegal kidney action pops up on eBay's site," *The New York Times on the Web*, 3 September 1999.

78. Ravi S. Achrol and Philip Kotler, "Marketing in the network economy," *Journal of Marketing* 63 (Special Issue 1999): 146–63.

79. Bob Tedeschi, "Product reviews from anyone with an opinion," *The New York Times on the Web*, 25 October 1999.

80. "Dunkin' Donuts buys out critical website," *The New York Times on the Web*, 27 August 1999.

81. Bradley Johnson, "febrezekilldogs.com (and birds too)," *Advertising Age*, 10 May 1999: 8.

82. Terry Poulton, "Canadian blog for sled heads finds its way to India," *Media in Canada*, accessed 8 July 2007.

83. Michelle Halpern, "Uncapping consumer generated content," *Marketing Magazine*, 17 July 2006.

84. Kate DeBevois, "Target marketing," *Philadelphia*, August 2007: 13.

Chapter 6

1. Roger Parloff, "China's newest export: Lawsuit," *Fortune*, 23 July 2007: 48.
2. US Statistical Abstract, 2007: 762.
3. B. Charles Ames and James D. Hlaracek, *Managerial Marketing for Industrial Firms*, New York: Random House Business Division, 1984; Edward F. Fern and James R. Brown, "The industrial/consumer marketing dichotomy: A case of insufficient justification," *Journal of Marketing*, Spring 1984: 68–77.
4. www.census.gov/pub/epcd/www/naics/html.
5. Terry Lefton, "Sprint positions as biz solution," *Brandweek*, 11 July 1994: 6.
6. Statistics Canada, Consolidated federal, provincial, territorial, and local government revenue and expenditures, www.statcan.ca/english/pgdb/State/Government.
7. Government of Canada website, www.canada.gc.ca/depts.
8. MERX homepage, www.merx.ca/english2/about.html.
9. Daniel H. McQuiston, "Novelty, complexity, and importance as causal determinants of industrial buyer behavior," *Journal of Marketing*, April 1989: 66–79.
10. J. Joseph Cronin Jr. and Michael H. Morris, "Satisfying customer expectations: The effect on conflict and repurchase intentions in industrial marketing channels," *Journal of the Academy of Marketing Science*, Winter 1989: 41–9; Thomas W. Leigh and Patrick F. McGraw, "Mapping the procedural knowledge of industrial sales personnel: A script-theoretic investigation," *Journal of Marketing*, January 1989: 16–34; William J. Qualls and Christopher P. Puto, "Organizational climate and decision framing: An integrated approach to analyzing industrial buying," *Journal of Marketing Research*, May 1989: 179–92.
11. Ruby Roy Dholakia, "Decision-making time in organizational buying behavior: An investigation of its antecedents," *Journal of the Academy of Marketing Science*, Fall 1993: 281–92.
12. Neville Nankivell, "Total change: Canadian companies reach out online," *Financial Post*, 26 April 2000: E3.
13. Eve Lazarus, "Cafeteria Blues," *Marketing Magazine Online*, 19 January, 2004.
14. Steve Zurier, "Supply Chain Progress," *Builder* 30(7), May 2007: 107.
15. Tom Venetis, "Extranets take over for EDI," *Computer Dealer News*, 15(39), 15 October 1999: 15.
16. *AgDealer Magazine*, www.agdealer.com/index.cfm, 17 July 2007.
17. www.worldbid.com.
18. Debbie Barrett, "Taking a page from efficiency's book: Tiny technology tools save city workers lots of frustration and create new ways to bond," *Technology in Government* 6(9), Spring 1999: 29.
19. Grant Buckler, "3Com rolls the dice on OSN," *Computer Dealer News* 23(4), 23 March 2007: 6.
20. Tom Venetis, "Extranets take over for EDI," *Computer Dealer News*, 15(39), 15 October 1999: 15.
21. Kimberly Chapman, "A matter of life and death," *Network World Canada* 9(15), 13 August 1999: 20.
22. Erik Heinrich, "What can work: One buyer, many sellers," *Toronto Star*, 23 October 2003: K.02.
23. Wendy Stueck, "Onvia lets small firms buy like big business," *The Globe and Mail*, 22 June 2000: T9.
24. B. Joseph Pine II, Don Peppers, and Martha Rogers, "Do you want to keep your customers forever?" *Harvard Business Review*, March–April 1995: 103.
25. "A crash course in customer relationship management," *Harvard Management Update*, March 2000: HBS reprint #U003B.
26. Quoted in Cara B. DiPasquale, "Navigate the maze," Special Report on 1:1 Marketing, *Advertising Age*, 29 October 2001: S1(2).
27. Jim Middlemiss, "Users say CRM is worth the effort," www.wallstreetandtech.com (Third Quarter 2001): 17–8.
28. Mel Duvall, "Charting customers: Why CRM spending remains strong even in tight times," *Interactive Week* 8, 20 August 2001: 23.
29. Kate Fitzgerald, "Events a big 1st step," *Advertising Age*, 29 October 2001: S4.
30. Susan Fournier, Susan Dobscha, and David Glen Mick, "Preventing the premature death of relationship marketing," *Harvard Business Review*, January–February 1998.
31. Mel Duvall, "Charting customers: Why CRM spending remains strong even in tight times," *Interactive Week* 8, 20 August 2001: 23.
32. Robert C. Blattberg, Gary Getz, and Mark Pelofsky, "Want to build your business? Grow your customer equity," *Harvard Management Update*, August 2001: HBS reprint #U0108B, 3.
33. Tonia Bruyns, "Banking on targeted marketing," *Business 2.0*, 7 November 2001.

Chapter 7

1. Information obtained from the Woodstream Corporation.
2. David Todd, "Dentyne Ice locks lips with youth target," *Strategy Magazine*, 8 May 2000: B14.
3. Wendy Cuthbert, "Big Rock brews up marketing push: Alberta brewer wants stronger foothold in Ontario and B.C.," *Marketing Magazine*, 20 July 1998: 1.

4. Ian P. Murphy, "All-American icon gets a new look," *Marketing News*, 18 August 1997: 6.

5. Brian Dunn, "Taking on Tropicana," *Marketing Magazine*, 2 November 1998: 16.

6. Astrid Van Den Broek, "Germ warfare," *Marketing Magazine*, 29 November 1999: 15.

7. Lee D. Dahringer, "Marketing services internationally: Barriers and management strategies," *Journal of Services Marketing* 5, Summer 1991: 5–17, Table 2.

8. Jim Carlton, "Support lines' busy signals hurt PC makers," *Wall Street Journal*, 6 July 1995: B1(2).

9. Lou W. Turkey and Douglas L. Fugate, "The multidimensional nature of service facilities: Viewpoints and recommendations," *Journal of Services Marketing* 6, Summer 1992: 37–45.

10. David H. Maister, "The psychology of waiting lines," in J.A. Czepiel, M.R. Solomon, and C.F. Surprenant (eds.), *The Service Encounter: Managing Employee/Customer Interaction in Service Businesses*, Lexington, MA: Lexington Books, 1985: 113–24.

11. Richard Gibson, *Wall Street Journal Interactive Edition*, 3 September 1998.

12. Norma Ramage, "Flames score with marketing plan," *Marketing Magazine*, 6 December 1999: 4.

13. Astrid Van Den Broek, "ING expansion includes cafés and web," *Marketing Magazine*, 5 April 1999: 4.

14. Michael T. Kaufman, "About New York: The nail salon of the 90s: Massages for the clothed," *The New York Times*, 1 December 1993: B3.

15. Rachel Lipton, "You don't have to be a celebrity . . . to live like one," *National Post*, 24 April 1999: 25.

16. "Employment by industry, population 15 years of age and over," Statistics Canada, CANSIM, Matrix 3472, www.statcan.ca/english/pgdb/Economy/Economic/econ40.htm.

17. John A. Czepiel, Michael R. Solomon, and Carol F. Surprenant, eds., *The Service Encounter: Managing Employee/Customer Interaction in Service Businesses*, Lexington, MA: D.C. Heath and Company, 1985.

18. *The Economist*, 13–19 December 2003: 79.

19. Caryne Brown, "Making money making toys," *Black Enterprise*, November 1993: 68–77.

20. Roman G. Hiebing and Scott W. Copper, *Instructor's Manual: The Successful Marketing Plan*, Lincolnwood, IL: NTC Business Books, 1992.

21. Lindsay Elliott, "What were they thinking?" *Realm*, Winter 1998: 29; James Dao, "From a collector of turkeys, a tour of a supermarket zoo," *The New York Times*, 24 September 1995: F12.

22. Scott Allen, "Entrepreneur success story: Brian Scudamore of 1800-GOT-JUNK?," FREE Newsletter, 2006.

23. John Gray, "U.S. optical company eyes Vancouver market," *Strategy Magazine*, 15 February 1999: 7.

24. Craig Saunders, "Canada test ground for Korean appliance manufacturer," *Strategy Magazine*, 5 June 2000: 5.

25. "Test marketing a new product: When it's a good idea and how to do it," *Profit Building Strategies for Business Owners*, March 1993: 14.

26. George Anders, "Vital statistic: Disputed cost of creating a drug," *The Wall Street Journal*, 9 November 1993: B1.

27. Edmund L. Andrews, "When imitation isn't the sincerest form of flattery," *The New York Times*, 9 August 1990: 20.

28. William M. Bulkeley, "PictureTel to introduce $6,000 system to make PCs work as video telephones," *The Wall Street Journal*, 16 July 1993: B8.

29. Mark De Wolf, "Barq's bites into Canadian root beer market," *Strategy Magazine*, 7 July 1997: 8.

30. Everett Rogers, *Diffusion of Innovations*, New York: Free Press, 1983: 247–51.

31. Beth Hitchcock, "Pore wars," *Marketing Magazine*, 12 April 1999: 16–7.

32. Christopher Power, Kathleen Kerwin, Ronald Grover, Keith Alexander, and Robert D. Hof, "Flops," *Business Week* 3332, 16 August 1993: 77.

33. Everett Rogers, *Diffusion of Innovations*, New York: Free Press, 1983: Chapter 6.

34. Statistics Canada, *Market Research Handbook*, www.statcan.ca; and Statistics Canada, "Selected dwelling characteristics and household equipment," 1995, 1993, 1991, 1990, 1987, 1984, 1981, www.statcan.ca.

35. Thomas S. Robertson and Yoram Wind, "Organizational psychographics and innovativeness," *Journal of Consumer Research* 7, June 1980: 24–31.

Chapter 8

1. Jo Marney, "Too much of a good thing," *Marketing Magazine*, 24 January 2000: 21.

2. www.ford.com/archive/edselhistory.html; www.lvrj.com/lvrjhome/1998/Mar-29-Sun=1998/news/; www.theautochannel.

3. "Warner-Lambert strips Listerine," *Marketing Magazine*, 3 July 2000: 2.

4. Cornelius Herstatt and Eric von Hippel, Developing New Product Concepts Via the Lead User Method: A Case Study in a "Low Tech Field," 2006; www.hilti.ca.

5. Gail Tom, Teresa Barnett, William Lew, and Jodean Selmonts, "Cueing the consumer: The role of salient cues in consumer perception," *Journal of Consumer Marketing*, 1987: 23–27.

6. Suzanne Steel, "Hudson's Bay Company set to join KFC, CIBC, IBM, O&Y and TD," *Financial Post*, 11 February 1999.

7. Hugh Graham, "Launch annals of marketing," *Report on Business Magazine*, October 1998: 16–7.

8. Cindy Waxer, "Dogfight," *Canadian Business* 79(6), March 2006.

9. David Aaker and Erich Joachimsthaler, "Brand leadership," *Brandweek*, 21 February 2000.

10. Kevin Lane Keller, "The brand report card," *Harvard Business Review*, January–February 2000.

11. Lesley Daw, "Pillsbury turnover," *Marketing Magazine*, 14 July 1997: 11–2.

12. Susan Caminiti, "How to win back customers," *Fortune*, 14 June 1993: 118; Craig Saunders, "Holt's launches private label promo blitz," *Strategy Magazine*, 31 July 2000: 3.

13. Kusum L. Ailawadi, Donald R. Lehmann, and Scott A. Neslin, "Revenue premium as an outcome measure of brand equity," *Journal of Marketing* 67, October 2003: 1–17.

14. Betsy Spethmann and Karen Benezra, "Co-branding or be damned," *Brandweek*, 21 November 1994: 21–4.

15. Keith McArthur, "Co-branding roulette," *The Globe and Mail*, 14 June 2000, www.theglobeandmail.com.

16. "Campaigners up and arms with Nestlé Fair Trade move," *Marketing Week*, September 2005.

17. Jack Neff, "P&G redefines the brand manager," *Advertising Age*, 13 October 1997: 1,18,20.

18. Pam Weisz, "Lever plans P&G-like moves," *Brandweek*, 10 January 1994: 1,6.

19. Gary Hoover, Alta Campbell, and Patrick J. Spain, *Hoover's Handbook of American Business 1994*, Austin: The Reference Press, 1994.

20. James B. Treece, "The great refrigerator race," *Business Week*, 15 July 1993: 78–81; "Whirlpool wins prize of $30 million to build efficient refrigerator," *The Wall Street Journal*, 30 June 1993: B8.

21. Zachary Schiller, "Frigidaire's run for the cold cash," *Business Week*, 15 July 1993: 81.

Chapter 9

1. Laura Pratt, "Trading places," *Financial Post Magazine*, March 1998: 97–100.

2. Eileen Travers, "Your money's no good here," *The Montreal Gazette*, 2 July 2005: G3.

3. Glenda Luymes, "Blogger trades up from paper clip to house in rural Saskatchewan," *National Post*, 10 July 2006: A2.

4. Michael L. Rothschild, "Marketing communications in nonbusiness situations or why it's so hard to sell brotherhood like soap," *Journal of Marketing*, Spring 1979: 11–20.

5. Kenneth Labich, "What will save the U.S. airlines," *Fortune*, 14 June 1993: 98–101.

6. Chris Sorensen, "Are airlines taking off . . . or heading for a rough landing?" *National Post*, 15 July 2006: FP1.

7. Leslie Vreeland, "How to be a smart shopper," *Black Enterprise*, August 1993: 88.

8. Melissa Campanelli, "The price to pay," *Sales and Marketing Management*, September 1994: 96.

9. Andrew E. Serwer, "What price brand loyalty?" *Fortune*, 10 January 1994: 103–4; Richard Gibson, "General Mills to cut prices of 3 cereals and curb discounts," *The Wall Street Journal* 222(116), 14 December 1993: A10; Richard Gibson, "Kellogg boosts prices on many cereals; average 2.6% rise may meet resistance," *The Wall Street Journal*, 8 February 1994: A3, A8.

10. Judann Pollack, "Post's price play rocked category, but did it work," *Advertising Age*, 1 December 1997: 24.

11. Betsy McKay, "Coca-Cola sets prices at premium," *The Globe and Mail*, 16 November 1999: B18; Matthew Grimm, *American Demographics*, February 2000: 62–63.

12. Joseph Pereira, "Early coupon campaign by Toys "R" Us may spark price war among discounters," *The Wall Street Journal*, 29 October 1993: B1.

13. Norma Ramage, "Nevada Bob's tries new brand stance," *Marketing Magazine*, 13 September 1999.

14. Steward Washburn, "Pricing basics: Establishing strategy and determining costs in the pricing decision," *Business Marketing*, July 1985, reprinted in Valerie Kijewski, Bob Donath, and David T. Wilson (eds.), *The Best Readings from Business Marketing Magazine*, Boston: PWS-Kent Publishing Co., 1993: 257–69.

15. Norihiko Shirouzu and Gina Chon, "Toyota plays coy with Tundra Plush; new line priced less than Big Three's comparably equipped trucks," *Wall Street Journal*, 5 February 2007: A11.

16. Ken Popovich and Mary Jo Foley, "Dell remains committed to pricing strategy," *eWeek*, 9 April 2001, accessed at www.eweek.com/articles/0,3658,s=701&a=9334,00.asp, 22 February 2002.

17. Tony Wong, "Some like it hot at Coca-Cola: Soft-drink maker exploring vending machines that raise the price of a can of pop when the weather warms up," *The Toronto Star*, 29 October 1999: Section Head, NEWS.

18. Jennifer Merritt, "The belle of the golf balls," *Business Week*, 29 July 1996: 6.

19. Zachary Schiller, "'Value pricing' pays off," *Business Week*, 1 November 1993: 32–3.

20. Jack Neff, "Diaper battle puts EDLP on injured list," *Advertising Age*, 14 August 1995: 3, 33.

21. Sebastian Rupley, "The PowerPC revolution," *PC/Computing*, February 1994: 129–31; Marc

Dodge, "New power chips," *PC/Computing*, February 1994: 116–7.

22. Jim Carlton, "Apple to launch Macintosh PowerPCs priced at level to gain market share," *Wall Street Journal*, 14 March 1994: B4.

23. Michael D. Mondello, "Naming your price," *Inc.*, July 1992: 159.

24. Annette Bourdreau, "Via targets future biz travel," *Strategy Magazine*, April 2007: 29

25. Paul Marck, "Telus pilot program serves up everything but the popcorn," *Edmonton Journal*, 22 February 2000: A-1.

26. Susanne Craig, "Wal-Mart has radically changed the retail scene," *The Financial Post*, 21 December 1996: 41.

27. "Challenging the high price at the pumps: Consumers force an inquiry on the gas industry," *Maclean's* 109(23), 3 June 1996: 17,19; Michael MacDonald, "Charge against Irving Oil just a distraction: Liberal MP," *Canadian Press Newswire*, 1 October 1999.

28. Betsy McKay, "Coca-Cola sets prices at premium," *The Globe and Mail*, 16 November 1999: B18.

29. William M. Bulkeley, "Kodak's strategy for first printer—cheaper cartridges," *Wall Street Journal*, 6 February 2007: B1.

30. Douglas Lavin, "Goodbye to haggling: Savvy consumers are buying their cars like refrigerators," *Wall Street Journal*, 20 August 1993: B1, B3.

31. Paul Brent, "Best friend in business," *The Toronto Star*, 10 May 2007; "Canadians spending record dollars on pet food, vet care and luxury items," *National Post*, 17 August 2006: A7

32. "Bogus bargains cost Suzy Shier $1 million," *The Times Colonist*, 14 June 2003: E2.

33. "Sears Canada Inc: Ads violated Competition Act by overstating regular prices," *The Wall Street Journal*, 25 January 2005: 1.

34. Mike Roberts, "World beats a path to Vancouver's cheap CDs," *The Province (Vancouver)*, 1 August 1999: B1.

35. Rebecca Wigod, "Harry Potter 7: Wizard of a loss leader," *The Vancouver Sun*, 7 July 2007: C8.

36. "Price discrimination enforcement guidelines," news release, Competition Bureau, Industry Canada, 17 August 1992.

37. Chris Flanagan, "Gas price group takes on the giants," *The Telegram* (St. John's), 20 May 1999: 1; Ryan Cleary, "Price-fixing charge dismissed," *The Telegram* (St. John's), 21 March 2000: 1.

38. "Canadian participant in an international price-fixing conspiracy for a feed additive fined $2.25 million," news release, Competition Bureau, Industry Canada, 24 September 1999.

39. "Former Roche executive convicted and fined for international conspiracies under the *Competition Act*," news release, Competition Bureau, Industry Canada, 27 September 1999.

40. "Korean Air posts loss after U.S. price-fixing fine," *The Globe and Mail*, 3 August 2007: B5

41. "Federal watchdog has concerns over airline merger, says Globe," *Canadian Press Newswire*, 7 October 1999.

42. "Predatory pricing dispute settled," *Expositor*, 20 October 2004: A9.

43. Jim Carlton, "Microsoft takes aim at Novell by cutting software price $35,000," *The Wall Street Journal* 222, 22 September 1993: B6.

44. Anita Lahey, "Wholesale war," *Marketing Magazine*, 27 April 1998.

45. Peter Verburg, "His party, your hangover," *Canadian Business*, 27 August 1999: 36–9.

46. Rahul Jacob, "The economy: Girding for worse," *Fortune*, 18 October 1993: 10.

47. Yumiki Ono, "As discounting rises in Japan, people learn to hunt for bargains," *The Wall Street Journal*, 31 December 1993: 1, 8.

48. Jacob Rahul, "Beyond quality and value," *Fortune*, Autumn/Winter 1993: 8(3).

49. George Burns, "McDonald's: Now it's just another burger joint," *Business Week*, 17 March 1997: 38; Bill McDowell and Laura Petrecca, "Burger King ads take slap at McD's," *Advertising Age*, 10 February 1997: 12.

50. Alisa Priddle, "Japanese car makers gaining ground," *The Edmonton Journal*, 8 December 1998: 18.

51. Lloyd Robertson, "Prairie farmers say they need as much as one billion dollars in aid to deal with a looming crisis in farm income," broadcast transcript, CTV National News, 4 November 1998.

52. Steve Mertl, "Forest industry battles switch to boardroom," *Times Colonist* (Victoria), 12 October 1999: E1.

53. William G. Flanagan, "Thanks for the subsidies," *Forbes*, 7 July 1997: 120–7.

54. Amy E. Cortese and Marcia Stepanek, "Good-bye to fixed pricing?" *Business Week*, 4 May 1998: 71–84.

55. Walter Baker, Mike Marn, and Craig Zawada, "Price smarter on the Net," *Harvard Business Review*, February 2001, accessed at www.hbsp.harvard.edu/rcpt/filestream.asp?otype=s&ey=69541836&prodno=R0102J&order_id=1136431&type.pdf, 22 February 2002.

56. Jennifer Gilbert, "Drugstores wage a pricey online battle," *Advertising Age*, 30 August 1999: 26.

57. Greg Winter, "What keeps a bottom line healthy? Weight loss," *The New York Times*, 2 January 2001,

accessed at www.nytimes.com/2001/01/02/business/02WEIG.html, 3 January 2001.

Chapter 10

1. Robert D. Tamilia et al., "Robert Bartels and the history of marketing thought," *Journal of Macromarketing* 21(2), 2001.
2. Thu Hien Dao, "Banks jump on kiosk bandwagon," *Financial Post* 2(58), 1 January 2000: C6.
3. G. Bruce Knecht, "Banks bag profits with supermarket branches," *The Wall Street Journal*, 20 May 1994: B1, B8.
4. Melanie Godsell, "Walking a distinctive path," *Precision Marketing*, 18 May 2007.
5. Jeffery A. Tannenbaum, "Chain reactions," *The Wall Street Journal*, 15 October 1993: R6.
6. Charise Clark, "The new face of franchising methods: From cool concepts to creative financing methods, franchising offers hot new growth opportunities," *Profit: The Magazine for Canadian Entrepreneurs* 18(8), December 1999/January 2000: 36–40.
7. Robert L. Rose and Bridget O'Brian, "United, Lufthansa form marketing tie, dealing a setback to American Airlines," *The Wall Street Journal*, 4 October 1993: A4.
8. Gundlach et al., "The changing landscape of supply chain management, marketing channels of distribution, logistics and purchasing," *The Journal of Business & Industrial Marketing* 21(7), 2006.
9. D. Vrontis et al., "Strategic marketing planning for a supplier of liquid food packaging products in Cyprus," *The Journal of Business & Industrial Marketing* 21(4), 2006.
10. Steve Breaton, "Lower your ATM fees," *Chatelaine*, 80(6), 2007.
11. Nancy Kwon, "Know thy enemy," *Canadian Grocer*, 121(1), 2007.
12. Qin Geng and Suman Malik, "Inventory competition and allocation in a multi-channel distribution system," *European Journal of Operational Research* 182(2), 2007.
13. Allan J. Magrath, "The gatekeepers," *Across the Board*, April 1992: 43–6.
14. Scott Woolley, "The new distribution," *Forbes*, 4 November 1996: 164–5.
15. Richard Norman and Rafael Ramirez, "From value chain to value constellation: Designing interactive strategy," *Harvard Business Review*, July–August 1993.
16. Thomas L. Friedman, *The World Is Flat: A Brief History of the Twenty-first Century*, New York: Farrar, Straus and Giroux, 2006.
17. Ewan Nettleton and Andrew Hill, "Specific performance of outsourcing contracts," *Journal of Database Marketing & Customer Strategy Management* 14(2), 2007.

18. Scott Woolley, "Replacing inventory with information," *Forbes*, 24 March 1997: 54–8.

Chapter 11

1. Jennifer Steinhauer, "Interactive stores make shopping an experience," *New York Times News Service* online, 28 February 1998.
2. Jacobson Consulting Inc., *The Retail Sector in Canada*, report prepared for the Retail Council of Canada, www.retailcouncil.org.
3. Michael Levy and Barton A. Weitz, *Retailing Management*, 3rd ed., Boston: Irwin/McGraw-Hill, 1998.
4. Stanley C. Hollander, "The wheel of retailing," *Journal of Retailing*, July 1960: 41.
5. William R. Davidson, Albert D. Bates, and Stephen J. Bass, "The retail life cycle," *Harvard Business Review*, November–December 1976: 89.
6. Gail DeGeorge, "Dilbert to the rescue," *Business Week*, 4 May 1998: 166.
7. "Safeway gas stations pose challenge to big oil," *The Globe and Mail*, 15 August 2000: B10.
8. Gina Morrison, "Retailing in a world of extremes," *The Globe and Mail*, IBM Global Services, 2007.
9. Julia Flynn, "IKEA's new game plan," *Business Week*, 6 October 1997: 99(2).
10. Astrid van den Broek, "Speaking the same language: Burger King cooks up a multicultural marketing menu," *Marketing Magazine*, 21 June 1999.
11. Judy Waytiuk, "The new native niche," *Marketing Magazine*, 22 May 2000: 13.
12. Robert E. Calem, "Coming to a cash register near you: Multimedia," *The New York Times*, 31 July 1994: F7.
13. Marianne Meyer, "Attention shoppers!" *Marketing and Media Decisions*, May 1988: 67–70.
14. Gary Robins, "Wireless POS systems," *STORES*, February 1994: 47(2).
15. Raju Mudhar, "Food for future thought: New database technology puts supermarkets in the high-tech fast lane," *Marketing Magazine*, 18 October 1999.
16. Diane Forget, chief systems, POS, Henry Birks & Sons, personal communication.
17. Alfred F. Lynch, "Training for a new ball game: Retailing in the 21st century," *The Futurist*, July/August 1992: 36–40.
18. Arthur Good and Stephen Granovsky, "Retail goes global," *Canadian Business Review* 22(2), Summer 1995: 31–3.
19. Norma Ramage, "Canadian cinnamon buns savoured in Asia," *Marketing Magazine*, 19 June 2000: 6.
20. Mitchell Russell, "The Gap dolls itself up," *Business Week*, 21 March 1994: 46.

21. Julie Liesse, "Welcome to the club," *Advertising Age* 2, 1 February 1993: 3(2).

22. Debra Hazel, "The factory outlets' best of times: Belz's and other centers beat the recession," *Chain Store Age Executive*, November 1992: 39–42.

23. Michael Levy and Barton A. Weitz, *Retailing Management*, 3rd ed., Boston: Irwin/McGraw-Hill, 1998.

24. Jennifer Steinhauer, "Interactive stores make shopping an experience," *New York Times News Service Online*, 28 February 1998.

25. "A wide world of sports shoes: Fixtures enhance appeal of world foot locker," *Chain Store Age Executive*, January 1993: 176–81.

26. Wendy Marx, "Shopping 2000," *Brandweek* 20(2), 9 January 1995: 20.

27. Chris Eby, "A toast to opening of booze behemoth," *National Post*, 24 February 1999: B1.

28. "The sound of retail," *Chain Store Age*, January 1996: 3C–6C.

29. "Lobbyists against noise pollution pick up some unexpected allies," *Wall Street Journal*, 1 June 1990: B1.

30. "Design therapy: New trends in supermarket design can create moods that can enhance sales," *Canadian Grocer* 107(2), February 1993: 102–10.

31. George Condon, "Retailing as entertainment!: Is it fun to shop in your store?" *Canadian Grocer* 112(6), July/August 1998: 14–9.

32. "Service: Retail's no. 1 problem," *Chain Store Age*, 19 January 1987.

33. Elaine Underwood, "Mall busters, like crime, a boon for home shopping," *Brandweek*, 17 January 1994: 18(2).

34. Stephanie Strom, "Bold stroke in Japan's art of retailing," *The New York Times*, 23 April 1993: D1(2).

35. Zena Olijnyk, "Supermarket chic. He's been raising food retailing to new heights: Architect Leslie Rebanks has transformed what used to be big boxes that sold groceries into cultural phenomena," *Financial Post*, 24 April 2000: C1,C4.

36. Kate Fitzgerald, "All roads lead to . . . ," *Advertising Age*, 1 February 1993: S-1.

37. "Service memorial for Jacob Ghermazian," *Canadian Press Newswire*, 4 January 2000.

38. Michael Levy and Barton A. Weitz, *Retailing Management*, 3rd ed., Boston: Irwin/McGraw-Hill, 1998.

39. Pat Sloan, "Avon looks beyond direct sales," *Advertising Age*, 22 February 1993: 32; Seema Nayyar, "Avon calling, by fax, phone, and infomercial," *Brandweek*, 22 February 1993: 22–3.

40. John Browning and Spencer Reiss, "Encyclopedia of the new economy, Part I," *Wired*, March 1998: 105(8).

41. Stratford Sherman, "Will the information super-highway be the death of retailing?" *Fortune*, 18 April 1994: 99(5), 110.

42. Boston Consulting Group and Retail Council of Canada, *The Canadian Online Retailing Report*, joint research project, June 19, 2000, www.bcg.com/media_center; "E-commerce: Shopping around the Web," *The Economist*, 26 February 2000: 65–93; ACNielsen, *The Canadian Internet Survey*, Industry Canada, 12 April 2000.

43. Boston Consulting Group and Retail Council of Canada, *The Canadian Online Retailing Report*, joint research project, 19 June 2000, www.bcg.com/media_center.

44. http://www.shop.org/research/summary.htm.

45. Danny Kucharsky, "Log-ons & lace," *Marketing Magazine*, 24 January 2000.

46. Richard Covington, "Companies find the net helps trap surprising source of revenue," *International Herald Tribune*, accessed via ssnewslink, 23 February 1998.

47. Timothy J. Mullaney, "Jewellery Heist," *Business Week*, 10 May 2004: 82.

48. Patricia Sellers, "Inside the first e-Christmas," *Fortune*, 1 February 1999: 71; Boston Consulting Group and Retail Council of Canada, *The Canadian Online Retailing Report*, joint research project, 19 June 2000, www.bcg.com/media_center.

49. Boston Consulting Group and Retail Council of Canada, *The Canadian Online Retailing Report*, joint research project, 19 June 2000, www.bcg.com/media_center.

50. Lisa Napoli, *New York Times News Service Online*, 26 February 1998, accessed via ssnewslink.

51. Andrew Tausz, "The Internet rewards Dell's directness," *Financial Post*, 17 April 2000: E1.

52. John Browning and Spencer Reiss, "Encyclopedia of the new economy, Part I," *Wired*, March 1998: 105(8).

53. Richard Mackie, "Ontario unveils e-biz act," *The Globe and Mail*, 14 June 2000: B5.

54. Industry Canada report, International research on the jewelry industry, 2006.

55. "Future Shop is a veteran of the e-commerce world," *The Globe and Mail*, 30 November 1999: E21.

56. Dana Canedy, "Buying Barbie, Legos and Beanie Babies online," *New York Times News Service*, 27 July 1998.

57. Frances Huffman, "Special delivery," *Entrepreneur*, February 1993: 81(3).

58. Paul Hughes, "Profits due," *Entrepreneur*, February 1994: 74(4).

59. Margaret Nearing, "A comfy place to shop: Canadians' increasing fondness for catalogue ordering is spurring red-hot sales growth," *Marketing Magazine*, 7 December 1998.

60. Zena Olinjnyk, "Sears shuts call centre: Internet more profitable," *Financial Post*, 12 May 2000: C6.

61. "Zellers delivers baby catalogue," *Marketing Magazine*, 21 June 1999: 3.

62. David Carr, "The limits of e-mail," *Marketing Magazine*, 24 April 2000.

63. Kate Ballen, "Get ready for shopping at work," *Fortune*, 15 February 1988: 95.

64. Michael Levy and Barton A. Weitz, *Retailing Management*, 3rd ed., Boston: Irwin/McGraw-Hill, 1998; Len Strazewski, "Tupperware locks in new strategy," *Advertising Age*, 8 February 1988: 30.

65. Peter Wilkinson, "For your eyes only," *Savvy Woman*, January 1989: 68.

66. Mario Brossi and Joseph Marino, *Multilevel Marketing: A Legal Primer*, Washington, DC: Direct Selling Association, 1990.

67. Linda Lipp, "Telephones ringing off the hook," *Journal and Courier*, 19 May 1994.

68. James Sterngold, "Why Japanese adore vending machines," *The New York Times*, 5 January 1992: A1(2).

69. Ian French, "Brand-based DRTV that sells: Rules to live by in the brave new world of direct response," *Marketing Magazine*, 24 April 2000.

70. "How Videotex offers special potential in France," *Business Marketing Digest* 17, 1992: 81–4.

Chapter 12

1. Rob Pashko, "No more yawns," *Marketing Magazine*, 31 January 2000.

2. J. Grunig, *Excellence in Public Relations and Communications Management*, New Jersey: Lawrence Erlbaum Associates, Inc., 1992.

3. J. Grunig, *Excellence in Public Relations and Communications Management*, New Jersey: Lawrence Erlbaum Associates, Inc., 1992.

4. Leiss et al., *Social Communication*; George Stigler, "The economics of information," *Journal of Political Economy*, 1961: 69.

5. William D. Wells, John Burnett, and Sandra Moriarty, *Advertising: Principles and Practice*, London: Prentice Hall, 2002.

6. Scott Hume, "Integrated marketing: Who's in charge here?" *Advertising Age*, 22 March 1993: 3(2).

7. Don E. Schultz, Stanley I. Tannenbaum, and Robert F. Lauterborn, *Integrated Marketing Communications: Pulling It Together and Making It Work*, Chicago: NTC Business Books, 1993; Melanie Wells, "Purposeful grazing in ad land," *Advertising Age*, 11 April 1994: S-12.

8. Annette Bourdeau, "Brilliant," *Strategy Magazine*, August 2007: 9.

9. Tom Eppes, "From theory to practice," Price/McNabb corporate presentation, Charlotte, NC, 2002.

10. Danny Kucharsky, "Ads on demand," *Marketing*, May 15, 2006, 9.

11. "NBC to hold online vote for top *Friends* episodes," 7 January 2004, www.wsj.com.

12. Curt Barry, "Building a database," *Catalog Age*, August 1992: 65–68.

13. Martin Everett, "This one's just for you," *Sales & Marketing Management*, June 1992: 119–26.

14. Ian P. Murphy, "*Reader's Digest* links profits directly to research," *Marketing News*, 31 March 1997: 7.

15. Elaine Santoro, "NBO markets with style," *Direct Marketing*, February 1992: 28–31, quoted on p. 30.

16. Gary Levin, "Package-goods giants embrace databases," *Advertising Age*, 2 November 1992: 1.

17. Carol Krol, "New window of opportunity in Hershey Direct's elf push," *Advertising Age*, 10 May 1999: 30, 34.

18. Martin Everett, "This one's just for you," *Sales & Marketing Management*, June 1992: 119–26.

19. Gert Assmus, "An empirical investigation into the perception of vehicle source effects," *Journal of Advertising* 7, Winter 1978: 4–10; Stephen Baker, *Systematic Approach to Advertising Creativity*, New York: McGraw-Hill, 1979.

20. Patricia Sellers, "The best way to reach your buyers," *Fortune*, Autumn/Winter 1993: 15(4).

21. John R. Rossiter, Larry Percy, and Robert J. Donovan, "A better advertising planning grid," *Journal of Advertising Research*, New York: Oct/Nov 1991, 31(5): 11.

22. John R. Rossiter, Larry Percy, and Robert J. Donovan, "A better advertising planning grid," *Journal of Advertising Research*, New York: Oct/Nov 1991, 31(5): 11.

23. George E. Belch and Michael A. Belch, *Introduction to Advertising & Promotion: An Integrated Marketing Communications Perspective*, 2nd ed., Homewood, IL: Irwin, 1993.

24. Scott Hume, "Integrated marketing: Who's in charge here?" *Advertising Age*, 22 March 1993: 3(2).

25. Matt Semansky, "LG tees up HD campaign in Montreal," *Marketing Daily*, 14 September 2007.

26. Emily Rayson, "Capturing the joy of online experiences," *Marketing Magazine Online*, 1 March 2004.

27. Annette Bourdeau, "Subaru's jealous Germans," *Strategy Magazine*, September 2007: 23.

28. Michael Lev, "For car buyers, technology or Zen," *The New York Times*, 22 May 1989: D1.

29. Linda L. Golden and Mark I. Alpert, "Comparative analysis of the relative effectiveness of one- and two-sided communication for contrasting products," *Journal of Advertising* 16, 1987:

18–25; Kamins, "Celebrity and non-celebrity advertising in a two-sided context,"; Robert B. Settle and Linda L. Golden, "Attribution theory and advertiser credibility," *Journal of Marketing Research* 11, May 1974: 181–5.

30. Frank R. Kardes, "Spontaneous inference processes in advertising: The effects of conclusion omission and involvement on persuasion," *Journal of Consumer Research* 15, September 1988: 225–33.

31. Juliette Walker, "Pepsi-Coke spat raises questions about ad policies," *Japan Times Weekly International Edition*, 24–30 June 1991: 7.

32. "Green promotes 'handyman's helper,'" *Marketing Magazine*, 3 July 2000: 3.

33. Joanne Laucius, "Celine Dion and Chrysler make for a bad mix, ad experts say," *The Times Colonist*, 27 November 2003: A3.

34. Kevin Goldman, "Ad with disabled children stirs controversy," *The Wall Street Journal*, 3 September 1993: B8.

35. Katsumi Hoshino, "Semiotic marketing and product conceptualization," in Jean Umiker-Sebeok (ed.), *Marketing and Semiotics: New Directions in the Study of Signs for Sale*, Berlin: Mouton de Bruyter, 1987: 41–56.

36. Annette Bourdeau, "Sid Lee: Artists, not ad guys," *Strategy Magazine*, June 2007: 13; Danny Kucharsky, "Sid Lee wins big at Boomerangs," *Marketing Daily*, 11 December 2006; Danny Kucharsky, "Who is Sid Lee," *Marketing Magazine*, 11 December 2006.

37. D. Schultz and B. Barnes, *Strategic Brand Communication Campaigns*, 5th ed., Lincolnwood, IL: NTC Publishing, 1999.

38. Michael Wilke, "A radio entrepreneur reaches for the interactive age," *The New York Times*, 4 September 1994: F7.

39. Sarah Dobson, "The main event," *Marketing Magazine*, 13 September 2004.

40. "Place your ad here, and here," *The New York Times*, 23 July 2006: WK 2.

41. Catharine P. Taylor, "What's in a word?" *Brandweek*, 24 October 2005: 30.

42. Lois Geller, "Wow—what a buzz," *Target Marketing*, June 2005: 21.

43. Matthew Creamer, "In era of consumer control, marketers crave the potency of word of mouth," *Advertising Age*, 28 November 2005: 32.

44. Todd Wasserman, "Word games," *Brandweek*, 24 April 2006: 24.

45. "Word of mouth: Brands of the unexpected," *Brand Strategy*, 5 December 2005: 24.

46. Ibid.

47. Ibid.

48. Ibid.

49. Ibid.

50. Todd Wasserman, "Blogs cause word of mouth business to spread quickly," *Brandweek*, 3 October 2005: 9.

51. Todd Wasserman, "Word games," *Brandweek*, 24 April 2006: 24.

52. Suzanne Vranica, "Getting buzz marketers to fess up," *The Wall Street Journal*, 9 February 2005: B9.

53. Ibid.

54. Todd Wasserman, "Blogs cause word of mouth business to spread quickly," *Brandweek*, 3 October 2005: 9.

55. Suzanne Vranica, "Getting buzz marketers to fess up," *The Wall Street Journal*, 9 February 2005: B9.

56. Todd Wasserman, "Word games," *Brandweek*, 24 April 2006: 24.

57. Ibid.

58. Todd Wasserman, "Blogs cause word of mouth business to spread quickly," *Brandweek*, 3 October 2005: 9.

59. Ibid.

60. T.L. Stanley, "Guerrilla marketers of the year," *Brandweek*, 27 March 2000: 28; Jeff Green, "Down with the Dirt Devils," *Brandweek*, 27 March 2000: 41–44; Stephanie Thompson, "Pepsi favors sampling over ads for fruit drink," *Advertising Age*, 24 January 2000: 8.

61. Jaimie Seaton, "Burger King guns for rivals in guerilla push," *Media*, 9 September 2005: 6.

62. Louella Miles, "Words' worth," *Marketing*, 25 January 2006: 35; "Brand metrics: The net-promoter score movement," *Brand Strategy*, 16 April 2007: 40; Roland T. Rust, "Weighing in on Net Promoter," *Advertising Age*, 10 September 2007: 26.

63. Chris Powell, "Get in the game," *Marketing Magazine*, 28 July/3 August 2003: 11.

64. Ibid.

65. Neil Davidson, "Canada's got game," *New Brunswick Telegraph Journal*, 17 March 2007: G7.

66. Danny Kucharsky, "Ah! Ha!: How a brilliant ad concept sparked a pop culture sensation and pumped up the profile of Quebec's Familiprix," *Marketing Magazine*, 9 June 2003: 8–10.

67. "The man from Glad—He's back," *Marketing Magazine*, 20 March 2000.

68. Jonathan Berry, "Wilma! What happened to the plain old ad?" *Business Week*, 6 June 1994: 54–5.

69. Tom Buerkle, "Advertisers find a formula they like in auto racing," *International Herald Tribune* [on-line] 10 March 1998, accessed via ssnewslink.

70. Patricia Sellers, "Winning over the new consumer," *Fortune*, 27 July 1991: 113.

71. "P&G stages live advertising," *Marketing Magazine*, 1 May 2000.

72. Barb Grant, "Getting the right balance," *Marketing Magazine*, 22 September 2003.

73. Gert Assmus, "An empirical investigation into the perception of vehicle source effects," *Journal of Advertising* 7, Winter 1978: 4–10; Stephen Baker, *Systematic Approach to Advertising Creativity*, New York: McGraw-Hill, 1979.

74. Patricia Sellers, "The best way to reach your buyers," *Fortune*, Autumn/Winter 1993: 15(4).

75. James P Masciarelli, "Are you managing your relationships?" *Management Review New York* 87(4): 41–5.

76. Charles Goodrum and Helen Dalrymple, *Advertising in America: The First 200 Years*, New York: Harry N. Abrams, 1990.

77. Kevin Goldman. "The message, clever as it may be, is lost in a number of high profile campaigns," *Wall Street Journal*, 27 July 1993: B1(2).

78. Charles Goodrum and Helen Dalrymple, *Advertising in America: The First 200 Years*, New York: Harry N. Abrams, 1990.

79. Kevin Goldman "Knock, knock. Who's there: The same old funny ad again," *The Wall Street Journal*, 2 November 1993: B10.

80. Curt Barry, "Building a database," *Catalog Age*, August 1992: 65–8.

81. John F. Yarbrough, "Putting the pieces together," *Sales and Marketing Management*, September 1996: 70.

82. Bruce MacDonald, "The art of the brief," *Marketing Magazine*, 27 October 2003: 36–38.

83. Ibid.

84. Ibid.

Chapter 13

1. Danielle D'Agostino, "Teaching brands new tricks: Fido's PR campaign worked by leveraging off the visual icon of the dog," *Marketing Magazine*, 28 February 1999: 28.

2. William Wells, John Burnett, and Sandra Moriarty, *Advertising Principles and Practice*, 2nd ed., Engelwood Cliffs, NJ: Prentice Hall, 1992.

3. Television Bureau of Canada, 2005.

4. Bob D. Cutler and Darrel D. Muehling, "Another look at advocacy advertising and the boundaries of commercial speech," *Journal of Advertising* 20, December 1991: 49–52.

5. Lara Mills, "Campaigns with legs," *Marketing Magazine*, 15 May 2000: 12–4.

6. Canadian Media Directors' Council, *2007 Canadian Media Directors' Council Media Digest*: 17.

7. Ibid.: 18.

8. James Careless, "Where's the price tag?" *Marketing Magazine*, 31 January 2000.

9. Philip Hart, "Product placement comes of age in Canada," *Marketing Magazine*, 18 November 1996: 20.

10. Phil Hall, "Make listeners your customers," *Nation's Business*, June 1994:53R.

11. Canadian Media Directors' Council, *1999/2000 Canadian Media Directors' Council Media Digest*: 27.

12. Ibid.: 34.

13. Terry Poulton, "TD Canada Trust launches mega-prize contest," *Media in Canada*, 2 August 2007.

14. Canadian Media Directors' Council, *1999/2000 Canadian Media Directors' Council Media Digest*: 35.

15. Ibid.: 70.

16. Ibid.: 71.

17. Michael McCarthy, "Companies are sold on interactive ad strategy," *USA Today*, 3 March 2000: 1B.

18. Lisa Marie Petersen, "Outside chance," *MediaWeek*, 15 June 1992: 20–3.

19. Canadian Media Directors' Council, *1999/2000 Canadian Media Directors' Council Media Digest*: 73.

20. Ann M. Mack, "Got e-mail," *Brandweek*, 20 March 2000, 84–8.

21. Written by Rian Bowden.

22. William Safire, "M-Commerce," *The New York Times Magazine*, accessed at www.nytimes.com/library/magazine/home/20000319mag-onlanguage.html on 27 February 2002.

23. Michael Bociurkiw, "Text messaging thrives in the Philippines," *Forbes*, 10 September 2001: 28.

24. "MTV adds wireless ads to mix," CNN.com, 23 August 2001, http://cnn.career.printthis.clickability.com/pt/printThis?clickMap=p.

25. "Mobile Marketing Handbook," *Marketing Magazine*, 10, January 2007.

26. "Lancôme runs texty campaign for eye shadow," Marketing Daily e-mail update, *Marketing Magazine*, 13 February 2006.

27. Patti Summerfield, "OMD Canada: Txt in to get toasted," *Strategy Magazine*, April 2007: 51.

28. Dana James, "RU PYNG ATTN?: Europeans find text messaging the right marketing call," *Marketing News*, 7 January 2000: 4.

29. Olga Karif, "Online extra: Mobile commerce is coming—modestly, eventually," *Business Week Online*, E-Biz, 14 May 2001, accessed 26 February 2002.

30. Ibid.

31. Mike Dano, "M-commerce will outperform e-commerce," *RCR Wireless News*, 20, 2 April 2001: 4.

32. Gene Koprowsky, "Eyeball to eyeball," *Critical Mass*, Fall 1999: 32(5).

33. Astrid Van De Broek, "TV network's ads go to the movies," *Marketing magazine*, 3 April 2000: 3.

34. Altaf M. Khan, "New ways to get in faces," *Marketing Magazine*, 10 April 2000: 33.

35. Michael Bernard, "The great house sale," *Marketing Magazine*, 23 February 1998.

36. Michelle Halpern, "Burger King debuts *Apprentice*," *Marketing Daily*, 24 January 2005.

37. Anita Lahey, Michael McCullough, and Gail Chiasson, "Placing products," *Marketing Magazine*, 12 August 1996.

38. Patrick Allossery, "Petro-Canada to list its costs per litre in public relation bid: Posted on the pumps," *Financial Post*, 14 March 2000: C6.

39. Ni Chen and Hugh M. Culbertson, "Two contrasting approaches of government public relations in mainland China," *Public Relations Quarterly*, Fall 1992: 36–41.

40. John Swinimer, "Untarnished: Rolling up their sleeves to polish up what is widely seen as a muddied image, insurance companies and industry associations are cleaning it off by getting involved in worthy causes and community projects," *Canadian Underwriter*, February 1993: 12–3.

41. "Ericsson, Manifest team on aid," *Marketing Magazine*, 8 May 2000.

42. Anita Lahey, Michael McCullough, and Gail Chiasson, "Placing products," *Marketing Magazine*, 12 August 1996.

43. Patrick Allossery, "Petro-Canada to list its costs per litre in public relation bid: Posted on the pumps," *Financial Post*, 14 March 2000: C6.

44. Tony Van Alphen, "Husky injection molding adds altruism to the mix," *Canadian Press Newswire*, 21 January 2000.

45. Roma Luciw, "Bridgestone recalls Canadian tires: About a million of affected brands are on selected SUVs and trucks," *The Globe and Mail*, 11 August 2000: A1.

46. Rick Hall, "Lessons of the McLibel case," *Marketing Magazine*, 25 January 1999.

47. Anita Lahey, Michael McCullough, and Gail Chiasson, "Placing products," *Marketing Magazine*, 12 August 1996.

48. Paul-Mark Rendon, "The AVEs and the AVE nots," *Marketing Magazine*, 12 March 2007.

49. Annette Bourdeau, "Going for gold," *Strategy Magazine*, August 2007: 37.

50. Patti Summerfield, "Canadian tourism taps peer-to-peer media scene," *Strategy Magazine*, August 2007: 39.

51. Howard Stumpf and John M. Kawula, "Point of purchase advertising," in S. Ulanoff (ed.), *Handbook of Sales Promotion*, New York: McGraw Hill, 1985; Karen A. Berger, *The Rising Importance of Point-of-Purchase Advertising in the Marketing Mix*, Englewood, NJ: Point-of-Purchase Advertising Institute.

52. Terry Poulton, "Hockey star contest resets bar for prizing," *Media in Canada*, accessed 14 September 2007.

53. Liza Finlay, "Perpetual promotions," *Marketing Magazine*, 31 May 1999: 11–2.

54. Jeromy Lloyd, "Wake up and smell the lead," *Marketing Magazine*, 10 September 2007: 15; Allison Jones, "Over 900,000 Canadian toys recalled," *TheStar.com*, 14 August 2007.

55. Melinda Grenier Guiles, "Wooing press and public at auto shows," *Wall Street Journal*, 8 January 1990: B1.

56. Fawzia Sheikh, "Do your own thing," *Marketing Magazine*, 14 July 1997: 14.

57. Jennifer Lawrence, "Tracy-Locke division works for the big event," *Advertising Age*, 17 May 1993: S-2, S-7.

58. Louise Gagnon, "The big one," *Marketing Magazine*, 14 April 1997: 12.

59. Coupon Industry Association of Canada, *Coupon Fact Sheet for 2006*.

60. Don E. Schultz, William A. Robinson, and Lisa A. Petrison, *Sales Promotion Essentials*, 2nd ed., Lincolnwood, IL: NTC Business Books, 1993.

61. "Sampling debuts PowerBar in East," *Marketing Magazine: Newsline*, 7 June 1999.

62. Kate Fitzgerald, "Guinness looks to its past to fresh 5th pub giveaway," *Advertising Age*, 30 March 1998: 46.

63. Liza Finlay, "Perpetual promotions," *Marketing Magazine*, 31 May 1999: 11–2.

64. Kerry J. Smith, "It's for you," *PROMO: The International Magazine for Promotion Marketing*, August 1994: 41(4); Sharon Moshavi, "Please deposit no cents," *Forbes*, 16 August 1993: 102; *The Point-of-Purchase Advertising Industry Fact Book*, Englewood, NJ: The Point-of-Purchase Advertising Institute, 1992.

65. Lesley Young, "Smart sampling wins award and new cat owners," *Marketing Magazine*, 3 November 2003: 14.

66. Kerry J. Smith, "It's for you," *PROMO: The International Magazine for Promotion Marketing*, August 1994: 41(4); Sharon Moshavi, "Please deposit no cents," *Forbes*, 16 August 1993: 102; *The Point-of-Purchase Advertising Industry Fact Book*, Englewood, NJ: The Point-of-Purchase Advertising Institute, 1992.

67. "Bausch & Lomb makes eyes with consumers in Spain," *PROMO: The International Magazine for Promotion Marketing*, October 1994: 93.

68. Patricia Sellers, "Winning over the new consumer," *Fortune*, 29 July 1991: 113.

69. Lara Mills, "Marketers face up to new challenges," *Marketing Magazine*, 24 May 1999: 4.

70. Lara Mills, "Too much of a good thing," *Marketing Magazine*, 19/26 August 1996.

71. "Rocky Mountaineer's direct mail response goes off the rails," *Marketing Direct*, 16 April 2001.

72. Sarah Dobson, "Cara's winning combo," *Marketing Magazine*, 28 October 2002: 10–12.

560 | Endnotes

Chapter 14

73. "Hewlett-Packard's S.A.S. reseller and end user promotion," Promo Report, *Marketing Magazine*, 29 October 2001.

74. Jaclyn Fierman, "The death and rebirth of the salesman," *Fortune*, 25 July 1994: 38(7), 88.

75. "A user's guide to the sales manager's budget planner," *Sales and Marketing Management*, 28 June 1993: 6–10.

76. Greg Weatherdon, "The telemarketing edge: Combining it with broadcast faxing creates a powerful tool for drug companies," *Marketing Magazine*, 19 October 1998: 25.

77. www.salesforce.com, accessed 18 July 2006; Daniel Tynan, "CRM software: who needs it?" *Sales & Marketing Management*, July 2003: 30; Daniel Tynan, "CRM: Buy or rent?" *Sales & Marketing Management*, March 2004: 41–5.

78. www.skype.com, accessed 13 July 2006; Daniel Tynan, "Tech advantage," *Sales & Marketing Management*, April 2004: 47–51.

79. Dan C. Weilbaker, "The identification of selling abilities needed for missionary type sales," *Journal of Personal Selling & Sales Management* 10, Summer 1990: 45–58.

80. W. David Gibson, "Fielding a force of experts," *Sales and Marketing Management*, April 1993: 88–92; Henry Canaday, "Team selling works!" *Personal Selling Power*, September 1994: 53–8.

81. Jack Branswell, "The gadget king," *Marketing Magazine*, 12 June 2000.

82. Martin Everett, "This is the ultimate in selling," *Sales and Marketing Management*, August 1989: 28.

83. Maurice G. Clabaugh Jr. and Jessie L. Forbes, *Professional Selling: A Relationship Approach*, New York: West, 1992.

84. André Mazerolle and Eva A. Lau, "A teleconference on steroids: Web-push technology offers the next best thing to being there at a press conference," *Marketing Magazine*, 15 March 1999.

85. Melissa Campanelli, "Reshuffling the deck," *Sales and Marketing Management*, June 1994: 83–90.

86. W. David Gibson, "Fielding a force of experts," *Sales and Marketing Management*, April 1993: 88–92.

87. Ibid.

Chapter 14

1. Nitin Nohria, William Joyce, and Bruce Roberson, "What really works," *Harvard Business Review*, July 2003: 42.

2. Ajay Sirsi, *Marketing Led, Sales Driven: How Successful Businesses Use the Power of Marketing Plans and Sales Execution to Win in the Marketplace*, Trafford Publishing, 2004.

3. "Firing Your Customer," CBC *Venture*, Episode #710, 26 January 1999.

4. Ibid.

5. Jim Collins, *Good to Great*, Harper Business, 2001.

6. Thomas Bonoma, "Market success can breed 'marketing inertia,'" *Harvard Business Review*, September–October 1981: 115.

7. Frederick F. Reichheld and W. Earl Sasser, Jr., "Zero defections: Quality comes to services," *Harvard Business Review*, September–October 1990.

8. Philip Kotler and Ronald E. Turner, *Marketing Management: Analysis, Planning, Implementation and Control*, Canadian Ninth Edition, Toronto: Prentice-Hall Canada.

9. Richard L. Oliver, *Satisfaction: A Behavioral Perspective on the Consumer*, New York: McGraw-Hill, 1997.

10. A. Parasuraman, Valerie A. Zeithaml, and Len L. Berry, "A conceptual model of service quality and its implications for future research," *Journal of Marketing* 49, Fall 1985: 41–50.

11. Thomas O. Jones and W. Earl Sasser, Jr., "Why satisfied customers defect," *Harvard Business Review*, November–December 1995: 88.

GLOSSARY

acceleration principle (multiplier effect) A marketing phenomenon in which a small percentage change in consumer demand can create a large percentage change in business-to-business demand. *209*

actual product The physical good or the delivered service that supplies the desired benefit. *243*

advertising Non-personal, paid communication from an identified sponsor, primarily using mass media. *435*

advertising appeal The central idea or theme of a communication message. *431*

advertising campaign A coordinated, comprehensive plan that carries out promotion objectives and results in a series of advertisements placed in media over a period of time. *463*

advertising exposure The degree to which the target market will see an advertising message placed in a specific vehicle. *448*

advocacy advertising A type of public service advertising provided by an organization that is seeking to influence public opinion on an issue because it has some stake in the outcome. *462*

AIDA model The communication goals of attention, interest, desire, and action. *424*

aided recall A research technique that uses clues to prompt answers from people about advertisements they might have seen. *450*

aperture The best place and time to reach a person in the target market group. *447*

approach The first step of the actual sales presentation in which the salesperson tries to learn more about the customer's needs, create a good impression, and build rapport. *489*

atmospherics The use of colour, lighting, scents, furnishings, and other design elements to create a desired store image. *394*

attitude A learned predisposition to respond favourably or unfavourably to stimuli based on relatively enduring evaluations of people, objects, and issues. *179*

attitudinal measures A research technique that probes a consumer's beliefs or feelings about a product before and after being exposed to messages about it. *450*

augmented product The actual product plus other supporting features such as a warranty, credit, delivery, installation, and repair service after the sale. *243*

baby boomers The largest age segment in Canada, it includes people who were born between 1947 and 1966. *86*

bait and switch An illegal marketing practice in which an advertised price special is used as bait to get customers into the store with the intention of switching them to a higher-priced item. *316*

banners Internet advertising in the form of rectangular graphics at the top or bottom of webpages. *467*

bartering The practice of exchanging a good or service for another good or service of like value. *295*

behavioural learning theories Theories of learning that focus onhow consumer behaviour is changed by external events or stimuli. *178*

behavioural segmentation Technique that divides consumers into segments on the basis of how they act toward, feel about, or use a product or service. *79*

benefit The outcome sought by acustomer that motivates buying behaviour (that satisfies a need or want). *9*

benefit segmentation A segmentation approach that groups consumers or customers based on the benefits or value they seek in buying and using products. *79*

bid rigging Collusion between suppliers responding to bid requests to lessen competition and secure higher margins. *318*

blue ocean strategy A positioning strategy where you create a new market and get to define the playing field before competitors enter. *102*

bots Electronic robots or shopping agents that help consumers find products and prices on the Internet. *400*

bottom-up budgeting techniques Allocation of the promotion budget that is based on identifying promotional goals and allocating enough money to accomplish them. *444*

brand A name, term, symbol, or any other unique element of a product that identifies one firm's product(s) and sets it apart from the competition. *280*

brand concept How the marketer wants the brand to be positioned. *97*

brand equity The value of a brand to an organization. *282*

brand extension A new product sold with the same brand name as a strong existing brand. *282*

brand image How consumers perceive the positioning of the brand. *97*

brand loyalty A pattern of repeat product purchases, accompanied by an underlying positive attitude toward the brand, which is based on the belief that the brand makes products superior to its competition. *172*

brand manager A manager who is responsible for developing and implementing the marketing plan for a single brand. *285*

brand personality A distinctive image that captures a product or service's character and benefits. *105*

break-even analysis A method for determining the number of units that a firm must produce and sell at a given price to cover all its costs. *337*

bulk breaking Dividing larger quantities of goods into smaller lots to meet the needs of buyers. *356*

business-to-business (B2B) e-commerce Internet exchanges between two or more businesses or organizations. *221*

business-to-business marketing The marketing of goods and services that business and organizational customers need in order to produce other goods and services for resale or to support their operations. *206*

business ethics Rules of conduct for an organization. *60*

business portfolio The group of different products or brands owned by an organization and characterized by different income-generating and growth capabilities. *48*

buttons Small banner-type advertisements that can be placed anywhere on a webpage. *467*

buy class One of three classifications of business buying situations that characterize the degree of time and effort required to make a decision in a buying situation. *213*

buying centre The group of people in an organization who influence and participate in purchasing decisions. *216*

buying group The coordination of purchasing among member organizations to realize economies of scale and other efficiencies. *222*

buzz Word of mouth communication that is viewed as authentic and generated by customers. *439*

buzz marketing Using high-profile entertainment or news to get people to talk about your brand. *439*

cannibalization The loss of sales of an existing product when a new item in a product line or product family is introduced. *245*

capacity management The process by which organizations adjust their offerings in an attempt to match demand. *249*

captive pricing A pricing tactic for two items that must be used together; one item is priced very low and the firm makes its profit on another, high-margin item essential to the operation of the first item. *311*

case allowance A discount to the retailer or wholesaler based on the volume of product ordered. *480*

case study A comprehensive examination of a particular firm or organization. *137*

catalogue A collection of products offered for sale in book form, usually consisting of product descriptions accompanied by photos or illustrations of the items. *405*

causal research Techniques that attempt to understand cause-and-effect relationships. *138*

cause marketing A marketing strategy in which an organization serves its community by promoting and supporting a worthy cause or by allying itself with a not-for-profit organization to tackle a social problem. *66*

centralized purchasing A business buying practice in which an organization's purchasing department does all the buying for the company. *215*

channel captain A firm at one level of distribution that takes a leadership role, establishing operating norms and processes that reduce channel conflicts, reduce costs, and enhance delivered customer value. *367*

channel intermediaries Firms or individuals such as wholesalers, agents, brokers, and retailers that help move a product from the producer to the consumer or business user. *352*

channel length The number of levels or different types of intermediaries used in a distribution strategy. *364*

channel levels The number of distinct categories of intermediaries that populate a channel of distribution. *360*

channel of distribution The series of firms or individuals that facilitates the movement of a product from the producer to the final customer. *352*

channel width The extent to which a channel covers a market either by distributing the product through the largest number of intermediaries or to only one in the market. *364*

classical conditioning Learning that occurs when a stimulus eliciting a response is paired with another stimulus that initially does not elicit a response on its own but will cause a similar response over time because of its association with the first stimulus. *178*

clickstream analysis A means of measuring a website's success by tracking customers' movement around the company website. *171*

co-branding An agreement between two brands to work together in marketing new or existing products. *283*

code of ethics Written standards of behaviour to which everyone in the organization must subscribe. *62*

cognitive dissonance The regret or remorse buyers may feel after making a purchase. *173*

cognitive learning theory A theory of learning that stresses the importance of internal mental processes and that views people as problem solvers, who actively use information from the world around them to master their environment. *179*

communication mix The major elements of marketer-controlled communications, including advertising, sales promotions, marketing public relations, direct marketing, and personal selling. *434*

communication model The elements necessary for meaning to be transferred from a sender to a receiver. *423*

communication plan A framework that outlines the strategies for developing, implementing, and controlling the firm's communication activities. *427*

competitive advantage The ability of a firm to outperform the competition, providing customers with a benefit the competition cannot. *26, 54, 503*

competitive bids A business buying process in which two or more suppliers submit proposals (including price and associated data) for a proposed purchase and the firm providing the better offer gets the bid. *213*

competitive effect objective Pricing that is intended to have an effect on the marketing efforts of the competition. *298*

component parts Manufactured goods or subassemblies of finished items that organizations need to complete their own products. *257*

concentrated targeting strategy Focusing a firm's efforts on offering one or more products to a single segment. *96*

conformity A change in beliefs or actions as a reaction to real or imagined group pressure. *190*

consideration set The set of alternative brands the consumer is considering for the decision process. *172*

consumer The ultimate user of a good or service. *9*

consumer-generated media (CGM) Posts (including video, audio, and multimedia posts) created by consumers in support or against products, brands, and corporate institutions. *194*

consumer-generated value Customers functioning in marketing roles, such as participating in creating advertisements, providing input to new product development, or serving as wholesalers or retailers. *28*

consumer-to-consumer (C2C) e-commerce Communications and purchases that occur among individuals without directly involving the manufacturer or retailer. *192*

consumer addiction A physiological or psychological dependency on goods or services. *29*

consumer behaviour The process individuals or groups go through to select, purchase, and use goods, services, ideas, or experiences to satisfy their needs and desires. *167*

consumer interviews One-on-one discussions between a consumer and a researcher. *135*

consumer orientation A management philosophy that focuses on being proactive and responsive in identifying and satisfying consumer needs and wants. *23*

consumer satisfaction/dissatisfaction The overall feelings or attitude a person has about a product after purchasing it. *173*

consumerism A social movement that attempts to protect consumers from harmful business practices. *62*

continuous innovation A modification of an existing product thatsets one brand apart from its competitors. *259*

contribution margin (CM) The price an organization receives less its variable costs. *337*

convenience product A consumer good or service that is usually low-priced, widely available, and purchased frequently with a minimum of comparison and effort. *255*

conventional marketing system A multiple-level distribution channel in which channel members work independently of one another. *353*

cookies Text files inserted by a website sponsor into a web surfer's hard drive that allow the site to track the surfer's moves. *150*

copy testing A marketing research method that seeks to measure the effectiveness of ads by determining whether consumers are receiving, comprehending, and responding to the ad according to plan. *471*

core product All the benefits the product will provide for consumers or business customers. *243*

cost-plus pricing A method of setting prices in which the seller totals all the unit costs for the product and then adds the desired profit per unit. *300*

cost of ownership A pricing strategy that considers the lifetime cost of using the product. *308*

cost per thousand (CPM) A measure used to compare the relative cost-effectiveness of different media vehicles that have different exposure rates: the cost to deliver a message to 1000 people or homes. *449*

creating assortments Providing a variety of products in one location to meet the needs of buyers. *356*

creative concept How the advertising appeal will be expressed through visuals, text, music, and other design elements. *431*

creative selling process The process of seeking out customers, analyzing their needs, determining how product attributes might provide benefits for them, and then communicating that information. *489*

creative strategy The process that turns a concept into an advertisement. *446*

cross-promotion Two or more companies combining forces and using a single promotional tool to create interest in their products or services. *483*

cross-sectional design Type of descriptive technique that involves the systematic collection of quantitative information at one point in time. *137*

cultural diversity A management practice that actively seeks to include people of different sexes, races, ethnic groups, religions, and sexual preferences in an organization's employees, customers, suppliers, and distribution channel partners. *67*

culture The values, beliefs, customs, and tastes that a group of people value. *184*

cumulative quantity discounts Discounts based on the total quantity bought within a specified time period. *314*

custom marketing strategy Approach that tailors specific products and the messages about them to individual customers. *97*

customer equity The financial value of a customer relationship throughout the lifetime of the relationship. *226*

Customer Relationship Management (CRM) A strategy and process used by companies to identify their best customers, stay on top of their needs, and increase their satisfaction. *223*

customer satisfaction The difference between a customer's needs and expectations and the customer's perception that the good or service has met those needs and expectations. *512*

customer satisfaction objective Pricing that is intended to maximize customer satisfaction and retention. *298*

customer value What the customer gets in the purchase, use, and ownership of a product relative to the costs and sacrifices incurred. *8*

customer's lifetime value The potential profit generated by a single customer's purchase of a firm's products over the customer's lifetime. *226*

data mining Sophisticated analysis techniques to take advantage of the massive amount of transaction information now available. *128*

database marketing The creation of an ongoing relationship with a set of customers who have an identifiable interest in a good or service and whose responses to promotional efforts become part of future communication attempts. *422*

decline stage The final stage in the product life cycle, in which sales decrease as customer needs change. *278*

decoding The process by which a receiver assigns meaning to the message. *425*

demand Customers' desire for products coupled with the resources to obtain them. *10*

demand-based pricing A price-setting method based on estimates of demand at different prices. *302*

demand curve A plot of the quantity of a product that customers will buy in a market during a period of time at various prices if all other factors remain the same. *302*

demographics Variables that describe objective characteristics of a population or group. *84*

derived demand The demand for business or organizational products that is derived from demand for consumer goods or services. *208*

descriptive research Tool that probes more systematically into the problem and bases its conclusions on large numbers of observations. *137*

differential benefit Properties of products that set them apart from competitors' products by providing unique customer benefits. *26*

differentiated targeting strategy Developing one or more products for each of several distinct customer groups and making sure these offerings are kept separate in the marketplace. *96*

diffusion The process by which the use of a product spreads throughout a population. *261*

direct-response marketing Marketing activity aimed at generating a measurable response via marketing communications. *485*

direct-response TV Television programming, such as infomercials or shopping channels, which elicits direct orders for products from the viewing public. *407*

direct mail A brochure or pamphlet offering a specific product or service at one point in time. *405*

direct marketing Exposing a consumer to information about a good or service through a non-personal medium and convincing the customer to respond with an order. *399*

direct selling An interactive sales process in which a salesperson presents a product to one individual or a small group, takes orders, and delivers the merchandise. *406*

discontinuous innovation A totally new product that creates major changes in the way we live. *260*

disintermediation The process of eliminating interaction between customers and service providers. *250*

distinctive competency A superior capability of a firm in comparison to its direct competitors. *26*

diversification strategies Growth strategies that emphasize both new products and new markets. *49*

dumping Pricing products lower in a foreign market than they are offered in the home market. *59*

durable goods Consumer products that provide benefits over a long period of time, such as cars, furniture, and appliances. *255*

dynamic pricing Pricing strategy in which the price can easily be adjusted to meet changes in the marketplace. *326*

dynamically continuous innovation A change in an existing product that requires a moderate amount of learning or behaviour change. *260*

e-mail A process of sending messages in electronic form. *468*

early adopters Those who adopt an innovation early in the diffusion process but later than the innovators. *263*

early majority Those whose adoption of a new product signals a general acceptance of the innovation. *264*

80/20 rule A marketing rule of thumb that 20 percent of purchasers typically account for 80 percent of a product's sales. *80*

embodying The inclusion of a service with a purchase of a physical good. *247*

emergency products Products we purchase when we're in dire need. *256*

encoding The process of translating an idea into a form of communication that will convey meaning. *424*

environmental stewardship A position taken by an organization to protect or enhance the natural environment as it conducts its business activities. *66*

equipment Expensive goods that an organization uses in its daily operations that last for a long time. *257*

etailing Offering products for sale directly to consumers via the Internet. *399*

ethnography A detailed report on observations of people in their own homes or communities. *137*

evaluative criteria The dimensions that consumers use to compare competing product alternatives. *172*

exchange The process by which some transfer of value occurs between a buyer and a seller. *9*

exclusive distribution Selling a product through only a single outlet in a particular region. *364*

experiential marketing A holistic approach to marketing predicated on the fact that consumers make both rational and emotional buying decisions. *393*

experimental pricing A strategy of experimenting with prices until the price that generates the highest profitability is found. *305*

experiments Techniques that test prespecified relationships among variables in a controlled environment. *139*

exploratory research Technique that marketers use to generate insights for future, more rigorous studies. *135*

external environment The uncontrollable elements outside of an organization that may affect its performance either positively or negatively. These include macro environment factors like regulatory or technology factors, consumer behaviour trends, industry factors such as industry concentration, and competitive factors such as the number and sophistication of competitors. *44*

f.o.b. delivered pricing A pricing tactic in which the cost of loading and transporting the product to the customer is included in the selling price, paid by the manufacturer. *311*

f.o.b. origin pricing A pricing tactic in which the cost of transporting the product from the factory to the customer's location is the responsibility of the customer. *311*

facilitating functions Functions of channel intermediaries that make the purchase process easier for customers and manufacturers. *357*

fair trade A strategy that creates opportunities for producers of goods and commodities who have been economically disadvantaged or marginalized by conventional distribution systems. *366*

family brand A brand that a group of individual products or individual brands share. *282*

family life cycle A means of characterizing consumers based on the different family stages they pass through as they grow older. *181*

fast-moving consumer goods (FMCG) Products that exhibit consistently high velocity of sales in the consumer marketplace. *256*

feedback Receivers' reactions to the message. *425*

fixed costs Costs of production that do not change with the number of units produced. *301*

focus group A product-oriented discussion among a small group of consumers led by a trained moderator. *136*

form utility All activities used to change the appearance or composition of a good or service with the intent of making it more attractive to potential and actual users. *355*

freight absorption pricing A pricing tactic in which the seller absorbs the total cost of transportation. *311*

frequency The number of times a person in the target group will be exposed to the message. *448*

frequent discounting A strategy of frequently using sale prices to increase sales volume. *306*

geodemography Segmentation technique that combines geography with demographics. *91*

goods Tangible products we can see, touch, smell, hear, or taste. *242*

government markets Federal, provincial, and local governments that buy goods and services to carry out public objectives and to support their operations. *213*

green marketing A marketing strategy that supports environmental stewardship by creating an environmentally founded differential benefit in the minds of consumers. *66*

grey market The importing of products by an unauthorized party, who then sells them for a fraction of the price. *59*

gross rating points (GRPs) A measure used for comparing the effectiveness of different media vehicles: average reach times frequency. *448*

growth stage The second stage in the product life cycle, during which the product is accepted and sales rapidly increase. *277*

guerrilla marketing Promotional strategies that "ambush" consumers with promotional content in places they are not expecting it. *441, 477*

heuristics A mental rule of thumb that leads to a speedy decision by simplifying the process. *172*

hierarchy of needs An approach that categorizes motives according to five levels of importance, the more basic needs being on the bottom of the hierarchy and the higher needs at the top. *178*

horizontal marketing system An arrangement within a channel of distribution in which two or more firms at the same channel level work together for a common purpose. *354*

hypermarkets Retailers with the characteristics of both warehouse stores and supermarkets; hypermarkets are several times larger than other stores and offer virtually everything from grocery items to electronics. *391*

image enhancement objective Pricing intended to establish a desired image or positioning to prospective customers. *299*

impressions The number of people who will be exposed to a message placed in one or more media vehicles. *448*

impulse product A product people often buy on the spur of the moment. *256*

independent intermediaries Channel intermediaries that are not controlled by any manufacturer but rather do business with many different manufacturers and many different customers. *357*

industrial psychographics The application of psychographics to the business-to-business context. *92*

inelastic demand The demand for products does not change because of increases or decreases in price. *208*

information search The process whereby a consumer searches for appropriate information needed to make a reasonable decision. *170*

information utility The value given to a product that provides the user with useful information. *355*

innovation A product that consumers perceive to be new and different from existing products. *258*

innovators The first segment (roughly 2.5 percent) of a population to adopt a new product. *263*

institutional advertising An advertising message that promotes the activities, personality, or point of view of an organization or company. *462*

integrated marketing communications (IMC) IMC is the practice of unifying all marketing communication tools and corporate and brand messages to communicate in a consistent way to and with stakeholder audiences. *418*

intensive distribution Selling a product through all suitable wholesalers or retailers that are willing to stock and sell the product. *364*

interactive marketing A promotion practice in which customized marketing communications elicit a measurable response from individual receivers. *422, 437*

internal environment The controllable elements inside an organization, including its people, its facilities, and how it does things that influence the operations of the organization. *44*

internal reference price A set price or a price range in consumers' minds that they refer to in evaluating a product's price. *321*

intranet An internal corporate communication network that uses Internet technology to link company departments, employees, and databases. *123, 222*

introduction The first stage of the product life cycle, in which slow growth follows the introduction of a new product in the marketplace. *275*

inventory control Activities to ensure that goods are always available to meet customers' demands. *373*

inventory turnover The average number of times a year a retailer expects to sell its inventory. *389*

involvement The relative importance of perceived consequences of the purchase to a consumer. *168*

joint demand The demand for two or more goods that are used together to create a product. *209*

judgment A pricing strategy that draws on past experience of the marketer in setting appropriate prices. *306*

just in time (JIT) Inventory management and purchasing processes that manufacturers and resellers use to reduce inventory to very low levels and ensure that deliveries from suppliers arrive only when needed. *219*

knock-off A new product that copies with slight modification the design of an original product. *260*

laggards The last consumers to adopt an innovation. *264*

late majority The adopters who are willing to try new products when there is little or no risk associated with the purchase, when the purchase becomes an economic necessity, or when there is social pressure to purchase. *264*

learning A relatively permanent change in behaviour caused by acquired information or experience. *178*

licensing An agreement in which one firm sells another firm the right to use a brand name for a specific purpose and for a specific period of time. *283*

lifestyle The pattern of living that determines how people choose to spend their time, money, and energy that reflects their values, tastes, and preferences. *182*

lifetime value of a customer How much profit companies expect to make from a particular customer, including each and every purchase he or she will make from them now and in the future. To calculate lifetime value, companies estimate the amount the person will spend and then subtract what it will cost the company to maintain this relationship. *25*

list price The price the end customer is expected to pay as determined by the manufacturer. *312*

logistics The process of designing, managing, and improving the movement of products through the supply chain. *368*

long tail A new approach to segmentation based on the idea that companies can make money by selling small amounts of items that only a few people want, provided they sell enough different items. *80*

longitudinal design Technique that tracks the responses of the same sample of respondents over time. *138*

loss-leader pricing The pricing strategy of setting prices below cost to attract customers into a store. *317*

m-commerce Promotional and other e-commerce activities transmitted over mobile phones and other mobile devices such as personal digital assistants (PDAs). *469*

maintenance, repair, and operating (MRO) products Goods that a business customer consumes in a relatively short time. *257*

margin The difference between the cost of the product and the selling price of the product. *318*

marginal analysis A method that uses costs and demand to identify the price that will maximize profits. *339*

market development strategies Growth strategies that introduce existing products to new markets. *48*

market fragmentation Creation of many consumer groups due to a diversity of distinct needs and wants in modern society. *75*

market manager A manager who is responsible for developing and implementing the marketing plans for products sold to a specific customer group. *285*

market penetration strategies Growth strategies designed to increase sales of existing products to current customers, nonusers, and users of competitive brands in served markets. *48*

market potential The maximum demand expected among consumers in a segment for a product or service. *94*

market segment A distinct group of customers within a larger market who have similar needs, wants, preferences, and behaviours, who seek similar product solutions, and whose needs differ from other customers in the larger market. *13*

market segmentation A process of dividing the overall market into groups of consumers who are sufficiently similar within the group to want a similar value offer and different enough from other groups to want a different value offer than those other groups. *13*

marketing An organizational function and a set of processes for creating, communicating, and delivering value to customers and for managing customer relationships in ways that benefit the organization and its stakeholders. *7*

marketing communications Informing consumers and customers about the relative value of products, and developing trust and other relational bonds that facilitate ongoing exchange relationships. *417*

marketing concept A business orientation that focuses on achieving organizational objectives by understanding customer needs, and creating and delivering value in exchanges that satisfy the needs of all parties. *9*

marketing decision support system (MDSS) The data, analysis software, and interactive software that allow managers to conduct analyses and find the information they need. *127*

marketing information system (MIS) Procedure developed by a firm to continuously gather, sort, analyze, store, and distribute relevant and timely marketing information to its managers. *122*

marketing intelligence A method by which marketers get information about everyday happenings in the marketing environment. *123*

marketing mix A combination of the product itself, the price of the product, the place where it is made available, and the activities that introduce it to consumers, which creates a desired response among a set of predefined consumers. *15*

marketing plan A document that describes the marketing environment, outlines the marketing objectives and strategy, identifies who will be responsible for carrying out each part of the marketing strategy, and describes how the strategy will be adjusted to respond to a changing marketplace. *50, 503*

marketing research The process of collecting, analyzing, and interpreting data about customers, competitors, and the business environment to make a specific marketing decision. *125*

marketplace Any location or medium used to conduct an exchange. *10*

mass customization Approach that modifies a basic product or service to meet the needs of an individual. *97*

mass market All possible customers in a market, regardless of the differences in their specific needs and wants. *14*

materials handling The moving of products into, within, and out of warehouses. *372*

maturity stage The third and longest stage in the product life cycle, in which sales peak and profit margins narrow. *277*

media planning The process of developing media objectives, strategies, and tactics for use in an advertising campaign. *447*

media schedule The plan that specifies the exact media to use and when. *447*

medium A communication vehicle through which a message is transmitted to a target audience. *424*

merchandise agents or brokers Channel intermediaries that provide services in exchange for commissions but never take title to the product. *359*

merchandise allowance A promotion that reimburses the retailer for in-store support of the product. *480*

merchandise assortment The range of products sold. *388*

merchandise breadth The number of different product lines available. *388*

merchandise depth The variety of choices available for each specific product. *388*

merchandise mix The total set of all products offered for sale by a firm, including all product lines sold to all consumer groups. *388*

merchant wholesalers Intermediaries that buy goods from manufacturers (take title to them) and sell to retailers and other business-to-business customers. *357*

message The communication in physical form that goes from a sender to a receiver. *424*

mission statement A formal statement in an organization's strategic plan that describes the overall purpose of the organization and what it intends to achieve in terms of its customers, products, and resources. *44*

missionary salesperson A salesperson who promotes the firm and tries to stimulate demand for a product but does not actually complete a sale. *487*

modified rebuy A buying situation classification that business buyers use to categorize a previously made purchase that involves some change and that requires limited decision making. *214*

motivation An internal state that drives us to satisfy needs by activating goal-oriented behaviour. *177*

multicultural marketing The practice of recognizing and targeting the distinctive needs and wants of one or more ethnic subcultures. *187*

multilevel marketing A system in which a master distributor recruits other people to become distributors, sells the company's product to the recruits, and receives a commission on all the merchandise they sell. *407*

multiple sourcing The business practice of buying a particular product from many suppliers. *220*

national or manufacturer brands Brands that the manufacturer of the product owns. *282*

need The recognition of any difference between a consumer's actual state and some ideal or desired state. *9*

new-task buy A new business-to-business purchase that is complex or risky and that requires extensive decision making. *214*

new product failure A new product that does not reach expectations for success, failing to reach sales objectives set. *241*

niche marketing A type of concentrated targeting strategy where the market segment chosen is relatively small. *96*

noise Anything that interferes with effective communication. *425*

non-cumulative quantity discounts Discounts based only on the quantity purchased in individual orders. *314*

nondurable goods Consumer products that provide benefits for a short time because they are consumed (such as food) or are no longer useful (such as newspapers). *255*

non-probability sample A sample in which personal judgment is used in selecting respondents. *145*

non-store retailing Any method used to complete an exchange with a product end user that does not require a customer visit to a store. *399*

North American Industry Classification System (NAICS) The numerical coding system that the United States, Canada, and Mexico use to classify firms into detailed categories according to their business activities and shared characteristics. *210*

not-for-profit institutions Organizations with charitable, educational, community, and other public service goals that buy goods and services to support their functions and to attract and serve their members. *213*

objective-task method A promotion budgeting method in which an organization first defines the specific communication goals it hopes to achieve and then tries to calculate what kind of promotional efforts it must take to meet these goals. *444*

off-price retailers Retailers that buy excess merchandise from well-known manufacturers and pass the savings on to customers. *391*

online auctions E-commerce that allows shoppers to purchase products through online bidding. *327*

operant conditioning Learning that occurs as the result of rewards or punishments. *179*

operating costs Costs involved in using a product. *295*

operating variables The production technology used, the business customer's degree of technical, financial, or operations expertise, and whether the prospect is a current user or non-user of the product. *91*

opinion leader A person who is frequently able to influence others' attitudes or behaviours by virtue of his or her active interest and expertise in one or more product categories. *191*

opportunity cost The value of something that is given up to obtain something else. *295*

order getter A salesperson who works creatively to develop relationships with customers or to generate new sales. *487*

order taker A salesperson whose primary function is to facilitate transactions that the customer initiates. *487*

out-of-home media Communications media that reach people in public places. *470*

outsourcing The business buying process of obtaining outside vendors to provide goods or services that otherwise might be supplied in-house; transferring a firm's task to an external supplier at a cheaper price. *220, 369*

party plan system A sales technique that relies heavily on people getting caught up in the "group spirit," buying things they would not normally buy if alone. *406*

penetration pricing A pricing strategy in which a firm introduces a new product at a very low price to encourage more customers to purchase it. *306*

perceived risk The belief that use of a product has potentially negative consequences, either financial, physical, or social. *168*

percentage-of-sales method A method for promotion budgeting, in which the promotion budget is based on a percentage of either last year's sales or on estimates for this year's sales. *444*

perception The process by which people select, organize, and interpret information from the outside world. *176*

perceptual map A picture of where products or brands are "located" in consumers' minds. *101*

perishability management A strategy that considers the characteristics of any given product or service that is perishable, that cannot be stored, and that must be sold at particular moments in time. *362*

permission-based marketing E-mail advertising in which online consumers have the opportunity to accept or refuse the unsolicited e-mail. *468*

personal selling The part of the promotion mix that involves direct contact between a company representative and a customer. *485*

personality The psychological characteristics that consistently influence the way a person responds to situations in the environment. *179*

place The availability of the product to the customer at the desired time and location. Also known as channels of distribution. *17*

place utility Increased usefulness created by making a product available at a location preferred by consumers. *355*

point-of-purchase (POP) promotion The use of signs or displays to influence purchases at the store. *482*

point-of-sale (POS) systems Retail computer systems that collect sales data and are hooked directly into the store's inventory control system. *386*

pop-up ad An advertisement that appears on the screen while a webpage is being loaded or after it has loaded. *468*

portals Gateways to the Internet that assist consumers in navigating the Internet and customizing their experience. *401*

positioning Strategies to establish the unique value proposition of an offering and sustain its superiority in the eyes of target customers; developing a marketing strategy aimed at influencing how a particular market segment perceives a product or service as being differentiated in comparison to the competition. *15, 97*

possession (ownership) utility Increased usefulness created by making it possible for a consumer to own, use, and consume a product. *355*

post-testing Research conducted on consumers' responses to actual advertising messages they have seen or heard. *449*

pre-approach A part of the selling process that includes developing information about prospective customers and planning the sales interview. *489*

pre-testing A research method that seeks to minimize mistakes by getting consumer reactions to ad messages before they appear in the media. *470*

predatory pricing The strategy of selling products at unreasonably low prices to drive competitors out of business. *316*

premium An item included without charge with a purchased product. *482*

press release Information that an organization distributes to the media about its activities, intended to appear as publicity. *476*

prestige pricing A strategy where prices are set significantly higher than competing brands. *309*

price The seller's assignment of value to a product; the value that customers give up, or exchange, to obtain a desired product. *17, 295*

price-floor pricing A method for calculating price in which, to maintain full plant operating capacity, a portion of a firm's output may be sold at a price that covers only marginal costs of production. *301*

price bundling Selling two or more goods or services as a single package for one price. *308*

price discrimination The illegal practice of offering the same product of like quality and quantity to different business customers at different prices, thus lessening competition. *317*

price elastic When a percentage change in price results in a larger percentage change in the quantity demanded. *322*

price elasticity of demand The percentage change in unit sales that results from a percentage change in price. *322*

price fixing An illegal business practice in which firms decide in advance on a common price for their product. *64*

price inelastic When a percentage change in price results in a smaller percentage change in the quantity demanded. *322*

price leadership (follower) The firm that sets prices first in an industry; other major firms in the industry follow the leader by staying in line. *307*

price lining The practice of setting a limited number of different specific prices, called price points, for items in a product line. *312*

price maintenance The collaboration of two or more firms in setting prices, usually to keep prices high. *317*

price subsidies Government payments made to protect domestic businesses or to reimburse them when they must price at or below cost to make a sale. The subsidy can be a cash payment or tax relief. *326*

primary research Research conducted by or for a single firm to provide information for a specific marketing decision. *127*

private exchanges Systems that link an invited group of suppliers and partners over the web. *222*

probability sample A sample in which each member of the population has some known chance of being included in the sample. *145*

problem recognition The process that occurs whenever the consumer sees a significant difference between his or her current state of affairs and some desired or ideal state. This recognition initiates the decision-making process. *169*

processed materials Products created when firms transform raw materials from their original state. *257*

procurement management Procuring goods and services from external suppliers in a strategic fashion. *368*

producers The individuals or organizations that purchase products for use in the production of other goods and services. *213*

product A tangible good, a service, an idea, or some combination of these that, through the exchange process, satisfies consumer or business customer needs; a bundle of attributes including features, functions, benefits, and uses. *16*

product adoption The process by which a consumer or business customer begins to buy and use a new good, service, or idea. *261*

product advertising An advertising message that focuses on a specific good or service. *462*

product category manager A manager who is responsible for developing and implementing the marketing plan for all the brands and products within a product category. *285*

product development strategies Growth strategies that focus on selling new products in served markets. *49*

product life cycle Concept that explains how products go through four distinct stages from birth to death: introduction, growth, maturity, and decline. *275*

product line A firm's total product offering designed to satisfy a single need or desire of target customers. *244*

product mix The total set of all products a firm offers for sale. *246*

product orientation A management philosophy that emphasizes the most efficient ways to produce and distribute products. *23*

product usage segmentation A segmentation approach that groups consumers or business customers based on the amount of a product purchased or consumed or how the product is used. *79*

profit objective Pricing products with a focus on a target level of profit growth or a desired net profit margin. *297*

projective techniques Tests that marketers use to explore people's underlying feelings about a product, especially appropriate when consumers are unable or unwilling to express their true reactions. *136*

promotion The coordination of a marketer's communication efforts to influence attitudes or behaviour toward a product or service. *17, 417*

prospecting A part of the selling process that includes identifying and developing a list of potential or prospective customers. *489*

psychographic segmentation A segmentation approach that groups people based on their attitudes, beliefs, values, lifestyles, or other psychological orientations. *81*

public relations (PR) Communications strategies to build good relationships and corporate image with an organization's stakeholders, including consumers, stockholders, and legislators. *437, 472*

public service advertisements Advertising run by the media without charge for not-for-profit organizations or to champion a particular cause. *462*

publicity Unpaid communication about an organization appearing in the mass media. *437, 476*

pull strategy Moving products through the channel by building desire for the products among consumers, who convince retailers to stock the items. *430*

push money A bonus paid by a manufacturer to a salesperson for selling its product. *481*

push strategy Moving products through the channel by convincing channel members to offer them. *430*

push technology Internet tools that allow marketers to send information they think is relevant to consumers directly to their computers. *401*

pyramid schemes An illegal sales technique in which the initial distributors profit by selling merchandise to other distributors, with the result that consumers buy very little product. *407*

qualify prospects A part of the selling process that determines how likely prospects are to become customers. *489*

quantity discounts A pricing tactic of charging reduced prices for larger quantities of a product. *313*

raw materials Products of the fishing, lumber, agricultural, and mining industries that organizational customers purchase to use in their finished products. *257*

reach The percentage of the target market that will be exposed to the media vehicle. *448*

rebates Sales promotions that allow the customer to recover part of the product's cost from the manufacturer. *481*

receiver The organization or individual that intercepts and interprets the message. *425*

reciprocity A trading partnership in which two firms agree to buy from one another. *220*

reference group An actual or imaginary individual or group that has a significant effect on an individual's evaluations, aspirations, or behaviour. *190*

relationship selling A form of personal selling in which the salesperson seeks to develop a mutually satisfying relationship with the consumer so that they can work together to satisfy each other's needs. *488*

reliability The extent to which research measurement techniques are free of errors. *144*

repositioning Redoing a product's position to respond to marketplace changes. *110*

representativeness The extent to which consumers in a study are similar to a larger group in which the organization has an interest. *144*

research design A plan that specifies what information marketers will collect and what type of study they will do. *134*

resellers The individuals or organizations that buy finished goods for the purpose of reselling, renting, or leasing to others to make a profit and to maintain their business operations. *213*

retail life cycle A process that focuses on the various retail life cycle stages from introduction to decline. *384*

retailing The final stop in the distribution channel by which goods and services are sold to consumers for their personal use. *383*

reverse marketing A business practice in which a buyer firm attempts to identify suppliers who will produce products according to the buyer firm's specifications. *220*

sales closing The stage of the selling process in which the salesperson asks the customer to buy the product. *491*

sales follow-up After-sales activities that provide important services to customers. *491*

sales management The process of planning, implementing, and controlling the personal selling function of an organization. *491*

sales or market share objective Pricing products to maximize sales or to attain a desired level of sales or market share. *298*

sales presentation The part of the selling process in which the salesperson seeks to persuasively communicate the product's features and the benefits it will provide after the sale. *490*

sales promotion A program designed to build interest in or encourage purchase of a product during a specified time period. *479*

sales territory A set of customers often defined by geographic boundaries, for whom a particular salesperson is responsible. *491*

sampling The process of selecting respondents who statistically represent a larger population of interest, *144*; distributing trial-size versions of a product for free to encourage people to try it. *482*

scalability The ability of organizations to get bigger without a big rise in expenses. *403*

scenarios Possible future situations that futurists use to assess the likely impact of alternative marketing strategies. *124*

scrambled merchandising A merchandising strategy that offers consumers a mixture of merchandise items that are not directly related to each other. *388*

search engines Internet tools that maintain databases of websites and use programs to collect information in order to help users find webpages on a given subject. *401*

secondary research Research collected for a purpose other than the decision at hand. *125*

segment profile A description of the "typical" customer in a segment. *93*

segment profiles Detailed descriptions of the characteristics, behaviours, and thinking of a market segment that help marketers design and present a valued offer. *13*

segmentation The process of dividing a larger market into smaller pieces, based on one or more meaningful, shared characteristics. *76*

segmentation variables Bases for dividing the total market into fairly homogenous groups, each with different needs and preferences. *78*

selective distribution Distribution using fewer outlets than in intensive distribution but more than in exclusive distribution. *365*

self-concept An individual's self-image that is composed of a mixture of beliefs, observations, and feelings about personal attributes. *181*

selling orientation A managerial view of marketing as a selling function, or a way to move products out of warehouses to reduce inventory. *23*

sensitivity analysis An analytic technique of testing how important an assumption is. Financial analysis is conducted under different assumptions for a key value. If the same marketing decision would be made under any assumption of the value, then the results are not sensitive to that value. If your decision would change depending on the number used, then research is needed to determine the correct value. *509*

service encounter The actual interaction between the customer and the service provider. *250*

services Intangible products that are exchanged directly from the producer to the customer. *249*

sex roles Society's expectations about the appropriate attitudes, behaviours, and appearance for men and women. *191*

share of customer The percentage of an individual customer's purchase of a product that is a single brand. *226*

shopping product A good or service for which consumers spend considerable time and effort gathering information and comparing alternatives before making a purchase. *256*

single-source data Information that is integrated from multiple sources in order to monitor the impact of marketing communications on a particular customer group over time. *148*

single sourcing The business practice of buying a particular product from only one supplier. *219*

skimming price Charging a very high, premium price for a new product. *305*

slotting allowance A fee paid by a manufacturer to a retailer in exchange for agreeing to place products on the retailer's shelves. *65*

social class The overall rank or social standing of groups of people within a society according to the value assigned to such factors as family background, education, occupation, and income. *188*

social marketing concept A marketing philosophy that emphasizes that customer needs must be satisfied in ways that also benefit society. *20*

social profit The benefit an organization and society receive from the organization's ethical practices, community service, efforts to promote cultural diversity, and concern for the natural environment. *60*

social responsibility A management practice in which organizations seek to engage in activities that have a positive effect on society and promote the public good. *65*

source An organization or individual that sends a message. *424*

spam Unsolicited electronic massages sent in bulk. *407*

spamming Sending unsolicited e-mail to five or more people not personally known to the sender. *468*

specialty products A good or service with unique characteristics that are important to the buyer and for which the buyer will devote significant effort to acquire. *256*

sponsorship A PR activity through which companies provide financial support to help fund an event in return for publicized recognition of the company's contribution. *476*

stakeholder People or organizations who influence or are influenced by marketing decisions. *9*

staples Basic or necessary items that are available almost everywhere. *256*

status symbols Products that consumers purchase to signal membership in a desirable social class. *188*

stimulus generalization Behaviour caused by a reaction to one stimulus that occurs in the presence of other similar stimuli. *179*

store image The way a retailer is perceived in the marketplace relative to the competition. *393*

store or private-label brands Brands that are owned and sold by a specific retailer or distributor. *282*

straight rebuy A buying situation in which business buyers make routine purchases that require minimal decision making. *214*

strategic planning A managerial decision process that matches an organization's resources and capabilities to its market opportunities for long-term growth and survival. *42*

strategy What a firm is going to do to achieve an objective. *42*

subculture A group within a society whose members share a distinctive set of beliefs, characteristics, or common experiences. *186*

supply chain All the firms that engage in activities necessary to turn raw materials into a good or service and put it in the hands of the consumer or business customer. *368*

supply chain management The management of flows among firms in the supply chain to maximize profitability. *368*

survey A questionnaire that asks participants about their beliefs or behaviours. *140*

switching costs Costs involved in moving from one brand to another. *295*

SWOT analysis An analysis of an organization's strengths and weaknesses and the opportunities and threats in its external environment. *50*

syndicated research Research by firms that collect data on a regular basis and sell the reports to multiple firms. *127*

tactics How a strategy is going to be implemented. *42*

take title To accept legal ownership of a product and the accompanying rights and responsibilities of ownership. *357*

target audience A highly segmented group of people who receive and respond similarly to marketing messages. *427*

target costing A process in which firms identify the quality and functionality needed to satisfy customers and what price they are willing to pay before the product is designed; the product is manufactured only if the firm can control costs to meet the required price. *303*

target market The market segment on which an organization focuses its marketing plan and toward which it directs its marketing efforts. *13, 94*

target marketing strategy Dividing the total market into different segments based on customer characteristics, selecting one or more segments, and developing products to meet the needs of those specific segments. *75*

technical specialist Sales support personnel with a high level of technical expertise who assist in product demonstrations. *487*

telemarketing The use of the telephone or fax to sell directly to consumers and business customers. *407, 486*

test marketing Testing the complete marketing plan in a small geographic area that is similar to the larger market the firm hopes to enter. *252*

time utility All activities that increase satisfaction by making products available at the time consumers want them. *355*

tipping point In the context of product diffusion, the point when a product's sales spike from a slow climb to an unprecedented new level, often accompanied by a steep price decline. *261*

top-down budgeting techniques Allocation of the promotion budget that is based on the total amount to be devoted to marketing communications. *444*

total contribution Contribution margin multiplied by the number of units sold. *337*

total unit cost Variable costs plus average fixed costs per unit. *337*

trade area A geographic zone that accounts for the majority of a store's sales and customers. *399*

trademark The legal term for a brand name, brand mark, or trade character; a trademark legally registered by a government obtains protection for exclusive use in that country. *280*

trade or functional discounts Discounts off the list price of products to members of the channel of distribution that perform various marketing functions. *313*

trade shows Events at which many companies set up exhibits to show their products, give away samples, distribute product literature, and troll for new business contacts. *480*

traffic flow The direction in which shoppers move through the store and what areas they pass or avoid. *394*

transactional selling A form of personal selling that focuses on making an immediate sale with little or no attempt to develop a relationship with the customer. *488*

trial pricing Pricing a new product low for a limited period of time to lower the risk for a customer. *307*

triple bottom line A business perspective that measures economic, social, and environmental value creation. *22*

umbrella pricing A strategy of ducking under a competitor's price by a fixed percentage. *308*

unaided recall A research technique conducted by telephone survey or personal interview that asks how much of an ad a person remembers during a specified period of time. *450*

undifferentiated (mass) targeting strategy Appealing to a broad spectrum of people. *95*

uniform delivered pricing A pricing tactic in which a firm adds a standard shipping charge to the price for all customers regardless of location. *311*

unsought products Goods or services for which a consumer has little awareness or interest until the product or a need for the product is brought to his or her attention. *257*

usage occasions Indicator used in one type of market segmentation based on when consumers use a product most. *80*

validity The extent to which research actually measures what it was intended to measure. *144*

VALS™ (Values and Lifestyles) A psychographic system that divides people into eight segments. *83*

value The benefits a customer receives from buying and using a good or service in relation to the costs and sacrifices of buying and using it. *5*

value-in-use analysis Analysis that quantifies the cost-benefit analysis from the customer's perspective, specifying what the customer will gain or save by using the product relative to the cost of buying, using, and disposing of the product. After the plan has been implemented, markets track customer satisfaction and retention as indicators of customer value creation. *510*

value chain A series of activities involved in designing, producing, marketing, delivering, and supporting any product. Each link in the chain has the potential to either add or remove value from the product the customer eventually buys; the concept of a supply chain that looks at how each firm receives inputs, adds value to these inputs, and then passes them along to the next firm in the value chain. *26, 368*

value pricing or everyday low pricing (EDLP) A pricing strategy in which a firm sets prices that provide ultimate value to customers. *306*

value proposition A marketplace offering that fairly and accurately sums up the value that will be realized if the good or service is purchased. *24*

variable costs The costs of production (raw and processed materials, parts, and labour) that are tied to, and vary depending on, the number of units produced. *301*

variable pricing A flexible pricing strategy that reflects what individual customers are willing to pay. *305*

venture teams Groups of people within an organization who focus exclusively on the development of a new product. *285*

vertical marketing system (VMS) A channel of distribution in which there is cooperation among members at the manufacturing, wholesaling, and retailing levels. *353*

viral marketing Creating entertaining or informative messages that are designed to be passed along in an exponential fashion, often electronically or by e-mail. *439*

want The desire to satisfy needs inspecific ways that are culturally and socially influenced. *9*

warehousing Storing goods in anticipation of sale or transfer to another member of the channel of distribution. *371*

wheel-of-retailing hypothesis A theory that explains how retail firms change, becoming more upscale as they go through their life cycle. *383*

wholesaling intermediaries Firms that handle the flow of products from the manufacturer to the retailer or business user. *357*

word of mouth (WOM) The act of consumers providing information to other consumers. *439*

word-of-mouth marketing Giving people a reason to talk about your products and making it easier for that conversation to take place. *439*

yield-management pricing A practice of charging different prices to different customers to manage capacity while maximizing revenues. *304*

zone pricing A pricing tactic in which customers in different geographic zones pay different transportation rates. *311*

CREDITS

204, 228 Courtesy of Deborah McKenzie; **205** Courtesy of Moosehead Breweries Limited; **207** Courtesy of DALSA Corporation; **208** Photograph reprinted courstey of Caterpillar Inc.; **209** BMW of North America, Inc.; **212 (top)** Courtesy of MTS Allstream; **212 (bottom)** Greater Vancouver Transportation Authority; **214** Federal Express; **215** Courtesy of Canon Canada; **216** Ralf-Finn Hestoft/SABA Press Photos, Inc.; **219** CP Photo; **221** Courtesy of Future Shop; **222** The Canadian Press (Steve White); **223** Used with permission of Excelon; **224** Federal Express; **225** Jupiter/Goodshoot.

Chapter 7

238 Churchill & Klehr Photography; **240, 266** Courtesy of Dee Dee Gordon; **241 (top)** © 2007 ProhibitOnions; **241 (bottom)** The Canadian Press (AP/Ted S. Warren); **244 (top)** Volkswagen of America, Inc.; **244 (bottom)** Volkswagen of America/FPG International LLC; **245** Photo used with permission of Bombardier Inc. Traxter™ XT are trademarks of Bombardier Inc. and/or its subsidiaries; **246 (top)** Courtesy of Procter & Gamble Inc.; **246 (bottom)** Victorinox® and Swiss Army™ are registered trademarks; **249** Norm Betts/Bloomberg News/Landov; **250** Courtesy of Johnson Research and Development Co., Inc.; **252** Procter & Gamble, Inc.; **260** Courtesy of Mastercard International; **262 (top)** Courtesy of Cadbury Adams Canada Inc.; **262 (bottom)** "Barq's" trademarks are used with permission; **264** Jergens Canada Inc.; **265** Denis Cahill/CP Photo Archive; **266 (top)** Courtesy of SAIC; (bottom) Renaissance Cosmetics, Inc.

Chapter 8

272 Dick Hemingway; **274, 286** Courtesy of Julie Desrosier; **275** © David Michael Zimmerman/Corbis; **277** Ad courtesy of Hitachi, Ltd.; **278** Warner-Lambert Canada, Inc.; **279** Courtesy of © WaiterPad POS Systems.; **280 (top)** Kraft Canada Inc.: **280 (bottom)** © Clarica Life Insurance Company. All rights reserved; **281** The A&W Rootbeer Company; **284** The Canadian Press (Andre Forget); **285** AP/Wide World Photos.

Chapter 9

292 TELUS advertisement used with permission. ©TELUS. All rights reserved; **294, 328 (bottom)** Courtesy of Leonard Hendricks; **296** Jim Young/Reuters/Landov; **298** © 1996–2008 Travelocity.com LP. All rights reserved. Travelocity, Travelocity.com, The Roaming Gnome and Stars Design are registered trademarks of Travelocity.com LP; **299** Courtesy of Burton Snowboards;

301 Michael Newman/PhotoEdit; **303** Used with permission of Dell Computer Corporation; **304** Tibor Bognar/CORBIS/MAGMA; **305** REUTERS/Yuriko Nakao/Landov; **306** Trademark reproduced with the permission of Zellers Inc.; **308** Malaysia Airlines/Albert Pointdexter; **309 (top)** Courtesy of Kodak Canada Inc.; **309 (bottom)** Lee Valley Tools Ltd.; **310** Suzuki; **311** Used with permission of Gillette Inc.; **312** Majorie Farrell/The Image Works; **313** Mongoose; **314** Tourism P.E.I.; **316** Dick Hemingway; **319** Gucci America Inc.; **320** Tursack Incorporated; **321 (top)** Dick Hemingway; **321 (bottom)** Blair Seitz/Photo Researchers, Inc.; **323** Cliff Otto/Lost Angeles Times; **324** Issei Kato/Landov; **325** Terri Stratford; **327** Used with permission of Eddie Bauer Inc.; **328 (top)** Courtesy of Priceline.com.

Chapter 10

348 Weldwood of Canada; **350, 374** Courtesy of Mike Nomura; **351** Courtesy of Expedia Canada Corp.; Alene M. McNeil; **355** Jupiter/Comstock; **356** Courtesy of Canadian Tire; **357** MATTHEW STAVER/Bloomberg News/Landov; **359 (top)** AP World Wide Photos; **359 (bottom)** These materials have been reproduced with the permission of Paypal, Inc. COPYRIGHT © 2007 PAYPAL, INC. ALL RIGHTS RESERVED; **362** Courtesy of ING Direct Canada; **363** PhotoEdit/Spencer Grant; **366** Courtesy of Planet Bean Coffee; **369** Copyright © Bob Daemmrich/Photo Edit; **370 (top)** DANIEL KARMANN/dpa/Landov; **370 (bottom)** GEORGE FREY/Bloomberg News/Landov; **371** Superstock, Inc.; **373** Arnold Bros. Transport Ltd.

Chapter 11

380, 409 Used with permission of Macy's Corporation; **382, 408** Courtesy of Dawn Robertson; **384** Courtesy of lululemon athletica; **385** Courtesy of Petro-Canada; **386** The Canadian Press (Toronto Star/Dick Loek); **387 (top)** R.A. Flynn, Inc./TC2; **388** Elnora Stuart; **390** Photo by David Young-Wolff/PhotoEdit; **391** Courtesy of The Running Room; **392** Elnora Stuart; **393 (top)** Photo by David Whittaker, Design Firm: Fiorino Design, LCBO Bayview Village; **393 (bottom)** Courtesy of Holt Renfrew; **396** Dick Hemingway; **397 (top left)** Toronto Corporate Services; **397 (top right)** Canapress/Dave Buston; **397 (bottom left)** AP/Wide World Photos; **397 (bottom right)** PhotoEdit, Jim Mone; **398** Samcor Communications Company; **401** Courtesy of La Senza; **403** Courtesy of Google; **404** Just White Shirts & Black Socks; **406** Cheryl Jackson.

Chapter 12

414 Henry Ausloos/AGE/firstlight.ca;
416, 451 Courtesy of David Chidley; 419 Courtesy
of Liz Claiborne Canada; 426 Courtesy of Bell
Canada, the WWE, and Rethink Communications;
426 Halifax Regional Police; 429 Courtesy of General Mills Canada Corporation; 432 Courtesy of
Procter & Gamble; 433 Courtesy of Goodyear;
434 Courtesy Procter & Gamble Company;
436 Courtesy of Procter & Gamble; 437 REUTERS/
Ho New; 445 David Duprey/CP Photo Archive;
446 Courtesy of Novell; 447 Sun-Rype Products
Ltd.; 450 Adobe and the Adobe logo are trademarks
of Adobe Systems Incorporated; 451 Under permission by V&S Vin & Spirit AB (publ). ABSOLUT
COUNTRY OF SWEDEN VODKA & LOGO,
ABSOLUT, ABSOLUT BOTTLE DESIGN AND
ABSOLUT CALLIGRAPHY ARE TRADEMARKS
OWNED BY V&S VIN & SPIRIT AB (publ).

Chapter 13

458 Courtesy of Saputo; 460, 493 Courtesy of
Mario Demers; 461 Microcell Solutions Inc.;
462 Pfizer Canada Inc.; 463 Courtesy of the
Canadian Red Cross; 464 Courtesy of Smith &
Nelson; 466 The Canadian Press (AP Photo/Mark
Lennihan, file); 470 Frank Gunn/CP Photo;
471 Tom Lyle/Medichrome/The Stock Shop, Inc.;
472 Cinemaxx; 474 Paul Chiasson/CP Photo
Archive; 476 Boivin Consulting Group; 477 Ron
Stroud/Masterfile; 478 FRANCIS SPECKER/
Landov; 481 Used with permission of 3M;
482 Labatt Breweries of Canada; 483 Courtesy of
Gillette Canada Company and CAFC; 484 Val-Pak
DMS, Inc.; 487 Used with permission of Tupperware;
488 John Kenney, The Gazette (Montreal);
490 Tourism Queensland (Australia); 492 The
Southwestern Company; 493 Used with permission
of Omaha Steaks.

Chapter 14

500, 502, 517 Photographer and Creative Director:
Jorden Barry; 504 Courtesy of Sony Canada;
512 Courtesy of TeamOne Advertising. Photograph
by Rick Rusing; 513 Creative Agency: Low and
Partners. Photographer: Richard Pullar;
515 Courtesy of Harry Rosen Inc.

COMPANY/NAME INDEX

SUBJECT INDEX

online games, 192–193
online research
  cookies, 150
  described, 150
  disadvantages, 152–153
  exploratory research, 151–152
  focus groups, 151–153
  market response estimates, 151
  new-product development, 151
  questionnaires, 151–153
  self-selection bias, 153
  testing, 151–153
  tracking, 150–151
online shopping. *See* etailing
online survey, 142
operant conditioning, 179
operating costs, 295
operating expense ratio, 343
operating expenses, 340
operating income, 340
operating plans, 43
operating ratios, 342–343
operating statement, 340
operating supplies, 257
operating variables, 91
operational excellence, 99–100
operational factors, 248
opinion leaders, 191–192
opportunities
  assessment, 508
  assumptions, 508
  identification of, 50, 508
  understanding, 12–15, 50–52
opportunity costs, 295
order getter, 487
order processing, 371
order processing cost, 344
order taker, 487
organizational buying behaviour. *See* business buying; business markets
organizational demographics, 92
organizational differences, 265–266
organizational objectives, 46–47
other revenue and expenses, 340
out-of-home media, 470
outlet mall, 391
outsourcing, 220, 369
over-redemption, 483
overcoming customer objections, 490

P

paradigm shift, 20
partner relationship management (PRM), 486
party plan system, 406
passive methods of data collection, 142–143
payment pricing, 310
payout plan, 445
Pearson correlation coefficient, 160
peer-to-peer e-commerce, 192–195
penetration pricing, 306–307

people-based services, 248
perceived risk, 168–169
percentage-of-sales method, 444
perception, 176–177
perceptual map, 101–102, 101f
perceptual selection, 177
performance goals, 491
performance measurement, 19, 49
perishability, 249
perishability management, 362
permission-based marketing, 468
persistence over time, 51
Personal Information Protection and Electronic Documents Act (PIPEDA), 146–147, 147t, 408
personal observation, 142
personal selling
  advantages of, 485
  the approach, 489
  approaches, 488
  creative selling process, 489–491, 489f
  defined, 485
  described, 435–436
  motivation, 492–493
  overcoming customer objections, 490
  pre-approach, 489
  prospecting, 489
  qualify prospects, 489
  recruitment, 492
  relationship selling, 488
  rewards, 492–493
  role of, 485–486, 488–491
  sales closing, 491
  sales follow-up, 491
  sales force objectives, 491
  sales force strategy, 491–492
  sales management, 491–493
  sales presentation, 490
  sales training, 492
  and technology, 486–487
  telemarketing, 486
  transactional selling, 488
personality, 179–180
p.e.s.t.o., 44
physical distribution. *See* logistics
physical environment, 182–184
piggyback services, 373
pioneering brand, 307
pipelines, 373
place, 17
  see also distribution
place-based media, 184, 470
place utility, 355
planning. *See* business planning; strategic planning
planning and development phase, 252
pleasure, 182
point-of-purchase (POP) promotion, 482
point-of-sale (POS) systems, 386

pop-up ad, 467
portals, 170–171, 401
portfolio analysis, 48
positioning
  analysis of competitors' positions, 101–102
  blue ocean strategy, 102
  brand personality, 105–107
  customer intimacy, 99
  defined, 15, 97
  described, 97
  evaluation of target market responses, 109–110
  implementation of strategy, 108–110
  operational excellence, 99–100
  perceptual map, 101–102, 101f
  and product leadership strategy, 99
  repositioning, 110
  strategy implementation, 104t
  symbolic-expressive value, 100
positioning maps, 102f, 102, 103f
positioning objectives, 299, 309
positioning statement, 430–431
possession utility, 355
post-purchase evaluation, 173–175, 220
post-testing, 449–450
pre-approach, 489
pre-testing, 470
Precious Metals Marking Act, 315
predatory pricing, 316–317, 318
Predicasts PROMT, 126
premium pricing, 308
premiums, 482
press release, 476
prestige products, 302, 302f
price
  defined, 17, 295
  fair pricing, 64–65
  internal reference price, 321
  list price, 313
  lowest-priced products, 296
  in marketing mix, 17
  monetary price, 295–296
  non-monetary price, 295–296
price-based consumer promotions, 481–482
price bundling, 308
price deals, 481
price discounts, 313–314
price discrimination, 64, 317, 328–329
price elastic, 322
price elasticity, 344
price elasticity of demand, 322–324
price fixing, 64, 307–308, 317–318
price-floor pricing, 301
price gouging, 65
price inelastic, 322
price leadership (follower), 307
price lining, 312–313, 313f